MICHIGAN'S EARLY

MILITARY FORCES

MICHIGAN'S EARLY

MILITARY FORCES

A ROSTER AND HISTORY OF TROOPS
ACTIVATED PRIOR TO THE AMERICAN CIVIL WAR

ROSTERS COMPILED BY LE ROY BARNETT

WITH HISTORIES BY ROGER ROSENTRETER

WAYNE STATE UNIVERSITY PRESS
DETROIT

Great Lakes Books

A complete listing of the books in this series can be found at the back of this volume.

Philip P. Mason, Editor
Department of History, Wayne State University

Dr. Charles K. Hyde, Associate Editor
Department of History, Wayne State University

COPYRIGHT © 2003 BY WAYNE STATE UNIVERSITY PRESS,

DETROIT, MICHIGAN 48201. ALL RIGHTS ARE RESERVED.

NO PART OF THIS BOOK MAY BE REPRODUCED WITHOUT FORMAL PERMISSION.

MANUFACTURED IN THE UNITED STATES OF AMERICA.

07 06 05 04 03   1 2 3 4 5

Library of Congress Cataloging-in-Publication Data

Michigan's early military forces : a roster and history of troops
activated prior to the American Civil War / rosters compiled by Le Roy
Barnett ; with histories by Roger Rosentreter.
        p. cm. — (Great Lakes books)
Includes bibliographical references and index.
    ISBN 0-8143-3081-9 (alk. paper)
  1. Michigan—Militia—History—18th century. 2.
Michigan—Militia—History—19th century. 3.
Michigan—Militia—Bibliography. 4. Michigan—Militia—Registers. 5.
Michigan—History, Military—18th century. 6. Michigan—History,
Military—19th century. 7. Michigan—Genealogy. 8.
Soldiers—Michigan—Genealogy. I. Barnett, LeRoy. II. Rosentreter,
Roger. III. Series.

    UA260 .M53 2003
    355.3'7'09774—dc21   2002152375

∞ THE PAPER USED IN THIS PUBLICATION MEETS THE MINIMUM REQUIREMENTS

OF THE AMERICAN NATIONAL STANDARD FOR INFORMATION SCIENCES—PERMANENCE

OF PAPER FOR PRINTED LIBRARY MATERIALS, ANSI Z39.48-1984.

Published with the assistance of the Michigan Genealogical Council.

To our parents . . .

. . . Who developed in us the curiosity

to ask questions

and the

determination to find correct answers.

CONTENTS

Contents

FOREWORD

SINCE FRENCH COLONIAL TIMES, the area that now constitutes Michigan has been protected by local militia. Whether from domestic or foreign threats, these citizen-soldiers were ready to defend their communities and governments whenever called upon to do so.

In time, these local militia units became collectively known as the Michigan State Troops and, later, as the Michigan National Guard. Many people are aware that some elements of this home defense force, under their more modern names, were activated to serve in the Mexican Border Campaign, World Wars I and II, as well as in Korea and the Persian Gulf War.

But while the more recent activities of the Michigan militia are fairly well chronicled and remembered, little is known about the earlier contributions of these Wolverine warriors. To partially fill this gap in our state's military history, Drs. Barnett and Rosentreter—with the help of Dennis Au—have created this account of Michigan's soldiery in the last quarter of the eighteenth century and the first half of the nineteenth century.

During this seventy-five-year period, Michigan's equivalent of the "Minutemen" were called to active duty numerous times during real or perceived crisis situations. On a few other occasions of lesser significance or alarm, the citizen soldiers were placed on alert until threatening circumstances returned to normal. In all of these instances, our troops served with distinction and honor in fulfilling their missions.

Because these early engagements were poorly documented, the accomplishments of our pioneer fighting men have been mostly forgotten and unappreciated. Now, for the first time, this book describes the conflicts in which the old Michigan militia participated and identifies each soldier who is known to have sacrificed his time (and in some cases his life) to keep the peace or preserve freedom. This volume, then, is more than the story of Michigan's military activities of long ago. It is also a roll of honor giving overdue recognition to those early residents of our State who answered the call to defend and maintain the American way of life that we enjoy today. Furthermore, the book can serve as an unofficial record of the organized and activated reserve within the borders of present-day Michigan.

My predecessors—in conjunction with crown, state, or federal authorities—ordered the Michigan militia to arms when conditions required between 1775 and 1850. The muster rolls, rosters, and papers generated by these crises have been (insofar as possible) tracked down by the authors of this work after years of research. Their findings are brought together here as a record of operations undertaken and successfully discharged by the first Michigan armies in the field.

In order for the Michigan Department of Military Affairs to keep alive this state's martial traditions, it must be aware of what has transpired in the past. This book will help my agency and the people it serves to learn more about and pay tribute to the active role of the early Michigan militia.

E. Gordon Stump,
Maj. Gen. MIANG, Adjutant General of Michigan

PREFACE

WHILE WORKING AS REFERENCE ARCHIVIST at the State Archives of Michigan from 1974 to 1997, I was impressed with the frequency with which I and others consulted the forty-six-volume *Record of Service of Michigan Volunteers in the Civil War.* Because this source is such a useful compilation, it disappointed me that similar books did not exist for the other wars in which Michigan men participated. After years of waiting for such a publication to appear, I decided to undertake the job myself.

I planned to identify every soldier who served on active duty from Michigan prior to the Civil War. In an attempt to be as inclusive as possible, I also decided to cite those individuals who volunteered to serve in combat during this period but were not activated at the time of crisis. Along with each name, I tried to track down some basic data about these soldiers, like rank, unit, and dates of muster. In the case of troops participating in the Mexican War, government sources enabled a wider range of information to be included. These data were gleaned from records found in the National Archives, the State Archives of Michigan, official government documents, county histories, and private letters and diaries.

I had hoped that by creating this reference tool I would finally be able to answer requests by patrons for information about their ancestors who participated in Michigan's military engagements during the British, territorial, and early statehood eras. However, as the project developed it became clear that other purposes could be served by this enterprise. For one thing, the work would finally permit us to recognize those individuals who served Michigan and the nation in times of perceived or actual danger.

Beyond standing as a tribute to veterans, this compilation also gives proper credit to Michigan for its participation in the antebellum wars. For example, the *American State Papers*[1] claim that about six hundred Michigan men fought in the War of 1812. I have discovered that the actual count is closer to one thousand. Additionally, some men are listed two or more times in the rosters, having served multiple tours of duty or with more than a single unit. And while the "Index to Compiled Service Records of Volunteer Soldiers Who Served From the State of Michigan During the Patriot War, 1838–1839"[2] shows about one hundred activated Michigan soldiers, the correct number is over four hundred.

Besides a more accurate record of the state's military personnel, this production has other benefits. It can, for instance, stand as a partial enumeration of adult male residents in selected areas during various intercensal periods. For example, the accompanying roster for the War of 1812 lists practically every white male of fighting age in the Lower Peninsula.

The degree to which this book identifies adult males in the population can be made clear by a few statistics. During the War of 1812, the residents of the United States totaled about 7,700,000. Of this number, approximately 450,000 served with militia units, a figure that represents close to 6 percent of the nation's population. In Michigan, on the other hand, the number of white inhabitants approached 4,000. If one accepts as accurate the low government estimate of 600 militia enrollments from the area now encompassed by our state, then at least 15 percent of the enumerated Michigan population fought in the War of 1812.

Another benefit of this book is the way its rosters show the degree to which "foreigners" have come forth to serve our state and territory when the call to battle sounded. For example, a disproportionate number of men of French descent aided Michigan's cause during the War of 1812, while those of Irish ancestry are overly represented in the Wolverine contingent serving in the Mexican-American War.

While this information is interesting, to present readers with just some names and related facts seemed inadequate. In an effort to address this deficiency, I decided to include organizational charts showing the military units involved in each conflict and their home base when known. Furthermore, to enable users to understand the activities associated with each conflict, Sherm Hollander prepared maps to show all theaters of operations for Michigan troops. Finally, Roger Rosentreter and Dennis Au wrote historical descriptions to help readers understand why Michigan men had to be activated and what they accomplished during their service.

Dennis Au's introductory essay and Roger Rosentreter's descriptive accounts of each war, coupled with my listings of individual soldiers, make this work the only known extensive treatment of Michigan's military performance prior to the Civil War. As such, the book is bound to be of great interest and benefit to genealogists, military enthusiasts, librarians, historians, archivists, and political scientists. It is hoped that these and other users will, through an examination of the following pages, come to know and appreciate the contributions of men who were involved in Michigan's early martial engagements.

There are two "wars" that involved the early nineteenth-century Michigan militia that will not appear in this work. The first is the Winnebago War, which took place in the summer of 1827. During this period, four companies of the Michigan militia under Captains Dickinson, Johnston, McNair, and Smith were activated in an effort to defend the frontier against Indian hostilities. Since the men serving in these units were from the area of Michigan Territory that is now part of Wisconsin (mainly around Green Bay), they have been excluded from the scope of this book. The rosters of the troops who participated in this conflict can be found on reel three of microfilm set number M1505 from Record Group 94 at the National Archives.

The other conflict that will not be found in this volume is an action grandiloquently or facetiously known as "The Lowell War." This inflated event occurred on

November 21, 1857, at the town named in the title of the engagement. The disturbance there resulted in the partial call-up of the Grand Rapids militia, but the activated units never performed any service.

The martial alert was caused by a riot on the part of about 250 Irish railroad laborers who were working in and around Lowell building the Detroit & Milwaukee Railroad. When the men had not been paid as promised, they threatened the construction engineer and company property with violence. Fearing that the angry crowd could not be controlled, the company appealed to the county sheriff for help. The sheriff, in turn, considering the size and anger of the mob, requested that some of the local civilian soldiery go with him to the site of the strife as part of a *posse comitatus*. This assembled force had marched to a point just short of Ada when it learned that everything had quieted down in Lowell. Upon hearing that peace had been restored up the road, the sheriff, his deputies, and the militia performed an about-face and returned to Grand Rapids.

While it is questionable whether the Kent County sheriff had the authority to activate the local militia, the fact remains that some troops were called to duty by a public official. The units that were partially activated for a day were elements of the Valley City Guards and the Ringgold Light Artillery. While rosters do not exist identifying those common soldiers from each unit who responded to the sheriff's call to arms, it appears from newspaper accounts of the time that the rank and file was probably led by the following officers:

Field and Staff—Major Christopher W. Leffingwell (Brigade Inspector);

Ringgold Light Artillery—Captain Stephen Gardner Champlin, 1st Lt. John J. Fay, 1st Lt. Edward H. Lockwood Jr., 2nd Lt. Tobias B. Borst, and 2nd Lt. Carlton Neal Jr.;

Valley City Guards—Captain Daniel McConnell, 1st Lt. John H. Earle, 2nd Lt. Robert M. Collins, and 3rd Lt. Milton S. Littlefield.

IN CLOSING, it is perhaps appropriate to say a few words about the Michigan citizens who served in every conflict prior to the Toledo War yet are largely missing from this volume. I am referring, of course, to the Native Americans of this state. These warriors served their cause valorously, sometimes fighting with U.S. forces and sometimes against them. No matter what side they were on, they proved to be formidable combatants. Unfortunately, these braves were mostly anonymous individuals, usually not appearing on any rosters or muster rolls.

Even when such records exist—as in the case of the ninety-five Potawatomi scouts organized during the Black Hawk War—it is difficult to tell which of the volunteers were Michigan residents. Within the company of "friendly" Indians raised in June of 1832 to fight against the forces of Black Hawk, only Chief White Pigeon can be said with some degree of confidence to have a connection with the Lower Peninsula tribes.[3] It is unfortunate that so many Michigan men must be excluded from this book, but circumstances dictate that they remain our state's unknown soldiers.

Michigan has long been proud of its record of military service. When these accomplishments are unknown, however, recognition cannot be given nor tribute paid. Now, with the compilation of this volume, we are at last made aware of the roles our forebears played in our state's earliest armed operations. May this book be a memorial to those citizen-soldiers who answered the call of their government when its leaders deemed a resort to battle was necessary.

Le Roy Barnett, April 2002

Notes

1. Military Affairs, Class 5, vol. 2, p. 281.
2. National Archives Microcopy No. 630.
3. *The Black Hawk War, 1831–1832*, vol. 1, p. 560

ACKNOWLEDGMENTS

THIS VENTURE TOOK TWO DECADES to complete. During this twenty-year period we became indebted to many institutions and people who helped contribute to this book. Besides the staffs of the various libraries and archives we visited, we wish to thank the Bureau of History, Michigan Department of State, which generously supported this project in a variety of ways; the Military Affairs Subcommittee of the Michigan Sesquicentennial Commission, which endorsed this undertaking as an official project of our state's 150th birthday celebration; the Michigan Genealogical Council, which, in conjunction with the Library of Michigan, worked to have this compilation shared with the public; and the staff of the Wayne State University Press who contributed to making this volume a reality.

At the individual level, recognition is due Roland Gurk and Debbie Christiansen of the Michigan Department of State; Carey Draeger and the late John Rummel, Library of Michigan; Albert Castel, Western Michigan University; James Clifton, University of Wisconsin-Green Bay; Frederick D. Williams, Michigan State University; Sandra S. Clark and Richard Geer from the Michigan Bureau of History; Harry Bosveld, Fort Malden National Park; Major Mike Johnson, formerly with the Michigan Department of Military Affairs; Matt Switlick, director of the Monroe County Historical Commission; David Finney of Howell; John Sturm of Ann Arbor; Arlynn Gantz of Orlando, Florida; and the Crossman family of Stielacoom, Washington.

Some special words of appreciation are in order for a few select individuals who played a very significant part in this book's creation. First, a place of honor is due Dennis Au for writing the outstanding overview of the Michigan militia from 1775 to 1811 that appears in chapter 1. Neither of the main authors felt qualified to address this subject, so Dennis graciously volunteered to create the three-part summary of this crucial period in our state's early military history. Second, tribute is in order for Pam Epple, who devoted a substantial numbers of hours to editing the text to make it ready for publication. Much of what is good about the layout and organization of this work is attributable to her, while any errors or omissions are our sole responsibility.

When distributing notes of appreciation we are required to mention Wayne Mann, formerly director of the Archives at Western Michigan University, who took a greater active interest in this undertaking than any information provider encountered in the course of our research. Kudos are in order to our wives, who made many sacrifices so this volume could be produced. We hope this book will be some compensation for the numerous hours its development took from our family life. Finally, it is with gratitude and sadness that we recognize Martin McLaughlin. Though he was not a partner in this endeavor, for years he freely gave of his time in helping with our many computer needs. We regret that he did not live to see the fruits of his labors in print. We think he would be pleased to know that the following pages are in his memory.

A User's Guide to the Listings

AGE: The figure given is years at the time of enlistment. In the Mexican-American War, hereafter referred to as the Mexican War, the average Michigan soldier was about 25.5 years old. During the American Civil War, the typical enlisted man in federal service was 25.8 years old.

BIRTHPLACE: The name given may be a county or a settlement. Of those Michigan soldiers who provided such information, 46 percent were born in New York State, 9 percent in Ireland, 6 percent in Canada, 6 percent in Germany, 5 percent in Michigan, 4 percent each in England, Ohio, and Vermont, 3 percent in Pennsylvania, and 2 percent in both Connecticut and New Jersey. In the American Civil War, about 9 percent of the U.S. troops were natives of Germany, 7 percent from Ireland, and 2 percent from England. With respect to Michigan troops in the Civil War, 24 percent were born in the state, 5 percent in Germany, and 4 percent each in England and Ireland.

DISCHARGE DATE AND PLACE: While the data entered here and elsewhere can be considered valid, for definitive information one should always have recourse to the original sources. Dates are listed month/day/year, the year being indicated by its last two digits. Years before "50" reference the nineteenth century, years after "50" reference the eighteenth century.

ENROLLED DATE AND PLACE: The individuals included in this work had to meet at least one of the following criteria to qualify for consideration:

> A. be living in Michigan at the time of enrollment in a military force slated for active duty in wartime.
>
> B. be admitted into a Michigan military unit that was activated (or intended to be activated) for service during a period of hostilities.

During the War of 1812, Canadians living in U.S.-occupied portions of what is now southwestern Ontario were considered to be Michigan residents. Dates are listed month/day/year, the year being indicated by its last two digits. Years before "50" reference the nineteenth century, years after "50" reference the eighteenth century.

MUSTERED DATE AND PLACE: This category indicates when a soldier was actually brought into the service, as opposed to enrollment, which is when a person made a commitment to join. Dates are listed month/day/year, the year being indicated by its last two digits. Years before "50" reference the nineteenth century, years after "50" reference the eighteenth century.

NAME: Though this effort has attempted to be as comprehensive as possible, it is known that some veterans (particularly those who served in the Revolutionary War, the War of 1812, and the Patriot War) have not been identified. Because of an absence of records, for example, we have not been able to list most Michiganians who served with British forces in the War of 1812. Furthermore, some of the records upon which this book is based are difficult to read or fragmentary. Therefore, if the name of the person being sought is not found, look for variant spellings or consider the possibility that the rosters no longer exist. We were able to identify 365 Michigan soldiers who served in the Revolutionary War, 1,535 soldiers in the War of 1812, 1,838 for the Black Hawk War, 1,181 for the Toledo War, 437 for the Patriot War, and 2,096 for the Mexican War. All told, more than 7,000 veterans are accounted for in this compilation, though some names are duplicated since a few men were associated with more than one military unit, particularly during the early conflicts.

OCCUPATION: Shows profession at the time of entry into service. Of those who provided such details, 35 percent were farmers, 20 percent laborers, 6 percent carpenters, 4 percent blacksmiths, 3 percent coopers, 3 shoemakers, 2 percent clerks, 2 percent sailors, 2 percent soldiers, 2 percent tailors, and the remainder in fifty other vocations. By comparison, during the U.S. Civil War 48 percent of the Yankee soldiers were farmers, 24 percent mechanics, 16 percent laborers, 5 percent in "commercial pursuits," 3 percent professional men, and 4 percent miscellaneous.

PHYSICAL CHARACTERISTICS: If some details on a given individual are absent, it is because the facts are unavailable. It is especially difficult to obtain such data for officers and deserters.

    A. COMPLEXION: Of those soldiers for whom such information is available, 39 percent were light, 28 percent dark, 22 percent fair, 6 percent florid, 2 percent ruddy, 2 percent sandy, and 1 percent sallow. During the Civil War it was observed that those men with florid complexions were best suited to the military life. The authors have noticed that, in the Mexican War, a disproportionate number of the Michigan officers and noncommissioned officers were dark-complected.

    B. EYES: Based upon the statistics available, 45 percent of the Michigan soldiers had blue eyes, 23 percent gray, 13 percent hazel, 11 percent black, 4 percent dark, and 3 percent brown. Similar figures for U.S. forces in the Civil War are 45 percent blue, 24 percent gray, 13 percent hazel, 10 percent dark, and 8 percent black.

    C. HAIR: Given the data at hand, 42 percent of the Michigan contingent had brown hair, 17 percent light, 14 percent black, 14 percent dark, 6 percent sandy, 2 percent fair, 2 percent gray, 1 percent auburn, and 1 percent red. For federal troops in the Civil War, the figures are 30 percent brown, 24 percent light, 13 percent black, 25 percent dark, 4 percent sandy, 3 percent red, and 1 percent gray. During the Civil War it was observed that those men with brown or red hair were best suited to the military life.

D. HEIGHT: The figure to the left of the decimal is feet, to the right of the decimal is inches. Fractions have been rounded off to the nearest whole number. The average Michigan soldier was almost 5 feet, 8 inches in height. A representative soldier serving with federal forces in the War Between the States was 5 feet, 8.25 inches tall.

RANK: The numbers before some of the ranks show grade within a particular classification. The ratio of enlisted men to officers (all of the troops were volunteers, except for a handful of men in the Revolutionary War and the War of 1812) can be seen in the chart below.

WAR	COMMISSIONED	NONCOMMISSIONED	RANK AND FILE	TOTAL
1812 War	88 (5.7%)	158 (10.3%)	1289 (84%)	1535
Black Hawk	159 (8.6%)	243 (13.3%)	1436 (78.1%)	1838
Toledo War	185 (15.6%)	169 (14.4%)	827 (70%)	1181
Patriot War	25 (5.7%)	45 (10.3%)	367 (84.0%)	437
Mexican War	119 (5.7%)	154 (7.3%)	1823 (87.0%)	2096

The Revolutionary War has not been included in this table because of insufficient data. It should be noted that, in the Toledo War, the commissioned officers outnumbered the noncommissioned officers. This may be the only time in military history that such an imbalance occurred, making the forces in that "conflict" inordinately top-heavy.

In the Revolutionary War one will find "ranks" that are uncommon by contemporary standards and, thus, possibly misunderstood. Those persons designated as "Clerks" were essentially people responsible for handing out arms and ammunition to the Indians. A closely related occupational title—and in some cases an identical one—was "Storekeeper." These latter individuals were responsible for seeing that British forces (red and white) were supplied with the necessary materials for making war, including food for their families while the men were in the field. The "Blacksmiths" were in reality armorers, many of whom were assigned to live with the Natives and keep their weapons in good working order. An "Extra" was someone who was not formally a member of a regular military body but was retained as an addition to the force in case of necessity.

REMARKS: Sometimes the restrictions of space have prevented all remarks pertaining to an individual from being included. For a complete list of particulars, refer to the original records. The information relating to pension status did not come from the same military sources that provided data on the soldiers. The following indexes were consulted in the course of identifying those persons who were on the pension rolls:

Troxel, Navena Hembree. *Mexican War Index to Pension Files, 1886–1926.* Gore, Okla.: VT Publications, 1983–97.

White, Virgil D. *Index to Indian Wars Pension Files, 1892–1926*. Waynesboro, Tenn.: National Historical Publishing Company, 1987.

———— *Index to Mexican War Pension Files*, [1887–1926]. Waynesboro, Tenn.: National Historical Publishing Company, 1989.

————. *Index to Old Wars Pension Files, 1815–1926*. Waynesboro, Tenn.: National Historical Publishing Company, 1987.

————. *Index to War of 1812 Pension Files*. Waynesboro, Tenn.: National Historical Publishing Company, 1989.

Wolfe, Barbara Schull. *An Index to Mexican War Pension Applications*. Indianapolis: Heritage House, 1985.

Michigan forces in the antebellum period had men killed in action during just three conflicts. One soldier is said to have been killed during the Revolutionary War and at least four died in the ensuing Indian Wars. Seventeen soldiers are known to have died in combat in the War of 1812, and twenty-six troops were similarly lost in the Mexican War (in this latter conflict, 329 died of disease or accident). Losses due to desertion were more widespread, with eight men lost in this fashion during the War of 1812, nine during the Black Hawk War, and 228 during the Mexican-American War.

RESIDENCE: Where the soldier is said to have lived before being admitted to a military unit or called to active duty.

UNIT: See organizational charts preceding the rosters in each chapter for more details. During the Mexican War, most of the soldiers from Michigan served in the First Michigan Volunteer Infantry Regiment, often shortened to the First Michigan Volunteers. Because of space limitations and a desire to include only the most important facts, this unit is cited as the 1st Michigan Infantry.

ABBREVIATIONS USED
IN THE ROSTERS

ADC	Aide-de-camp	CDM	Company disbanded before muster	DIV	Division
ADJ	Adjutant			DMB	Bass drummer
AJG	Adjutant general	CDT	Commandant	DMM	Drum major
AKA	Also known as . . .	CHP	Chaplin	DMR	Drummer
ANW	Army of the Northwest	CIC	Commander in chief	DMT	Detachment
		CLK	Clerk	DOD	Died of disease at/on . . .
ARF	Artificer	CLR	Clear		
ARM	Armorer	CLT	Lieutenant colonel	DOW	Died of wounds at/on . . .
ART	Artillery	CMD	Commander		
ASD	Also served during period . . .	CML	Lieutenant commander	DRG	Dragoon or dragoons
				DRK	Dark
ASG	Assigned to . . .	CMO	Commanding officer	DSC	Discharged on surgeon's certificate
AUB	Auburn	COL	Colonel		
AUS	Austria	COM	Company	DSU	Date(s) of service uncertain
AWOL	Absent without leave	COR	Cornet		
		COS	Chief of staff	DUC	Died of unknown causes at/on . . .
BAT	Battalion	CPL	Corporal (also CP as in 1CP, etc.)		
BEL	Belgium				
BKS	Barracks	CPT	Captured at . . .	EGN	Engineer
BLK	Black	CPX	Complexion	EGT	Engagement
BLS	Blacksmith	CSA	Assistant commissary	ENA	Assistant engineer
BLU	Blue	CSI	Issuing commissary	ENG	England
BOT	Boat master	CSS	Commissary sergeant	ENS	Ensign
BRG	Brigade	CST	Chestnut	ETO	Escaped to Ohio
BSN	Boatswain	CSY	Commissary	EXN	Expressman
BTY	Battery	CTY	County (also Co)	EXP	Expedition
BUG	Bugler			EXT	Extra
BVT	Brevet	DCA	Discharged by civil authority		
BWN	Brown			FAR	Farrier
		DES	Deserted	FED	Federal
CAN	Canada	DET	Detached to or as . . .	FIF	Fifer
CAP	Captain	DFD	Discharged for disability	FIM	Fife major
CAR	Carpenter			FIR	Fair
CAV	Cavalry	DIS	Discharged	FLD	Florid
CDL	Lieutenant commandant	DIT	Variously surnamed or called . . .	FLX	Flaxen
				FRA	France

21

F&S	Field & staff	**MUS**	Musician (also MU)	**SAD**	Saddler
FUR	Furlough			**SAL**	Sallow
		NOR	Claims to have served but not on roster	**SCO**	Scotland
GDE	Guide			**SCT**	Scout
GDS	Guards	**NRE**	Name on rolls may be error	**SCU**	Service claimed but unproven
GEB	Brigadier general				
GEL	Lieutenant general	**NTH**	Northern	**SDY**	Sandy
GEM	Major general			**SEA**	Seaman
GEN	General	**OAS**	On alert status	**SGM**	Sergeant major
GER	Germany	**ODS**	On detached service at . . .	**SGT**	Sergeant (also SG as in 1SG, etc)
GOA	Governor's aide				
GOS	Governor's staff	**ORD**	Ordnance	**SMA**	Assistant surgeon's mate
GRY	Gray				
GUN	Gunner	**PAL**	Pale	**SOB**	Served on board ship(s) . . .
		PAY	Paymaster		
HGT	Height	**PEN**	Received pension	**SPY**	Spy
HMS	His Majesty's Ship	**PFG**	Promoted for gallantry	**SQD**	Squadron
HOA	Hospital attendant			**SRA**	Surrendered at . . .
HOL	Holland	**PHY**	Physician	**STH**	Sent to hospital at . . .
HOS	Hospital steward	**PIL**	Navigation pilot	**STO**	Staff officer
HZL	Hazel	**PMT**	Promoted to . . .	**STR**	Storekeeper
		POW	Prisoner of war on/at . . .	**SUA**	Assistant surgeon
INB	Brigade inspector			**SUB**	Substitute for . . .
IND	Division inspector	**PRO**	Provost	**SUM**	Surgeon's mate
INF	Infantry	**PVT**	Private	**SUP**	Supernumerary
ING	Inspector general			**SUR**	Surgeon
INS	Inspector	**QUA**	Assistant quartermaster	**SWR**	Swarthy
INT	Interpreter			**SWT**	Switzerland
IRE	Ireland	**QUB**	Brigade quartermaster		
		QUD	Division quartermaster	**TEA**	Teamster
KIA	Killed in action on/at . . .			**TEB**	Baggage teamster
		QUG	Quartermaster general	**TRA**	Transferred to . . .
		QUR	Regimental quartermaster	**TRM**	Trumpeter
LAN	Landsman			**TWP**	Township
LGT	Light	**QUS**	Quartermaster sergeant		
LIH	Left in hospital on/at . . .			**UNA**	Unassigned
		QUT	Quartermaster	**UNK**	Unknown
LTD	Light dragoons			**US**	United States
LUT	Lieutenant (also LT as in 1LT, etc.)	**RAN**	Rangers	**USS**	United States Ship
		RBL	Received bounty land		
				VOL	Volunteer
MAC	Master carpenter	**RCT**	Recruit	**VTG**	Voltigeurs
MAJ	Major	**RED**	Red	**VTS**	Volunteered to serve if needed in U.S. forces
MAS	Master (Marine)	**REG**	Regiment		
MBL	Military bounty land grant	**REJ**	Rejected from service		
		RES	Resigned		
MEX	Mexico	**RIF**	Rifles (unit, not weapon)	**WAG**	Wagoner
MIA	Missing in action on/at . . .			**WHT**	White
		ROC	Relieved of command	**WIA**	Wounded in action at/on . . .
MID	Midshipman	**RTR**	Reduced to ranks		
MNI	Middle name is . . .	**RUD**	Ruddy		
MTD	Mounted	**RUS**	Russia	**YEL**	Yellow

MICHIGAN'S EARLY
MILITARY FORCES

Theater of Operations, Revolutionary War. *(Cartography by Sherm Hollander)*

ONE

INTRODUCTION TO THE PRE-TERRITORIAL MILITIA

Michigan in the Revolutionary War, 1775–1783

"A few men, well conducted," George Rogers Clark boldly bragged to Virginia's governor Patrick Henry; that was the secret to the conquest of the Old Northwest. When we look at the map, we see that Clark's conquest only encompassed a fraction of this territory. At the end of the Revolution, and indeed until the British evacuated the area in 1796, hostile Indians, British garrisons at Detroit and Mackinac, and a few Michigan men, well placed, held sway over the majority of the Northwest. During this dramatic era, Michigan men had an impact over an immense area from Montreal and western Pennsylvania to the east, reaching as far west as St. Louis and the Upper Mississippi River, and south going well into Kentucky.

There was no such entity as Michigan during this time, but within the present boundaries of the state there were two major population centers, Detroit and Michilimackinac, and a fortified trading post, St. Joseph (now Niles). Detroit and Michilimackinac were military posts and seats of civil authority. Companies of the King's Eighth Regiment constituted the bulk of the garrisons at these forts. The Quebec Act of 1774 placed a lieutenant governor at both settlements with authority in civilian matters. The non-Native population within this territory was very fluid. Well over four-fifths of the people claimed French Canadian heritage. English-speaking traders, while prominent, were few in number and had to be conversant in French.

Michilimackinac was a fur-trading entrepôt. At the beginning of the Revolution the settlement centered on the fort at the very tip of Michigan's Lower Peninsula (now Mackinaw City). Within its walls were military barracks and officer's quarters and as many as thirty private residences. Beyond the gates the "suburbs" boasted almost a hundred seasonally occupied dwellings. Michilimackinac guarded the strategic waterway crossroads of the fur trade. Its population swelled and waned with the cycles of that trade. Only about two hundred people resided at the Straits year round.

The authority of the lieutenant governor and the realm of the traders went far beyond the Straits. In Michilimackinac's sphere were the settlements at Sault Ste. Marie,

Green Bay (Wisconsin), St. Joseph (present Niles, Michigan), and, to some extent, Prairie du Chien (Wisconsin). Because Michilimackinac was the focal point for these outlying settlements, it is possible to consider them as part of a "greater Michigan."

Detroit, too, centered around a British fort. Unlike Michilimackinac, the fort was exclusively a military establishment. Like its sister post to the north, most of its settlers had some connection to the fur trade. At the opening of the Revolution, Detroit had one of the largest populations in the interior of British North America. In addition to the fort and the actual village, the settlement encompassed farms strung along both sides of the river from Lake St. Clair in the north to the Ecorse River in the south as well as farms on both sides of the River Rouge. A census taken in 1778 counted 2,144 people in the region, 736 of whom were militia-aged males. The area's farms supplied the local population and the fur traders.

The Detroit officials had authority and traders had influence over most of present-day Ohio and over the traders at Kekionga—Fort Wayne, Indiana. Ouiatenon, a fortified trading center on the Wabash near where West Lafayette, Indiana, is now, and the before mentioned St. Joseph were at the fringes of its official influence.

Not only in the immediate vicinity of Detroit and Michilimackinac, but also throughout the orbits of their respective influence, the fur trade dominated. This does not mean that Native people always came to fur-trading posts at these settlements. While some trading was done at the settlements, most traders did the bulk of their business in the Indian villages. At least a third of the adult males at Detroit and practically everyone at Michilimackinac wintered in the Indian country. These men lived with the Native people, intimately knew their customs, and fluently spoke their languages. They generally developed strong associations with particular Indians, villages, and tribes. Contact with the Indians continued in the summer. Many of the traders then were employed in the other leg of the business, transporting furs by ship and canoe to Montreal and returning with British trade goods.

The fur trade had a profound effect on the nature of the armed struggle in and around eighteenth-century Michigan and on the role its citizens played in these hostilities. From the Revolution and the Indian wars through the War of 1812, while the actors in the conflicts changed, the fight was basically the same.

The service of Michigan men during this period is little understood and difficult to document. Both Michilimackinac and Detroit had militias. Because of the transitory nature of the population, Michilimackinac's militia was rather amorphous. Detroit, on the other hand, was more organized. In 1776 there were six militia companies with an estimated total strength of 350 men. In 1782, documents list six companies with 448 men available. On occasion these militia units did march and there are muster rolls to read.

The most important role the Michigan men played was not militia duty but acting as cultural intermediaries between the British and the Indians. Throughout this period the Native people had their own agendas and strategies. Michigan men had their feet in both worlds and wielded much influence in the British-Indian alliance. In addition to their intimate knowledge of the Native people, they also had a familiarity with the territory matched only by the indigenous population. They were ideal scouts, informants, and couriers. Because they did much of this service on an ad hoc basis, documenting it involves pouring over correspondence, journals, and official papers looking for a chance passing mention of a name.

By no means was all of the liaison between the British and the Indians on an ad hoc basis. The British Indian Departments at Detroit and Michilimackinac put some of the relationship on a more formal level. During this entire era the departments recruited Michigan men to serve as translators, store keepers, gunsmiths, blacksmiths, and officers, all assigned to court the Native people and carry out British policy as it involved the Indians. A handful of the men serving in these departments came to Michigan from other regions. In this group were the most notorious of the veterans: Simon Girty, Alexander McKee, Matthew Elliott, and William Caldwell.

At the time of the first shots at Lexington and Concord in April of 1775, all was quiet at Detroit and Michilimackinac. This was the season when the traders returned from wintering in the Indian country. The British commanders at both posts—Captain Arent Schuyler De Peyster at Michilimackinac and Captain Richard Beringer Lernoult at Detroit—routinely questioned the traders to ascertain the state of affairs among the tribes. Preventing intertribal rivalries from disrupting the fur trade was the British authorities' prime concern.

The Revolution soon impacted these distant posts. The Americans' capture of Montreal in November 1775 meant the Rebels had a stranglehold on the fur trade at Detroit, Michilimackinac, and other western posts. When this news reached Michilimackinac in June 1776, De Peyster sent trader James Stanley Goddard to La Baye (Green Bay) to call the Menominee and Winnebago Indians to action. Similarly, interpreter Joseph Louis Ainsse was told to gather the Ottawa and Chippewa in the vicinity of Michilimackinac. Once assembled, De Peyster sent both parties off to Montreal. Ainsse and the Ottawa and Chippewa warriors arrived in time to help drive the Americans from Montreal. Goddard and the famed Indian Department interpreter Charles Langlade arrived at Montreal with the La Baye Indians after the Americans had retreated. This would be the first of many instances during the Revolution where the British called on Michigan men to recruit and lead Native people on expeditions against the Rebels.

News of the Americans' capture of Montreal came to Detroit from its own lieutenant governor. On his way to Detroit, Lieutenant Governor Henry Hamilton slipped through the American sentries at Montreal by disguising himself. He arrived at Detroit 9 November 1775. Though he liked the beauty of the Detroit River region, he quickly discovered it was not insulated from the revolution. American agents were among the Native people in the Ohio Valley, and in August of 1776 some even came to Detroit. Hamilton needed every resource at hand to manage the Indian situation and to check Rebel advances.

On 6 October 1776 the governor of Quebec, General Guy Carleton, penned an order to both Hamilton and De Peyster that established the future course of the war in the West. Carleton commanded De Peyster to send "200 chosen Indians" to Quebec in the spring, and he instructed Hamilton to assemble the Ohio Valley tribes and organize raids on the Virginia and Pennsylvania frontiers. Hamilton regretted this "deplorable sort of war," but he remarked that this is what "the arrogance, disloyalty and imprudence of the Virginians had justly drawn down upon them."

To carry out these orders, both commanders drew upon Michigan men who knew both the Native people and the terrain. De Peyster sent word out to his most trusted Indian contacts. In response to this call, Charles Langlade journeyed among the Menominee in the vicinity of La Baye (Green Bay), and Charles Gautier gathered Sac and Fox braves from further north and west. The elderly Louis Chevallier of St. Joseph (Niles), a man long influential with the Potawatomis, stepped forward to recruit braves from that tribe.

Langlade's warriors arrived at the rendezvous first. On 4 June 1777 his Indian party left for Canada. They arrived in time to join General John Burgoyne's thrust down Lake Champlain. These Indians were under the strict watch of Langlade and British officers to prevent feared incendiary depredations. Still, the braves proved difficult to control, and after the much publicized killing of loyalist Jane McCrae by an Indian, Burgoyne dismissed his Native auxiliaries. This was fortunate for the Mackinac contingent because two months later the Americans soundly defeated Burgoyne at the Battle of Saratoga. De Peyster also dispatched both Gautier's and Chevallier's forces to Canada, but they did not participate in Burgoyne's campaign.

At Detroit, Hamilton first sent runners off to the distant tribes to encourage them to take up the tomahawk. As a part of this effort, he wrote to his superior in London that he intended to raise a company of "Chasseurs" (light infantry or scouts) "by gentle or other means" from the young men of the best of Detroit's French families. It is likely that the Lieutenant Governor at least partially carried through on this plan. Although we do not know whom he recruited, it is probable that he tapped Charles Beaubien, Pierre Drouillard, Charles Reaume, Guillaume Lamothe, Isidore Chene, and the three Dequindre brothers Charles (*dit* Fontenay), Antoine (*dit* Ponchartrain), and François (*dit* Lipiconiere). These were men who had an early association with the Indian Department and who were among the most active operatives in that department to the end of the war.

The Indian council at Detroit June 17, 1777, set the tone of the Indian war in the West for the next several years. In a scene repeated more than thirty times before the war ended, a British commander (in this case Hamilton) addressed the assembled Natives through Indian Department interpreters. Hamilton urged the Native warriors to strike the American frontier, and he liberally distributed presents and promised the Indians supplies, support, ransom for prisoners, and rewards for killing Rebels. Many took to the warpath, and in the month that followed no less than fifteen raiding parties left Detroit, spreading terror from Kentucky to Pittsburgh. By fall the Indian Department supervisor at Detroit, Jehu Hay, counted 1,150 braves in his service. In most instances Indian Department personnel—Michigan men—accompanied the Native warriors on the raids.

The British also considered their Great Lakes supply lines crucial and took steps to keep these maritime routes in their control. Captain Alexander Grant, a man who would have a long association with Michigan, commanded three armed vessels for His Majesty on the Lakes. To supplement his force, in the spring of 1777 the British pressed into the King's service the first of what became a small fleet of private vessels. The first instance of this was De Peyster taking John Askin's ship the *Welcome* on 8 May 1777. It is likely that the British drafted both the ship and the crew of this prominent Detroit merchant.

Seventeen seventy-eight proved to be a most eventful year in the fight for control of the Lakes region. In the north, Charles Langlade and Charles Gautier rallied 550 braves from the distant Sioux, Fox, and Winnebago tribes to serve the cause of "John Bull." De Peyster ordered the traders to take these allies to Montreal in their canoes. The British commandants there had no use for so many warriors, however, and consequently sent them back.

On the Ohio frontier, 28 March was a watershed. That day a party of five men, disgusted with the Rebels, deserted their compatriots at Pittsburgh and headed for Detroit where they cast their lot with the Crown. Among them were Simon Girty, Alexander McKee, and Matthew Elliott. These frontiersmen had longstanding trade and blood ties with the Ohio tribes. All but Elliott immediately joined the Detroit Indian Department. Along with William Caldwell, another frontier Loyalist, these men wielded great influence with the Native people. For over two decades they held claim to being the most famous and reviled British Indian agents in the West. From this point on, the Detroit River region was their home.

Early in the spring of 1778 Colonel Hamilton made preparations to intensify the Indian warfare. He sent Captain Henry Bird with some British regulars to Sandusky to construct a forward post. Although we do not know if Michiganians helped build the enclosure, Detroit Indian Department men often used it as an advanced station for military activities.

When the raids on Kentucky and western Pennsylvania resumed that spring, the Indians brought the frontier to its knees. A mark of their effectiveness was Charles Beaubien and Charles Lorimer returning to Detroit with a band of Indians and none other than Daniel Boone as their captive. Boone confessed to Hamilton that "the people of the frontier have been incessantly harassed by parties of Indians, they have not been able to sow grain and at Kentucke [sic] will not have a morsel of bread by the middle of June."

The Americans could not stand this. They believed capturing Detroit was the key to putting a halt to the raids. Detroit, though, was just beyond the reach of the Rebel forces. This insuperable distance did not stop Colonel George Rogers Clark from taking the situation in hand. In a bold stroke that caught the British and Indians off guard, in July 1778 he and a band of Kentuckians and Virginians seized Kaskaskia, Prairie du Rocher, and Cahokia on the Mississippi River and then Vincennes on the Wabash.

This news stunned Detroit. Hamilton resolved to dislodge Clark with all dispatch. First, to ensure the continued allegiance of the vital Wabash tribes, he sent Jean Celoron, the son of a former French military commander at Detroit, to Post Ouiatenon (present Lafayette, Indiana) on the upper Wabash. Celoron arrived too late. One of Clark's lieutenants was already there. Observing this now unsalvageable situation, Celoron returned home and reported the bad news.

Meanwhile, Hamilton received permission from his superior in Canada to organize an assault on Vincennes and the Illinois Country. The lieutenant governor planned to ferry a force of 200 men up the Maumee River and then swiftly descend the Wabash to catch Clark's men by surprise. Runners went to De Peyster at Michilimackinac and Louis Chevallier at St. Joseph (Niles) advising them of his plans and asking them to rally what

Native people they could to come to his support. Hamilton's Indian Department went to the Indian villages in the Detroit region alerting them to be ready to join the effort.

Since Hamilton could only spare thirty-eight British regulars from the Detroit garrison, he needed the help of the Detroit militia to carry out his attack. The ambivalence of the people of Detroit to the British war effort was reflected in the attitudes of this home defense force. For example, the British arrested Captain James Sterling in 1777 for his suspected sympathy for the Rebels and sent him under guard to Canada. In 1778 Captain Jean Baptiste Chapoton resigned because his loyalty was doubted, and Captain Pierre Reaume was dismissed for similar reasons.

To select the most loyal, willing, and able men for his planned expedition, Hamilton mustered the Detroit militia and asked for volunteers. At least 125 men under Captains Normand McLeod, Guillaume LaMothe, and Alexis Maisonville volunteered for the mission. The Detroit Indian Department added seventeen men—officers, interpreters, and armorers. Indians, at least sixty in number, rounded out this army.

Captain McLeod and about fifty militiamen left for Vincennes on 24 September 1778, fourteen days before Hamilton and the main force. McLeod had orders to prepare the vital portage between the Maumee and Wabash Rivers. Enlisting the help of the traders who lived there, they cleared the upper reaches of these rivers and improved the portage trail.

Once Hamilton's force cleared the portage and began their descent, men from the Indian Department under one of the Dequindre brothers went ahead gathering intelligence, looking for enemy outposts, and seizing anyone who might alert the Americans of their advance. Other Indian Department men fanned out, eliciting support of additional Native warriors.

The Indian Department did its job well. On 17 December Hamilton's army swept into Vincennes unopposed and captured the two-man American garrison without a fight. To secure his position, Hamilton sent out Indian Department parties in several directions. Matthew Elliot, for instance, took an Indian war party down to the Ohio River, and Charles Beaubien went to scout the French towns on the Mississippi.

Hamilton intended to strike Clark at Cahokia and Kaskaskia next. However, the season for military activities was at an end. With winter coming on, the lieutenant governor decided to wait for spring before continuing his offensive. Sure he was beyond Clark's reach, he sent fifty-seven Detroit militiamen home.

Though Clark lacked supplies and men, he did not want for boldness to counter Hamilton's moves. To augment his force, he recruited a company of men from the French settlements along the Mississippi. Then the American colonel pushed his soldiers to Vincennes on a forced march. He arrived there on 22 February 1779 and caught Hamilton off guard. Clark's daring assault gave Hamilton the impression he was outnumbered. Clark took advantage of this notion and demanded that the British surrender.

The lieutenant governor assembled his men, more than half of whom were French militiamen from Detroit, and asked if they would "defend the King's colours to the last extremity." The British regulars, Hamilton wrote, "to a man declared they would stand to the last for the honour of their Country. . . . The French hung their heads . . . some said it was hard they should fight against their friends and relations [Illinois French] who they could see had joined the Americans." With the majority of his garrison ill-disposed to fight, Hamilton surrendered.

Clark sent Hamilton and several key Indian Department men off to prison in Virginia. The Detroit militiamen expected the same fate. Instead, Clark allowed them to return home if they took an oath of neutrality. They were even promised boats, supplies, and arms if they accepted the offer. The vast majority of the Detroit men took advantage of these generous terms, foreswore participating in further hostilities, and left for their respective points of origin.

This magnanimous gesture left a favorable impression on the Detroiters. Clark noted that from this point on he "had Spies, disguised as traders, constant to and from Detroit[.] I learnt they answered every purpose that I could have wished for, by prejudicing their friends in favour of America."

Clark's decisive victory dampened Indian enthusiasm for action. Bands of warriors recruited by Charles Langlade and Charles Gautier and by Louis Chevallier—who were on their way to join Hamilton and who were poised to strike Cahokia—turned around and went home.

Clark's victory at Vincennes put the British on alert. Detroit was vulnerable. The British officer left in charge at Detroit after Hamilton's departure, Captain Richard Lernoult, felt concerned about this situation and began to shore up his defenses as early as the fall of 1778. This is when he commenced building a new and more formidable fort. Through the winter and into the spring he hurried construction along, pressing all able-bodied men in town to work three days out of every nine. The British merchants and traders willingly pitched in; the French had to be coerced. By April of 1779 they finished building the stronghold and christened it Fort Lernoult.

Through the spring and summer of 1779, Lernoult sent Indian Department scouts out to gather intelligence of American movements. The Indian Department also worked tirelessly to keep the Ohio Indians loyal and to restore the allegiance of the Wabash Indians who had been disaffected by Hamilton's defeat.

Lernoult believed he needed reinforcements. In March he wrote De Peyster at Michilimackinac asking for assistance. In response, De Peyster directed his Indian Department to send Ottawa and Chippewa braves to Detroit.

De Peyster also had concerns about Clark coming north. The Michilimackinac Indian Department concentrated on reconnoitering the American colonel. In June their contacts told them that Clark's men at Cahokia and Vincennes were on the way to Detroit. To stall the Cahokia contingent, De Peyster sent Charles Gautier and a few Indians to burn the "fort" at Peoria.

Just after Gautier's departure, De Peyster received word that Clark's men were going to rendezvous at St. Joseph (Niles) before striking Detroit. Taking quick action, the British commander assembled at the Straits a force of twenty of his soldiers, sixty traders and militiamen, and two hundred warriors. Commanded by one of De Peyster's officers, Lieutenant Thomas Bennet, and by Charles Langlade, this little army shoved off by canoe for the St. Joseph River valley. They arrived there and scouted around for Clark. The only thing they discovered was that Clark was not on the move to Detroit. This sortie was one of the few times the Michilimackinac militia is mentioned. Unfortunately, no names are given.

On 4 October 1779 Michilimackinac's lieutenant governor, Patrick Sinclair, finally arrived at his post and relieved De Peyster, who in turn had orders to take command at Detroit. Sinclair had been appointed to the post back in 1775 but on his journey there was arrested in New York. The day after Sinclair arrived at Michilimackinac he made a momentous decision: he would move the fort to a more defensible position on Mackinac Island. Like the building of Fort Lernoult in Detroit, the British utilized civilian labor in the construction. This project involved more than just building a fort, however. The entire town of Michilimackinac would be moved to the island too.

It was not long before the war touched Sinclair. Early in February 1780 London sent a directive instructing the western British posts to strike Spanish territory. Spain controlled the mouth of the Mississippi and everything to the west of the river. From the beginning of the war Spanish agents from St. Louis actively courted Indian favor on the British side of the river. Now Spain was in the war against the British. Mackinac, and to a lesser extent, Detroit, were the only British posts in striking distance of the upper reaches of Spanish territory.

Sinclair decided on a bold stroke—the capture of St. Louis. He planned a two-pronged operation. First, from Detroit De Peyster would launch an assault on the Americans in Kentucky to draw Clark's forces east from the Illinois Country. Then Sinclair's men would overrun St. Louis in a surprise attack.

In March of 1780 De Peyster assembled a detachment commanded by Captain Henry Bird from the King's Eighth Regiment. Out of a force of 150 whites, 86 were Detroit militiamen under Captains Louis de Joncaire de Chabert and Isidore Chene. Thirty-one of these militiamen volunteered; the remainder were "ordered to go."

Augmenting the soldiers and militia were as many as a thousand warriors. The objective was Clark's supply depot at the Falls of the Ohio (Louisville, Kentucky). On the journey down, the Native people balked at attacking this fort on hearing it had just been reinforced. Instead, they had a mind to attack settlements on the Licking River in Kentucky. As always, the Indians were not pawns of the British in these operations but independent agents at best under the council of the Indian Department. Captain Bird judged he had to acquiesce to the Indians' plan. They attacked and easily captured Martin's Station and Ruddle's Station before returning to Detroit laden with plunder.

Sinclair set the attack on St. Louis in motion in February 1780. Only able to spare a token number of soldiers, Sinclair had to count on his Indian Department men, the traders, and the Native people to carry out his plan. In the first move, in February Jean Baptiste Cadot and Alexander Kay, both prominent traders, went among the Indians along the south shore of Lake Superior. Joseph Rocque gathered the more distant Sioux. Emanuel Hesse—a trader who operated out of Prairie du Chien and a man who seems to have held the rank of captain in the militia—had orders to round up Winnebago, Sac, and Fox warriors. Hesse had an entourage of traders and the traders' employees, many of whom were members of the militia. After Chief Matchekewis and his Mackinac braves as well as a sergeant and two privates from Sinclair's garrison rendezvoused at Prairie du

Chien, the motley force of about twelve hundred descended the Mississippi to St. Louis. They expected this to be a surprise attack and an easy conquest.

The Spanish and the Americans knew of the coming attack. When Hesse's men assaulted St. Louis on 26 May 1780, to their horror they faced a strengthened stockade and a tower equipped with artillery. Native warriors were masters at raid and ambush, not direct frontal assault. This was not their kind of fight. So in the face of a stiff defense and large-bore weapons, they retreated. The traders followed the Indians, and the engagement turned into a plundering foray. Hesse next turned his contingent to the American stockade across the Mississippi River at Cahokia. They, too, were ready and handily repulsed him. The British forces had no recourse but to turn for home.

Before Sinclair knew the outcome of the St. Louis expedition, he decided to remove a thorn in his side: the residents of St. Joseph (Niles). They and their Potawatomis neighbors had evidenced too many inclinations to the Rebels' ally, the French. Therefore, in May, Sinclair dispatched Joseph Louis Ainsse to bring Louis Chevallier Sr. and forty-eight settlers there to Mackinac where they would be under his watchful eyes.

Traders still used St. Joseph as a depot, and the Americans saw it as a target. Early in December, 1780, Jean Baptiste Hamelin led a body of sixty men from Cahokia in a raid on what was left of St. Joseph. They captured a handful of traders and got away with fifty bales of merchandise. Hot on their trail, though, was Lieutenant Louis Dequindre from the Detroit Indian Department. Rallying warriors to his aid, they caught up with Hamelin's forces. In the resulting skirmish Dequindre's men killed four of their foes, wounded two, and captured seven.

The next month the Spanish headed off for St. Joseph too. Leaving from St. Louis, Captain Eugene Pouré commanded a troop of sixty-five militiamen and sixty Indians. The liaison to the Native warriors was none other than Louis Chevallier Jr., whose father served with the British Indian Department! In the early morning of 12 February 1781 Pouré's men took the post by surprise, capturing everyone there. Pouré and his men lingered only one day, just long enough for the captain to raise the Spanish flag and claim St. Joseph and the surrounding territory for the Spanish king. Again, Lieutenant Dequindre was nearby. He tried but could not convince the local Potawatomis to rally behind him and give chase.

The only other major action in the Old Northwest in 1781 was to the southeast of Detroit. Along the Tuscarawas River in present-day Ohio, Moravian missionaries had three villages of Christian Delaware Indians. These Native people declared themselves neutral in the British/American conflict; the missionaries, however, had pro-Rebel leanings. In early spring De Peyster sent Matthew Elliott with a handful of loyalists, a few Detroit French, and about 140 Indians to bring these Native converts closer to Detroit.

The Indians and the missionaries moved to their assigned new home near present-day Mount Clemens, but many of the Indians returned to their old quarters by the following year. This proved to be their undoing. Out to put a stop to the endless Indian raids and ambushes, in March 1782 the Pennsylvania militia massacred the Christian Delaware Indians living in Ohio. This wanton killing enraged the Native population. As a result, 1782 saw some of the fiercest raids led out of Detroit during the entire war.

This massacre was fresh in everyone's mind in May when Colonel William Crawford led a detachment from Pennsylvania toward Sandusky to strike the Indians again. British Captain William Caldwell with a company of Butler's Rangers, several hundred warriors, and certainly a good representation from the Detroit Indian Department, went out to meet Crawford. The two day engagement started on 1 June. By the night of the fifth the Americans felt they were in a desperate position and planned an orderly retreat. This exit degenerated into a rout, with the Indians falling on the stragglers. Among the prisoners was Colonel Crawford himself. In a famous incident witnessed by both Simon Girty and Matthew Elliott, revenge-hungry Delaware slowly tortured the American colonel to death.

The successes of the British and Indians goaded the Americans to strike at Indian villages along the Ohio. In turn, the British and Indians launched a major attack into Kentucky once again. With Captain William Caldwell in charge, a force of thirty "rangers"—undoubtedly Indian Department men—and more than two hundred Indians from as far away as Mackinac, struck Bryan's Station (near present-day Lexington) in central Kentucky in mid-August. The Americans put up a stiff defense and obliged Caldwell to retreat. The Americans pursued.

Hoping to turn the tables on the Americans, Caldwell chose an Indian tactic. He placed his men on advantageous ground and then lured the Americans into an ambush. The result was wholesale slaughter. Caldwell's "rangers" and the Indians mowed down the flower of the Kentucky militia while suffering only minor casualties. The victory was so complete that Battle of the Blue Licks, 19 August 1782, would long be remembered in the annals of frontier warfare.

William Caldwell, Simon Girty, and Matthew Elliott are the men from Detroit who are mentioned in all of the literature as being there. There were some Michigan French there too. As is the case with most actions, these individuals are seldom mentioned by name. In this fight, though, a couple of names are known. Claude Labutte of Detroit died in the battle, and Charles Langlade Jr. and Antoine Ignace from Mackinac accompanied the Mackinac Indians on the expedition.

Blue Licks was the last major action in the Great Lakes theater during the Revolutionary War. In April of 1783 De Peyster received notice to cease all hostilities, as negotiations were successfully drawing to a close in Europe. An agreement ending hostilities was soon reached, and by September De Peyster had a copy of the peace treaty in hand. The document contained bad news for the British and devastating terms for the Native people. Although the Americans only had a toehold in Vincennes and the Illinois Country, the treaty negotiators awarded the Americans the entire Northwest—including Detroit and even the Mackinac region.

The burden of closing out the war in the Old Northwest fell on the Mackinac and Detroit Indian Departments. They had to spread this bitter notice among the tribes and convince them to halt the fighting. This was no small task. The Indians were incredulous. Why the British conceded anything to the Rebels, especially since their operations in the Northwest during 1782 were so overwhelmingly successful, could not be comprehended. The Native people were confused and felt abandoned by their white allies.

To add insult to injury, the various tribes were incensed when the Indian Department men told them that the British were going to reduce the rations and presents that had been a keystone of their military alliance with the British.

At the end of the Revolutionary War the Indian Department was greatly reduced but not disbanded. Most of the Michigan men who served the Crown returned to rather anonymous lives in the Indian fur trade. In this occupation they still trod the expanses of the Northwest territory and kept their close association with the Native people, traits that made them key players during the war. These Michigan men and the Native people still held on to the conceded land. Both hoped the Americans would leave them to live and trade undisturbed, as they had for generations.

Michigan in the Indian War, 1783–1796

The Revolutionary War resolved nothing in the Northwest. The Indian war of 1783–96 was, in reality, a continuation of that conflict. Indeed, with the exception of a few changes in personalities, essentially the same cast of characters came to center stage in this struggle.

A potent mix of factions made the Northwest a tinderbox. On top of the old enmities simmering from the Revolution, now the United States had standing as a sovereign nation and the British held several strategic posts—among them Detroit and Mackinac—within its borders. The British kept these posts in retaliation for what they claimed was American noncompliance of the 1783 Treaty of Paris. Lingering at these posts gave the British time to better consolidate the defenses of Canada, to appease their Native allies in the Northwest, and to continue to reap the wealth of the fur trade there. The Native people had even more at stake. They understood that the peace treaty agreed to by their British partner forfeited their lands to the Americans. The Indians stood firm in their resolve that the Ohio River was the border between red and white.

In the vortex of this storm, the people of what was to be Michigan worked and traded. Just as in the days of the Revolution, the livelihood of nearly every settler here—the fur trade—brought Michigan's people into constant contact with both the British and the Indians. On one end of the cycle, the Natives supplied the furs, and on the other end, the British merchants in Montreal purchased the furs and supplied trade goods.

This was not a matter of the Indians coming to settlements to trade. The traders, fluent in Indian tongues and knowledgeable of Native customs, spent entire seasons in Indian villages. Just as in the days of the Revolutionary War, this meant that a large number of Michigan men had an intimate familiarity with the Indians, had economic ties with the English, and knew the disputed terrain better than any other whites. This also meant that at any time there was a minimum of one hundred Michigan traders in Indian villages scattered all over the disputed area north of the Ohio River.

Taking these factors into account, it might seem certain that the people of Michigan would automatically side with the British and Indians if hostilities arose with the Americans. The experiences of the Revolutionary War proved that this was not assured. The settlers of Michigan had their own agenda.

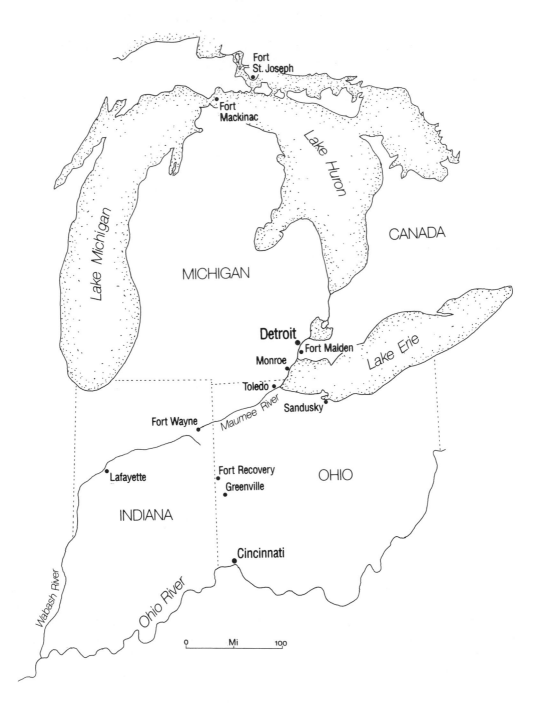

Theater of Operations, Indian War. (*Cartography by Sherm Hollander*)

The character of the settlements since the Revolution was only slightly different. Over four-fifths of the people still claimed French-Canadian parentage, and the French language and culture still dominated. Just as before, Detroit and Mackinac were the primary population centers. The major differences now were that St. Joseph (Niles) no longer existed as a white emplacement, and a major new settlement area, the River Raisin, had come on the scene. The River Raisin settlement (now Monroe), centered on the river of that name about forty miles south of Detroit. Founded in the mid-1780s, this was a fast-growing community composed almost exclusively of French families from Detroit and Quebec.

Just before the close of the Revolution, a census taken of Detroit (both sides of the river) enumerated 2,191 residents. It is estimated that at the same time there were about 200 people residing year round at Mackinac Island and vicinity. When the Americans took control in 1796, they counted 1,765 people living on the American side of the Detroit River and another 450 individuals at the River Raisin. Mackinac Island still had approximately 200 people.

The British organized militia companies at Mackinac, Detroit, and the River Raisin. Several of these companies did see action in the Indian Wars. Precise numbers of Michigan men or companies at Detroit and Mackinac at the close of the Revolution are not known. This information is available for the Indian Department, however.

Muster rolls show eight men in the Indian Department at Mackinac and twenty-six at Detroit in May 1783. Just as in the days of the Revolution, this quasi-military branch of the British colonial establishment wielded more influence and power among the Native people than the militia and the British military.

The Indian Department men were far more than just messengers, support artisans keeping weapons repaired, scouts, translators, and commissary clerks distributing presents; these men orchestrated councils, mediated intertribal quarrels, built tribal alliances, and acted as cultural intermediaries between the red and white worlds. In war and peace, the Indian Department had the daunting task of convincing the Native people to conform to official British policy.

Both hopes of peace and ominous portents of war clouded the treaty ending the American Revolution. In April of 1783, Colonel Arent Schuyler De Peyster, British commandant at Detroit, received orders to cease hostilities. Negotiations abroad had just brought an end to the Revolutionary War. Now De Peyster and his counterpart at Mackinac, Captain Daniel Robertson, had to rein in the Native warriors who were anxious to repeat their stunning victories of 1782. This job called for all of the skill and finesse the Indian Department could muster as it was obvious to all that the Natives would be incredulous of the settlement terms and would probably take offense that their British allies had bargained away their homeland.

To spread the news of peace, the Indian Department had orders to summon several intertribal councils. The council held at Sandusky beginning 5 September 1783 was typical of these meetings. Alexander McKee and his compatriot Indian Department men gathered the lower Great Lakes tribes together at the behest of Sir John Johnson, British superintendent of Indian Affairs. At the council the Indian Department liberally distributed "presents," and alcohol was available. The culmination was Sir Johnson's speech to the Natives. Johnson could not be there, so McKee, the most prominent of the Detroit Indian Department men, both translated and delivered his speech.

Johnson's words to the assembled nations summed up the tenuous situation and foretold coming problems. Johnson told the Native allies that he would "take the tomahawk out of their hand, though he would not remove it out of sight or far from them, but lay it down carefully by their side, that they might have it convenient to use in defense of their rights and property if they were invaded or molested by the Americans."

The Indian Department skillfully scripted the council, and Johnson's proposal was well received. Reassured that the British would not totally abandon them to the Americans, the Indians conformed to the British wishes and abandoned the warpath. The British, on the other hand, hoped their Indian councils would result in continued peaceful association with the indigenous people. They could not afford to alienate these allies, whom they still considered as a key to the defense of Canada.

The British did have some fear that the Indians might turn on them. This was potentially a problem at Mackinac, where the garrison was reduced to a skeleton force in 1783. To police the walled town below the fort, the British utilized the Mackinac militia from 1783 to 1784. Nothing came of the perceived threat, and Mackinac remained relatively quiet even through the height of the fighting in the Ohio Country in the next decade.

The Americans made the first move in the conflict in the Ohio Country. They had designs on this Indian land. They considered the Native people and their land as conquered. In a series of treaties with the Indians from 1784 to 1786, the Americans sought to break the Indian unity and obtain land in a piecemeal fashion.

First came the 1784 Treaty of Fort Stanwix. In this treaty, negotiated in upstate New York, the Americans convinced the Iroquois to cede Algonkian Indian land in the upper reaches of the Ohio River. The next year the Americans held a treaty council at Fort McIntosh in extreme western Pennsylvania. In the resulting agreement pro-American leaders from the Wyandot, Delaware, and Ojibwa tribes ceded territory north of the Ohio River. A peace faction of the Shawnee made similar concessions in the Treaty of Fort Finney in 1786.

These treaties set off a whole chain of events. American backwoodsmen thought this immediately opened up Indian lands. The result was an irreversible tide of settlers crossing the Ohio River. The treaties also broke Indian unity. The majority of the Shawnee and the upper Wabash tribes thought their brethren who had signed the treaties violated their sacred land. The Indians who had not agreed to surrender their territory pledged their blood to defend the Ohio River boundary. To push the Americans back, in 1786 the nonsignatory tribes opened up guerrilla warfare on American settlements. In a swift response to these raids, Kentuckians organized two expeditions aimed at the hostile Indians in the fall of 1786. A column under George Rogers Clark targeting the Wabash tribes failed miserably. Men under Benjamin Logan did capture and burn two principal Shawnee towns.

In the midst of all of the activity in 1786, several of the former key officers in the Detroit Indian Department emerged from their "semi-retirement" in the fur trade and resumed active duty. Among these were Matthew Elliott and William Caldwell. Elliott and most likely the other Indian Department officers held frequent parlays with the Native people, counseling them on their dealings with the Americans, promoting British policy, and gathering intelligence.

Just before 1786 drew to a close, the Indians held a grand council at Detroit. General Logan's raid on the Shawnee villages was fresh on their minds. Joseph Brant, famed Iroquois sachem, presided at the meeting. Brant sized up the situation and eloquently argued for Indian unity in the face of the encroaching Americans. Brant's arguments won the day, but the resulting Indian confederation lacked strength.

Two years after the Detroit council, Brant met with the Americans to discuss the Ohio boundary line. Brant stood firm on this question, and the talks broke off. A month later, in January of 1789, the Americans called a treaty council that excluded the intractable Shawnee, Miami, and Mohawk nations. The agreement that resulted, the Treaty of Fort Harmar, did nothing more than reconfirm previous boundary settlements.

The summer and fall of 1789 saw the disaffected tribes take up the tomahawk again. The raids were so fierce that President Washington could not ignore them. He ordered his Revolutionary War compatriot, General Josiah Harmar, to retaliate in force. Assembling a motley army of undisciplined militia and ill-trained regulars at Fort Washington (modern Cincinnati) in the autumn of 1790, Harmar set off for the Miamis' villages at the headwaters of the Maumee.

The chief of the Miamis, Little Turtle, watched Harmar's plodding army inch north. Outnumbered by the Americans, Little Turtle ordered the abandonment of his villages and the small settlement of Detroit based traders at Kikionga (present-day Fort Wayne). Harmar's soldiers were spoiling for a fight, but all that greeted them when they arrived at Kikionga on 15 October were empty lodges. The disappointed soldiers turned the expedition into a pillaging foray. The Americans congratulated themselves on this handy victory.

On the night of 17 October, however, the Indians retaliated by driving off most of Harmar's packhorses and some cavalry mounts. Anxious to strike back at the Miamis, Harmar ordered out two reconnaissance patrols. The first, commanded by Lieutenant Colonel James Trotter, encountered only two braves. The second foray went out on 19 October. In this mission Colonel John Hardin took 180 soldiers out on a sortie to locate the Indians. Little Turtle's warriors ambushed Hardin's men. Nearly to a man the militia fled in mortal fear. A company of regulars in the troop held their ground, but without support the Indians annihilated them. This turn of events so demoralized Harmar's army that it destroyed the effectiveness of his force, and Harmar withdrew.

One day's march out of Kikionga, Harmar received intelligence that the Miami were filtering back into their destroyed towns. Anxious to salvage his army's honor, Harmar ordered a midnight raid to catch the Indians by surprise. The vigilant Natives were watching Harmar's moves, and his 400-man detachment rode into an ambush at Kikionga. The fighting was desperate. The U.S. regulars, suffering 83 percent casualties, bore the brunt of the clash. After Little Turtle's braves had done their worst, the remnants of the regulars and the militia beat back an Indian advance. The Americans could not hold on to their temporary advantage, however, and they retired from the field leaving behind their dead and even some wounded.

Harmar's expedition was a disaster that gave all sides pause to think. Little Turtle and the Shawnee chief Blue Jacket went to Detroit to plead to Major John Smith to provision their people made destitute of food by Harmar's raid. They also demanded the arms, ammunition, and soldiers the British alluded would be forthcoming to their Native American allies. Although providing food was no problem, on the question of other support Smith was officially evasive.

While Smith, in Detroit, dodged the question of military aid, McKee—representing the British Indian Department from his headquarters at the Rapids of the Maumee (modern Toledo)—openly supported the tribal forces. Indeed, McKee's house at the Rapids became a focal point for Indian councils and for the war itself. For example, here in November of 1790 the Delaware expressed their determination that they were "going off to the [American] forts on this side of the Ohio River to see what we can do in defense of our lands." This ushered in a winter season of raids on American settlements. The Indian Department (Detroit men) supported these raids, many times sending advisors along. Simon Girty, the most reviled man in the Indian Department, took a visible role in these attacks.

While the Indian Department supported Native belligerence, it did realize that there were propitious times for peace. In the wake of the Indian victories, the official British policy was to promote improved relations with the United States. The British and Indians now could negotiate from a position of strength. At a tribal council at McKee's headquarters at the Maumee Rapids in June 1791, McKee encouraged a negotiated settlement. The Shawnee and Miamis rejected the idea because this would surely mean concessions of land to the Americans.

In June 1791, as the Indian war moved ever closer to Detroit, the British took stock of the forces available to them. At Detroit they counted seven militia companies and a total of 631 men on the muster rolls. On the River Raisin there was one company of 110 militiamen.

The captains of these militia companies mustered their men to gauge their readiness. The resulting muster was very revealing. First, only about two-thirds of the men turned out. A third of the men were in the Indian country. The captains asked each man two questions. Would extended service do irreparable damage to crops or business? Would they be willing to provide a mount and serve as cavalry? The answers to these questions exposed divisions in the community. In Detroit, no one in the three predominantly French Canadian companies stepped forward to volunteer in any capacity. The other Detroit companies, such as John Askin's, seem to have been more Anglo-oriented and were markedly more responsive to the call. Among these companies, sixty-seven men announced they could serve as infantry and seventy-eight were ready to go as cavalry.

Reflecting on the differences between the French-Canadian *habitants* and the English-speaking residents revealed by this muster in Detroit, a correspondent to the Canadian lieutenant governor observed,

> The result [of this militia muster] strongly marks the genius of the two people. The British and Irish traders, flattered with an appearance of con-

fidence, declared themselves ready to march and would not even offer an individual excuse. . . . The idea of a cavalry being suggested, one company agreed to mount themselves. The [French] Canadians on the other hand . . . to a man refused voluntarily to encounter fatigue or danger without further inducement.

The correspondent went on to say, however, that the French Canadians "would, on receiving their orders, obey without a murmur, . . . and once in the field a single example of severity for breach of discipline would make them useful partisans."

The results of the muster on the River Raisin were different. In general, Joseph Porlier *dit* Benac's company of French-Canadians were receptive to the call. Perhaps the closer geographic proximity to the turmoil had something to do with this. Or it could have been that the people here were more tied to the well-being of the Indians and the fur trade.

The British and Indians did have reason to be concerned. The new commander of the American forces—none other than the governor of the Northwest Territory, Arthur St. Clair, had ambitious plans to reverse the previous year's humiliating losses. While he trained a cadre of regulars, assembled militia auxiliaries, and accumulated supplies, he sent a detachment of mounted Kentucky militiamen to capture and burn the Wea Indian/French post of Ouiatenon (modern Lafayette, Indiana). Brigadier General Charles Scott accomplished this with ease in June of 1791. In August another detachment of mounted Kentuckians forayed north to destroy several Miami towns on the Wabash upriver from Ouiatenon. As in the previous raid, they handily captured the villages, killed a handful of braves, and took a score or more Indian women and children captive before destroying the villages and burning the cornfields.

The Native warriors anticipated another season of success too. In August a full force of the tribes assembled at McKee's headquarters at the Maumee Rapids. Generously provisioned and armed from the British commissary in Detroit, they saw the presence of their longtime Indian Department advisors McKee, Elliott, and Girty as official support of their endeavor against the Americans.

Joseph Brant and six other chiefs went to Quebec, where they asked the British governor to build a fort at the Rapids of the Maumee and questioned the officials as to how much support from the British they could expect. Considering their position strong, the Indians also talked to the British about suing for peace. They even expressed a willingness to concede the upper reaches of the Ohio River.

Peace was not to be. The American raids on the Wabash River villages in June and August and the departure of St. Clair's army north in early September made the Indians fearful for their villages. Red tobacco, a sign for warriors to gather, circulated among the tribes. With Simon Girty as their advisor, braves under the leadership of Little Turtle and Blue Jacket followed the progress of St. Clair's army and waited for a favorable opportunity to strike.

Ill equipped, full of questionably useful militia, and plagued by desertions, St. Clair's cumbersome army of 2,300 marched north toward the Miami towns. On 3 November 1791 this brigade, now reduced to 1,400 men, made camp near the headwaters of the

Wabash River in what is now extreme western Ohio. Under cover of night, just over a thousand of Little Turtle's and Blue Jacket's warriors took up positions and waited for dawn.

At first light there was a hideous din, the war cry of a thousand braves, followed by volleys that seemed to come from nowhere. The Indians quickly pressed a militia unit, which fled through the American camp, throwing all into disorder. By the time the Americans responded with their artillery, volley fire, and fixed bayonets, the Indians had enveloped the entire camp. It was pure panic as the battle became a rout. Abandoning everything—artillery, provisions, weapons, and even the wounded—the Americans were a terrified pack in a headlong retreat.

The Indians completely destroyed St. Clair's army in a loss unequaled even by the Custer massacre of 1876. The Americans reported about 650 dead and missing; somewhere near 500 did manage to escape. The Indians counted 21 killed and 40 wounded. St. Clair's defeat was a masterful execution of the Indians' tactic of surprise and envelope. In this maneuver their overwhelming success was usually assured if they could throw their opponent into a panic. Among the victorious warriors was at least one Indian Department officer. Simon Girty reportedly led the Wyandot in combat and shared the spoils of war.

After this stunning Indian victory, all sides poised themselves for the next move and actually talked about peace. At Indian councils—usually held under the eyes of Indian Department officers—the divisive question still was whether to compromise on the Ohio River boundary. The Miami, Delaware, and Shawnee held firm against any concession. Joseph Brant and other peace-minded Natives were willing to concede this in return for a settlement.

The Americans attempted to lure Brant and the more concession-minded tribes into negotiations. They realized that these negotiations themselves would drive a wedge in the Indian alliance. While there was no meeting, there was a growing schism in Indian unity. The Americans also tried sending spies, scouts, and peace emissaries into the Indian country. Some of these were killed or captured.

The British also thought this might be a time to promote peace. Perhaps with a few concessions they might be able to convince the Americans to establish an Indian buffer state in the Ohio country. This would satisfy the British feelings of duty toward the Indians as well as provide security for the western Canadian frontier.

In the end the Indians decided to invite the Americans to a treaty council to be held at Lower Sandusky in the summer of 1793. The Americans accepted the invitation and even agreed to allow the British Indian Department to organize the meeting and have advisors present. In June 1793, just before the treaty council convened, the Detroit Indian Department, under McKee's direction, assembled a grand council of the tribes at the Rapids of the Maumee to discuss strategy. The question of compromise on the Ohio boundary proved too divisive, however, and Indian unity faltered. The situation was so bad that when the American peace commissioners sailed in on Lake Erie from Niagara, the British kept them at the mouth of the Detroit River and only allowed exchanges of notes. The Americans never met with the Indians, and this last hope for peace evaporated.

While there was a chance that the peace initiatives would succeed, the Americans ordered a cessation of military activity. When the negotiations failed to materialize, though, the Americans were ready for action. General Anthony Wayne, a soldier with a reputation for tactical genius and stern discipline, now had the reins of the army. He personally supervised nearly a year of rigorous training of this new force of 1,200 soldiers, known as the Legion of the United States. In October the Legion marched north out of Cincinnati to well-supplied depots, and by Christmas Wayne's soldiers were building a fort (called Recovery) at the site of St. Clair's defeat. From these well-secured positions Wayne prepared for the 1794 campaign.

Wayne's movements caused great concern for the British and the Indians. Not wanting to meet Wayne at the very gates of Detroit, in April the British commenced constructing a forward position at the Rapids of the Maumee. The building of Fort Miamis (as the British named it) emboldened the Native warriors and enraged Wayne. The Indians saw it as tangible evidence of British support, and the Americans interpreted it as a flagrant violation of the 1783 Treaty of Paris.

Late in the spring large numbers of Indians came down from the Mackinac region and the area west of Lake Michigan. At a council at the Glaize River on the upper reaches of the Maumee, they made two momentous decisions: they would strike Wayne's supply column, and they would demand that the British officials and traders who sat in the council with them prove their solidarity by putting on Indian garb and fighting alongside them. Matthew Elliott of the Indian Department, an unnamed British officer, and a group of French and British Detroit-based traders agreed.

On the morning of 30 June 1794 the fight started with a commotion and random firing in the packhorse herd grazing outside Fort Recovery. The Americans sent their dragoons and a company of riflemen to reconnoiter and bring in the herd. In fierce combat, the Indians slaughtered them. Having tasted easy victory, the warriors foolishly stormed the fort itself. The Americans handily repulsed them, reversing their fortunes on the battlefield. The Indians kept up a desultory fire until the next morning when they retired, disappointed there was no easy conquest. Elliott, the British officer, and the traders did take part in the action; one "French-Canadian" trader was wounded. This French Canadian at the very least had Detroit connections. It was probably not unusual that a French Canadian trader was in the ranks in a fight. It was also not unusual that the British failed to mention his name.

Realizing the demoralizing effect this defeat had on the Native warriors, Wayne moved forward. By early August he poised his army on the Maumee, ready to strike. The British did all they could to prepare their tribal allies and Fort Miamis to receive the blow from Wayne's Legion. McKee and his Indian Department men did their utmost to gather, provision, and arm the indigenous combatants. From the lowest echelon in the Indian Department to the highest levels of the British government, the hope was that the Indians would be able to defeat the Federal troops.

The British now did everything they could to speed the construction of Fort Miamis. The building of this fort gave the British cause to consider the role of the Michigan militia in this unfolding affair. The 120 British regulars at Miamis were not enough to keep the construction on schedule. The British looked to the Detroit militia and especially to the unit on the River Raisin as the most available source of labor. Earlier, militia lieutenant François Baby had ordered the River Raisin militia to the fort to assist with building. The majority refused to go. They told Baby they only answered to "the orders of the King." However, as Wayne approached closer to the Maumee Rapids in August, the British had about 100 militiamen from Detroit and the River Raisin there on corvee duty.

Ever since the reverses at Fort Recovery, the Indians' fortunes seemed on the wane. Disheartened, large numbers of western and northern braves returned home. Wayne's first conquest of the huge Indian villages and fields at the Glaize River bode ill for the Miamis and Shawnee. The Federals' destruction of the winter food and homes of hundreds of Native families was a severe blow.

As Wayne continued pressing forward, the situation at the Maumee Rapids grew urgent. McKee and the Indian Department did all they could to rally even more warriors and to feed the braves and the Indian families there. The Indians, in turn, looked to McKee and asked if the British were going to honor their promise to support them. At McKee's bequest, his son Thomas accompanied Matthew Elliott on a trip to Detroit in August 1794 to impress the commander there, Lieutenant Colonel Richard England, of the desperate need for more men, provisions, and ammunition and to apprise him of the impending threat.

The British were in a dilemma. Authorizing regular British soldiers to join the Native ranks was a flagrant act of war. The British hoped the Michigan militia could get them out of this predicament. Wayne's advance to the Glaize River arguably constituted an invasion of the territory. In such an event the British commandant could call out the entire home guard. Thinking this might further provoke Wayne, Colonel England at first activated one company of militiamen—fifty-three men under Lieutenant Colonel William Caldwell—and sent them to Fort Miamis with orders to stand by the Native warriors. England held the remainder of the Detroit militia in readiness. Four days before the battle with Wayne, England called on the River Raisin militia to send an armed detachment to the Maumee Rapids. Captain Charles Reaume and thirty-seven men responded.

The Indians planned to engage Wayne using one of their most effective maneuvers—ambush. On the approach to Fort Miamis and just a few miles from the post, there was a perfect setting to stage this trap. Several years before a tornado had turned this place into a morass of twisted and fallen trees. A couple years of growth on top of this provided perfect cover. Here Blue Jacket deployed his 1,300 braves and about 70 Detroit and River Raisin militiamen.

On 20 August 1794 Wayne's army marched into the area of Fallen Timbers, about two miles southwest of present-day Maumee, Ohio, a suburb of Toledo. While advancing in battle order, the Kentucky militia at the point took a withering fire as they came to the thicket. In a repeat of the disasters that befell Harmar and St. Clair, these militiamen bolted and in a panic fell back in great disorder. Smelling easy victory, impetuous Ottawa and Potawatomis warriors charged forward.

Instead of fear-stricken soldiers, the braves came squarely into Wayne's well-disciplined Legion. With bayonets fixed, the Federals turned the Indians back and pressed on into the tangled vegetation. In the fallen timbers they came face-to-face with the Wyandot and Michigan militia. These Natives and their allied militia poured heavy volleys into Wayne's men. The Legion reeled for only a moment before they returned fire, inflicting heavy casualties and forcing their opponents to retreat.

From this point on the battle was more of a skirmish as Wayne's army scattered the Indians. The only serious rear guard action involved the Wyandot and the Michigan militia again. These forces stood briefly, covering the Indians' retreat. This deed done, they too scattered.

The retreating Indians fell back to Fort Miamis, where they expected the British to harbor them. Here, in their hour of greatest need, the British firmly shut them out. This betrayal would be remembered for generations.

At the commencement of the action, about one hundred Michigan militia laborers were outside the fort clearing the perimeter. When the sound of the fighting drew near, they abandoned their work and withdrew into the defenses. From inside the fort they and the 160 British regulars witnessed Wayne's men scour the countryside, destroying everything in their path. Wayne himself taunted the British to open fire on him and his soldiers. The British could only hurl back insults, as they had strict orders not to create an international incident.

Three days after the fight, Wayne withdrew his army. Though not a fierce battle, Wayne thoroughly and decisively scattered and demoralized the Indians at what came to be called the Battle of Fallen Timbers. The Indian challenge to the Americans was gone.

The major British casualties were the loss of the confidence of the Indians and the elimination of the warriors as an effective force to shield the Crown's hold on Detroit, Mackinac, Niagara, and Oswego. Now it was only a matter of time before Great Britain surrendered these posts to the Americans as the treaty that ended the American Revolution stipulated.

The Michigan militia's conduct in the battle received mixed reviews. Teamed up with the Wyandot, they did provide some of the stiffest resistance in the fight and their rearguard action allowed many braves to escape. In the battle they lost four killed and one captured. Major William Campbell, the British commander at Fort Miamis, probably thinking of those militiamen on corvee duty who ran from their work detail as the battle approached the fort, said of the other Michigan men, "from the natural indolence and listlessness of some, and the timidity of others who ran away when things were likely to become serious, they have not afforded the assistance which might have been expected."

Those few militiamen and Indian Department men who are known to have been present at Fallen Timbers have interesting stories. Indian Department officers Alexander McKee, Matthew Elliott, and Simon Girty all participated in the battle only by observing it from a safe distance. All of these men had a track record with the Department that went back to the Revolution, and all three were the most active officers of the Department in the Indian Wars.

Captain Charles Reaume of the River Raisin militia served as an interpreter for the British Indian Department during the Revolution and probably was still associated with the Department in some way. Although we do not know what service he performed in the battle of Fallen Timbers, Major Campbell lauded him for his conduct.

Major William Caldwell, the British officer in charge at the Battle of the Blue Licks years before, received credit for commanding the militia at Fallen Timbers. One of his former sergeants at that Kentucky victory, Daniel McKillop (McKillip), was also present at the battle against Anthony Wayne. Now serving as a captain of the militia, he was one of the four to be mortally wounded in the Battle of Fallen Timbers. Another of the four was Charles Smith, who in civilian life was clerk of the court at Detroit.

The story of the one captured militiaman, Antoine Lasselle, is particularly interesting and gives insights into the militia in this action. Since before the American Revolution Lasselle, his brothers, and then his nephews plied the Indian fur trade in the Maumee-Wabash valleys. Just before Fallen Timbers, the British authorities questioned Antoine's loyalty. To prove where he stood, he, his nephew Jacques Lasselle, and seven or eight of his employees came to Fort Miamis to lend their hand in construction there.

As Wayne's army approached Fort Miamis, Antoine Lasselle became entangled in the Battle of Fallen Timbers. Antoine claimed to be a part of Caldwell's "Company of Refugees" during the engagement. Captured by the Americans, he was convicted of being a spy on the grounds he was found to be a white man in Indian garb. Jacques Lasselle, the future son-in-law of Blue Jacket, saved his uncle from execution by exchanging him for several Americans whom he had rescued from the Indians.

The Battle of Fallen Timbers proved a watershed for the Indians. This shattered their confederacy, temporarily eliminated them as a threat to the Americans, and embittered them toward the British. Just surviving the coming winter—not protecting their ancestral lands from the incursion of settlers—was the Indians' most immediate problem. Their fields destroyed, they had to look to the British Indian Department for provisions.

With remarkable unity the Native people recognized the ascendancy of the Americans. One by one the warriors, factions, and Indian nations came to make peace with Wayne. This does not mean that there was no maneuvering and machinations on all sides. Wayne, for example, selectively courted the tribesmen. To do this effectively, the General needed men familiar with the Native people. For the purpose of acquiring people with these backgrounds and contacts, Wayne created an informal Indian Department of his own.

A very high percentage of the men working for Wayne in this capacity were French traders from Detroit and the River Raisin. They intimately knew the Indians, and for the sake of the fur trade would do all they could to promote peace. One of Wayne's first recruits was Antoine Lasselle, the Detroit militiaman captured at Fallen Timbers. As a condition for his release, Lasselle went among both the Native people and the traders promoting a settlement with Wayne.

Among the other Michigan traders who worked for Wayne's unofficial Indian Department were Antoine's brother Hyacinthe and his nephews Jacques and François. The former captain of the British militia at the River Raisin, Joseph Porlier *dit* Benac, as well as François Pepin, Jean Baptiste Romaine *dit* Sanscrainte, François Navarre, George MacDougall, Pierre Menard, François La Fountaine, Chevalier Chabert, and Joseph Bourdeau were also associated with Wayne's department.

The people of the River Raisin settlement were particularly receptive to overtures from Wayne. Indeed, the British probably knew that even before Fallen Timbers several of the settlement's prominent citizens had made contact with Wayne and that a pro-American priest by the name of Thomas LeDru had gained favor there. Calling the Raisin's French *sans culottes,* a derogatory term used to describe the Paris revolutionaries, Colonel England sought to keep an eye on them.

Since soldiers were not a viable option for this job, Governor Simcoe himself convinced the Bishop of Quebec to assign a loyal priest there. Father Edmund Burke, a University of Paris-educated Irishman, was that loyal priest. He later admitted that his mission at the Raisin was "expressly to counteract the mackinations [sic] of Jacobin Emissaries whose influence amongst the settlers and numerous tribes . . . would have caused an insurrection."

Burke arrived at his parish in November of 1794. It was not long before his "violent" diatribes against the Americans, open counseling of the Natives, and his distribution of Indian Department provisions gave him away as a partisan. All but a small minority at the River Raisin hated him. It came to the point that Burke feared for his life so much that, as he wrote a friend in Ireland, he was "obliged to keep two Christian Indians well armed, who slept in my room together with a hardy Canadian."

Burke and the Indian Department both hoped to dissuade the Indians from attending the grand peace council Wayne scheduled for Greenville in June 1795. It was an impossible task. In October of 1794 word spread that the British and American treaty commissioners had initialed a treaty in which the Red Coats agreed to evacuate Detroit, Mackinac, Niagara, and Oswego in June 1796. Then, the most effective officer of the British Indian Department—Alexander McKee—fell ill in the spring of 1795 and, upon recovering a few months later, was sent east to serve in another post. Lacking leadership, and with the Crown's withdrawal a certainty, British-sponsored Indian councils failed and their influence waned.

Conversely, Wayne and his Indian Department met with great success in gathering the tribes for the peace conference at Greenville. At the council, Wayne proposed the Indians' acceptance of the 1789 Treaty of Fort Harmar as the basis for a document of peace. Though Little Turtle eloquently argued that this was not entirely equitable, the indigenous people had little choice but to accept Wayne's terms. In exchange for peace and guaranteed annuities from the federal government, they basically ceded their lands to the United States. Of the disputed territory, this left roughly only the northwestern corner of the present state of Ohio and most of Indiana in Native hands.

Michigan men in Wayne's service from Detroit and the River Raisin played important roles in the negotiations for this, the Treaty of Greenville. Eight of them—François La Fontaine, Antoine Lasselle, Jean Baptiste Beaubien, Louis Beaufait, Romaine Lachambre, François Pepin, Jean Baptiste Couture, and Pierre Navarre—were among the signed witnesses to the document. Jacques Lasselle, Maurice Moran, and Jean Baptiste Sanscrainte are the recognizable Michigan names on the list of official interpreters. Other Michigan men were there but did not sign the treaty.

After Wayne made peace with the Native tribes, next came the formalities of the British evacuation from Detroit and Mackinac. The Jay Treaty set a date of June 1796 for this transfer. In preparation, the Crown offered land on the Canadian side of the border for any loyal British subject who wished to leave the territory about to come under U.S. control. Many active partisans who fought under the Union Jack—and especially those in the British Indian Department—took advantage of this offer.

Because of logistical problems, the Americans did not raise their flag at Detroit until 11 July. Owing to similar difficulties, it was 1 September 1796 before the Stars and Stripes flew over the post at Mackinac. This tardy changing of the guard established a watershed in the history of Michigan territory. The act at once officially concluded a series of eighteenth-century Indian wars, signaled the end of British colonial rule in the Old Northwest, and marked the beginning of the American era in the region.

Quite obviously, the British surrendered posts vital to defense and commerce on the Great Lakes. The British also lost the confidence and trust of their Native allies—nations the British considered the cornerstone for the defense of western Canada. This had tremendous impact on British interests in the fur trade and caused them to rethink their military strategy.

The Indians lost more than just the land ceded in the Treaty of Greenville. Their relationship with the white population was altered. More and more, the whites with whom they now dealt—the Americans—did not seek Indian furs. They wanted Indian land.

This war put to rest the dispute the Americans had with the Indians about settlement on the right bank of the Ohio River. From this point on there would be no stopping the American tide of pioneers spilling over the Ohio River boundary. The posts the Americans gained were valuable real estate, giving the United States a firm grasp on the Great Lakes. Clearly, the new Federal Republic came out a winner.

The outcome for the people of Michigan was not so clear. The proceedings at Greenville did mean peace, and the people hoped peace translated into a return of prosperity in the fur trade. But a bright future was not certain because the trade remained dependent on business connections with British-held Montreal. At Mackinac many traders also interacted commercially with the Native people in British territory. This new economic relationship was unpredictable. For the French settlers here, this was still another government where their language and culture had no enduring place.

The Indian war of the 1790s was fought on Michigan's southern doorstep, and thus the residents of the territory could not help but get entangled in the conflict. In their many roles, they certainly had a significant impact on affairs. Those Michigan men in the British Indian Department—and especially those in the Detroit company of that establishment—were deeply involved in the struggle. They had direct contact with the Indians and were assigned to bring Indian actions into line with British policy regarding hostilities with the Americans. Though the Indian Department failed in the end, it is hard to imagine its members doing a better job under the circumstances. It is interesting to note that when Wayne assembled his own Indian Department, he recruited many Michigan agents who served him very effectively.

In the one instance where the Michigan militia is known to have served in combat during the late eighteenth-century Indian Wars—at Fallen Timbers—they received mixed reviews. The British accused those activated for corvee duty of cowardice in the face of aggressive enemy action. The militia units activated to bear arms, however, were one of the few bright spots in the entire battle for the British and Indian forces.

The sad thing is that this was not the last chapter in the Indian wars in the Northwest. A little more than a decade and a half later, many of the same partisans fighting for the same countries and causes took up arms on many of the same battlefields in the War of 1812.

The Period of Growing Tension, 1797–1811

Although the British vacated the area that is now Michigan in 1796, they continued to have a great deal of influence over the Indian population of the realm. This was accomplished in two principal ways. First, the British maintained nearly complete control of the mid-continent fur trade. The British and the Indians had, for three and a half decades, developed an economic relationship that did not cease with a change in landlords. The commercial ties between the two populations remained in place after the Union Jack had departed, giving the British a substantial amount of leverage with the tribes in the Great Lakes region.

British traders still wintered among the tribes in the Old Northwest where they bartered for the Indian's animal harvests from the rivers and forests. Additionally, traders of American citizenship were still largely dependent upon British connections in Montreal. Merchants at this Canadian commercial center bought the furs carried in by traders, and then supplied the men with goods for exchange with the Native people.

Two new British forts—Fort Malden near the mouth of the Detroit River and Fort St. Joseph on the eastern approach to the St. Mary's River—were the foci of the other British connection to the Indians on American soil. There were still British Indian Department officers at these posts. Indeed, many of these officers resided on the American side of the border before the British withdrew in 1796. The British used these officers to promote and maintain their ties with the red men. These officers regularly communicated with Native leaders and welcomed the American tribesmen to annual councils at these forts where they received food and presents.

The Yankees were deeply suspicious of British traders wintering on American soil. Furthermore, the British explanation that their gift giving to the Native people was an innocent exchange between old friends did not wash at all with the Americans. It was no secret that at the very least the British wanted to see the Old Northwest left as a preserve for Indians and fur-bearing creatures. To American eyes, then, British agents in Upper Canada were arming the Indians and encouraging the Native cause in an effort to realize this economic goal.

Canadian officials still figured the Northwestern tribes to be strategic to the defense of Canada, and a few British officials even mused over the possibility that the territory they had lost by the Treaty of 1783 could eventually be regained for the Crown. This ambition was promoted by deeds that could be interpreted as actively inciting Indian unrest by representatives of a foreign government. Though this kind of behavior was not very open or widespread, it did contribute to growing Anglo-American friction in the post-Indian War period.

While the Indians certainly relied upon the British for moral support and a variety of manufactured articles, they did not need any stimulus from outside sources to be upset with the Americans. All along the Ohio River and its northern tributaries white settlers continued to push into the lands that the Native people once called home. To further this migration, between 1800 and 1809 William Henry Harrison (governor of Indiana Territory) convinced some carefully selected Indian chiefs to cede large portions of Ohio and Indiana (33,000,000 acres) to the United States. In the eyes of dissident tribesmen, this surrender of ancestral lands and the ensuing advance of American pioneers was a creeping cancer destroying the very fabric of their culture.

Those seeking to halt this trend found their spokesman in Tenskwatawa, a Shawnee messiah and half brother to the famed Tecumseh. The Prophet, as Tenskwatawa was known, began spreading his revelations to the tribes in 1805. This was an Indian revival movement. The Prophet called his Native brethren to unite and return to the values and ways of their ancestors. He rejected white culture. Tenskwatawa preached that Indian lands were sacred and that those red men who bartered them away violated the precepts of "The Master of Life."

At a time when Indian culture was in chaos and disintegration, the Prophet's message hit a receptive chord. Native people by the hundreds flocked to him. This revitalization of the Indians of the Great Lakes and Ohio Valley region unnerved the Americans. Always suspicious of the British, many Yankees mistakenly saw their hand in this revival movement.

On the River Raisin this threat was acutely felt. Many of the French on the Raisin apparently knew Tecumseh well. Yet, in spite of this acquaintance they were very uneasy about the situation and decided to consider defensive measures. In the face of increased incidences of Indian depredations, on 6 June 1806, a council of officers of the Second Regiment met to decide on a course of action. The council resolved that all of the citizens of the River Raisin who wanted to express their determination to fight for the United States in any ensuing struggle should express this determination by wearing an eagle emblem and feather in their hat. More important though, the officers resolved to petition the territorial government to assist them in building a stockade with two blockhouses in the center of the settlement on the Raisin. This stockade would be called Wayne Stockade, and it would stand on the Raisin as the major defensive works there until the British would burn it in August 1812.

This uneasiness about peace in the Old Northwest was compounded by a crisis in Anglo-American relations. The two countries had been at odds for years over the British practice of stopping U.S. merchant vessels on the high seas and checking their crews in search of deserters from His Majesty's Navy. Whenever Royal Navy officers found such men on board vessels flying the stars and stripes, they arrested the offenders and either hanged them or sentenced them to a lifetime of service on a British warship.

Unfortunately, some British maritime officers were not willing to limit their searches to escaped seamen from His Majesty's navy. In addition to deserters from their own ranks, ship captains on occasion arrested and impressed into service our native-born sailors as well as naturalized American citizens. This gross violation of international law and U.S. sovereignty had many residents of Britain's former colonies ready for another war with their mother country.

This anger at the way Britain treated our merchant vessels on the high seas reached the limits of tolerance on 22 June 1807. On that day the HMS *Leopard* ordered the USS *Chesapeake* to stop and be searched for suspected deserters from the Royal Navy. When the American frigate refused to submit, the *Leopard* fired several broadsides into the *Chesapeake,* inflicting twenty casualties among the crew. The U.S. vessel, its rigging in shambles, struck its colors and was boarded by the British, who removed four sailors (one Englishman and three Americans) from the ship.

When the *Chesapeake* returned to its port at Norfolk and reported this affront, war between the two countries seemed inevitable. In anticipation of this event, Congress quickly passed an act authorizing the president to raise volunteer companies totaling up to thirty thousand men for action in the expected hostilities with Great Britain.

Upon hearing of this call to arms, the governor of Michigan Territory, William Hull, offered the services of the Legionary Corps. This force consisted of one company each of cavalry, artillery, light infantry, and riflemen. While the governor waited to hear if the tendered troops were needed, he daily activated "about one hundred of the Militia [to be] at work on [improving] the stockade and block houses [at Detroit]."

These and other military preparations were mirrored by similar activities on the Canadian side of the river. Furthermore, the British were showing success in encouraging the Indians to take their side in any engagements that might result from the growing crisis. In recognition of this threatening situation, on 16 October 1807 the Secretary of War ordered Governor Hull "to call out for constant duty three companies of the militia of Michigan territory, under the immediate command of a Major, to be posted within the town of Detroit."

These orders reached Hull at 5:00 P.M. on 5 December 1807. Later that evening the governor wrote the secretary of war. Regarding the militia, "I shall immediately order them into actual service, and shall give the command to Major [John] Whipple, formerly a Captain in the Army of the U. States [and] now the Major of the Legionary Corps."

Keeping his word, on 7 December Governor Hull—acting as commander in chief of the Territory—issued general orders to the Michigan Militia. These directives called upon "the officers, non-commissioned officers and privates of Captain [William McDowell] Scott's company of Riflemen, and Captain [Harris Hampden] Hickman's company of Light Infantry, who have voluntarily offered their services to the President, for this duty."

To obtain the third unit requested by the president, Hull gave to the First Regiment of Michigan militia "the honor to furnish a company of volunteers consisting of four serjeants [sic], four corporals, four musicians, and sixty-four privates, to be commanded by Captain Jacob Visger, the senior Captain of the Regiment." The governor noted that "these troops will be subject to the same regulation and entitled to the same pay, rations &c. as the regular troops of the United States."

The men of these three companies, totaling about two hundred individuals, could not stay in their respective residences while serving on active duty. Therefore, most of them were housed in three blockhouses at the fort. They remained billeted in these quarters until late March of 1808, by which time the threat of war had diminished to the point that they could be discharged from their military obligations.

The muster and pay rolls of those called up for duty were supposed to be sent to Washington, D.C. While there is no reason to believe that Hull did not comply with this requirement, the records cannot be found today. From secondary sources, however, it is possible to identify a few of the Detroiters who played a part in the active militia of 1807–8. Their names are recorded in the list of soldiers at the end of this chapter.

When the government released these soldiers and the other militiamen from active service, they were encouraged to remain in a state of readiness. This alert status was finally withdrawn nationally by a presidential proclamation of 10 June 1809. But in the Great Lakes region matters remained rather tense, even though the military was told to be at ease. The British were still viewed with distrust because they advised and supplied the Natives from their posts in Upper Canada. And the Indians that they increasingly supported seemed to be growing in belligerence.

The *Chesapeake* affair made it clear to all in the Northwest that in any conflict between the United States and Britain, the Natives would most likely fight with the redcoats. Even without open hostilities between John Bull and Uncle Sam, the Indians were bold enough to attack sporadically various points on the frontier in an effort to check the advance of white settlement. After Tecumseh came to the fore as the leader of the Indian revival movement in 1810, he even went so far as to threaten war if American pioneers attempted to occupy his stronghold in the Wabash Valley of Indiana.

Seeking to force the issue and awe the Native population, William Henry Harrison invaded the Wabash River basin in the autumn of 1811. On the morning of 7 November his force of army regulars and non-Michigan militia was encamped at the mouth of Tippecanoe Creek near present-day Lafayette. Shortly before dawn on that day the Indians—led by Tecumseh's brother, the Prophet—launched a surprise attack against the American troops.

The Indians caught Harrison's soldiers off guard, and more than sixty white men were killed and a hundred wounded in the sharp engagement. Eventually, the general rallied his forces and repulsed the assailants. To retaliate for his heavy losses, Harrison burned a nearby Shawnee village called Prophet's Town—the gathering point for the Prophet's and Tecumseh's followers—and then left the battlefield claiming victory.

News of the Battle of Tippecanoe increased the demand for war throughout much of the trans-Appalachian region. There were cries for vengeance against the offending Indians and the British who supported them. Both adversaries, it was clear, would have to be dealt with in a definitive way before the frontier could be secure. Increasingly, the American residents of the Great Lakes realm wanted to initiate action that would settle the problem once and for all. The commencement of that final struggle for control of the Northwest was less than one year away.

Dennis M. Au, M.A.

BIBLIOGRAPHIC NOTE

Sources that prove most revealing about Michigan and the Revolutionary War are:

Armour, David. "Remnants of the Revolutionary War in Michigan." *Chronicle* 10, no. 1 (1974): 1–11.

Armour, David, and Keith Widder. *At the Crossroads: Michilimackinac During the American Revolution.* Lansing: Mackinac Island State Park Commission, 1978.

Ash, Edith Worley. *Wafting Winds of the Revolution in Michigan Literature.* Grand Marais: Voyager Press, 1976.

Burton, Clarence M. "Detroit in the Revolution." *The City of Detroit,* vol. 1 (Chicago: Clarke Publishing Company, 1922), pp. 905–63.

Dunbar, Willis. "Michigan and the American Revolution." *Michigan Through the Centuries,* vol. 1 (New York: Lewis Historical Publishing Company, 1995), pp. 94–105.

Evans, William A., and Elizabeth Skiar, eds. *Detroit to Fort Sackville, 1778–1779: The Journal of Normand MacLeod.* Detroit: Wayne State University Press, 1978.

Horsman, Reginald. *Matthew Elliott, British Indian Agent.* Detroit: Wayne State University Press, 1964.

James, James Alton, ed. *George Rogers Clark Papers, 1771–1781.* Springfield: Illinois State Historical Library, 1912.

Mason, Philip. *Detroit, Fort Lernoult, and the American Revolution.* Detroit: Wayne State University Press, 1964.

Michigan Pioneer and Historical Collections (esp. vols. 3, 9, 10, 11, and 19). Lansing: Michigan Pioneer and Historical Society, 1881–91.

"Michigan's Role in the Revolution: A Bibliography for the Bicentennial," Pamphlet. Lansing: The State Library, 1974.

Nelson, Russell. *The British Regime in Michigan, 1760–1796.* Northfield, Minn.: Carleton College, 1939.

Quaife, Milo, ed. *The John Askin Papers.* Detroit: Detroit Library Commission, 1928, 1931.

Skaggs, David Curtis, and Larry L. Nelson, eds. *The Sixty Years' War for the Great Lakes, 1754–1814.* East Lansing: Michigan State University Press, 2001.

Widder, Keith. "Michigan in the American Revolution." *Family Trails* 5, no. 2 (Summer 1976): 2–3.

For information about the Indian War period, in addition to the sources listed above one should consult:

Bird, Harrison. *War for the West, 1790–1813.* New York: Oxford University Press, 1971.

Cruikshank, Ernest, ed. *The Correspondence of Lieutenant Governor John Graves Simcoe.* Toronto: Ontario Historical Society, 1923–31.

Sword, Wiley. *President Washington's Indian War: The Struggle for the Old Northwest, 1790–1795,* Norman: University of Oklahoma Press, 1985.

White, Richard. *The Middle Ground.* Cambridge: Cambridge University Press, 1991.

The best sources of information about the period of growing tension during the first decade of the nineteenth century are:

Carter, Clarence. *The Territorial Papers of the United States,* vol. 10. Washington, D.C.: Government Printing Office, 1942.

Michigan Historical Collections, vol. 40. Lansing: Michigan Historical Commission, 1929.

RELATED HISTORIC SITES AND MONUMENTS IN MICHIGAN

American Flag Raising County Historic Tablet, Monroe County
American Flag Raising Tablet, Detroit Security Trust Building
Cob-moo-sa (Chief) DAR Historic Bronze Tablet, Oceana County
Colonel John Francis Hamtramck Historical Marker, Wayne County

Colonial Boat Yard, Mackinaw City Historic Marker, Emmet County
Fort Lernoult Bronze Tablet, Old Post Office Building, Detroit
Fort Lernoult State Historic Marker, Wayne County
Fort Michilimackinac, Mackinaw City Historic Marker, Emmet County
Fort Michilimackinac State Historic Marker, Emmet County
Fort Pontchartrain State Historic Marker, Wayne County
Fort St. Joseph Historical Society Marker, Niles, Berrien County
Fort St. Joseph State Historic Marker, Berrien County
General Anthony Wayne Bronze Tablet, Wayne County Courthouse
Historic Fort Mackinac State Marker, Mackinac County
Livonia Revolutionary War Veterans Historical Marker, Wayne County
Mackinac City State Historic Marker, Cheboygan County
Mackinac Island State Historic Marker, Mackinac County
Moravian Road State Historic Marker, Macomb County
Old Council House Bronze Tablet, Water Works Building, Detroit
Revolutionary War Memorial Bronze Tablet, Caledonia, Kent County
U.S. Troops Arrival Bronze Tablet, Griswold and Atwater St., Detroit

LIST OF RELEVANT MICHIGAN ILLUSTRATIONS

Revolutionary and Indian War—Representative Soldiers

Atwell, Willis. *Do You Know.* [Grand Rapids]: Booth Newspapers, 1937. Pp. 255, 256, 259, 261, 269, 296, 307, 310–12, 345, 346, 350. Representations of various scenes that occurred during this conflict.

Bald, F. Clever. *Michigan in Four Centuries.* New York: Harper & Brothers, 1954. P. 76. Sketch of American prisoners being marched by Indians to Detroit.

Coleman, J. Winston Jr., ed. *Kentucky: A Pictorial History.* Lexington: University Press of Kentucky, 1971. P. 15. A drawing of the Battle of Blue Licks.

Company of Military Historians. *Military Uniforms in America: The Era of the American Revolution, 1755–1795.* San Rafael Calif.: Presidio Press, 1974. After p. 48. An illustration of the uniforms for British Rangers.

Dillon, Richard H. *North American Indian Wars.* New York: Facts on File, 1983. P. 71. Cartoon showing activities of "Detroit Hair Buyers."

Downey, Fairfax. *Indian Wars of the U.S. Army, 1776–1865.* Garden City, N.Y.: Doubleday & Company, 1963. Between pp. 104–5. A scene showing the Battle of Tippecanoe.

Dunnigan, Brian Leigh. *King's Men at Mackinac.* Lansing: Mackinac Island State Park Commission, 1973. Pp. [20], 31. Depictions of a member of the Mackinac Militia.

Ellis, Edward S. *The History of Our Country.* Indianapolis: J. H. Woolling & Company, 1905. Opposite p. 610. Shows frontiersmen at Battle of Fallen Timbers.

Lawson, Cecil C. P. *A History of the Uniforms of the British Army.* New York: Barnes & Company, 1979. P. 79. Representation of British uniforms during the period.

Miles, Richard D. *The Stars and Stripes Come to Detroit.* Detroit: Wayne University Press, 1951. Pages 16, 18. Illustrations of U.S. forces taking over Detroit from the British.

Mollo, John. *Uniforms of the American Revolution in Color.* New York: Macmillan Publishing Company, 1975. P. [121] item 144, p. [137] item 190. Typical dress for Indian combatants.

Quaife, Milo M. *This is Detroit, 1701–1951.* Detroit: Wayne State University Press, 1951. Page [22]. Also David A. Armour and Keith R. Widder, *At the Crossroads.* Lansing: Mackinac Island State Park Commission, 1978. P. 95. An artist's conception of the surrender of Vincennes by the British to George Rogers Clark.

Werstein, Irving. *The Adventure of the American Revolution Told With Pictures.* New York: Cooper Square Publishers, 1965. P. 86. Also William Cullen Bryant and Sydney Howard Gay, *A Popular History of the United States.* New York: Charles Scribner's Sons, 1879. P. 612. Drawing of surrender of Fort Sackville to Detroit forces.

Windrow, Martin, and Gerry Embleton. *Military Dress of North America, 1665–1970.* New York: Scribner's Sons, 1973. P. 41, plate 5, no. 21. This colonial militiaman was probably attired in a fashion similar to his Caucasian adversaries.

Revolutionary and Indian War—Specific Soldiers

Grant, Alexander. In Photograph Collection, Burton Historical Collections, Detroit Public Library.

Langlade, Charles. In Raymond Arthur McCoy, *The Massacre of Old Fort Mackinac.* 1939. Opposite p. 94.

Revolutionary and Indian War—Theater of Operations

Detroit Committee on Centennial Celebration. *The Centennial Celebration of the Evacuation of Detroit by the British.* Detroit: John F. Eby, 1896. Opposite pp. 21, 80, 168. Various views of the fort at Detroit.

ROSTER OF MICHIGAN MEN IN THE
REVOLUTIONARY AND EARLY INDIAN WARS

Name	Rank	Military Unit	Service Dates	Remarks
Abbott, Robert	UNK	Askin's Company	06/07/91–??/??/91	VTS WNA. Occupation merchant
Adehemar, Tousaint A.	CSY	Indian Department	??/??/78–03/05/79	POW Vincennes. AKA T. St. Martin
Ainsse, Joseph Louis	INT	Indian Department	??/??/76–??/??/76	
Allard, James	PVT	Scott's Company	12/??/07–??/??/08	Deserted
Allard, Pierre	PVT	Scott's Company	12/??/07–??/??/08	
Anderson, James	CAP	Detroit Militia	8/13/07–??/??/??	VTS
Ansley, Amos	MAC	Field & Staff, Militia	09/15/78–02/15/80	SRA Fort Sackville. POW
Arquoite, François	PVT	Lamothe's Company	09/17/78–03/05/79	SRA Fort Sackville
Askin, John Jr.	UNK	Askin's Company	06/07/91–??/??/91	VTS WNA. Occupation trader
Askin, John Sr.	CAP	Askin's Company	06/07/91–??/??/91	VTS WNA
Aunger, Henry	PVT	Chabert's Company	05/25/80–06/18/80	
Babant, Francis	SGT	Chabert's Company	03/24/80–05/24/80	
Baby, Baptiste	UNK	Askin's Company	06/07/91–??/??/91	VTS WNA. Occupation clerk
Baby, Duperon	CAP	Indian Department	??/??/78–??/??/83	Also interpreter for the Shawnee
Baby, Henry	VOL	Indian Department	03/24/79–??/??/83	
Baby, Jacques	STR	Indian Department	??/??/82–??/??/83	
Baker, Melcher	VOL	Indian Department	??/??/82–??/??/83	
Ballard, Etienne	BLS	Indian Department	??/??/78–??/??/78	
Baron, Joseph	SGT	Lamothe's Company	09/17/78–03/05/79	SRA Fort Sackville
Bartelett, Francis	LUT	Detroit Militia	??/??/??–??/??/??	

NAME	RANK	MILITARY UNIT	SERVICE DATES	REMARKS
Barth, Louis	UNK	Askin's Company	06/07/91–??/??/91	VTS WNA. Occupation clerk
Baubault	SGT	Chabert's Company	05/25/80–08/04/80	Forename unknown
Baubin, Charles	INT	Indian Department	??/??/78–??/??/83	AKA Braubin/Beaubien. Miami INT
Beaubien, Antoine	PVT	Maisonville's Company	10/07/78–12/24/78	
Beaubien, Pierre	PVT	Maisonville's Company	09/17/78–12/24/78	
Beaubin, Jean Baptiste	LUT	Detroit Militia	??/??/??–??/??/??	
Beaudouin, J. B.	PVT	Lamothe's Company	09/17/78–03/05/79	SRA Fort Sackville
Bellefeuille, Antoine	INT	Field & Staff, Militia	09/17/78–05/24/81	POW
Bellefeuille, L. F.	INT	Indian Department	??/??/??–03/05/79	SRA Fort Sackville. POW
Belton, David	CAP	Royal Navy	??/??/??–??/??/??	Stationed at Detroit
Benault, Regis	CPL	Maisonville's Company	09/17/78–12/24/78	
Bennett, John	CAP	Royal Navy	??/??/??–??/??/??	Stationed at Detroit
Bergeron, Joseph	PVT	Chabert's Company	03/24/80–08/04/80	Drafted
Bergeron, Simon	PVT	Chabert's Company	03/24/80–05/24/80	Drafted
Bertiaume, Andrew	PVT	Chabert's Company	03/24/80–08/04/80	AKA Andre Berthiaume
Bigras, Alexander	CPL	Lamothe's Company	09/17/78–03/05/79	SRA Fort Sackville
Billette, Ignace	PVT	Chene's Company	03/24/80–05/24/80	Drafted
Bisonnet, Etiene	CPL	Maisonville's Company	09/17/78–12/24/78	
Blay, Joseph	PVT	Chene's Company	03/24/80–05/24/80	Drafted
Bogarts, Jacob	CAR	Detroit Militia	??/??/??–??/??/79	SRA Fort Sackville, AKA Jacob Bogard
Bondy, Joseph Douaire	CAP	Detroit Militia	??/??/76–??/??/??	AKA Joseph de Bondy
Bondy, Joseph	LUT	Indian Department	??/??/78–??/??/78	
Boulanger, Charles	EXT	Indian Department	??/??/82–10/24/82	
Bourrassa, Louis	CPL	Maisonville's Company	09/17/78–12/24/78	
Bray, William	BSN	Royal Navy	??/??/??–??/??/??	Stationed at Detroit
Brazau, Baptiste	PVT	Chabert's Company	03/24/80–08/04/80	AKA Jean Baptiste Baazau/Barau

NAME	RANK	MILITARY UNIT	SERVICE DATES	REMARKS
Bribonne, John	PVT	Lamothe's Company	09/17/78–03/05/81	SRA Fort Sackville. AKA John Brebane
Brooks, Leonard	LUT	Detroit Militia	07/03/07–??/??/??	VTS Artillery
Brown, William	SUR	F&S Detroit Militia	12/11/07–??/??/08	
Brush, Elijah	CLT	Detroit Militia	07/03/07–??/??/??	VTS Commandant
Bylair, François	PVT	Chabert's Company	03/24/80–05/24/80	Drafted. AKA François Belaire
Caffee, Samuel	PVT	Lamothe's Company	09/17/78–03/05/79	SRA Fort Sackville
Caldwell, William	CLT	Detroit Militia	??/??/94–??/??/94	In action at Fallen Timbers
Campau, Charles	PVT	Chabert's Company	03/24/80–05/24/80	Drafted
Campeau, Jacques Jr.	CAP	Detroit Militia	??/??/76–??/??/78	Resigned
Campeau, Jean Baptiste	CAP	Detroit Militia	??/??/78–??/??/82	
Cardinal, Joseph	LUT	Detroit Militia	??/??/??–??/??/??	
Carrier, Joseph	CPL	Chabert's Company	03/24/80–08/04/80	AKA Joseph Carrie
Cassety, James	LUT	Detroit Militia	??/??/??–??/??/??	
Chabert, Chevallier	LUT	Maisonville's Company	09/17/78–12/24/78	
Chabert, François	LUT	Indian Department	??/??/78–??/??/78	
Chabert, Jencaise	LUT	McLeod's Company	09/17/78–12/24/78	AKA Joncaire Chabert
Chabert, Joncaire	CAP	Detroit Volunteers	??/??/??–??/??/83	
Chabert, Louis J.	CAP	Chabert's Company	03/24/80–08/04/80	AKA Louis Chabert de Joncaire
Chanon	SGT	Chabert's Company	05/25/80–08/04/80	Forename unknown
Chapanton, Jean B. Jr.	LUT	Detroit Militia	??/??/??–??/??/??	MNI Baptiste
Chapaw, Lefevre	BLS	Indian Department	??/??/78–??/??/78	
Chapman	QUT	Field & Staff, Militia	09/17/78–12/24/78	End-of-service date uncertain
Chapoton, Jean B.	CAP	Detroit Militia	??/??/??–??/??/78	RES. Accused of favoring Rebels
Chapue, Benjamin	PVT	Chabert's Company	03/24/80–08/04/80	Drafted. AKA Benjamin Chafrue
Charleboy, Touissant	PVT	Chabert's Company	03/24/80–08/04/80	Drafted
Charon, Antoine	SGT	Chabert's Company	03/24/80–05/24/80	

NAME	RANK	MILITARY UNIT	SERVICE DATES	REMARKS
Chartier, Jacques	PVT	Chabert's Company	03/24/80–05/24/80	Drafted
Chauvin, Charles	PVT	Maisonville's Company	09/17/78–12/24/78	
Chauvin, Jacques	PVT	Chene's Company	03/24/80–05/24/80	Drafted
Chauvin, Jacques	BLS	Indian Department	??/??/82–??/??/83	Blacksmith at Detroit
Chene, Antoine	VOL	Indian Department	??/??/82–??/??/83	
Chene, Isidore	CAP	Chene's Company	??/??/80–??/??/80	AKA Isidore Chaine or Chesne
Chesne, Isidore	CAP	Indian Department	??/??/78–??/??/83	Also interpreter for Ottawas
Chevalier, Pierre	EXT	Indian Department	??/??/82–10/24/82	
Chevallier, Louis Jr.	INT	Spanish Militia	01/02/81–03/??/81	On expedition to Fort St. Joseph
Chinchett, Pierre	PVT	Chabert's Company	05/25/80–08/04/80	
Cissne, John	CAP	Detroit Militia	08/13/07–??/??/??	VTS
Cissne, Joseph	UNK	Detroit Militia	08/13/07–??/??/??	VTS
Cissne, William	UNK	Detroit Militia	08/13/07–??/??/??	VTS
Clenchette, Pierre	PVT	Chene's Company	03/24/80–05/24/80	Drafted
Compari, F.	PVT	Maisonville's Company	09/17/78–12/24/78	
Connally, Thomas	PVT	Lamothe's Company	09/17/78–03/05/79	SRA Fort Sackville
Conner, John	ENS	Detroit Militia	07/03/07–??/??/??	VTS Infantry
Constant, J. B.	INT	Indian Department	??/??/82–??/??/83	
Cote, Joseph	PVT	Chabert's Company	03/24/80–05/24/80	Drafted
Daine, Jean	PVT	Lamothe's Company	09/17/78–03/05/79	SRA Fort Sackville. AKA John Dain
Daunois, J. B.	PVT	Lamothe's Company	09/17/78–03/05/79	SRA Fort Sackville
Degagne, Joseph	PVT	Chene's Company	03/24/80–05/24/80	Drafted
Dejean, Philip	CAP	Detroit Militia	??/??/??–??/??/79	
Dejean, Philip	CSY	Indian Department	02/??/79–??/??/79	POW at Vincennes
Delisle, François	UNK	Detroit Militia	08/13/07–??/??/??	VTS
Demerk, Pierre	PVT	Chabert's Company	03/24/80–05/24/80	AKA Pierre Denuere

Name	Rank	Military Unit	Service Dates	Remarks
Demoushelle, Louis	PVT	Lamothe's Company	09/17/78–03/05/79	SRA Fort Sackville
Dequendre, Dagneau	LUT	Indian Department	06/24/79–??/??/83	AKA Dagneau Duquinder
Dequindie, Antoine Jr.	LUT	Detroit Militia	07/03/07–??/??/??	VTS Rifles
Dequindre, Antoine	LUT	Indian Department	??/??/78–??/??/78	
Dequindre, François	LUT	Indian Department	??/??/78–??/??/78	
Dequindre, Frontenay	LUT	Indian Department	??/??/78–??/??/79	AKA Fontenoy de Quindre
Dequindre, Lepiconier	LUT	Indian Department	??/??/78–??/??/78	
Dequindre, Pontchartrain	LUT	Indian Department	??/??/78–??/??/78	
Desaunier, Louis	PVT	Chabert's Company	03/24/80–08/04/80	Drafted. AKA Louis Dezonier
Desnoyers, Pierre Jr.	PVT	Maisonville's Company	09/17/78–12/24/78	
Desnoyers, Pierre Sr.	PVT	Maisonville's Company	09/17/78–12/24/78	
Diel, Francis	BLS	Indian Department	03/24/79–??/??/83	AKA Francis Deloeuil. At Shawaneetown
Dodemead, James	CAP	Dodemead's Company	12/??/07–??/??/08	Artillery
Dodemead, John	UNK	Askin's Company	06/07/91–??/??/91	VTS WNA. Occupation shopkeeper
Dolphin, Pierre	PVT	Lamothe's Company	09/17/78–03/05/79	SRA Fort Sackville
Drouillard, Francis	LUT	Detroit Militia	??/??/??–??/??/??	
Drouillart, Pierre	INT	Indian Department	??/??/78–??/??/83	AKA Pierre Drouillard. Huron INT
Drouilliart, Joseph	PVT	Chabert's Company	03/24/80–05/24/80	AKA Joseph Drouillard
Druillard, Nicholas	PVT	Maisonville's Company	09/17/78–12/24/78	
Dubord, J. B.	PVT	Lamothe's Company	09/17/78–03/05/79	SRA Fort Sackville
Duplesis, Louis	BLS	Indian Department	??/??/78–??/??/78	
Duplessis, Joseph	BLS	Indian Department	03/24/79–??/??/83	Blacksmith at Miamis Towns
Durucher, Martin	PVT	Maisonville's Company	09/17/78–12/24/78	
Dyelle, François	BLS	Indian Department	??/??/78–??/??/78	AKA Francis Deloeuil
Elliott, Mathew	VOL	Indian Department	??/??/79–??/??/83	
Faverau, J. B.	PVT	Chabert's Company	05/25/80–08/04/80	
Fleury, John	PVT	Chabert's Company	03/24/80–08/04/80	AKA John Flurry

NAME	RANK	MILITARY UNIT	SERVICE DATES	REMARKS
Forton, James Jr.	PVT	Scott's Company	12/??/07–??/??/08	Deserted
Fraser, James	UNK	Askin's Company	06/07/91–??/??/91	VTS WNA. Occupation merchant
Gaffee, J. B.	CSY	Indian Department	??/??/78–03/05/79	SRA Fort Sackville
Gagnier, Jacques	PVT	Lamothe's Company	09/17/78–03/05/79	SRA Fort Sackville
Gaigvin, Augustin	BLS	Indian Department	??/??/82–??/??/83	AKA Augustin Gagnier
Gamelin, Francis	LUT	Detroit Militia	??/??/??–??/??/??	
Gamelin, Medard	LUT	Detroit Militia	??/??/??–??/??/??	PMT CAP about September 1778
Gamelin, Paul	PVT	Maisonville's Company	09/17/78–12/24/78	
Gamelin, Paul	VOL	Detroit Militia	??/??/??–??/??/79	SRA Fort Sackville
Gautier, Charles	INT	Indian Department	??/??/77–??/??/77	
Girty, George	INT	Indian Department	??/??/82–??/??/83	INT for Delaware Indians
Girty, James	VOL	Indian Department	??/??/79–??/??/83	
Girty, Simon	INT	Indian Department	??/??/78–??/??/83	INT for Six Nations
Godette, Francis M.	LUT	Detroit Militia	??/??/??–??/??/??	MNI Marantete
Godfroy, Gabriel	LUT	Detroit Militia	07/03/07–??/??/??	VTS Cavalry
Godraux, Jaquez	PVT	Maisonville's Company	09/17/78–12/24/78	
Gouin, Charles	LUT	Detroit Militia	??/??/??–??/??/??	
Graham, M.	LUT	Royal Navy	??/??/??–??/??/??	Stationed at Detroit
Grant, Alexander	CMD	Royal Navy	??/??/78–01/??/12	Commanded on Upper Great Lakes
Greg, William	EXT	Indian Department	??/??/82–10/24/82	
Gregg, William	PVT	Chabert's Company	03/24/80–08/04/80	SGT from 05/25/80–08/04/80
Griffard, Louis	PVT	Scott's Company	12/??/07–??/??/08	
Grimard, Joseph	PVT	Chene's Company	03/24/80–05/24/80	Drafted
Guilbault, Jean	PVT	Maisonville's Company	09/17/78–12/24/78	
Guilbeaux, Joseph	PVT	Chabert's Company	05/27/80–07/01/80	AKA Joseph Guilleaux
Gunner, Abraham	UNK	Detroit Militia	08/13/07–??/??/??	VTS
Hamilton, Henry	CMD	Field & Staff	09/17/78–03/05/79	SRA Fort Sackville. POW

NAME	RANK	MILITARY UNIT	SERVICE DATES	REMARKS
Hands, William	UNK	Askin's Company	06/07/91–??/??/91	VTS WNA. Occupation merchant
Hay, Jehu	MAJ	Detroit Militia	09/15/78–12/24/80	Also Deputy Agent, Indian Dept.
Hay, Jehu	MAJ	Field & Staff, Regiment	09/15/78–05/24/81	SRA Fort Sackville. POW
Herbert, Michel	VOL	Indian Department	??/??/82–02/24/83	
Hickman, Harris	CAP	Hickman's Company	12/??/07–??/??/08	MNI Hampden
Higgins, John	VOL	Indian Department	??/??/82–02/24/83	
Home, M.	MAS	Royal Navy	??/??/??–??/??/??	Stationed at Detroit
Hull, Abijah	MAJ	F&S Detroit Militia	12/10/07–??/??/08	ADC
Hull, William	CIC	Michigan Militia	12/??/07–??/??/08	Governor
Hunt, Henry Jackson	MAJ	F&S Detroit Militia	12/11/07–??/??/08	ADC
Ignace, Antoine	LUT	Indian Department	??/??/82–??/??/82	At Battle of Blue Licks
Jencaire, Louis	LUT	Indian Department	??/??/78–??/??/78	AKA Louis Chabert
Jitter, Amable	PVT	Chabert's Company	03/24/80–05/24/80	Drafted. AKA Amable Jetter
Johnson, Alexander	PVT	Chabert's Company	03/24/80–08/04/80	Drafted
Johnson, Alexander	EXT	Indian Department	??/??/82–10/24/82	
Jones, Isaac	UNK	Detroit Militia	08/13/07–??/??/??	VTS
Jones, John	PVT	Chabert's Company	03/24/80–08/04/80	AKA John Johnes
Knaggs, Whitmore	LUT	Visger's Company	12/??/07–??/??/08	
Labadie, Antoine	PVT	Maisonville's Company	09/17/78–12/24/78	
Labady, Jean B.	PVT	Chabert's Company	03/24/80–08/04/80	Drafted
Labady, Jean B. Jr.	PVT	Chene's Company	03/24/80–05/24/80	Drafted
Labate, Claude	LUT	Indian Department	??/??/78–??/??/79	AKA Claud Lubute or Labutte
Labuie, Alexis	PVT	Maisonville's Company	09/17/78–12/24/78	
Labutte, Julien	PVT	Chabert's Company	03/24/80–08/04/80	Drafted. AKA Julian Labute
Labutte, Pierre	PVT	Chabert's Company	03/24/80–08/04/80	Drafted. AKA Pierre Laluette
Laduke, Baptiste	PVT	Chabert's Company	05/25/80–08/04/80	
Laflur, Joseph P.	CPL	Maisonville's Company	09/17/78–12/24/78	MNI Poinerelit

NAME	RANK	MILITARY UNIT	SERVICE DATES	REMARKS
Lafoy, Augustin	LUT	Detroit Militia	??/??/??–??/??/??	
Lajeunesse, Jean B.	PVT	Chabert's Company	03/24/80–05/24/80	Drafted
Lajeunesse, Jean B.	PVT	Chene's Company	03/24/80–05/24/80	Drafted
Laliberte, Joseph	PVT	Chabert's Company	03/24/80–08/04/80	AKA Joseph Laliberty
Lamothe, Guillaume	CAP	Field & Staff Militia	09/17/78–??/??/83	SRA Ft Sackville. POW. AKA William
Langlade, Charles Michel	CAP	Indian Department	??/??/76–??/??/77	Led force to Montreal
Langlade, Charles Jr.	LUT	Indian Department	??/??/82–??/??/82	At Battle of Blue Licks
Lapont, Joseph	PVT	Chabert's Company	03/24/80–08/04/80	AKA Joseph Laforest or Laforet
Lariviere, Bonaventu	PVT	Chabert's Company	03/24/80–08/04/80	Drafted
Laronde, Joseph	PVT	Lamothe's Company	09/17/78–03/05/79	SRA Fort Sackville
Lasaline, Paul	PVT	Chabert's Company	03/24/80–05/24/80	Drafted
Lasselle, Nicholas	STR	Indian Department	??/??/78–03/05/79	SRA Fort Sackville
Latourneau, Pierre	PVT	Maisonville's Company	09/17/78–12/24/78	
Latourneur, Jean Baptiste	CPL	Maisonville's Company	09/17/78–12/24/78	
Laughton, Peter	UNK	Askin's Company	06/07/91–??/??/91	VTS WNA. Occupation trader
Lazon, Pierre	PVT	Chabert's Company	05/25/80–08/04/80	
Lebeau, Etienne	PVT	Chene's Company	03/24/80–05/24/80	Drafted
Leblanc, Charles	PVT	Chene's Company	03/24/80–05/24/80	Drafted
Leclair, Francis	BLS	Indian Department	06/24/79–??/??/83	BLS at St. Joseph. AKA Francis L'Coellie
LeCerp, Jean M.	PVT	Chabert's Company	03/24/80–08/04/80	Drafted. AKA Jean Marie L'Lerf
Ledaux, Jean B.	PVT	Chabert's Company	03/24/80–05/24/80	Drafted
Ledue, Jean B.	PVT	Chene's Company	03/24/80–05/24/80	Drafted
Lefoi, Augustin	ARM	Indian Department	??/??/78–??/??/78	
Lepage, Joseph	PVT	Maisonville's Company	09/17/78–12/24/78	
Leroux, John Baptiste	PVT	Lamothe's Company	09/17/78–03/05/79	SRA Fort Sackville
Lesucier, Joseph	EXT	Indian Department	??/??/82–10/24/82	
Licot, Jean B.	LUT	Detroit Militia	??/??/??–??/??/??	MNI Baptiste

NAME	RANK	MILITARY UNIT	SERVICE DATES	REMARKS
Longueville, Pierre	PVT	Lamothe's Company	09/17/78–03/05/79	SRA Fort Sackville
Longuiel, Joseph	PVT	Chabert's Company	03/24/80–08/04/80	AKA Joseph Longite
Lortie, J. B.	EXT	Indian Department	??/??/82–10/24/82	
Loson, Jacques	PVT	Chabert's Company	03/24/80–08/04/80	Drafted. AKA Jacque Lozen
Loson, Pierre	PVT	Chabert's Company	03/24/80–08/04/80	AKA Pierre Lazon or Loxon
Lovain, Charles	CSY	Field & Staff, Militia	09/17/78–??/??/??	Provisioner at the Miami
MacComb, John	UNK	Detroit Militia	08/13/07–??/??/??	VTS
Mackintosh, James	UNK	Askin's Company	06/07/91–??/??/91	VTS WNA. Occupation clerk
MacNay, Juhg	UNK	Detroit Militia	08/13/07–??/??/??	VTS
Magnian, François	SGT	Lamothe's Company	09/17/78–03/05/79	SRA Fort Sackville
Maisonville, Alexis	CAP	Maisonville's Company	09/17/78–12/24/78	WIA & POW at Vincennes 1779
Maisonville, Francois	BOT	Field & Staff, Militia	09/17/78–12/24/78	Dates of service uncertain
Makie, John	CSA	Indian Department	??/??/79–??/??/83	AKA John Mackay
Mallet, Guillaume	PVT	Chabert's Company	03/24/80–08/04/80	AKA Guilliame Mellet
Marcheierre, François	SGT	Maisonville's Company	09/17/78–12/24/78	
Marion, Jean M.	PVT	Chabert's Company	03/24/80–08/04/80	MNI Marie
Martell, Antoine	PVT	Chabert's Company	03/24/80–08/04/80	AKA Antoine Martelle
Martin, Hugh R.	LUT	F&S Detroit Militia	12/21/07–??/??/08	QUT
Maw, Andre	PVT	Chene's Company	03/24/80–05/24/80	Drafted. AKA Vincent Maw
May, James	UNK	Askin's Company	06/07/91–??/??/91	VTS WNA. Occupation merchant
McAlpine, James	SGT	Chabert's Company	05/25/80–08/04/80	
McBeath, John	SUR	Field & Staff, Militia	09/15/78–05/24/81	SRA Fort Sackville. POW
McDonald, John	SEA	Royal Navy	??/??/??–12/??/79	Drowned at Detroit
McDonald, Ronald	UNK	Askin's Company	06/07/91–??/??/91	VTS WNA. Occupation trader
McDonell, James	UNK	Askin's Company	06/07/91–??/??/91	Occupation merchant
McDougall, George	UNK	Askin's Company	06/07/91–??/??/91	VTS WNA. Occupation merchant
McDougall, George	COL	F&S Detroit Militia	12/??/07–??/??/08	QUG

NAME	RANK	MILITARY UNIT	SERVICE DATES	REMARKS
McGregor, Gregor	CAP	Detroit Militia	03/24/79–06/21/84	
McGregor, John	UNK	Askin's Company	06/07/91–??/??/91	VTS WNA. Occupation trader
McKay, Mark	GUN	Royal Navy	??/??/??–??/??/??	Stationed at Detroit
McKee, Alexander	CAP	Indian Department	??/??/78–??/??/79	Also served as interpreter
McKee, Thomas	UNK	Askin's Company	06/07/91–??/??/91	VTS WNA
McKillip, Daniel	CAP	Detroit Militia	08/10/94–08/24/94	KIA at Fallen Timbers
McKindlar, Patrick	PVT	Lamothe's Company	09/17/78–06/06/80	SRA Fort Sackville. AKA Patrick McKindley
McKinzee, Alexander	UNK	Askin's Company	06/07/91–??/??/91	VTS WNA. Occupation merchant
McKivors, John	SGT	Lamothe's Company	09/17/78–03/05/79	
McLeod, Normond	CAP	McLeod's Company	09/17/78–12/24/78	
McMichel, John	PVT	Lamothe's Company	09/17/78–03/05/79	SRA Fort Sackville
McPhee, James	PVT	Chene's Company	03/24/80–05/24/80	Drafted
Metez, Janette Joseph	CPL	Maisonville's Company	09/17/78–12/24/78	
Mince, François	CPL	Lamothe's Company	09/17/78–03/05/79	SRA Fort Sackville. AKA Lenfant
Miney, Pierre	PVT	Chene's Company	03/24/80–05/24/80	Drafted
Misee, Pierre	PVT	Chabert's Company	03/24/80–08/04/80	Drafted. AKA Pierre Mizie
Moine, Louis	PVT	Chabert's Company	03/24/80–08/04/80	Drafted. AKA Louis Morran
Monforton, William	CAP	Detroit Militia	??/??/78–??/??/??	
Moran, Bazil	PVT	Chabert's Company	03/24/80–08/04/80	
Moran, Jean B.	UNK	Askin's Company	06/07/91–??/??/91	VTS WNA. Occupation trader
Moran, Pierre	UNK	Askin's Company	06/07/91–??/??/91	VTS WNA. Occupation clerk
Morand, Charles	CAP	Detroit Militia	??/??/??–??/??/??	
Mouinerel, Jean B.	PVT	Chene's Company	03/24/80–05/24/80	Drafted. AKA Jean B. Monmuel
Murray, John	PVT	Chabert's Company	03/24/80–08/04/80	
Newland, Benjamin	VOL	Indian Department	??/??/82–??/??/83	
Nickervas, William	BSN	Royal Navy	??/??/??–??/??/??	Stationed at Detroit
Niger, Andre	PVT	Chene's Company	03/24/80–05/24/80	

NAME	RANK	MILITARY UNIT	SERVICE DATES	REMARKS
Ouimette, Jean B.	PVT	Lamothe's Company	09/17/78–03/05/79	SRA Fort Sackville
Palmer, John	ENS	Detroit Militia	07/03/07–??/??/??	VTS Rifles
Pauget, Joseph	PVT	Maisonville's Company	09/17/78–12/24/78	
Peltier, Antoine	UNK	Askin's Company	06/07/91–??/??/91	VTS WNA
Peltier, Jacque Jr.	UNK	Askin's Company	06/07/91–??/??/91	VTS WNA
Peltier, Jacque Sr.	UNK	Askin's Company	06/07/91–??/??/91	VTS WNA. Occupation trader
Peltier, Jean B.	PVT	Chabert's Company	03/24/80–08/04/80	Drafted. AKA Baptiste Peltier
Pinard, Joseph	PVT	Scott's Company	12/??/07–??/??/08	
Plant, Jean M.	PVT	Chabert's Company	03/24/80–08/04/80	AKA Jean Mary Plaute
Pollard, Richard	UNK	Askin's Company	06/07/91–??/??/91	VTS WNA. Occupation merchant
Pommanville, Joseph	PVT	Maisonville's Company	09/17/78–12/24/78	
Price, James	UNK	Detroit Militia	08/13/07–??/??/??	VTS
Prudhomme, François	PVT	Chene's Company	03/24/80–05/24/80	Drafted
Prudhomme, Jacques	PVT	Chabert's Company	03/24/80–08/04/80	Drafted
Rankine, William	BSN	Royal Navy	??/??/??–??/??/??	Stationed at Detroit Yard
Rapin, John Baptiste	PVT	Lamothe's Company	09/17/78–03/05/79	SRA Fort Sackville
Reagh, Joseph	PVT	Chabert's Company	03/24/80–08/04/80	CPL starting 05/25/80. AKA Joseph Rough
Reaume, Banaventu	LUT	Detroit Militia	??/??/??–??/??/??	
Reaume, Charles	CAP	Indian Department	??/??/78–??/??/79	Also an INT. SRA Fort Sackville
Reaume, Charles	CAP	River Raisin Militia	??/??/94–??/??/94	
Reaume, Claude	LUT	Detroit Militia	??/??/??–??/??/??	
Reaume, Jean Baptiste	LUT	Detroit Militia	??/??/??–??/??/??	
Reaume, Joseph	LUT	Detroit Militia	??/??/??–??/??/??	
Reaume, Pierre	CAP	Detroit Militia	??/??/76–??/??/78	Dismissed from service
Renkin, James	LUT	Detroit Militia	??/??/??–??/??/??	
Reynolds, Caleb	PVT	Chabert's Company	03/24/80–08/04/80	Drafted. AKA Calib Reyn

NAME	RANK	MILITARY UNIT	SERVICE DATES	REMARKS
Richard, Claude	PVT	Chabert's Company	03/24/80–08/04/80	
Rix, John	PVT	Chabert's Company	05/25/80–06/23/80	
Robert, J.	PVT	Lamothe's Company	09/17/78–03/05/79	SRA Fort Sackville
Robert, Pierre	PVT	Chene's Company	03/24/80–05/24/80	Drafted
Robertson, David	UNK	Askin's Company	06/07/91–??/??/91	VTS WNA. Occupation merchant
Rocque, Joseph	INT	Indian Department	??/??/79–??/??/80	
Roseau, Charles	PVT	Chene's Company	03/24/80–05/24/80	Drafted
Ruland, Isaac	UNK	Detroit Militia	08/13/07–??/??/??	VTS
Ruland, John	ENS	Detroit Militia	08/13/07–??/??/??	VTS
Russel, Spencer	UNK	Detroit Militia	08/13/07–??/??/??	VTS
Russell, William	UNK	Detroit Militia	07/03/07–??/??/??	VTS Cavalry
Saint Andre, Pierre	PVT	Lamothe's Company	09/17/78–03/05/79	SRA Fort Sackville
Saint Aubin, Claude	CPL	Maisonville's Company	09/17/78–12/24/78	
Saint Aubin, Jacques	CPL	Maisonville's Company	09/17/78–12/24/78	
Saint Cosme, Amable	ARM	Indian Department	??/??/78–??/??/78	
Saint Cosme, Pierre	LUT	Detroit Militia	??/??/??–??/??/??	
Saint Etienne, Amable	PVT	Chabert's Company	03/24/80–05/24/80	Drafted
Saint Lorne, Pierre	LUT	Detroit Militia	??/??/??–??/??/??	
Saint Louis, Christome	PVT	Chene's Company	03/24/80–05/24/80	Drafted
Saint Louis, Pierre	PVT	Chabert's Company	03/24/80–05/24/80	Drafted
Saint Martin, Adhemar	CSY	Field & Staff, Militia	09/17/78–12/24/78	DSU. AKA Toussaint A. Adhemar
Saint Pierre, Jean B.	PVT	Lamothe's Company	09/17/78–03/05/79	SRA Fort Sackville
Saliberte, Joseph	PVT	Chabert's Company	03/24/80–05/25/80	
Scheiffelin, Jonathan	LUT	Chabert's Company	03/24/80–08/04/80	
Schieffelin, Jacob	LUT	Indian Department	09/15/78–??/??/83	SRA Fort Sackville. POW
Schieffelin, Jacob	CAP	Detroit Militia	??/??/94–??/??/94	

Name	Rank	Military Unit	Service Dates	Remarks
Scott, William	PVT	Lamothe's Company	09/17/78–03/05/79	SRA Fort Sackville
Scott, William	CAP	Scott's Company	12/??/07–??/??/08	MNI McDowell
Seek, Conrad	LUT	Detroit Militia	08/13/07–??/??/??	VTS
Shags, John	UNK	Detroit Militia	08/13/07–??/??/??	VTS
Shee, Edward	UNK	Unknown	??/??/??–??/??/79	SRA Fort Sackville
Shehe, Edward	PVT	Chabert's Company	03/24/80–08/04/80	
Shelly, Edward	PVT	Lamothe's Company	09/17/78–03/05/79	SRA Fort Sackville
Shepherd, William	UNK	Askin's Company	06/07/91–??/??/91	VTS WNA. Occupation clerk
Smith, Charles	UNK	Askin's Company	06/07/91–??/??/91	VTS WNA. Occupation clerk
Smith, Charles	UNK	Detroit Militia	08/10/94–08/24/94	KIA at Fallen Timbers
Smith, Richard	CAP	Detroit Militia	07/03/07–??/??/??/	VTS Cavalry
Somlers, Louis	PVT	Chabert's Company	03/24/80–05/24/80	AKA Louis Sowters
Sterling, James	CAP	Detroit Militia	??/??/76–??/??/77	Suspected of supporting Rebels
Sterling, William	LUT	Detroit Militia	??/??/??–??/??/??	
Stevens, Robert	UNK	Askin's Company	06/07/91–??/??/91	VTS WNA. Occupation clerk
Stockwell, John	PVT	Chabert's Company	03/24/80–08/04/80	
Surphlet, Robert	VOL	Indian Department	??/??/79–??/??/83	
Swan, [James]	UNK	Askin's Company	06/07/91–??/??/91	VTS WNA. Occupation clerk
Tavuan, Jean B.	PVT	Chabert's Company	03/24/80–08/04/80	Drafted. AKA Jean B. Faverau
Taylor, William	PVT	Lamothe's Company	09/17/78–05/25/81	SRA Fort Sackville. POW
Tessier, François	PVT	Chabert's Company	03/24/80–08/04/80	AKA Francis Tizier
Tessier, Pierre	PVT	Chabert's Company	03/24/80–08/04/80	AKA Pierre Tizier
Tramblay, Etienne	PVT	Chabert's Company	03/24/80–08/04/80	Drafted. AKA Etienne Tromble
Tramblay, Jean B.	PVT	Chabert's Company	03/24/80–08/04/80	Drafted. AKA Jean B. Tramble
Tramblay, Michel	PVT	Chene's Company	03/24/80–05/24/80	Drafted
Trap, Martin	EXT	Indian Department	??/??/82–10/24/82	

NAME	RANK	MILITARY UNIT	SERVICE DATES	REMARKS
Tremble, Gagette	PVT	Scott's Company	12/??/07–??/??/08	Deserted
Trouillier, Joseph	CPL	Chabert's Company	05/25/80–08/04/80	AKA Joseph Touillier
Trudelle, Francis	PVT	Chabert's Company	03/24/80–08/04/80	AKA Francis Trudell
Truttie, Antoine	PVT	Chabert's Company	03/24/80–08/04/80	AKA Antoine Trottier
Tucker, William	INT	Indian Department	??/??/78–??/??/83	INT for Ottawa and Chippewa
Tussy, James	PVT	Chabert's Company	03/24/80–08/04/80	AKA James Tressey
Vailette, Alexandre	PVT	Maisonville's Company	09/17/78–12/24/78	
Valade, John B.	PVT	Lamothe's Company	09/17/78–03/05/79	SRA Fort Sackville. MNI Baptist
Venette, Nicolas	PVT	Lamothe's Company	09/17/78–03/05/79	SRA Fort Sackville
Viaux, Louis	PVT	Lamothe's Company	09/17/78–03/05/79	SRA Fort Sackville
Viger, Andre	PVT	Chene's Company	??/??/80–??/??/80	Drafted
Villier, F.	SGT	Maisonville's Company	09/17/78–12/24/78	
Visger, Jacob	CAP	Visger's Company	12/??/07–??/??/08	AKA Jacob Visgar
Watson, John	LUT	Detroit Militia	07/03/07–??/??/??	VTS Infantry
Watson, Joseph	LUT	F&S Detroit Militia	12/21/07–??/??/08	ADJ
Welsh, Roger	PVT	Chabert's Company	05/25/80–06/23/80	
Whaler, Daniel	PVT	Chabert's Company	05/25/80–06/20/80	
Whipple, John	MAJ	F&S Detroit Militia	12/??/07–??/??/08	
Wickham, Samuel	LUT	Royal Navy	??/??/??–??/??/??	Stationed at Detroit
Wilkinson, Patrick	GUN	Royal Navy	??/??/??–??/??/??	Stationed at Detroit
Woodward, Augustus	CDT	F&S Detroit Militia	08/13/07–??/??/??	VTS MNI Brevoort
Yax, J. B.	PVT	Chene's Company	03/24/80–05/24/80	Drafted. AKA J. B. Yacks
Yax, Simon	PVT	Chene's Company	03/24/80–05/24/80	Drafted. AKA Simon Yacks
Young, Andrew	CAR	Detroit Militia	??/??/??–??/??/79	SRA Fort Sackville
Yvon, Simon	PVT	Maisonville's Company	09/17/78–12/24/78	

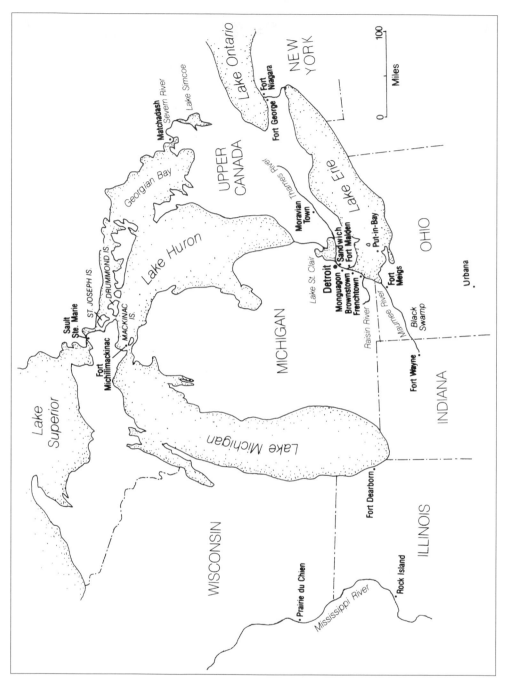

Theater of Operations, War of 1812. (*Cartography by Sherm Hollander*)

TWO

WAR OF 1812

Michigan in the War of 1812

In mid-1812, Brigadier General William Hull, Michigan's territorial governor and the commander of the newly created North Western Army, left Urbana, Ohio, for Detroit—some two hundred miles north. Deteriorating relations between the United States and Great Britain had led the U.S. War Department to reinforce the small garrison at Fort Detroit. Unbeknownst to Hull, a few days later, the United States declared war on Great Britain.

Hull's army of fifteen hundred Ohio militiamen and five hundred U.S. regulars moved slowly through the Great Black Swamp in northwestern Ohio. Finally, two weeks after leaving Urbana, the army reached the rapids of the Maumee River, sixty miles southwest of Detroit. Hull arranged to have the schooner *Cayauga* transport the officers' wives and any sick soldiers, along with much of the army's baggage, to Detroit. By mistake, the army's official papers, including Hull's general campaign plans, were also placed on board. The British at Fort Malden, already aware of the outbreak of hostilities, captured the *Cayauga* before it reached Detroit. American officials in Washington had sent word of the outbreak of hostilities to Hull via the regular mail. An alert postmaster in Cleveland, Ohio, forwarded the dispatch to Hull by special courier. Still, Hull did not discover that war had been declared until he reached Frenchtown (present-day Monroe).

In 1812, the United States' hatred and fear of Great Britain, as well as the hope of territorial gain, made war between the two countries appear inevitable. The deep-seated hostility many Americans felt for their former colonial rulers had many causes. For years the British navy had violated U.S. neutrality on the high seas. The British were also accused of encouraging Indians in the Ohio River Valley to oppose the advance of American settlement. But the desire to annex the vast and agriculturally rich lands of Upper Canada (present-day Ontario) proved more important to many Americans than defending U.S. pride or frontier safety. Confident that Canada could be captured quickly and with little bloodshed, Congressman Henry Clay of Kentucky and other "War Hawks" pushed the United States toward its second war with Great Britain in thirty years.

In 1812 the Michigan Territory, which shared a common border with Upper Canada, had fewer than five thousand settlers; most were French-Canadian and lived along the Detroit River. With a population of about eight hundred people, Detroit was the territorial capital. On the east side of the Detroit River lay Upper Canada. Amherstburg, sixteen miles below Detroit, was slightly smaller and the largest Canadian community along the Detroit River.

The defenses of Detroit and Amherstburg were similar. Fort Detroit was enclosed by a six-foot-deep, twelve-foot-wide ditch and surrounded by a row of eleven-foot-high cedar pickets. Because Fort Detroit was located away from the river it was necessary to fire over the town to control river traffic effectively. Fort Malden at Amherstburg had four bastions with an advanced redoubt, and it was surrounded by a ditch and a row of fourteen-foot-high pickets. Located above Amherstburg, the Canadian fort was ideally situated on the Detroit River's deepest channel and within musket range of passing ships. The major difference between U.S. and British defenses was their naval forces. At Amherstburg the British had at least one brig (sixteen guns), two schooners (six and ten guns), several lightly armed merchant vessels, and numerous bateaux. At Detroit the Americans had one fourteen-gun vessel, which was inoperative. Considering the importance of controlling the waterways—the vital communication and supply lines to the East—the difference in naval strength posed a serious problem for the United States.

The arrival of Hull's army in Detroit on July 6 relieved the town's residents. As early as May the detention of Americans by Canadian authorities and increased military activity across the Detroit River had led the authorities to mobilize part of the Michigan militia and order each company commander to drill his men daily for two hours. In case of a surprise attack, three rounds were to be fired from a cannon to signal the militia to assemble at the town's south gate.

Hull's army consisted of about 450 regulars, 1,450 Ohio militia, and 200 men from the Michigan Detached Militia, which was commanded by Major James Witherell. The majority of Hull's men were ill-equipped, untrained, and undisciplined. Given discretionary orders to attack Fort Malden, and pressed by zealous Ohio militia officers, especially Colonels Duncan McArthur and Lewis Cass, Hull moved his army across the Detroit River in the early morning darkness of July 12. Hull's force included his regulars and most of the Ohio militia. The Michigan militia, one Ohio regiment, and about one hundred other Ohioans, who refused to leave their nation's borders, remained at Detroit. Hull's invasion was part of the U.S. strategy to invade Canada simultaneously at Detroit, Niagara, and Montreal.

Hull's opponent, Lieutenant Colonel Thomas St. George, possessed a force of 1,500 men—300 British regulars and an equal number of Canadian militia and Indians under Shawnee chief Tecumseh. With fewer troops, Colonel St. George feared he could not prevent the fall of Fort Malden. However, Hull, recognizing that the capture of Malden was essential before his army moved inland, delayed an attack on the fort until carriages were constructed for his heavy artillery. In the meantime, American raiding parties wreaked havoc on the Canadian countryside. Hull also issued a bombastic proclamation offering Canadians liberty from British tyranny. The U.S. general claimed he was not seeking

Canadian assistance against the British, but added that no quarter would be given to any white man fighting next to an Indian. The decree apparently worked since the British force, now commanded by Colonel Henry Proctor, was seriously affected by desertion.

Two weeks after the American invasion of Upper Canada, Hull's leadership and the chances of U.S. success along the Detroit River showed signs of imminent demise. British naval supremacy on the upper Great Lakes had kept Hull from sending reinforcements to Fort Mackinac, which was located on Mackinac Island and guarded the passageway between Lakes Huron and Michigan. Hull had not even informed the fort's commandant, Lieutenant Porter Hanks, and his sixty-one men that war had broken out.

British forces on St. Joseph Island, forty miles northeast of Mackinac, were commanded by Captain Charles Roberts. Roberts, who knew that war had been declared, led a command that totaled only forty-six officers and men. Augmenting his force with employees of the North West Company and their numerous Indian allies, Roberts moved quickly. During the early morning hours of July 17 his men landed on the northwest shore of Mackinac Island near present-day British Landing. They then dragged a cannon to the high ground overlooking the rear of Fort Mackinac.

While the British got into position, Michael Dousman, a former Michigan militia captain who lived on the island, informed the villagers that they should move to the distillery west of town to avoid the wrath of Roberts' Indian allies. Dousman had been captured by Roberts the previous night and had agreed to inform the village of the impending battle in exchange for his freedom. Dousman kept his pledge not to inform Lieutenant Hanks that the British had landed on the island. Hanks learned of the British arrival at dawn and made all possible preparations, but he was outnumbered ten to one. Because the fort's water supply was located beyond the range of its guns, Hanks could not withstand a siege. As he looked up at the British cannon and the several hundred Indians waiting to attack, Hanks realized he had no option but surrender. Americans on Mackinac either took the British oath of allegiance or left the island. Lieutenant Hanks and most of his men were paroled and arrived in Detroit on August 2.

The fall of Fort Mackinac disheartened General Hull, who believed it would "open the northern hive of Indians." Two days after Hanks reached Detroit an American force of two hundred Ohio militia was sent to the River Raisin where a supply expedition, commanded by Ohio Militia Captain Henry Brush, awaited an escort to Detroit. The Americans ignored warnings of a possible ambush and did not even take the precaution of sending scouts ahead of their main force. A group of approximately twenty-five Indians, led by Tecumseh, attacked and routed the Ohioans. This skirmish, called the Battle of Brownstown, left seventeen Ohioans dead and at least a dozen wounded. It also left Hull more apprehensive. The American general knew that U.S. efforts against Montreal and Niagara had stalled, which would allow British general Isaac Brock to turn his attention to the Detroit theater. With the gun carriages finally completed, Hull agreed to an attack on Fort Malden. A few hours later, he reversed his decision when news reached him that Brock and British reinforcements were headed towards Amherstburg. Over the protests of Cass and others, Hull returned his army to Detroit on August 8.

The day after he returned to Detroit, Hull dispatched another force to aid Brush's stranded relief expedition. Commanded by Lieutenant Colonel James Miller, a regular army officer, the force of approximately six hundred men, including Captain Antoine Dequindre's company of Michigan Detached Militia and Captain Richard Smyth's troop of Michigan cavalry, defeated a smaller British/Indian force near Monguagon (present-day Trenton). The victory opened up the way for Miller to reach Brush's relief expedition at the River Raisin. But the fear of another ambush and a shortage of supplies delayed Miller until Hull ordered him back to Detroit. American casualties at Monguagon were eighteen killed and sixty-four wounded; British casualties were at least six killed, twenty-one wounded, and two taken prisoner.

On August 13, General Brock arrived at Fort Malden and moved to attack Detroit. Brock ordered artillery batteries built opposite Detroit, and on August 15 he demanded Hull's surrender. Hull defiantly responded, "I am ready to meet any force which may be at your disposal." Equally determined, Brock ordered an artillery bombardment of Detroit that damaged many dwellings in the city and led residents to pack up and bury "valuables of every sort." The Americans returned the fire, which continued for several hours.

At dawn on August 16, Brock's force of 330 regulars, 400 militia, and 600 Indians crossed the Detroit River uncontested. The British resumed their artillery barrage but directed it toward Fort Detroit, not the town. After learning that Colonel Elijah Brush's First Michigan Militia, stationed outside the fort, had deserted, Hull ordered his troops to retire within the fort's walls. (The Michigan Detached Militia held their ground.) According to one observer, with so many soldiers as well as women and children inside the stockade, "it was almost impossible for a ball to strike on the fort without killing someone." Among those killed was Lieutenant Hanks, the former commandant of Fort Mackinac.

Lacking sufficient gunpowder and cannon shells to withstand a long siege and having an exaggerated idea of the number of Indians in the British ranks, Hull surrendered without consulting his fellow officers. Hoping to avert an Indian massacre, he reasoned that he had no other choice. Shortly after noon, the British entered Fort Detroit, lowered the Stars and Stripes, and, with their band playing "God Save the King," hoisted the Union Jack.

Hull's decision to surrender without a fight was influenced by the actions of Colonels Cass and McArthur. The two men had left Detroit on August 14 with four hundred men on another expedition to advance Brush's much-needed supplies to Hull's army. They never reached Brush. Earlier, the two colonels had worked to remove Hull from his command, and on the morning of the surrender they were camped three miles outside of Detroit. Aware of the British bombardment of the fort, Cass and McArthur did not inform Hull of their location, nor did they initiate any action that might have aided the Detroit garrison. To protect Cass and McArthur from possible Indian attacks, Hull also surrendered these forces. When informed that they had been surrendered, the Ohioans cursed Hull but returned to Fort Detroit and laid down their arms.

Some Americans would not surrender. Captain Brush, whose expedition still sat at the River Raisin, refused to acknowledge that Hull had also surrendered his troops. Instead, Brush withdrew to Ohio. One resourceful militiaman, A. C. Traux, after discarding his musket in Detroit, picked up a trunk and under the watchful eye of British and American officers, both of whom supposed him to be detailed to carry the trunk, walked out of Detroit and eventually reached freedom. Hull's regular soldiers were sent to Montreal, and the Ohio and Michigan militia were paroled and allowed to go home. Hull was paroled in October 1812. Two years later, a board of inquiry found him guilty of cowardliness and neglect of duty. He was sentenced to be executed, but President James Madison pardoned him because of his record during the American Revolution.

Too cautious to command in a situation that required decisiveness and imagination, Hull was the wrong man to lead the North Western Army. Instead, he was a scapegoat for an administration that had plunged into a war with too little preparation. Besides failing to inform Hull of the outbreak of hostilities, the War Department should have discouraged him from invading Canada before his army was properly trained and supplied. Finally, Hull might have been successful if the government had not rejected his prewar suggestion that a U.S. naval force be built on the Great Lakes.

The loss of Detroit shocked residents of the Northwest Territory. One month after Hull's capitulation, Indiana territorial governor William Henry Harrison organized a new North Western Army. Harrison's orders included the capture of Detroit and the invasion of Upper Canada. During the remainder of 1812, his forces harassed Indians in Ohio and Indiana and gathered supplies for an expedition against Fort Malden.

In early January 1813, General James Winchester, a veteran of the American Revolution, left his encampment on the Maumee River and moved down the river to the rapids with a force of 1,100 men. He immediately began receiving pleas for relief from residents at Frenchtown, forty miles away. According to the reports, the British were rounding up all American sympathizers and sending them to Fort Malden. Winchester also learned that substantial grain stores were located at Frenchtown. On January 17, against Harrison's direct orders and against the advice of Colonel Samuel Wells, who commanded Winchester's regulars, Winchester ordered half his force to Frenchtown. The Americans beat back a smaller British force, and Winchester arrived to take command of the American force, now reinforced to approximately nine hundred men—seven hundred Kentuckians and two hundred U.S. regulars. Besides being a great distance from its base, Winchester's army was haphazardly encamped in a poor defensive position with its back to the River Raisin. Winchester failed to improve his position or dispatch scouts to check reports of an imminent British attack. Many of the American soldiers had insufficient ammunition, and their extra powder was stored at the general's headquarters—a mile away and on the other side of the river.

At dawn on January 22, 1813, British colonel Henry Proctor and a force of five hundred British regulars and militia, plus eight hundred Indians, fell upon the unsuspecting Americans. Winchester's regulars, who had been placed behind a rail fence despite pleas from Colonel Wells to move them, suffered heavily from British artillery fire. However, on the left flank, the Kentucky militia repulsed three British assaults and inflicted heavy casualties. Winchester reached the battlefield just in time to watch the Indians outflank and rout his regulars. Winchester was captured and—convinced by the British that an Indian massacre was imminent—he surrendered his army.

Fearing the arrival of American reinforcements, Colonel Proctor moved his army and most of the American prisoners away from the River Raisin. Proctor left behind approximately eighty wounded Americans, a handful of interpreters, and several dozen Indians. The Indians came back the next morning and murdered approximately sixty wounded Americans. Those who were not killed were taken to Indian camps; some were later ransomed by Detroit citizens.

The disaster at Frenchtown left about 220 Americans dead and more than 500 taken prisoner; only 33 Americans escaped. British losses were 24 killed and more than 160 wounded. Indian casualties are unknown. Winchester's defeat provided Americans, especially Kentuckians, with the war cry, "Remember the River Raisin!" But the loss of more than 900 men, bad weather, restrictive orders from U.S. Secretary of War John Armstrong, and the expiration of militia enlistments kept Harrison from continuing his winter campaign in early 1813.

A shortage of troops prevented Proctor, recently promoted to brigadier general for his success at River Raisin, from pursuing the Americans after his victory. He did garrison one hundred British regulars at Detroit. Concerned the Detroiters might subvert British authority, Proctor ordered at least thirty of the town's prominent citizens to leave the Michigan Territory. The British general planned to send Elijah Brush, Conrad Ten Eyck, J. McDonnell, and others to Fort George at Niagara. The Detroiters protested that such an action would violate the August 1812 Articles of Capitulation, and Proctor temporarily delayed implementing his order. He did, however, place Michigan under martial law.

British occupation during the winter of 1812–13 proved difficult for many Michiganians. In Detroit, a shortage of food, an influx of both Indians and settlers, and disease took a frightful toll on the residents of the territorial capital. Indian depredations presented another problem. Canadians living in Detroit painted their cattle and houses with a red mark to keep Indians from pillaging their possessions. But according to Silas Farmer, Detroiters "were plundered in every possible way." One resident recounted,

> On a beautiful Sunday morning in Detroit, I heard the scalp-whoop of a war party coming up the river. When they came near, I discovered that they were carrying a woman's scalp upon a pole, and they had with them, as prisoners, a family of nine children, from three years old up to two girls full grown. These little captives had nothing on their heads, and their clothes were torn into shreds by the brushwood and the bushes in the way by which they had come. I went to meet them, brought them into my house, gave them and their Indian captors a meal, with a few loaves of bread for further use, and told the children not to be frightened or uneasy, for that my brother would buy them from the Indians. . . . My brother, H. J. Hunt, paid five hundred dollars for their ransom, and sent them home.

In late April 1813, Proctor invaded northwestern Ohio and laid siege to Fort Meigs. Recently constructed, Fort Meigs lay on the Maumee River, twelve miles from Lake Erie, where it threatened British control of western Lake Erie. Proctor was eventually forced to withdraw, but not before his forces ambushed and killed or captured an American force of more than eight hundred men.

British offensive movements and American setbacks had kept Harrison on the defensive during 1813. But on September 10, Lieutenant Oliver Perry's decisive victory over the British fleet at Put-in-Bay, near Sandusky, Ohio, ended British naval superiority on Lake Erie and allowed Harrison to resume the offensive. On September 27 Harrison's army of more than four thousand men made an unopposed landing three miles below Amherstburg. At the same time, Colonel Richard Johnson's five hundred mounted Kentuckians were taking an overland route via the River Raisin to Detroit. On September 29, Harrison's troops reached Sandwich, opposite Detroit, and General Duncan McArthur crossed the river and liberated Detroit, which had been evacuated by the British on the previous day. On September 30, Colonel Johnson's men arrived in Detroit. Detroiters were overjoyed with the arrival of American troops. British troops had no sooner left the town than one resident hoisted a U.S. flag atop the Mansion House. According to Silas Farmer, "The Kentucky soldiers—with their blue hunting shirts, red belt, and blue pantaloons fringed with red—met with a hearty welcome." Fort Detroit was renamed after Kentucky Governor Isaac Shelby, who had accompanied Harrison's invasion force.

Short of supplies, General Proctor realized that Perry's destruction of the British fleet placed his troops in a precarious situation. On September 27 the British evacuated Fort Malden and slowly retreated up the Thames River. Harrison pursued Proctor, whose retreating army destroyed or abandoned vast quantities of supplies and ammunition.

On October 5, several miles west of Moravian Town on the Thames River, Proctor turned to fight. The British general carelessly placed his regulars in an exposed position where Harrison's cavalry routed them in a matter of minutes. Tecumseh's eight hundred Indians, who had opposed Proctor's retreat, vigorously resisted the Americans before they were overwhelmed. Tecumseh was killed, but Proctor, who fled at the first sign of defeat, reached safety. He was later court-martialed and convicted of showing poor leadership at Moravian Town. British casualties at the Battle of the Thames were at least forty-five killed, thirty-six wounded, and six hundred taken prisoner. American losses were seven killed and twenty-two wounded. The Americans also captured eight cannon and supplies that exceeded one million dollars in value.

The day after the Battle of the Thames, the British schooner *Nancy* reached the head of the St. Clair River en route to Amherstburg to get supplies for the garrison at Mackinac. The captain of the ship, exercising caution, anchored at the rapids near what is now Port Huron and inquired about the status of the war in that area. He learned from local residents about the outcome of the fight at Moravian Town but because of unfavorable winds did not move his vessel. About noon the following day, the commander of the St. Clair River militia ordered the captain to surrender the *Nancy* or be fired upon by fifty of his men. The captain chose to try an escape, an action that brought fire from the Michigan forces upon the shore. Although the schooner suffered serious damage from the engagement, the ship managed to return to the safety of Mackinac.

After burning Moravian Town, Harrison returned his army to Detroit. Since it was too late in the season to mount an expedition to recapture Fort Mackinac, he sailed to Niagara. Before Harrison left, an armistice was signed with various Michigan Indians, which allowed them to return to their normal camping grounds until a formal peace conference could be held. Lewis Cass, promoted to brigadier general earlier in the year, was left in command at Detroit. On October 29, 1813, President Madison appointed Cass governor of the Michigan Territory.

Except for an occasional raid into Upper Canada, the Michigan/Canadian frontier was quiet until the summer of 1814. In June 1814 a ragtag force of Michigan Fencibles (Mackinac Island and Sault Ste. Marie residents in British service), three hundred Indians, and two companies of *voyageurs* and Canadian militiamen was organized at Mackinac Island to capture Prairie du Chien. Located on the Mississippi River in present-day Wisconsin, Prairie du Chien was a key to returning the fur trade in the upper Mississippi River region to British control. The British expedition left Mackinac on June 28. It was led by Lieutenant Colonel William McKay, a former captain in the Michigan Fencibles, whose "entire knowledge of war matters," according to one observer, "consisted of his predilection for rum." Outnumbering the U.S. garrison at Prairie du Chien, McKay forced its surrender on July 20. In September a group of the Fencibles helped defeat an American force at present-day Rock Island, Illinois, before returning to Prairie du Chien to help garrison that post.

The British on Mackinac Island had waited all spring for the inevitable American effort to recapture Fort Mackinac. It came at daybreak on July 26, 1814, when British sentries sighted an American fleet off Mackinac Island. The U.S. naval squadron included the *Lawrence* and the *Niagara,* ships that saw action at Put-in-Bay, and was commanded by Captain Arthur Sinclair. On board was an army force of seven hundred men, which included five companies of regulars led by twenty-two-year-old Lieutenant Colonel George Croghan.

In a manner reminiscent of earlier American debacles, the joint navy-army operation suffered repeated setbacks. Even before leaving Detroit on July 3, the expedition had been plagued by disputes within the U.S. high command. The fleet had been ordered to destroy British installations at Matchadash, at the mouth of the Severn River in northeastern Lake Huron, but no one aboard the vessels knew how to reach the British supply base. After wandering aimlessly for several days, the American fleet sailed to St. Joseph Island and Sault Ste. Marie, where miscellaneous British property was destroyed.

Arriving off Mackinac Island, the Americans remained confused. Since the fleet's guns could not be elevated to reach Fort Mackinac, the Americans dismissed the notion of a frontal attack. Finally, on August 4, the American ships bombarded the spot where the British had landed two years earlier. Colonel Croghan then led his men ashore, hoping to entice the British to leave Fort Mackinac and fight in the open. Colonel Robert McDougall, the British commandant at Fort Mackinac, left the fort and selected a strong defensive position of his force of 140 soldiers and 350 Indians. Captain Andrew Holmes led the American attack, but the British position and the placement of Indians on the American flanks resulted in heavy U.S. casualties, including the death of Captain Holmes. The Americans withdrew and gave up the idea of recapturing Fort Mackinac. Sinclair and Croghan returned to Detroit with part of the fleet. They left the *Scorpion* and the *Tigress,* under the command of Lieutenant Daniel Turner, to prevent supplies from reaching Fort Mackinac. Before leaving, Sinclair warned Turner to keep shifting the position of his ships to avoid possible enemy capture. Turner ignored the advice.

Facing starvation if supplies were not received, the British on Mackinac Island decided on a desperate move. On the night of September 3, Lieutenant Miller Worsley, of the Royal Navy, silently led a force of approximately fifty men to Drummond Island, where the *Tigress* was anchored. Worsley's men moved within one hundred yards of the unsuspecting *Tigress* before they were seen. After a brief struggle, the thirty-man crew was overpowered. On September 5 the *Scorpion* approached the *Tigress*, which was still flying the American flag, and anchored two miles away. That night, Worsley pulled up anchor and got within ten yards of the *Scorpion* before the Americans realized what had happened. The British quickly seized the *Scorpion*. Worsley and his men then sailed to Mackinac Island where they were hailed as heroes. Food, supplies, and Indian trading goods soon began arriving to take the islanders through another winter. The capture of the *Scorpion* and the *Tigress*, which Captain Sinclair described as "mortifying," ended the war on the upper Great Lakes.

A few days after the *Scorpion* and *Tigress* encounter, a minor incident occurred near Detroit. On the morning of that day William McMillan, a farmer, went out on the commons to find his cows. Upon reaching a point now marked by the intersection of Grand River Avenue and Griswold Street, he was fired upon by Indians waiting in ambush. McMillan was killed and scalped. Angered by this and earlier outrages, Governor Cass roused the settlers to action. A party of about two dozen mounted men was raised, which rode "up the river to the Witherell farm and through the lane northward to the woods." Coming to the back of what was then the Macomb farm, the body of citizen troops encountered and killed several Indians. After driving off all of the other Native Americans in sight, Governor Cass and his squad marched to the Rouge River, where they drove out another band of Indians before returning to Detroit in the evening. According to one observer, this engagement "gave quiet to the settlement until the end of the war in 1815." William McMillan's body was buried in Elmwood Cemetery, "and on his gravestone may be read a short account of his violent death."

Also during 1814, American spies were active along the Detroit frontier. Though little is known of their activities, spies were organized into at least two companies, commanded by James H. Audrain and Andrew Westbrook, and gathered intelligence about British and Indian activities in the Detroit River area.

In late 1814 new Indian depredations outside of Detroit and a fear of a British attack led Governor Cass to request that reinforcements be sent to Detroit. On October 9, 1814, Brigadier General McArthur arrived from Ohio with more than six hundred mounted Kentucky volunteers. On October 23, McArthur's force, accompanied by fifty mounted Michigan militia, began a twenty-four-day raid into Upper Canada. McArthur defeated two separate British forces and destroyed numerous gristmills and other public property in one of the war's most devastating raids. McArthur's foray into Upper Canada marked the last important military action on the Detroit frontier before the Treaty of Ghent on December 24, 1814.

The Treaty of Ghent restored all conquered territory to both countries. On July 1, 1815, the British returned to Fort Malden. Seventeen days later, after repeatedly stalling to avoid damaging relations with their former Indian allies, the British finally relinquished control of Fort Mackinac.

The Americans had failed in their conquest of Canada, but they enjoyed certain gains from their second war with Great Britain. After the war, white pioneers continued their march westward with a substantially reduced fear of encountering Indian resistance. The war increased the power and prestige of the United States, and it more clearly delineated the boundaries between this country and Canada.

Such positive effects were less visible in Michigan. Two years of warfare and enemy occupation had devastated the territory's settlements, especially along the River Raisin. On March 5, 1815, Territorial Justice Augustus B. Woodward painted a dismal picture of conditions:

> The desolation of this territory is beyond all conception. No kind of flour or meal [is] to be procured, and [there is] nothing for the subsistence of the cattle. No animals for slaughter, and more than half of the population destitute of any [livestock] for domestic or agricultural purposes. The fencing of their farms [was] entirely destroyed by the incursions of the enemy, and for fuel for the military. Their houses [were] left without glass, and in many instances even the flooring burnt. Their clothing [was] plundered from them by the Indians.

Woodward added that residents along the River Raisin were so short of provisions that they were eating boiled hay.

Unlike other regions in the Northwest, Michigan did not attract flocks of settlers after the war, nor was the War of 1812 the last time Michiganians and Canadians exchanged gunfire. In 1838, hostilities, on a smaller scale, would erupt again along the Detroit River. If Michigan experienced a positive result from the War of 1812 it was the appointment of Lewis Cass as territorial governor. Cass may have been an overzealous and at times uncooperative militia officer, but he proved to be an enthusiastic governor who gave his adopted home of Michigan over a half-century of devoted service.

BIBLIOGRAPHIC NOTE

Sources used in preparing this chapter, or recommended for further reading, include:

Abbott, John Roblin. *The History of Fort St. Joseph.* Toronto: Dundurn Group, 2000. 87–110.

Anderson, Fanny J. "Medical Practices in Detroit During the War of 1812." *Bulletin of the History of Medicine* 16, no. 3 (Oct. 1944): 261–75.

Au, Dennis M. "Best Troops in the World: The Michigan Territorial Militia in the Detroit River Theater During the War of 1812." In Robert J. Holden, ed., *Selected Papers from the 1991 and 1992 George Rogers Clark Trans-Appalachian Frontier History Conferences.* Vincennes, Ind.: 1994. 105–26.

———. *War on the Raisin.* Monroe, Mich.: Monroe County Historical Commission, 1981.

Bulkley, John M. *History of Monroe County.* Chicago: Lewis Publishing Company, 1913. 1:57–136.

Burton, Clarence M. "The War of 1812," *The City of Detroit.* Detroit: Clarke Publishing Company, 1922, 1:979–1051.

Clarke, James Freeman. *William Hull and the Surrender of Detroit.* Boston: George H. Ellis, [1912].

Clift, Garrett Glenn. *Remember the Raisin!* Frankfort: Kentucky Historical Society, 1961.

Cruikshank, Ernest A. "General Hull's Invasion of Canada in 1812." *Proceedings and Transactions of the Royal Society of Canada.* Ottawa: The Society, 1907. Section 2, pp. 211–90.

———, ed. *Documents Relating to the Invasion of Canada and the Surrender of Detroit, 1812.* New York: Arno Press, 1971.

Darnell, Elias. *A Journal, Containing an Accurate and Interesting Account of the . . . Years 1812–1813.* Philadelphia: Lippincott, Grambo, 1854.

Douglas, R. Alan. *Uppermost Canada: The Western District and the Detroit Frontier, 1800–1850.* Detroit: Wayne State University Press, 2001. 33–85.

———. "Yankee Doodle Upset." *Detroit Historical Society Bulletin* 20, no. 2 (Nov. 1963): 4–8.

Dunbar, Willis. "Early Territorial Days and the War of 1812." *Michigan Through the Centuries.* New York: Lewis Historical Publishing Company, 1955. 129–52.

Dunnigan, Brian Leigh. "Michigan Fencibles." *Michigan History Magazine* 57, no. 4 (Winter 1973): 277–95.

———. "To Make a Military Appearance: Uniforming Michigan's Militia and Fencibles." *Michigan Historical Review* 15, no. 1 (Spring 1989): 29–43.

Durocher, Laurent. *Laurent Durocher's Account of the Battles and Massacre of the River Raisin.* Monroe, Mich.: Monroe County Community College, 1987.

Farmer, Silas. *History of Detroit and Wayne County and Early Michigan.* 1890; rpt., Detroit: Gale Research Co., 1969. 274–98.

Forbes, James G. *The Trial of Brig. General William Hull.* New York: Eastburn, Kirk & Co., 1814.

Fuller, George N. "Michigan in the War of 1812." *Historic Michigan.* Dayton: National Historical Association, 1924. 1:223–34.

———. "War of 1812," *Michigan, A Centennial History.* Chicago: Lewis Publishing Company, 1939. 1:120–38.

Gilpin, Alec R. *The War of 1812 in the Old Northwest.* East Lansing: Michigan State University Press, 1958.

Hamil, Fred C. *Michigan in the War of 1812.* Lansing: Michigan History Division, 1977.

Herndon, Nell G. "Detroit Under British Rule, 1812–1813," M.A. thesis, Wayne State University, 1933.

Hull, William. *Memoirs of the Campaign of the Northwestern Army.* Boston: True & Greene, 1824.

"An Indian Skirmish," *Michigan Pioneer Collections* 28 (1897–98): 633.

Lossing, Benson John. *Hull's Surrender of Detroit.* Philadelphia: J. E. Potter & Co., 1875.

———. *Pictorial Fieldbook of the War of 1812.* New York: Harper & Bros., 1869. 251–96, 338–64.

Mason, Philip P., ed. *After Tippecanoe.* East Lansing: Michigan State University Press, 1963.

May, George S. *War of 1812.* Kalamazoo: Mackinac Island State Park Commission, 1962.

———. *War of 1812 in Michigan.* Lansing: Michigan Historical Commission, 1964.

Monroe County Historical Commission. *The Battles and Massacre of the River Raisin Archaeological Survey.* Monroe, Mich.: The Commission, 1976.

Moore, Charles. "Michigan in the War of 1812." *History of Michigan.* Chicago: Lewis Publishing Company, 1915. 1:290–312.

"A Muster Roll of 1812," *Michigan Pioneer Collections* 5 (1882): 553–57.

Quaife, Milo M. "An Artilleryman of Old Fort Mackinac." *Burton Historical Collection Leaflet* 6, no. 3 (Jan. 1928): 33–48.

Rahn, Adele E. *The Events at Brownstown.* Lansing: Historical Society of Michigan, 1962.

Robertson, John. "The War of 1812–13," *Michigan in the War.* Lansing: W. S. George & Co., 1882. 1005–22.

Rosentreter, Roger. "Remember the Raisin." *Michigan History Magazine* 82, no. 6 (Nov./Dec. 1998): 40–51.

State Library. "Three Years of War—150 Years of Peace." *Michigan in Books* 5, no. 1 (Summer 1962): 75–79.

Utley, Henry M. *Michigan as a Province, Territory, and State.* New York: American Press, 1906. 2:171–239.

Vorderstrasse, Alfred B. *Detroit in the War of 1812.* Detroit: Wayne State University Press, 1951.

Zeisler, Karl F. "The Battle of the River Raisin." *Detroit Historical Society Bulletin* 18, no. 7 (Apr. 1962): 4–10.

WAR OF 1812 RELATED HISTORIC SITES AND MONUMENTS IN MICHIGAN

Alexander Macomb State Historic Marker, Macomb County
American Surrender County Historic Marker, Monroe County
Anderson Trading Post County Historic Marker, Monroe County
Battle of Brownstown State Historic Marker, Wayne County
Battle of Monguagon State Historic Marker, Wayne County
Battlefield of 1814 Brass Marker, U.S. Daughters of 1812, Mackinac County
Battlefield of 1814 State Historic Marker, Mackinac County
British Cannon State Historic Marker, Mackinac Island, Mackinac County
British Landing State Historic Marker, Mackinac Island, Mackinac County
British Victory at Frenchtown County Historic Marker, Monroe County
Capture of General Winchester County Historic Marker, Monroe County
Death of Captain Woolfolk County Historic Marker, Monroe County
Death of Colonel John Allen County Historic Marker, Monroe County
First Battle of the River Raisin County Historic Marker, Monroe County
Fort de Baude State Historic Marker, Mackinac County
Fort Drummond State Historic Marker, Chippewa County
Fort Holmes Brass Marker, Mackinac Island Commission, Mackinac County
Fort Holmes State Historic Marker, Mackinac Island, Mackinac County
Fort Lernoult State Historic Marker, Wayne County
Fort Shelby Bronze Tablet, Old Fort Street Post Office, Detroit
Fort St. Joseph State Historic Marker, St. Clair County
Historic Fort Mackinac State Marker, Mackinac Island, Mackinac County
Historic River Raisin County Historic Marker, Monroe County
Indian Ambush County Historic Marker, Monroe County
Indian Fields Bronze Tablet, Airport Terminal, Kalamazoo
Indian Massacre Bronze Tablet, State and Griswold Streets, Detroit
John Johnston House State Historic Marker, Chippewa County
Johnston Homestead City Historic Marker, Sault Ste. Marie
Kentucky Troops State Monument at Memorial Place, Monroe
LaPlaisance Bay Settlement County Historic Marker, Monroe County
Lewis Cass Bronze Tablet, Mackinac Island, Mackinac County
Mackinac Island State Historic Marker, Mackinac County
Mackinac Straits State Historic Marker, Mackinac County
Mansion House and Survey Tree State Historic Marker, Wayne County
Memorial Place County Historic Marker, Monroe County
Michigan: Historic Crossroads State Historic Marker, Monroe County
Military Outpost 1815–1817 State Historic Marker, Wayne County
Monroe State Historic Marker, Monroe County
Murder of Captain Hart County Historic Marker, Monroe County
Navarre-Anderson Trading Post Registered Historic Site, Monroe
Old Hull Road County Historic Marker, Monroe County
Raisin Massacre of 1813 County Historic Marker, Monroe County
Redford Cemetery State Historic Marker, Wayne County
River Raisin Blockhouse County Historical Tablet, Monroe County
River Raisin Massacre Site, Woman's Civic Improvement Society Monument, Monroe
Sandy Creek Settlement County Historic Marker, Monroe County
Storied Homestead County Historic Marker, Monroe County
Tecumseh's Headquarters County Historic Marker, Monroe County
U.S. 17th Infantry Campsite County Historic Marker, Monroe County
War of 1812 Dead State Historic Marker, Wayne County
War of 1812 Memorial Bronze Tablet, Byron Center, Kent County

War of 1812 Memorial Bronze Tablet, Caledonia, Kent County
War of 1812 Memorial Bronze Tablet, Moffat Building, Detroit
Wayne Stockade County Historic Marker, Monroe County

LIST OF RELEVANT MICHIGAN ILLUSTRATIONS

War of 1812—Representative Soldiers

Atwell, Willis. *Do You Know.* [Grand Rapids]: Booth Newspapers, 1937. Pp. 360, 362, 366, 368–70, 374, 375, 377–81, 391, 393, 397, 401. Representations of events that occurred during the war.

Au, Dennis M. *War on the Raisin.* Monroe, Mich.: Monroe County Historical Commission, 1981. P. 89. British cartoon showing the conclusion of the battle at the River Raisin.

Bald, F. Clever. *Michigan in Four Centuries.* New York: Harper & Brothers, 1961. P. 116. Original in Photograph Collection, State Archives of Michigan, Lansing. Drawing of Indian depredations after battle of the River Raisin.

Barry, James P. *Old Forts of the Great Lakes.* Lansing: Thunder Bay Press, 1994. P. 56. Hull surrendering Detroit to General Brock.

Clements Library, University of Michigan, Ann Arbor. Also Dennis M. Au, *War on the Raisin.* Monroe, Mich.: Monroe County Historical Commission, 1981. P. 90. Color print of the massacre following the battle at the River Raisin.

Company of Military Historians. *Military Collector and Historian* 37, no. 3 (Fall 1985): 140–41. Color rendition of the Michigan Legionary Corps.

———. *Military Uniforms in America: Years of Growth, 1796–1851.* San Rafael, Calif.: Presidio Press, 1977. After p. 34. Color print showing uniforms of U.S. Infantry during period.

———. *Military Uniforms in America: Years of Growth, 1796–1851.* San Rafael, Calif.: Presidio Press, 1977. After p. 48. Color portrayal of the Kentucky Militia at the River Raisin.

———. *Military Uniforms in America: Years of Growth, 1796–1851.* San Rafael, Calif.: Presidio Press, 1977. After p. 50. Color depiction of Colonel Richard M. Johnson's mounted volunteers.

Cooper, James Fennimore. *Works of J. Fennimore Cooper.* Vol. 8: Oak Openings. New York: P. F. Collier, 1891. Frontispiece and opposite page 217. Shows fictitious scenes of Michigan Indians in action around southwestern Michigan.

Downey, Fairfax. *Indian Wars of the U.S. Army, 1776–1865.* Garden City, N.Y.: Doubleday & Company, 1963. P. 92. Depiction of the Kentucky Militia at the River Raisin.

Dunnigan, Brian Leigh. *The British Army at Mackinac, 1812–1815.* Lansing: Mackinac Island State Park Commission, 1980. Pp. 24–25. Hostile action on Mackinac Island.

———. *The British Army at Mackinac, 1812–1815.* Lansing: Mackinac Island State Park Commission, 1980. Pp. 28–29, 44–45. Color illustrations of the typical militiaman and Michigan Fencible.

Ellis, Edward S. *The History of Our Country,* vol. 2. Indianapolis: Woolling & Company, 1900. Opposite p. 666. The surrender of Detroit.

Elting, John R. *Amateurs, to Arms!* Chapel Hill, N.C.: Algonquin Books, 1991. After p. 174. Hull's march to Detroit, 1812.

Gurney, Gene. *A Pictorial History of the United States Army.* New York: Crown Publishers, 1966. P. 98. A caricature of the caliber of men available to military recruiters.

Hamil, Fred C. *Michigan in the War of 1812.* Lansing: Michigan Historical Commission, 1960. Opposite p. 20. Also Benson J. Lossing. *Our Country.* New York: Amies Publishing Company, 1888. P. 1207. Hull pondering the fate of Detroit.

———. *Michigan in the War of 1812.* Lansing: Michigan Historical Commission, 1960. Opposite p. 27. Also Benson J. Lossing. *Our Country.* New York: Amies Publishing Company, 1888. P. 1233. Representation of the River Raisin massacre.

Holden, Robert J., ed. *Selected Papers from the 1991 and 1992 George Rogers Clark Trans-Appalachian Frontier History Conferences.* Vincennes, Ind., 1994. Page 104. Likeness of a Michigan Territorial Militiaman.

Katcher, Philip R. N. *The American War, 1812–1814*. New York: Hippocrene Books, 1974. Plate G. Shows a volunteer with the British forces, probably clothed much like his American counterparts.

McConnell, David B. *Discover Michigan*. Hillsdale, Mich.: Hillsdale Educational Publishers, 1981. P. 49. A cannonball falls through the roof of a house in Detroit.

Marsh, Harriet A., and Florence A. Marsh. *History of Detroit*. Chicago: R. R. Donnelley & Sons, 1935. P. 129. The surrender of Detroit.

May, George S. *War, 1812*. Lansing: Mackinac Island State Park Commission, 1962. Pp. [4], 13, 17, 37, 41. Action scenes at contest for control of fort on Mackinac Island.

May, George S. *The War of 1812 in Michigan*. Lansing: Michigan Historical Commission, 1964. Filmstrip and accompanying booklet devoted to this conflict.

Nelson, William H., and Frank E. Vandiver. *Fields of Glory*. New York: Dutton & Company, 1960. P. 38. Lithograph showing the Battle of the Thames.

Nursey, Walter R. *The Story of Isaac Brock*. Toronto: McClelland & Stewart, 1923. Opposite p. 124. Brock and Tecumseh observing Detroit before its surrender.

Otis, James. *The Boy Spies at the Siege of Detroit*. New York: Burt Company, 1904. Frontispiece. Fictional scene in woods during 1812 battle for Detroit.

Reeder, Red. *The Story of the War of 1812*. New York: Duell, Sloan and Pearce, 1960. P. 66. Image of soldiers being maltreated after battle of the River Raisin.

Stanley, George F. G. *The War of 1812*. Toronto: Macmillan, 1983. P. 298. Fort MacKay, at Prairie du Chien, including the Michigan Fencibles.

Thomson, John Lewis. *History of the War of the United States with Great Britain in 1812*. Philadelphia: Lippincott Company, 1887. Opposite p. 28. Drawing of the Battle of Monguagon.

———. *History of the War of the United States with Great Britain in 1812*. Philadelphia: Lippincott Company, 1887. Opposite p. 106. Indignation of U.S. troops at the surrender of Detroit. Opposite p. 130. Illustration of the massacre at the River Raisin.

Vorderstrasse, Alfred B. *Detroit in the War of 1812*. Detroit: Wayne University Press, 1951. Pp. 6, 10, 12. Drawings of events that occurred in and around Detroit.

Windrow, Martin, and Gerry Embleton. *Military Dress of North America, 1665–1970*. New York: Charles Scribner's Sons, 1973. P. 59. Image of a Maryland Rifle Volunteer may give a rough idea of how Michigan men appeared.

War of 1812—Specific Soldiers

Anderson, John. In Photograph Collection, Monroe County Historical Museum, Monroe. Also Dennis M. Au, *War on the Raisin*. Monroe, Mich.: Monroe County Historical Commission, 1981. P. 83.

Bentley, James. In Photograph Collection, Monroe County Historical Museum, Monroe, Mich.

Bisonette, Gabriel. In Talcott E. Wing, *History of Monroe County, Michigan*. New York: Munsell & Company, 1890. Opposite p. 121.

Brush, Elijah. In Photograph Collection, Burton Historical Collections, Detroit Public Library.

Campau, Joseph. In Sarah Lieb. History of Michigan. Chicago: Belford, Clarke & Company, 1889. P. 168.

Guyor (Goire), Joseph. In John M. Bulkley, *History of Monroe County, Michigan*. Chicago: Lewis Publishing Company, 1913. P. 127.

Johnston, John. *In Michigan Pioneer and Historical Collections,* vol. 32. Lansing: Robert Smith Printing Company, 1903. Opposite p. 305.

Knaggs, James. In Benson J. Lossing, *The Pictorial Field-Book of the War of 1812*. New York: Harper & Brothers, 1869. P. 363.

Lacroix, Hubert. In Talcott E. Wing, *History of Monroe County, Michigan*. New York: Munsell & Company, 1890. Opposite p. 106.

Marsac, Joseph. In Kresge Art Center, *Early Michigan Paintings*. East Lansing: Michigan State University, 1976. P. 103.

McKay, William. In Brian Leigh Dunnigan, *The British Army at Mackinac*. Lansing: Mackinac Island State Park Commission, 1980. P. 17.

Navarre, Peter. In Photograph Collection, Monroe County Historical Museum, Monroe. Also Talcott E. Wing, *History of Monroe County, Michigan*. New York: Munsell & Company, 1890. Opposite p. 127. Also Dennis M. Au, *War on the Raisin*. Monroe, Mich.: Monroe County Historical Commission, 1981. P. 92. Also Benson J. Lossing, *The Pictorial Field-Book of the War of 1812*. New York: Harper & Brothers, 1869. P. 490.

Navarre, Robert F. *In Pageant of Historic Monroe*. Monroe, Mich.: Lamour Printing Company, 1926. P. [17].

Sibley, Solomon. In Photograph Collection, State Archives of Michigan, Lansing. Also Clarence M. Burton, *History of Wayne County and the City of Detroit, Michigan*. Detroit: Clarke Publishing Company, 1930. P. [561].

Veterans Reunion 1871. In Photograph Collection, Monroe County Historical Museum, Monroe. Also Talcott E. Wing, *History of Monroe County, Michigan*. New York: Munsell & Company, 1890. Opposite p. 82. Print and engraving of about nineteen men who fought in the conflict.

Witherell, James. In Photograph Collection, State Archives of Michigan, Lansing. Also Clarence M. Burton, *History of Wayne County and the City of Detroit, Michigan*. Detroit: Clarke Publishing Company, 1930. P. [555]. Also Silas Farmer, *The History of Detroit and Michigan*. Detroit: Silas Farmer & Company, 1889. After p. 1132. Also Western Biographical Publishing Company, *American Biographical History of Eminent and Self-Made Men*. Michigan volume. Cincinnati, 1878. Opposite p. 148.

War of 1812—Theater of Operations

Au, Dennis M. *War on the Raisin*. Monroe, Mich.: Monroe County Historical Commission, 1981. Pp. 85–88. Various maps of the River Raisin battlefield. Also p. 91. Lasselle (Francois) home at River Raisin settlement.

Barry, James P. *Old Forts of the Great Lakes*. Lansing: Thunder Bay Press, 1994. P. 40. Michilimackinac on Lake Huron.

Burton, Clarence M. *The City of Detroit, Michigan*. Detroit: Clarke Publishing Company, 1922. Opposite p. 1024. Map of fortifications in and near Detroit.

Michigan Pioneer and Historical Collections, vol. 35. Lansing: Wynkoop Hallenbeck Crawford Company, 1907. P. 203. General Winchester's headquarters at Navarre house, River Raisin.

Monroe County Historical Society. River Raisin Massacre and Battles of the War of 1812 in Historic Monroe. Monroe, 1988. Brochure identifying related historic markers and sites.

Peterson, Charles J. *The Military Heroes of the War of 1812*. Philadelphia: Smith & Company, 1859. P. 130. Also John Frost, *The Pictorial History of the United States of America*. Hartford, Conn.: Case, Tiffany and Burnham, 1847. P. 122. General Harrison's Army Crossing Lake Erie.

Utley, Henry M.. and Byron M. Cutcheon. *Michigan as a Province, Territory and State*. New York: Americana Press, 1906. Vol. 2, opposite p. 194. Maguaga battle ground.

ORGANIZATIONAL CHART OF PARTICIPATING MICHIGAN UNITS

The number of Michigan men, extracted from the rosters, is listed after each company.

1st Regiment Michigan Militia, Elijah Brush Commanding (Detroit)

Jacques Campau's Company of Infantry	51
Whitmore Knaggs' Company of Infantry	57
Soloman Sibley's Company of Infantry	49

2nd Regiment of Michigan Militia, John Anderson Commanding (Monroe)

Jean Baptiste Couture's Company of Infantry	44
Dominique Drouillard's Company of Infantry	34
Joseph Jobean's Company of Light Horsemen	21
Jean Baptiste Lasselle's Company of Infantry	27

Jacques Martin's Company of Infantry	21
Joseph Menard's Company of Infantry	44
Daniel Mulholland's Company of Infantry	27

Legionary Corps of Michigan, James Witherell Commanding (Detroit)

Antoine Dequindre's Company of Riflemen	66
Hubert Lacroix's Company of Infantry (Stationed at Monroe)	86
Stephen Mack's Company of Artillery	104
Richard Smyth's Company of Cavalry (A detachment at Monroe)	108

Independent Companies in the Service of the United States

James H. Audrain's Company of Spies (Detroit)	134
James H. Audrain's Company of U.S. Rangers (Detroit)	99
Isaac Lee's Company of Michigan Militia Cavalry (Monroe)	58
John McDonell's Troop of Michigan Militia Cavalry (Malden)	52
Andrew Westbrook's Company of Spies (Detroit)	27

Federal Units with Significant Michigan Representation

James Ball's Squadron of Light Dragoons	20
Joel Collins' Company of 19th Infantry	61
Henry Crittenden's Company of 17th Infantry	8
Thomas Edmondson's Company of 28th Infantry	30
Porter Hanks' Company of 1st Artillery	22
Martin Hawkins' Company of 17th Infantry	29
Benjamin Johnson's Company of 2nd Rifles	10
William Whistler's Company of 1st Infantry	16

State Units with Significant Michigan Representation

John Reading's Company of Kentucky Mounted Infantry	20

Michigan Units Serving with British Forces

John Johnston's Company of Volunteers (Sault Ste. Marie)	(unknown)
Michigan Fencibles, William McKay Commanding (Mackinac)	19

Miscellaneous Unit Affiliations	**186**

Total Number of Michigan Soldiers in the War of 1812	**1,535***

*Some men served with multiple units during the War so they will appear more than once in the listings.

ROSTER OF MICHIGAN MEN
IN THE WAR OF 1812

Name	Rank	Military Unit	Service Dates	Remarks
Abott, George	PVT	Collins' COM 19 US INF	03/17/14–10/13/14	Died in service
Abbott, James	QUT	F&S Legionary Corps	05/11/12–08/16/12	Surrendered at Detroit
Adams, William	CPL	Audrain's Rangers	12/01/14–08/31/15	
Adaret, Louis	PVT	Audrain's Spies	07/01/14–07/31/14	
Albert, Joseph	PVT	Mack's Company	06/03/12–08/16/12	SUB Antoine Labadi. SRA Detroit
Albin, Robert	PVT	Westbrook's Company	05/12/14–06/11/14	
Aleshire, William	4SG	Collins' COM 19 US INF	03/10/14–??/??/??	
Allard, Joseph	PVT	Audrain's Spies	07/01/14–07/31/14	
Allard, Joseph	PVT	Mack's Company	05/28/12–08/16/12	Surrendered at Detroit. PEN
Allard, Louis	PVT	Mack's Company	06/03/12–08/16/12	SUB Louis Ledue. SRA Detroit.
Allard, Pierre	PVT	Audrain's Spies	07/01/14–07/31/14	
Allaways, Joseph	PVT	Collins' COM 19 US INF	03/15/14–07/20/15	
Allen, Aaron	PVT	Audrain's Rangers	10/20/14–11/30/15	PEN
Allen, Hiram	CPL	McDonell's Company	01/01/14–03/10/14	
Allen, Moses	PVT	Audrain's Rangers	10/20/14–11/30/15	
Allen, Price	GDE	Harrison's ANW	08/02/13–08/13/13	SCU
Allen, William	GDE	Harrison's ANW	08/02/13–08/13/13	SCU
Allen, William	PVT	Campau's Company	07/02/12–08/16/12	Surrendered at Detroit
Ambrose, Joseph	PVT	Mack's Company	05/12/12–08/16/12	Surrendered at Detroit
Anderson, Amos	PVT	Audrain's Rangers	12/23/14–08/31/15	

Name	Rank	Military Unit	Service Dates	Remarks
Anderson, James	PVT	Westbrook's Company	05/12/14–06/11/14	
Anderson, James	SAD	Lee's Company	12/16/13–04/21/14	
Anderson, John	COL	F&S 2nd MI Regiment	08/04/12–08/18/12	CMO SRA Monroe.
Anderson, John	SUP	Johnson's KY MTD INF	09/??/13–10/??/13	Appointed sheriff of occupied Canada
Andre, Joseph	DRG	Smyth's Company	04/21/12–08/16/12	Surrendered at Detroit
Andre, Joseph	VOL	Lewis Cass Expedition	09/15/14	SCU
Arheart , Robert	PVT	Dequindre's Company	07/13/12–08/16/12	Surrendered at Detroit
Armstrong, Henry	PVT	Edmondson's COM 28 US INF	03/28/14–06/30/15	TRA Stockton's Company
Arnold, John	PVT	Edmondson's COM 28 US INF	03/26/14–06/30/15	TRA Stockton's Company
Ashbrook, Thomas	PVT	Sibley's Company	07/02/12–08/16/12	Surrendered at Detroit
Atwater, Reuben	CIC	F&S Michigan Militia	04/21/12–08/11/12	
Audrain, François	1LT	Audrain's Rangers	07/01/14–07/31/14	
Audrain, François	1LT	Collins' COM 7 US RAN	08/04/14–09/03/15	
Audrain, James	SCT	Campbell's Expedition	12/17/12–12/18/12	GDE to Mississinewa. SCU
Audrain, James H.	CAP	Audrain's Spies	07/01/14–07/31/14	
Audrain, James H.	CAP	Audrain's Rangers	05/01/14–11/30/15	
Audrain, John	1LT	Audrain's Rangers	05/01/14–11/30/15	
Audrain, Peter F.	PVT	Sibley's Company	07/02/12–08/16/12	Surrendered at Detroit
Austin, Peter J.	SMA	F&S Legionary Corps	06/09/12–08/18/12	DET River Raisin. SRA Monroe
Babcock, Henry	PVT	Collins' COM 19 US INF	03/17/14–07/20/15	
Bacon, John	SAD	McDonell's Company	12/20/13–03/10/14	
Bailey, James	PVT	Edmondson's COM 28 US INF	04/24/14–06/30/15	TRA Stockton's Company
Bailey, Joshua	PVT	Collins' COM 19 US INF	06/28/14–07/19/15	TRA Van Horn's COM 27 US INF
Baker, Dennis	PVT	Hickman's COM 17 US INF	08/19/08–??/??/??	
Baker, Jacob	PVT	Hawkins' COM 17 US INF	03/07/14–03/07/19	
Baker, Jacob	PVT	Lee's Company	10/22/13–03/15/14	

NAME	RANK	MILITARY UNIT	SERVICE DATES	REMARKS
Baker, James W.	5CP	Audrain's Rangers	12/23/14–08/31/15	
Bancroff, Samuel	HOA	Unassigned	10/16/13–01/23/14	Stationed at Detroit
Baptiste, John	CPL	Edmondson's COM 28 US INF	03/23/14–06/30/15	TRA Stockton's Company
Baril, Joseph	PVT	Lacroix's Company	05/18/12–08/16/12	Surrendered at Detroit
Barnard, Joshua	PVT	Audrain's Rangers	10/20/14–08/31/15	
Barnard, Pierre	CPL	Dequindre's Company	04/21/12–08/16/12	PMT CPL 06/17/12. SRA Detroit
Barnes, Hiram	PVT	Mulholland's Company	08/04/12–08/18/12	Surrendered at Monroe
Barreau, Antoine	DRG	Smyth's Company	04/26/12–08/16/12	Surrendered at Detroit
Barree, Lewis	PVT	Drouillard's Company	08/04/12–08/18/12	Surrendered at Monroe
Barreow, Joseph	PVT	Audrain's Spies	07/01/14–07/31/14	
Barrien, Joseph	PVT	Mack's Company	06/10/12–08/16/12	Surrendered at Detroit
Barron, Alexis	PVT	Lacroix's Company	05/18/12–08/16/12	Surrendered at Detroit
Barron, Gasante	PVT	Drouillard's Company	08/04/12–08/18/12	Surrendered at Monroe
Bartelow, Claudius	PVT	Jobean's Company	08/04/12–08/18/12	Surrendered at Monroe
Barthelet, Henry	PVT	Sibley's Company	07/02/12–08/16/12	Surrendered at Detroit
Basines, Joseph	PVT	Audrain's Rangers	10/20/14–10/19/15	
Basome, Alexander	PVT	Couture's Company	08/04/12–08/18/12	Surrendered at Monroe
Baubien, Joseph Jr.	4CP	Knaggs' Company	07/02/12–08/16/12	Surrendered at Detroit
Bayonne, Baptiste	PVT	Menard's Company	08/04/12–08/18/12	Surrendered at Monroe
Beach, William	PVT	Edmondson's COM 28 US INF	04/03/14–06/30/15	TRA Stockton's Company
Beasonette, Alexis	PVT	Martin's Company	08/04/12–08/18/12	Surrendered at Monroe. PEN
Beasonette, Joseph Jr.	CPL	Martin's Company	08/04/12–08/18/12	Surrendered at Monroe. PEN
Beasonette, Joseph Sr.	SGT	Martin's Company	08/04/12–08/18/12	Surrendered at Monroe
Beaubien, Alexis	PVT	Knaggs' Company	07/02/12–08/16/12	Surrendered at Detroit
Beaubien, Antoine	PVT	Campau's Company	07/02/12–08/16/12	Surrendered at Detroit
Beaubien, Antoine	PVT	Knaggs' Company	07/02/12–08/16/12	Surrendered at Detroit

Name	Rank	Military Unit	Service Dates	Remarks
Beaubien, Antoine	PVT	Mack's Company	05/28/12–08/16/12	Drafted. Surrendered at Detroit.
Beaubien, Jean Baptiste	3SG	Campau's Company	07/02/12–08/16/12	Surrendered at Detroit
Beaubien, Jean Marie	CLT	St. Clair Militia	10/06/13–10/07/13	HMS Nancy EGT. SCU
Beaubien, John B.	VOL	Lewis Cass Expedition	09/15/14	SCU
Beaubien, John M.	PVT	Knaggs' Company	07/02/12–08/16/12	Surrendered at Detroit
Beaubien, Joseph Jr.	CPL	Knaggs' Company	07/02/12–08/16/12	Surrendered at Detroit
Beaubien, Lambert Jr.	2CP	Campau's Company	07/02/12–08/16/12	Surrendered at Detroit
Beaubien, Lambert Jr.	VOL	Lewis Cass Expedition	09/15/14	SCU
Beaubien, Lambert Sr.	LUT	Campau's Company	07/02/12–08/16/12	Surrendered at Detroit
Beaufort, Louis	CAP	Michigan Militia	??/??/??–??/??/14	DUC 1814. AKA Louis Beufait. SCU
Beauhome, Jean Baptiste	PVT	Lee's Company	10/22/13–03/26/14	Died in service
Beauhome, Joseph	PVT	Lee's Company	10/22/13–12/31/13	
Beaulieu, Charles	SGT	McDonell's Company	12/20/13–03/10/14	PEN
Beauxhome, Jean B.	DRG	Smyth's Company	05/25/12–08/16/12	DET River Raisin. MNI Baptiste
Beigraft, Moses	PVT	Westbrook's Company	05/12/14–06/11/14	
Bellair, Amable	PVT	Jobean's Company	08/04/12–08/18/12	Surrendered at Monroe
Bellair, Gabriel	DRG	Smyth's Company	04/26/12–08/16/12	Surrendered at Detroit
Bellair, Jean Louis	PVT	Jobean's Company	08/04/12–08/18/12	Surrendered at Monroe
Bellair, Joseph	PVT	Knaggs' Company	07/02/12–08/16/12	Surrendered at Detroit
Bellair, Oliver	UNK	Unknown	??/??/12–08/16/12	SUR Detroit. SCU Palmer p.551
Bellair, Pierre	PVT	Knaggs' Company	07/02/12–08/16/12	Surrendered at Detroit
Bellan, Charles	PVT	Mack's Company	06/06/12–08/16/12	Surrendered at Detroit
Bellanger, Gregorie	PVT	Martin's Company	08/04/12–08/18/12	Surrendered at Monroe
Bellanges, Babtiste	DRG	Smyth's Company	04/23/12–08/16/12	Surrendered at Detroit
Bellmare, Alexis	PVT	Lacroix's Company	05/18/12–08/16/12	Surrendered at Detroit
Bellville, Peter	PVT	Whistler's COM 1 US INF	02/02/12–12/31/15	Discharged for disability

NAME	RANK	MILITARY UNIT	SERVICE DATES	REMARKS
Bennet, Martin	4SG	Smyth's Company	04/21/12–08/16/12	Surrendered at Detroit
Bentley, James	2SG	Lee's Company	10/22/13–04/21/14	PEN
Bentley, James	2SG	Reading's COM KY MTD INF	08/15/13–11/19/13	PEN
Bentley, James	DRG	Smyth's Company	04/29/12–09/30/12	DET River Raisin 05/01/12. ETO
Bentley, James	SGT	Ball's SQD US LTD	09/30/12–05/10/13	
Bernard, Peter	CPL	Audrain's Spies	07/01/14–07/31/14	
Best, William	PVT	Dequindre's Company	04/22/12–08/16/12	Surrendered at Detroit
Biggs, Josiah	PVT	Collins' COM 19 US INF	03/10/14–07/20/15	
Bilan, Joseph	DRG	Smyth's Company	04/21/12–08/16/12	Surrendered at Detroit
Bissonette, Jean Baptiste	PVT	Lacroix's Company	05/18/12–08/16/12	Surrendered at Detroit
Blackmoor, Simeon	PVT	Mulholland's Company	08/04/12–08/18/12	Surrendered at Monroe
Blackmoor, William	ENS	Mack's Company	05/20/12–08/16/12	Surrendered at Detroit
Blain, Pierre	PVT	Mack's Company	06/12/12–08/16/12	Surrendered at Detroit
Blake, Henry	DMR	Collins' COM 19 US INF	03/21/14–07/20/15	
Blanchard, Moses	PVT	Hopkins' COM 2 US LTD	10/14/13–05/02/15	
Blay, Francis	PVT	Mack's Company	05/20/12–08/16/12	Surrendered at Detroit
Bleekman, Nathan	SGT	Herron's COM 17 US INF	04/02/14–06/07/15	
Bodrie, Noah	PVT	Hanks' COM 1 US ART	04/08/11–06/01/16	TRA Pierce's Company
Boinnes, Baptist	PVT	Audrain's Rangers	10/12/14–11/30/15	
Boismier, Jean Baptiste	PVT	Lee's Company	10/22/13–04/21/14	
Boismore, Jean Baptiste	PVT	Lacroix's Company	05/18/12–08/16/12	Surrendered at Detroit
Bomier, Baptist	PVT	Audrain's Spies	07/01/14–07/31/14	
Bondvielle, Noel	CPL	Michigan Fencibles	??/??/13–??/??/15	
Bondy, Joseph	PVT	Knaggs' Company	07/02/12–08/16/12	Surrendered at Detroit
Boner, James	PVT	Audrain's Rangers	12/01/14–10/31/15	
Bonhomme, Francis	UNK	St. Clair Militia	10/06/13–10/07/13	HMS Nancy EGT. SCU

Name	Rank	Military Unit	Service Dates	Remarks
Bonhomme, Michael	PVT	McDonell's Company	01/14/14–03/10/14	
Bonhomme, Michel	CPL	Mack's Company	05/28/12–08/16/12	Drafted. SRA Detroit
Bonnai, Antoine	PVT	Michigan Fencibles	??/??/13–??/??/15	
Bono, Jean Baptiste	PVT	Couture's Company	08/04/12–08/18/12	Surrendered at Monroe
Bono, Lewis	PVT	Couture's Company	08/04/12–08/18/12	Surrendered at Monroe
Bonville, Lewis	PVT	Watson's COM 25 US INF	10/05/13–03/26/16	Discharged for lame hip
Bosome, Joseph	PVT	Couture's Company	08/04/12–08/18/12	Surrendered at Monroe
Bouchard, Ignace	CPL	Lasselle's Company	08/04/12–08/18/12	Surrendered at Monroe
Bouchard, Jean Baptiste	PVT	Lasselle's Company	08/04/12–08/18/12	Surrendered at Monroe
Boudrie, Noah	PVT	Hanks' COM 1 US ART	04/08/11–06/01/16	TRA Pierce's Company
Bouete, Louis C.	1CP	Dequindre's Company	04/21/12–05/27/12	
Bougard, Antoine Jr.	PVT	Lacroix's Company	05/18/12–08/16/12	Surrendered at Detroit
Bougard, Antoine Sr.	PVT	Lacroix's Company	05/18/12–08/16/12	Surrendered at Detroit
Boulard, Anthony	PVT	Edmondson's COM 28 US INF	03/21/14–06/30/15	TRA Stockton's Company
Boulard, Antoine	PVT	Lacroix's Company	05/18/12–08/16/12	Surrendered at Detroit
Bourassa, Antoine	DRG	Smyth's Company	04/26/12–08/16/12	Surrendered at Detroit
Bourassa, François	PVT	Lacroix's Company	05/18/12–08/16/12	Surrendered at Detroit
Bourdau, François	PVT	Jobean's Company	08/04/12–08/18/12	Surrendered at Monroe
Bourdeau, Pierre	PVT	Menard's Company	08/04/12–08/18/12	Surrendered at Monroe
Bourdeaux, Jean Baptiste	PVT	Menard's Company	08/04/12–08/18/12	Surrendered at Monroe
Bourdeaux, Joseph Jr.	PVT	Couture's Company	08/04/12–08/18/12	Surrendered at Monroe
Bourdeaux, Joseph Sr.	PVT	Couture's Company	08/04/12–08/18/12	Surrendered at Monroe
Bourdignon, Clement	PVT	Knaggs' Company	07/02/12–08/16/12	Surrendered at Detroit
Bourgas, Jacques	DRG	Smyth's Company	04/21/12–08/16/12	Surrendered at Detroit
Bourgon, Pierre	PVT	Dequindre's Company	04/21/12–08/16/12	Surrendered at Detroit
Bourgue, Joseph	PVT	Lacroix's Company	05/18/12–08/16/12	Surrendered at Detroit
Bourk, James	PVT	Couture's Company	08/04/12–08/18/12	Surrendered at Monroe

NAME	RANK	MILITARY UNIT	SERVICE DATES	REMARKS
Bourre, Louis	PVT	Campau's Company	07/02/12–08/16/12	Surrendered at Detroit
Bouvieu, Baptiste	PVT	Menard's Company	08/04/12–08/18/12	Surrendered at Monroe
Bowidan, Peter	PVT	Hanks' COM 1 US ART	05/16/12–01/30/16	
Boye, Antoine	PVT	Audrain's Spies	07/01/14–07/31/14	
Boye, Francis	PVT	Mack's Company	05/20/12–08/16/12	Surrendered at Detroit
Boyer, François	PVT	McDonell's Company	12/21/13–03/10/14	
Boyer, Medard	PVT	McDonell's Company	01/14/14–03/10/14	
Boyles, Andrew	DRG	Smyth's Company	04/21/12–08/16/12	Surrendered at Detroit
Boyles, Thomas	PVT	Collins' COM 19 US INF	03/15/14–07/20/15	
Bradley, William	PVT	Collins' COM 19 US INF	03/16/14–07/19/15	
Brady, Eli	PVT	Collins' COM 19 US INF	03/31/14–07/20/15	
Brady, Josiah	LUT	Dequindre's Company	05/11/12–08/16/12	Surrendered at Detroit
Braunchau, Peter	PVT	Menard's Company	08/04/12–08/18/12	Surrendered at Monroe
Brevoort, Henry Bregaw	CAP	COM ?, 2nd US INF	05/01/11–03/08/14	CPT Detroit 08/16/12
Brevoort, Henry Bregaw	MAJ	COM ?, 45th US INF	03/09/14–06/15/15	
Briggs, Daniel	PVT	Collins' COM 19 US INF	03/18/14–07/20/15	
Bristow, George	PVT	Edmondson's COM 28 US INF	03/22/14–??/??/??	
Brown, Joseph	2CP	Knaggs' Company	07/02/12–08/16/12	Surrendered at Detroit
Brown, William	4CP	Smyth's Company	04/21/12–08/16/12	Surrendered at Detroit
Brown, William	SUM	F&S Legionary Corps	05/29/12–08/16/12	Surrendered at Detroit
Brown, William	UNK	St. Clair Militia	10/06/13–10/07/13	HMS Nancy EGT. SCU
Brunet, Jean Baptiste	DRG	Smyth's Company	05/02/12–08/16/12	DET River Raisin
Bruno, John B.	PVT	Reading's COM KY MTD INF	08/15/13–11/19/13	
Brush, Elijah	COL	F&S 1st REG MI Militia	??/??/??–08/16/12	CMD. Surrendered at Detroit
Bryan, Aaron	PVT	Collins' COM 19 US INF	03/02/14–??/??/??	
Bucklin, William	PVT	Mack's Company	05/??/12–08/16/12	SRA Detroit. PEN
Bucklin, William	GDE	Harrison's ANW	08/02/13–08/11/13	SCU

Name	Rank	Military Unit	Service Dates	Remarks
Bullard, Anthony	PVT	Edmondson's COM 28 US INF	03/21/14–06/30/15	TRA Stockton's Company
Bumard, Bazil	DRG	Smyth's Company	04/29/12–09/30/12	DET River Raisin 05/01/12
Bumard, Bazil	PVT	Ball's SQD US LTD	09/30/12–05/10/13	
Bunnell, Levi	3CP	Lee's Company	10/22/13–04/04/14	Killed in Battle
Bunnell, Levi	DRG	Smyth's Company	04/21/12–08/16/12	Surrendered at Detroit
Burdinaw, Charles	PVT	Collins' COM 19 US INF	03/16/14–07/20/15	
Burdon, Peter	PVT	Hanks' COM 1 US ART	05/16/12–01/30/16	
Burnett, Isaac	PVT	Sibley's Company	07/02/12–08/16/12	Surrendered at Detroit
Burnett, James	PVT	Sibley's Company	07/02/12–08/16/12	Surrendered at Detroit
Burris, John	PVT	Collins' COM 19 US INF	05/19/14–07/20/15	
Butler, John	PVT	Audrain's Rangers	10/20/14–11/30/15	
Butler, John	PVT	Westbrook's Company	05/12/14–06/11/14	
Cadaret, Louis	PVT	Audrain's Spies	07/01/14–07/31/14	
Cadarette, Joseph	PVT	Collins' COM 19 US INF	05/30/14–05/12/19	Reenlisted
Cadieu, Pierre	PVT	Mack's Company	07/10/12–08/16/12	Surrendered at Detroit
Cadoret, Charles	PVT	Dequindre's Company	04/22/12–08/16/12	Surrendered at Detroit
Cadoret, Joseph	PVT	Dequindre's Company	04/21/12–08/16/12	Surrendered at Detroit
Cain, Daniel	PVT	Collins' COM 19 US INF	03/21/14–03/24/19	
Calhoun, Abner	PVT	Mulholland's Company	08/04/12–08/18/12	Surrendered at Monroe
Calhoun, Andrew Jr.	PVT	Mulholland's Company	08/04/12–08/18/12	SRA Monroe. PEN
Calhoun, Andrew Sr.	PVT	Mulholland's Company	08/04/12–08/18/12	Surrendered at Monroe
Calin, Joseph	PVT	Knaggs' Company	07/02/12–08/16/12	Surrendered at Detroit
Cambell, Ducan	PVT	Audrain's Spies	07/01/14–07/31/14	
Campaign, Joseph	PVT	Audrain's Rangers	10/20/14–10/19/15	
Camparet, Jean B. Jr.	PVT	Campau's Company	07/02/12–08/16/12	SRA Detroit. MNI Baptiste
Camparet, Jean B. Sr.	PVT	Campau's Company	07/02/12–08/16/12	SRA Detroit. MNI Baptiste
Campau, Alexis	PVT	Knaggs' Company	07/02/12–08/16/12	Surrendered at Detroit

Name	Rank	Military Unit	Service Dates	Remarks
Campau, Antoine P.	PVT	Knaggs' Company	07/02/12–08/16/12	Surrendered at Detroit
Campau, Baptiste B.	PVT	Mack's Company	06/10/12–08/16/12	Surrendered at Detroit
Campau, Barnabas	PVT	Sibley's Company	07/02/12–08/16/12	Surrendered at Detroit
Campau, Dennis	ENS	Campau's Company	07/02/12–08/16/12	Surrendered at Detroit
Campau, Glode	PVT	Crittenden's COM 17 US INF	12/01/13–12/01/18	
Campau, Henry	PVT	Campau's Company	07/02/12–08/16/12	Surrendered at Detroit
Campau, Jacques Jr.	2SG	Campau's Company	07/02/12–08/16/12	Surrendered at Detroit
Campau, Jacques Sr.	CAP	Campau's Company	07/02/12–08/16/12	Surrendered at Detroit
Campau, John Baptiste	PVT	Knaggs' Company	07/02/12–08/16/12	Surrendered at Detroit
Campau, Joseph	PVT	Audrain's Spies	07/01/14–07/31/14	
Campau, Joseph	PVT	Sibley's Company	07/02/12–08/16/12	Surrendered at Detroit
Campau, Joseph Jr.	PVT	Lacroix's Company	05/18/12–08/16/12	Surrendered at Detroit
Campau, Joseph Sr.	PVT	Lacroix's Company	05/18/12–08/16/12	Surrendered at Detroit
Campau, Louis	PVT	Sibley's Company	07/02/12–08/16/12	Surrendered at Detroit
Campau, Pierre	PVT	Audrain's Rangers	01/13/15–11/30/15	
Campbell, Duncan	PVT	Audrain's Rangers	10/12/14–08/31/15	
Campeau, Claud	PVT	Audrain's Spies	07/01/14–07/31/14	
Campeau, Jacques	DRG	Smyth's Company	04/29/12–08/16/12	DET to River Raisin. SRA Monroe
Campeau, Pierre	PVT	Audrain's Spies	07/01/14–07/31/14	
Carman, Caleb	PVT	Amberson's COM 22 US INF	02/16/13–02/16/18	TRA Lawrence's COM 12/07/13
Carman, Caleb	PVT	Dequindre's Company	07/07/12–??/??/??	TRA Hickman's COM 07/20/12
Carman, Caleb	PVT	Mack's Company	07/10/12–08/16/12	Surrendered at Detroit
Carpenter, John	PVT	Mack's Company	07/10/12–08/16/12	Surrendered at Detroit
Carrie, Jean	PVT	Knaggs' Company	07/02/12–08/16/12	Surrendered at Detroit
Carrier, Augustan	PVT	Audrain's Spies	07/01/14–07/31/14	
Cartright, John	PVT	Audrain's Rangers	10/20/14–10/19/15	PEN
Cartwright, George	PVT	Robinson's COM 17 US INF	04/16/14–??/??/??	CPT 09/03/14, POW at Halifax

NAME	RANK	MILITARY UNIT	SERVICE DATES	REMARKS
Cass, Lewis	CMD	F&S MI Militia	10/29/13–12/24/14	
Cecil, Henry B.	PVT	Hawkins' COM 17 US INF	04/04/14–06/09/15	TRA Herron's Company
Cecile, Antoine	PVT	Campau's Company	07/02/12–08/16/12	Surrendered at Detroit
Cere, Charles	PVT	McDonell's Company	12/20/13–03/10/14	
Chabert, François	PVT	Knaggs' Company	07/02/12–08/16/12	Surrendered at Detroit
Chabert, George	PVT	Knaggs' Company	07/02/12–08/16/12	Surrendered at Detroit
Chabert, George	PVT	Mack's Company	05/28/12–08/16/12	Drafted. Surrendered at Detroit
Chabert, Isadore	PVT	Knaggs' Company	07/02/12–08/16/12	Surrendered at Detroit
Chabert, Philip	PVT	Knaggs' Company	07/02/12–08/16/12	Surrendered at Detroit
Chamberland, Laurant	PVT	Lee's Company	11/01/13–12/28/13	Died in Service
Chamberland, Louis	PVT	Audrain's Spies	07/01/14–07/31/14	
Chamberlin, Young	PVT	Johnson's COM 2 US RIF	05/09/14–06/30/15	
Chamland, Louis	PVT	Knaggs' Company	07/02/12–08/16/12	SRA Detroit. PEN
Champaign, Francis	PVT	Audrain's Spies	07/01/14–07/31/14	
Champaign, Isedore	PVT	Audrain's Rangers	10/20/14–10/19/15	
Champaign, Joseph	PVT	Audrain's Rangers	10/20/14–10/19/15	PEN
Champaign, Pierre	PVT	Audrain's Rangers	10/20/14–10/19/15	PEN
Champaigne, Lambert	PVT	Collins' COM 19 US INF	05/06/14–01/18/19	Reenlisted
Champaigne, Lambert	PVT	Lasselle's Company	08/04/12–08/18/12	Surrendered at Monroe
Champaigne, Lewis	PVT	Lacroix's Company	05/18/12–08/16/12	Surrendered at Detroit
Champaigne, Lewis	PVT	Lee's Company	10/22/13–04/21/14	
Champaigne, Lewis	PVT	Martin's Company	08/04/12–08/18/12	Surrendered at Monroe
Champaigne, Louis	PVT	Collins' COM 19 US INF	05/07/14–06/30/18	
Chapaton, Eustache	PVT	McDonell's Company	01/14/14–03/10/14	
Chapaton, Henry	SGT	McDonell's Company	01/14/14–03/10/14	
Charland, Ambrose C.	3SG	Lacroix's Company	05/18/12–08/16/12	Surrendered at Detroit

NAME	RANK	MILITARY UNIT	SERVICE DATES	REMARKS
Charland, Ambrose C.	GDE	Winchester's ANW	01/22/13–??/??/??	Taken prisoner. SCU
Charland, Ambrose C.	CAP	Independent COM VOLS	01/18/13–??/??/??	SCU
Charties, Francois	PVT	Audrain's Rangers	10/20/14–10/19/15	
Chatillon, Dominique	PVT	Knaggs' Company	07/02/12–08/16/12	Surrendered at Detroit
Chatilrau, Pascal	PVT	Menard's Company	08/04/12–08/18/12	Surrendered at Monroe
Chauvin, Henri	GDE	Winchester's ANW	01/22/13–??/??/??	KIA at Monroe. SCU
Chauvin, Henry	DRG	Smyth's Company	04/29/12–08/16/12	Detached to River Raisin
Chesne, Gabriel	PVT	Campau's Company	07/02/12–08/16/12	Surrendered at Detroit
Chevalier, Joseph	PVT	Dequindre's Company	04/21/12–08/16/12	Surrendered at Detroit
Chevallies, Joseph	PVT	Audrain's Spies	07/01/14–07/31/14	
Chinn, Charles	PVT	Edmondson's COM 28 US INF	03/18/14–06/30/15	TRA Stockton's Company
Chittenden, Benjamin	PVT	Sibley's Company	07/02/12–08/16/12	Surrendered at Detroit
Chittenden, George R.	PVT	Campau's Company	07/02/12–08/16/12	Surrendered at Detroit
Chorkie, Charles	PVT	Audrain's Spies	07/01/14–07/31/14	
Chorkie, Francis	PVT	Audrain's Spies	07/01/14–07/31/14	
Chorkie, Joseph	PVT	Audrain's Spies	07/01/14–07/31/14	
Chorkie, Louis	PVT	Audrain's Spies	07/01/14–07/31/14	
Choven, Baptist	PVT	Audrain's Rangers	10/20/14–11/30/15	
Choven, Nicholas	PVT	Audrain's Rangers	10/20/14–11/30/15	PEN
Choven, Pierre	PVT	Audrain's Rangers	10/20/14–11/30/15	
Choven, Simon	PVT	Audrain's Rangers	10/20/14–10/19/15	PEN
Chovin, Baptist	PVT	Audrain's Spies	07/01/14–07/31/14	
Chovin, Colas	PVT	Audrain's Spies	07/01/14–07/31/14	
Chovin, Joseph	PVT	Audrain's Spies	07/01/14–07/31/14	PEN
Chovin, Peter	PVT	Martin's Company	08/04/12–08/18/12	Surrendered at Monroe
Chovin, Pierre	PVT	Audrain's Spies	07/01/14–07/31/14	

NAME	RANK	MILITARY UNIT	SERVICE DATES	REMARKS
Churchill, Philemon	PVT	Dequindre's Company	07/03/12–08/09/12	Killed at Brownstown
Cicile, Antoine	PVT	Campau's Company	07/02/12–08/16/12	Surrendered at Detroit
Cicotte, Edward	PVT	Knaggs' Company	07/02/12–08/16/12	Surrendered at Detroit
Cicotte, Edward	VOL	Lewis Cass Expedition	09/15/14	SCU
Cicotte, Francis	CAP	Cicotte's Company	06/09/12–08/16/12	SRA Detroit. SCU. PEN
Cicotte, Francis	VOL	Lewis Cass Expedition	09/15/14	SCU
Cicotte, George	PVT	Knaggs' Company	07/02/12–08/16/12	Surrendered at Detroit
Cicotte, George	VOL	Lewis Cass Expedition	09/15/14	SCU
Cicotte, James	VOL	Lewis Cass Expedition	09/15/14	SCU
Cicotte, John Baptiste Jr.	LUT	Knaggs' Company	07/02/12–08/16/12	Surrendered at Detroit
Cicotte, Joseph	PVT	Knaggs' Company	07/02/12–08/16/12	Surrendered at Detroit
Clapp, Silas	PVT	Sibley's Company	07/02/12–08/16/12	Surrendered at Detroit
Clark, Amos	PVT	Collins' COM 19 US INF	03/15/14–07/20/15	
Clark, Joseph	DRG	Smyth's Company	04/21/12–08/16/12	Surrendered at Detroit
Clark, Joseph D.	PVT	Hawkins' COM 17 US INF	04/02/14–04/03/15	
Clark, Thomas	PVT	Audrain's Rangers	12/01/14–06/14/15	
Clement, Joseph	PVT	Mack's Company	05/28/12–08/16/12	Drafted. Surrendered at Detroit
Clements, William	PVT	Whistler's COM 1 US INF	08/22/10–01/09/14	Died of disease 01/09/14
Cloutier, Baptiste	DRG	Smyth's Company	05/01/12–08/16/12	Detached to River Raisin
Clucky, Jacob	PVT	Drouillard's Company	08/04/12–08/18/12	Surrendered at Monroe
Clucky, Joseph	PVT	Drouillard's Company	08/04/12–08/18/12	Surrendered at Monroe
Clucky, Peter	PVT	Drouillard's Company	08/04/12–08/18/12	Surrendered at Monroe
Clutier, Romain	PVT	Collins' COM 19 US INF	05/19/14–05/19/19	
Cluture, Thomas	PVT	Lacroix's Company	05/18/12–08/16/12	Surrendered at Detroit
Cob, Samuel B.	3CP	Sibley's Company	07/02/12–08/16/12	Surrendered at Detroit
Cochois, Alexis	PVT	Mack's Company	05/20/12–08/16/12	Surrendered at Detroit
Cochois, Jean B.	PVT	Mack's Company	06/12/12–08/16/12	Surrendered at Detroit

NAME	RANK	MILITARY UNIT	SERVICE DATES	REMARKS
Cockiard, Alexis	PVT	Audrain's Spies	07/01/14–07/31/14	
Coffey, Richard	PVT	Johnson's COM 2 US RIF	06/09/14–06/30/15	
Cofrin, William	DRG	Smyth's Company	04/29/12–08/16/12	Detached to River Raisin
Cole, Joseph	CPL	Mack's Company	05/28/12–08/16/12	Surrendered at Detroit
Collier, John	PVT	Knaggs' Company	07/02/12–08/16/12	Surrendered at Detroit
Columbe, Augustin	PVT	Lacroix's Company	05/18/12–08/16/12	Surrendered at Detroit
Comparet, Baptiste	CPL	Audrain's Spies	07/01/14–07/31/14	
Comparet, Francis	PVT	Mack's Company	05/28/12–08/16/12	Surrendered at Detroit
Comparet, Jean Baptiste	PVT	Campau's Company	07/02/12–08/16/12	Surrendered at Detroit
Compau, Antoine	PVT	Knaggs' Company	07/02/12–08/16/12	Surrendered at Detroit
Conant, Shubael	VOL	Lewis Cass Expedition	09/15/14	SCU
Conant, Shubal	2SG	Sibley's Company	07/02/12–08/16/12	Surrendered at Detroit
Conkey, Thomas	PVT	Mack's Company	06/25/12–08/16/12	Surrendered at Detroit
Conkey, Thomas	PVT	Westbrook's Company	05/12/14–06/11/14	
Conner, Rodrick	PVT	Westbrook's Company	05/12/14–06/11/14	
Contoua, Joseph	PVT	McDonell's Company	12/21/13–03/10/14	
Cook, Abraham	UNK	Michigan Militia	??/??/12–08/16/12	WIA left hand. SUR Detroit. SCU
Cook, George G.	PVT	Dequindre's Company	05/22/12–??/??/??	TRA Hickman's COM 07/18/12
Cook, Giles	SGT	Audrain's Spies	07/01/14–07/31/14	
Cook, Jacob	SGT	Crittenden's COM 17 US INF	05/04/12–06/30/17	
Cooper, David	2SG	Knaggs' Company	07/02/12–08/16/12	Surrendered at Detroit
Corbus, John	PVT	Dequindre's Company	05/20/12–08/16/12	Surrendered at Detroit
Coshway, Alexis	PVT	Audrain's Spies	07/01/14–07/31/14	
Coshway, Baptist	CPL	Audrain's Spies	07/01/14–07/31/14	
Coshway, Lambert	PVT	Audrain's Spies	07/01/14–07/31/14	
Cota, Joseph	PVT	Audrain's Spies	07/01/14–07/31/14	
Cote, Joseph	CPL	Mack's Company	05/28/12–08/16/12	Surrendered at Detroit

NAME	RANK	MILITARY UNIT	SERVICE DATES	REMARKS
Cote, Prisque	PVT	Sibley's Company	07/02/12–08/16/12	Surrendered at Detroit
Cottrell, George	UNK	St. Clair Militia	10/06/13–10/07/13	HMS Nancy EGT. SCU
Cottrelle, John	SGT	Audrain's Spies	07/01/14–07/31/14	
Couchoix, Baptist	PVT	Audrain's Rangers	10/20/14–11/30/15	
Couchoix, Lambert	PVT	Audrain's Rangers	10/20/14–11/30/15	
Cousano, Alexis	PVT	Audrain's Spies	07/01/14–07/31/14	
Cousinau, Antoine	PVT	Lacroix's Company	05/18/12–08/16/12	Surrendered at Detroit
Cousinau, Tousaint	PVT	Jobean's Company	08/04/12–08/18/12	Surrendered at Monroe
Cousineau, François	SCT	Harrison's ANW	02/??/13–10/??/13	SCU. PEN
Cousinotte, Basille	PVT	Lasselle's Company	08/04/12–08/18/12	Surrendered at Monroe
Cousinou, Francis	PVT	Drouillard's Company	08/04/12–08/18/12	Surrendered at Monroe
Cousman, Alexis	PVT	Lacroix's Company	05/18/12–08/16/12	Surrendered at Detroit
Couture, Antoine	GDE	Winchester's ANW	01/??/13–01/??/13	SCU
Couture, Antoine	PVT	Jobean's Company	08/04/12–08/18/12	Surrendered at Monroe
Couture, Antoine	SCT	Harrison's ANW	02/??/13–04/??/13	Died in service. SCU
Couture, Claude	PVT	Lacroix's Company	05/18/12–08/16/12	Surrendered at Detroit
Couture, Claude	PVT	Lee's Company	10/22/13–04/21/14	
Couture, Etienne	PVT	Menard's Company	08/04/12–08/18/12	Surrendered at Monroe
Couture, Jean Baptiste Sr.	CAP	Couture's Company	08/04/12–08/18/12	Surrendered at Monroe
Couture, Jean Baptiste Sr.	GDE	Winchester's ANW	01/22/13–??/??/??	KIA at Monroe
Couture, Jean Baptiste Jr.	LUT	Couture's Company	08/04/12–08/18/12	Surrendered at Monroe
Couture, Lewis Jr.	PVT	Menard's Company	08/04/12–08/18/12	Surrendered at Monroe
Couture, Lewis Sr.	PVT	Menard's Company	08/04/12–08/18/12	Surrendered at Monroe
Couture, Louis	PVT	Drouillard's Company	08/04/12–08/18/12	Surrendered at Monroe
Couture, Medore	DRG	Smyth's Company	04/29/12–08/16/12	Detached to River Raisin
Couture, Medore	PVT	Lee's Company	10/22/13–12/31/13	

Name	Rank	Military Unit	Service Dates	Remarks
Couzeneau, Alexsi	SGT	Audrain's Spies	07/01/14–07/31/14	
Craig, Samuel	PVT	Collins' COM 19 US INF	03/19/14–07/20/15	
Cramer, John	PVT	Lee's Company	10/22/13–04/21/14	
Crandell, Joshua	SGT	Mack's Company	05/28/12–08/16/12	Surrendered at Detroit
Crandell, Samuel	CPL	Mack's Company	05/28/12–08/16/12	Surrendered at Detroit
Crawford, David	PVT	Audrain's Rangers	10/20/14–11/30/15	PEN
Crawford, David	PVT	Audrain's Spies	07/01/14–07/31/14	
Creamer, John	3CP	Audrain's Rangers	10/20/14–11/20/15	
Creamer, John	CPL	Audrain's Spies	07/01/14–07/31/14	
Cremer, John	PVT	Reading's COM KY MTD INF	08/15/13–11/19/13	
Cremor, John Jr.	PVT	Lacroix's Company	05/18/12–08/16/12	Surrendered at Detroit
Cremor, John Sr.	PVT	Lacroix's Company	05/18/12–08/16/12	Surrendered at Detroit
Crempayt, Daniel	PVT	Reading's COM KY MTD INF	05/20/13–08/15/13	
Creque, Baptist	PVT	Audrain's Spies	07/01/14–07/31/14	
Cross, Jonathan	PVT	Johnson's COM 2 US RIF	05/09/14–06/30/15	PEN
Crosset, John	PVT	Dequindre's Company	04/22/12–08/16/12	Surrendered at Detroit
Cummins, James	PVT	Audrain's Rangers	11/01/14–08/31/15	
Cummins, Thomas	PVT	Wadsworth's COM 1 US RIF	10/30/13–??/??/??	
Curjotte, Francis	PVT	Lasselle's Company	08/04/12–08/18/12	Surrendered at Monroe
Curtis, Daniel	ENS	Whistler's COM 1 US INF	01/03/12–??/??/??	Promoted to 2LT 12/31/12
Datson, Peter	2CP	Lee's Company	12/16/13–04/21/14	
Davis, John	PVT	Hanks' COM 1 US ART	??/??/??–07/17/12	SRA Fort Michilimackinac
Day, Isaac	GDE	Winchester's ANW	01/??/13–01/??/13	SCU
Day, Isaac	PVT	Drouillard's Company	08/04/12–08/18/12	Surrendered at Monroe
Day, Isaac W.	1SG	Audrain's Rangers	10/12/14–11/30/15	
Dear, George	PVT	Whistler's COM 1 US INF	03/01/10–??/??/??	POW

Name	Rank	Military Unit	Service Dates	Remarks
Defont, Paul	PVT	Dequindre's Company	04/21/12–08/16/12	Surrendered at Detroit
Degerdin, Oliver	PVT	Michigan Fencibles	??/??/13–??/??/15	
Deleosierre, François	PVT	Martin's Company	08/04/12–08/18/12	Surrendered at Monroe
Delisle, Alexis B.	PVT	Mack's Company	05/28/12–08/16/12	Drafted. SRA Detroit. PEN
Delisle, Jean Baptiste	PVT	Campau's Company	07/02/12–08/16/12	Surrendered at Detroit
Delisle, John Baptiste	PVT	Knaggs' Company	07/02/12–08/16/12	Surrendered at Detroit
Delorie, Francis	PVT	Dequindre's Company	04/21/12–08/16/12	Surrendered at Detroit
Delorme, Pierre	PVT	Mack's Company	05/28/12–08/16/12	Surrendered at Detroit
Deloy, Francis	PVT	Lasselle's Company	08/04/12–08/18/12	Surrendered at Monroe
Delylle, Charles	PVT	Mack's Company	05/28/12–08/16/12	Drafted. SRA Detroit
Demairaix, Solomon	PVT	Michigan Fencibles	??/??/13–??/??/15	
Demarchmais, Antoine	PVT	Dequindre's Company	04/22/12–08/16/12	Surrendered at Detroit
Deningsburg, William	PVT	Hawkins' COM 17 US INF	04/01/14–06/27/15	Was POW
Dennis, Anthony	PVT	Hawkins' COM 17 US INF	03/07/14–??/??/??	TRA Stockton's Company
Dennis, William	HOA	Unassigned	10/20/13–01/23/14	Stationed at Detroit
Denott, Augustin	PVT	Lasselle's Company	08/04/12–08/18/12	Surrendered at Monroe
Denoyer, François	PVT	Audrain's Spies	07/01/14–07/31/14	
Denoyer, Joseph	PVT	Audrain's Spies	07/01/14–07/31/14	
Denton, John	PVT	Edmondson's COM 28 US INF	03/21/14–??/??/??	
Deplanes, Jacques	PVT	Smyth's Company	04/21/12–08/16/12	Surrendered at Detroit
Depuy, Joseph	PVT	McDonell's Company	12/18/13–03/10/14	
Dequindre, Antoine	CAP	Dequindre's Company	04/21/12–08/16/12	Surrendered at Detroit
Dequindre, Benjamin	4CP	Campau's Company	07/02/12–08/16/12	Surrendered at Detroit
Dequindre, Louis	1SG	Campau's Company	07/02/12–08/16/12	Surrendered at Detroit
Dequindre, Louis	VOL	Lewis Cass Expedition	09/15/14	SCU
Dequindre, Pierre	4SG	Campau's Company	07/02/12–08/16/12	Surrendered at Detroit

NAME	RANK	MILITARY UNIT	SERVICE DATES	REMARKS
Dequindre, Timothy	PVT	Campau's Company	07/02/12–08/16/12	Surrendered at Detroit
Desnoyer, Francois	PVT	Knaggs' Company	07/02/12–08/16/12	Surrendered at Detroit
Desnoyer, Jean Baptiste	PVT	Campau's Company	07/02/12–08/16/12	Surrendered at Detroit
Desnoyer, Joseph	PVT	Campau's Company	07/02/12–08/16/12	SRA Detroit. PEN
Desnoyers, Pierre Jean	LUT	Sibley's Company	07/02/12–08/16/12	Surrendered at Detroit
Desplait, Jacque Jr.	PVT	Audrain's Spies	07/01/14–07/31/14	
Desplait, Jacquis Sr.	PVT	Audrain's Spies	07/01/14–07/31/14	
Desplats, Joseph	PVT	Knaggs' Company	07/02/12–08/16/12	Surrendered at Detroit
Devour, Enos	PVT	Collins' COM 19 US INF	03/16/14–07/20/15	
Dibble, Elisha	2SG	Smyth's Company	04/29/12–08/16/12	Detached to River Raisin
Dibble, Samuel	DRG	Smyth's Company	05/16/12–09/30/12	Detached to River Raisin. ETO
Dibble, Samuel	PVT	Ball's SQD US LTD	09/30/12–05/05/13	
Dibble, Samuel	PVT	Lee's Company	10/22/13–04/21/14	
Dinkins, John	PVT	Collins' COM 19 US INF	03/15/14–07/20/15	
Disjardin, Hyacinthe	PVT	Sibley's Company	07/02/12–08/16/12	Surrendered at Detroit
Dobbins, Daniel	UNK	Sibley's Company	08/02/12–08/16/12	Surrendered at Detroit. SCU
Dodelain, Andrew	PVT	Knaggs' Company	07/02/12–08/16/12	Surrendered at Detroit
Dodemead, Isaac	3CP	Dequindre's Company	04/21/12–08/16/12	Surrendered at Detroit
Dodemead, James	SGT	Mack's Company	05/28/12–08/16/12	Drafted. SRA Detroit
Dolson, Matthew	SCT	Harrison's Army	??/??/13–??/??/13	SCU
Dolson, Peter	PVT	Westbrook's Company	05/12/14–06/11/14	
Donais, Michel	PVT	Michigan Fencibles	??/??/13–??/??/15	
Dosson, John H.	PVT	Westbrook's Company	05/12/14–06/11/14	
Doty, Prince	PVT	Sibley's Company	07/02/12–08/16/12	Surrendered at Detroit
Dougherty, Dennis	PVT	Dyson's COM 1 US ART	02/27/12–02/27/17	POW
Douseau, Etiene	PVT	Audrain's Rangers	10/12/14–11/30/15	

Name	Rank	Military Unit	Service Dates	Remarks
Downing, Rufus	DRG	Smyth's Company	04/29/12–08/16/12	Detached to River Raisin
Downing, Stephen	DRG	Smyth's Company	05/04/12–08/16/12	Detached to River Raisin
Downing, Stephen Jr.	PVT	Mulholland's Company	08/04/12–08/18/12	Surrendered at Monroe
Downing, Stephen H. Sr.	SGT	Mulholland's Company	08/04/12–08/18/12	SRA Monroe. MNI Holmes
Doyl, Samuel	PVT	Westbrook's Company	05/12/14–06/11/14	
Dreward, Neni	PVT	Reading's COM KY MTD INF	05/20/13–08/15/13	
Dreweard, Louis	4SG	Reading's COM KY MTD INF	05/20/13–11/19/13	
Drouillard, Dennis	PVT	Lacroix's Company	05/18/12–08/16/12	Surrendered at Detroit
Drouillard, Dominique Jr.	SGT	Drouillard's Company	08/04/12–08/18/12	Surrendered at Monroe
Drouillard, Dominique Sr.	CAP	Drouillard's Company	08/04/12–08/18/12	Surrendered at Monroe
Drouillard, Jean Baptiste	PVT	Lacroix's Company	05/18/12–08/16/12	Surrendered at Detroit
Drouillard, Louis	DRG	Smyth's Company	05/16/12–09/30/12	Detached to River Raisin. ETO
Drouillard, Louis	ENS	Audrain's Rangers	05/01/14–11/30/15	
Drouillard, Louis	PVT	Ball's SQD US LTD	09/30/12–05/10/13	
Drouillard, Louis	PVT	Lee's Company	10/22/13–04/21/14	
Drouilliard, Louis	PVT	Audrain's Spies	07/01/14–07/31/14	
Droullard, Charles	PVT	Lasselle's Company	08/04/12–08/18/12	Surrendered at Monroe
Dubay, François	PVT	Audrain's Spies	07/01/14–07/31/14	
Dubay, Jean Marie	PVT	Audrain's Rangers	10/20/14–11/30/15	PEN
Dubay, Jean Marie	PVT	Audrain's Spies	07/01/14–07/31/14	
Dubay, Simon	PVT	Tucker's Company	06/01/12–08/16/12	SRA Detroit. SCU. PEN
Dube, François	PVT	Mack's Company	05/21/12–08/16/12	Surrendered at Detroit
Dubey, Jean Baptiste	CPL	Drouillard's Company	08/04/12–08/18/12	Surrendered at Monroe
Dubruille, Louis	PVT	Michigan Fencibles	??/??/13–??/??/15	
Ducatte, Joseph	PVT	Drouillard's Company	08/04/12–08/18/12	Surrendered at Monroe
Duchesne, Etienne	PVT	Mack's Company	06/25/12–08/16/12	Surrendered at Detroit

NAME	RANK	MILITARY UNIT	SERVICE DATES	REMARKS
Duchesne, François	PVT	Mack's Company	05/21/12–08/16/12	Surrendered at Detroit
Duchesne, Pierre	PVT	Lacroix's Company	05/18/12–08/16/12	Surrendered at Detroit
Dufour, Louis	PVT	Audrain's Rangers	10/12/14–11/30/15	
Dufour, Peter	PVT	Couture's Company	08/04/12–08/18/12	Surrendered at Monroe
Dugate, Paul	PVT	Lacroix's Company	05/18/12–08/16/12	Surrendered at Detroit
Dulack, Joseph	PVT	Audrain's Rangers	10/20/14–11/30/15	
Dumais, François	PVT	Knaggs' Company	07/02/12–08/16/12	Surrendered at Detroit
Dumay, Baptiste	CPL	Audrain's Spies	07/01/14–07/31/14	
Dumay, Baptiste	PVT	Mack's Company	06/04/12–08/16/12	Surrendered at Detroit
Dummett, Robert	PVT	Edmondson's COM 28 US INF	03/28/14–06/30/15	TRA Stockton's Company
Dupais, Lewis	PVT	Jobean's Company	08/04/12–08/18/12	Surrendered at Monroe
Dupeis, Charles	PVT	Dequindre's Company	04/21/12–08/16/12	Surrendered at Detroit
Duplaire, Jean Baptiste	DRG	Smyth's Company	04/26/12–08/16/12	Surrendered at Detroit
Duplat, Jacques	PVT	Mack's Company	05/28/12–08/16/12	Surrendered at Detroit
Dupre, Francis	PVT	Dequindre's Company	07/03/12–08/16/12	Surrendered at Detroit
Dupre, Francis	PVT	Hawkins' COM 17 US INF	04/14/14–09/12/14	KIA on USS Scorpion near Mackinac
Dupre, Jean Baptiste	DRG	Smyth's Company	04/21/12–08/16/12	Surrendered at Detroit
Dupre, Louis	PVT	Dequindre's Company	04/22/12–08/16/12	Surrendered at Detroit
Dupree, John B.	PVT	Hawkins' COM 17 US INF	04/14/14–04/14/19	
Dupret, Joseph	PVT	Audrain's Rangers	10/20/14–11/30/15	
Duprey, Francis	PVT	Audrain's Spies	07/01/14–07/31/14	
Duprey, Louis	PVT	Audrain's Spies	07/01/14–07/31/14	
Dupuis, Lacenne	PVT	Michigan Fencibles	??/??/13–??/??/15	
Dupuoy, Charles	PVT	Harris' COM 2 US LTD	07/13/13–??/??/??	TRA Hopkins' Company
Dupuy, Joseph	PVT	Campau's Company	07/02/12–08/16/12	Surrendered at Detroit
Durett, Baptist	CPL	Audrain's Spies	07/01/14–07/31/14	

NAME	RANK	MILITARY UNIT	SERVICE DATES	REMARKS
Durgate, François	PVT	Couture's Company	08/04/12–08/18/12	Surrendered at Detroit
Durocher, Laurent	COR	Lee's Company	10/22/13–04/21/14	
Durocher, Laurent	DRG	Smyth's Company	04/29/12–08/16/12	DET River Raisin 05/01/12
Durocher, Laurent	PVT	Ball's SQD US LTD	09/30/12–05/10/13	
Durocher, Laurent	SCT	Harrison's ANW	02/??/13–10/??/13	SCU
Duseau, Etienne	PVT	Audrain's Rangers	10/20/14–11/30/15	
Dusow, Atien	SGT	Drouillard's Company	08/04/12–08/18/12	Surrendered at Monore
Dusow, Joseph	LUT	Drouillard's Company	08/04/12–08/18/12	Surrendered at Monroe
Dusseau, Joseph	SCT	Harrison's ANW	01/22/13–07/04/13	WIA 04/08/13 Ft. Meigs. SCU. PEN
Duval, Francis	PVT	Whistler's COM 1 US INF	09/13/11–??/??/??	POW
Duvalle, Antoine	PVT	Menard's Company	08/04/12–08/18/12	Surrendered at Monroe
Duvalle, Daniel	PVT	Menard's Company	08/04/12–08/18/12	Surrendered at Monroe
Duvalle, Joseph	PVT	Menard's Company	08/04/12–08/18/12	Surrendered at Monroe
Eaves, Ransom	PVT	Edmondson's COM 28 US INF	03/21/14–06/30/15	TRA Stockton's Company
Edwine, John G.	PVT	Hawkins' COM 17 US INF	04/01/14–12/19/14	Died at Buffalo
Egnew, George	PVT	Mulholland's Company	08/04/12–08/18/12	Surrendered at Monroe
Egnew, Samuel	DRG	Smyth's Company	04/29/12–08/16/12	Surrendered at Detroit
Ellis, William	PVT	Hawkins' COM 17 US INF	05/12/14–??/??/??	TRA Herron's Company
Ermatinger, Charles O.	UNK	British Volunteers	??/??/??–??/??/??	Apparently served at Mackinac
Evans, William	CPL	Johnson's COM 2 US RIF	05/09/14–06/30/15	
Ewing, Alexander	PVT	Reading's COM KY MTD INF	05/20/13–11/19/13	
Fairchild, Hiram	PVT	Audrain's Spies	07/01/14–07/31/14	
Farmer, Amasa	PVT	Mack's Company	07/07/12–08/16/12	Surrendered at Detroit
Faviro, Jean Baptiste	DRG	Smyth's Company	04/29/12–08/16/12	Surrendered at Detroit
Finley, John	PVT	Dequindre's Company	07/09/12–08/16/12	Surrendered at Detroit
Fish, Richard	2CP	Collins' COM 19 US INF	06/09/14–07/20/15	

Name	Rank	Military Unit	Service Dates	Remarks
Fisher, Brice	PVT	Collins' COM 19 US INF	05/21/14–07/19/15	
Fisher, Leven	PVT	Collins' COM 19 US INF	03/16/14–07/19/15	
Fitzgerald, Edward	PVT	Hanks' COM 1 US ART	12/20/10–07/17/12	SRA Fort Michilimackinac
Fleury, Francis	PVT	Hawkins' COM 17 US INF	05/01/14–05/07/19	Was POW
Foille, Jean Baptiste	PVT	Martin's Company	08/04/12–08/18/12	Surrendered at Monroe
Fontain, Gabriel	PVT	Lacroix's Company	05/18/12–08/16/12	Surrendered at Detroit. PEN
Fontenoy, Antoine	PVT	Campau's Company	07/02/12–08/16/12	Surrendered at Detroit
Fontenoy, Antoine	PVT	McDonell's Company	01/14/14–03/10/14	
Ford, George	SGT	Edmondson's COM 28 US INF	03/28/14–06/30/15	TRA Stockton's Company
Forgeau, David	PVT	Lasselle's Company	08/04/12–08/18/12	Surrendered at Monroe
Forsyth, Robert	CPL	McDonell's Company	12/18/13–03/10/14	
Forsyth, Robert A.	2CP	Sibley's Company	07/02/12–08/16/12	Surrendered at Detroit
Forsyth, Robert A.	LUT	Mack's Company	05/25/12–08/16/12	Surrendered at Detroit
Fortier, Joseph	PVT	Couture's Company	08/04/12–08/18/12	Surrendered at Monroe. PEN
Fortin, Augustus	PVT	Chunn's COM 3 US INF	02/04/14–11/15/15	TRA Stockton's Company. DFD
Forton, Francis Jr.	PVT	Hawkins' COM 17 US INF	05/07/14–02/21/16	TRA Stockton's COM AKA Furtow/Fortune
Forton, Francis Sr.	PVT	Crittenden's COM 17 US INF	05/07/14–11/22/15	DFD. MBL. AKA Furtow /Fortune
Forton, John	PVT	Hawkins' COM 17 US INF	05/07/14–??/??/??	Absent 08/16/14
Fortress, John	PVT	Dequindre's Company	04/24/12–08/16/12	Surrendered at Detroit
Foster, William	PVT	Sibley's Company	07/02/12–08/16/12	Surrendered at Detroit
Foucreau, Alexis	SCT	Harrison's ANW	02/??/13–??/??/??	WIA 04/08/13 near Ft. Meigs. SCU
Foucreau, Joseph	VOL	Harrison's ANW	01/22/13–??/??/??	SCU
Foucrow, Alexander	PVT	Lasselle's Company	08/04/12–08/18/12	Surrendered at Monroe
Fountain, Joseph	GDE	Winchester's ANW	01/18/13–01/22/13	SCU
Fountain, Joseph	SCT	Harrison's ANW	02/??/13–10/??/13	SCU
Fountaine, Baptiste	PVT	Lasselle's Company	08/04/12–08/18/12	Surrendered at Monroe

NAME	RANK	MILITARY UNIT	SERVICE DATES	REMARKS
Fountaine, Charles	PVT	Couture's Company	08/04/12–08/18/12	Surrendered at Monroe
Fountaine, Lewis	PVT	Couture's Company	08/04/12–08/18/12	Surrendered at Monroe
Fouragge, Joseph	DRG	Smyth's Company	04/21/12–08/16/12	Surrendered at Detroit
Fourtier, Joseph	GDE	Winchester's ANW	01/18/13–01/22/13	SCU
Fourtier, Joseph	SCT	Harrison's ANW	02/??/13–10/??/13	SCU
Fox, Michael	PVT	Dequindre's Company	04/21/12–06/10/12	
Freshet, Antoine	UNK	Unknown	??/??/??–??/??/??	SCU Palmer p. 608
From, Pierre	PVT	Michigan Fencibles	??/??/13–??/??/15	
Gage, Robert	PVT	Dequindre's Company	04/22/12–08/16/12	Surrendered at Detroit
Gagnies, Charles	PVT	Knaggs' Company	07/02/12–08/16/12	Surrendered at Detroit
Gagnies, François	PVT	Knaggs' Company	07/02/12–08/16/12	Surrendered at Detroit
Gaines, François	PVT	Audrain's Rangers	10/25/14–10/19/15	PEN
Gamelin, Francis	PVT	Audrain's Spies	07/01/14–07/31/14	
Gamelin, François Jr.	PVT	Knaggs' Company	07/02/12–08/16/12	Surrendered at Detroit
Gamer, Pierce	PVT	Lacroix's Company	05/18/12–08/16/12	Surrendered at Detroit
Gandon, Francis	PVT	Lacroix's Company	05/18/12–08/16/12	Surrendered at Detroit
Gard, Jobe	PVT	Audrain's Rangers	11/01/14–11/30/15	
Gardner, John	PVT	Audrain's Spies	07/01/14–07/31/14	
Garlow, John	PVT	Hanks' COM 1 US ART	05/13/11–06/15/15	Was POW
Garren, Joseph	PVT	Audrain's Rangers	10/25/14–11/30/15	
Garren, Louis	PVT	Audrain's Rangers	11/15/14–11/30/15	
Garren, Louis	PVT	Audrain's Spies	07/01/14–07/31/14	
Garvey, John	PVT	Dequindre's Company	07/07/12–08/16/12	Surrendered at Detroit. PEN
Gassaway, Benjamin	SGT	Gill's COM 19 US INF	05/15/14–03/27/15	TRA Kissling's Company
Gassett, David	PVT	Collins' COM 19 US INF	03/16/14–07/20/15	
Gates, Wilson Lee	PVT	Collins' COM 19 US INF	03/17/14–07/20/15	PEN

Name	Rank	Military Unit	Service Dates	Remarks
Gattis, Robert	PVT	Collins' COM 19 US INF	05/18/14–04/05/15	
Gause, Samuel	PVT	Collins' COM 19 US INF	04/23/14–07/20/15	
Geaurow, Joshua	PVT	Menard's Company	08/04/12–08/18/12	Surrendered at Monroe
Gee, Alexander Jr.	PVT	Couture's Company	08/04/12–08/18/12	Surrendered at Monroe
Gee, Alexander Sr.	PVT	Couture's Company	08/04/12–08/18/12	Surrendered at Monroe
Gee, Antoine Jr.	PVT	Couture's Company	08/04/12–08/18/12	Surrendered at Monroe
Geel, Abraham	1LT	Smyth's Company	04/21/12–08/16/12	Surrendered at Detroit
Gegave, Antoine	RCT	Collins' COM 19 US INF	05/10/14–??/??/??	
Geradin, Jacques	PVT	Lacroix's Company	05/18/12–08/16/12	Surrendered at Detroit
Germain, Andrew	DRG	Smyth's Company	05/21/12–08/16/12	Surrendered at Detroit
German, Joseph	PVT	Crittenden's COM 17 US INF	07/31/12–07/31/17	
Gibau, François	PVT	Menard's Company	08/04/12–08/18/12	Surrendered at Monroe
Gibson, John	PVT	Collins' COM 19 US INF	04/23/14–07/19/15	
Gibson, John	PVT	McDonell's Company	12/26/13–03/10/14	DES 01/27/14; retaken 02/03/14
Gibson, William	PVT	Edmondson's COM 28 US INF	03/23/14–07/08/15	TRA Stockton's Company
Gile, John	PVT	Dequindre's Company	04/21/12–08/16/12	Surrendered at Detroit
Giles, John	PVT	Lee's Company	11/01/13–04/21/14	
Gill, Abraham	1LT	Smyth's Company	04/21/12–08/16/12	Surrendered at Detroit
Gillet, James	PVT	Hawkins' COM 17 US INF	03/24/14–??/??/??	Deserted 03/25/15
Giradin, Jacques	PVT	Lacroix's Company	05/18/12–08/16/12	Surrendered at Detroit
Gireux, Joachin	PVT	Lee's Company	10/22/13–04/21/14	
Glass, Robert	2SG	Lacroix's Company	05/18/12–08/16/12	Surrendered at Detroit
Glass, Robert	PVT	Lee's Company	10/22/13–04/21/14	
Glover, Thomas	PVT	Johnson's COM 2 US RIF	05/09/14–06/30/15	
Gobby, François	PVT	Audrain's Spies	07/01/14–07/31/14	
Gobiel, François	PVT	McDonell's Company	12/21/13–03/10/14	

NAME	RANK	MILITARY UNIT	SERVICE DATES	REMARKS
Gobielle, Francis	4CP	Dequindre's Company	04/21/12–08/16/12	Surrendered at Detroit
Goby, John B.	PVT	Crittenden's COM 17 US INF	04/30/12–04/30/17	
Goddard, Louis	DRG	Smyth's Company	04/21/12–08/16/12	Surrendered at Detroit
Godfroy, Gabriel	INT	Unassigned	??/??/??–??/??/??	For Potawatomie and French
Godfroy, Gabriel	CLT	F&S 1st MI Regiment	??/??/??–??/??/??	SCU
Godfroy, John	PVT	Dequindre's Company	04/22/12–08/16/12	Surrendered at Detroit
Godfroy, John Baptiste Jr.	3SG	Knaggs' Company	07/02/12–08/16/12	Surrendered at Detroit
Godfroy, Peter	PVT	Knaggs' Company	07/02/12–08/16/12	Surrendered at Detroit
Goire, Joseph	PVT	Lasselle's Company	08/04/12–08/18/12	Surrendered at Monroe
Golais, Joseph	PVT	Dequindre's Company	04/21/12–08/16/12	Surrendered at Detroit
Gomer, Pierre	PVT	Lacroix's Company	05/18/12–08/16/12	Surrendered at Detroit
Gonia, Augustin	PVT	Drouillard's Company	08/04/12–08/18/12	Surrendered at Monroe
Gonia, Bartimie	PVT	Drouillard's Company	08/04/12–08/18/12	Surrendered at Monroe
Gonia, Lewis	PVT	Drouillard's Company	08/04/12–08/18/12	Surrendered at Monroe. PEN
Goodell, John	3SG	Lee's Company	10/22/13–04/01/14	Died in service
Goodill, Daniel	PVT	Mack's Company	06/25/12–08/16/12	Surrendered at Detroit. PEN
Goodman, Miles	GDE	Harrison's ANW	08/02/13–08/11/13	SCU
Goodrich, Samuel B.	PVT	Mack's Company	07/10/12–08/16/12	Surrendered at Detroit
Goodspeed, Joseph	PVT	Mulholland's Company	08/04/12–08/18/12	Surrendered at Monroe
Gooley, Baptiste	PVT	Sibley's Company	07/02/12–08/16/12	Surrendered at Detroit
Gordon, John	SGT	Hickman's COM 17 US INF	03/25/11–03/25/16	TRA Stockton's Company
Gossett, David	PVT	Collins' COM 19 US INF	03/16/14–07/20/15	
Goudon, Francis	PVT	Lacroix's Company	05/18/12–08/16/12	Surrendered at Detroit|
Gouin, Leon	ENS	Audrain's Spies	07/01/14–07/31/14	
Gouin, Medard	PVT	Campau's Company	07/02/12–08/16/12	Surrendered at Detroit
Goulebout, Joseph	PVT	Lacroix's Company	05/18/12–08/16/12	Surrendered at Detroit

Michigan Men in the War of 1812

Name	Rank	Military Unit	Service Dates	Remarks
Goulet, Louis	PVT	Audrain's Rangers	10/12/14–11/30/15	
Graham, Ebenezer A.	2SG	Collins' COM 19 US INF	03/16/14–07/20/15	
Graham, John	DRG	Smyth's Company	04/26/12–08/16/12	Surrendered at Detroit
Graham, William	PVT	Johnson's COM 2 US RIF	05/07/14–06/30/15	
Gratiot, Charles Jr.	COL	F&S Michigan Militia	10/??/14–02/09/15	Rank was BVT. SCU
Graverat, Henry	GDE	Harrison's ANW	08/02/13–08/11/13	SCU
Graves, Beamon	PVT	Edmondson's COM 28 US INF	04/25/14–09/07/15	TRA Stockton's Company
Gravet, Joseph	PVT	McDonell's Company	12/26/13–03/10/14	
Green, Martin	DMR	Hawkins' COM 17 US INF	03/23/14–03/23/19	TRA Stockton's Company
Griffard, Dominique	PVT	Audrain's Spies	07/01/14–07/31/14	
Griffier, Lorick	PVT	McDonell's Company	12/21/13–03/10/14	
Griffith, Ann	HOA	Unassigned	10/20/13–01/23/14	Stationed at Detroit
Griffith, William	1LT	Reading's COM KY MTD INF	05/20/13–11/19/13	WIA 10/04/13 at McGregor's Creek
Grifford, Antoine	PVT	Audrain's Spies	07/01/14–07/31/14	
Grossbeck, James	PVT	Audrain's Rangers	10/12/14–11/30/15	PEN
Grossbeck, William	PVT	Audrain's Spies	07/01/14–07/31/14	
Gubby , Baptist	PVT	Whistler's COM 1 US INF	03/30/11–??/??/??	
Guiles, Joseph	PVT	Whistler's COM 1 US INF	04/08/12–05/31/15	Was POW
Guy, William	CPL	Dequindre's Company	04/25/12–08/16/12	PMT CPL 08/13/12. SRA Detroit
Guyor, Joseph	PVT	Lasselle's Company	08/04/12–08/18/12	Surrendered at Monroe. SCU
Guyor, Joseph	PVT	Michigan Militia	??/??/??–??/??/??	SCU
Haines, Benjamin	PVT	Edmondson's COM 28 US INF	03/20/14–06/30/15	TRA Stockton's Company
Hall, William	PVT	Edmondson's COM 28 US INF	03/29/14–06/30/15	TRA Stockton's Company
Hamilton, William	PVT	Dequindre's Company	04/26/12–08/16/12	Surrendered at Detroit
Harper, George	PVT	Collins' COM 19 US INF	05/14/14–07/20/15	
Harris, Cage	PVT	Audrain's Rangers	10/12/14–11/30/15	

NAME	RANK	MILITARY UNIT	SERVICE DATES	REMARKS
Harris, Cage	PVT	Audrain's Spies	07/01/14–07/31/14	
Harrison, Charles	SGT	Vance's COM Riflemen	08/19/12–08/29/12	Attached to 2 Ohio Militia
Harrison, Charles	PVT	Cullom's COM 2 Ohio INF	09/04/13–03/02/14	Stationed at Detroit
Harrison, Charles	PVT	Audrain's Rangers	11/01/14–11/30/15	Stationed at Brownstown. PEN
Harrison, Leonard	1SG	Dequindre's Company	04/21/12–08/16/12	Surrendered at Detroit
Harter, Charles	PVT	Audrain's Rangers	10/20/14–08/31/15	
Hartley, Joseph	PVT	Edmondson's COM 28 US INF	03/24/14–06/30/15	TRA Stockton's Company
Hartly, Abijah	PVT	Audrain's Rangers	??/??/??–07/07/15	Deserted at River Rouge
Hartshorn, George	PVT	Collins' COM 19 US INF	03/17/14–07/20/15	
Hatch, Roswell	2CP	Lacroix's Company	05/18/12–08/16/12	Surrendered at Detroit
Hatris, Charles	PVT	Audrain's Spies	07/01/14–07/31/14	
Hawkersmith, William	PVT	Edmondson's COM 28 US INF	03/30/14–06/30/15	TRA Stockton's Company
Haynes, Benjamin	PVT	Edmondson's COM 28 US INF	03/20/14–06/30/15	TRA Stockton's Company
Hebert, Jacques	PVT	Michigan Fencibles	??/??/13–??/??/15	
Henderson, Joseph	PVT	Sibley's Company	07/02/12–08/16/12	Surrendered at Detroit
Henry, Stephen Chambers	SUR	Smyth's Company	05/21/12–08/16/12	Surrendered at Detroit. PEN
Herrington, Harvey	PVT	Collins' COM 19 US INF	03/17/14–07/20/15	
Hickman, Harris Hampton	CAP	Hickman's COM 19 US INF	03/12/12–06/15/15	TRA 17 US INF 05/12/14.
Hicks, Jesse	PVT	Audrain's Spies	07/01/14–07/31/14	
Hicks, William	PVT	Michigan Militia	??/??/??–??/??/??	SCU
Hill, Daniel	DRG	Smyth's Company	04/24/12–08/16/12	Surrendered at Detroit
Hill, David	DMR	Edmondson's COM 28 US INF	07/17/14–06/30/15	TRA Stockton's Company
Hivon, Charles	PVT	Martin's Company	08/04/12–08/18/12	Surrendered at Monroe. PEN
Hivon, Joseph	SGT	Jobean's Company	08/04/12–08/18/12	Surrendered at Monroe. PEN
Hizer, John	2CP	Dequindre's Company	04/21/12–08/16/12	Broken to PVT 08/13/12. SRA Detroit
Howard, Joseph	PVT	Audrain's Rangers	??/??/??–02/??/15	Deserted at Detroit

NAME	RANK	MILITARY UNIT	SERVICE DATES	REMARKS
Hubbard, Diodate	PVT	Cullom's COM 2 OH INF	09/04/13–03/02/14	AKA Dodate/Vivdate Hubbard. PEN
Hubbard, Edward	DRG	Smyth's Company	04/21/12–08/16/12	Surrendered at Detroit
Hubbard, Edward	UNK	Ball's SQD US LTD	??/??/12–??/??/13	SCU
Hudson, Henry	SGT	Mack's Company	05/28/12–08/16/12	Drafted. Surrendered at Detroit
Hughett, John K.	PVT	Kisling's COM 19 US INF	03/25/14–03/27/15	
Hull, David	PVT	Lee's Company	10/22/13–04/21/14	
Hull, Levi	GDE	Harrison's ANW	08/02/13–08/11/13	SCU
Hull, Levi	SGT	McDonell's Company	12/26/13–03/10/14	
Hull, William	GEB	F&S Michigan Militia	01/11/05–08/16/12	Commander in Chief
Hunt, Henry Jackson	VOL	Lewis Cass Expedition	09/15/14	SCU
Hunt, Thomas	SGM	F&S, Legionary Corps	05/29/12–07/20/12	
Hunt, Thomas	SGM	Smyth's Company	04/20/12–05/28/12	Detached by General Hull
Hunter, Cyrus	DRG	Smyth's Company	05/16/12–09/30/12	Detached to River Raisin. ETO
Hunter, Cyrus	PVT	Ball's SQD US LTD	09/30/12–05/10/13	
Hunter, Cyrus	PVT	Lee's Company	10/22/13–04/21/14	WIA at Mississinewa
Hunter, Joshua	PVT	Westbrook's Company	05/12/14–06/11/14	
Hunter, Thomas	PVT	Collins' COM 19 US INF	03/22/14–07/20/15	PEN
Hunter, William	DRG	Smyth's Company	04/29/12–09/30/12	DET River Raisin 05/01/12. ETO
Hunter, William	PVT	Ball's SQD US LTD	09/30/12–05/05/13	
Hunter, William	PVT	Lee's Company	10/22/13–04/21/14	
Hunter, William	PVT	Whistler's COM 1 US INF	10/21/11–06/10/15	Was POW
Huntington, Joseph	PVT	Mulholland's Company	08/04/12–08/18/12	Surrendered at Monroe
Imick, John	PVT	Lee's Company	10/22/13–04/21/14	Substitute for Jean St. Clouture
Jack, Peter	PVT	Lee's Company	11/07/13–04/21/14	
Jacob, Jacques	CPL	Menard's Company	08/04/12–08/18/12	Surrendered at Monroe
Jacob, Jean	PVT	Drouillard's Company	08/04/12–08/18/12	Surrendered at Monroe

Name	Rank	Military Unit	Service Dates	Remarks
Jacob, Joseph	PVT	Drouillard's Company	08/04/12–08/18/12	Surrendered at Monroe
Jacob, Louis	PVT	Lacroix's Company	05/18/12–08/16/12	WIA Brownstown 08/05/12. SRA Detroit
Jacob, Pierre	PVT	Lacroix's Company	05/18/12–08/16/12	Surrendered at Detroit
Jacob, Simon	DRG	Smyth's Company	04/29/12–08/16/12	Detached to River Raisin
Jamison, John	MUS	Mack's Company	06/10/12–08/16/12	Surrendered at Detroit
Jamison, John	PVT	Hawkins' COM 17 US INF	04/21/14–04/03/19	
Jassman, Tousaint	PVT	Mack's Company	06/10/12–08/16/12	Surrendered at Detroit
Joachim, Jean Baptiste	PVT	Lacroix's Company	05/18/12–08/16/12	Surrendered at Detroit
Jobean, Joseph	CAP	Jobean's Company	08/04/12–08/18/12	Surrendered at Monroe
John, Thomas	PVT	Westbrook's Company	05/12/14–06/11/14	
Johnson, George	2LT	Lee's Company	10/22/13–04/21/14	
Johnson, George	2LT	Smyth's Company	04/21/12–08/16/12	Surrendered at Detroit
Johnson, George	PVT	Edmondson's COM 28 US INF	03/23/14–06/30/15	
Johnston, George	PVT	Audrain's Spies	07/01/14–07/31/14	
Johnston, John	CAP	British Volunteers	??/??/12–??/??/14	Served at Michilimackinac
Johnston, John	CAP	Michigan Fencibles	??/??/??–??/??/??	Served at Michilimackinac
Johnston, Lewis Saurin	MID	HMS Lady Prevost	07/15/12–09/10/13	CPT Put-in-Bay
Jolia, Joseph	PVT	Couture's Company	08/04/12–08/18/12	Surrendered at Monroe
Jones, Benjamin	PVT	Hawkins' COM 17 US INF	04/21/14–06/09/15	
Jones, Elijah	1CP	Collins' COM 19 US INF	05/07/14–07/20/15	
Jones, John	MUS	Reed's COM 2 US LGT ART	08/13/12–08/12/17	Was POW
Jones, Richard H.	PVT	Sibley's Company	07/02/12–08/16/12	Surrendered at Detroit
Jubenville, Francis	DRG	Smyth's Company	04/26/12–08/16/12	Surrendered at Detroit
Jubenville, Jean Baptiste	DRG	Smyth's Company	04/21/12–08/16/12	Surrendered at Detroit
Kelly, Charles	SGT	Mack's Company	05/20/12–08/16/12	Surrendered at Detroit
Kelly, Palmer	PVT	Mack's Company	05/20/12–08/16/12	Surrendered at Detroit

Michigan Men in the War of 1812

Name	Rank	Military Unit	Service Dates	Remarks
Kent, Datas	CPL	Mulholland's Company	08/04/12–08/18/12	Surrendered at Monroe
Kent, Joseph	PVT	Mulholland's Company	08/04/12–08/18/12	Surrendered at Monroe
Kesler, John	PVT	Collins' COM 19 US INF	03/16/14–07/20/15	
Kilbourn, Johnston	PVT	Audrain's Rangers	11/02/14–11/30/15	Stationed at Brownstown
Kilbourn, Johnston	PVT	Audrain's Spies	07/01/14–07/31/14	
Kilburn, Anthony	PVT	Westbrook's Company	05/12/14–06/11/14	
King, Joseph	PVT	Campau's Company	07/02/12–08/16/12	Surrendered at Detroit
King, Robert	PVT	Collins' COM 19 US INF	03/17/14–07/20/15	
Kingsland, Daniel	PVT	Collins' COM 19 US INF	04/16/14–07/19/15	
Kingsland, Daniel	PVT	McDonell's Company	12/21/13–03/10/14	
Kipp, Isaac	PVT	Westbrook's Company	05/12/14–06/11/14	
Kipp, John	PVT	Westbrook's Company	05/12/14–06/11/14	
Kipp, Johnathan	PVT	Westbrook's Company	05/12/14–06/11/14	
Kittridge, Ebenezer	UNK	Unknown	??/??/??–??/??/??	SCU
Knaggs, James	DRG	Smyth's Company	04/21/12–09/30/12	DET River Raisin 05/01/12. ETO
Knaggs, James	PVT	Ball's SQD US LTD	09/30/12–05/10/13	PEN
Knaggs, James	PVT	Lee's Company	10/22/13–04/21/14	
Knaggs, James	PVT	Reading's COM KY MTD INF	08/15/13–11/19/13	
Knaggs, Thomas	GDE	Winchester's ANW	01/22/13–??/??/??	Taken prisoner. SCU
Knaggs, Thomas	PVT	Martin's Company	08/04/12–08/18/12	Surrendered at Monroe
Knaggs, Whitmore	CAP	Knaggs' Company	07/02/12–08/16/12	Surrendered at Detroit
Knaggs, Whitmore	GDE	Winchester's ANW	01/22/13–??/??/??	POW, sent to Quebec SCU
Knaggs, William	PVT	Martin's Company	08/04/12–08/18/12	Surrendered at Monroe
Knaggs, William G.	PVT	Mulholland's Company	08/04/12–08/18/12	Surrendered at Monroe
Knap, Isaac	CPL	McDonell's Company	12/22/13–03/10/14	
Knap, James	PVT	McDonell's Company	01/01/14–03/10/14	

Name	Rank	Military Unit	Service Dates	Remarks
Knapp, Walter	PVT	McDonell's Company	01/14/14–03/10/14	
Knight, Stephen	PVT	Harris' COM 1 US LTD	10/14/13–04/14/15	
L'enfant, Benjamin	SCT	Harrison's ANW	01/11/13–10/??/13	AKA Joseph Benjamin L'enfant. SCU
Labadi, Antoine	PVT	Mack's Company	05/28/12–08/16/12	Surrendered at Detroit
Labadie, Alexis	SGT	Jobean's Company	08/04/12–08/18/12	Surrendered at Monroe
Labadie, Medard	GDE	Winchester's ANW	01/22/13–??/??/??	Taken prisoner. SCU
Labadie, Medard	SCT	Harrison's ANW	02/??/13–10/??/13	SCU
Labadie, Medore	CPL	Jobean's Company	08/04/12–08/18/12	Surrendered at Monroe
Labadie, Pierre	PVT	Audrain's Spies	07/01/14–07/31/14	
Laberosh, Benjamin	PVT	Couture's Company	08/04/12–08/18/12	Surrendered at Monroe
Labidi, Madore	PVT	Menard's Company	08/04/12–08/18/12	Surrendered at Monroe
Labidi, Pierre	ENS	Knaggs' Company	07/02/12–08/16/12	Surrendered at Detroit
Labranche, Pierre	PVT	Lacroix's Company	05/18/12–08/16/12	Surrendered at Detroit
Lacissoire, Augustine	PVT	McDonell's Company	12/30/13–03/10/14	
LaCourciere, Augustine	PVT	Jobean's Company	08/04/12–08/18/12	Surrendered at Monroe
Lacroix, Hubert	CAP	Lacroix's Company	05/18/12–08/16/12	Surrendered at Detroit. PEN
Lacroix, Hubert	GDE	Winchester's ANW	01/22/13–??/??/??	POW, sent to Quebec. SCU
Lacroix, Peter	PVT	Couture's Company	08/04/12–08/18/12	Surrendered at Monroe
Ladarot, J.	PVT	Audrain's Spies	07/01/14–07/31/14	
LaDuc, Peter	PVT	Mack's Company	05/28/12–08/16/12	SRA Detroit. AKA Peter Percy. PEN
LaDuc, Peter	PVT	Holmes' COM 26 US INF	??/??/14–??/??/15	POW Mackinac. AKA Peter Percy. SCU
Ladue, Louis	PVT	McDonell's Company	01/14/14–03/10/14	
Laduke, Jean Baptiste	PVT	Couture's Company	08/04/12–08/18/12	Surrendered at Monroe
Laduke, Louis	PVT	Campau's Company	07/02/12–08/16/12	Surrendered at Detroit
Laferty, Joseph	PVT	Knaggs' Company	07/02/12–08/16/12	Surrendered at Detroit
Laferty, Louis	PVT	Campau's Company	07/02/12–08/16/12	Surrendered at Detroit

NAME	RANK	MILITARY UNIT	SERVICE DATES	REMARKS
Laferty, Pierre	PVT	Knaggs' Company	07/02/12–08/16/12	Surrendered at Detroit
Lafleur, Raphael	PVT	Mack's Company	05/20/12–08/16/12	Surrendered at Detroit
Laflore, Andrew	SGT	Couture's Company	08/04/12–08/18/12	Surrendered at Monroe
Lafond, Antoine	PVT	Martin's Company	08/04/12–08/18/12	Surrendered at Monroe
Laforge, Charles	PVT	Sansfacon's Company	08/01/12–08/16/12	SRA Detroit. SCU. PEN
LaForge, George	PVT	Audrain's Company	02/??/13–??/??/13	SCU. PEN
Laforge, Louis	PVT	Audrain's Spies	07/01/14–07/31/14	
Lafort, Joshua	PVT	McDonell's Company	01/14/14–03/10/14	
Lafountaine, Antoine	PVT	Drouillard's Company	08/04/12–08/18/12	Surrendered at Monore
Lafountaine, Antoine	PVT	Reading's COM KY MTD INF	09/15/13–11/19/13	
Lafoy, Augustus	PVT	Campau's Company	07/02/12–08/16/12	Surrendered at Detroit
LaFoy, Lambert	VOL	Lewis Cass Expedition	09/15/14	SCU
Lajeunesse, François	PVT	McDonell's Company	01/14/14–03/10/14	PEN
Lajeunesse, Louis	PVT	McDonell's Company	12/28/13–03/10/14	
Lajoie, Bazile	PVT	Lee's Company	10/22/13–02/10/14	
Lajoie, Charles	PVT	Lee's Company	10/22/13–12/14/13	Died in service
Lajore, Bazil	DRG	Smyth's Company	05/01/12–08/16/12	Detached to River Raisin
Lajoy, Charles	PVT	Lacroix's Company	05/18/12–08/16/12	Surrendered at Detroit
Lajoy, Hyacinth	1SG	Lacroix's Company	05/18/12–08/16/12	Surrendered at Detroit
Lajoy, Louis	1CP	Lacroix's Company	05/18/12–08/16/12	Surrendered at Detroit
Lalon, George	PVT	Edmondson's COM 28 US INF	03/02/14–??/??/??	
Lalona, George	PVT	McDonell's Company	12/28/13–03/10/14	
Laluminger, Lewis	SGT	Couture's Company	08/04/12–08/18/12	Surrendered at Monroe
Lamphare, Elisha	DRG	Smyth's Company	03/21/12–08/16/12	Surrendered at Detroit
Lampher, Elisha	PVT	Audrain's Rangers	10/20/14–11/30/15	Stationed at Brownstown
Landroch, Andre	PVT	Mack's Company	06/26/12–08/16/12	Surrendered at Detroit

Michigan Men in the War of 1812

Name	Rank	Military Unit	Service Dates	Remarks
Landroche, Andre	PVT	McDonell's Company	12/21/13–03/10/14	
Landroche, Pierre	PVT	Mack's Company	06/12/12–08/16/12	Surrendered at Detroit. PEN
Landry, Louis	PVT	Whistler's COM 1 US INF	03/13/12–??/??/??	POW
Langervan, Jean Baptiste	PVT	Martin's Company	08/04/12–08/18/12	Surrendered at Monroe
Lantroff, Andrew	PVT	Collins' COM 19 US INF	03/16/14–??/??/??	DUC 08/28/15. TRA Hawkins' COM
Laparte, Alexander	PVT	Hawkins' COM 17 US INF	03/30/14–03/30/19	
Laperle, Antoine	PVT	Mack's Company	07/10/12–08/16/12	Surrendered at Detroit
Lapoint, Baptiste	PVT	Drouillard's Company	08/04/12–08/18/12	Surrendered at Monroe
Lapoint, Gabriel	PVT	Mack's Company	05/28/12–08/16/12	Drafted. Surrendered at Detroit
Lapoint, Geome	PVT	Drouillard's Company	08/04/12–08/18/12	Surrendered at Monroe
Lapoint, Nicholas	PVT	Lacroix's Company	05/18/12–08/16/12	Surrendered at Detroit
Lapointe, Arthur	PVT	Lee's Company	10/22/13–04/21/14	
Larabee, John	PVT	Mack's Company	07/10/12–08/16/12	Surrendered at Detroit
Larange, Antoine	PVT	Reading's COM KY MTD INF	09/15/13–11/19/13	
Lariviere, Joseph	PVT	Michigan Fencibles	??/??/13–??/??/15	
Larned, Charles	VOL	Lewis Cass Expedition	08/15/14	SCU
Laroche, Charles	PVT	McDonell's Company	12/20/13–03/10/14	
Lasselle, Antoine	PVT	Jobean's Company	08/04/12–08/18/12	Surrendered at Monroe
Lasselle, François	UNK	Unknown	??/??/13–??/??/13	POW at Fort Malden as spi. SCU
Lasselle, François	LUT	Lacroix's Company	05/18/12–08/16/12	Surrendered at Detroit
Lasselle, Jean Baptiste	1LT	Lasselle's Company	08/04/12–08/18/12	Surrendered at Monroe
Lasselle, Jean Baptiste	SGT	Lasselle's Company	08/04/12–08/18/12	Surrendered at Monroe
Lassivore, Augustine	PVT	Lacroix's Company	05/18/12–08/16/12	Surrendered at Detroit
Latour, Jean Marie	PVT	Lacroix's Company	05/18/12–08/16/12	Surrendered at Detroit
Latour, Jean M.	PVT	Lee's Company	10/22/13–04/21/14	
Latoure, Jean Baptiste	PVT	Couture's Company	08/04/12–08/18/12	Surrendered at Monroe

NAME	RANK	MILITARY UNIT	SERVICE DATES	REMARKS
Laurenger, Alexis	ENS	Martin's Company	08/04/12–08/18/12	Surrendered at Monroe
Laurent, Antoine	PVT	Mack's Company	05/28/12–08/16/12	Surrendered at Detroit
Laurent, Louis	PVT	Mack's Company	05/28/12–08/16/12	Drafted. Surrendered at Detroit
Lauzon, François	PVT	Lacroix's Company	05/18/12–08/16/12	Surrendered at Detroit
Lavine, Lewis	PVT	Drouillard's Company	08/04/12–08/18/12	Surrendered at Monroe
Lavoilette, François	PVT	Lacroix's Company	05/18/12–08/16/12	Surrendered at Detroit
Leach, Ichabod	PVT	Mack's Company	05/28/12–08/16/12	Drafted. Surrendered at Detroit
Leaparl, Joseph	PVT	Audrain's Spies	07/01/14–07/31/14	
Lebeau, Baptiste	PVT	Mack's Company	06/15/12–08/16/12	Surrendered at Detroit
Lebeau, Etienne	PVT	Lacroix's Company	05/18/12–08/16/12	Surrendered at Detroit
LeBeau, Joseph	PVT	Audrain's Spies	07/01/14–07/31/14	
LeBlanche, Joseph	DRG	Smyth's Company	04/26/12–08/16/12	Surrendered at Detroit
LeClair, Joseph (1	PVT	Mack's Company	05/28/12–08/16/12	Surrendered at Detroit
LeClair, Joseph (2	PVT	Mack's Company	06/02/12–08/16/12	SUB Isidore Chabert. SRA Detroit
Leduc, Hyacinth	PVT	Lacroix's Company	05/18/12–08/16/12	Surrendered at Detroit
Leduc, Pierre	PVT	Mack's Company	05/28/12–08/16/12	Surrendered at Detroit
Leduick, Pierre	PVT	Collins' COM 19 US INF	05/04/14–??/??/??	
Leduke, Louis	1CP	Audrain's Rangers	10/20/14–10/19/15	
Lee, Isaac	CAP	Lee's Company	10/22/13–05/14/14	
Lee, Isaac	COR	Smyth's Company	04/29/12–09/30/12	CMD at River Raisin 05/01/12. ETO
Lee, Isaac	LUT	Ball's SQD US LTD	09/30/12–05/10/13	
LeGros, Amable	SCT	Harrison's ANW	01/22/13–04/08/13	KIA near Ft. Meigs. SCU
LeGross, Amable	PVT	Mack's Company	06/02/12–08/16/12	Surrendered at Detroit
Lelavre, Charlow	PVT	Audrain's Spies	07/01/14–07/31/14	
Lelavre, Fonfon	PVT	Audrain's Spies	07/01/14–07/31/14	
Lelavre, Louis	PVT	Audrain's Spies	07/01/14–07/31/14	

119

Name	Rank	Military Unit	Service Dates	Remarks
Lemay, Alexis	PVT	Knaggs' Company	07/02/12–08/16/12	Surrendered at Detroit
Leonard, Collan	PVT	Drouillard's Company	08/04/12–08/18/12	Surrendered at Monroe
Leonard, François	CPL	Drouillard's Company	08/04/12–08/18/12	Surrendered at Monroe
Leonard, François	PVT	Lacroix's Company	05/18/12–08/16/12	Surrendered at Detroit
Leonard, Louis	PVT	Lacroix's Company	05/18/12–08/16/12	Surrendered at Detroit
Leonard, Martin	SGT	Dyson's COM 1 US ART	06/24/09–10/14/14	Was POW
Leonard, Stephen	PVT	Collins' COM 19 US INF	03/15/14–??/??/??	
Leparl, Alexis	PVT	Audrain's Spies	07/01/14–07/31/14	
Lesperance, Antoine	PVT	Audrain's Spies	07/01/14–07/31/14	
Lesperance, Antoine	PVT	Campau's Company	07/02/12–08/16/12	Surrendered at Detroit
Lesperance, François	PVT	McDonell's Company	12/28/13–03/10/14	
Lewis, Hiram	PVT	McDonell's Company	02/02/14–03/10/14	
Lewis, Silas	SCT	Hull's Army	??/??/12–??/??/12	SCU
Lewis, Silas	PVT	Lee's Company	10/22/13–04/21/14	
Lievre, Charles Jr.	PVT	Dequindre's Company	04/22/12–08/16/12	Surrendered at Detroit
Lievre, Charles Sr.	PVT	Dequindre's Company	04/22/12–08/16/12	Surrendered at Detroit
Lievre, Louis	PVT	Dequindre's Company	04/22/12–08/16/12	Surrendered at Detroit
Lifive, Joffroy	DRG	Smyth's Company	04/21/12–08/16/12	Surrendered at Detroit
Little, William	2LT	McDonell's Company	12/20/13–03/10/14	
Little, William	DRG	Smyth's Company	04/21/12–08/16/12	Surrendered at Detroit
Little, William	SGM	F&S Legionary Corps	07/21/12–08/16/12	Surrendered at Detroit
Little, William T.	PVT	Tucker's Company	06/01/12–08/16/12	SRA Detroit. SCU. PEN
Livernois, Etienne	PVT	Knaggs' Company	07/02/12–08/16/12	Surrendered at Detroit
Livernois, Joseph	3CP	Knaggs' Company	07/02/12–08/16/12	Surrendered at Detroit
Livernois, Joseph	SCT	Harrison's ANW	02/??/13–??/??/??	WIA near Ft. Meigs 04/08/13. SCU
Livingston, Robert	LUT	Mackinac Volunteers	??/??/12–08/08/12	WIA & CPT Monguagon

NAME	RANK	MILITARY UNIT	SERVICE DATES	REMARKS
Lobeille, François	2CP	Audrain's Rangers	10/20/14–11/30/15	
Lognan, Augustine	1CP	Smyth's Company	04/21/12–08/16/12	Surrendered at Detroit
Lognan, Louis	DRG	Smyth's Company	04/21/12–08/16/12	Surrendered at Detroit
Lonfon, Joseph	PVT	Couture's Company	08/04/12–08/18/12	Surrendered at Monroe
Lonfont, Benjamin	CPL	Lasselle's Company	08/04/12–08/18/12	Surrendered at Monroe
Lonfont, Joseph	SGT	Lasselle's Company	08/04/12–08/18/12	Surrendered at Monroe
Loran, Amable	PVT	Audrain's Spies	07/01/14–07/31/14	
Loran, Antoine	PVT	Audrain's Spies	07/01/14–07/31/14	
Loran, Baptist	PVT	Audrain's Rangers	10/20/14–11/30/15	Stationed at Brownstown
Loran, Baptist	PVT	Audrain's Spies	07/01/14–07/31/14	
Loran, François	PVT	Audrain's Spies	07/01/14–07/31/14	
Loran, Joseph	PVT	Audrain's Rangers	10/20/14–11/30/15	
Loran, Joseph	PVT	Audrain's Spies	07/01/14–07/31/14	
Loran, Louis	PVT	Audrain's Rangers	10/20/14–11/30/15	Stationed at Brownstown
Loran, Louis	PVT	Audrain's Spies	07/01/14–07/31/14	
Lorrell, John	PVT	Campau's Company	07/02/12–08/16/12	Surrendered at Detroit
Louis, John	PVT	Dequindre's Company	04/22/12–08/16/12	Surrendered at Detroit
Louis, Silas	DRG	Smyth's Company	04/29/12–09/30/12	DET River Raisin 05/01/12. ETO
Louis, Silas	PVT	Ball's SQD US LTD	09/30/12–05/10/13	
Louson, Francis	PVT	Audrain's Spies	07/01/14–07/31/14	
Lucas, Ben	VOL	Lewis Cass Expedition	09/15/14	SCU
Luker, Benjamin	PVT	Hanks' COM 1 US ART	05/18/11–07/17/12	SRA Fort Michilimackinac
Lusone, Dominique	PVT	Menard's Company	08/04/12–08/18/12	Surrendered at Monroe
Lusore, Baptiste	PVT	Menard's Company	08/04/12–08/18/12	Surrendered at Monroe
Luster, John	PVT	Westbrook's Company	05/12/14–06/11/14	
Lutes, Daniel	PVT	Mulholland's Company	08/04/12–08/18/12	Surrendered at Monroe

Name	Rank	Military Unit	Service Dates	Remarks
Mack, Stephen	CAP	Mack's Company	06/29/12–08/16/12	Surrendered at Detroit
Madox, Joshua	PVT	Hawkins' COM 17 US INF	04/02/14–06/09/15	
Magaw, William	PVT	Sibley's Company	07/02/12–08/16/12	Surrendered at Detroit
Magee, Hugh	PVT	Audrain's Rangers	10/20/14–11/30/15	
Mahoney, Thomas	ARF	Dyson's COM 1 US ART	02/26/12–02/26/17	Was POW
Maison, Nicholas	PVT	Mack's Company	06/26/12–08/16/12	Surrendered at Detroit. PEN
Major, Jean Baptiste	PVT	Audrain's Rangers	10/20/14–11/30/15	
Major, Jean Baptiste	PVT	Lee's Company	10/22/13–04/21/14	
Majore, Jean Baptiste	PVT	Lasselle's Company	08/04/12–08/18/12	Surrendered at Monroe
Mallard, Augustus	PVT	Stockton's COM 28 US INF	01/20/13–12/06/16	
Mallette, Joseph	3CP	Lacroix's Company	05/18/12–08/16/12	Surrendered at Detroit
Mallory, Timothy P.	PVT	Audrain's Rangers	12/23/14–08/31/15	
Manason, Dennis	PVT	Couture's Company	08/04/12–08/18/12	Surrendered at Monroe
Marr, James	PVT	Hawkins' COM 17 US INF	04/02/14–06/09/15	
Marsac, Baptiste	PVT	Mack's Company	06/20/12–08/16/12	Surrendered at Detroit
Marsac, Joseph F.	PVT	Tucker's Company	06/01/12–08/16/12	SRA Detroit. SCU. PEN
Marsac, Joseph F.	PVT	Gouin's Company	09/??/13–05/01/14	SCU. PEN
Martin, Carr	PVT	Wadsworth's COM 1 US RIF	08/06/12–06/10/15	
Martin, Jacques	1LT	Martin's Company	08/04/12–08/18/12	Surrendered at Monroe
Martin, Toussaint	PVT	Martin's Company	08/04/12–08/18/12	Surrendered at Monroe. PEN
Massack, John B.	PVT	Crittenden's COM 17 US INF	10/04/13–??/??/??	
Massico, Jean Baptiste	DRG	Smyth's Company	04/21/12–08/16/12	Surrendered at Detroit
Masters, William	PVT	Collins' COM 19 US INF	04/17/14–07/20/15	
Matavia, Francis	PVT	Hawkins' COM 17 US INF	03/02/14–01/29/19	TRA Whistler's Company
Mattocks, Ebenezer	FIF	Adair's COM 17 US INF	10/15/13–06/04/15	
Mattox, Joshua	PVT	Hawkins' COM 17 US INF	04/02/14–06/09/15	

NAME	RANK	MILITARY UNIT	SERVICE DATES	REMARKS
Maxwell, William	ARF	Hanks' COM 1 US ART	02/12/06–07/17/12	SRA Fort Michilimackinac
Mayrs, Francis	PVT	Watson's COM 25 US INF	10/04/13–05/15/15	Died in service
Mayrs, George	PVT	Watson's COM 25 US INF	10/15/13–??/??/??	
McCarty, Edward	PVT	Audrain's Spies	07/01/14–07/31/14	
McCarty, William	3LT	Audrain's Rangers	05/01/14–11/30/15	
McCarty, William	3LT	Audrain's Spies	07/01/14–07/31/14	
McCluer, Thomas	3SG	Dequindre's Company	04/21/12–08/16/12	Surrendered at Detroit
McClung, John	PVT	Collins' COM 19 US INF	03/17/14–07/20/15	
McCombs, John	ENS	Dequindre's Company	04/21/12–08/16/12	Surrendered at Detroit
McConais, John Baptiste	PVT	Knaggs' Company	07/02/12–08/16/12	Surrendered at Detroit
McCune, Samuel	PVT	Audrain's Rangers	12/23/14–08/31/15	
McDermott, Michael	PVT	Lee's Company	10/22/13–04/21/14	WIA at Mississinewa. PEN
McDonald, John	SGT	Johnson's COM 2 US RIF	01/18/14–06/30/15	
McDonell, John	CAP	McDonell's Company	12/20/13–03/10/14	COM raised at Malden, Canada?
McDonell, John	PVT	Sibley's Company	07/02/12–08/16/12	Surrendered at Detroit
McDougall, George Jr.	AJG	F&S Michigan Militia	04/21/12–08/16/12	Surrendered at Detroit
McDougall, George Jr.	COL	Duncan McArthur's Exped.	10/23/14–11/17/14	SCU
McDowel, John	SGT	Johnson's COM 2 US RIF	01/18/14–06/30/15	
McDowns, Michael	DRG	Smyth's Company	04/29/12–09/30/12	DET River Raisin 05/01/12. ETO
McDowns, Michael	PVT	Ball's SQD US LTD	09/30/12–05/10/13	
McGarry, Barney	PVT	Mack's Company	07/10/12–08/16/12	Surrendered at Detroit
McGarvey, Morris	PVT	Collins' COM 19 US INF	03/15/15–07/20/15	
McGee, Henry	DRG	Smyth's Company	05/01/12–08/16/12	Surrendered at Detroit
McGee, Hugh	DMR	Dequindre's Company	04/24/12–08/16/12	Surrendered at Detroit
McGee, John	FIF	Dequindre's Company	04/24/12–08/16/12	Surrendered at Detroit
McGill, John	PVT	Audrain's Rangers	12/23/14–08/31/15	PEN

Name	Rank	Military Unit	Service Dates	Remarks
McGill, Michael	PVT	Hanks' COM 1 US ART	03/04/12–07/17/12	SRA Fort Michilimackinac
McKay, William	CAP	Michigan Fencibles	??/??/13–02/25/14	
McLean, David	PVT	Sibley's Company	07/02/12–08/16/12	Surrendered at Detroit
McMahon, Hugh	DRG	Smyth's Company	04/21/12–08/16/12	Surrendered at Detroit
McMannis, Joseph	PVT	Collins' COM 19 US INF	03/24/14–??/??/??	
McNally, Patrick	PVT	Whistler's COM 1 US INF	02/23/12–??/??/??	
McNil, William	PVT	Audrain's Rangers	??/??/14–??/??/??	DES 02/14/15 at Sandwich, Canada
McPeck, Thomas	3CP	Collins' COM 19 US INF	03/18/14–07/20/15	
Meem, John	MUS	Whistler's COM 1 US INF	04/15/12–06/10/15	Was POW
Meile, Peter	PVT	Martin's Company	08/04/12–08/18/12	Surrendered at Monroe
Meldrum, James	VOL	Duncan McArthur's Exped.	10/23/14–11/17/14	SCU
Meldrum, James	VOL	Lewis Cass Expedition	09/15/14	SCU
Meldrum, John	VOL	Lewis Cass Expedition	09/15/14	SCU
Meldrum, William	2LT	Audrain's Rangers	05/01/15–11/30/15	
Meldrum, William	2LT	Audrain's Spies	07/01/14–07/31/14	
Meldrum, William	COR	McDonell's Company	12/20/13–03/10/14	
Meldrum, William	DRG	Smyth's Company	04/21/12–08/16/12	Surrendered at Detroit
Meldrum, William	VOL	Lewis Cass Expedition	09/15/14	SCU
Melloche, Françoise	PVT	Mack's Company	06/26/12–08/16/12	Surrendered at Detroit
Menard, François Jr.	PVT	Menard's Company	08/04/12–08/18/12	Surrendered at Monroe. PEN
Menard, François Sr.	PVT	Menard's Company	08/04/12–08/16/12	Surrendered at Detroit. PEN
Menard, Jean Marie	PVT	Martin's Company	08/04/12–08/18/12	Surrendered at Monroe
Menard, John	PVT	Reading's COM KY MTD INF	06/20/13–07/19/13	
Menard, Joseph	CAP	Menard's Company	08/04/12–08/18/12	SRA Monroe. AKA Joseph Montoore
Menard, Joseph	DRG	Smyth's Company	05/16/12–08/16/12	Detached to River Raisin
Menare, Gabriel	PVT	Menard's Company	08/04/12–08/18/12	Surrendered at Monroe

NAME	RANK	MILITARY UNIT	SERVICE DATES	REMARKS
Menie, Leo	PVT	Hawkins' COM 17 US INF	10/20/13–??/??/??	Deserted 04/09/15
Menow, Joshua	PVT	Menard's Company	08/04/12–08/18/12	Surrendered at Monroe
Mercier, John	PVT	Dequindre's Company	04/21/12–08/16/12	Surrendered at Detroit
Metia, Jean M.	PVT	Lacroix's Company	05/18/12–08/16/12	SRA Detroit. MNI Marie
Metog, François	PVT	Lacroix's Company	05/18/12–08/16/12	Surrendered at Detroit
Metta, Bazile	PVT	Audrain's Spies	07/01/14–07/31/14	
Metta, Theoplis	PVT	Audrain's Spies	07/01/14–07/31/14	
Mettes, Bazile	PVT	Audrain's Rangers	12/20/14–11/30/15	
Mettez, Rene	PVT	Knaggs' Company	07/02/12–08/16/12	Surrendered at Detroit
Mettez, Theofilus	PVT	Dequindre's Company	04/21/12–08/16/12	Surrendered at Detroit
Mettez, Theofilus Jr.	1SG	Knaggs' Company	07/02/12–08/16/12	Surrendered at Detroit
Mettivie, Francis	PVT	Dequindre's Company	04/21/12–08/16/12	Surrendered at Detroit
Michel, Joseph	PVT	Mack's Company	05/28/12–08/16/12	Surrendered at Detroit
Miles, Elizabeth	HOA	Unassigned	10/15/13–01/23–14	Stationed at Detroit
Miles, William	HOA	Unassigned	10/15/13–01/23/14	Stationed at Detroit
Millar, Miles	PVT	Mack's Company	06/20/12–08/16/12	Surrendered at Detroit
Miller, Abraham	PVT	Audrain's Rangers	12/23/14–08/31/15	
Miller, Bush G.	4CP	Audrain's Rangers	10/20/14–11/20/15	PEN
Miller, David	PVT	Dequindre's Company	04/21/12–06/10/12	
Miller, John	PVT	Audrain's Spies	07/01/14–07/31/14	
Miller, John S.	PVT	Mack's Company	06/02/12–08/16/12	Surrendered at Detroit
Miller, Richee	PVT	Audrain's Rangers	11/01/14–11/13/15	
Miller, Thomas	PVT	McDonell's Company	01/14/14/03/10/14	
Miller, William	PVT	Audrain's Rangers	11/01/14–09/24/15	
Millrow, Antoine	PVT	Lacroix's Company	05/18/12–08/16/12	Surrendered at Detroit
Minarre, François Jr.	PVT	Menard's Company	08/04/12–08/18/12	Surrendered at Monroe

Name	Rank	Military Unit	Service Dates	Remarks
Minarre, François Sr.	PVT	Menard's Company	08/04/12–08/18/12	Surrendered at Monroe
Mine, François	PVT	Audrain's Spies	07/01/14–07/31/14	
Mingo, Joseph	PVT	Whistler's COM 1 US INF	03/28/11–??/??/??	
Mini, François	PVT	Knaggs' Company	07/02/12–08/16/12	Surrendered at Detroit
Mini, Gajite	PVT	Menard's Company	08/04/12–08/18/12	Surrendered at Detroit
Mini, Joseph	UNK	St. Clair Militia	10/06/13–10/07/13	HMS Nancy EGT. AKA Minnie. SCU
Mini, Pierre	UNK	St. Clair Militia	10/06/13–10/07/13	HMS Nancy EGT. AKA Minnie. SCU
Minni, Louis	PVT	Mack's Company	07/10/12–08/16/12	Surrendered at Detroit
Miron, Antoine	PVT	Lacroix's Company	05/18/12–08/16/12	Surrendered at Detroit
Mitchell, David	SUM	British Army	??/??/11–??/??/15	POW 10/06/13 near Port Huron
Mitchell, James	4SG	Dequindre's Company	04/23/12–08/16/12	PMT SGT 06/17/12. SRA Detroit
Mocaby, John	PVT	Whistler's COM 1 US INF	06/17/10–07/01/15	
Moffit, Francis	PVT	Lee's Company	10/22/13–04/21/14	
Momeni, Antwain	PVT	Reading's COM KY MTD INF	05/20/13–11/19/13	PEN
Momeni, Peter	PVT	Reading's COM KY MTD INF	08/15/13–11/19/13	
Momine, Antoine	PVT	Lee's Company	10/22/13–04/21/14	
Momine, François	PVT	Drouillard's Company	08/04/12–08/18/12	Surrendered at Monroe
Momine, Joseph	PVT	Drouillard's Company	08/04/12–08/18/12	Surrendered at Monroe
Momini, Lewis	PVT	Jobean's Company	08/04/12–08/18/12	Surrendered at Monroe
Momini, Peter	PVT	Jobean's Company	08/04/12–08/18/12	Surrendered at Monroe
Mominie, Antoine	PVT	Lacroix's Company	05/18/12–08/16/12	Surrendered at Detroit
Monett, John S.	PVT	Whistler's COM 1 US INF	01/24/11–??/??/??	
Montgomery, Joseph	PVT	Dequindre's Company	04/22/12–08/16/12	Surrendered at Detroit
Montgomery, Richard	PVT	Edmondson's COM 28 US INF	03/19/14–06/30/15	TRA Stockton's Company
Moore, Louis	PVT	Mack's Company	06/20/12–08/16/12	Surrendered at Detroit
Moore, Morris	PVT	Dequindre's Company	04/21/12–08/16/12	Surrendered at Detroit

NAME	RANK	MILITARY UNIT	SERVICE DATES	REMARKS
Moore, William	CPL	Mulholland's Company	08/04/12–08/18/12	Surrendered at Monroe
Moore, William	DRG	Smyth's Company	04/21/12–08/16/12	Surrendered at Detroit
Moore, William	PVT	Audrain's Rangers	10/20/14–11/30/15	
Moran, Charles Jr.	3CP	Campau's Company	07/02/12–08/16/12	Surrendered at Detroit
Moran, Charles Jr.	VOL	Lewis Cass Expedition	09/15/14	SCU
Moran, Louis Jr.	VOL	Duncan McArthur's Exped.	10/23/14–11/17/14	SCU
Moran, Louis Jr.	VOL	Lewis Cass Expedition	09/15/14	SCU
Moran, Louis Jr.	1CP	Campau's Company	07/02/12–08/16/12	Surrendered at Detroit
Moran, Morris	PVT	Campau's Company	07/02/12–08/16/12	Surrendered at Detroit
Moran, Patrick	PVT	Holder's COM 17 US INF	11/26/14–11/26/19	TRA Whistler's Company
Morass, Joseph	PVT	Campau's Company	07/02/12–08/16/12	Surrendered at Detroit
Morasse, Joseph	PVT	Lasselle's Company	08/04/12–08/18/12	Surrendered at Monroe
Morrison, Ephraim	PVT	Dequindre's Company	07/10/12–08/16/12	Surrendered at Detroit
Morrow, Lewis	DRG	Smyth's Company	04/21/12–08/16/12	Surrendered at Detroit
Morse, Canfield	PVT	Knaggs' Company	07/02/12–08/16/12	Surrendered at Detroit
Morton, Morris	PVT	Hanks' COM 1 US ART	07/??/11–07/12/16	
Mouton, François	LUT	Jobean's Company	08/04/12–08/18/12	Surrendered at Monroe
Muffett, Francis	PVT	Smyth's Company	08/04/12–09/30/12	Detached to River Raisin
Mulholland, Daniel	LUT	Mulholland's Company	08/04/12–08/18/12	Surrendered at Monroe
Mullen, Thomas	PVT	Hanks' COM 1 US ART	??/??/??–07/17/12	SRA Fort Michilimackinac
Mullin, James	PVT	Audrain's Rangers	12/23/14–08/31/15	
Murdock, George L.	DRG	Smyth's Company	06/11/12–08/16/12	Surrendered at Detroit. PEN
Murphy, John	DRG	Smyth's Company	04/21/12–09/30/12	DET River Raisin 05/01/12. ETO
Murphy, John	PVT	Audrain's Rangers	10/12/14–11/31/15	
Murphy, John	PVT	Audrain's Spies	07/01/14–07/31/14	
Murphy, John	PVT	Ball's SQD US LTD	09/30/12–05/10/13	

NAME	RANK	MILITARY UNIT	SERVICE DATES	REMARKS
Murphy, John	PVT	Lee's Company	10/22/13–04/21/14	
Murphy, Thomas	DRG	Smyth's Company	04/21/12–08/16/12	Surrendered at Detroit
Murphy, Thomas	PVT	Hanks' COM 1 US ART	??/??/??–07/17/12	SRA Fort Michilimackinac
Murray, Peter J.	PVT	Dequindre's Company	04/21/12–06/10/12	
Murray, William	PVT	Crittenden's COM 17 US INF	04/11/14–??/??/??	
Myers, George	PVT	Dequindre's Company	06/07/12–08/16/12	Surrendered at Detroit
Myers, Ignace	PVT	Mack's Company	05/28/12–08/16/12	Surrendered at Detroit
Myers, Michael	PVT	Hawkins' COM 17 US INF	02/28/14–02/24/19	Was POW
Naddo, Alexis	DRG	Smyth's Company	05/16/12–08/16/12	DET River Raisin. AKA Alexis Nadeau
Naddo, Antoine	PVT	Lee's Company	10/22/13–04/21/14	AKA Nadeau
Naddo, Antoine(1	DRG	Smyth's Company	04/29/12–08/16/12	DET River Raisin. AKA Nadeau
Naddo, Antoine(2	DRG	Smyth's Company	05/01/12–08/16/12	DET River Raisin. AKA Nadeau
Naddo, Jean Baptiste	PVT	Couture's Company	08/04/12–08/18/12	Surrendered at Monroe
Naddo, Joseph	CPL	Couture's Company	08/04/12–08/18/12	SRA Monroe. AKA Joseph Nadeau
Naddo, Joseph	PVT	Couture's Company	08/04/12–08/18/12	SRA Monroe. AKA Joseph Nadeau
Naddo, Joseph	PVT	Lacroix's Company	05/18/12–08/16/12	SRA Detroit. AKA Joseph Nadeau
Naddo, Martin	ENS	Couture's Company	08/04/12–08/18/12	SRA Monroe. AKA Martin Nadeau
Namailin, Lewis	PVT	Lasselle's Company	08/04/12–08/18/12	Surrendered at Monroe
Navarre, Alexander Jr.	PVT	Lasselle's Company	08/04/12–08/18/12	Surrendered at Monroe
Navarre, Alexander Sr.	PVT	Lasselle's Company	08/04/12–08/18/12	Surrendered at Monroe
Navarre, Alexis P.	DRG	Smyth's Company	04/29/12–08/16/12	Detached to River Raisin. PEN
Navarre, Antoine	SCT	Harrison's ANW	02/??/13–10/??/13	SCU
Navarre, François Jr.	SGT	Menard's Company	08/04/12–08/18/12	Surrendered at Monroe
Navarre, François Sr.	UNK	Johnson's KY MTD INF	??/??/13–08/??/13	Captured at Brownstown. SCU
Navarre, François Sr.	CLT	F&S 2nd MI Regiment	??/??/12–08/25/14	
Navarre, Frishette	DRG	Smyth's Company	05/16/12–08/16/12	DET River Raisin. AKA Antoine

Name	Rank	Military Unit	Service Dates	Remarks
Navarre, Isidore	SGT	Menard's Company	08/04/12–08/18/12	Surrendered at Monroe
Navarre, Jacques	GDE	Winchester's ANW	01/18/13–01/22/13	Escaped to Ohio. SCU
Navarre, Jacques	LUT	Menard's Company	08/04/12–08/18/12	Surrendered at Monroe
Navarre, Jacques	SCT	Harrison's ANW	02/??/13–10/??/13	SCU
Navarre, Jacques Utro	PVT	Jobean's Company	08/04/12–08/18/12	Surrendered at Monroe
Navarre, Jean May	CPL	Menard's Company	08/04/12–08/18/12	Surrendered at Monroe
Navarre, John Marie	PVT	Knaggs' Company	07/02/12–08/16/12	Surrendered at Detroit
Navarre, Pierre	UNK	Menard's Company	08/04/12–08/18/12	SCU. PEN
Navarre, Pierre	GDE	Winchester's ANW	01/18/13–01/22/13	Escaped to Ohio. SCU
Navarre, Robert	PVT	Lasselle's Company	08/04/12–08/18/12	Surrendered at Monroe
Navarre, Robert F.	DRG	Smyth's Company	05/16/12–08/16/12	Detached to River Raisin. PEN
Navarre, Robert F.	GDE	Winchester's ANW	01/18/13–01/22/13	Escaped to Ohio. SCU
Navarre, Robert H.	PVT	Jobean's Company	08/04/12–08/18/12	Surrendered at Monroe. PEN
Navarre, Robert H.	SCT	Harrison's ANW	02/??/13–10/??/13	SCU
Navarre, Pierre	SCT	Harrison's ANW	02/??/13–10/??/13	SCU
Nelson, George	CPL	Mack's Company	05/28/12–08/16/12	Surrendered at Detroit
Neview, Joseph	PVT	Mack's Company	06/11/12–08/16/12	Surrendered at Detroit. PEN
Nevill, Henry	PVT	Betts' COM 28 US INF	03/17/14–??/??/??	
Newland, George	PVT	Audrain's Rangers	12/23/14–08/31/15	
Nicholas, William	PVT	Mulholland's Company	08/04/12–08/18/12	Surrendered at Monroe
Nichols, Charles	SGT	Mack's Company	05/28/12–08/16/12	Drafted. Surrendered at Detroit
Nichols, William	PVT	Audrain's Rangers	10/20/14–11/30/15	
Nicholson, William	CPL	McDonell's Company	02/08/14–03/10/14	
Nicket, Michel	PVT	Audrain's Spies	07/01/14–07/31/14	
Nickles, James	PVT	Collins' COM 19 US INF	03/15/14–07/20/15	
Niquette, Michel	DRG	Smyth's Company	04/21/12–08/16/12	Surrendered at Detroit

NAME	RANK	MILITARY UNIT	SERVICE DATES	REMARKS
Nolin, Jean B.	UNK	British Volunteers	??/??/??–??/??/??	Apparently served at Mackinac
Norman, Joseph	PVT	Couture's Company	08/04/12–08/18/12	Surrendered at Monroe
Norton, Daniel	PVT	Mack's Company	06/05/12–08/16/12	SUB J.B. Piquette. SRA Detroit
Norton, John B.	DMR	Stockton's COM 3 US INF	04/15/12–11/22/15	Discharged for disability
Noyear, Joseph	PVT	Lasselle's Company	08/04/12–08/18/12	Surrendered at Monroe
Null, Samuel	PVT	Hawkins' COM 17 US INF	04/29/14–06/09/15	
O'Hara, John	PVT	Whistler's COM 1 US INF	07/22/12–??/??/??	Surrendered at Detroit 08/16/12
Oben, Joseph	PVT	Audrain's Rangers	05/01/15–11/30/15	
Odren, Alexander	PVT	2nd U.S. Rifles	07/??/14–04/30/15	AKA Odrien, Odrian, Audrienne
Ogden, Anamas	PVT	Westbrook's Company	05/12/14–06/11/14	
Ogden, Ananias	1SG	Lee's Company	10/22/13–04/21/14	
Ogden, Annanias	PVT	Audrain's Spies	07/01/14–07/31/14	
Ogden, Reshor	PVT	Mack's Company	05/28/12–08/16/12	Surrendered at Detroit
Ogden, Richard	PVT	McDonell's Company	02/18/14–03/10/14	
Osterhout, Charles	GDE	Harrison's ANW	09/02/13–08/11/13	SCU
Ousterhout, Charles	1CP	Lee's Company	10/22/13–04/21/14	
Palmer, John	3SG	Smyth's Company	04/21/12–08/16/12	PMT SGT 06/02/12. SRA Detroit
Palmer, Thomas	PVT	MI Legionary Corps	??/??/12–08/16/12	SRA Detroit. SCU
Palnode, Jean Baptiste	PVT	Couture's Company	08/04/12–08/18/12	Surrendered at Monroe
Palnode, Lewis	PVT	Couture's Company	08/04/12–08/18/12	Surrendered at Monroe
Parisiens, Jacques	PVT	Michigan Fencibles	??/??/13–??/??/15	
Parker, Thomas	TRM	Smyth's Company	04/21/12–08/16/12	Surrendered at Detroit
Parnies, Paul	PVT	Knaggs' Company	07/02/12–08/16/12	Surrendered at Detroit
Parsons, Robert	PVT	Edmondson's COM 28 US INF	03/21/14–09/04/15	TRA Stockton's Company
Patrick, Joshua	DRG	Smyth's Company	04/24/12–08/16/12	Surrendered at Detroit
Paulin, François	PVT	Menard's Company	08/04/12–08/18/12	Surrendered at Monroe

NAME	RANK	MILITARY UNIT	SERVICE DATES	REMARKS
Paxton, John	DRG	Smyth's Company	05/08/12–08/16/12	Detached to River Raisin
Paxton, John	GDE	Winchester's ANW	01/18/13–01/22/13	SCU
Paxton, John	SCT	Harrison's ANW	02/??/13–10/??/13	SCU
Peltier, Baptist	PVT	Audrain's Spies	07/01/14–07/31/14	
Peltier, Charles Jr.	PVT	Campau's Company	07/02/12–08/16/12	Surrendered at Detroit. PEN
Peltier, Charles Sr.	PVT	Campau's Company	07/02/12–08/16/12	Surrendered at Detroit
Peltier, Ezekeial	PVT	Audrain's Spies	07/01/14–07/31/14	
Peltier, Francis	PVT	Dequindre's Company	04/21/12–08/16/12	Surrendered at Detroit
Peltier, Isadore	4SG	Dequindre's Company	04/21/12–08/16/12	RTR 06/12/12. SRA Detroit
Peltier, Isadore	SGT	Audrain's Spies	07/01/14–07/31/14	
Peltier, Isedore	PVT	Audrain's Rangers	11/20/14–03/26/15	
Peltier, John	PVT	Knaggs' Company	07/02/12–08/16/12	Surrendered at Detroit
Peltier, Louis	2SG	Dequindre's Company	04/21/12–08/16/12	Surrendered at Detroit
Peltier, Louis	SGT	Audrain's Spies	07/01/14–07/31/14	
Pelties, Louis	4SG	Audrain's Rangers	10/12/14–11/30/15	
Pelton, James	PVT	Westbrook's Company	05/12/14–06/11/14	
Penard, Joseph	PVT	Audrain's Spies	07/01/14–07/31/14	
Penny, John	SGT	Howard's COM 1 US ART	01/13/09–01/31/14	POW
Peno, Peter	PVT	McDonell's Company	12/22/13–03/10/14	
Pepin, Bazile	PVT	Audrain's Spies	07/01/14–07/31/14	
Pernier, François	PVT	Audrain's Spies	07/01/14–07/31/14	
Pernier, Jacques	PVT	Audrain's Spies	07/01/14–07/31/14	
Pernier, Joseph	PVT	Audrain's Spies	07/01/14–07/31/14	
Pernier, Pierre	PVT	Audrain's Spies	07/01/14–07/31/14	
Pernil, James	PVT	Audrain's Spies	07/01/14–07/31/14	
Petere, François	PVT	Audrain's Spies	07/01/14–07/31/14	

NAME	RANK	MILITARY UNIT	SERVICE DATES	REMARKS
Petit, Charles	PVT	Audrain's Rangers	11/14/14–11/30/15	
Petit, Charles	PVT	Mack's Company	05/20/12–08/16/12	Surrendered at Detroit
Petre, François	PVT	Campau's Company	07/02/12–08/16/12	Surrendered at Detroit. PEN
Pettit, Louis	PVT	Lasselle's Company	08/04/12–08/18/12	Surrendered at Monroe
Philimore, Robert	PVT	Audrain's Rangers	11/02/14–11/30/15	
Phillion, Joseph	PVT	Mack's Company	05/28/12–08/16/12	Drafted. Surrendered at Detroit
Phillips, Daniel	PVT	Collins' COM 19 US INF	03/15/14–03/14/19	
Picotte, Joseph	DRG	Smyth's Company	04/26/12–08/16/12	Surrendered at Detroit
Pierce, James	PVT	Collins' COM 19 US INF	05/02/14–07/20/15	
Pierre, John T.	PVT	Sibley's Company	07/02/12–08/16/12	Surrendered at Detroit
Pinon, Joseph	PVT	Dequindre's Company	04/21/12–08/16/12	Surrendered at Detroit
Piquot, Joseph	PVT	McDonell's Company	12/26/13–03/10/14	
Piter, William	PVT	Lee's Company	10/22/13–04/21/14	
Plaunte, Antoine	PVT	Dequindre's Company	04/25/12–??/??/??	Deserted 05/12/12
Plumb, Caleb	PVT	Mulholland's Company	08/04/12–08/18/12	Surrendered at Monroe
Plumb, Ignominin	PVT	Mulholland's Company	08/04/12–08/18/12	Surrendered at Monroe
Plumb, Merlin	PVT	Lacroix's Company	05/18/12–08/16/12	Surrendered at Detroit
Plumb, Parys M.	DRG	Smyth's Company	05/16/12–08/16/12	Detached to River Raisin
Plumb, Prisque	SGT	Mulholland's Company	08/04/12–08/18/12	Surrendered at Monroe
Poirer, Charles	PVT	Audrain's Spies	07/01/14–07/31/14	
Polepard, Charles	PVT	Lacroix's Company	05/18/12–08/16/12	Surrendered at Detroit
Polepard, Joseph	PVT	Lacroix's Company	05/18/12–08/16/12	Surrendered at Detroit
Pomaville, Joseph	PVT	Audrain's Spies	07/01/14–07/31/14	
Ponpard, Charles	PVT	Mack's Company	06/21/12–08/16/12	Surrendered at Detroit
Porgers, David	PVT	Lee's Company	10/22/13–04/21/14	
Porlier, Joseph Jacques	LUT	Michigan Fencibles	??/??/13–02/25/15	

NAME	RANK	MILITARY UNIT	SERVICE DATES	REMARKS
Pouget, Dominique	PVT	Lacroix's Company	05/18/12–08/16/12	Surrendered at Detroit
Pouget, Joseph	PVT	Lacroix's Company	05/18/12–08/16/12	Surrendered at Detroit
Poupard, Joseph	GDE	Winchester's ANW	01/19/13–01/22/13	SCU
Poupard, Joseph	SCT	Harrison's ANW	02/??/13–10/??/13	SCU
Poupard, Lewis	PVT	Couture's Company	08/04/12–08/18/12	Surrendered at Monroe
Pourien, Joseph	PVT	Lacroix's Company	05/18/12–08/16/12	Surrendered at Detroit
Praux, Etienne	PVT	Campau's Company	07/02/12–08/16/12	Surrendered at Detroit
Price, George	PVT	Audrain's Spies	07/01/14–07/31/14	
Price, George	PVT	Lee's Company	10/22/13–04/21/14	
Proux, Etienne	SCT	Harrison's ANW	02/??/13–??/??/??	WIA near Ft. Meigs 04/08/13. SCU
Provost, Jean Baptiste	PVT	McDonell's Company	12/28/13–03/10/14	
Prudhome, Jean Baptiste	PVT	Lee's Company	10/22/13–04/21/14	
Pullman, James	LUT	Michigan Fencibles	07/25/13–??/??/15	
Pupord, Lewis	PVT	Couture's Company	08/04/12–08/18/12	Surrendered at Monroe
Ramon, Pierre	PVT	Audrain's Spies	07/01/14–07/31/14	
Randall, Aguilla A.	PVT	Michigan Volunteers	??/??/??–09/14/14	KIA. SCU
Rankin, David	PVT	Audrain's Rangers	12/23/14–08/31/15	
Rano, Jacques	PVT	Audrain's Spies	07/01/14–07/31/14	
Rasbury, Coleman	PVT	Martin's Company	08/04/12–08/18/12	Surrendered at Monroe
Rattelle, Paul	PVT	McDonell's Company	02/18/14–03/10/14	
Rayome, Babtiste	PVT	Menard's Company	08/04/12–08/18/12	Surrendered at Monroe
Reaume, Charles	INT	British Army	??/??/12–12/20/13	POW 10/06/13 near Port Huron
Reaume, Joseph	DRG	Smyth's Company	04/29/12–08/16/12	Detached to River Raisin
Reaume, Joseph Jr.	PVT	Couture's Company	08/04/12–08/18/12	Surrendered at Monroe
Reaume, Joseph Sr.	CPL	Couture's Company	08/04/12–08/18/12	Surrendered at Monroe
Reaume, Stephen	PVT	Couture's Company	08/04/12–08/18/12	SRA Monroe. SCU. PEN

NAME	RANK	MILITARY UNIT	SERVICE DATES	REMARKS
Reavo, Baptist	PVT	Audrain's Spies	07/01/14–07/31/14	
Redding, John	PVT	Betts' COM 28 US INF	03/24/14–03/31/15	
Redman, William	PVT	Hanks' COM 1 US ART	06/01/12–07/17/12	SRA Fort Michilimackinac
Redstone, John H.	2SG	Audrain's Rangers	10/20/14–08/31/15	
Reed, Duncan	1LT	McDonell's Company	12/20/13–03/10/14	
Reid, Duncan	ENS	Lacroix's Company	05/18/12–08/16/12	Surrendered at Detroit
Reopelle, Joseph	PVT	Knaggs' Company	07/02/12–08/16/12	Surrendered at Detroit
Reople, Joseph	PVT	Audrain's Spies	07/01/14–07/31/14	
Rhodes, Oliver	ENS	Mulholland's Company	08/04/12–08/18/12	Surrendered at Monroe
Rhodes, Oren	DRG	Smyth's Company	04/29/12–09/30/12	DET River Raisin 05/01/12. ETO
Rhodes, Oren	PVT	Ball's SQD US LTD	09/30/12–05/05/13	
Rhodes, Orin	PVT	Lee's Company	10/22/13–04/21/14	PEN
Rhodes, Simon	PVT	Mulholland's Company	08/04/12–08/18/12	Surrendered at Monroe
Rhody, Stuart	PVT	Lacroix's Company	05/18/12–08/16/12	Surrendered at Detroit
Richard, Gabriel	PVT	Drouillard's Company	08/04/12–08/18/12	Surrendered at Monroe
Rickard, Joseph	PVT	Audrain's Spies	07/01/14–07/31/14	
Riddle, John	PVT	Lee's Company	10/22/13–04/21/14	
Riley, James	VOL	Lewis Cass Expedition	09/15/14	SCU
Riley, John	VOL	Lewis Cass Expedition	09/15/14	SCU
Riley, Peter	VOL	Lewis Cass Expedition	09/15/14	SCU
Riopelle, Dominique	PVT	Knaggs' Company	07/02/12–08/16/12	Surrendered at Detroit
Riopelle, Joseph	PVT	Mack's Company	05/28/12–08/16/12	Drafted. Surrendered at Detroit
Riopelle, Joseph	VOL	Lewis Cass Expedition	09/15/14	SCU
Rivard, Antoine	PVT	Campau's Company	07/02/12–08/16/12	Surrendered at Detroit
Rivard, Augustin	PVT	Jobean's Company	08/04/12–08/18/12	Surrendered at Monroe
Rivard, Colas	PVT	Audrain's Spies	07/01/14–07/31/14	

NAME	RANK	MILITARY UNIT	SERVICE DATES	REMARKS
Rivard, Jean Baptiste	CPL	Jobean's Company	08/04/12–08/18/12	Surrendered at Monroe. PEN
Rivard, John Baptiste	PVT	Knaggs' Company	07/02/12–08/16/12	Surrendered at Detroit
Rivard, Louis B.	SGT	Marsac's Company	??/??/12–??/??/15	SCU. PEN
Robair, Antoine	PVT	Audrain's Spies	07/01/14–07/31/14	
Robare, Isidore	PVT	Menard's Company	08/04/12–08/18/12	Surrendered at Monroe
Robb, Andrew	DRG	Smyth's Company	04/29/12–09/30/12	DET River Raisin 05/01/12. ETO
Robb, Andrew	PVT	Ball's SQD US LTD	09/30/12–05/10/13	
Robb, James	DRG	Smyth's Company	04/29/12–09/30/12	DET River Raisin 05/01/12. ETO
Robb, James	PVT	Ball's SQD US LTD	09/30/12–05/10/13	
Robb, James	PVT	Lee's Company	10/22/13–04/21/14	
Robb, James	PVT	Reading's COM KY MTD INF	09/15/13–11/19/13	
Robb, Scott	DRG	Smyth's Company	04/29/12–09/30/12	DET River Raisin 05/01/12. ETO
Robb, Scott	PVT	Ball's SQD US LTD	09/30/12–05/10/13	
Robb, Scott	PVT	Lee's Company	10/22/13–04/21/14	PEN
Robb, Thomas	PVT	Lee's Company	10/22/13–04/21/14	
Robb, Thomas	PVT	Reading's COM KY MTD INF	08/15/13–11/19/13	
Robb, William	DRG	Smyth's Company	05/16/12–08/16/12	Detached to River Raisin
Robedoux, Stien	PVT	Drouillard's Company	08/04/12–08/18/12	Surrendered at Monroe
Roberson, James	PVT	Audrain's Spies	07/01/14–07/31/14	
Robert, Antoine	PVT	Lacroix's Company	05/18/12–08/16/12	Surrendered at Detroit
Robert, François	PVT	Menard's Company	08/04/12–08/18/12	Surrendered at Monroe
Robert, Ignace	PVT	Menard's Company	08/04/12–08/18/12	Surrendered at Monroe. PEN
Robert, Isaac	PVT	Lacroix's Company	05/18/12–08/16/12	Surrendered at Detroit
Robert, Joseph	ENS	Menard's Company	08/04/12–08/18/12	Surrendered at Monroe
Robert, Pierre	PVT	Menard's Company	08/04/12–08/18/12	Surrendered at Monroe
Robertson, James	PVT	McDonell's Company	02/18/14–03/10/14	

NAME	RANK	MILITARY UNIT	SERVICE DATES	REMARKS
Robertson, William	DRG	Smyth's Company	05/16/12–08/16/12	Detached to River Raisin
Robideau, Pierre	SCT	Harrison's ANW	01/22/13–04/08/13	KIA near Ft. Meigs. SCU
Robideaux, Etienne	PVT	Lacroix's Company	05/18/12–08/16/12	Surrendered at Detroit
Robideaux, Jean Marie	PVT	Lacroix's Company	05/18/12–08/16/12	Surrendered at Detroit
Robideaux, Joseph	PVT	Lacroix's Company	05/18/12–08/16/12	Surrendered at Detroit
Robideaux, Louis	PVT	Lacroix's Company	05/18/12–08/16/12	Surrendered at Detroit
Robideaux, Pierre	PVT	Lacroix's Company	05/18/12–08/16/12	Surrendered at Detroit
Robinson, James	PVT	McDonell's Company	12/??/13–03/??/14	SCU
Robinson, James	PVT	Anderson's Company	??/??/14–??/??/14	SCU
Robinson, Tobias	PVT	Edmondson's COM 28 US INF	03/23/14–07/08/15	TRA Stockton's Company
Robinson, William	DRG	Smyth's Company	04/21/12–08/16/12	Surrendered at Detroit
Robitaille, Joseph	PVT	Mack's Company	05/28/12–08/16/12	Surrendered at Detroit
Roby, John S.	PVT	Sibley's Company	07/02/12–08/16/12	Surrendered at Detroit
Rod, Alexander	PVT	Audrain's Spies	07/01/14–07/31/14	
Rodd, Alexander	PVT	Campau's Company	07/02/12–08/16/12	Surrendered at Detroit
Rolo, Jean Baptiste	PVT	Couture's Company	08/04/12–08/18/12	Surrendered at Monroe
Ronde, Peter L'isle	PVT	Menard's Company	08/04/12–08/18/12	Surrendered at Monroe
Root, Charles C.	4CP	Sibley's Company	07/02/12–08/16/12	Surrendered at Detroit
Rosseau, Jean B.	PVT	Mack's Company	06/15/12–08/16/12	Surrendered at Detroit
Rosseau, Pierre	DRG	Smyth's Company	05/02/12–08/16/12	Detached to River Raisin
Rosseau, Pierre	PVT	Ball's SQD US LTD	09/30/12–05/10/13	
Rouleau, John	PVT	McDonell's Company	12/20/13–03/10/14	
Roulo, Charles	SGT	Mack's Company	06/18/12–08/16/12	SRA Detroit. SCU. PEN
Roulon, Jean Baptiste	PVT	Couture's Company	08/04/12–08/18/12	Surrendered at Monroe
Rouson, Baptist	PVT	Audrain's Spies	07/01/14–07/31/14	
Row, Baptiste Jr.	PVT	Drouillard's Company	08/04/12–08/18/12	Surrendered at Monroe

NAME	RANK	MILITARY UNIT	SERVICE DATES	REMARKS
Row, Dominique	PVT	Drouillard's Company	08/04/12–08/18/12	Surrendered at Monroe
Row, Jean Baptiste	ENS	Drouillard's Company	08/04/12–08/18/12	Surrendered at Monroe
Rowley, Thomas	PVT	Collins' COM 19 US INF	03/17/14–07/20/15	
Roy, Francis	SGT	Michigan Fencibles	??/??/13–??/??/15	
Rucker, Thomas	PVT	Edmondson's COM 28 US INF	03/20/14–06/30/15	TRA Stockton's Company
Ruff, Francis	PVT	Westbrook's Company	05/12/14–06/11/14	PEN
Ruland, Isaac	GDE	Winchester's ANW	01/22/13–??/??/??	POW to Ft. George. SCU. PEN
Ruland, Isaac	PVT	Mulholland's Company	08/04/12–08/18/12	SRA Monroe. POW 01/22/13–05/27/13
Ruland, Isaac	VOL	Harrison's ANW	??/??/13–??/??/14	Served as ship pilot and EXN. SCU
Ruland, Israel	5SG	Audrain's Rangers	10/20/14–11/30/15	
Ruland, Israel	CPL	McDonell's Company	02/08/14–03/10/14	
Ruland, Israel	PVT	Mulholland's Company	08/04/12–08/18/12	Surrendered at Monroe
Ruland, John	1LT	Lee's Company	10/22/13–04/21/14	
Ruland, John	2CP	Smyth's Company	04/29/12–09/30/12	DET River Raisin 05/01/12. ETO
Ruland, John	LUT	Audrain's Rangers	10/20/14–11/30/15	
Ruland, John	PVT	Reading's COM KY MTD INF	06/20/13–11/19/13	
Ruland, John	SGT	Ball's SQD US LTD	09/30/12–05/10/13	
Ruland, John	VOL	Lewis Cass Expedition	09/15/14	SCU
Ruland, Joseph	PVT	Mulholland's Company	08/04/12–08/18/12	Surrendered at Monroe
Russar, Alexander	DRG	Smyth's Company	05/08/12–??/??/??	Deserted to the enemy
Russell, Joseph	PVT	Campau's Company	07/02/12–08/16/12	Surrendered at Detroit
Russell, William	PVT	Campau's Company	07/02/12–08/16/12	Surrendered at Detroit
Ryan, Edward	PVT	Sibley's Company	07/02/12–08/16/12	Surrendered at Detroit
Rylie, Pierre	PVT	Campau's Company	07/02/12–08/16/12	Surrendered at Detroit
Saintcroint, Alexis	PVT	Lacroix's Company	05/18/12–08/16/12	Surrendered at Detroit
Saintcroint, François	PVT	Couture's Company	08/04/12–08/18/12	Surrendered at Monroe

NAME	RANK	MILITARY UNIT	SERVICE DATES	REMARKS
Saintcroint, Jean Baptiste	PVT	Couture's Company	08/04/12–08/18/12	Surrendered at Monroe
Saintcroint, Peter	PVT	Couture's Company	08/04/12–08/18/12	Surrendered at Monroe
Saintobin, Gabriel	PVT	Mack's Company	06/21/12–08/16/12	Surrendered at Detroit
Sanes, Erastus	PVT	Mack's Company	06/02/12–08/16/12	Surrendered at Detroit
Sargeant, Antoine	GDE	Winchester's ANW	01/18/13–01/22/13	SCU
Sargeant, Antoine	PVT	Jobean's Company	08/04/12–08/18/12	Surrendered at Monroe
Sargeant, Antoine	SCT	Harrison's ANW	02/??/13–10/??/13	SCU
Sargeant, John	PVT	Lee's Company	11/07/13–04/21/14	
Sargeant, Thomas	PVT	Lee's Company	10/22/13–04/21/14	
Sarriot, Alexis	PVT	Audrain's Spies	07/01/14–07/31/14	
Sauer, Adam	PVT	Collins' COM 19 US INF	03/31/14–07/19/15	
Savignac, Francis	DRG	Smyth's Company	04/21/12–08/16/12	Surrendered at Detroit
Savignac, Jean Baptiste	3CP	Smyth's Company	04/21/12–08/16/12	Surrendered at Detroit
Sayen, Pierre	PVT	Audrain's Spies	07/01/14–07/31/14	
Scott, Merit	PVT	Audrain's Rangers	11/01/14–08/31/15	
Scott, Noah	PVT	Hanks' COM 1 US ART	02/27/11–07/17/12	SRA Fort Michilimackinac
Scott, William McDowell	SUM	Unassigned	04/02/14–12/12/14	POW Quebec
Seek, Conrad S.	PVT	Sibley's Company	07/02/12–08/16/12	Surrendered at Detroit
Selare, Baptist	PVT	Hawkins' COM 17 US INF	03/17/14–??/??/??	TRA Stockton's Company
Senecal, Hypolite	PVT	Michigan Fencibles	??/??/13–??/??/15	
Senture, Antoine	PVT	Reading's COM KY MTD INF	09/15/13–11/19/13	
Sessions, Benjamin	PVT	Lee's Company	10/22/13–04/21/14	
Sharp, David	PVT	Audrain's Spies	07/01/14–07/31/14	
Shepherd, David	PVT	Edmondson's COM 28 US INF	03/28/14–09/07/15	TRA Stockton's Company
Shover, Simon	PVT	Westbrook's Company	05/12/14–06/11/14	
Shovin, Simon	4SG	Lee's Company	01/14/14–04/21/14	

Michigan Men in the War of 1812

Name	Rank	Military Unit	Service Dates	Remarks
Shuirick, Ulrick	PVT	Audrain's Rangers	11/19/14–11/30/15	
Sibley, Soloman	CAP	Sibley's Company	07/10/12–08/16/12	AKA Solomon Sibley. SRA Detroit
Sly, John	PVT	Westbrook's Company	05/12/14–06/11/14	
Smart, Robert	PVT	Sibley's Company	07/02/12–08/16/12	Surrendered at Detroit
Smick, John	PVT	Lee's Company	10/22/13–04/21/14	SUB Jean St. Cloutur
Smith, Ann	HOA	Unassigned	10/01/13–01/23/14	Stationed at Detroit
Smith, Isaac	PVT	Mulholland's Company	08/04/12–08/18/12	Surrendered at Monroe
Smith, Jack	VOL	Lewis Cass Expedition	09/15/14	SCU
Smith, Jacob	DRG	Smyth's Company	06/30/12–08/16/12	Surrendered at Detroit
Smith, Joel	PVT	Hawkins' COM 17 US INF	03/24/14–??/??/??	Died at Buffalo 02/28/15
Smith, John R.	PVT	Audrain's Rangers	12/01/14–08/31/15	
Smith, John (1)	PVT	Collins' COM 19 US INF	03/15/14–07/20/15	
Smith, John (2)	PVT	Collins' COM 19 US INF	04/30/14–07/20/15	
Smith, Osborn	ARF	Hanks' COM 1 US ART	01/10/08–07/17/12	SRA Fort Michilimackinac
Smith, Younger	PVT	Audrain's Rangers	12/01/14–08/31/15	
Smyth, Richard	CAP	Smyth's Company	04/21/12–08/16/12	Surrendered at Detroit
Snay, Enos	PVT	McDonell's Company	01/14/14–03/10/14	PEN
Socier, Baptiste	PVT	Mack's Company	06/12/12–08/16/12	Surrendered at Detroit
Socier, Etienne	PVT	Mack's Company	05/20/12–08/16/12	Surrendered at Detroit
Solau, Joseph	PVT	Menard's Company	08/04/12–08/18/12	Surrendered at Monroe
Soleau, Touisaint	PVT	Lacroix's Company	05/18/12–08/16/12	Surrendered at Detroit
Solo, Jean Baptiste	PVT	Couture's Company	08/04/12–08/18/12	Surrendered at Monroe
Solo, Pierre	PVT	Mack's Company	06/22/12–08/16/12	SUB Nicholas Campau. SRA Detroit
Soloro, Baptist	PVT	Hawkins' COM 17 US INF	03/17/14–??/??/??	TRA Stockton's Company
Sordoret, Joseph	PVT	Lacroix's Company	05/18/12–08/16/12	Surrendered at Detroit
Spencer, Joseph	PVT	Campau's Company	07/02/12–08/16/12	Surrendered at Detroit

Name	Rank	Military Unit	Service Dates	Remarks
St. Bernard, Henry	PVT	Mack's Company	06/15/12–08/16/12	SUB Dominique Riopelle. SRA Detroit
St. Bernard, Joseph	PVT	Lacroix's Company	05/18/12–08/16/12	Surrendered at Detroit
St. Clair, Joseph (1	PVT	Mack's Company	05/28/12–08/16/12	Surrendered at Detroit
St. Clair, Joseph (2	PVT	Mack's Company	06/02/12–08/16/12	SUB Isidore Chabert. SRA Detroit
St. George, Peter	PVT	Dequindre's Company	05/04/12–08/16/12	Surrendered at Detroit. PEN
St. George, Pierre	PVT	Audrain's Company	07/01/14–07/31/14	
St. Obin, Gabriel	PVT	Audrain's Spies	07/01/14–07/31/14	
Steers, John	PVT	Mack's Company	06/02/12–08/16/12	Surrendered at Detroit
Stephens, Elminer	PVT	Sibley's Company	07/02/12–08/16/12	Surrendered at Detroit
Stephenson, Luther	3SG	Audrain's Rangers	10/20/14–11/30/15	
Stewart, Charles	GDE	Harrison's ANW	08/02/13–08/11/13	SCU
Stewart, Henry	GDE	Harrison's ANW	08/02/13–08/11/13	SCU
Stewart, Johnathan	PVT	Westbrook's Company	05/12/14–06/11/14	
Stockwell, Isaac	PVT	Hawkins' COM 17 US INF	04/10/12–??/??/15	Deserted sometime in 1815
Supernant, François	PVT	Michigan Fencibles	??/??/13–??/??/15	
Susore, Baptiste	PVT	Menard's Company	08/04/12–08/18/12	SRA Monroe. AKA John Bte Susore
Susore, Dominique	PVT	Menard's Company	08/04/12–08/18/12	Surrendered at Monroe
Sutton, Amariah	PVT	Hawkins' COM 17 US INF	04/30/14–06/09/15	PEN
Suzor, Dominique	GDE	Winchester's ANW	01/18/13–01/22/13	SCU
Suzor, Dominique	SCT	Harrison's ANW	02/??/13–10/??/13	SCU
Tanner, Joseph	PVT	Mulholland's Company	08/04/12–08/18/12	Surrendered at Monroe
Tavis, Jean Baptiste	DRG	Smyth's Company	04/29/12–08/16/12	Surrendered at Detroit
Taylor, Benonia	PVT	Mack's Company	06/01/12–08/16/12	SUB Joseph Weaver. SRA Detroit
Taylor, Daniel F.	PVT	Westbrook's Company	07/01/14–07/31/14	
Tebo, Ignace	PVT	Audrain's Spies	07/01/14–07/31/14	
Tebo, Louis	PVT	Audrain's Rangers	??/??/14–11/30/15	SCU. PEN

Name	Rank	Military Unit	Service Dates	Remarks
Ten Eyck, Conrad	PVT	Sibley's Company	07/05/12–08/16/12	Surrendered at Detroit
Tessier, Antoine	PVT	Laselle's Company	08/04/12–08/18/12	Surrendered at Monroe
Tessier, Augustin	PVT	Lacroix's Company	05/18/12–08/16/12	Surrendered at Detroit
Tessier, François	PVT	Lasselle's Company	08/04/12–08/18/12	Surrendered at Monroe
Thebean, James	PVT	Beaufait's Company	??/??/12–08/16/12	SRA Detroit. SCU. PEN
Theboutte, Louis	PVT	Audrain's Spies	07/01/14–07/31/14	
Thibault, Lewis	PVT	Lacroix's Company	05/18/12–08/16/12	Surrendered at Detroit
Thibault, Louis	1SG	Smyth's Company	04/21/12–08/16/12	Surrendered at Detroit
Thibault, Prosper	PVT	Sibley's Company	07/02/12–08/16/12	Surrendered at Detroit
Thibeault, Louis	SGT	Audrain's Spies	07/01/14–07/31/14	
Thibedeaux, Lambert	PVT	Campau's Company	07/02/12–08/16/12	Surrendered at Detroit
Thibodo, Lambert	PVT	McDonell's Company	01/14/14–03/10/14	
Thomas, Felix	PVT	Mack's Company	05/20/12–08/16/12	Surrendered at Detroit
Thomas, Joel	PVT	Sibley's Company	07/02/12–08/16/12	Surrendered at Detroit
Thomas, Joel	PVT	Westbrook's Company	05/12/14–06/11/14	
Thomas, Robert	PVT	Audrain's Spies	07/01/14–07/31/14	
Thorn, John	PIL	Unknown	??/??/14–??/??/14	With EXP against Fort Mackinac. SCU
Tibbetts, Allen	PVT	Lacroix's Company	05/18/12–08/16/12	Surrendered at Detroit
Tibbetts, William	PVT	Lacroix's Company	05/18/12–08/16/12	Surrendered at Detroit
Tibodo, John Baptiste	PVT	Dequindre's Company	04/21/12–08/16/12	Surrendered at Detroit
Torrence, William B.	PVT	Sibley's Company	07/02/12–08/16/12	Surrendered at Detroit
Tourange, Joseph	DRG	Smyth's Company	04/21/12–08/16/12	Surrendered at Detroit
Tourjot, Francis	PVT	Audrain's Spies	07/01/14–07/31/14	
Tramblay, Jean Baptiste	PVT	McDonell's Company	12/28/13–03/10/14	
Travarcie, Ambrose	SGT	Martin's Company	08/04/12–08/18/12	Surrendered at Monroe
Travarcie, Joseph	CPL	Martin's Company	08/04/12–08/18/12	Surrendered at Monroe

Name	Rank	Military Unit	Service Dates	Remarks
Tremble, Andrew	PVT	Audrain's Spies	07/01/14–07/31/14	
Tremble, Benoit Louis	UNK	Unknown	10/27/14–??/??/??	SCU
Tremble, Joseph Jr.	PVT	Mack's Company	05/20/12–08/16/12	SRA Detroit. AKA Trombly PEN
Tremble, Joseph Sr.	PVT	Mack's Company	05/20/12–08/16/12	SRA Detroit. AKA Joseph Trombly
Tremble, Louis	PVT	Audrain's Spies	07/01/14–07/31/14	
Tremble, Pierre	PVT	Audrain's Spies	07/01/14–07/31/14	PEN
Tremble, Venjile	PVT	Audrain's Spies	07/01/14–07/31/14	
Trembles, Vangile	PVT	Audrain's Rangers	12/20/14–11/30/15	
Trembley, Baptiste	PVT	Sibley's Company	07/02/12–08/16/12	Surrendered at Detroit
Trembley, Michael	PVT	Sibley's Company	07/02/12–08/16/12	Surrendered at Detroit
Trombley, Banoit	PVT	Mack's Company	??/??/12–08/16/12	SRA Detroit. PEN. AKA Trembley
Tromley, John W.	PVT	Crittenden's COM 17 US INF	05/08/14–01/06/19	PEN. AKA John Trembley
Troutwine, Nimrod H.	PVT	Audrain's Rangers	10/20/14–08/31/15	PEN
Truax, Abraham Caleb	3SG	Sibley's Company	07/02/12–08/16/12	Surrendered at Detroit
Trudell, Jean Baptist	PVT	Audrain's Rangers	10/20/14–11/30/15	
Trudelle, Jean Baptiste	PVT	Audrain's Spies	07/01/14–07/31/14	
Truedell, Jean Baptiste	PVT	Campau's Company	07/02/12–08/16/12	Surrendered at Detroit
Truedell, Joseph	PVT	Mack's Company	06/12/12–08/16/12	Surrendered at Detroit
Tucker, Harry	PVT	Audrain's Rangers	11/01/14–11/30/15	
Tucker, Henry	PVT	Mack's Company	05/20/12–08/16/12	Surrendered at Detroit
Tucker, Willis	PVT	Audrain's Spies	07/01/14–07/31/14	
Tuotte, Jacque	PVT	Lacroix's Company	05/18/12–08/16/12	Surrendered at Detroit
Tuotte, Michel	PVT	Menard's Company	08/04/12–08/18/12	Surrendered at Monroe
Tuotte, Peter	PVT	Menard's Company	08/04/12–08/18/12	Surrendered at Monroe
Turner, Amasa	PVT	Mack's Company	05/20/12–08/16/12	Surrendered at Detroit
Tyler, John	PVT	Dequindre's Company	04/28/12–08/16/12	Surrendered at Detroit
Tyler, Morris	PVT	Audrain's Rangers	10/20/14–11/30/15	

Name	Rank	Military Unit	Service Dates	Remarks
Tyler, Morris	PVT	Audrain's Spies	07/01/14–07/31/14	
Tyler, Morris	PVT	Dequindre's Company	04/28/12–08/16/12	Surrendered at Detroit
Ulylder, Joshua	PVT	Westbrook's Company	05/12/14–06/11/14	
Vailencourt, Henry	MUS	Hanks' COM 1 US ART	03/01/12–07/17/12	Boy MUS. SRA Michilimackinac
Vailencourt, Jean Baptiste	MUS	Hanks' COM 1 US ART	05/01/11–07/17/12	SRA Michilimackinac.
Vailencourt, Joseph	SGT	Hanks' COM 1 US ART	05/01/11–07/17/12	SRA Fort Michilimackinac
Valicate, Joseph	PVT	Reading's COM KY MTD INF	05/20/13–11/19/13	
Valiquette, Joseph	PVT	Lee's Company	10/22/13–04/21/14	
Vallequette, Joseph	PVT	Lacroix's Company	05/18/12–08/16/12	Surrendered at Detroit
Vallicate, Jean Baptiste	PVT	Reading's COM KY MTD INF	07/20/13–11/19/13	PEN
Vallicatte, Jean Baptiste	PVT	Drouillard's Company	08/04/12–08/18/12	Surrendered at Monroe
Van Avery, Peter	UNK	Unknown	??/??/??–??/??/12	SUR Detroit. POW. SCU
Vandousen, William	PVT	Audrain's Rangers	11/01/14–11/30/15	PEN
Varmette, Antoine	PVT	Dequindre's Company	04/21/12–08/09/12	Killed at Brownstown
Vasseur, Louis	PVT	Michigan Fencibles	??/??/13–??/??/15	
Velaire, Cleustome	PVT	Drouillard's Company	08/04/12–08/18/12	Surrendered at Monroe
Venier, Joseph	PVT	Mack's Company	06/26/12–08/16/12	Surrendered at Detroit
Verboncours, Jacques	PVT	Lacroix's Company	05/18/12–08/16/12	Surrendered at Detroit
Vermet, Joseph	PVT	Mack's Company	06/26/12–08/16/12	Surrendered at Detroit
Visgar, Joseph	1CP	Knaggs' Company	07/02/12–08/16/12	Surrendered at Detroit
Visgar, Joseph	VOL	Lewis Cass Expedition	09/15/14	SCU
Wade, Parks	PVT	Edmondson's COM 28 US INF	03/21/14–06/30/15	TRA Stockton's Company
Waggoner, Michael	PVT	Hawkins' COM 17 US INF	04/02/14–06/09/15	PEN
Walden, Eli	PVT	Audrain's Spies	07/01/14–07/31/14	
Walden, Elisha	PVT	Audrain's Rangers	10/20/14–08/31/15	PEN
Walker, John	DRG	Smyth's Company	05/01/12–08/16/12	Surrendered at Detroit. PEN

Name	Rank	Military Unit	Service Dates	Remarks
Walker, Joseph	PVT	Campau's Company	07/02/12–08/16/12	Surrendered at Detroit
Walker, William	SPY	Unknown	??/??/12–??/??/??	Identified by William Atherton
Warner, Elijah	PVT	Sibley's Company	07/02/12–08/16/12	Surrendered at Detroit
Warren, John	PVT	Campau's Company	07/02/12–08/16/12	Surrendered at Detroit
Washburn, Jacob	PVT	McDonell's Company	12/21/13–03/10/14	
Washburn, John	PVT	Johnson's COM 2 US RIF	04/14/14–06/30/15	
Watson, Joseph	COL	F&S Michigan Militia	04/21/12–08/16/12	Aide to CIC. SRA Detroit
Watson, William	DRG	Smyth's Company	04/21/12–08/16/12	Surrendered at Detroit
Watt, David	3SG	Collins' COM 19 US INF	03/28/14–07/02/15	
Weaver, Joseph	4SG	Sibley's Company	07/02/12–08/16/12	Surrendered at Detroit
Welch, Thomas	PVT	Dequindre's Company	04/21/12–08/16/12	Surrendered at Detroit
Wells, John	DRG	Smyth's Company	04/26/12–08/16/12	Surrendered at Detroit
Welsh, George	SGT	McDonell's Company	12/22/13–03/10/14	
Wendell, Abraham	1SG	Sibley's Company	07/02/12–08/16/12	Surrendered at Detroit
Wendell, Josiah	1CP	Sibley's Company	07/02/12–08/16/12	Surrendered at Detroit
Westbrook, Andrew	CDT	Westbrook's Company	05/12/14–06/11/14	
Whelpley, John	ARF	Hanks' COM 1 US ART	11/27/08–11/27/13	SRA Fort Michilimackinac
Whistler, John Jr.	ENS	Whistler's COM 19 US INF	03/07/12–??/??/??	POW at Detroit 08/16/12
White, Bath	PVT	Sibley's Company	07/02/12–08/09/12	KIA near Brownstown
White, James	PVT	Sibley's Company	07/02/12–08/16/12	Surrendered at Detroit
White, John	PVT	Audrain's Rangers	10/20/14–08/31/15	
White, John	PVT	Hanks' COM 1 US ART	04/30/11–07/17/12	SRA Fort Michilimackinac
Wilder, Joshua	PVT	Audrain's Rangers	11/01/14–11/30/15	
Willett, Elijah	PVT	Dequindre's Company	07/07/12–08/16/12	Surrendered at Detroit
Willett, Isaac	PVT	Dequindre's Company	07/07/12–08/16/12	Surrendered at Detroit
Williams, John	PVT	Audrain's Rangers	10/20/14–11/30/15	
Williams, John R.	PVT	Sibley's Company	07/02/12–08/16/12	Surrendered at Detroit

Name	Rank	Military Unit	Service Dates	Remarks
Wilson, George	PVT	Sibley's Company	07/02/12–08/16/12	Surrendered at Detroit
Wilson, William	PVT	Smyth's Company	04/21/12–08/16/12	Surrendered at Detroit
Windell, Simeon	PVT	Hanks' COM 1 US ART	??/??/??–07/17/12	SRA Fort Michilimackinac
Witherell, James Sr.	MAJ	F&S Legionary Corps	05/11/12–08/16/12	SRA Detroit. POW Kingston
Witherell, James C. Jr.	LUT	F&S Legionary Corps	??/??/??–08/16/12	SRA Detroit. MNI Cullen Columbus. POW
Wood, George T.	SGT	Edmondson's COM 28 US INF	04/28/14–??/??/??	
Woods, William	PVT	Collins' COM 19 US INF	03/13/14–03/14/19	
Woodworth, Benjamin	ENS	Sibley's Company	07/02/12–08/16/12	Surrendered at Detroit
Woolcut, Justice	PVT	Audrain's Rangers	12/01/14–08/31/15	
Worrel, John	PVT	Audrain's Rangers	12/23/14–08/31/15	
Wortsbaugh, John	PVT	Collins' COM 19 US INF	03/15/14–07/20/15	
Wydle, John	CPL	Dyson's COM 1 US ART	02/09/12–08/26/15	Was POW
Wyman, James	DRG	Smyth's Company	04/26/12–08/16/12	Surrendered at Detroit
Wyncore, John B.	MUS	Rochester's COM 29 US INF	05/01/10–11/07/13	
Yanger, Peter	DRG	Smyth's Company	04/26/12–08/16/12	Surrendered at Detroit
Yax, Eber	PVT	Gouin's Company	06/??/12–08/16/12	SRA Detroit. SCU. PEN
Yax, Michael	PVT	Audrain's Rangers	10/20/14–11/30/15	
Yax, Pierre	PVT	Audrain's Spies	07/01/14–07/31/14	
Yax, Pierre	PVT	Mack's Company	05/20/12–08/16/12	Surrendered at Detroit. PEN
Young, Samuel	DRG	Smyth's Company	05/25/12–09/30/12	Detached to River Raisin. ETO
Young, Samuel	PVT	Ball's SQD US LTD	09/30/12–05/10/13	
Young, Samuel	PVT	Lee's Company	10/22/13–04/21/14	
Younglove, Ezra	PVT	Butler's COM 28 US INF	01/01/14–04/30/14	SOB as marine with Perry's fleet
Younglove, Ezra	PVT	Westbrook's Company	05/12/14–06/11/14	

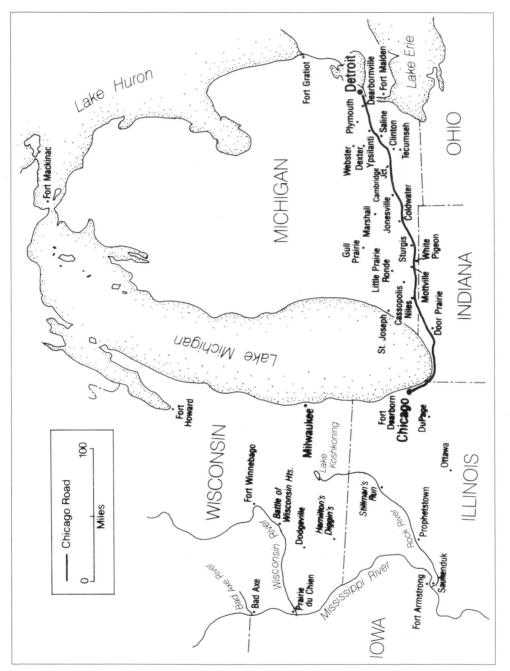

Theater of Operations, Black Hawk War. (*Cartography by Sherm Hollander*)

THREE

Black Hawk War, 1832

Michigan in the Black Hawk War

Colonel Zachary Taylor described it as "a tissue of blunders miserably managed from start to finish," and historian Reuben Thwaites characterized it as "a tale fraught with dishonor to the American name." The last Indian war in the Old Northwest, the Black Hawk War was a tragedy that might have been avoided. The conflict brought death to hundreds of Sauk and Fox Indians who followed Black Hawk, and it left these Indian tribes racked with serious internal dissension. The war also caused the deaths of a small number of Americans, created great anxiety, especially in Illinois and the western Michigan Territory (present-day Wisconsin), engendered considerable economic loss in the area, and contributed to the casualties resulting from the choleric plague that spread across North America in 1832.

Antecedents of the Black Hawk War date to 1804 when Sauk and Fox Indians ceded to the United States approximately fifty million acres of land, most notably areas of southwestern Wisconsin and northwestern Illinois. The treaty, however, allowed the Indians to live and hunt on the land as long as it remained in the public domain. The ceded land included Saukenuk, a Sauk village near the confluence of the Rock and Mississippi Rivers (present-day Rock Island, Illinois).

Makataimeshekiakiak, or Black Sparrow Hawk, was neither a hereditary nor an elected Sauk chief, but he was an important leader at Saukenuk. Like many Sauk, Black Hawk had sided with the British in the War of 1812. In 1813 he had fought with Tecumseh at the Battle of the Thames northeast of Detroit. During the late 1820s, Americans began settling near Saukenuk—lands that the federal government had neither surveyed nor sold. They grazed their livestock in the Indians' cornfields, erected fences, beat Indian women and children, and plowed up Indian graves. On at least two occasions when the Sauk were away from Saukenuk, they returned to find that their vacant lodges had been burned.

During the summer of 1830 the main body of Saukenuk Indians moved across the Mississippi River. Keokuk, a prominent Sauk chief, vowed never to return and declared that if any Indians continued to reside on the Rock River "they must take their chances."

The following year, Black Hawk, whose supporters had earlier "very fiercely" announced that "the land was theirs . . . and [they] . . . would defend it as long as they existed," demanded that the Americans quit selling whiskey to the Indians and ordered them to leave his people's land or be forcibly evicted. The Americans demanded protection. In late June a force of more than one thousand U.S. regulars and Illinois militia reached Saukenuk only to discover that it had been abandoned. Black Hawk's faction had fled to the west bank of the Mississippi River. On June 30 the Sauk signed articles of capitulation that recognized the 1804 cession of land. Black Hawk also agreed to remain west of the Mississippi River. A month after the treaty signing, a Sauk party crossed the Mississippi River to gather food. Near Prairie du Chien they ambushed and massacred a group of Menominee Indians to avenge the deaths of fellow tribesmen who had been murdered by the Menominee the previous year. American officials demanded that the murderers be surrendered; the Sauk refused.

During the winter of 1831–32, a Winnebago shaman named Wabokishek (White Cloud) invited Black Hawk's band to join him at his village forty miles up the Rock River. White Cloud, better known as the Winnebago Prophet, also shared with Black Hawk visions that, if the Americans attempted to dispose Black Hawk's supporters from the Rock River, Indian tribes from the region would rise to their defense. The Winnebago Prophet even prophesied that the British would send guns and supplies to Milwaukee to support Black Hawk if he were attacked. (The British had actually advised Black Hawk not to fight.)

On April 5, 1832, Black Hawk's band of one thousand men, women, and children crossed the Mississippi River; they arrived at the Winnebago Prophet's village two weeks later. Three weeks later, Black Hawk received a communique from U.S. brigadier general Henry Atkinson ordering him to recross the Mississippi. Atkinson also warned, "You will be sorry if you do not come back." The chieftains of the Sauk and Fox Indians also urged Black Hawk to return before it was too late. Black Hawk, however, responded that his intentions were peaceful and he would not return. By early May, Black Hawk's band had begun to run short of provisions. They discovered that, since local Indians expressed no intention of supporting them, the visions of the Winnebago Prophet had been "vain imaginings."

Illinois governor John Reynolds responded to Black Hawk's action by mobilizing the state militia. On May 7 approximately fifteen hundred mounted Illinoisans, commanded by Brigadier General Samuel Whiteside, moved up the Rock River to the Winnebago Prophet's village. As one Illinois newspaper declared, "These Indians must be taught to respect their treaties." Following Whiteside on steamboats were four hundred regular infantry and several hundred additional militia commanded by General Atkinson. When Whiteside's men reached the Winnebago Prophet's village they found it deserted. Black Hawk had moved up the Rock River away from the advancing soldiers. The Sauk leader also decided that because of a lack of supplies, as well as of Indian support, he would meet with General Atkinson and announce his intent to return west of the Mississippi River. That soon became an impossibility.

On May 14 a detachment of approximately three hundred Illinois militiamen commanded by Major Isaiah Stillman made their camp about eight miles from Black Hawk's camp. Black Hawk immediately sent three unarmed men under a flag of truce to, in his words, "meet them, and conduct them to our camp, that we might hold a council with them, and descend the Rock River again." The three Indians were escorted to the disorderly Illinois camp where many of the militiamen were drunk. However, when five additional Indians sent by Black Hawk to observe the negotiations were discovered, the militiamen opened fire. One truce bearer was killed, the other two escaped. Two of the Sauk observers were also killed. The Illinoisans pursued the Indians. Back in the Sauk camp, an enraged Black Hawk ordered his forty braves to avenge the murder of his peace party. The Sauk hid in the bushes until the militia neared; then they charged and sent the Illinoisans fleeing. Some of the militiamen, many of whom never fired a volley, rode twenty-five miles before stopping. This skirmish, soon known as Stillman's "Run," left eleven militiamen and three Indians dead. It also made war unavoidable. Black Hawk's band retreated to Lake Koshkonong in the western Michigan Territory, there they were visited by a small number of Winnebago and Potawatomi.

Following the defeat of Major Stillman's command, a panicky J. V. Owen, Indian agent at Chicago, urged Michigan Territorial militia colonel Almanson Huston at Niles to send "a force of some magnitude" to Chicago. Owen, an elderly and ailing man, also predicted that "hostile Sauk" would advance into Michigan's Lower Peninsula via the Chicago Road (present-day U.S. 12).

Owen's request also reached acting Michigan Territorial governor Stevens T. Mason, who ordered Major General John R. Williams to raise a force of three hundred volunteers. The order was posted on May 22. The following day, because no one had volunteered, Mason allowed Williams to mobilize the militia. In a stirring declaration, Mason urged Williams not to "return to this place, until every shadow of danger from hostile Indians on the frontier is removed." Mason advised Williams to move quickly because "delay is only calculated to give rise, to false and unfounded reports, which may possibly have an injurious effect upon the emigration to our Territory." Williams was ordered to rendezvous with Brigadier General Joseph W. Brown, who commanded the territory's Third Brigade of militia. (Without awaiting orders, Brown, who lived in Tecumseh, had mobilized his brigade and was on his way to Niles.) Born in Detroit in 1782, John R. Williams had been active in the city's development. He had served as a militia private during the War of 1812, and following the war operated a mercantile business. Elected mayor of Detroit in 1824, Williams was reelected five times. In 1829, President Andrew Jackson appointed him major general in the territorial militia.

On May 24 the territory's First Regiment of militia, the Detroit City Guards, a company of Detroit-area cavalry and two separate battalions commanded by Major Jonathan D. Davis and Major Henry Hollbrook, gathered at Ten Eyck's Tavern in Dearborn. Of the assembled troops, Joseph Marsac's company (First Regiment), Captain Isaac Rowland's Detroit City Guards, and Captain Charles Jackson's cavalry volunteered for service. Williams drafted an additional two hundred men from the First Regiment, including companies commanded by Josiah Burton (Ypsilanti), Albert Stevens (Plymouth), Anthony R. Swarthout (Ypsilanti) and Nahum Thayer (Detroit).

The militia organization was complete, but General Williams' problems were only beginning. His request for arms and accouterments to Lieutenant J. Howard, commandant of the U.S. Ordnance Depot in Detroit, was rejected because Howard refused to "acknowledge the authority of any Militia Officer." Finally, the situation was resolved after Williams reassured Howard that he had Governor Mason's permission to request the supplies. Williams also promised the concerned quartermaster that he would "prevent, so far as it was possible . . . any injury or loss of the public property."

Mobilization of the Michigan militia received little support in Detroit. On May 25 the city's most prominent citizens held a public meeting to criticize the "premature and ill-advised" call to arms. Labeling the fears of an Indian uprising threatening the Lower Peninsula "groundless," the assemblage contended that hostile Indians were more than 250 miles away from "the most remote settlements in Michigan." The Detroiters confidently added that even if "all the Indians" east of the Mississippi River reached Chicago, there existed five times more Illinois and Indiana militia to handle the problem. The Detroiters were primarily concerned that the call to arms might adversely affect immigration to Michigan. According to the *Detroit Journal and Michigan Advertiser,* too much panic would make it difficult "to convince emigrants that they could proceed into the interior, without being exposed to the tomahawk and skalpingknife [sic]."

Regardless of such concerns, Williams' detachment left Dearborn at noon on May 26. The first day the militiamen marched seventeen miles to Willow Run; the second day they marched to Saline. Williams reported that though his men lacked tents and blankets, they exhibited high spirits. The march was made arduous by heavy rains that at times forced the men to halt. Before Williams could leave the Saline encampment, Governor Mason ordered the militiamen back to Detroit, where they were discharged. Williams was ordered to continue to Niles and dismiss General Brown's troops unless he found "it necessary, to continue part of his Regiment in the field, for the purpose of quieting the fears of the timid." Mason's actions were motivated in part by the Detroit rally. More important was a dispatch from Chicago Indian Agent Owen, who declared that his earlier apprehensions had been "greatly exaggerated [sic]" and that the troops from the Lower Peninsula would not be needed.

No sooner had Williams sent the militia back to Detroit under Colonel Edward S. Brooks than Owen again requested troops. According to the Indian agent, "our whole frontier Country is invaded and presents one Continued Scene of desolation." Mason ordered Colonel Brooks to enlist volunteers and join General Williams. On May 31, Williams reached Niles. Convinced that the Sauk were headed toward Fort Malden in Amherstburg, Ontario, where they would receive arms and ammunition from the British, Williams moved to block that route. Williams had also heard that two "parties of Warriors" (eleven and eight men each) had been spotted near Jonesville in St. Joseph County. Reports indicated that both groups were furnished with new rifles from Malden. (Williams' fears were not unwarranted. For years the Sauk, Fox, and other western Indian parties had traveled the Sauk Trail to Amherstburg for their annual "presents," which included firearms and ammunition.)

While urging Mason to increase his command to one thousand men, Williams discovered that General Brown had dismissed the Eighth Regiment, approximately three hundred men from Lenawee County. Despite Brown's unusual action, Williams still commanded approximately 350 volunteers at Niles. Williams and Brown conferred and decided that Brown should lead a force to the Door Prairie (present-day LaPorte, Indiana) to prevent Indian travel into the Lower Peninsula. Williams would wait in Niles for Colonel Brooks' detachment to join him.

The situation soon worsened. Brown's men still needed cartridge boxes, and one company of St. Joseph volunteers had to be dismissed for lack of weapons. Tents were nonexistent and food was in short supply. Mason did not respond to Williams' letters detailing plans on how best to protect the southwestern Lower Peninsula; however, the general received a letter from a White Pigeon militia colonel criticizing the "exaggerated reports of danger from hostile bands of Indians." Colonel Abraham Edwards, a personal friend of Williams, argued that since the territory had neither been invaded nor placed in imminent danger, there was no reason to mobilize the militia. Edwards feared that calling out the militia took men away from their farms and fields and guaranteed a famine.

On June 2, Colonel Brooks arrived in Niles accompanied by only twenty-six men. On the same day, General Brown, who had left Niles the day before with a direct order from Mason to advance to Chicago, returned to Niles and dismissed his entire force. Brown then received permission to return home to tend to his children, who were sick with the measles. A frustrated General Williams vowed to have Brown court-martialed, and countermanded Brown's order dismissing his command. A small body of men from Colonel Huston's Seventh Regiment remained in service, but most of the militiamen—arguing that they had been marched and countermarched until they were worn out—went home. Williams' dilemma was compounded by local businessmen who were unwilling to furnish supplies to the militiamen on credit.

In the midst of this chaos, Williams finally received a dispatch from Mason. It declared, "It is impossible for me to advise which course should be pursued. . . . I therefore depend upon you to take some steps as circumstances may require." The governor added that Williams would have critics in Detroit but hoped that the general would do what he thought was correct, "regardless of any thing [sic] they can say." It is no surprise that Williams described Mason's actions as "contradictory, inconsistent and incompatible."

Despite all these setbacks and embarrassments, Williams continued with his plans. On June 5 he moved his small force of 115 men to the stockade on the Door Prairie. There he reorganized his force into two companies and readied to advance to Chicago.

The response of Lower Peninsula communities to the Sauk uprising was varied. Some settlers fled their farms for a safer refuge, even going back to New York State. Others took up arms, planned a defense, and displayed a fierce determination to resist any Indian incursion. Forts were planned in Dexter and Gull Prairie (present-day Richland). Cass County settlers considered moving to and fortifying an island in Diamond Lake near Cassopolis. A committee of public safety in St. Joseph County ordered a fort built in Colon Township. Fifty men gathered one afternoon, and by nightfall several furrows had been plowed along the westernmost traverse of an area that was to encompass five acres. Located on the land of Daniel H. Hogan, the defensive work was named Fort Hogan. At dark the workers returned home under orders to report at dawn to continue their efforts. The next morning only a few men returned, and the fort was abandoned.

Many other Michigan communities responded to the war scare by organizing militia companies. Although all able-bodied men in Dexter mustered into a company, they lacked a commander and went home. In Marshall a citizens' meeting led twelve men, including future Congressman Isaac Crary, to march off to Prairie Ronde in Cass County, where they were discharged and returned home. At Gull Prairie, a dozen men gathered, and one man, who had claimed he was a sergeant, organized and drilled those present. The next day the group headed to Prairie Ronde for a militia rendezvous. Between one and two hundred militiamen trained at the rendezvous for ten days before being sent home because of a lack of information from the theater of war. Ten days later, the men were reformed and marched to the St. Joseph River. But since there were no canoes, the men returned home.

It was readily apparent that the militia lacked the necessary training to be good soldiers. John Adam of Clinton recalled that the first night his company bivouacked near Cambridge Junction a sentry killed a neighbor's hog because "it insisted on coming within the lines, without giving the countersign." Adam also remembered how local Indians laughed at the militiamen as they took target practice "with some of the old flint-lock muskets, which had been sent along for us to use." But the militiamen did not lack enthusiasm. Two Gull Prairie men who volunteered for service without weapons exchanged "high words and fierce threatenings" over a rifle both claimed to have borrowed from its owner.

Left alone while their men went off to war, Michigan women also prepared their defenses. In Volina Township in Cass County the women erected fortifications. Plymouth women all gathered at one house at night. While most slept, several stood guard with a cauldron of water "ready to scald the first head that thrust itself unpermitted into the castle."

Less courageous settlers left their fields uncultivated, hid their valuables and headed east. One Washtenaw County family deserted its house, which lay on the edge of the settlement, and moved into a neighbor's barn until the war excitement ceased. Gardner Bird, who had just moved to Webster in Washtenaw County, packed his household goods in a wagon and with his wife and three children started for New York. At Ypsilanti, Bird realized that the dangers had been exaggerated. Following a good night's rest, the Birds returned to their Michigan home. A Sturgis family was less fortunate. Late one night the apprehensive settlers placed all their dishes, mirrors, and other valuables in a tub and began lowering it into the well. The rope broke, and all the family's valuables, many of which had been carefully carried over hundreds of miles from Pennsylvania to Michigan, dropped to the well floor with a loud crash.

Besides being concerned about a Sauk invasion, settlers in the southwest Lower Peninsula were apprehensive about a possible uprising of local Potawatomi. As rumors and reports of the distant war reached the Lower Peninsula, white-Indian relations became strained. In Kalamazoo County, settlers confiscated the Potawatomi's rifles despite Indian protests that this action would precipitate starvation.

Notwithstanding such preparations and fears, some Michigan residents denied that there was reason for anxiety. Newspapers in the territorial capital emphasized that the chances of an Indian raid on the Lower Peninsula were remote. On June 13, 1832, the *Detroit Journal and Michigan Advertiser* noted that there was "no more probability of an invasion by Black Hawk's party than there is from the emperor of Russia." In St. Joseph County, S. E. Coffinberry recalled that those who urged patience were subjected to "indignant, reprehension and outright curses" because they would not participate in their neighbors' fears. At least one St. Joseph County resident, Cyrus Shellhous, sought to reduce his neighbors' fears. Shellhous visited the Nadowesippe (or Nottawayseppe) Potawatomi reservation in the northern part of the country. He found the Indians destitute and certain that the Americans planned to use the Black Hawk excitement to drive them off their land. Shellhous arranged an interview between leading Potawatomi and Captain Henry Powers, who commanded the local militia. Powers asked the Potawatomi what the whites had done "to induce you to set about cutting our throats and scalping our women and children?" The Potawatomi explained that they had no such intentions. Powers discovered that his defensive measures appeared to the Potawatomi to be preliminaries for an offensive against their village. The Potawatomi added that they were Sauk enemies and would fight on the side of the Americans if Black Hawk invaded the Lower Peninsula. Both parties appeared relieved after the meeting.

On June 9, General Williams and his one hundred men left the Door Prairie for Chicago. Before leaving, Williams had been assured that at the suggestion of General Brown, who had recently arrived in Detroit, Governor Mason was sending muskets to Tecumseh, Niles, and White Pigeon. Inhabitants would be able to arm themselves at a moment's notice. Mason added that as soon as Williams was satisfied that his presence was no longer needed, he should return to Michigan.

Williams, however, was not ready to come home. Instead, he ordered Colonel Henry Stewart to assemble three hundred men of his Eleventh Regiment and march to the Door Prairie to "prevent the passing of any hostile Bands of Sacs through the Territory of Michigan to the British province of Upper Canada." On June 12, Williams reached Chicago. In response to pleas for protection, he sent Colonel Brooks with thirty-five mounted militiamen to assist in the defense of Du Page, a settlement twenty-eight miles west of Chicago. The Michiganians traveled all night and arrived at Du Page at 5:00 A.M. on June 14. The reports of nearby Sauk were exaggerated, and Brooks' men returned to Chicago the following day. Williams also ordered that the defenses of Fort Dearborn be upgraded and that all efforts be made for the comfort and convenience of the many white families residing there. The general's orders concluded, "Our duty as Citizen Soldiers is to protect and defend—But not to molest or offend."

Williams' plans went beyond the defense of Fort Dearborn. He hoped to organize a force of up to eight hundred Michigan militiamen to move against Black Hawk. In communiques to Governor Mason, Williams observed that his force was closer to the Sauk band than General Atkinson's troops. Furthermore, neither Atkinson nor Illinois Governor Reynolds had been able to catch the Sauk leader. Arguing that "concert and energy" were needed to return tranquility to the frontier, Williams asked Mason to send him three hundred men from Detroit via steamboat, as well as several artillery pieces. The Michigan general concluded, "Give me men and means and you will see that I am determined to try my best to do something for the service and honor of Our Country." Williams also ordered Colonel Huston to muster one hundred men from the Seventh Regiment and march to Chicago.

Williams did not get an opportunity to lead a campaign against Black Hawk. On June 16, Colonel Stewart informed Williams that he could not raise three hundred men either from volunteers or through a draft. Furthermore, Stewart had received new orders from Governor Mason and General Brown to raise ninety men to prevent any Indians in the southwestern Lower Peninsula from proceeding to Fort Malden. Stewart apologetically noted that he had no difficulty finding men to serve at home, but the volunteers feared what the Potawatomi might do to their women if they left home. Colonel Huston conveyed similar sentiments from Niles.

On June 17, Major William Whistler, who had sailed from Fort Niagara, New York, with two companies of U.S. regulars, arrived at Chicago and assumed command. The following day Chicago residents gathered and passed a resolution thanking General Williams and the Michigan militia "for the prompt and efficient aid they gave us when we were without protection, and had not the means of defending ourselves; And also for their Urbane and polite deportment toward the Citizens Generally during their Stay among us as Citizen Soldiers."

On June 22 fresh reinforcements arrived at Fort Dearborn—a detachment of three hundred Indiana militiamen. With Chicago adequately defended and no additional Michigan men available, Williams ordered his militia men home. The infantry boarded the steamer *Napoleon* for St. Joseph and then marched to Niles, while the mounted men returned overland. The militiamen were discharged, but Williams ordered the Seventh and Eleventh regiments "to be held in readiness to assemble and Act as circumstances may require." Except for two militiamen wounded by the discharge of a loaded musket during instruction in the manual of arms, the Michigan militia had suffered no casualties during the Black Hawk War. However, the Lower Peninsula soon witnessed its share of death and suffering.

Dissatisfied with the progress of the war against the Sauk, President Andrew Jackson ordered General Winfield Scott to proceed to Chicago with nine companies of regulars. On June 26, 1832, Scott's men reached Buffalo from Fort Monroe, Virginia. There, Scott hired four lake steamers to transport his troops to Chicago. The *Henry Clay* and the *Sheldon Thompson* sailed on July 2. The two vessels carrying the men's supplies left later.

The *Henry Clay* reached Detroit on July 4. Soon after arriving, two recruits on the *Clay* developed cholera symptoms—vomiting and diarrhea. Cholera had first been noted on the North American continent in Montreal a month earlier. On June 25 the Detroit Board of Health had issued instructions for the prevention and treatment of the dreaded disease. At the same time the city's mayor forbade vessels from any other port to land until an examination by a health officer had been made. This stipulation must have been overlooked for the *Henry Clay*. During the night of July 4, sixteen cases of cholera developed among the soldiers. By morning, eleven men had died. On July 5 the *Sheldon Thompson* and the *Henry Clay* left Detroit. The boats may have left, but cholera remained behind. On July 6 two deaths were reported among Detroit residents. The upper floor of the state capitol was converted into a hospital, but by mid-July twenty-six of fifty-eight victims had died.

Terror-stricken neighboring communities mustered their militia to keep travelers from passing through their towns. Ypsilanti militiamen stopped a westbound stage and shot one of its horses when the driver insisted on passing. Even Territorial Secretary Mason was halted along the Chicago Road and arrested for trying to pass a quarantine on his way to Mottville. (Governor George Porter had returned to Detroit and resumed control of the territorial government in mid-July.) Roadblocks could not halt the disease. In only eight days, eight of Marshall's seventy residents died. In Detroit the ringing of the passing bell was discontinued because it only served to panic the populace. Among the many courageous individuals who ministered to the sick was Father Gabriel Richard, who became one of the plague's victims. When the cholera epidemic ended in mid-August about one hundred Detroiters had died.

Conditions aboard Scott's troop ships were equally frightening. Sanitary facilities were primitive, and men vomited and defecated wherever they could. The *Thompson* stopped at Fort Gratiot near Port Huron and dropped off two companies of regulars before proceeding. These companies returned to Detroit, much to the consternation of some Detroiters who associated cholera with soldiers. Then they marched overland to St. Joseph, where they boarded a vessel for transport to Chicago. Aboard the *Henry Clay*, the captain noted, "The disease had become so violent . . . that nothing like discipline could be observed." The *Henry Clay* also stopped at Fort Gratiot where many of the recruits fled inland. The remaining troops, commanded by Colonel David Twiggs, camped south of the fort. Disease and desertion ravaged the encampment. In the three days after his arrival, Twiggs lost 230 men from his original command of 360 (175 from desertion and 55 from cholera). A letter from Detroit that appeared in the *Niles Weekly Register* noted: "Of the deserters, scattered all over the country, some have died in the woods, and their bodies have been devoured by the wolves. . . . Straggling survivors are occasionally seen marching, some of them know not wither, with their knapsacks on their backs, shunned by the terrified inhabitants." The dead also included the son of Kentucky congressman Henry Clay.

Scott and the *Thompson* stopped at Fort Mackinac for fuel before heading to Chicago. Death plagued the *Thompson* on the entire three-hundred-mile journey from Mackinac. Scott's surgeon became drunk, and the general attended to his ill soldiers. He kept panic aboard the vessel in check, and when opium and calomel failed to arrest the disease, Scott simply ordered the sick to get well. Many did not. As the soldiers died, they were wrapped in blankets, weighed down and buried at sea. Few were immune. The sergeant who supervised the first burial died only six hours later. The *Thompson* reached Chicago on July 10. An excited populace crowded the beach to greet the soldiers until it was announced that there was cholera aboard the vessels. Although Fort Dearborn was evacuated, disease made Chicago a ghost town, and settlers who had flocked there to escape the Sauk now fled, according to one observer, with "precipitant haste and terror."

The army's official report on the Black Hawk War proudly noted that Scott had moved 1,800 miles in eighteen days, a "rapidity which is believed to be unprecedented." However, out of the more than 700 men who left Buffalo, only 135 served in Chicago.

As General Scott's men lay dying at Fort Dearborn, a newly formed army of Illinois militiamen, U.S. regulars, and Michigan Territorial militia from the lead-mining region north of the Illinois border, moved against Black Hawk's Sauk. Although General Williams and the Lower Peninsula militia had gone home, several Michiganians from that part of the territory that would become Wisconsin played important roles in the Black Hawk War.

Williams S. Hamilton, the fifth son of the nation's first secretary of the treasury, Alexander Hamilton, had come west following a year at the U.S. Military Academy at West Point. In 1828, he lived in the lead-mining region and operated a smelting establishment known as Hamilton Diggin's in present-day Wiota, Wisconsin. Hamilton spent most of the Sauk conflict commanding bands of Indians friendly to the Americans.

Henry Dodge, one of the most important men in the lead-mining region, entered the Black Hawk War by leading a group of twenty-seven men to Illinois. Born in Vincennes, Indiana, in 1782, Dodge had fought Indians in Missouri during the War of 1812 and participated in quelling Wisconsin's Winnebago Indian Uprising in 1827. During the late 1820s, Dodge violated U.S. treaty obligations by intruding on Winnebago land near present-day Dodgeville, Wisconsin, where he established a thriving mining operation. Though U.S. Indian agents sought to have him evicted, Dodge's power in the western Michigan Territory went unchallenged. Indeed, the absence of any orders or even communiques between Dodge and General Williams or Governor Mason during the Black Hawk War confirm Dodge's independence. By 1831, Dodge had been elected to the Michigan Territorial Legislative Council and appointed militia colonel. Following Stillman's defeat, Dodge met with leaders of the thousands of Winnebago Indians living between the Wisconsin and Rock Rivers and helped persuade them not to join the Sauk. During the war's final campaign, Dodge commanded a force of two hundred "rangers" mustered from the lead-mining region.

Another Michigan resident who played a role in the Black Hawk War was Brevet Brigadier General Hugh Brady. Commandant of the Department of the Upper Great Lakes and headquartered in Detroit, Brady, with one aide, left the territorial capital for Fort Winnebago (near present-day Portage, Wisconsin) in late April 1832. Asked what he thought of the war, the sixty-four-year-old veteran, who had seen action with "Mad" Anthony Wayne in 1793–94 and in the War of 1812, declared, "Give me two infantry companies mounted, and I will . . . whip the Sauks out of the country in one week." In June, Brady led two companies of regulars from Fort Winnebago to northern Illinois to rendezvous with General Atkinson's army. Brady was given a larger command, but a bout with dysentery in early July sidelined him for the rest of the war.

In late June, General Atkinson's army of approximately four thousand men moved against Black Hawk, who had remained near Lake Koshkonong. After several skirmishes, including one on the Pecatonica River where Colonel Dodge routed a party of Kickapoo Indians, Atkinson's main body moved north into the Michigan Territory. In mid-July, Winnebago Indian guides leading Dodge's rangers and the Illinois militia discovered Black Hawk's band moving northwestward toward the Mississippi River. On July 21 the soldiers overtook the Sauk as they crossed the Wisconsin River near present-day Sauk City. Black Hawk bravely directed his outnumbered warriors but lost the Battle of Wisconsin Heights. That night the Sauk tried to communicate with the army. They proposed that if left alone they would harm no one and recross the Mississippi River. But their pleas could not be understood since the army's Winnebago translators and guides had left the encampment.

Black Hawk attempted to save some of his band's women and children by sending them down the Wisconsin River. At the confluence of the Wisconsin and Mississippi Rivers a detachment of regulars spotted the raft and opened fire. Many of the Sauk were killed or drowned; thirty-two women and children were taken prisoner. Those who eluded the soldiers were tracked down and killed by William Hamilton's band of Menominee Indians.

Black Hawk's flight to the Mississippi River was a nightmare. Starving Sauk stragglers, described by one soldier as "the most miserable poor creatures you can imagine," were often killed and scalped by Menominee and Dakota Indians aiding the troops. On August 1, Black Hawk reached the Mississippi River, two miles below the mouth of the Bad Axe tributary. That afternoon the *Warrior* appeared on the Mississippi. Holding a white flag, Black Hawk asked the ship's captain if he would send a small boat to bring him aboard so he could surrender. (The few canoes the Sauk possessed were transporting women and children across the river.) The whites feared a trick and opened fire with the vessel's small cannon. Twenty-three Sauk were killed. The Indians were delayed in crossing the Mississippi, and the army was closing in.

On August 2 the army attacked. An attempt to decoy the soldiers away from the main body failed, and as Sauk resistance weakened, the battle became a massacre. Described by one American as "wild beasts" who were being subjected to God's vengeance for "the horrid deeds they had done," the Sauk were killed unmercifully. Those who attempted to swim across the Mississippi River became easy targets for American and Indian riflemen shooting from the riverbanks. The slaughter lasted three hours and left 150 Indians killed and an equal number drowned. The army lost approximately a dozen killed. (Colonel Dodge's force suffered six wounded.) Many of the approximately three hundred Sauk who successfully reached the west bank of the Mississippi River were hunted down and massacred by Indians aiding the Americans. Of the one thousand Indians who had crossed into Illinois with Black Hawk in April, only 150 survived. Black Hawk, who hid himself while his followers were being massacred at Bad Axe, survived and escaped. He was captured and turned over to government authorities at Prairie du Chien. In late September a treaty of peace was signed at Fort Armstrong in which the Sauk ceded six million acres of land along the western bank of the Mississippi River for less than a dime an acre.

In the spring of 1833, Black Hawk, his son, and several others were imprisoned at Fort Monroe, Virginia. President Jackson released Black Hawk's party in June but ordered them to visit several eastern cities to impress the defeated Sauk with the strength and wealth of the white man. On July 4, 1833, Black Hawk reached Detroit on his way back to Iowa where the September treaty had established a small reservation for the remaining Sauk. During his brief visit at the Michigan territorial capital, Black Hawk expressed disappointment in not being able to visit with Lewis Cass, who he claimed had always given him "good advice" and treated him with "friendship." Black Hawk, whose activities had dishonored him among the main body of Sauk and Fox Indians, died in 1838 near present-day Eldon, Iowa.

The Black Hawk War caused approximately seventy American fatalities, excluding the hundreds of deaths from cholera and a reported one hundred soldiers who died at

Prairie du Chien after hostilities ended. The war temporarily halted immigration to Illinois and the Michigan Territory. (The flow of white settlers resumed the following year.) Besides destroying Black Hawk's band of Sauk and embarrassing the main body of Sauk and Fox Indians who opposed his actions, the Black Hawk War humbled the Winnebago Indians. During the winter of 1832–33, they suffered terribly. The passage of the army through their lands in the western Michigan Territory had delayed the harvesting of crops, scattered much of the area's game and depleted emergency provisions at Fort Howard. Annuities were delayed through bureaucratic bungling at Detroit. The Black Hawk War also renewed American demands to remove the remaining northwestern Indians west of the Mississippi River. In the fall of 1833 the earlier fears of the St. Joseph County Potawatomi were realized when they were forced to cede their lands and prepare to remove to "a new reservation" on the Great Plains.

BIBLIOGRAPHIC NOTE

Sources used in preparing this article include various Michigan county histories and the following:

"Black Hawk War." *Constantine Weekly Mercury and St. Joseph County Advertiser,* May 25–June 8, 1871.

"Black Hawk War." *Niles Republican,* May 19, 1870.

"The Black Hawk War." *Tecumseh Herald,* July 22–Sept. 16, 1875.

Bulkley, John M. "The Black Hawk War." *History of Monroe County.* Chicago: Lewis Publishing Co., 1913. 1:167–69.

Burton, Clarence M. "The Black Hawk War." *The City of Detroit.* Detroit: Clarke Publishing Company, 1922. 1:1052–57.

Coffinberry, S. C. "Incidents and History of the Pottawatamie Indians." *Three Rivers Western Chronicle,* Oct. 13–Nov. 10, 1859.

Eby, Cecil. *That Disgraceful Affair: The Black Hawk War.* New York: Norton and Co., 1973.

Farmer, Silas. *History of Detroit, Wayne County and Early Michigan.* 1890; rpt., Detroit: Gale Research, 1969. 48–49, 299, 962.

Jackson, Donald, ed. *Black Hawk: An Autobiography.* Urbana: University of Illinois Press, 1964.

"John R. Williams Papers." *Michigan Pioneer and Historical Collections* 31 (1901): 313–471.

Little, Henry. "A History of the Black Hawk War." *Michigan Pioneer and Historical Collections* 5 (1882): 152–78.

Lowry, Thomas J. "Michigan in the Blackhawk War." *Niles Republican,* May 19, 1870.

McGrain, Gertrude C. "Michigan's Role in the Black Hawk War." M.A. thesis, University of Detroit, 1937.

Miller, Stanley. "Massacre at Bad Axe." *American History Illustrated* 19, no. 2 (Apr. 1964): 30–35.

Nichols, Roger L., ed. "The Battle of Bad Axe: General Atkinson's Report." *Wisconsin Magazine of History* 50, no. 1 (Autumn 1966): 54–58.

Robertson, John. "The Black Hawk War." *Michigan in the War.* Lansing: W. S. George & Co., 1882. 1023–27.

"Roll of Volunteers for Black Hawk War." *Michigan Pioneer and Historical Collections* 37 (1909): 240–50.

Stevens, Frank E. *The Black Hawk War.* Chicago: Frank Stevens, 1903.

Thwaites, Reuben G. "The Story of the Black Hawk War." *Wisconsin Historical Collections* 12 (1892): 217–65.

Wallace, Anthony F. C. *The Course of Indian-White Relations Which Led to the Black Hawk War of 1832.* Springfield: Illinois State Historical Society, 1970.

Weissert, Charles A. "Michigan and the Black Hawk War." *An Account of Southwest Michigan and St. Joseph County.* Dayton: National Historical Association, 1900. 113–20.

Zackem, Mathilde Z. "Michigan's Aid in the Black Hawk War." M.A. thesis, Wayne State University, 1943.

BLACK HAWK WAR RELATED HISTORIC SITES AND MONUMENTS IN MICHIGAN

General John R. Williams Bronze Tablet, Grand River and Woodward Avenues, Detroit

LIST OF RELEVANT MICHIGAN ILLUSTRATIONS

Black Hawk War—Representative Soldiers

Elting, John R., ed. *Military Uniforms in America: Years of Growth, 1796–1851*. San Rafael, Calif.: Presidio Press, 1977. P. 101. Color image of four Illinois militiamen in the Black Hawk War.

Geer. Richard. Michigan militia marching west on the Chicago Road. Artist's depiction of volunteer troops en route to rendezvous point. Michigan State Historical Museum, Lansing, Accession 98.0.2.

Mac, Alle. *True Tales of the Pioneers*. Sturgis, Mich.: Sturgis Junior Woman's League, 1967. P. 21. Image from mural depicting the history of Sturgis that shows typical militiaman from the area.

Nelson, William H., and Frank E. Vandiver. *Fields of Glory*. New York: Dutton & Company, 1960. P. 46. Image of early nineteenth-century militiamen.

Todd, Frederick P. *Soldiers of the American Army, 1775–1954*. Chicago: Henry Regnery Company, 1954. Plate 9. Image of men typical of the general militia, ca. 1830.

Black Hawk War—Specific Soldiers

Adam, John J. In Chapman Brothers, *Portrait and Biographical Album of Lenawee County, Michigan*. Chicago, 1888. P. [464]. Also Everts and Stewart, *Combination Atlas Map of Lenawee County, Michigan*. Chicago, 1874. P. 9.

Barnes, Carlos. In Everts and Abbott, *History of Kalamazoo County, Michigan*. Philadelphia, 1880. P. 458.

Beeson, William B. In Photograph in the collections of the Fort St. Joseph Museum, Niles, Mich.

Black Hawk. In Willis Atwell, *Do You Know.* [Grand Rapids]: Booth Newspapers, 1937. P. 414.

Brown, Ebenezer Lakin. In *Kalamazoo Gazette,* Sept. 8, 1946, p. 11. Also *Michigan Pioneer and Historical Collections,* vol. 30. Lansing, 1906. P. [425].

Brown, Joseph W. In John I. Knapp and R. I. Bonner, *Illustrated History and Biographical Record of Lenawee County, Michigan*. Adrian, Mich.: Times Printing Company, 1903. P. 66.

Calhoun, Alvin. In L. H. Everts and Company, *History of St. Joseph County, Michigan*. Philadelphia, 1877. P. 134.

Carpenter, Guy. In Everts and Stewart, *Combination Atlas Map of Lenawee County, Michigan*. Chicago, 1874. P. 27.

Edwards, Asa G. In Everts and Abbott, *History of Hillsdale County, Michigan*. Philadelphia, 1879. Between pp. 216 and 217.

Harrison, Bazel. In *Kalamazoo Gazette,* June 16, 1929, p. 6. Also Larry B. Massie and Peter J. Schmitt, *Kalamazoo*. Woodland Hills, Calif.: Windsor Publications, 1981. P. 18.

Huston, Hosea B. In *Kalamazoo Gazette,* Sept. 8, 1946, p. 11.

Marsac, Joseph F. In Charles Richard Tuttle, *General History of the State of Michigan*. Detroit: Tyler & Company, 1873. P. 469. Also Frank E. Stevens, *The Black Hawk War.* Chicago: Frank E. Stevens, 1903. Opposite p. 255. Also Photograph Collection, State Archives of Michigan, Lansing.

McCrary, Preston J. In Everts and Abbott, *History of Kalamazoo County, Michigan*. Philadelphia, 1880. P. 444.

Shurte, Isaac. In Waterman, Watkins and Company, *History of Cass County, Michigan*. Chicago, 1882. Opposite p. 64.

Stewart, Hart L. In Frank E. Stevens, *The Black Hawk War.* Chicago: Frank E. Stevens, 1903. Opposite p. 235.

Townsend, Gamaliel. In Waterman, Watkins and Company, *History of Cass County, Michigan*. Chicago, 1882. After p. 56.

Warner, Harvey. In Everts and Abbott. *History of Branch County, Michigan*. Philadelphia, 1879. P. 160.
Whipple, Charles W. In Photograph Collection, State Archives of Michigan, Lansing.
Williams, John R. In *Michigan Pioneer and Historical Collections,* vol. 31. Lansing, Mich.: Wynkoop Hallenbeck Crawford Company, 1902. Opposite p. 313. Also Western Biographical Publishing Company, *American Biographical History of Eminent and Self Made Men*. Michigan volume. Cincinnati, 1878. Opposite p. 155. Also Frank E. Stevens, *The Black Hawk War.* Chicago: Frank E. Stevens, 1903. Opposite p. 255. Also Photography Collection, State Archives of Michigan, Lansing.

ORGANIZATIONAL CHART OF PARTICIPATING MICHIGAN UNITS

The number of Michigan men, extracted from the rosters, is listed after each company.

1st Regiment, 3rd Brigade, 1st Division (Wayne and Washtenaw Counties)
Colonel Edward S. Brooks, commanding (Detroit)

Companies:	
Josiah Burton (Ypsilanti)	63
Joseph F. Marsac (Detroit)	62
Isaac Rowland (Detroit)	57
Albert Stevens (Plymouth?)	50
Anthony R. Swarthout (Ypsilanti)	56
Nahum Thayer (Detroit)	65

7th Regiment, 3rd Brigade, 1st Division (Berrien and Cass Counties)
Major General John R. Williams, commanding (Detroit)

Companies:	
Job Brookfield, 5th Company (Niles)	15
John Curry (Little Prairie Ronde)	22
Joseph Gardner, 1st Company (Pokagon Prairie?)	34
Fowler Preston, 7th Company (St. Joseph)	36
Isaac Shurte, 2nd Company (LaGrange)	62
John White (Cass County)	48

Detachments Assigned to the 7th Regiment
Colonel Almanson Huston, commanding (Niles)

Companies:	
Isaac Butler, 4th Company (Edwardsburg)	43
Benoni Finch, Infantry (Niles)	43
Charles Jackson, Cavalry (Detroit)	25
John Silsbe, Cavalry (Edwardsburg)	32

8th Regiment, 3rd Brigade, 1st Division (Lenawee County)
Colonel William McNair, commanding (Tecumseh)

Companies:	
Appollos Drown (Tecumseh)	77
William Edmunds (Adrian)	25
Sewal Goff, 3rd Company, Cavalry (Blissfield)	33

Lt. Colonel Daniel Pittman, commanding (Tecumseh)

Companies:	
Asahel Finche, Rifle Grenadiers (Tecumseh)	52
Daniel Hixson (Clinton)	50
Richard Lewis (Palmyra)	72

11th Regiment, 3rd Brigade, 1st Division (St. Joseph County)
Colonel Hart L. Stewart, commanding (Mottville)

Companies: John Anderson, Cavalry (White Pigeon)	54
Alvin Calhoun (Florence)	49
William Hunter (Sturgis)	29
Andrew Jackson, Mounted (Flowerfield)	06
Henry Powers, 4th Company (Nottawa Prairie)	63
Alanson Stewart, 1st Company (Centerville?)	52

12th Regiment, 3rd Brigade, 1st Division (Kalamazoo County)
Colonel David E. Brown, commanding (Schoolcraft)

Companies: Carlos Barnes (Richland)	52
Ephraim Harrison (Schoolcraft)	65
James Noyes (Gourdneck Prairie)	42

[14th Regiment], 3rd Brigade, 2nd Division (Branch & Hillsdale)
Major Beniah Jones, commanding (Jonesville)

Companies: Abraham Bolton, 1st Company (Girard)	50
Seth Dunham, 3rd Company (Bronson)	26
James Olds, 2nd Company (Jonesville)	31

400 Mounted United States Volunteers (Never Activated)
Major Joseph W. Brown, commanding (Tecumseh)

Companies: John W. Anderson (White Pigeon)	14
Lyman I. Daniels (Schoolcraft)	55
Charles C. Hascall (Pontiac)	45
Levi S. Humphrey (Monroe)	73
Almanson Huston (Niles)	32

Miscellaneous units	78
Total Number of Michigan Soldiers in the Black Hawk War	1,838

ROSTER OF MICHIGAN MEN
IN THE BLACK HAWK WAR

Name	Rank	Military Unit	Service Dates	Remarks
Abbott, James	PVT	Marsac's Company	05/22/32–05/30/32	
Abbott, Robert H.	DMB	Burton's Company	05/22/32–05/31/32	
Abby, J.	PVT	Harrison's Company	05/21/32–06/09/32	
Ackerman, Benjamin P.	VOL	Hascall's Company	07/2?/32–07/29/32	VTS OAS WNA
Ackle, Stephen	VOL	Daniels' Company	07/2?/32–07/29/32	VTS OAS WNA NRE
Ackle, William	VOL	Daniels' Company	07/2?/32–07/29/32	VTS OAS WNA
Adam, John J.	PVT	Hixson's Company	05/21/32–06/07/32	
Adams, Henry	4SG	Calhoun's Company	05/21/32–06/21/32	
Adams, Isa O.	PVT	Anderson's Company	06/16/32–06/21/32	
Adams, John H.	2SG	Barnes' Company	05/21/32–06/03/32	
Adams, Wales	ENS	Dunham's Company	??/??/32–??/??/32	Absent sick
Adams, William	PVT	Anderson's Company	07/28/32–07/29/32	VTS WNA
Adams, William H.	QUS	F&S 11th Regiment	05/21/32–06/21/32	
Aiken, Daniel	1SG	Olds' Company	05/21/32–06/03/32	
Aiken, Marcus G.	PVT	Olds' Company	??/??/32–??/??/32	Absent
Akins, A. William	PVT	Thayer's Company	05/22/32–05/31/32	
Akins, Arenius	PVT	Bolton's Company	06/14/32–06/21/32	
Alcott, John	PVT	Powers' Company	05/21/32–07/21/32	
Aldrich, Erastus	PVT	Lewis' Company	06/13/32–06/19/32	
Aldrich, Hyram	PVT	Lewis' Company	06/13/32–06/19/32	

NAME	RANK	MILITARY UNIT	SERVICE DATES	REMARKS
Aldrich, Roswell	PVT	Barnes' Company	05/21/32–06/03/32	
Alexander, Hugh	PVT	Bolton's Company	??/??/32–??/??/32	Absent
Alexander, James	PVT	Rowland's Company	05/22/32–05/31/32	
Alford, Martin	PVT	Powers' Company	05/21/32–06/21/32	
Allen, George	PVT	Rowland's Company	05/22/32–05/31/32	
Allen, Hiram H.	PVT	Finche's Company	05/21/32–06/05/32	
Allen, Horace	2CP	Noyes' Company	05/21/32–06/09/32	
Allen, James	PVT	Lewis' Company	05/21/32–06/06/32	ASD 06/13/32–06/19/32
Allen, John	1LT	Bolton's Company	05/21/32–06/03/32	
Allen, Solon	PVT	Drown's Company	05/21/32–06/21/32	
Amick, Jacob	PVT	White's Company	05/19/32–06/21/32	
Anderson, John W.	CAP	Anderson's Company	05/21/32–06/21/32	VTS WNA 07/26/32–07/29/32
Andress, Frederick	PVT	Swarthout's Company	05/22/32–05/31/32	
Andress, Nathan	SGT	Swarthout's Company	05/22/32–05/31/32	
Andrews, Charles	UNK	Unknown	??/??/32–??/??/32	SCU History of Kalamazoo p. 327
Andrews, Daniel	PVT	Stevens' Company	05/22/32–05/31/32	
Armstrong, Thomas	PVT	Stewart's Company	05/21/32–06/21/32	
Arrison, William	PVT	Preston's Company	05/21/32–06/21/32	
Arwood, William	PVT	Swarthout's Company	05/22/32–05/31/32	
Ashbery, Abram	PVT	White's Company	05/19/32–05/23/32	
Ashbey, Abraham	PVT	Huston's Company	07/26/32–07/29/32	VTS WNA
Ashbey, Thompson	PVT	Stewart's Company	05/21/32–06/06/32	
Atkinson, G. E.	PVT	Burton's Company	05/22/32–05/31/32	
Audrain, Abbott	1SG	Jackson's Company	05/22/32–06/05/32	Left sick at Clinton
Austin, Abel	PVT	Humphrey's Company	07/27/32–07/29/32	VTS OAS WNA
Babcock, Russel	PVT	Finch's Company	05/19/32–06/25/32	

163

NAME	RANK	MILITARY UNIT	SERVICE DATES	REMARKS
Bacon, Thomas	PVT	Hunter's Company	05/21/32–06/06/32	
Bailey, Isaac G.	PVT	Powers' Company	05/21/32–06/21/32	
Bailey, Lewis E.	4SG	Humphrey's Company	07/27/32–07/29/32	VTS OAS WNA
Bair, Joseph	1SG	Noyes' Company	05/21/32–06/21/32	
Bair, Joseph	VOL	Daniels' Company	07/2?/32–07/29/32	VTS OAS WNA
Baker, Clark	PVT	Olds' Company	??/??/32–??/??/32	Absent
Baker, James	PVT	Humphrey's Company	07/27/32–07/29/32	VTS OAS WNA
Baker, Josiah	PVT	Lewis' Company	05/21/32–06/06/32	ASD 06/13/32–06/19/32
Baker, Peter	PVT	Hunter's Company	05/21/32–06/06/32	
Baldwin, David	PVT	Silsbe's Company	05/29/32–06/27/32	
Baldwin, Horatio N.	1LT	Hixson's Company	05/21/32–06/07/32	ASD 06/12/32–06/19/32
Baldwin, Joel	PVT	Silsbe's Company	05/29/32–06/27/32	
Baldwin, Silas	ENS	Butler's Company	05/19/32–06/25/32	
Baldwin, Walter	VOL	Hascall's Company	07/2?/32–07/29/32	VTS OAS WNA
Ball, Charles	PVT	Swarthout's Company	05/22/32–05/31/32	
Ballard, Jesse	PVT	Drown's Company	05/21/32–06/21/32	
Ballard, William A.	3SG	Burton's Company	05/22/32–05/31/32	
Ballow, George W.	PVT	Swarthout's Company	05/22/32–05/31/32	
Bangs, Smith	SGT	Drown's Company	05/21/32–06/21/32	
Banner, Phineas	PVT	Bolton's Company	05/24/32–06/03/32	
Barber, Ames	PVT	Thayer's Company	05/22/32–05/31/32	
Barber, Daniel	PVT	Harrison's Company	05/21/32–06/09/32	
Barber, Jonas	PVT	Harrison's Company	05/21/32–06/09/32	
Barber, Phineas	PVT	Humphrey's Company	07/27/32–07/29/32	VTS OAS WNA
Barber, Samuel	PVT	Humphrey's Company	07/27/32–07/29/32	VTS OAS WNA
Barker, Daniel	VOL	Daniels' Company	07/2?/32–07/29/32	VTS OAS WNA

Name	Rank	Military Unit	Service Dates	Remarks
Barker, Francis	PVT	Finch's Company	05/19/32–06/25/32	
Barlow, Milton	PVT	Swarthout's Company	05/22/32–05/31/32	
Barnes, Carlos	CAP	Barnes' Company	06/13/32–06/21/32	
Barnes, Hamilton	PVT	Anderson's Company	05/27/32–06/21/32	VTS WNA 07/28/32–07/29/32
Barnes, Isaac	CLT	F&S 12th Regiment	05/21/32–06/21/32	Adjutant
Barnes, John B.	PVT	Barnes' Company	05/21/32–06/03/32	
Barney, Warren	ENS	Burton's Company	05/22/32–05/31/32	
Barnhart, Martin	PVT	Bolton's Company	05/21/32–06/03/32	ASD 06/14/32–06/21/32
Barnhart, Peter	PVT	Finch's Company	05/19/32–06/25/32	
Barns, Reuben	PVT	Stevens' Company	05/22/32–05/31/32	
Barns, William	PVT	Stewart's Company	05/21/32–06/06/32	
Barrett, Chris	PVT	Drown's Company	05/21/32–06/21/32	
Barron, Hezekiah	MUS	Finch's Company	05/19/32–06/25/32	
Barron, Hezekiah	PVT	Huston's Company	07/26/32–07/29/32	VTS WNA
Bartlett, Calvin	1CP	Preston's Company	05/21/32–06/21/32	
Bartlett, Samuel A.	SAD	Humphrey's Company	07/27/32–07/29/32	VTS OAS WNA
Bates, George L	FIF	Burton's Company	05/22/32–05/31/32	
Baum, Jesse	PVT	Anderson's Company	05/21/32–06/21/32	VTS WNA 07/28/32–07/29/32
Beach, Rodney	PVT	Humphrey's Company	07/27/32–07/29/32	VTS OAS WNA
Beach, Rufus	VOL	Hascall's Company	07/2?/32–07/29/32	VTS OAS WNA
Beach, William	VOL	Hascall's Company	07/2?/32–07/29/32	VTS OAS WNA
Beadle, David Jr.	VOL	Daniels' Company	07/2?/32–07/29/32	VTS OAS WNA
Beardsley, Elam	TEA	Unknown	05/31/32–??/??/??	
Beardsley, Eldridge	SGT	Butler's Company	05/19/32–06/25/32	PEN
Bears, Ephraim	PVT	Anderson's Company	05/27/32–06/21/32	VTS WNA 07/28/32–07/29/32
Beatty, John	SGT	Butler's Company	05/19/32–06/25/32	

Michigan Men in the Black Hawk War

Name	Rank	Military Unit	Service Dates	Remarks
Beaubein, Alexis	PVT	Humphrey's Company	07/27/32–07/29/32	VTS OAS WNA
Beaubien, Joseph	PVT	Humphrey's Company	07/27/32–07/29/32	VTS OAS WNA
Beaufet, Lewis	PVT	Jackson's Company	05/22/32–07/22/32	
Beck, Harry	PVT	Drown's Company	05/21/32–06/21/32	
Beckwith, Albert	SGT	Stewart's Company	05/21/32–06/06/32	
Bedle, David	PVT	Harrison's Company	05/21/32–06/09/32	
Beebe, Andrew	PVT	Burton's Company	05/22/32–05/31/32	
Beebe, D.	CLK	Lewis' Company	05/21/32–06/06/32	ASD 06/13/32–06/19/32
Beeby, John	PVT	Noyes' Company	05/21/32–06/21/32	
Beers, Harvey	PVT	Thayer's Company	05/22/32–05/31/32	Deserter
Beerwan, David	PVT	Finch's Company	05/19/32–06/25/32	
Beeson, Jacob	COL	F&S 3rd Brigade	05/21/32–06/20/32	Paymaster. PEN
Beeson, William B.	SUM	F&S 7th Regiment	05/19/32–06/21/32	PEN
Beisel, Peter Jr.	PVT	Anderson's Company	06/16/32–06/21/32	VTS WNA 07/27/32–07/29/32
Bell, H. G.	PVT	Burton's Company	05/22/32–05/31/32	
Bell, H. M.	PVT	Burton's Company	05/22/32–05/31/32	
Bell, William	PVT	Olds' Company	05/21/32–06/03/32	
Bellips, John	PVT	Stewart's Company	05/21/32–06/06/32	
Bendour, Thomas	VOL	Daniels' Company	07/2?/32–07/29/32	VTS OAS WNA
Bendure, H.	PVT	Harrison's Company	05/21/32–06/21/32	
Bendure, I.	PVT	Harrison's Company	05/21/32–06/21/32	
Bendure, William	PVT	Harrison's Company	05/21/32–06/09/32	
Benedict, R. R.	PVT	Burton's Company	05/22/32–05/31/32	
Bennet, Hiram	PVT	Huston's Company	07/26/32–07/29/32	VTS WNA
Bennett, George	PVT	Burton's Company	05/22/32–05/31/32	Deserter

Name	Rank	Military Unit	Service Dates	Remarks
Bennett, Henry	PVT	Burton's Company	05/22/32–05/31/32	Deserter
Bennett, Luke K.	PVT	Lewis' Company	06/13/32–06/19/32	
Bennett, M. P.	3CP	Preston's Company	05/21/32–06/21/32	
Bennett, T. J.	QUS	F&S 12th Regiment	05/21/32–06/21/32	
Bennett, Thomas J.	3SG	Daniels' Company	07/2?/32–07/29/32	VTS OAS WNA
Benson, Peter	PVT	Olds' Company	05/21/32–06/03/32	
Benson, Silas	1LT	Olds' Company	05/21/32–06/03/32	
Benson, Silus	1LT	Bolton's Company	06/14/32–06/21/32	
Berthlett, Calvin	1CP	Preston's Company	05/21/32–06/21/32	
Bertrand, Joseph Jr.	INT	F&S MI Militia	05/26/32–06/02/32	
Bertrand, Samuel	PVT	Brookfield's Company	05/21/32–05/31/32	
Beson, Cyrus	2SG	Noyes Company	05/21/32–06/09/32	
Beusell, Charles	PVT	Butler's Company	05/20/32–06/25/32	
Billops, William	PVT	Butler's Company	05/20/32–06/25/32	
Bills, William	PVT	Bolton's Company	06/14/32–06/21/32	
Billups, Richard M.	PVT	Calhoun's Company	05/21/32–06/06/32	PEN
Billups, Silas G.	PVT	Calhoun's Company	05/21/32–06/21/32	PEN
Billups, William	2SG	Calhoun's Company	05/21/32–06/06/32	PEN
Bingham, Lemuel	PVT	Bolton's Company	05/21/32–06/03/32	
Bingham, Lenov L.	PVT	Bolton's Company	06/14/32–06/21/32	
Bingham, Seymour	PVT	Bolton's Company	05/24/32–06/03/32	
Bird, Hiram	FIM	Burton's Company	05/22/32–05/31/32	PEN
Birdsley, Philo G.	PVT	Lewis' Company	05/21/32–06/06/32	
Bishop, William	2SG	Harrison's Company	05/21/32–06/09/32	
Bishop, William	VOL	Daniels' Company	07/2?/32–07/29/32	VTS OAS WNA

Name	Rank	Military Unit	Service Dates	Remarks
Bishop, William A.	PVT	Harrison's Company	05/21/32–06/09/32	
Blackman, James C.	1CP	Edmund's Company	05/22/32–06/06/32	Left Company at Beardsley's Prairie
Blackmer, Osborn	2CP	Olds' Company	05/21/32–06/03/32	
Blair, James C.	1SG	Thayer's Company	05/22/31–05/31/32	
Blanchard, Farnum	SGT	Drown's Company	05/21/32–06/21/32	
Bliss, Weston W.	PVT	Anderson's Company	05/21/32–06/21/32	VTS WNA 07/28/32–07/29/32
Bliss, Weston W.	PVT	Jackson's Company	05/21/32–06/04/32	
Blood, Leonard C.	PVT	Finche's Company	05/21/32–06/05/32	
Bloss, Lyman	PVT	Stevens' Company	05/22/32–05/31/32	Absent without leave
Bodin, George	PVT	Stevens' Company	05/22/32–05/31/32	
Bolster, Thomas	PVT	Drown's Company	05/21/32–06/21/32	
Bolton, Abraham F.	CAP	Bolton's Company	05/21/32–06/03/32	ASD 06/14/32–06/21/32
Bond, Franklin	PVT	Humphrey's Company	07/27/32–07/29/32	VTS OAS WNA
Bondie, John	PVT	Marsac's Company	05/22/32–05/30/32	
Bonner, Phineas	PVT	Bolton's Company	05/24/32–06/03/32	
Boon, George	PVT	Gardner's Company	05/19/32–06/21/32	
Boon, George	PVT	Huston's Company	07/26/32–07/29/32	VTS WNA
Boon, John	3SG	Huston's Company	07/26/32–07/29/32	VTS WNA
Boon, John	PVT	Gardner's Company	05/19/32–06/21/32	
Boon, Lewis	PVT	White's Company	05/19/32–05/23/32	
Booth, C. N.	PVT	Stevens' Company	05/22/32–05/31/32	
Borris, Joseph	PVT	Marsac's Company	05/22/32–05/30/32	
Borris, Soloman	PVT	Marsac's Company	05/22/32–05/30/32	
Bostick, Daniel	PVT	Bolton's Company	06/14/32–06/21/32	
Bourasan, Louis	PVT	Marsac's Company	05/22/32–05/30/32	
Bowen, John	PVT	White's Company	05/19/32–05/27/32	

Name	Rank	Military Unit	Service Dates	Remarks
Bowten, Samuel	PVT	Swarthout's Company	05/22/32–05/31/32	
Boyd, James	PVT	Rowland's Company	05/22/32–05/31/32	
Bradish, Currin	PVT	Lewis' Company	05/21/32–06/06/32	
Bradish, John	PVT	Lewis' Company	05/21/32–06/06/32	
Bradish, Nelson	PVT	Lewis' Company	05/21/32–06/06/32	
Bradly, H.	PVT	Calhoun's Company	05/21/32–06/06/32	
Bradner, Ezra	2CP	Stevens' Company	05/22/32–05/31/32	
Bradner, Ira	1CP	Stevens' Company	05/22/32–05/31/32	
Bradnew, Enos	3CP	Stevens' Company	05/22/32–05/31/32	
Brazie, Hiram	DMR	Rowland's Company	05/22/32–05/31/32	
Brears, John	PVT	Hixson's Company	05/21/32–06/07/32	
Breck, Philip H.	LUT	Hunter's Company	05/21/32–06/21/32	
Brewer, I.	PVT	Stevens' Company	05/22/32–05/31/32	
Brewer, John	PVT	Lewis' Company	06/13/32–06/19/32	
Brice, William H.	2SG	Silsbe's Company	05/29/32–06/27/32	
Briggs, Richmond	PVT	Thayer's Company	05/22/32–05/31/32	
Brigham, A.	PVT	Swarthout's Company	05/22/32–05/31/32	
Bristol, C. L.	PVT	Jackson's Company	05/22/32–07/22/32	
Britan, Joseph	PVT	Preston's Company	05/28/32–06/21/32	
Britton, Sanford	1CP	Thayer's Company	05/22/32–05/31/32	
Brockway, Sylvester	PVT	Dunham's Company	??/??/32–??/??/32	Absent without leave
Bromley, Roswell	VOL	Hascall's Company	07/2?/32–07/29/32	VTS OAS WNA
Brookfield, Job	1LT	Brookfield's Company	05/21/32–06/21/32	PEN. RBL
Brooks, Daniel S.	1CP	Hixson's Company	05/21/32–06/07/32	ASD 06/12/32–06/19/32
Brooks, Edward S.	COL	F&S 7th Regiment	05/22/32–07/22/32	Inspector General
Brooks, George W.	SGT	Powers' Company	05/21/32–06/06/32	

Name	Rank	Military Unit	Service Dates	Remarks
Brooks, Tate	SGT	Stewart's Company	05/21/32–06/21/32	
Brooks, William	PVT	Lewis' Company	05/21/32–06/06/32	
Broughton, Richard	1LT	Stevens' Company	05/22/32–05/31/32	
Brower, Daniel	PVT	Finch's Company	05/19/32–06/25/32	
Brown, Aaron	PVT	Butler's Company	05/20/32–06/25/32	
Brown, David E.	COL	F&S 12th Regiment	05/21/32–06/21/32	
Brown, Ebenezer Lakin	PVT	Noyes' Company	05/21/32–06/09/32	PEN
Brown, Egbert B.	ENS	Lewis' Company	05/21/32–06/06/32	
Brown, G.	PVT	Harrison's Company	05/21/32–06/09/32	
Brown, George	ENS	Drown's Company	05/21/32–06/21/32	
Brown, Jacob Kingery	PVT	Finch's Company	05/19/32–06/25/32	RBL
Brown, Joseph White	GEB	F&S 3rd Brigade	05/21/32–06/21/32	Commander
Brown, Mahlon	PVT	Edmund's Company	06/12/32–06/19/32	
Brown, S. S.	PVT	Burton's Company	05/22/32–05/31/32	
Brown, Thomas M.	4CP	Lewis' Company	05/21/32–06/06/32	
Brownell, Garden T.	PVT	Stewart's Company	05/21/32–06/21/32	
Brusell, Charles	PVT	Butler's Company	05/20/32–06/25/32	
Buck, Peter H.	SGT	Stewart's Company	05/21/32–06/21/32	PEN
Buck, William	PVT	Gardner's Company	05/19/32–05/27/32	
Buckman, Cyrus	PVT	Drown's Company	05/21/32–06/21/32	
Buel, James M.	2CP	Anderson's Company	05/27/32–06/21/32	VTS OAS WNA 07/26/32–07/29/32
Buel, Josiah	PVT	Drown's Company	05/21/32–06/21/32	
Bull, Charles M.	4SG	Rowland's Company	05/22/32–05/31/32	
Bumgardner, Bolsor	2SG	Hunter's Company	05/21/32–06/06/32	
Bunker, Stephen	PVT	Curry's Company	05/19/32–05/23/32	
Bunnell, Eli P.	1SG	Shurte's Company	05/19/32–06/21/32	

NAME	RANK	MILITARY UNIT	SERVICE DATES	REMARKS
Burch, Addison	PVT	Humphrey's Company	07/27/32–07/29/32	VTS OAS WNA
Burch, Ethel	3SG	Humphrey's Company	07/27/32–07/29/32	VTS OAS WNA
Burch, Ethel	VOL	Daniels' Company	07/2?/32–07/29/32	VTS OAS WNA
Burch, John H.	PVT	Humphrey's Company	07/27/32–07/29/32	VTS OAS WNA
Burch, Morris	PVT	Goff's Company	05/22/32–05/??/32	Deserted at Coldwater MI
Burden, William	PVT	Finch's Company	05/19/32–06/25/32	
Burdick, Ambrose L.	PVT	Olds' Company	??/??/32–??/??/32	Absent
Burdick, Ichebod	4SG	Bolton's Company	06/14/32–06/21/32	
Burdick, James M.	PVT	Olds' Company	05/21/32–06/03/32	
Burgett, Thomas	PVT	Stewart's Company	05/21/32–06/21/32	
Burk, Thomas	PVT	Gardner's Company	05/19/32–05/27/32	
Burk, William	PVT	Gardner's Company	05/19/32–05/27/32	
Burke, Andrew L.	PVT	Finch's Company	05/19/32–06/25/32	
Burnell, Samuel	PVT	Anderson's Company	05/27/32–06/21/32	
Burns, Michael	PVT	Burton's Company	05/22/32–05/31/32	
Burns, Thomas	CPL	Stewart's Company	05/21/32–06/21/32	PEN
Burson, Abner	3CP	Noyes' Company	05/21/32–06/09/32	PEN
Burson, James	PVT	Noyes' Company	05/21/32–06/09/32	
Burton, Josiah	CAP	Burton's Company	05/22/32–05/31/32	
Busby, James	PVT	Swarthout's Company	05/22/32–05/31/32	
Butler, Bela	VOL	Daniels' Company	07/2?/32–07/29/32	VTS OAS WNA
Butler, Bely	PVT	Noyes' Company	05/21/32–06/21/32	
Butler, Isaac	CAP	Butler's Company	05/19/32–06/25/32	
Butler, Joseph	PVT	Powers' Company	05/21/32–06/06/32	
Butterfield, E.	PVT	Swarthout's Company	05/22/32–05/31/32	
Butterfield, Edward	3SG	Hunter's Company	05/21/32–06/06/32	

Name	Rank	Military Unit	Service Dates	Remarks
Butterfield, Edward	PVT	Butler's Company	05/20/32–06/25/32	
Butterfield, Jonathan	PVT	Humphrey's Company	07/27/32–07/29/32	VTS OAS WNA
Cabbesha, Joseph	PVT	Jackson's Company	05/22/32–07/22/32	
Cable, George W.	3SG	Dunham's Company	05/21/32–06/03/32	
Cade, Thomas Jr.	BUG	Anderson's Company	05/21/32–06/21/32	VTS OAS WNA 07/26/32–07/29/32
Cahill, A.	PVT	Stewart's Company	05/21/32–06/06/32	
Calhoun, Abner	PVT	Harrison's Company	05/21/32–06/09/32	
Calhoun, Abner	VOL	Daniels' Company	07/2?/32–07/29/32	VTS OAS WNA
Calhoun, Alvin	CAP	Calhoun's Company	06/07/32–06/21/32	Took over COM from Seldon Martin
Campbell, George	1CP	Finche's Company	05/21/32–05/30/32	Deserted at Niles MI
Campbell, Harry	PVT	Drown's Company	05/21/32–06/21/32	
Campeau, James	PVT	Marsac's Company	05/22/32–05/30/32	
Canfield, Elnathan	PVT	Stevens' Company	05/22/32–05/31/32	
Capcan, Michael	PVT	Marsac's Company	05/22/32–05/30/32	
Carkins, Edward	PVT	Humphrey's Company	07/27/32–07/29/32	VTS OAS WNA
Carmack, William	PVT	Hixson's Company	05/21/32–06/07/32	
Carmel, Bellone	PVT	Marsac's Company	05/22/32–05/30/32	
Carpenter, Elias	PVT	Drown's Company	05/21/32–06/21/32	
Carpenter, Guy	PVT	Goff's Company	05/22/32–06/06/32	
Carpenter, John C.	PVT	Noyes' Company	05/21/32–06/21/32	PEN
Carpenter, John R.	4CP	Edmund's Company	05/22/32–06/06/32	ASD 06/12/32–06/19/32. PEN
Carpenter, John T.	PVT	Edmund's Company	05/22/32–06/06/32	
Carpenter, Joshua	2CP	Lewis' Company	05/21/32–06/06/32	
Carpenter, Mordecai	PVT	Edmund's Company	05/22/32–06/06/32	ASD 06/12/32–06/19/32
Carpenter, William L.	3CP	Edmund's Company	05/22/32–06/06/32	

NAME	RANK	MILITARY UNIT	SERVICE DATES	REMARKS
Carter, Uri M.	PVT	Hixson's Company	05/21/32–06/07/32	
Carwin, William U.	PVT	Hixson's Company	05/21/32–06/07/32	
Case, Harrison	PVT	Humphrey's Company	07/27/32–07/29/32	VTS OAS WNA
Case, Horrace	PVT	Drown's Company	05/21/32–06/21/32	
Cassady, James	PVT	Humphrey's Company	07/27/32–07/29/32	VTS OAS WNA
Castin, Seldan	PVT	Stevens' Company	05/22/32–05/31/32	
Cathcart, Charles W.	QUS	F&S 7th Regiment	05/29/32–06/25/32	
Cathkert, John	PVT	Stewart's Company	05/21/32–06/06/32	
Cathkert, William	PVT	Stewart's Company	05/21/32–06/21/32	
Cavender, John	3CP	Burton's Company	05/22/32–05/31/32	
Cays, John	2CP	Shurte's Company	05/19/32–06/21/32	
Cedorus, Frederick	PVT	Stewart's Company	05/21/32–06/06/32	
Chace, Alvin	VOL	Daniels' Company	07/2?/32–07/29/32	VTS OAS WNA
Champion, Nathan	PVT	Thayer's Company	05/22/32–05/31/32	
Champlin, Elisha P.	CAP	F&S 3rd Brigade	05/21/32–06/20/32	Aide-de-camp
Chapin, Adolphus	LUT	Stewart's Company	05/21/32–06/06/32	
Chapin, N. B.	PVT	Stewart's Company	05/21/32–06/06/32	
Chapin, Samuel A.	ENS	Stewart's Company	06/07/32–06/21/32	
Chapin, Samuel A.	PVT	Anderson's Company	05/21/32–06/06/32	
Chapin, Samuel A.	PVT	Jackson's Company	05/21/32–06/04/32	
Chapman, John Jr.	PVT	Lewis' Company	06/13/32–06/19/32	
Charles, Jacob	PVT	Curry's Company	05/19/32–06/21/32	
Charles, John	PVT	Butler's Company	05/20/32–06/25/32	
Charles, John	PVT	Preston's Company	05/21/32–06/21/32	
Chase, Alvin	1SG	Humphrey's Company	07/27/32–07/29/32	VTS OAS WNA

Name	Rank	Military Unit	Service Dates	Remarks
Chase, Enoch	SUR	F&S 3rd Brigade	05/21/32–06/20/32	Also served as Adjutant
Chaudonois, Jean B.	INT	F&S 7th Regiment	06/04/32–06/26/32	MNI Baptiste
Chess, William	PVT	White's Company	05/19/32–05/27/32	
Chiefbrough, David A.	1SG	Lewis' Company	05/21/32–06/06/32	
Chipman, Daniel C.	VOL	Hascall's Company	07/2?/32–07/29/32	VTS OAS WNA
Chipman, Samuel F.	VOL	Hascall's Company	07/2?/32–07/29/32	VTS OAS WNA
Chowen, John	PVT	Swarthout's Company	05/22/32–05/31/32	
Church, Nelson	PVT	Anderson's Company	05/27/32–06/21/32	VTS OAS WNA 07/27/32–07/29/32
Churchill, Randall	PVT	Powers' Company	05/21/32–06/21/32	
Cicotte, James Jr.	PVT	Marsac's Company	05/22/32–05/30/32	
Cisco, Henry	PVT	Humphrey's Company	07/27/32–07/29/32	VTS OAS WNA
Cisco, Henry	VOL	Daniels' Company	07/2?/32–07/29/32	VTS OAS WNA
Clark, Daniel A.	MUS	Goff's Company	05/22/32–06/06/32	PEN
Clark, Duncan R.	MAJ	F&S 11th Regiment	05/21/32–06/21/32	
Clark, Henry	PVT	Olds' Company	05/21/32–06/03/32	AKA Harvey Clark
Clark, John	PVT	Gardner's Company	05/19/32–05/27/32	
Clark, John A.	PVT	Humphrey's Company	07/27/32–07/29/32	VTS OAS WNA
Clark, Lewis	PVT	Stevens' Company	05/22/32–05/31/32	
Clark, Major	VOL	Daniels' Company	07/2?/32–07/29/32	VTS OAS WNA
Clark, Orrin	PVT	Finche's Company	05/21/32–06/05/32	
Clark, Richard	PVT	Hunter's Company	05/21/32–06/06/32	
Clark, Robert Jr.	2LT	F&S 11th Regiment	05/21/32–06/21/32	Assistant Quartermaster
Clark, Rowland	2SG	Brookfield's Company	05/21/32–06/21/32	
Clark, Rowland	PVT	Huston's Company	07/2?/32–07/29/32	VTS OAS WNA
Clarke, David	PVT	Dunham's Company	05/21/32–06/03/32	
Claypole, H. M.	PVT	Finch's Company	05/19/32–06/25/32	

Michigan Men in the Black Hawk War

Name	Rank	Military Unit	Service Dates	Remarks
Cleveland, Joseph N.	PVT	Lewis' Company	06/13/32–06/19/32	
Clews, Joseph	PVT	Powers' Company	05/21/32–06/06/32	
Clifton, John	2SG	Shurte's Company	05/19/32–06/21/32	
Cline, Cornelius	PVT	Lewis' Company	06/13/32–06/19/32	
Clune, A. S.	PVT	Swarthout's Company	05/22/32–05/31/32	
Clyborne, William L.	PVT	Finch's Company	05/19/32–06/25/32	
Coastin, Sheldin	PVT	Stevens' Company	05/22/32–05/31/32	
Coats, Jacon	PVT	Shurte's Company	05/19/32–05/23–32	
Coats, John Jr.	PVT	Calhoun's Company	05/21/32–06/06/32	
Coats, Thomas	PVT	Calhoun's Company	05/21/32–06/06/32	
Cobb, Alonzo	PVT	Noyes' Company	05/21/32–06/09/32	
Cobb, Stephen G.	PVT	Lewis' Company	05/21/32–06/06/32	ASD 06/13/32–06/19/32
Cochran, Stewart	PVT	Stewart's Company	05/21/32–06/06/32	
Cody, Isaac	PVT	Thayer's Company	05/22/32–05/31/32	
Coffinberry, Jacob W.	ENS	Calhoun's Company	05/21/32–06/06/32	
Cole, Abram	PVT	Shurte's Company	05/19/32–05/27/32	
Cole, Daniel B.	PVT	Rowland's Company	05/22/32–05/31/32	Absent without leave
Cole, James W.	PVT	Hixson's Company	05/21/32–06/07/32	
Coleman, John	PVT	Butler's Company	05/20/32–06/25/32	
Colliar, Jonathan	CPL	Butler's Company	05/19/32–06/25/32	
Collier, George	CPL	Butler's Company	05/19/32–06/25/32	
Collins, Michael	PVT	White's Company	05/19/32–05/27/32	
Colt, Samuel D.	LUT	Rowland's Company	05/22/32–05/31/32	
Colton, Henry	1SG	Stevens' Company	05/22/32–05/31/32	
Colvin, Absalim	PVT	Shurte's Company	05/19/32–05/27/32	
Colvin, Josiah	PVT	Drown's Company	05/21/32–06/21/32	

Michigan Men in the Black Hawk War

Name	Rank	Military Unit	Service Dates	Remarks
Colvin, Stephen	2SG	Edmund's Company	05/22/32–06/06/32	ASD 06/12/32–06/19/32
Colvin, Wilkinson	PVT	Shurte's Company	05/19/32–05/23/32	
Comparet, O.	PVT	Swarthout's Company	05/22/32–05/31/32	
Comstock, William	PVT	Thayer's Company	05/22/32–05/31/32	Deserter
Conner, Richard	1CP	Rowland's Company	05/22/32–05/31/32	
Conner, William	PVT	Powers' Company	05/21/32–06/06/32	
Cook, Peter	1LT	F&S 11th Regiment	05/21/32–06/21/32	Adjutant. PEN
Cook, Vaness	PVT	Humphrey's Company	07/27/32–07/29/32	VTS OAS WNA
Cook, Warren	PVT	Humphrey's Company	07/27/32–07/29/32	VTS OAS WNA
Cooper, James R.	SGT	Drown's Company	05/21/32–06/21/32	
Cooper, Justin	PVT	Powers' Company	05/21/32–06/06/32	PEN
Corbus, Joseph C.	PVT	Bolton's Company	05/24/32–06/03/32	
Cornish, John	PVT	Bolton's Company	06/14/32–06/21/32	
Cory, John B.	PVT	Powers' Company	05/21/32–06/06/32	
Cotten, William	PVT	Brookfield's Company	05/19/32–06/21/32	RBL
Coutson, Uriah	SGT	Swarthout's Company	05/22/32–05/31/32	
Cowin, James	PVT	Powers' Company	05/21/32–06/21/32	
Cowin, Robert	PVT	Powers' Company	05/21/32–06/06/32	
Cox, Corman	PVT	Stewart's Company	05/21/32–06/06/32	
Cox, David	PVT	Thayer's Company	05/22/32–05/31/32	
Cox, John Jr.	PVT	Drown's Company	05/21/32–06/21/32	
Cox, John Sr.	PVT	Drown's Company	05/21/32–06/21/32	
Cox, Julian	PVT	Finch's Company	05/19/32–06/25/32	
Coykendall, Collins	PVT	Stevens' Company	05/22/32–05/31/32	
Craig, Louis	PVT	Bolton's Company	05/21/32–06/03/32	AKA James Craig
Crampton, James	PVT	Hixson's Company	05/21/32–06/07/32	

NAME	RANK	MILITARY UNIT	SERVICE DATES	REMARKS
Crane, Ichabod	MUS	Butler's Company	05/19/32–06/25/32	
Crane, John B.	FIF	Hixson's Company	05/21/32–06/07/32	
Crane, Leonard	PVT	Curry's Company	05/19/32–06/21/32	
Crary, Isaac Edwin	LUT	Unknown	??/??/32–??/??/32	SCU History of Calhoun Co. p. 232
Crawford, John H.	PVT	Rowland's Company	05/22/32–05/31/32	
Cressy, Alonzo	UNK	F&S 8th Regiment	??/??/32–??/??/32	Surgeon?
Crispin, Joshua	PVT	White's Company	05/19/32–06/21/32	
Crisple, Henry	PVT	Swarthout's Company	05/22/32–05/31/32	
Crook, Zacheriah	PVT	Olds' Company	05/21/32–06/03/32	
Cross, Amanda	DMM	Burton's Company	05/22/32–05/31/32	
Cross, Robert G.	PVT	Bolton's Company	05/21/32–06/03/32	
Cross, William	3CP	Hixson's Company	05/21/32–06/07/32	
Cross, William H	3SG	Bolton's Company	06/14/32–06/21/32	MNI Hanna
Croy, Jacob	PVT	Butler's Company	05/20/32–06/25/32	
Croy, Jacob	PVT	Calhoun's Company	05/21/32–06/06/32	
Cruper, Josiah	PVT	Huston's Company	07/2?/32–07/29/32	VTS OAS WNA
Cuddy, John	PVT	Powers' Company	05/21/32–06/06/32	
Cuddy, Samuel	PVT	Powers' Company	05/21/32–06/21/32	
Curry, A.	PVT	Powers' Company	05/21/32–06/21/32	
Curry, John	CAP	Curry's Company	05/19/32–06/21/32	
Curtis, Sylvanus W.	PVT	Humphrey's Company	07/27/32–07/29/32	VTS OAS WNA
Cusper, Josiah	PVT	Huston's Company	07/2?/32–07/29/32	VTS OAS WNA
Custis, Stephen	VOL	Daniels' Company	07/2?/32–07/29/32	VTS OAS WNA
Cyrus, Nathan	PVT	Stewart's Company	05/21/32–06/06/32	
Daan, Elisha	3SG	Noyes' Company	05/21/32–06/09/32	
Daily, W.	PVT	Harrison's Company	05/21/32–06/21/32	

Name	Rank	Military Unit	Service Dates	Remarks
Daily, William	VOL	Daniels' Company	07/2?/32–07/29/32	VTS OAS WNA
Daines, Ira A.	PVT	Burton's Company	05/22/32–05/31/32	
Dakins, Samuel R.	PVT	Thayer's Company	05/22/32–05/31/32	
Daniel, G. S.	PVT	Harrison's Company	05/21/32–06/09/32	
Daniels, Garratt I.	VOL	Daniels' Company	07/2?/32–07/29/32	VTS OAS WNA
Daniels, John	VOL	Hascall's Company	07/2?/32–07/29/32	VTS OAS WNA
Daniels, Lyman I.	CAP	Daniels' Company	07/2?/32–07/29/32	VTS OAS WNA
Daniels, Lyman I.	CLT	F&S 12th Regiment	05/21/32–06/21/32	
Dare, Thomas	3SG	Rowland's Company	05/22/32–05/31/32	PEN
Dare, Thomas	4SG	Jackson's Company	05/22/32–07/22/32	PEN
Darrow, Francis	VOL	Hascall's Company	07/2?/32–07/29/32	VTS OAS WNA
Davenport, Lewis	CAP	F&S 1st Regiment	05/21/32–06/20/32	Adjutant
Davidson, Simeon	PVT	Drown's Company	05/21/32–06/21/32	
Davis, Benjamin	VOL	Hascall's Company	07/2?/32–07/29/32	VTS OAS WNA
Davis, Ebenezer	PVT	Hixson's Company	05/21/32–06/07/32	ASD 06/12/32–06/19/32
Davis, Jacob	PVT	Noyes' Company	05/21/32–06/09/32	
Davis, John	2CP	Hixson's Company	05/21/32–06/07/32	ASD 06/12/32–06/19/32
Davis, John	PVT	Harrison's Company	05/21/32–06/21/32	
Davis, Jonathan D.	CLT	F&S 1st Regiment	??/??/32–??/??/32	
Davis, Samuel F.	PVT	Goff's Company	05/22/32–06/06/32	ASD 06/12/32–06/19/32. PEN
Debo, John C.	PVT	Swarthout's Company	05/22/32–05/31/32	
Deerduff, Peter	PVT	Gardner's Company	05/19/32–05/23/32	
Defoe, James	2SG	Jackson's Company	05/22/32–07/22/32	
Demestroy, Winthrop	FIF	Rowland's Company	05/22/32–05/31/32	
Densmore, John	2SG	Lewis' Company	05/21/32–06/06/32	ASD 06/13/32–06/19/32
Derfy, Allen	PVT	Swarthout's Company	05/22/32–05/31/32	

NAME	RANK	MILITARY UNIT	SERVICE DATES	REMARKS
Desnoyas, Francis	4CP	Rowland's Company	05/22/32–05/31/32	
Desnoyer, Charles R.	ENS	Rowland's Company	05/22/32–05/31/32	
Devenport, Lewis	LUT	Thayer's Company	05/22/32–05/31/32	
Devine, David M.	PVT	Olds' Company	05/21/32–06/03/32	
Devoe, William	PVT	Bolton's Company	??/??/32–??/??/32	Absent
Dewey, Francis A.	DMB	F&S 8th Regiment	05/21/32–06/20/32	MNI Asbury
Dewey, Isaac	PVT	Shurte's Company	05/19/32–05/27/32	
Dewey, Soloman	PVT	Shurte's Company	05/19/32–05/23/32	
Dickison, Miller M.	PVT	Burton's Company	05/22/32–05/31/32	
Dickison, Silas	PVT	Burton's Company	05/22/32–05/31/32	
Dilly, George W.	PVT	Powers' Company	05/21/32–06/06/32	
Dingley, Daniel	PVT	Preston's Company	06/05/32–06/21/32	
Dixon, D.	PVT	Harrison's Company	05/21/32–06/09/32	
Doan, Elisha	VOL	Daniels' Company	07/2?/32–07/29/32	VTS OAS WNA
Dobson, Richard	PVT	Drown's Company	05/21/32–06/21/32	PEN
Dodge, Daniel O.	VOL	Daniels' Company	07/2?/32–07/29/32	VTS OAS WNA
Dodge, Hiram	PVT	Hixson's Company	06/12/32–06/19/32	
Dodge, J. E.	2CP	Finche's Company	05/21/32–06/05/32	
Donalds, John	PVT	White's Company	05/19/32–05/23/32	
Doty, Enos	PVT	Edmund's Company	05/22/32–06/06/32	
Dougherty, Thomas	PVT	Humphrey's Company	07/27/32–07/29/32	VTS OAS WNA
Downard, Luther	PVT	Thayer's Company	05/22/32–05/31/32	
Downer, Cyrus	PVT	Lewis' Company	06/13/32–06/19/32	
Downer, I. or J.	PVT	Swarthout's Company	05/22/32–05/31/32	
Downing, Nelson	PVT	Anderson's Company	06/16/32–06/21/32	VTS OAS WNA 07/29/32
Drake, Nathaniel	PVT	Humphrey's Company	07/27/32–07/29/32	VTS OAS WNA

Name	Rank	Military Unit	Service Dates	Remarks
Dranillard, Simon	PVT	Butler's Company	05/20/32–06/25/32	
Drayton, Thomas	3SG	Stevens' Company	05/22/32–05/31/32	
Drew, Henry	PVT	Finch's Company	05/19/32–06/25/32	
Drew, Henry	PVT	Huston's Company	07/2?/32–07/29/32	VTS OAS WNA
Driggs, Alfred S.	PVT	Dunham's Company	05/24/32–06/03/32	Absent without leave
Drown, Appollos	CAP	Drown's Company	05/21/32–06/21/32	
Drum, David M.	PVT	Olds' Company	05/21/32–06/03/32	
Drumum, David M.	PVT	Silsbe's Company	05/29/32–06/27/32	
Druyer, Simeon	FIF	Calhoun's Company	05/21/32–06/06/32	
Duba, Joseph	PVT	Marsac's Company	05/22/32–05/30/32	
Ducket, Isaac W.	PVT	Gardner's Company	05/19/32–05/27/32	
Duluc, Jean B.	PVT	Marsac's Company	05/22/32–05/30/32	MNI Baptiste
Duluc, Lewis	PVT	Marsac's Company	05/22/32–05/30/32	
Dumond, Archibald G.	PVT	Calhoun's Company	05/21/32–06/06/32	
Dun, Nehemiah	PVT	White's Company	05/19/32–05/27/32	
Dunham, Seth	CAP	Dunham's Company	05/21/32–06/03/32	
Dunkin, Joshua B.	1LT	Noyes' Company	05/21/32–06/21/32	
Dunn, Jonathan	VOL	Hascall's Company	07/2?/32–07/29/32	VTS OAS WNA
Dupra, Louis	PVT	Marsac's Company	05/22/32–05/30/32	
Duret, Gabriel	PVT	Marsac's Company	05/22/32–05/30/32	
Duto, Francis	PVT	Marsac's Company	05/22/32–05/30/32	
Dychus, James	PVT	Noyes' Company	05/21/32–06/09/32	
Eanos, Jehiel	4SG	Preston's Company	05/21/32–06/21/32	
Earl, Morris	PVT	Olds' Company	05/21/32–06/03/32	
Eastburn, Samuel	PVT	Noyes' Company	05/21/32–06/09/32	
Eaton, Alexander S.	PVT	Barnes' Company	05/21/32–06/03/32	PEN

NAME	RANK	MILITARY UNIT	SERVICE DATES	REMARKS
Eaton, Clement C.	PVT	Finche's Company	05/21/32–06/05/32	ASD 06/12/32–06/18/32
Eaton, Sloan	VOL	Daniels' Company	07/2?/32–07/29/32	VTS OAS WNA
Eaton, W. G.	PVT	Finche's Company	05/21/32–06/05/32	
Eayers, John W.	PVT	Goff's Company	06/12/32–06/19/32	
Ebi, Daniel	PVT	Stewart's Company	05/21/32–06/06/32	PEN
Eckler, William	PVT	Harrison's Company	05/21/32–06/21/32	
Eddy, William	PVT	Swarthout's Company	05/22/32–05/31/32	
Edmunds, William	CAP	Edmund's Company	05/22/32–06/06/32	ASD 06/12/32–06/19/32
Edwards, Alexander H.	1LT	Anderson's Company	05/21/32–06/21/32	VTS WNA 07/26/32–07/29/32. PEN
Edwards, Asa	PVT	Drown's Company	05/21/32–06/21/32	
Edwards, Joseph	PVT	Dunham's Company	05/21/32–06/03/32	
Edwards, Lewis	PVT	Gardner's Company	05/19/32–06/21/32	
Edwards, Thomas A.	CLT	F&S 7th Regiment	05/22/32–07/22/32	
Elison, James	VOL	Daniels' Company	07/2?/32–07/29/32	VTS OAS WNA
Elliot, Anthony	PVT	Rowland's Company	05/22/32–05/30/32	
Ellis, William	PVT	Burton's Company	05/22/32–05/31/32	
Elliston, James	PVT	Humphrey's Company	07/27/32–07/29/32	VTS OAS WNA
Enas, Joab	PVT	Drown's Company	05/21/32–06/21/32	
England, Thomas	PVT	White's Company	05/19/32–05/27/32	
Engle, George	PVT	Powers' Company	05/21/32–06/06/32	
Engle, James	PVT	Powers' Company	05/21/32–06/06/32	
Engle, Jonathan M. Jr	LUT	Power's Company	05/??/32–06/??/32	SCU
Engle, Joseph	PVT	Powers' Company	05/21/32–06/06/32	
Englewright, Andrew	PVT	Finch's Company	05/19/32–06/25/32	
Enos, Jacob	PVT	Calhoun's Company	05/21/32–06/06/32	
Enos, Jehiel	4SG	Preston's Company	05/21/32–06/21/32	

Name	Rank	Military Unit	Service Dates	Remarks
Eslow, Isaac	3SG	Bolton's Company	05/21/32–06/03/32	ASD 06/14/32–06/21/32 as PVT
Estis, Selvenus	PVT	Lewis' Company	06/13/32–06/19/32	
Evans, Samuel B.	LUT	Drown's Company	05/21/32–06/21/32	
Evans, U. or V. L.	PVT	Finche's Company	05/21/32–06/05/32	
Evart, Nelson	PVT	Thayer's Company	05/22/32–05/31/32	
Evarts, Erastus S.	PVT	Thayer's Company	05/22/32–05/31/32	
Falconer, John	PVT	Unknown	05/??/32–??/??/32	SCU from Washtenaw County
Fales, Ebenezer	FIF	Thayer's Company	05/22/32–05/31/32	
Fall, Benazah	PVT	Swarthout's Company	05/22/32–05/31/32	
Farley, Amos	PVT	Preston's Company	05/29/32–06/21/32	
Farley, Daniel	PVT	Preston's Company	05/29/32–06/21/32	
Favoo, John	2LT	Jackson's Company	05/22/32–07/22/32	AKA John Farrar
Faxon, E. T.	PVT	Finche's Company	05/21/32–06/05/32	
Feakes, Joseph	PVT	Noyes' Company	05/21/32–06/21/32	
Featherly, Daniel	PVT	Stevens' Company	05/22/32–05/31/32	
Feathers, Joseph	4CP	Preston's Company	05/21/32–06/21/32	
Fellows, James M.	4SG	Harrison's Company	05/21/32–06/09/32	
Fellows, John	PVT	Harrison's Company	05/21/32–06/09/32	PEN
Fellows, Michael	SGM	F&S 11th Regiment	05/21/32–06/21/32	
Fellows, Simon S.	PVT	Harrison's Company	05/21/32–06/21/32	
Feltz, Aaron	PVT	Butler's Company	05/19/32–07/22/32	
Fenstermaker, Soloman	PVT	Finche's Company	05/21/32–06/05/32	ASD 06/12/32–06/18/32
Ferguson, Benjamin	PVT	White's Company	05/19/32–05/23/32	
Ferguson, William	PVT	Butler's Company	05/20/32–06/25/32	
Ferrington, George W.	PVT	Burton's Company	05/22/32–05/31/32	
Field, Chris	PVT	Lewis' Company	05/21/32–06/06/32	ASD 06/13/32–06/19/32

NAME	RANK	MILITARY UNIT	SERVICE DATES	REMARKS
Fifield, Osgood H.	CAP	Jackson Militia	05/??/32–??/??/32	CDM
Filkins, John D.	PVT	Hunter's Company	05/21/32–06/06/32	
Filson, James	3SG	Jackson's Company	05/19/32–07/22/32	
Finch, A. W.	ENS	Silsbe's Company	05/29/32–06/27/32	
Finch, Benoni W.	CAP	Finch's Company	05/19/32–06/25/32	
Finch, Charles B.	1LT	Silsbe's Company	05/29/32–06/27/32	
Finch, Doct	PVT	Preston's Company	05/21/32–06/21/32	
Finch, James B.	ENS	Brookfield's Company	05/21/32–06/21/32	
Finch, John	PVT	Silsbe's Company	05/29/32–06/27/32	
Finch, Marcellus	PVT	Preston's Company	05/21/32–06/21/32	
Finch, Nathaniel	PVT	Silsbe's Company	05/29/32–06/27/32	
Finch, Walter	CPL	Finch's Company	05/19/32–06/25/32	
Finche, Asahel	CAP	Finche's Company	05/21/32–06/05/32	ASD 06/12/32–06/18/32
Finney, John	PVT	Stewart's Company	05/21/32–06/06/32	
Finney, Thomas	PVT	Stewart's Company	05/21/32–06/21/32	
Fisher, Henry	PVT	Swarthout's Company	05/22/32–05/31/32	
Fitch, Charles B.	UNK	Unknown	??/??/32–??/??/32	SCU
Fitch, Frederick	PVT	Finche's Company	05/21/32–06/05/32	
Fitch, Joel	PVT	Lewis' Company	05/21/32–06/06/32	
Fitch, Samuel A.	PVT	Powers' Company	05/21/32–06/21/32	
Flack, George D.	PVT	Rowland's Company	05/22/32–05/31/32	
Fletcher, John W.	CPL	Powers' Company	05/21/32–06/06/32	PEN
Fluellen, John	PVT	Shurte's Company	05/19/32–05/27/32	
Ford, John T.	PVT	Finche's Company	05/21/32–06/05/32	ASD 06/12/32–06/18/32
Foreman, Alexander	PVT	Powers' Company	05/21/32–06/06/32	
Foster, Drury	PVT	Hunter's Company	05/21/32–06/21/32	

NAME	RANK	MILITARY UNIT	SERVICE DATES	REMARKS
Foster, George	PVT	Hunter's Company	05/21/32–06/21/32	
Foster, Hiram	PVT	Powers' Company	05/21/32–06/06/32	
Fournier, Abraim	PVT	Marsac's Company	05/22/32–05/30/32	
Fournier, Louis	PVT	Marsac's Company	05/22/32–05/30/32	
Fowle, James	PVT	Goff's Company	05/22/32–06/06/32	ASD 06/12/32–06/19/32
Fowler, Archibald	PVT	Finche's Company	05/21/32–06/05/32	PEN
Fowler, Henry H.	SUR	F&S 7th Regiment	05/19/32–06/21/32	
Fowler, Joseph H.	PVT	Bolton's Company	06/14/32–06/21/32	
Fowler, Lewman A.	PVT	Stevens' Company	05/22/32–05/31/32	
Fox, Benjamin F.	LUT	Burton's Company	05/22/32–05/31/32	
Fraiks, Joseph	VOL	Daniels' Company	07/2?/32–07/29/32	VTS OAS WNA
Franklin, S.	PVT	Calhoun's Company	05/21/32–06/06/32	
Franklin, Simeon	4CP	Anderson's Company	06/16/32–06/21/32	VTS OAS WNA 07/26/32–07/29/32
Fraser, Alexander D.	MAJ	F&S 1st Division	05/22/32–06/11/32	Division Quartermaster
Frazer, James B.	1SG	Burton's Company	05/22/32–05/31/32	
Freeland, Jonathan C.	PVT	Goff's Company	05/22/32–06/06/32	
Freeman, Daniel	PVT	Noyes' Company	05/21/32–06/09/32	
Freeman, David	PVT	Burton's Company	05/22/32–05/31/32	
Frost, Hiram	PVT	Hixson's Company	05/21/32–06/07/32	
Fuller, Andrew J.	PVT	Swarthout's Company	05/22/32–05/31/32	
Fuller, Samuel S.	PVT	Swarthout's Company	05/22/32–05/31/32	
Fuller, Suiel	PVT	Rowland's Company	05/22/32–05/31/32	
Fullerton, Almond	PVT	Burton's Company	05/22/32–05/31/32	
Fullerton, Henry	PVT	Burton's Company	05/22/32–05/31/32	
Fulton, Alexander	ENS	Curry's Company	05/19/32–06/21/32	
Gailord, William	VOL	Hascall's Company	07/2?/32–07/29/32	VTS OAS WNA

NAME	RANK	MILITARY UNIT	SERVICE DATES	REMARKS
Galaspie, James	PVT	Preston's Company	05/28/32–06/21/32	
Gamble, George W.	PVT	Dunham's Company	05/21/32–06/03/32	
Gamble, George W.	PVT	Stewart's Company	05/21/32–06/21/32	
Gard, John B.	PVT	Curry's Company	05/19/32–06/21/32	PEN
Gard, Jonathan	PVT	Curry's Company	05/19/32–06/21/32	
Gardinier, John	PVT	Burton's Company	05/22/32–05/31/32	
Gardner, Benjamin	VOL	Hascall's Company	07/2?/32–07/29/32	VTS OAS WNA
Gardner, David	SGT	Finch's Company	05/19/32–06/25/32	
Gardner, Joseph	CAP	Gardner's Company	05/19/32–06/21/32	
Gardner, Joseph	PVT	Huston's Company	07/2?/32–07/29/32	VTS OAS WNA
Gardner, R.	PVT	Calhoun's Company	05/21/32–06/06/32	
Gardner, Richard	PVT	Thayer's Company	05/22/32–05/31/32	
Garland, E D.	DMR	Rowland's Company	05/22/32–05/31/32	
Garron, Augustus	PVT	Marsac's Company	05/22/32–05/30/32	
Garron, Joseph	PVT	Marsac's Company	05/22/32–05/30/32	
Garver, Frederick	PVT	Silsbe's Company	05/29/32–06/27/32	
Garver, Henry	PVT	Noyes' Company	05/21/32–06/21/32	
Garwood, Joseph	PVT	Gardner's Company	05/19/32–06/21/32	
Garwood, William	PVT	Gardner's Company	05/19/32–06/21/32	
Gates, Hiram	ENS	Powers' Company	05/21/32–06/21/32	
Gates, Samuel	CPL	Swarthout's Company	05/22/32–05/31/32	
Gay, Simon	2CP	Humphrey's Company	07/27/32–07/29/32	VTS OAS WNA
Gay, Simon	VOL	Daniels' Company	07/2?/32–07/29/32	VTS OAS WNA
Gaynier, Charles	PVT	Rowland's Company	05/22/32–05/31/32	
Gibbs, Nathan Jr.	PVT	Goff's Company	05/22/32–06/06/32	PEN
Gibson, Henry	VOL	Hascall's Company	07/2?/32–07/29/32	VTS OAS WNA

NAME	RANK	MILITARY UNIT	SERVICE DATES	REMARKS
Giddens, Eli	PVT	Barnes' Company	05/21/32–06/03/32	
Giddens, William P.	ENS	Barnes' Company	05/21/32–06/21/32	
Giddings, William P.	VOL	Daniels' Company	07/2?/32–07/29/32	VTS OAS WNA
Gilbert, D. B.	DMR	Harrison's Company	05/21/32–06/21/32	
Gilbert, Harvey	3SG	Hixson's Company	05/21/32–06/07/32	
Giles, James	PVT	Goff's Company	05/22/32–06/06/32	
Gilkey, John L.	PVT	Barnes' Company	05/21/32–06/03/32	
Gill, James M.	1SG	Dunham's Company	05/21/32–06/03/32	AKA James M. Gile
Gillett, James A.	PVT	Silsbe's Company	05/29/32–06/27/32	
Gilmore, Asa	2SG	Finche's Company	05/21/32–06/05/32	
Gilmore, Samuel	PVT	Hunter's Company	05/21/32–06/21/32	
Girard, Augustus	PVT	Marsac's Company	05/22/32–05/30/32	
Gleason, Nathaniel Jr.	PVT	Edmund's Company	05/22/32–06/06/32	PEN
Goble, Elijah	1LT	Curry's Company	05/19/32–06/21/32	
Gobley, John B.	1CP	Curry's Company	05/19/32–06/21/32	
Godfrey, Alexander D.	PVT	Rowland's Company	05/22/32–05/31/32	
Godfrey, Horace	2SG	Preston's Company	05/21/32–06/21/32	
Godfrey, Levi	PVT	Shurte's Company	05/19/32–05/27/32	
Godfry, William	PVT	Huston's Company	07/2?/32–07/29/32	VTS OAS WNA
Goff, Sewell S.	1LT	Goff's Company	05/22/32–06/06/32	ASD 06/12/32–06/19/32
Gohun, Michael R.	PVT	Drown's Company	05/21/32–06/21/32	
Goodell, Brown	DMR	Stevens' Company	05/22/32–05/31/32	
Goodell, E. B.	MUS	Swarthout's Company	05/22/32–05/31/32	
Gooden, Cyrus	PVT	Stevens' Company	05/22/32–05/31/32	Absent without leave
Goodrich, Alanson	VOL	Hascall's Company	07/2?/32–07/29/32	VTS OAS WNA
Goodrich, Chester	VOL	Hascall's Company	07/2?/32–07/29/32	VTS OAS WNA

NAME	RANK	MILITARY UNIT	SERVICE DATES	REMARKS
Goodrich, David	VOL	Hascall's Company	07/2?/32–07/29/32	VTS OAS WNA
Goodrich, Ira	VOL	Hascall's Company	07/2?/32–07/29/32	VTS OAS WNA
Goodrich, Willard	VOL	Hascall's Company	07/2?/32–07/29/32	VTS OAS WNA
Goodspead, David	SGT	Swarthout's Company	05/22/32–05/31/32	
Gothrip, John	PVT	Shurte's Company	05/19/32–05/27/32	
Gouin, Francis	PVT	Marsac's Company	05/22/32–05/30/32	
Gouin, Nicholas	PVT	Marsac's Company	05/22/32–05/30/32	
Gould, William	PVT	Stewart's Company	05/21/32–06/06/32	
Gouldsbury, Benjamin F.	PVT	Edmund's Company	05/22/32–06/06/32	
Gragg, Jacob	PVT	Drown's Company	05/21/32–06/21/32	
Gragg, Robert	PVT	Finche's Company	05/21/32–06/05/32	
Graham, Alexander	VOL	Hascall's Company	07/2?/32–07/29/32	VTS OAS WNA
Grahem, Benjamin	VOL	Hascall's Company	07/2?/32–07/29/32	VTS OAS WNA
Grant, Christ	CPL	Stewart's Company	05/21/32–06/21/32	
Grant, John	ENS	Marsac's Company	05/22/32–05/30/32	
Gray, Jessie	PVT	Stewart's Company	05/21/32–06/06/32	
Gray, Joseph W.	1LT	Finche's Company	06/12/32–06/18/32	
Grefor, John	PVT	Marsac's Company	05/22/32–05/30/32	
Gregory, Samuel	1SG	Goff's Company	05/22/32–06/06/32	ASD 06/12/32–06/19/32
Griffin, Zadock	SGT	Finch's Company	05/19/32–06/25/32	
Griffis, William	PVT	Curry's Company	05/19/32–06/21/32	
Grimes, Hezekiah	PVT	Brookfield's Company	05/21/32–06/21/32	
Grouble, Pharent	PVT	Huston's Company	07/2?/32–07/29/32	VTS OAS WNA
Grub, Andrew	PVT	Finch's Company	05/19/32–06/25/32	
Grubb, Andrew	PVT	White's Company	05/19/32–06/21/32	
Grubb, William	PVT	White's Company	05/19/32–05/23/32	

Name	Rank	Military Unit	Service Dates	Remarks
Guile, James M.	2SG	Bolton's Company	06/14/32–06/21/32	
Guilford, Samuel	VOL	Daniels' Company	07/2?/32–07/29/32	VTS OAS WNA
Guilford, Voluntine	PVT	Harrison's Company	05/21/32–06/09/32	
Guning, James	PVT	Thayer's Company	05/22/32–05/31/32	
Gunsolley, James	LUT	Finch's Company?	??/??/32–??/??/32	Detachment Adjutant
Guoin, Francis	PVT	Marsac's Company	05/22/32–05/30/32	
Guoin, Nicholas	PVT	Marsac's Company	05/22/32–05/30/32	
Hachett, Edward S.	1SG	Bolton's Company	05/21/32–06/03/32	ASD 06/14/32–06/21/32
Hachett, George	PVT	Bolton's Company	05/21/32–06/03/32	ASD 06/14/32–06/21/32
Hacket, Samuel	2CP	Harrison's Company	05/21/32–06/09/32	
Hager, Andrew	VOL	Daniels' Company	07/2?/32–07/29/32	VTS OAS WNA NRE
Haggie, Robert H.	PVT	Hixson's Company	05/21/32–06/07/32	ASD 06/12/32–06/19/32
Hale, I. E.	3CP	Finche's Company	05/21/32–06/05/32	
Haliday, John	PVT	Huston's Company	07/2?/32–07/29/32	VTS OAS WNA
Hall, Clark	PVT	Noyes' Company	05/21/32–06/09/32	
Hall, Elisha	PVT	Barnes' Company	05/21/32–06/03/32	
Hall, George W.	PVT	Silsbe's Company	05/29/32–06/27/32	
Hall, Hiram	PVT	Burton's Company	05/22/32–05/31/32	
Hall, John	PVT	Humphrey's Company	07/27/32–07/29/32	VTS OAS WNA
Hall, Jonathan	PVT	Drown's Company	05/21/32–06/21/32	PEN
Hall, Thomas G.	PVT	Stewart's Company	05/21/32–06/21/32	
Hall, Thomas	PVT	Hunter's Company	05/21/32–06/21/32	
Halsted, John	PVT	Anderson's Company	06/06/32–06/21/32	VTS OAS WNA 07/29/32
Hamilton, David	LUT	Harrison's Company	05/21/32–06/31/32	
Hamilton, Robert	PVT	Jackson's Company	06/08/32–07/03/32	
Hammer, Isaac B.	PVT	Huston's Company	07/2?/32–07/29/32	VTS OAS WNA

188

NAME	RANK	MILITARY UNIT	SERVICE DATES	REMARKS
Hand, John G	2SG	Burton's Company	05/22/32–05/31/32	
Hanson, Abel	VOL	Daniels' Company	07/2?/32–07/29/32	VTS OAS WNA
Hanson, David M.	PVT	Noyes' Company	05/21/32–06/21/32	
Hanson, David M.	VOL	Daniels' Company	07/2?/32–07/29/32	VTS OAS WNA
Harlow, Jonathan	2LT	Humphrey's Company	07/27/32–07/29/32	VTS OAS WNA
Harmon, O. B.	PVT	Powers' Company	05/21/32–06/21/32	
Harper, Benjamin	PVT	Swarthout's Company	05/22/32–05/31/32	
Harper, William	CPL	Swarthout's Company	05/22/32–05/31/32	VTS OAS WNA 07/27/32–07/29/32
Harrington, Daniel B.	PVT	Rowland's Company	05/22/32–05/31/32	
Harrison, Almond	PVT	Goff's Company	05/22/32–06/06/32	
Harrison, Bazel	PVT	Harrison's Company	05/21/32–06/21/32	
Harrison, Elias	VOL	Daniels' Company	07/2?/32–07/29/32	VTS OAS WNA
Harrison, Elias S.	PVT	Harrison's Company	05/21/32–06/09/32	
Harrison, Ephraim	CAP	Harrison's Company	05/21/32–06/21/32	
Harrison, Epraim	1SG	Daniels' Company	07/2?/32–07/29/32	VTS OAS WNA
Harrison, Reuben N.	CAP	F&S 7th Regiment	05/19/32–06/21/32	Assistant Quartermaster
Harrison, Salmon	PVT	Goff's Company	05/22/32–06/06/32	ASD 06/12/32–06/19/32
Harrow, John O.	PVT	Hixson's Company	05/21/32–06/07/32	
Hart, William	PVT	Swarthout's Company	05/22/32–05/31/32	
Hartman, Rensaler C.	PVT	Powers' Company	05/21/32–06/06/32	
Hartman, Ruben	PVT	Stewart's Company	05/21/32–06/06/32	
Hartsough, David	PVT	Olds' Company	??/??/32–??/??/32	Absent
Hartsough, Elijah	PVT	Olds' Company	??/??/32–??/??/32	Absent
Hartsough, John	PVT	Olds' Company	??/??/32–??/??/32	Absent
Hartsough, Joseph	PVT	Bolton's Company	06/14/32–06/21/32	
Harwood, Heman	PVT	Powers' Company	05/21/32–06/21/32	PEN

189

NAME	RANK	MILITARY UNIT	SERVICE DATES	REMARKS
Harwood, Hiram	PVT	Powers' Company	05/21/32–06/21/32	PEN
Hasard, R. S.	PVT	Powers' Company	05/21/32–06/21/32	
Hascall, Charles C.	CAP	Hascall's Company	07/2?/32–07/29/32	VTS OAS WNA
Hascall, John	PVT	Barnes' Company	06/13/32–06/21/32	
Hatch, Ambrose Timothy	QUT	Eleventh Regiment	05/02/32–06/15/32	SCU
Hatch, Charles	PVT	Powers' Company	05/21/32–06/06/32	
Hathaway, William	PVT	Lewis' Company	06/13/32–06/19/32	
Havens, Merit S.	PVT	Rowland's Company	05/22/32–05/31/32	
Havens, Sylvanus	PVT	Finche's Company	05/21/32–06/05/32	
Haverlon, Alanson	PVT	Burton's Company	05/22/32–05/31/32	
Hawks, Isaac	PVT	Thayer's Company	05/22/32–05/31/32	Absent without leave
Haynes, John	PVT	Shurte's Company	05/19/32–05/23/32	
Hays, Andrew L.	PHY	Field & Staff	??/??/32–??/??/32	SCU
Hayward, Rosewell G.	PVT	Stevens' Company	05/22/32–05/31/32	MNI "J"?
Haywood, S. G.	CPL	Swarthout's Company	05/22/32–05/31/32	
Heacox, Adna	PVT	Anderson's Company	05/21/32–06/21/32	
Heacox, James	PVT	Anderson's Company	05/21/32–06/21/32	
Heacox, Joseph	PVT	Burton's Company	05/22/32–05/31/32	
Hecox, Adna A.	PVT	Powers' Company	05/21/32–06/21/32	
Hecox, Hiram A.	PVT	Anderson's Company	05/21/32–06/21/32	
Hecox, James	DMR	Powers' Company	05/21/32–06/06/32	
Hellen, George A.	PVT	Butler's Company	05/20/32–06/25/32	
Hendershott, Caleb	PVT	Drown's Company	05/21/32–06/21/32	
Henderson, Asue	PVT	Rowland's Company	05/22/32–05/31/32	
Henderson, George	ENS	Thayer's Company	05/22/32–05/31/32	
Henderson, Ira B.	PVT	Shurte's Company	05/19/32–05/23/32	

NAME	RANK	MILITARY UNIT	SERVICE DATES	REMARKS
Hendricks, Enos	3CP	Anderson's Company	05/21/32–06/21/32	VTS OAS WNA 07/27/32–07/29/32
Henricks, Peter	PVT	Stevens' Company	05/22/32–05/31/32	
Henshaw, Rheuben	PVT	Huston's Company	07/2?/32–07/29/32	VTS OAS WNA
Herick, Moses	PVT	Bolton's Company	05/21/32–06/03/32	
Herington, Rial	PVT	Swarthout's Company	05/22/32–05/31/32	
Herrington, Hiram	PVT	Stevens' Company	05/22/32–05/31/32	
Hickory, Stephen	PVT	Olds' Company	??/??/32–??/??/32	Absent
Highberger, Simeon	PVT	Powers' Company	05/21/32–06/06/32	
Higley, Philander	PVT	Finch's Company	05/19/32–06/25/32	
Hill, Alvin	4SG	Goff's Company	05/22/32–06/06/32	ASD 06/12/32–06/19/32
Hill, Marvin	PVT	Bolton's Company	05/24/32–06/03/32	
Hill, Nevil	PVT	Bolton's Company	06/14/32–06/21/32	
Hillick, Hugh	2LT	F&S 8th Regiment	05/21/32–06/21/32	CSA Rank uncertain
Hillman, Alvin	PVT	Calhoun's Company	05/21/32–06/06/32	
Hills, Henry	4SG	Hixson's Company	05/21/32–05/25/32	ASD 06/12/32–06/19/32
Hinckley, Adarial	PVT	Rowland's Company	05/22/32–05/31/32	
Hinckley, Luther G.	1CP	Goff's Company	05/22/32–06/06/32	ASD 06/12/32–06/19/32
Hines, John	PVT	Silsbe's Company	05/29/32–06/27/32	
Hinton, Jeremiah	PVT	Butler's Company	05/20/32–06/25/32	
Hitchcock, John B.	PVT	Calhoun's Company	05/21/32–06/07/32	
Hitten, Nathan	PVT	Humphrey's Company	07/27/32–07/29/32	VTS OAS WNA
Hixson, Daniel A.	CAP	Hixson's Company	05/21/32–06/07/32	ASD 06/12/32–06/19/32. PEN
Hizer, Peter H.	PVT	Finche's Company	05/21/32–06/05/32	
Hodge, Andrew	PVT	Humphrey's Company	07/27/32–07/29/32	VTS OAS WNA
Hodge, Horace	PVT	Barnes' Company	05/21/32–06/21/32	
Hodgkins, Silas	PVT	Lewis' Company	06/13/32–06/19/32	

NAME	RANK	MILITARY UNIT	SERVICE DATES	REMARKS
Hoeg, William H.	MAJ	F&S 3rd Brigade	05/21/32–06/20/32	Inspector
Hoffman, George W.	1LT	Huston's Company	07/2?/32–07/29/32	VTS OAS WNA
Hoffman, George William	MAJ	F&S 7th Regiment	05/19/32–06/21/32	Adjutant
Hogan, Daniel	PVT	Powers' Company	05/21/32–06/21/32	
Hogan, Henry	PVT	Powers' Company	05/21/32–06/06/32	
Hogue, James	PVT	Stewart's Company	05/21/32–06/21/32	
Hoistington, Washington	PVT	Stevens' Company	05/22/32–05/31/32	
Holbrook, Benajah	MAJ	F&S 1st Regiment	??/??/32–??/??/32	
Holden, William	PVT	Finch's Company	05/19/32–06/25/32	
Holmes, Dalus T.	PVT	Stewart's Company	05/21/32–06/21/32	
Holmes, Daufemus J.	PVT	Dunham's Company	05/21/32–06/03/32	
Holmes, Thomas	2SG	Dunham's Company	05/21/32–06/03/32	
Holmes, Thomas	FIF	Stevens' Company	05/22/32–05/31/32	
Holmes, Thomas	PVT	Bolton's Company	06/14/32–06/21/32	
Hom, Charles	PVT	Swarthout's Company	05/22/32–05/31/32	
Hooper, Samuel F.	PVT	Hixson's Company	05/21/32–06/07/32	
Hopgood, Dexter	PVT	Silsbe's Company	05/29/32–06/27/32	
Hopkins, James	PVT	Hunter's Company	05/21/32–06/06/32	PEN
Hopkins, William	2CP	Silsbe's Company	05/29/32–06/27/32	
Horton, Orsiman	PVT	Drown's Company	05/21/32–06/21/32	
Hottenstien, Phillip S.	PVT	Hixson's Company	05/21/32–06/07/32	
Hough, David	PVT	Shurte's Company	05/19/32–06/21/32	
Hough, Thomas James	PVT	Humphrey's Company	07/27/32–07/29/32	VTS OAS WNA
Hovey, Hiram S.	PVT	Burton's Company	05/22/32–05/31/32	
How, George E.	PVT	Finche's Company	05/21/32–06/05/32	ASD 06/12/32–06/18/32
Howard, John	TEA	Unknown	??/??/32–??/??/32	SCU With baggage wagon

Name	Rank	Military Unit	Service Dates	Remarks
Howard, John D.	DMR	Finche's Company	05/21/32–06/05/32	ASD 06/12/32–06/18/32
Howard, P.	PVT	Noyes' Company	05/21/32–06/09/32	
Howard, Rochester	PVT	Noyes' Company	05/21/32–06/21/32	PEN
Howe, George	CSA	F&S 8th Regiment	05/21/32–06/21/32	
Howell, Joseph Jr.	PVT	Drown's Company	05/21/32–06/21/32	
Howell, Robert	2CP	Thayer's Company	05/22/32–05/31/32	
Howland, A. M.	PVT	Burton's Company	05/22/32–05/31/32	
Howland, Job C.	FIF	Rowland's Company	05/22/32–05/31/32	
Howlett, Robert	PVT	Swarthout's Company	05/22/32–05/31/32	
Hoyt, Benjamin C.	1LT	Preston's Company	05/21/32–06/21/32	MNI Carlton. PEN
Hoyt, Ransford	4CP	Harrison's Company	05/21/32–06/09/32	
Huff, Abram V.	PVT	Shurte's Company	05/19/32–06/21/32	
Huff, Cornelius	CPL	Finch's Company	05/19/32–06/25/32	
Huff, David	UNK	Unknown	??/??/32–??/??/32	SCU Cass County History p. 287
Huff, Isaac Jr.	PVT	Shurte's Company	05/19/32–06/21/32	
Huff, Isaac Sr.	PVT	Shurte's Company	05/19/32–06/21/32	
Huff, John V.	PVT	Shurte's Company	05/19/32–06/21/32	
Huff, Peter	PVT	Shurte's Company	05/19/32–06/21/32	
Huff, William	PVT	Curry's Company	05/19/32–06/21/32	
Huffman, Martin	PVT	Preston's Company	05/21/32–06/21/32	
Hulard, George	PVT	Burton's Company	05/22/32–05/31/32	
Hultz, Hoglen	PVT	Butler's Company	05/30/32–06/25/32	
Hultz, William C.	PVT	Butler's Company	05/20/32–06/25/32	Wounded at Chicago. PEN
Humphrey, Levi S.	CAP	Humphrey's Company	07/27/32–07/29/32	VTS OAS WNA
Hunible, Thomas	PVT	Rowland's Company	05/22/32–05/31/32	
Hunt, George	PVT	Jackson's Company	05/19/32–07/22/32	

193

NAME	RANK	MILITARY UNIT	SERVICE DATES	REMARKS
Hunt, Hiram B.	ENS	Olds' Company	05/21/32–06/03/32	
Hunt, James M.	PVT	Calhoun's Company	05/21/32–06/06/32	
Hunter, Alexander	PVT	White's Company	05/19/32–05/31/32	
Hunter, John W.	2SG	Rowland's Company	05/22/32–05/31/32	
Hunter, John W.	PVT	Anderson's Company	05/21/32–06/21/32	
Hunter, John W.	PVT	Jackson's Company	06/01/32–07/22/32	
Hunter, Samuel	1SG	White's Company	05/19/32–06/21/32	
Hunter, Thomas	PVT	Silsbe's Company	05/29/32–06/27/32	
Hunter, William	CAP	Hunter's Company	05/21/32–06/21/32	
Hurd, Allan D.	PVT	Hixson's Company	06/12/32–06/19/32	
Huston, Almanson	CAP	Huston's Company	07/2?/32–07/29/32	VTS OAS WNA
Huston, Almanzon	COL	F&S 7th Regiment	05/19/32–06/21/32	
Huston, Hosea B.	LUT	Daniels' Company	07/2?/32–07/29/32	VTS OAS WNA
Huston, Hosea B.	MAJ	F&S 12th Regiment	05/21/32–06/21/32	
Huston, Robert	PVT	Swarthout's Company	05/22/32–05/31/32	
Hutchinson, Chester	PVT	Lewis' Company	06/13/32–06/19/32	
Hutchinson, John	PVT	Lewis' Company	05/21/32–06/06/32	PEN
Hutchinson, William	SGT	Finch's Company	05/19/32–06/25/32	
Huyck, Richard	VOL	Daniels' Company	07/2?/32–07/29/32	VTS OAS WNA
Ingle, Jonathan	LUT	Powers' Company	05/21/32–06/21/32	
Ingleright, Andrew	PVT	Finch's Company	05/19/32–06/25/32	PEN
Ingleright, Jacob	PVT	Jackson's Company	05/21/32–06/04/32	
Ingles, David P.	PVT	Burton's Company	05/22/32–05/31/32	
Isbell, Joel	DMR	Stewart's Company	05/21/32–06/21/32	
Jack, Fulton	PVT	Drown's Company	05/21/32–06/21/32	
Jacks, Joseph L.	3CP	Silsbe's Company	05/29/32–06/27/32	

Name	Rank	Military Unit	Service Dates	Remarks
Jackson, Andrew	CAP	Jackson's Company	05/21/32–06/04/32	
Jackson, Charles	CAP	Jackson's Company	05/22/32–07/22/32	
Jackson, Clark	PVT	Preston's Company	05/29/32–06/21/32	
Jackson, Gregory	PVT	Anderson's Company	07/28/32–07/29/32	VTA OAS WNA
Jackson, Gregory	PVT	Calhoun's Company	05/21/32–06/06/32	
Jackson, Gregory	PVT	Jackson's Company	06/16/32–06/21/32	
Jackson, I. C.	PVT	Burton's Company	05/22/32–05/31/32	
Jackson, Jabez H.	PVT	Edmund's Company	05/22/32–06/06/32	ASD 06/12/32–06/19/32. PEN
Jackson, John	PVT	Lewis' Company	05/21/32–06/06/32	ASD 06/13/32–06/19/32
Jackson, Walter	PVT	Stevens' Company	05/22/32–05/31/32	
Jacobs, Hiram	PVT	Hunter's Company	05/21/32–06/06/32	
James, John	PVT	Butler's Company	05/29/32–06/25/32	
James, Mason I.	VOL	Hascall's Company	07/2?/32–07/29/32	VTS OAS WNA
Jarvis, Lewis	PVT	Rowland's Company	05/22/32–05/31/32	
Jeffers, Charles	PVT	Humphrey's Company	07/27/32–07/29/32	VTS OAS WNA
Jenkins, M.	PVT	Harrison's Company	05/21/32–06/21/32	
Jerome, Orrin	3SG	Harrison's Company	05/21/32–06/09/32	
Jewell, James	PVT	Shurte's Company	05/19/32–06/21/32	
Jewell, Jerome	PVT	Olds' Company	05/21/32–06/03/32	
Jewell, William	PVT	Shurte's Company	05/19/32–06/21/32	
John, Joseph	PVT	Lewis' Company	05/21/32–06/06/32	
Johnson, Daniel	PVT	Finch's Company	05/19/32–06/25/32	PEN
Johnson, E. B.	4CP	Burton's Company	05/22/32–05/31/32	
Johnson, Henry	PVT	Rowland's Company	05/22/32–05/31/32	
Johnson, Horace	VOL	Hascall's Company	07/2?/32–07/29/32	VTS OAS WNA
Johnson, Joseph	PVT	Stevens' Company	05/22/32–05/31/32	

Michigan Men in the Black Hawk War

Name	Rank	Military Unit	Service Dates	Remarks
Johnson, Porter	PVT	Lewis' Company	05/21/32–06/06/32	ASD 06/13/32–06/19/32
Johnson, Richard	PVT	Butler's Company	05/26/32–06/25/32	
Johnson, Silander	PVT	Finche's Company	05/21/32–06/05/32	
Johnson, Wallace	PVT	Lewis' Company	05/21/32–06/06/32	
Johnson, William	VOL	Daniels' Company	07/2?/32–07/29/32	VTS OAS WNA
Johnson, Wilson	PVT	Finch's Company	05/19/32–06/??/32	SCU. RBL
Johnston, G. M.	PVT	Stevens' Company	05/22/32–05/31/32	
Johnston, Henry	PVT	Barnes' Company	05/21/32–06/03/32	
Johnston, Henry	PVT	Bolton's Company	05/21/32–06/03/32	
Jones, B.	PVT	Harrison's Company	05/21/32–06/09/32	
Jones, Beniah Jr.	MAJ	F&S 3rd Brigade	05/21/32–06/20/32	
Jones, Benjamine	VOL	Daniels' Company	07/2?/32–07/29/32	VTS OAS WNA
Jones, Drewrey	PVT	White's Company	05/19/32–05/23/32	
Jones, Edmund	QUA	F&S 3rd Brigade	05/21/32–06/20/32	
Jones, Nathan	1CP	Huston's Company	07/2?/32–07/29/32	VTS OAS WNA
Jordon, Henry C.	1SG	Edmund's Company	05/22/32–06/06/32	PEN
Joslin, Silas	PVT	Thayer's Company	05/22/32–05/31/32	
Joslyn, Charles	PVT	Humphrey's Company	07/27/32–07/29/32	VTS OAS WNA
Josslin, Carloss	4SG	Burton's Company	05/22/32–05/31/32	
Jubinville, Louis	PVT	Marsac's Company	05/22/32–05/30/32	
Judson, Horace D.	PVT	Dunham's Company	05/21/32–06/03/32	
Judson, Isaac B.	PVT	Anderson's Company	05/21/32–06/06/32	VTS OAS WNA 07/29/32
Judson, Lewis B.	PVT	Anderson's Company	05/21/32–06/06/32	
Kavanaugh, James	PVT	Shurte's Company	05/19/32–06/21/32	
Kedzie, James T.	PVT	Goff's Company	05/22/32–06/06/32	ASD 06/12/32–06/19/32. PEN
Keeler, H.	PVT	Harrison's Company	05/21/32–06/21/32	

Name	Rank	Military Unit	Service Dates	Remarks
Keeler, Henry	VOL	Daniels' Company	07/2?/32–07/29/32	VTS OAS WNA
Keith, Alpheus	SGT	Drown's Company	05/21/32–06/21/32	
Kell, Hiram	PVT	Silsbe's Company	05/29/32–06/27/32	
Kell, Hiram	PVT	Stewart's Company	05/21/32–06/21/32	
Keller, David	PVT	Thayer's Company	05/22/32–05/31/32	
Kellogg, Edwin	VOL	Daniels' Company	07/2?/32–07/29/32	VTS OAS WNA
Kelly, Christian	DMR	Thayer's Company	05/22/32–05/31/32	
Kelly, Daniel	PVT	Edmund's Company	05/22/32–06/06/32	ASD 06/12/32–06/19/32
Kelly, Dennis	VOL	Hascall's Company	07/2?/32–07/29/32	VTS OAS WNA
Kelly, Willis	PVT	Lewis' Company	05/21/32–06/06/32	
Kelsey, Abner	ENS	White's Company	05/19/32–06/21/32	
Kennedy, Frederick A.	PVT	Drown's Company	05/21/32–06/21/32	
Kent, James	PVT	Barnes' Company	05/21/32–06/21/32	
Ketchum, George	UNK	Unknown	??/??/32–??/??/32	SCU History of Calhoun Co. p. 232
Ketchum, Sidney	PVT	Barnes' Company	05/21/32–05/27/32	
Keyes, John	VOL	Hascall's Company	07/2?/32–07/29/32	VTS OAS WNA
Kidzie, James S.	PVT	Goff's Company	05/22/32–06/06/32	ASD 06/12/32–06/19/32. PEN
Kimble, Erastus	PVT	Barnes' Company	05/21/32–06/21/32	
Kimble, James L.	PVT	Barnes' Company	05/21/32–06/21/32	
King, Benjamin	PVT	Powers' Company	05/21/32–06/21/32	
King, Henry	PVT	Barnes' Company	05/21/32–06/21/32	
King, John	PVT	Thayer's Company	05/22/32–05/31/32	
King, William R.	2SG	Goff's Company	05/22/32–06/06/32	
Kinnicutt, Jeremiah	PVT	Finche's Company	05/21/32–06/05/32	
Kinzie, Jacob L.	PVT	Finch's Company	05/19/32–06/25/32	
Kinzie, William	PVT	Finch's Company	05/19/32–06/25/32	PEN

NAME	RANK	MILITARY UNIT	SERVICE DATES	REMARKS
Kirk, David	1SG	Finch's Company	05/19/32–06/25/32	
Kirk, David	1SG	Huston's Company	07/2?/32–07/29/32	VTS OAS WNA
Kirk, Elisha	PVT	Powers' Company	05/21/32–06/21/32	
Kirk, Joshua	PVT	White's Company	05/19/32–05/23/32	
Kirk, Thomas	1LT	White's Company	05/19/32–06/21/32	
Kirk, William	PVT	Gardner's Company	05/19/32–06/21/32	
Kirkindall, Isaac	PVT	Curry's Company	05/19/32–06/21/32	
Kitcham, Stephen	PVT	Finche's Company	05/21/32–06/05/32	ASD 06/12/32–06/18/32
Knaggs, Peter W.	PVT	Marsac's Company	05/22/32–05/30/32	
Knaggs, William G.	INT	Anderson's Company	05/21/32–06/21/32	VTS OAS WNA 07/26/32–07/29/32
Knapp, James	COR	Anderson's Company	05/21/32–06/21/32	VTS OAS WNA 07/26/32–07/29/32
Knight, Eli	PVT	Drown's Company	05/21/32–06/21/32	
Knight, James	PVT	Harrison's Company	05/21/32–06/21/32	
Knight, John	PVT	Harrison's Company	05/21/32–06/21/32	
Knight, Richard	VOL	Daniels' Company	07/2?/32–07/29/32	VTS OAS WNA
Knight, Warlin	PVT	Drown's Company	05/21/32–06/21/32	
Knisbite, Robert	PVT	Harrison's Company	05/21/32–06/21/32	
Knisbitt, J.	PVT	Harrison's Company	05/21/32–06/09/32	
Kniss, Peter	PVT	Noyes' Company	05/21/32–06/21/32	
Kniss, Peter	VOL	Daniels' Company	07/2?/32–07/29/32	VTS OAS WNA
Knowlton, James	PVT	Lewis' Company	05/21/32–06/06/32	
Knox, Charles	PVT	Hunter's Company	05/21/32–06/06/32	
Knox, Jacob	PVT	Anderson's Company	06/16/32–06/21/32	VTS OAS WNA 07/27/32–07/29/32
Knox, Jacob	PVT	Hunter's Company	05/21/32–06/06/32	
Knox, Lewis	1SG	Hunter's Company	05/21/32–06/21/32	
Krigger, Michael	1SG	Goff's Company	05/22/32–06/06/32	

Name	Rank	Military Unit	Service Dates	Remarks
Kromer, John	1SG	Anderson's Company	05/21/32–06/21/32	VTS OAS WNA 07/26/32–07/29/32
Kurry, David	PVT	Curry's Company	05/19/32–06/21/32	
Labada, Peter I.	VOL	Daniels' Company	07/2?/32–07/29/32	VTS OAS WNA NRE
Labadie, Peter D.	PVT	Humphrey's Company	07/27/32–07/29/32	VTS OAS WNA
Laduke, Mador	PVT	Marsac's Company	05/22/32–05/30/32	
Laferty, Laughlin	PVT	Stewart's Company	05/21/32–06/06/32	
Lafferty, James	3SG	Marsac's Company	05/22/32–05/30/32	
Lafferty, Joseph	PVT	Jackson's Company	05/22/32–07/22/32	
Lafontaine, Charles	PVT	Rowland's Company	05/22/32–05/31/32	
Lamb, Rufus	PVT	Humphrey's Company	07/27/32–07/29/32	VTS OAS WNA
Lambert, John	PVT	Rowland's Company	05/22/32–05/31/32	
Lancaster, Dennis	PVT	Hixson's Company	06/12/32–06/19/32	
Lancaster, Elizer	PVT	Dunham's Company	05/21/32–06/03/32	
Lancaster, William	PVT	Olds' Company	05/21/32–06/03/32	
Landers, Jacob	PVT	Gardner's Company	05/19/32–05/27/32	
Landers, Solomon	PVT	Gardner's Company	05/19/32–05/27/32	
Landes, Abram	PVT	Finch's Company	05/19/32–06/25/32	PEN
Lane, Jacob	PVT	Calhoun's Company	05/21/32–06/21/32	
Lane, Thomas J.	VOL	Daniels' Company	07/2?/32–07/29/32	VTS OAS WNA
Langdon, John C.	1SG	Marsac's Company	05/22/32–05/30/32	
Langley, William	PVT	Swarthout's Company	05/22/32–05/31/32	PEN
Langloss, Henry	PVT	Stewart's Company	05/21/32–06/21/32	
Langston, Hardy	PVT	White's Company	05/19/32–05/23/32	PEN
Lanning, Jonathan	PVT	Lewis' Company	05/21/32–06/06/32	ASD 06/13/32–06/19/32
Lapage, Andrew	PVT	Marsac's Company	05/22/32–05/30/32	AKA Andre Lapaguyers
Lard, James	PVT	Powers' Company	05/21/32–06/06/32	

NAME	RANK	MILITARY UNIT	SERVICE DATES	REMARKS
Latterell, Orange	PVT	Drown's Company	05/21/32–06/21/32	
LaValey, John	PVT	Preston's Company	05/21/32–06/21/32	
Lawrence, Jeremiah	PVT	Calhoun's Company	05/21/32–06/21/32	
Lazell, George	PVT	Hixson's Company	06/12/32–06/19/32	Absent without leave for 6 days
Leblan, Louis	PVT	Marsac's Company	05/22/32–05/30/32	
LeBlanc, Denis	PVT	Rowland's Company	05/22/32–05/31/32	
Ledaroot, Elaier	1CP	Marsac's Company	05/22/32–05/30/32	
Ledaroot, Enos	PVT	Marsac's Company	05/22/32–05/30/32	
Ledaroot, Lombari	PVT	Marsac's Company	05/22/32–05/30/32	
Ledaroot, Vangil	PVT	Marsac's Company	05/22/32–05/30/32	
Ledyard, Philip	PVT	Bolton's Company	05/21/32–06/03/32	
Lee, Benjamin	3SG	Thayer's Company	05/22/32–05/31/32	
LeRoy, Robert	VOL	Hascall's Company	07/2?/32–07/29/32	VTS OAS WNA
Lewis, Holsey	PVT	Finche's Company	06/12/32–06/18/32	
Lewis, Morgan	PVT	Finche's Company	05/21/32–06/05/32	
Lewis, Orren	3SG	Calhoun's Company	05/21/32–06/06/32	
Lewis, Owen	PVT	Butler's Company	05/20/32–06/25/32	
Lewis, Richard M.	CAP	Lewis' Company	05/21/32–06/06/32	ASD 06/13/32–06/19/32
Ligar, Charles	PVT	Thayer's Company	05/22/32–05/31/32	
Ligar, John	PVT	Thayer's Company	05/22/32–05/31/32	
Lightner, George	PVT	Stewart's Company	05/21/32–06/21/32	
Lindon, Samuel	PVT	Stevens' Company	05/22/32–05/31/32	
Lindsley, Timothy H.	PVT	Humphrey's Company	07/27/32–07/29/32	VTS OAS WNA
Lines, Frederick	PVT	Bolton's Company	06/14/32–06/21/32	
Litchard, Adam	PVT	Finche's Company	05/21/32–06/05/32	
Litchard, Jacob	PVT	Finche's Company	05/21/32–06/05/32	ASD 06/12/32–06/18/32. PEN

NAME	RANK	MILITARY UNIT	SERVICE DATES	REMARKS
Livesay, George	PVT	Lewis' Company	05/21/32–06/06/32	
Lockaby, Benjamin	PVT	Hixson's Company	05/21/32–06/07/32	
Locke, Thomas	PVT	Hunter's Company	05/21/32–06/06/32	
Long, Richard	PVT	Jackson's Company	05/22/32–07/22/32	
Longfellow, Thomas	PVT	Anderson's Company	05/21/32–06/21/32	
Longwell, Selleck	PVT	Harrison's Company	05/21/32–06/21/32	
Loomis, Hubull	SUR	F&S 11th Regiment	05/21/32–06/21/32	
Lothrop, Edwin H.	PVT	Noyes' Company	05/21/32–06/21/32	
Louden, John	PVT	Preston's Company	05/21/32–06/21/32	
Loukes, Sylvenus	PVT	Preston's Company	05/21/32–06/21/32	
Louks, John W.	PVT	Thayer's Company	05/22/32–05/31/32	
Loutt, Marquis	PVT	Shurte's Company	05/19/32–05/27/32	AKA Marquis Loux
Lovell, Cyrus	PVT	Barnes' Company	05/21/32–06/21/32	
Low, George W.	MUS	Butler's Company	05/19/32–06/25/32	
Low, Jacob	CPL	Butler's Company	05/19/32–06/25/32	
Low, Levi	CPL	Butler's Company	05/19/32–06/25/32	
Lowe, William C.	2CP	Edmund's Company	05/22/32–06/06/32	
Lowery, Thomas J.	PVT	Butler's Company	05/20/32–06/25/32	MNI Jefferson
Ludlow, Noah	PVT	Shurte's Company	05/19/32–05/23/32	
Lundt, Jason	PVT	Olds' Company	05/21/32–06/03/32	
Lybrook, Henley C.	PVT	Shurte's Company	05/19/32–05/23/32	
Lybrook, John	PVT	Shurte's Company	05/19/32–05/27/32	
Lynch, John	PVT	Hixson's Company	06/12/32–06/19/32	
Lynes, Frederick	2CP	Dunham's Company	05/21/32–06/03/32	
Lynn, Daniel Jr.	CPL	Stewart's Company	05/21/32–06/06/32	
Lynn, Daniel Jr.	PVT	Anderson's Company	07/29/32	VTS OAS WNA

Michigan Men in the Black Hawk War

NAME	RANK	MILITARY UNIT	SERVICE DATES	REMARKS
Lyon, Jacob	ENS	Stevens' Company	05/22/32–05/31/32	
Lyon, T. T.	PVT	Swarthout's Company	05/22/32–05/31/32	
Lyons, Aaron	PVT	Thayer's Company	05/22/32–05/31/32	
Lyons, Frederick	2CP	Dunham's Company	05/21/32–06/03/32	
Mack, Norman	CPL	Swarthout's Company	05/22/32–05/31/32	
Macklin, Jacob	PVT	Harrison's Company	05/21/32–06/21/32	
Madden, Hiram	VOL	Hascall's Company	07/2?/32–07/29/32	VTS OAS WNA
Maffit, John	PVT	Drown's Company	05/21/32–06/21/32	
Maloy, John T.	PVT	Calhoun's Company	06/07/32–06/21/32	
Maloy, Jon T.	PVT	Hixson's Company	05/21/32–06/01/32	
Mangus, Daniel	PVT	Drown's Company	05/21/32–06/21/32	
Mangus, Soloman	PVT	Drown's Company	05/21/32–06/21/32	
Mann, Lewis W.	VOL	Hascall's Company	07/2?/32–07/29/32	VTS OAS WNA
Manning, John	PVT	Thayer's Company	05/22/32–05/31/32	
Mapes, Barnabas	PVT	Stevens' Company	05/22/32–05/31/32	Substitute for John Miller
Marcuville, John L.	PVT	Shurte's Company	05/19/32–06/21/32	AKA John D. Marenville
Marmin, Stephen	PVT	White's Company	05/19/32–05/23/32	
Marmon, Peter	PVT	Shurte's Company	05/19/32–05/23/32	
Marsac, Joseph F.	CAP	Marsac's Company	05/22/32–05/30/32	AKA Joseph F. Marsarse
Martin, Alfred	PVT	Calhoun's Company	05/21/32–06/21/32	Promoted to Ensign 06/07/32
Martin, E.	PVT	Anderson's Company	05/21/32–06/21/32	
Martin, E.	PVT	Calhoun's Company	05/21/32–06/06/32	
Martin, James	PVT	Powers' Company	05/21/32–06/06/32	
Martin, Joseph	PVT	Calhoun's Company	05/21/32–06/06/32	
Martin, P.	1SG	Calhoun's Company	05/21/32–06/06/32	
Martin, Philamon	PVT	Butler's Company	05/20/32–06/25/32	

Michigan Men in the Black Hawk War

Name	Rank	Military Unit	Service Dates	Remarks
Martin, Seldon	CAP	Butler's Company	05/20/32–06/25/32	TRA Chicago June 6 ROC June 15
Masters, David S.	PVT	Calhoun's Company	05/21/32–06/06/32	
Mathews, George	PVT	Powers' Company	05/21/32–06/06/32	
Matison, Amos	PVT	Humphrey's Company	07/27/32–07/29/32	VTS OAS WNA
Matthews, James	PVT	Jackson's Company	05/22/32–07/22/32	
McBride, John H.	PVT	Rowland's Company	05/22/32–05/31/32	
McCall, Franklin	2SG	White's Company	05/19/32–07/01/32	
McCall, John	3SG	Preston's Company	05/21/32–06/21/32	
McCartney, Samuel	PVT	Rowland's Company	05/22/32–05/31/32	
McCartny, Patrick	PVT	Stevens' Company	05/22/32–05/31/32	
McCartny, William	ENS	Finch's Company	05/19/32–06/25/32	DIS as ENS 06/09/32, kept as SUP
McCarty, James	2SG	Bolton's Company	05/21/32–06/03/32	ASD 06/14/32–06/21/32 as PVT
McCay, Richard	PVT	Brookfield's Company	05/19/32–06/21/32	
McClarey, David	PVT	White's Company	05/19/32–05/31/32	
McClarey, Isaac	PVT	White's Company	05/19/32–05/31/32	
McClintley, William	PVT	Humphrey's Company	07/27/32–07/29/32	VTS OAS WNA
McCord, Cornahum	1CP	Burton's Company	05/22/32–05/31/32	
McCord, David	PVT	Burton's Company	05/22/32–05/31/32	
McCormick, James	PVT	Butler's Company	05/29/32–06/25/32	
McCorty, Owen	PVT	Thayer's Company	05/22/32–05/31/32	
McCoy, Archibald B.	PVT	Humphrey's Company	07/27/32–07/29/32	VTS OAS WNA
McCoy, Henry	PVT	Gardner's Company	05/19/32–05/29/32	
McCoy, Henry	PVT	Huston's Company	07/2?/32–07/29/32	VTS OAS WNA
McCoy, Richard	PVT	Gardner's Company	05/19/32–06/21/32	
McCoy, Russel	ENS	Finch's Company	06/09/32–06/25/32	
McCrary, Preston J.	1SG	Harrison's Company	05/21/32–06/09/32	AKA McCreary

NAME	RANK	MILITARY UNIT	SERVICE DATES	REMARKS
McDaniel, John	PVT	Gardner's Company	05/19/32–06/21/32	
McDaniel, John	PVT	Huston's Company	07/2?/32–07/29/32	
McDonald, Richard	PVT	Thayer's Company	05/22/32–05/31/32	
McDowell, Thomas	PVT	Humphrey's Company	07/27/32–07/29/32	VTS OAS WNA
McElvain, Thomas	PVT	Noyes' Company	05/21/32–06/09/32	
McEnterfee, Eli	PVT	Stewart's Company	05/21/32–06/06/32	
McFarlane, John	PVT	Rowland's Company	05/22/32–05/31/32	
McFarlin, Franklin	PVT	Stevens' Company	05/22/32–05/31/32	
McGraw, Edward M.	PVT	Rowland's Company	05/22/32–05/31/32	
McGraw, Virgil W.	PVT	Rowland's Company	05/22/32–05/31/32	
McIntosh, John	PVT	White's Company	05/19/32–07/06/32	
McIntosh, William	PVT	White's Company	05/19/32–05/23/32	
McKaleb, William	1LT	Humphrey's Company	07/27/32–07/29/32	VTS OAS WNA
McKee, Samuel	1CP	Thayer's Company	05/22/32–05/31/32	
McKee, Samuel	PVT	Powers' Company	05/21/32–06/06/32	
McKee, Samuel	PVT	Thayer's Company	05/22/32–05/31/32	
McKee, William	SGT	Powers' Company	05/21/32–06/06/32	
McKey, Anthony	PVT	Goff's Company	05/22/32–06/06/32	
McKinney, Micajah	1CP	Shurte's Company	05/19/32–06/21/32	
McKinstry, David C.	COL	F&S 3rd Brigade	05/30/32–06/20/32	QUG Rank uncertain
McKinzie, Charles M.	PVT	Lewis' Company	05/21/32–06/06/32	
McKinzie, George	PVT	Lewis' Company	06/13/32–06/19/32	
McLain, Maris	PVT	Humphrey's Company	07/27/32–07/29/32	VTS OAS WNA
McLary, David	PVT	Huston's Company	07/2?/32–07/29/32	VTS OAS WNA
McLevain, Thomas	VOL	Daniels' Company	07/2?/32–07/29/32	VTS OAS WNA
McLevain, William	VOL	Daniels' Company	07/2?/32–07/29/32	VTS OAS WNA

Name	Rank	Military Unit	Service Dates	Remarks
McLin, Samuel	PVT	Harrison's Company	05/21/32–06/21/32	
McLin, Thomas	PVT	Harrison's Company	05/21/32–06/09/32	
McMillen, Albert	CPL	Powers' Company	05/21/32–06/21/32	
McMillen, Anuncias	PVT	Rowland's Company	05/22/32–05/31/32	
McMillen, Franklin	1SG	Powers' Company	05/21/32–06/06/32	
McMillen, John	PVT	Powers' Company	05/21/32–06/06/32	
McNair, William	COL	F&S 8th Regiment	05/21/32–06/21/32	
McNeary, E.	SGT	Butler's Company	05/19/32–06/25/32	
McPharson, Joseph	PVT	Shurte's Company	05/19/32–05/23/32	
McQuillon, Edward	PVT	Humphrey's Company	07/27/32–07/29/32	VTS OAS WNA
McQuillon, Lyman	PVT	Humphrey's Company	07/27/32–07/29/32	VTS OAS WNA
McRay, James B.	PVT	Drown's Company	05/21/32–06/21/32	
Meacham, Lyman	1SG	Silsbe's Company	05/29/32–06/27/32	
Mead, Henry	PVT	Noyes' Company	05/21/32–06/21/32	
Meed, J.	PVT	Harrison's Company	05/21/32–06/09/32	
Meek, Andrew	PVT	Rowland's Company	05/22/32–05/31/32	
Meigs, Charles	PVT	Humphrey's Company	07/27/32–07/29/32	VTS OAS WNA
Meldrum, William	UNK	Unassigned	??/??/32–??/??/32	Expressman
Mercer, William	PVT	Noyes' Company	05/21/32–06/21/32	PEN
Merk, Johnson	PVT	Anderson's Company	05/27/32–06/21/32	
Merrick, Rufus	PVT	Edmund's Company	06/12/32–06/19/32	
Merwin, Chauncey C.	ENS	Noyes' Company	05/21/32–06/21/32	
Messmore, Joseph	PVT	Thayer's Company	05/22/32–05/31/32	
Mette, Antoine	LUT	Marsac's Company	05/22/32–05/30/32	
Metty, Charles	PVT	Thayer's Company	05/22/32–05/31/32	
Michael, Alonzo	PVT	Goff's Company	05/22/32–06/06/32	ASD 06/12/32–06/19/32

Michigan Men in the Black Hawk War

Name	Rank	Military Unit	Service Dates	Remarks
Michimin, Martin	PVT	Barnes' Company	05/21/32–06/21/32	
Mickley, Daniel	4SG	Edmund's Company	05/22/32–06/06/32	ASD 06/12/32–06/19/32
Milin, Samuel	PVT	Harrison's Company	05/21/32–06/21/32	
Milin, Thomas	PVT	Harrison's Company	05/21/32–06/09/32	
Millard, William	PVT	Powers' Company	05/21/32–06/06/32	
Millen, Jacob	PVT	Harrison's Company	05/21/32–06/21/32	
Miller, Anthony	4CP	Shurte's Company	05/19/32–06/21/32	
Miller, Jacob	PVT	Preston's Company	05/21/32–06/21/32	
Miller, John W.	PVT	Anderson's Company	05/27/32–06/21/32	VTS OAS WNA 07/28/32–07/29/32
Miller, John (1)	PVT	Calhoun's Company	05/21/32–06/06/32	
Miller, John (2)	PVT	Calhoun's Company	05/21/32–06/06/32	
Miller, Peter	PVT	Calhoun's Company	05/21/32–06/06/32	
Miller, William	1CP	Noyes' Company	05/21/32–06/09/32	
Millet, Martin	ENS	Edmund's Company	05/22/32–06/06/32	
Millet, Samuel P.	PVT	Drown's Company	05/21/32–06/21/32	
Mills, John	PVT	Drown's Company	05/21/32–06/21/32	
Mills, Simeon	PVT	Barnes' Company	05/21/32–06/21/32	
Mills, Sylvester	DMR	Barnes' Company	05/21/32–06/03/32	
Minchill, Elias	PVT	Barnes' Company	05/21/32–06/21/32	
Minor, Milo	DMR	Burton's Company	05/22/32–05/31/32	PEN
Mitchell, Alonzo	PVT	Goff's Company	05/22/32–06/06/32	ASD 06/12/32–06/19/32
Mitchell, Timothy	PVT	Drown's Company	05/21/32–06/21/32	
Mittez, Antoine	PVT	Humphrey's Company	07/27/32–07/29/32	VTS OAS WNA
Moffett, L. W.	PVT	Barnes' Company	05/21/32–06/21/32	
Mond, Archy D.	PVT	Butler's Company	05/20/32–06/25/32	
Mondingen, Jacob	PVT	Swarthout's Company	05/22/32–05/31/32	

NAME	RANK	MILITARY UNIT	SERVICE DATES	REMARKS
Montz, Joseph	PVT	Rowland's Company	05/22/32–05/31/32	
Moore, Benjamin B.	3CP	Thayer's Company	05/22/32–05/31/32	
Moore, George C.	PVT	Thayer's Company	05/22/32–05/31/32	Absent without leave
Moore, Samuel	PVT	Humphrey's Company	07/27/32–07/29/32	VTS OAS WNA
Morain, Denne	PVT	Marsac's Company	05/22/32–05/30/32	
Moran, George	PVT	Jackson's Company	05/19/32–06/20/32	
Moran, Peter	PVT	Marsac's Company	05/22/32–05/30/32	
More, Gideon	PVT	Harrison's Company	05/21/32–06/21/32	
More, Gideon	VOL	Daniels' Company	07/2?/32–07/29/32	VTS OAS WNA
More, Nelson	PVT	Rowland's Company	05/22/32–05/31/32	
More, Silas	PVT	Finche's Company	05/21/32–06/05/32	
Moreland, Jacob	PVT	Curry's Company	05/19/32–06/21/32	
Morgan, Chauncey	PVT	Bolton's Company	05/24/32–06/03/32	
Morgan, William	1CP	Humphrey's Company	07/27/32–07/29/32	VTS OAS WNA
Morris, Dolphin	PVT	Curry's Company	05/19/32–06/21/32	
Morris, James	PVT	Curry's Company	05/19/32–06/21/32	
Morris, John	1SG	Curry's Company	05/19/32–06/21/32	
Morris, Samuel	PVT	Curry's Company	05/19/32–06/21/32	
Morse, John	FIM	F&S 3rd Brigade	05/24/43–06/03/32	
Mortimer, Edward	PVT	Hunter's Company	05/21/32–06/06/32	
Morton, Samuel	LUT	Finch's Company	05/19/32–06/25/32	
Mountain, Samuel	PVT	Huston's Company	07/2?/32–07/29/32	VTS OAS WNA
Moyiers, Levi	PVT	Drown's Company	05/21/32–06/21/32	
Mudget, Myron	1SG	Finche's Company	05/21/32–06/05/32	
Mudgit, Truman M.	PVT	Drown's Company	05/21/32–06/21/32	PEN
Mukins, Henry	PVT	Jackson's Company	05/22/32–07/22/32	

NAME	RANK	MILITARY UNIT	SERVICE DATES	REMARKS
Mulkin, Allen	4CP	Thayer's Company	05/22/32–05/31/32	
Munger, Tilson	PVT	Thayer's Company	05/22/32–05/31/32	
Munroe, J. R.	ENS	Harrison's Company	05/21/32–06/21/32	
Munson, Samuel C.	VOL	Hascall's Company	07/2?/32–07/29/32	VTS OAS WNA
Murdock, Tilson	PVT	Hixson's Company	05/21/32–06/07/32	ASD 06/12/32–06/19/32
Murray, John	PVT	Stevens' Company	05/22/32–05/31/32	
Murry, Alfred H.	PVT	Anderson's Company	05/21/32–06/21/32	VTS OAS WNA 07/28/32–07/29/32
Murwin, Shelton	FIM	F&S 8th Regiment	05/21/32–06/21/32	
Myers, James	PVT	Thayer's Company	05/22/32–05/31/32	
Myers, Job	VOL	Daniels' Company	07/2?/32–07/29/32	VTS OAS WNA
Myers, John	PVT	Lewis' Company	05/21/32–06/06/32	ASD 06/13/32–06/19/32
Myres, Jobe	PVT	Barnes' Company	05/21/32–06/21/32	
Nash, Ira	DMM	F&S 7th Regiment	05/19/32–06/21/32	
Nash, Jefferson	PVT	Finche's Company	05/21/32–05/30/32	Deserted at Niles MI
Neice, Alvin	PVT	Finche's Company	05/21/32–06/05/32	
Newell, David	PVT	Rowland's Company	05/22/32–05/31/32	
Newell, Francis	PVT	Stewart's Company	05/21/32–06/21/32	
Newell, George	PVT	Humphrey's Company	07/27/32–07/29/32	VTS OAS WNA
Newell, William B.	PVT	Lewis' Company	05/21/32–06/06/32	ASD 06/13/32–06/19/32
Newhall, John S.	PVT	Anderson's Company	05/29/32–06/21/32	07/29/32 VTS OAS WNA
Nichols, William	FIF	Burton's Company	05/22/32–05/31/32	
Nicholson, Ambrose	STO	F&S 3rd Brigade	05/21/32–06/30/32	
Nicholson, David F.	PVT	Shurte's Company	05/19/32–06/21/32	
Nicholson, George	SGT	Butler's Company	05/19/32–06/25/32	
Nicholson, William	4SG	Silsbe's Company	05/29/32–06/27/32	
Nixon, James W.	PVT	Silsbe's Company	05/29/32–06/27/32	

NAME	RANK	MILITARY UNIT	SERVICE DATES	REMARKS
Nixon, William	FIF	Finche's Company	05/21/32–06/05/32	ASD 06/12/32–06/18/32
Nolen, H.	PVT	Harrison's Company	05/21/32–06/09/32	
Noris, Benjamin	PVT	Thayer's Company	05/22/32–05/31/32	
Norris, B. F.	PVT	Burton's Company	05/22/32–05/31/32	
Northrup, Cornelius	PVT	Barnes' Company	05/21/32–06/21/32	
Norton, Howel B.	PVT	Hixson's Company	05/21/32–06/07/32	
Norton, Levi D.	PVT	Butler's Company	05/20/32–06/25/32	
Norton, Silas	PVT	White's Company	05/19/32–05/23/32	
Noyce, Samuel	PVT	Powers' Company	05/21/32–06/06/32	
Noyes, James	CAP	Noyes' Company	05/21/32–06/21/32	
O'Brian, Elijah	DMM	F&S 11th Regiment	05/21/32–06/21/32	
O'Harro, J.	PVT	Harrison's Company	05/21/32–06/09/32	
O'Harrow, James	VOL	Daniels' Company	07/2?/32–07/29/32	VTS OAS WNA
Obair, Joseph	PVT	Thayer's Company	05/22/32–05/31/32	
Obrian, Elijah	PVT	Anderson's Company	07/27/32–07/29/32	VTS OAS WNA
Odell, James	PVT	Stewart's Company	05/21/32–06/06/32	
Odle, John	PVT	White's Company	05/19/32–05/23/32	
Odle, Josiah	PVT	White's Company	05/19/32–05/23/32	
Odle, Thomas	PVT	White's Company	05/19/32–05/27/32	
Olds, Abel	PVT	Olds' Company	05/21/32–06/03/32	
Olds, Dexter	3CP	Olds' Company	05/21/32–06/03/32	
Olds, James	CAP	Olds' Company	05/21/32–06/03/32	
Oliver, John C.	LUT	Calhoun's Company	05/21/32–06/21/32	
Oliver, Thomas	PVT	Calhoun's Company	05/21/32–06/06/32	
Olmstead, Israel	PVT	Burton's Company	05/22/32–05/31/32	
Omstead, Moses	PVT	Dunham's Company	05/21/32–06/03/32	

NAME	RANK	MILITARY UNIT	SERVICE DATES	REMARKS
Omstead, Philip	1CP	Dunham's Company	05/21/32–06/03/32	
Osborn, Nathaniel T.	SGT	Finche's Company	06/12/32–06/18/32	
Osmore, Henry	PVT	Burton's Company	05/22/32–05/??/32	Deserted
Overfield, John E.	CPL	Powers' Company	05/21/32–06/21/32	
Owlet, Robert	PVT	Swarthout's Company	05/22/32–05/31/32	
Oxtell, William	PVT	Butler's Company	05/27/32–06/25/32	
Page, Curtis	DMR	Finche's Company	06/12/32–06/18/32	
Page, David	PVT	Jackson's Company	05/21/32–06/04/32	
Page, Jefferson	PVT	Goff's Company	05/22/32–06/06/32	ASD 06/12/32–06/19/32
Page, Wilder	PVT	Calhoun's Company	05/21/32–06/06/32	
Palmer, Alexander	CPL	Drown's Company	05/21/32–06/21/32	
Palmer, Jesse	PVT	Calhoun's Company	05/21/32–06/21/32	
Pappin, Bazil	PVT	Rowland's Company	05/22/32–05/31/32	
Parker, Amasa S.	PVT	Barnes' Company	05/21/32–06/03/32	
Parker, James	PVT	Barnes' Company	05/21/32–06/21/32	
Parker, John	PVT	Barnes' Company	05/21/32–06/03/32	
Parker, John	PVT	Hunter's Company	05/21/32–06/21/32	
Parker, Joshua	PVT	Humphrey's Company	07/27/32–07/29/32	VTS OAS WNA
Parker, William	PVT	Drown's Company	05/21/32–06/21/32	
Parkinson, John	PVT	Bolton's Company	05/21/32–06/03/32	
Parks, Calvin C.	VOL	Hascall's Company	07/2?/32–07/29/32	VTS OAS WNA
Parrish, Lewis D.	PVT	Calhoun's Company	05/21/32–06/06/32	
Parrish, Lewis J.	PVT	Butler's Company	05/20/32–06/25/32	
Parshall, Luther	PVT	Swarthout's Company	05/22/32–05/31/32	
Parsols, Jacob	1CP	Hunter's Company	05/21/32–06/21/32	
Parsons, David J.	PVT	Dunham's Company	05/21/32–06/03/32	

Name	Rank	Military Unit	Service Dates	Remarks
Patchen, William H.	MAJ	F&S 8th Regiment	05/21/32–06/21/32	
Pate, Alva	PVT	Burton's Company	05/22/32–05/31/32	
Patrick, Johnson	2SG	Daniels' Company	07/2?/32–07/29/32	VTS OAS WNA
Patrick, Johnson	SGM	F&S 12th Regiment	05/21/32–06/21/32	
Patrick, Thomas	PVT	Shurte's Company	05/19/32–05/23/32	
Patten, John	PVT	Humphrey's Company	07/27/32–07/29/32	VTS OAS WNA
Patterson, Caleb	PVT	Drown's Company	05/21/32–06/21/32	
Patterson, Ellery	CPL	Drown's Company	05/21/32–06/21/32	
Patterson, Joseph	PVT	Lewis' Company	06/13/32–06/19/32	
Patterson, Michael A.	SUR	F&S 8th Regiment	05/21/32–06/21/32	
Patton, John	PVT	Humphrey's Company	07/27/32–07/29/32	VTS OAS WNA
Paul, James M.	2CP	Anderson's Company	05/27/32–06/21/32	VTS OAS WNA 07/26/32–07/29/32
Pease, Daniel	VOL	Hascall's Company	07/2?/32–07/29/32	VTS OAS WNA
Peck, Silas	2CP	Burton's Company	05/22/32–05/31/32	
Peck, Thomas	PVT	Noyes' Company	05/21/32–06/09/32	
Pedigrew, John	PVT	Finch's Company	05/19/32–06/25/32	
Pedigrue, James	ENS	Shurte's Company	05/19/32–06/21/32	
Pegg, Joseph	PVT	White's Company	05/19/32–05/23/32	
Pegg, Reuben	PVT	White's Company	05/19/32–05/23/32	
Peltier, Isadore T.	PVT	Humphrey's Company	07/27/32–07/29/32	VTS OAS WNA
Peltier, John	PVT	Jackson's Company	06/22/32–07/22/32	
Peltier, Simon	PVT	Marsac's Company	05/22/32–05/30/32	
Pendlim, Andrew	PVT	White's Company	05/19/32–05/23/32	
Pennock, George W.	SGT	Finche's Company	06/12/32–06/18/32	
Pepper, Edward	PVT	Swarthout's Company	05/22/32–05/31/32	
Perkison, John	PVT	Bolton's Company	05/21/32–06/03/32	

NAME	RANK	MILITARY UNIT	SERVICE DATES	REMARKS
Perrin, Horrace	PVT	Drown's Company	05/21/32–06/21/32	
Perrine, John	PVT	Harrison's Company	05/21/32–06/09/32	
Perry, Marvin	PVT	Goff's Company	06/12/32–06/19/32	
Perry, W. T.	PVT	Swarthout's Company	05/22/32–05/31/32	
Persons, David J.	PVT	Dunham's Company	05/21/32–06/03/32	
Persons, Hiram	2CP	Rowland's Company	05/22/32–05/31/32	
Persons, Jarid I.	PVT	Bolton's Company	06/14/32–06/21/32	
Pettibone, R.	PVT	Swarthout's Company	05/22/32–05/31/32	
Pettinbone, M.	PVT	Swarthout's Company	05/22/32–05/31/32	
Petty, Peleg	PVT	Goff's Company	05/22/32–06/06/32	AKA Peleg Pettis
Petty, R. K.	PVT	Lewis' Company	05/21/32–06/06/32	
Pettys, Daniel	PVT	Humphrey's Company	07/27/32–07/29/32	VTS OAS WNA
Phelps, Aurunah	PVT	Calhoun's Company	05/21/32–06/21/32	
Phelps, Hiram	PVT	Anderson's Company	06/16/32–06/21/32	VTS OAS WNA 07/28/32–07/29/32
Phelps, Hiram	PVT	Calhoun's Company	05/21/32–06/06/32	
Phelps, John	PVT	Calhoun's Company	05/21/32–06/06/32	
Philips, Asahel	CPL	Powers' Company	05/21/32–06/06/32	
Philips, Daniel	PVT	Gardner's Company	05/19/32–06/21/32	
Phillips, William	VOL	Hascall's Company	07/2?/32–07/29/32	VTS OAS WNA
Picket, Presley	PVT	Brookfield's Company	05/21/32–06/21/32	
Pierce, Richard	PVT	Hunter's Company	05/21/32–06/21/32	
Pillbean, Joseph	PVT	Finche's Company	05/21/32–06/05/32	ASD 06/12/32–06/18/32
Pine, Alvah	MUS	Swarthout's Company	05/22/32–05/31/32	
Pine, Ephraim	PVT	Swarthout's Company	05/22/32–05/31/32	
Piper, Asa	PVT	Burton's Company	05/22/32–05/31/32	
Pirams, Silas	PVT	White's Company	05/19/32–05/27/32	

NAME	RANK	MILITARY UNIT	SERVICE DATES	REMARKS
Pittman, Daniel	CLT	F&S 8th Regiment	05/21/32–06/21/32	PEN
Place, William A.	PVT	Burton's Company	05/22/32–05/31/32	
Plummer, Daniel A.	SGT	Barnes' Company	05/21/32–06/03/32	
Pomeroy, Charles W.	ENS	Hixson's Company	05/21/32–06/07/32	ASD 06/12/32–06/19/32. PEN
Pool, Isaac	PVT	Burton's Company	05/22/32–05/31/32	
Post, Russell	PVT	Powers' Company	05/21/32–06/21/32	
Postall, Charles	VOL	Hascall's Company	07/2?/32–07/29/32	VTS OAS WNA
Potter, Abiel	QUS	F&S 3rd Brigade	05/21/32–06/20/32	
Potter, John	QUS	F&S 3rd Brigade	05/21/32–06/20/32	
Potter, Z. B.	BUG	Burton's Company	05/22/32–05/31/32	
Powers, Henry	CAP	Powers' Company	05/21/32–06/21/32	
Powers, John	PVT	Lewis' Company	05/21/32–06/06/32	
Powers, William	PVT	Barnes' Company	05/21/32–06/03/32	
Prater, Jonathan	3SG	Shurte's Company	05/19/32–06/21/32	
Premo, Francis	PVT	Hunter's Company	05/21/32–06/06/32	
Preston, Asaph S.	PVT	Preston's Company	05/21/32–06/21/32	
Preston, Fowler	CAP	Preston's Company	05/19/32–06/21/32	
Preston, John Jr.	PVT	Goff's Company	06/12/32–06/19/32	
Price, John	PVT	Burton's Company	05/22/32–05/31/32	
Pricket, Presley	PVT	Brookfield's Company	05/21/32–06/21/32	
Prine, John	PVT	Harrison's Company	05/21/32–06/09/32	
Pritchette, Kintzing	CSY	F&S 7th Regiment	05/19/32–07/22/32	
Prymall, Brown	PVT	Silsbe's Company	05/29/32–06/27/32	
Purdy, Lewis	PVT	Stevens' Company	05/22/32–05/31/32	
Putnam, Benjamin F.	PVT	Shurte's Company	05/19/32–06/21/32	
Putnam, Ira H.	PVT	Shurte's Company	05/19/32–06/21/32	

Name	Rank	Military Unit	Service Dates	Remarks
Putnam, Orlean	PVT	Shurte's Company	05/19/32–06/21/32	
Quagley, John	VOL	Daniels' Company	07/2?/32–07/29/32	VTS OAS WNA
Quick, Elijah	PVT	Thayer's Company	05/22/32–05/31/32	
Quigly, J. H.	PVT	Noyes' Company	05/21/32–06/09/32	
Ramor, Francis	PVT	Marsac's Company	05/22/32–05/30/32	
Randal, J.	PVT	Harrison's Company	05/21/32–06/09/32	
Ransdell, Joshua	PVT	Dunham's Company	05/21/32–06/03/32	
Raymond, Oliver	ENS	Hunter's Company	05/21/32–06/06/32	
Reams, Moses	PVT	Shurte's Company	05/19/32–05/23/32	
Reams, Silas	PVT	White's Company	05/19/32–05/27/32	
Reddick, John B.	PVT	Silsbe's Company	05/29/32–06/27/32	
Redfield, Alexander H.	CLT	F&S 7th Regiment	05/19/32–07/22/32	Rank uncertain. QUT. MNI Heman
Reed, Don A.	PVT	Finche's Company	06/12/32–06/18/32	
Reed, Harvey	PVT	Shurte's Company	05/19/32–05/23/32	
Reed, John	PVT	Drown's Company	05/21/32–06/21/32	
Reed, John C.	1CP	Olds' Company	05/21/32–06/03/32	
Reed, Rufus D.	DMR	Finche's Company	05/21/32–06/05/32	ASD 06/12/32–06/18/32
Reeves, Isaac	2SG	Stevens' Company	05/22/32–05/31/32	
Reopell, Ambrose	2SG	Thayer's Company	05/22/32–05/31/32	
Reopell, Joseph	PVT	Thayer's Company	05/22/32–05/31/32	
Reopell, Tesant	PVT	Thayer's Company	05/22/32–05/31/32	
Revor, Joseph	PVT	Marsac's Company	05/22/32–05/30/32	
Reynolds, Buel	VOL	Daniels' Company	07/2?/32–07/29/32	VTS OAS WNA
Reynolds, Hiram	PVT	Hixson's Company	05/21/32–06/07/32	ASD 06/12/32–06/19/32
Reynolds, Samuel	PVT	Anderson's Company	05/21/32–06/21/32	VTS OAS WNA 07/27/32–07/29/32
Rhubart, Jacob Jr.	PVT	Thayer's Company	05/22/32–05/31/32	

Name	Rank	Military Unit	Service Dates	Remarks
Ribble, Chris	PVT	Gardner's Company	05/19/32–06/21/32	
Rice, Abner	PVT	Hixson's Company	05/21/32–06/07/32	
Rice, Ira	PVT	Anderson's Company	05/29/32–06/21/32	VTS OAS WNA 07/29/32
Rice, Moses	PVT	Anderson's Company	05/29/32–06/21/32	VTS OAS WNA 07/29/32
Rice, Paul	PVT	Hixson's Company	05/21/32–06/07/32	
Rich, Estes	PVT	Barnes' Company	05/21/32–06/21/32	
Rich, Samuel	PVT	Curry's Company	05/19/32–06/21/32	
Richard, Leonard	PVT	Stewart's Company	05/21/32–06/06/32	
Richardson, Hiram	PVT	White's Company	05/19/32–05/31/32	
Richardson, John G.	PVT	Dunham's Company	05/24/32–06/03/32	Absent without leave
Richardson, Nathaniel S.	PVT	Powers' Company	05/21/32–06/06/32	
Richardson, Oragin D.	VOL	Hascall's Company	07/2?/32–07/29/32	VTS OAS WNA
Rickkart, Frederick	PVT	Gardner's Company	05/19/32–05/27/32	
Rickstraw, Charles	PVT	Powers' Company	05/21/32–06/21/32	
Riggs, Alfred S.	PVT	Dunham's Company	05/24/32–06/03/32	Absent without leave
Right, Dennis	PVT	Huston's Company	07/2?/32–07/29/32	VTS WNA. AKA Dennis Wright
Rivard, Ferdinand	PVT	Marsac's Company	05/22/32–05/30/32	
Rivard, John B.	PVT	Marsac's Company	05/22/32–05/30/32	
Rivard, Lewis M.	PVT	Marsac's Company	05/22/32–05/30/32	
Rivard, Richard	PVT	Marsac's Company	05/22/32–05/30/32	
Rivor, Edward	2SG	Marsac's Company	05/22/32–05/30/32	
Rivor, Lambert	4SG	Marsac's Company	05/22/32–05/30/32	
Roads, Lyman	3CP	Lewis' Company	05/21/32–06/06/32	
Roady, Edmond	PVT	Lewis' Company	05/21/32–06/06/32	
Robbins, Moses	PVT	Anderson's Company	07/29/32	VTS OAS WNA
Robbs, Samuel	PVT	Thayer's Company	05/22/32–05/31/32	

NAME	RANK	MILITARY UNIT	SERVICE DATES	REMARKS
Robertjohn, Moses	PVT	Marsac's Company	05/22/32–05/30/32	
Roberts, Moses	PVT	Hunter's Company	05/21/32–06/06/32	
Roberts, Robert E.	1SG	Rowland's Company	05/22/32–05/31/32	
Robertson, Ambrose	PVT	Finche's Company	05/21/32–06/05/32	ASD 06/12/32–06/18/32
Robertson, Ashbell	1LT	F&S 8th Regiment	05/21/32–06/21/32	Assistant Quartermaster
Robertson, Socrates	PVT	Drown's Company	05/21/32–06/21/32	
Robins, Moses	PVT	Anderson's Company	05/27/32–06/21/32	
Robinson, Mitchel	PVT	Gardner's Company	05/19/32–05/27/32	
Robinson, Parley	PVT	Edmund's Company	06/12/32–06/19/32	
Rodes, Oliver	PVT	Goff's Company	05/22/32–06/06/32	AKA Oliver Roads
Rodgers, Samuel	PVT	Finch's Company	05/19/32–06/15/32	PEN
Rogers, John V.	PVT	Hixson's Company	05/21/32–06/07/32	
Root, Stephen W.	PVT	Stevens' Company	05/22/32–05/31/32	Absent without leave
Rose, John	PVT	Dunham's Company	05/24/32–06/03/32	Absent without leave
Ross, Jacob	PVT	Rowland's Company	05/22/32–05/31/32	
Rowen, Arthur	PVT	Anderson's Company	05/27/32–06/21/32	
Rowen, Mathew	3SG	Anderson's Company	05/21/32–06/21/32	VTS OAS WNA 07/26/32–07/29/32
Rowland, Isaac S.	CAP	Rowland's Company	05/22/32–05/31/32	
Rowley, Alvah	PVT	Humphrey's Company	07/27/32–07/29/32	VTS OAS WNA
Rowley, William H.	PVT	Humphrey's Company	07/27/32–07/29/32	VTS OAS WNA
Royce, Zachariah H.	VOL	Hascall's Company	07/2?/32–07/29/32	VTS OAS WNA
Ruland, William	PVT	Humphrey's Company	07/27/32–07/29/32	VTS OAS WNA
Rull, Daniel	PVT	Hixson's Company	05/21/32–06/06/32	
Rulons, Charles	4SG	Thayer's Company	05/22/32–05/31/32	
Russell, Clement	PVT	Powers' Company	05/21/32–06/21/32	
Russell, David	PVT	Humphrey's Company	07/27/32–07/29/32	VTS OAS WNA

NAME	RANK	MILITARY UNIT	SERVICE DATES	REMARKS
Russell, Jonathan	1LT	Barnes' Company	05/21/32–06/21/32	
Sabin, Josiah	PVT	Lewis' Company	06/13/32–06/19/32	
Sacia, David	PVT	Stevens' Company	05/22/32–05/31/32	
Sage, John	PVT	Drown's Company	05/21/32–06/21/32	
Sales, Samuel	PVT	Preston's Company	05/21/32–06/21/32	
Saliday, John	PVT	Huston's Company	07/2?/32–07/29/32	VTS OAS WNA
Saliot, Moses	PVT	Rowland's Company	05/22/32–05/31/32	
Salisbury, Jonathan	4SG	Lewis Company	05/21/32–06/06/32	
Salisbury, Osmyn	1CP	Lewis' Company	05/21/32–06/06/32	
Salsberry, D. L.	PVT	Burton's Company	05/22/32–05/31/32	
Salyer, George Z.	1CP	Anderson's Company	05/27/32–06/21/32	VTS OAS WNA 07/26/32–07/29/32
Sanborn, Daniel	PVT	Lewis' Company	06/13/32–06/19/32	
Sanders, Jacob	PVT	Gardner's Company	05/19/32–05/27/32	
Sanders, John P.	PVT	Silsbe's Company	05/29/32–06/27/32	
Sanders, Soloman	PVT	Gardner's Company	05/19/32–05/27/32	
Sanry, Cyrus	PVT	Anderson's Company	05/21/32–06/21/32	
Savage, F.	1CP	Harrison's Company	05/21/32–06/21/32	
Sawtell, Obadiah	3SG	Silsbe's Company	05/29/32–06/27/32	
Saxon, Cyrus	PVT	Barnes' Company	05/21/32–06/03/32	
Saxton, Cyrus	VOL	Daniels' Company	07/2?/32–07/29/32	VTS OAS WNA
Saxton, William	PVT	Drown's Company	05/21/32–06/21/32	
Scarborough, George	2LT	F&S 7th Regiment	05/22/32–07/22/32	QUA Rank uncertain
Schellhaus, Martin G.	PVT	Powers' Company	05/21/32–06/06/32	
Schellhaus, Roswell	PVT	Powers' Company	05/21/32–06/06/32	
Schnall, John I.	PVT	Hixson's Company	05/21/32–06/07/32	ASD 06/12/32–06/19/32
Schock, Jacob C.	PVT	Drown's Company	05/21/32–06/21/32	

Name	Rank	Military Unit	Service Dates	Remarks
Scholl, John	PVT	Hixson's Company	05/21/32–06/07/32	ASD 06/12/32–06/19/32
Schooly, William	PVT	White's Company	05/19/32–06/21/32	
Schreder, John F.	PVT	Drown's Company	05/21/32–06/21/32	MNI Ferdinand
Schwarz, John E.	AJG	F&S MI Militia	05/19/32–06/11/32	Acting Commander in Chief
Scott, Greenby	PVT	White's Company	05/19/32–05/27/32	
Scott, James	PVT	Thayer's Company	05/22/32–05/31/32	
Searl, H. B.	3CP	Harrison's Company	05/21/32–06/21/32	
Seek, John	PVT	Rowland's Company	05/22/32–05/31/32	
Seeley, Abijah C.	PVT	Calhoun's Company	05/21/32–06/21/32	
Seniz, Fabian	PVT	Marsac's Company	05/22/32–05/30/32	
Sesson, Ellery	PVT	Finche's Company	05/21/32–06/05/32	
Severy, John	PVT	Finch's Company	05/19/32–06/25/32	
Seymour, Rodney	PVT	Noyes' Company	05/21/32–06/09/32	
Seymour, Select	PVT	Drown's Company	05/21/32–06/21/32	
Shaffer, Peter	PVT	Silsbe's Company	05/29/32–06/27/32	
Shain, Tousaint	PVT	Marsac's Company	05/22/32–05/31/32	
Shampain, Lambert	PVT	Swarthout's Company	05/22/32–05/31/32	
Sharp, Nathan	PVT	White's Company	05/19/32–05/27/32	
Shattuck, Thomas	PVT	Thayer's Company	05/22/32–05/31/32	
Shaw, George	PVT	Harrison's Company	05/21/32–06/21/32	
Shaw, John	PVT	Curry's Company	05/19/32–06/21/32	
Shaw, Peter H.	PVT	Drown's Company	05/21/32–06/21/32	PEN
Sheldon, Theodore P.	2LT	Anderson's Company	05/21/32–05/28/32	VTS OAS WNA 07/26/32–07/29/32
Shelhammer, John	PVT	Stewart's Company	05/21/32–06/06/32	
Shellhammer, Daniel	PVT	Stewart's Company	07/??/32–??/??/32	SUB Hiram Kell. SCU
Shellhouse, George F.	PVT	Powers' Company	05/21/32–06/06/32	

Michigan Men in the Black Hawk War

NAME	RANK	MILITARY UNIT	SERVICE DATES	REMARKS
Shellhouse, Martin G.	PVT	Powers' Company	05/21/32–06/06/32	
Shellhouse, Roswell	PVT	Powers' Company	05/21/32–06/06/32	
Shepherd, John T.	PVT	Finche's Company	05/21/32–06/05/32	ASD 06/12/32–06/18/32
Sherer, I. or J.	PVT	Harrison's Company	05/21/32–06/09/32	
Sherman, Benjamin	PVT	Powers' Company	05/21/32–06/21/32	
Shermerhorn, N. V.	PVT	Hixson's Company	05/21/32–06/07/32	ASD 06/12/32–06/19/32
Sherwin, Ezra T.	PVT	Lewis' Company	06/13/32–06/19/32	
Sherwin, Lyman	PVT	Finche's Company	06/12/32–06/18/32	
Sherwood, Eber	PVT	Barnes' Company	06/13/32–06/21/32	
Shew, Jacob	3SG	Humphrey's Company	07/27/32–07/29/32	VTS OAS WNA
Shields, A. S.	PVT	Finch's Company	05/19/32–06/25/32	
Shields, George	PVT	Burton's Company	05/22/32–05/31/32	
Shields, Nelson	PVT	Finch's Company	05/19/32–06/25/32	
Shields, Nelson S.	PVT	White's Company	05/19/32–06/21/32	PEN
Shoemaker, Jacob	2CP	Preston's Company	05/21/32–06/21/32	PEN
Sholl, David	PVT	Drown's Company	05/21/32–06/21/32	
Sholl, Peter	PVT	Drown's Company	05/21/32–06/21/32	
Shurte, Isaac	UNK	Huston's Company	07/2?/32–07/29/32	VTS OAS WNA
Shurte, Isaac	CAP	Shurte's Company	05/19/32–06/21/32	
Sidener, Samuel	PVT	Hunter's Company	05/21/32–06/21/32	PEN
Sifford, Henry	PVT	Gardner's Company	05/19/32–06/21/32	
Sifford, John	PVT	Gardner's Company	05/19/32–06/21/32	
Silsbe, John	CAP	Silsbe's Company	05/29/32–06/27/32	
Simmons, David	PVT	Burton's Company	05/22/32–05/31/32	
Simms, Daniel	PVT	White's Company	05/19/32–05/27/32	
Simpson, Elias	PVT	Shurte's Company	05/19/32–06/21/32	

NAME	RANK	MILITARY UNIT	SERVICE DATES	REMARKS
Simpson, John	PVT	Shurte's Company	05/19/32–06/21/32	
Simpson, Thomas	PVT	Shurte's Company	05/19/32–06/21/32	
Sink, John	PVT	Calhoun's Company	05/21/32–06/06/32	
Sisson, Thomas	PVT	Silsbe's Company	05/29/32–06/27/32	
Skiff, Vinal	PVT	Humphrey's Company	07/27/32–07/29/32	VTS OAS WNA
Skinner, Benjamin L.	FIF	Hixson's Company	05/21/32–06/07/32	ASD 06/12/32–06/19/32
Skinner, Oramel D.	4CP	Hixson's Company	05/21/32–06/07/32	
Slater, H. J.	PVT	Brookfield's Company	05/21/32–06/21/32	
Slater, Henry J.	PVT	Drown's Company	05/21/32–06/21/32	PEN
Slater, Joseph	PVT	Drown's Company	05/21/32–06/21/32	
Smart, Richard	PVT	Calhoun's Company	06/07/32–06/21/32	
Smith, Aaron	VOL	Hascall's Company	07/2?/32–07/29/32	VTS OAS WNA
Smith, Allen	PVT	Barnes' Company	06/13/32–06/21/32	
Smith, Asa	4SG	Stevens' Company	05/22/32–05/31/32	
Smith, Aziel	PVT	Brookfield's Company	05/21/32–06/21/32	
Smith, Benjamin H.	PVT	Bolton's Company	05/21/32–06/03/32	ASD 06/14/32–06/21/32
Smith, Daniel	PVT	Bolton's Company	06/14/32–06/21/32	
Smith, Daniel	PVT	Dunham's Company	05/21/32–06/03/32	
Smith, Davis	1LT	F&S 8th Regiment	05/21/32–06/21/32	Adjutant
Smith, Ebenezer	VOL	Hascall's Company	07/2?/32–07/29/32	VTS OAS WNA
Smith, Edward	ENS	Preston's Company	05/21/32–06/21/32	PEN. MBL
Smith, Erastus	PVT	Barnes' Company	06/13/32–06/21/32	
Smith, George	CPL	Butler's Company	05/19/32–06/25/32	PEN
Smith, H.	PVT	Harrison's Company	05/21/32–06/09/32	
Smith, Horatio	PVT	Rowland's Company	05/22/32–05/31/32	
Smith, Ira	PVT	Barnes' Company	05/21/32–06/03/32	

Name	Rank	Military Unit	Service Dates	Remarks
Smith, Isaac	PVT	Bolton's Company	06/14/32–06/21/32	
Smith, Isaac	PVT	Dunham's Company	05/21/32–06/03/32	PEN
Smith, J. A.	4SG	Daniels' Company	07/2?/32–07/29/32	VTS OAS WNA
Smith, James	PVT	Noyes' Company	05/21/32–06/09/32	
Smith, Jeremiah	PVT	Lewis' Company	06/13/32–06/19/32	
Smith, John	PVT	Preston's Company	05/28/32–06/21/32	
Smith, John F.	LUT	Butler's Company	05/19/32–06/25/32	AKA John T. Smith. PEN
Smith, John H.	PVT	Barnes' Company	05/21/32–06/03/32	PEN
Smith, John R.	VOL	Hascall's Company	07/2?/32–07/29/32	VTS OAS WNA
Smith, Joseph	PVT	Preston's Company	05/28/32–06/21/32	
Smith, Niles F.	PVT	Anderson's Company	05/27/32–06/21/32	VTS OAS WNA 07/27/32–07/29/32
Smith, Robert D.	PVT	Rowland's Company	05/22/32–05/31/32	
Smith, Soloman	PVT	Drown's Company	05/21/32–06/21/32	
Smith, Thaddeus	MUS	Daniels' Company	07/2?/32–07/29/32	VTS OAS WNA
Smith, Thaddeus	MUS	Noyes' Company	05/21/32–06/09/32	
Smith, Wiley	1SG	Brookfield's Company	05/21/32–06/21/32	
Snay, Fabian	PVT	Marsac's Company	05/22/32–05/30/32	
Solerday, Henry	PVT	Curry's Company	05/19/32–06/21/32	
Solerday, Jacob	PVT	Gardner's Company	05/19/32–05/27/32	
Spafford, Ethan	PVT	Lewis' Company	06/13/32–06/19/32	
Spear, Stephen P.	PVT	Lewis' Company	05/21/32–06/06/32	ASD 06/13/32–06/19/32. PEN
Spears, Alexander	PVT	Rowland's Company	05/22/32–05/31/32	
Spencer, Garey	1LT	Jackson's Company	05/22/32–07/22/32	
Spencer, Simeon Jr	1SG	Hixson's Company	05/21/32–06/07/32	ASD 06/12/32–06/19/32
Sperry, Ammon	PVT	Hixson's Company	05/21/32–06/07/32	ASD 06/12/32–06/19/32
Spofford, Samuel L.	ENS	Finche's Company	05/21/32–06/05/32	ASD 06/12/32–06/18/32

NAME	RANK	MILITARY UNIT	SERVICE DATES	REMARKS
Spooner, Warner	PVT	Lewis' Company	06/13/32–06/19/32	
Springer, Samuel	PVT	Shurte's Company	05/19/32–06/21/32	
Springstead, Cornelius	PVT	Humphrey's Company	07/27/32–07/29/32	VTS OAS WNA
Squares, Daniel Conklin	PVT	Curry's Company	05/19/32–06/21/32	AKA Daniel Squier
St. Clair, William H.	PVT	Hixson's Company	05/21/32–06/07/32	ASD 06/12/32–06/19/32
St. John, David	BUG	Humphrey's Company	07/27/32–07/29/32	VTS OAS WNA
Stanburgh, Jacob	PVT	Stevens' Company	05/22/32–05/31/32	Absent without leave
Stanley, Alanson	PVT	Calhoun's Company	05/21/32–06/21/32	
Stanley, George	PVT	Calhoun's Company	05/21/32–06/21/32	PEN
Stanley, T.	PVT	Harrison's Company	05/21/32–06/09/32	
Starkwether, Nathaniel B.	1SG	Preston's Company	05/21/32–06/21/32	
Starr, Ruel	PVT	Noyes' Company	05/21/32–06/21/32	
Stearnes, Lyman	PVT	Drown's Company	05/21/32–06/21/32	
Stearns, John	PVT	Noyes' Company	05/21/32–06/21/32	PEN
Steele, James	VOL	Hascall's Company	07/2?/32–07/29/32	VTS OAS WNA
Stephens, Elisha	PVT	Thayer's Company	05/22/32–05/31/32	
Stephens, Walter G.	BUG	Anderson's Company	06/16/32–06/21/32	
Stephens, William	PVT	Noyes' Company	05/21/32–06/09/32	
Stetson, Turner	PVT	Lewis' Company	05/21/32–06/06/32	
Stevens, Albert	CAP	Stevens' Company	05/22/32–05/31/32	
Stevens, George	PVT	Swarthout's Company	05/22/32–05/31/32	
Stevens, Liman	PVT	Stevens' Company	05/22/32–05/31/32	
Stevens, Pelick	PVT	Noyes' Company	05/21/32–06/09/32	
Steward, John	PVT	Olds' Company	05/21/32–06/03/32	
Stewart, Alanson C.	CAP	Stewart's Company	05/21/32–06/21/32	
Stewart, Hart L.	COL	F&S 11th Regiment	05/21/32–06/21/32	

NAME	RANK	MILITARY UNIT	SERVICE DATES	REMARKS
Stewart, William	PVT	Drown's Company	05/21/32–06/21/32	
Stewart, William W.	PVT	Hunter's Company	05/21/32–06/06/32	PEN
Stewart, William C.	DMR	Calhoun's Company	05/21/32–06/21/32	
Stockwell, Alva	PVT	Stevens' Company	05/22/32–05/31/32	
Stoddard, Nathan	PVT	Drown's Company	05/21/32–06/21/32	
Stoddard, Orson	PVT	Humphrey's Company	07/27/32–07/29/32	VTS OAS WNA
Stone, Danforth	PVT	Goff's Company	06/12/32–06/19/32	
Stone, David	PVT	Humphrey's Company	07/27/32–07/29/32	VTS OAS WNA
Stone, Horatio O.	PVT	Hixson's Company	05/21/32–06/07/32	ASD 06/12/32–06/19/32
Stone, Warren	PVT	Stevens' Company	05/22/32–05/31/32	
Stoops, Washington	PVT	Finche's Company	05/21/32–06/05/32	
Stout, George	PVT	Goff's Company	05/22/32–06/06/32	ASD 06/12/32–06/19/32
Streck, Joseph	PVT	Gardner's Company	05/19/32–05/23/32	
Strevey, Daniel	PVT	Stewart's Company	05/21/32–06/06/32	
Sullivan, Calvin	PVT	Gardner's Company	05/19/32–06/21/32	
Sumner, Samuel H.	PVT	Hunter's Company	05/21/32–06/21/32	
Sutton, James W.	PVT	Rowland's Company	05/22/32–05/31/32	
Swain, Benjamin	PVT	White's Company	05/19/32–05/23/32	
Swarthout, Anthony R.	CAP	Swarthout's Company	05/22/32–05/31/32	
Tabey, Frederick	PVT	Stewart's Company	05/21/32–06/06/32	
Tabor, Paul	PVT	Lewis' Company	06/13/32–06/19/32	
Tacey, John	PVT	Shurte's Company	05/19/32–06/21/32	
Tailor, John	PVT	Bolton's Company	06/14/32–06/21/32	
Taylor, James	4SG	Noyes' Company	05/21/32–06/21/32	
Taylor, James	VOL	Daniels' Company	07/2?/32–07/29/32	VTS OAS WNA
Taylor, John	PVT	Olds' Company	05/21/32–06/03/32	

NAME	RANK	MILITARY UNIT	SERVICE DATES	REMARKS
Taylor, Levi	PVT	Edmund's Company	06/12/32–06/19/32	
Taylor, Rodman	PVT	Drown's Company	05/21/32–06/21/32	PEN
Taylor, William	3CP	Shurte's Company	05/19/32–06/21/32	PEN
Teeple, George	PVT	Stevens' Company	05/??/32–05/??/32	Absent without leave
Telepaw, Jonas	PVT	Bolton's Company	05/24/32–06/03/32	
Tenbrook, Jarret	PVT	Lewis' Company	05/21/32–06/06/32	
Tendall, Noah H.	PVT	Drown's Company	05/21/32–06/21/32	
Terhoon, John	DMB	Burton's Company	05/22/32–05/31/32	
Terril, Abraham	PVT	Humphrey's Company	07/27/32–07/29/32	VTS OAS WNA
Tharp, Nathan	PVT	White's Company	05/19/32–05/27/32	
Thayer, Nahum P.	CAP	Thayer's Company	05/22/32–05/31/32	
Thebault, Gabriel	2CP	Marsac's Company	05/22/32–05/30/32	
Thomas, Ebenezer	PVT	Shurte's Company	05/19/32–06/21/32	
Thomas, Enos	CPL	Stewart's Company	05/21/32–06/06/32	
Thomas, Ira E.	PVT	Thayer's Company	05/22/32–05/31/32	
Thomas, Jasper	PVT	Burton's Company	05/22/32–05/31/32	
Thomas, Jeremiah C.	PVT	Thayer's Company	05/22/32–05/31/32	
Thomas, Jonathan	PVT	Barnes' Company	05/21/32–06/21/32	
Thomas, William	VOL	Hascall's Company	07/2?/32–07/29/32	VTS OAS WNA
Thompson, Abner	PVT	Shurte's Company	05/19/32–06/21/32	
Thompson, M. B.	PVT	Finche's Company	05/21/32–06/05/32	
Thompson, Squire	EXN	F&S 7th Regiment	06/03/32–06/26/32	
Thompson, Syms	PVT	Swarthout's Company	05/22/32–05/31/32	
Thorn, Henry	PVT	Rowland's Company	05/22/32–05/31/32	Absent without leave
Thurman, Charles	PVT	Gardner's Company	05/19/32–06/21/32	
Thurston, Benjamin L.	PVT	Edmund's Company	05/22/32–06/06/32	ASD 06/12/32–06/19/32

224

Name	Rank	Military Unit	Service Dates	Remarks
Thurston, George	PVT	Anderson's Company	05/27/32–06/21/32	VTS OAS WNA 07/28/32–07/29/32
Thurston, Ira	PVT	Anderson's Company	05/29/32–06/21/32	VTS OAS WNA 07/29/32
Thurston, Washington	PVT	Olds' Company	05/21/32–06/03/32	
Tibbits, Benjamin	ENS	Goff's Company	05/22/32–06/06/32	ASD 06/12/32–06/19/32
Tilipan, Jonas	PVT	Bolton's Company	05/21/32–06/03/32	ASD 06/14/32–06/21/32
Tillotson, Jeremiah	1LT	Dunham's Company	05/21/32–06/03/32	
Tilton, Joseph B.	PVT	Finche's Company	05/21/32–06/05/32	
Tilton, William W.	PVT	Drown's Company	05/21/32–06/21/32	PEN
Timus, Daniel	PVT	White's Company	05/19/32–05/27/32	
Tindall, Jesse	CPL	Drown's Company	05/21/32–06/21/32	
Tinglepan, I. or J. I.	PVT	Stevens' Company	05/22/32–05/31/32	
Tisdale, Erastus	PVT	Noyes' Company	05/21/32–06/21/32	
Titsort, Abram	PVT	Huston's Company	07/2?/32–07/29/32	VTS OAS WNA. AKA Tietsort
Titsort, Abram Jr.	4SG	Shurte's Company	05/19/32–06/21/32	AKA Abram Tietsort
Titsort, Levi	PVT	Shurte's Company	05/19/32–06/21/32	AKA Levi Tietsort
Titsort, Peter	PVT	Shurte's Company	05/19/32–06/21/32	PEN. AKA Peter Tietsort
Titsworth, John	PVT	Thayer's Company	05/22/32–05/31/32	
Todd, Alfred	PVT	Lewis' Company	05/21/32–06/06/32	ASD 06/13/32–06/19/32
Todd, John	VOL	Hascall's Company	07/2?/32–07/29/32	VTS OAS WNA
Todd, Morris	PVT	Edmund's Company	05/22/32–06/06/32	ASD 06/12/32–06/19/32
Tole, Philip I.	3CP	Humphrey's Company	07/27/32–07/29/32	VTS OAS WNA
Tompkins, Abraham	PVT	Drown's Company	05/21/32–06/21/32	PEN
Tompkins, James D.	PVT	Bolton's Company	??/??/32–??/??/32	Absent
Toney, Sebert	CPL	Finch's Company	05/19/32–06/25/32	
Toney, Stephen	PVT	Gardner's Company	05/19/32–06/21/32	
Torry, Derastus	LUT	Lewis' Company	05/21/32–06/06/32	ASD 06/13/32–06/19/32. PEN

Michigan Men in the Black Hawk War

Name	Rank	Military Unit	Service Dates	Remarks
Town, Oka	1CP	Barnes' Company	05/21/32–06/21/32	PEN
Townsend, Gamaliel	1LT	Shurte's Company	05/19/32–06/21/32	PEN
Townsend, Gamaliel	PVT	Huston's Company	07/2?/32–07/29/32	VTS OAS WNA
Townsend, John	2CP	Huston's Company	07/2?/32–07/29/32	VTS OAS WNA
Trail, William	PVT	Humphrey's Company	07/27/32–07/29/32	VTS OAS WNA
Treiblebis, Martin	PVT	Silsbe's Company	05/29/32–06/27/32	
Trembley, Francis	PVT	Jackson's Company	05/22/32–07/22/32	
Trombla, Edward	PVT	Marsac's Company	05/22/32–05/30/32	
Trombla, Eustace	4CP	Marsac's Company	05/22/32–05/30/32	
Trombla, Francis	PVT	Marsac's Company	05/22/32–05/30/32	
Trombla, John	PVT	Marsac's Company	05/22/32–05/30/32	
Trombla, Joseph	PVT	Marsac's Company	05/22/32–05/30/32	
Trombla, Peter	3CP	Marsac's Company	05/22/32–05/30/32	
Trotter, John	PVT	Burton's Company	05/22/32–05/31/32	
True, Elias	PVT	Stewart's Company	05/21/32–06/21/32	
Trumbull, Edward A.	PVT	Anderson's Company	05/21/32–05/28/32	
Trumbull, Edward A.	PVT	Jackson's Company	06/04/32–07/22/32	
Trusdel, Stephen W.	PVT	Powers' Company	05/21/32–06/06/32	
Tuck, Charles	4CP	Stevens' Company	05/22/32–05/31/32	
Tucker, Charles B.	PVT	White's Company	05/19/32–06/21/32	
Tuller, Harry	PVT	Finche's Company	05/21/32–06/05/32	
Tuttle, Joel	PVT	Stevens' Company	05/22/32–05/31/32	
Tuttle, Ralph	PVT	Barnes' Company	05/21/32–06/03/32	
Ullman, Isaac J.	CAP	F&S 3rd Brigade	05/21/32–06/20/32	Quartermaster
Underwood, Elias S.	PVT	Finche's Company	05/21/32–06/05/32	
Vallois, Peter	PVT	Marsac's Company	05/22/32–05/30/32	

Name	Rank	Military Unit	Service Dates	Remarks
Van Antwerp, Daniel	VOL	Hascall's Company	07/2?/32–07/29/32	VTS OAS WNA
Van Hining, Henry	PVT	Bolton's Company	05/21/32–06/03/32	
Van Norwick, Ira	PVT	Rowland's Company	05/22/32–05/31/32	
Van Pool, Rufus	PVT	Bolton's Company	06/14/32–06/21/32	
Van Scoten, Ben	PVT	Drown's Company	05/21/32–06/21/32	
Van Vleet, John	PVT	Drown's Company	05/21/32–06/21/32	
Vandemark, John	PVT	Powers' Company	05/21/32–06/06/32	
Vanderhoof, Thomas	PVT	Shurte's Company	05/19/32–06/21/32	
Vanderwaler, Lawrence	PVT	Anderson's Company	05/21/32–06/21/32	VTS OAS WNA 07/26/32–07/29/32
Vanduser, E.	PVT	Harrison's Company	05/21/32–06/21/32	
Vanduser, G.	PVT	Harrison's Company	05/21/32–06/21/32	
Vanpool, Rufus	PVT	Olds' Company	05/21/32–06/03/32	
Vantassel, John	PVT	Hixson's Company	05/21/32–06/07/32	ASD 06/12/32–06/19/32
Vantine, David	PVT	Finche's Company	05/21/32–06/05/32	
Vesey, John D.	PVT	Brookfield's Company	05/21/32–06/21/32	
Vickery, Stephen	2LT	F&S 12th Regiment	05/21/32–06/21/32	QUA Rank uncertain
Vickory, Stephen	VOL	Daniels' Company	07/2?/32–07/29/32	VTS OAS WNA
Voorhes, J. N.	PVT	Swarthout's Company	05/22/32–05/31/32	
Wade, Robert	PVT	Anderson's Company	05/27/32–06/21/32	
Waid, John B.	PVT	Shurte's Company	05/19/32–05/23/32	
Wakefield, Abner	PVT	Thayer's Company	05/22/32–05/31/32	
Wall, John	PVT	Bolton's Company	06/14/32–06/21/32	
Wallace, John S.	2SG	Anderson's Company	05/21/32–06/21/32	VTS OAS WNA 07/26/32–07/29/32
Walten, Hiram	PVT	Swarthout's Company	05/22/32–05/31/32	PEN. AKA Hiram Walton
Walters, Amos	PVT	Barnes' Company	05/21/32–06/03/32	
Walters, Ebenezer	PVT	Barnes' Company	05/21/32–06/03/32	

NAME	RANK	MILITARY UNIT	SERVICE DATES	REMARKS
Walters, Elias T.	3CP	Barnes' Company	05/21/32–06/03/32	
Walters, Nathaniel	PVT	Barnes' Company	05/21/32–06/21/32	
Walton, Henry Jr.	1CP	Silsbe's Company	05/29/32–06/27/32	
Walworth, Cornelius	3SG	Lewis' Company	05/21/32–06/06/32	
Walworth, Joseph	PVT	Calhoun's Company	05/30/32–06/21/32	
Walworth, Joseph	PVT	Lewis' Company	05/21/32–06/06/32	
Walworth, William	PVT	Lewis' Company	05/21/32–06/06/32	ASD 06/13/32–06/19/32
Ward, Enoch	PVT	Drown's Company	05/21/32–06/21/32	
Warner, Cassius P.	PVT	Edmund's Company	05/22/32–06/06/32	ASD 06/12/32–06/19/32
Warner, Harvey	ENS	Bolton's Company	05/21/32–06/03/32	ASD 06/14/32–06/21/32
Warner, Joseph	PVT	Lewis' Company	06/13/32–06/19/32	
Warner, Stephen Jr.	3SG	Edmund's Company	05/22/32–06/06/32	ASD 06/12/32–06/19/32. PEN
Warsan, Joseph	PVT	Stewart's Company	05/21/32–06/21/32	
Warsan, Samuel	PVT	Stewart's Company	05/21/32–06/21/32	AKA Samuel Wasson
Washburn, Allen	PVT	Lewis' Company	06/13/32–06/19/32	
Wasson, John	PVT	Anderson's Company	07/29/32	VTS OAS WNA. AKA Warson
Wasson, Samuel	PVT	Anderson's Company	07/29/32	VTS OAS WNA
Wasson, Samuel	PVT	Silsbe's Company	05/29/32–06/27/32	
Watson, James	PVT	Rowland's Company	05/22/32–05/31/32	
Wearing, Daniel	PVT	Finche's Company	05/21/32–06/05/32	
Weaver, William	PVT	Stewart's Company	05/21/32–06/21/32	
Webber, Eli	PVT	Swarthout's Company	05/22/32–05/31/32	PEN
Webster, Luke	PVT	Brookfield's Company	05/21/32–06/21/32	
Weed, Orlando	2LT	Barnes' Company	05/21/32–06/21/32	
Weeks, James	VOL	Hascall's Company	07/2?/32–07/29/32	VTS OAS WNA
Welch, Walter	PVT	Drown's Company	05/21/32–06/21/32	

NAME	RANK	MILITARY UNIT	SERVICE DATES	REMARKS
Welling, Asa A.	DMR	Hixson's Company	05/21/32–06/07/32	ASD 06/12/32–06/19/32
Welling, William J.	DMR	Hixson's Company	06/12/32–06/19/32	
Wells, Charles	4CP	Silsbe's Company	05/29/32–06/27/32	
Wells, David	2SG	Hixson's Company	05/21/32–06/07/32	ASD 06/12/32–06/19/32
Wells, Jesse	PVT	Finch's Company	05/19/32–06/25/32	
Wells, John	PVT	Brookfield's Company	05/19/32–06/21/32	
Wells, Joseph	PVT	Gardner's Company	05/19/32–06/21/32	
Wells, Joseph	PVT	Huston's Company	07/2?/32–07/29/32	VTS OAS WNA
Wells, Lewis	COR	Humphrey's Company	07/27/32–07/29/32	VTS OAS WNA
Wenchell, Jesse H.	PVT	Anderson's Company	05/21/32–06/21/32	
Wenchell, John W.	PVT	Anderson's Company	05/21/32–06/21/32	
Wenchell, William	PVT	Anderson's Company	06/16/32–06/21/32	VTS OAS WNA 07/28/32–07/29/32
Wert, Martin	PVT	Preston's Company	05/21/32–06/21/32	
Wesner, Decay	PVT	Swarthout's Company	05/22/32–05/31/32	
Westfall, Jacob	PVT	Stevens' Company	05/22/32–05/31/32	
Westfall, James	PVT	Thayer's Company	05/22/32–05/31/32	
Weston, Chester	PVT	Thayer's Company	05/22/32–05/31/32	
Weston, William	PVT	Thayer's Company	05/22/32–05/31/32	
Wheeler, Samuel	PVT	Butler's Company	05/20/32–06/25/32	
Wheeler, Samuel M.	3SG	Goff's Company	05/22/32–06/06/32	
Wheeling, Herbert	PVT	Drown's Company	05/21/32–06/21/32	
Whinery, John V.	PVT	White's Company	05/19/32–06/21/32	
Whipple, Charles W.	MAJ	F&S 7th Regiment	05/22/32–07/22/32	Adjutant General
Whipple, Henry	PVT	Harrison's Company	05/21/32–06/21/32	
White, Calam C.	PVT	Barnes' Company	05/21/32–06/03/32	
White, Charles	PVT	Swarthout's Company	05/22/32–05/31/32	

Name	Rank	Military Unit	Service Dates	Remarks
White, George	PVT	Rowland's Company	05/22/32–05/31/32	
White, John	2SG	Huston's Company	07/2?/32–07/29/32	VTS OAS WNA
White, John	CAP	White's Company	05/19/32–06/21/32	
White, Josiah	CSI	Lewis' Company	06/13/32–06/19/32	
White, Lem S.	1SG	Barnes' Company	05/21/32–06/21/32	
White, Levi S.	PVT	Barnes' Company	06/13/32–06/21/32	
White, Nathan	CPL	Drown's Company	05/21/32–06/21/32	
White, Stacy	PVT	Goff's Company	05/22/32–06/06/32	ASD 06/12/32–06/19/32. PEN
White, Thomas J.	PVT	Drown's Company	05/21/32–06/21/32	PEN
Whitecar, James	PVT	Anderson's Company	05/27/32–06/21/32	VTS OAS WNA 07/27/32–07/29/32
Whited, George	PVT	Silsbe's Company	05/29/32–06/27/32	
Whiting, John L.	SUR	F&S 1st Regiment	??/??/32–??/??/32	
Whitman, Horas	PVT	Thayer's Company	05/22/32–05/31/32	
Whitmarsh, Horace	PVT	Goff's Company	05/22/32–06/06/32	
Whitmore, O.	PVT	Butler's Company	05/20/32–06/25/32	
Whitmore, O.	PVT	Calhoun's Company	05/21/32–06/06/32	
Whitney, Daniel S.	PVT	Lewis' Company	05/21/32–06/06/32	ASD 06/13/32–06/19/32
Whitney, Russell	PVT	Lewis' Company	06/13/32–06/19/32	
Whitney, Volney B.	PVT	Lewis' Company	06/13/32–06/19/32	
Wigant, Abraham	PVT	Harrison's Company	05/21/32–06/09/32	
Wigant, Peter	PVT	Harrison's Company	05/21/32–06/21/32	
Wilder, Elias	PVT	Lewis' Company	05/21/32–06/06/32	
Wilder, Levi	PVT	Calhoun's Company	05/21/32–06/06/32	
Wilkenson, B.	PVT	Calhoun's Company	05/21/32–06/21/32	
Wilkins, Thomas	CPL	Finch's Company	05/19/32–06/25/32	

NAME	RANK	MILITARY UNIT	SERVICE DATES	REMARKS
Wilkinson, Aloy D.	PVT	Thayer's Company	05/22/32–05/31/32	
Willard, Isaac W.	PVT	Anderson's Company	05/27/32–06/21/32	VTS OAS WNA 07/27/32–07/29/32
Willcox, Lewis N.	LUT	Edmund's Company	05/21/32–06/06/32	ASD 06/12/32–06/19/32
Willcox, Micagar	PVT	Thayer's Company	05/22/32–05/31/32	
Williams, Horace	PVT	Noyes' Company	05/21/32–06/21/32	
Williams, John R.	GEM	F&S MI Militia	05/22/32–07/22/32	
Williams, Richard	PVT	Burton's Company	05/22/32–05/31/32	
Williams, Spencer	PVT	Butler's Company	05/20/32–6/25/32	
Williams, Thomas	3CP	Rowland's Company	05/22/32–05/31/32	
Williams, Thomas	MUS	Jackson's Company	05/22/32–07/22/32	
Williams, Uzal	FIF	Burton's Company	05/22/32–05/31/32	
Williams, William	VT	Burton's Company	05/22/32–??/??/32	Deserted
Williver, Michael	PVT	Hunter's Company	05/21/32–06/21/32	
Wilson, David	MAJ	F&S 7th Regiment	05/19/32–06/21/32	
Wilson, David	PVT	Huston's Company	07/2?/32–07/29/32	VTS OAS WNA
Wilson, Francis	FAR	Humphrey's Company	07/27/32–07/29/32	VTS OAS WNA
Wilson, James	SGT	Jackson's Company	06/06/32–07/22/32	
Wilson, Jeremiah	PVT	Preston's Company	05/21/32–06/21/32	
Wilson, John	PVT	Bolton's Company	05/21/32–06/03/32	
Wilson, John M.	MAJ	F&S 7th Regiment	05/22/32–07/22/32	ADC to General Williams
Wilson, Samuel	PVT	Shurte's Company	05/19/32–06/21/32	
Wilson, Thomas	PVT	Humphrey's Company	07/27/32–07/29/32	VTS OAS WNA
Wilson, William	PVT	Preston's Company	05/21/32–06/21/32	
Winchell, David	4SG	Anderson's Company	05/21/32–06/21/32	VTS OAS WNA 07/26/32–07/29/32
Winchell, I. or J. H.	PVT	Stewart's Company	05/21/32–06/06/32	

NAME	RANK	MILITARY UNIT	SERVICE DATES	REMARKS
Winchell, John W.	PVT	Anderson's Company	07/28/32–07/29/32	VTS OAS WNA
Winchell, John W.	PVT	Jackson's Company	05/21/32–06/04/32	
Winchell, William	2CP	Barnes' Company	05/21/32–06/03/32	
Winnery, John	PVT	Finch's Company	05/19/32–06/25/32	
Winslow, Erasmus	SUA	F&S 7th Regiment	05/22/32–07/22/32	
Winter, James	PVT	Olds' Company	??/??/32–??/??/32	Absent
Wirt, Martin	PVT	Preston's Company	05/21/32–06/21/32	
Witherall, Ansel	PVT	Hixson's Company	05/21/32–06/07/32	ASD 06/12/32–06/19/32
Witherbee, Asa	PVT	Anderson's Company	05/21/32–06/21/32	PEN
Withington, Martin V.	MUS	Humphrey's Company	07/27/32–07/29/32	VTS OAS WNA
Wonchell, David	4SG	Anderson's Company	05/21/32–06/21/32	VTS OAS WNA 07/26/32–07/29/32
Wood, Alanson	PVT	Harrison's Company	05/21/32–06/09/32	
Wood, John	PVT	Lewis' Company	05/21/32–06/06/32	
Wood, John Jr.	PVT	Swarthout's Company	05/22/32–05/31/32	
Wood, Jonathan	FIF	Harrison's Company	05/21/32–06/21/32	
Woodruff, James	VOL	Hascall's Company	07/2?/32–07/29/32	VTS OAS WNA
Woods, George	PVT	Burton's Company	05/22/32–05/31/32	
Woods, James A.	PVT	Gardner's Company	05/19/32–05/27/32	
Woods, John	PVT	Gardner's Company	05/19/32–05/23/32	
Woolman, John	CSS	F&S 7th Regiment	05/19/32–06/25/32	
Wright, A.	PVT	Jackson's Company	05/22/32–07/22/32	
Wright, Charles	PVT	Humphrey's Company	07/27/32–07/29/32	VTS OAS WNA
Wright, Dennis	PVT	Shurte's Company	05/19/32–05/23/32	
Wright, Elijah W.	PVT	Shurte's Company	05/19/32–05/27/32	
Wright, Joel C.	PVT	Shurte's Company	05/19/32–05/27/32	
Wygant, Abram	VOL	Daniels' Company	07/2?/32–07/29/32	VTS OAS WNA

NAME	RANK	MILITARY UNIT	SERVICE DATES	REMARKS
Yates, William	PVT	Barnes' Company	05/21/32–06/03/32	
Young, James	PVT	Harrison's Company	05/21/32–06/21/32	
Young, Nathan	PVT	White's Company	05/19/32–06/21/32	
Yumans, John	PVT	Barnes' Company	05/21/32–06/03/32	
Zanes, Maxwell	PVT	Shurte's Company	05/19/32–05/27/32	
Zanes, William	PVT	Shurte's Company	05/19/32–06/21/32	

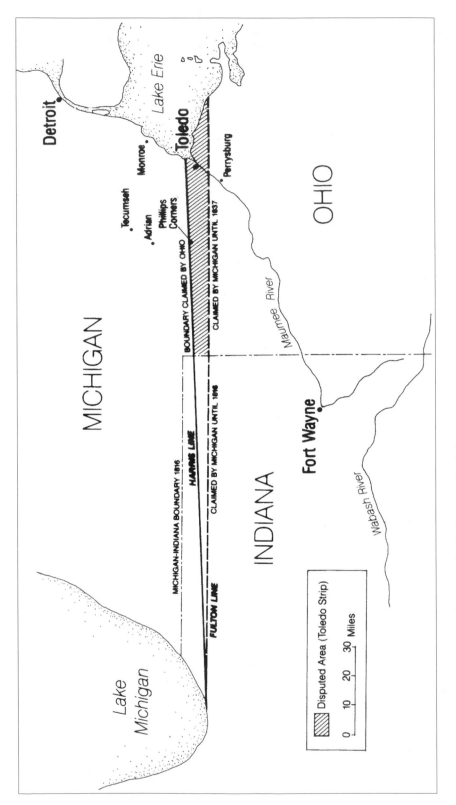

Theater of Operations, Toledo War. *(Cartography by Sherm Hollander)*

FOUR

TOLEDO WAR, 1835

Michigan in the Toledo War

On January 12, 1835, acting Michigan Territorial governor Stevens T. Mason announced to the Territorial Legislative Council that Michigan faced a crisis. According to Mason, Michigan's effort to join the Union as a state had failed. Its request to Congress for an enabling act—congressional permission to call a constitutional convention—had been rejected, despite a census that showed that enough people lived in the Lower Peninsula to qualify Michigan for statehood under the Northwest Ordinance. The twenty-three-year-old Virginia native declared that Michigan had a "right" to be admitted into the Union, and he asked the legislative council to call a constitutional convention. Twelve days later, the council concurred; delegates would be elected in April and gather in Detroit in early May. The decision to proceed toward statehood without congressional approval precipitated the Toledo War—a conflict between the Michigan Territory and the state of Ohio over a less-than-five-hundred-square-mile strip of land dominated by the community of Toledo.

Disagreement over who owned the Toledo Strip, especially the mouth of the Maumee River, which empties into Lake Erie, began in the early nineteenth century. According to the Northwest Ordinance of 1787, which established the government of the states of Ohio, Indiana, Illinois, Michigan, and Wisconsin, the boundary between the northern and southern states in the territory would be an east-west line that extended from the southern tip of Lake Michigan. Because of the uncertainty of the exact location of the lake's southernmost point, as well as the absence of a good survey marking the east-west line, Ohio included a provision in its 1803 state constitution that specified that the mouth of the Maumee River belonged to Ohio regardless of where the Northwest Ordinance placed it. For the next thirty years, both Michigan and Ohio claimed the Toledo Strip. A survey conducted by Ohio placed the strip in Ohio; several others, including one in 1834 by U.S. Army engineers, put the disputed land in Michigan. In 1827, Michigan organized the Toledo Strip, enforcing laws and collecting taxes there. Michigan even sought a compromise with Ohio, suggesting that Ohio take the land east of the river's mouth, while Michigan kept the land west and north of the river. Ohio refused.

Congress' refusal to grant Michigan an enabling act was directly tied to this border dispute. With twenty-one members of Congress, Ohio was the strongest state in the west; the Michigan Territory had one nonvoting congressional delegate. Ohio wanted to retain the mouth of the Maumee River because of a proposed canal that would connect Toledo with the Ohio River via the Maumee and Wabash Rivers. Some people believed that the canal would make Toledo a great commercial center. Until assured control over the Toledo Strip, Ohio planned to block Michigan's bid for admission into the Union.

Michigan's decision to call a constitutional convention left Ohioans, especially Governor Robert Lucas, uneasy. An irascible politician and War of 1812 veteran, Lucas realized that if the boundary issue was not resolved before Michigan joined the Union, Ohio would lose its congressional advantage. More important, once Michigan was a state it could submit the border dispute to the U.S. Supreme Court—something it could not do as a territory. Ohio responded to Michigan's call for a constitutional convention by annexing the disputed territory. Michigan retaliated with the Pains and Penalties Act, which made it illegal for any non-Michigan resident to exercise official jurisdiction in the Toledo Strip upon "pain" of a one-thousand-dollar fine and five years imprisonment. Describing Ohio's annexation of the disputed territory as "unjustifiable" and "high-handed," a confident Governor Mason declared, "We are the weaker party, it is true; but we are on the side of justice, and with the guidance of Him who never forsakes the weak, or hesitates to pursue with punishment the unjust, we cannot fail to maintain our rights against the encroachments of a powerful neighboring State."

Echoing Mason, Major General Joseph W. Brown, who commanded Michigan's territorial militia, issued the following address to his men:

> A Cause which has the sanction of the highest authority in the nation, as well as the laws of our Territory, must be sustained by us, and will meet the approbation of all our common country who respect our institutions and who are capable of appreciating the just claims of the injured and weaker party when they are sought to be trodden down and trampled upon by mere physical force. We cannot submit to an invasion of our soil; we are determined to repel with force whatever strength the State of Ohio may attempt to bring into our Territory to sustain her usurpations, and let the consequences which may follow rest on the guilty heads of those who attempt to deprive us by force of our rightful jurisdiction.

In early April, Ohio reacted to the Pains and Penalties Act by ordering the re-marking of the survey line known as the Harris Line.

The situation along the border intensified as Ohio and Michigan prepared to defend their perceived rights. In early March, Detroiters petitioned President Andrew Jackson to keep Ohio from annexing territory that operated under the jurisdiction of the federal government. The assemblage reasoned, "Are the rights and dignity of the United States less to be regarded than those of an individual member of the Confederacy?" The Detroiters added that they would not be deterred "by the disparity of strength in opposing by force the lawless aggression of Ohio." At about the same time, the Michigan Territorial Legislative Council declared that it was "the duty of every citizen to resist at all hazards" any Ohio effort to establish jurisdiction over the Toledo Strip. The council also approved Governor Mason's efforts to assert Michigan's claim.

On March 5, 1835, Mason urged U.S. secretary of war Lewis Cass to send two companies of U.S. regulars from Fort Gratiot to occupy the border area. Mason also informed U.S. secretary of state John Forsyth that if Ohio established jurisdiction over the Toledo Strip, he would, "without hesitation," arrest Governor Lucas and "meet his force by a force of a like character." The governor also placed the Michigan militia on alert. When too few men responded to a call for volunteers, Mason resorted to a draft to muster five hundred men, whom he planned to place under General Brown's command. To arm these men, Mason requested one thousand muskets and seventy-five thousand cartridges from Colonel Henry Whiting, acting quartermaster at the U.S. arsenal at Detroit. Feeling that the urgency of the situation required him to honor the request before notifying his superiors in Washington D.C., Colonel Whiting gave Mason the armaments. Colonel Whiting, however, did refuse to give Mason the cannon he requested. After being notified of Whiting's action, a distraught Secretary of War Cass ordered him to retrieve the weapons immediately.

While prepared to fight for the disputed territory, Mason claimed that he planned to avoid any "rash acts" and urged General Brown to undertake only preparatory actions. Brown was ordered to witness the April elections ever mindful to keep Ohio "in the wrong." However, if Lucas or an armed body of Ohioans entered the disputed territory, Brown was to arrest the trespassers. Although he authorized Brown to mobilize "any force" he thought necessary, Mason dismissed the militia to avoid looking like the aggressor.

On March 20, Governor Lucas declared that Ohio would "quietly and firmly" implement its jurisdiction over the strip and in so doing would "avoid all cause of offence to Michigan." Lucas added that Ohio wished Michigan "prosperity and happiness," but if it interfered with Ohio's enforcing its rights, the fault would lie with Michigan. A week later, Lucas, who reported that many volunteer companies had offered their services "to defend the soil of Ohio," ordered part of the 17th Division of Ohio militia mustered. At the same time, he cautioned that Governor Mason's actions "enkindled a martial feeling in Ohio, that . . . will require the utmost care to keep down."

The Ohio governor's determination was further evident when Michigan Territorial legislator James Doty stopped at the Ohio capital in late March. According to Doty, Lucas contended that the border controversy had been "brought on by Michigan by opposing the Officers of Ohio who were bound to see the statute to extend her jurisdiction executed." Doty reminded Lucas that the Toledo Strip was an area under territorial—hence federal government—jurisdiction. If Ohio opposed Michigan, it actually opposed the U.S. government. According to Doty, Lucas retorted that "Ohio would just as soon meet the United States as Michigan."

Secretary of State Forsyth heightened tensions when he informed Mason that if the Pains and Penalties Act remained in effect, Congress might use its prerogatives over a territory to force a compromise with Ohio. A dismayed Mason offered to resign if the president would not support him. Jackson did not ask for Mason's resignation; instead, he sought an opinion on the border dispute from his attorney general. To Jackson's consternation, Attorney General Benjamin Butler sustained Michigan's position and ruled that Ohio had no right to assume jurisdiction in the Toledo Strip without Congress' approval. Butler also argued that the Pains and Penalties Act was a legitimate measure for Michigan to use to resist excursions into its territory. Butler noted that since the president had jurisdiction over territorial officials, he could remove them; however, the same was not true with state officials. Jackson responded to Butler's opinion by appointing two commissioners to negotiate a resolution of the dispute: Congressman Benjamin C. Howard, a congressman from Maryland, and Richard Rush, a Pennsylvanian who had negotiated the 1817 Rush-Bagot Treaty that limited armaments between Great Britain and the United States on the Great Lakes.

The presidential commissioners arrived at Toledo in time to witness the Toledo War's first hostilities. On April 1, 1835, Michigan partisans, who represented a majority of Toledo's citizenry, went to the polls. One week later, Monroe County sheriff Nathan Hubble and a small posse arrived in Toledo to arrest George McKay and Naaman Goodsell for aiding another Toledoan who resisted Michigan authorities. Hubble found Goodsell at the home of Major Benjamin Stickney, an outspoken Ohio partisan. Goodsell threatened Hubble with bodily harm, and only after breaking down the door was the Monroe sheriff able to make his arrest. Hubble also arrested McKay after wrestling a gun from him. During these operations, Goodsell's wife and one of Stickney's daughters escaped from the house and ran toward town screaming for help. According to Hubble, Toledo came alive with gunfire and blowing horns. The Monroe posse was closely followed by fifty to sixty armed Ohioans, but it escaped with its prisoners. On April 10, Sheriff Hubble again journeyed to Toledo to arrest Ohio partisans who had violated the Pains and Penalties Act. Aware that, "at least" one hundred armed men waited at Toledo to resist any Michigan effort to enforce the law, Hubble formed a posse of more than 160 men. Under orders only to use their weapons in self-defense, Hubble's men discovered that the four Ohioans they sought had fled Toledo.

The events of early April prompted President Jackson's commissioners to travel between Monroe, where Mason was, and Perrysburg, Ohio, where Lucas was, in hopes of resolving the worsening border dispute. After meeting with Governor Lucas, Commissioner Howard observed that he was "very firm in character—and though doing what nine tenths of the nation will hereafter pronounce wrong . . . will listen to no argument upon the point." The commissioners found Mason equally determined. According to Howard, Mason agreed not to take "any step that will lead to a broil" as long as Ohio did not attempt to establish its jurisdiction over the territory. Mason also tried to reach an accord with Lucas by sending him a dispatch urging that Michigan and Ohio end their "sectional divisions." Lucas rejected Mason's request for a meeting and refused to respond to the Michigan governor's letter because it was filled, according to Lucas, with "menaces and threats."

Mason's efforts to preserve peace along the border did not relieve the commissioners' concerns. Describing the Ohio/Michigan border as suffering from "violent" excitement, Howard and Rush believed that while Mason opposed the use of military force, the real problem lay with the enforcement of the Pains and Penalties Act. Michigan courts—over which Mason claimed he had no control—found indictments against Ohio partisans in the disputed territory. Then an armed posse went into the district where it would meet with armed resistance. As the commissioners pointed out to Secretary Forsyth, it was difficult to distinguish the "army of armed men on horseback," raised and equipped for enforcing the Pains and Penalties Act, "from any other effective force under arms." According to Howard and Rush, Michigan's posses enjoyed "a military root" and operated "with military effect."

The commissioners hoped to use the president's influence to get Mason to suspend the law. Instead, Mason, who expressed great admiration for Jackson, described the president's request as "an act of executive usurpation and tyranny which would place every department of the government within the despotic control of a single officer." The commissioners then proposed a compromise: Michigan would suspend the Pains and Penalties Act and stop prosecuting those who had violated it, Ohio would rerun the Harris Line, and both Ohio and Michigan would establish joint jurisdiction in the disputed territory until the matter was resolved by Congress. Mason labeled the proposal "dishonorable and disreputable"; Lucas responded favorably to it.

The early April arrests of Toledoans by the Monroe County sheriff left the Ohio commissioners chosen to resurvey the Harris Line apprehensive. On April 20 the commissioners—still on Ohio soil—informed Lucas that their supplies were exhausted, the roads were impassable, and rumors were afloat that General Brown was gathering a force at Adrian "to act as exigencies may require, should Ohio attempt to run the line." Lucas urged them to move as rapidly as possible and, if confronted by a "superior force," to retreat "immediately" until forces "sufficient to protect them" could be collected. As a word of encouragement, the governor concluded, "Be cautious,—keep at sharp look out,—do not suffer yourselves to be surprised."

The surveyors apparently failed to heed Lucas' advice. At noon on April 26, fourteen miles south of Adrian, a posse of approximately thirty Michiganians, commanded by Lenawee County undersheriff William McNair, surprised the Ohioans, who were camped in a field owned by a "Mr. Phillips." The encounter began peacefully with McNair and an aide approaching the Ohio camp. But as the Ohioans, except for the commissioners who were not in camp, grabbed and loaded their rifles, McNair's men arrived on the scene. Some of the outnumbered Ohioans surrendered, while at least nine others sought refuge in a nearby cabin. McNair demanded their surrender, and after "a length of time" the Ohioans came out "with their rifles cocked." The Michigan and Ohio men faced each other almost eight rods apart. According to McNair, the Ohioans broke for the woods "in double quick time" as his men fired a volley over their heads and gave chase. Some of the Ohioans escaped, but nine were taken into custody and imprisoned at Tecumseh. Two of the prisoners were released for lack of evidence, and six others posted bail ranging from four to eight hundred dollars. One Ohioan, Colonel J. E. Fletcher, refused bail and remained a prisoner, under orders, he claimed, from Governor Lucas. No one was injured in the "Battle" of Phillips Corners, despite an Ohio claim that a Michigan musket ball "passed through the clothing" of a member of their party.

Professing that "an armed force of several hundred men" stretched across the Michigan/Ohio border, the three Ohio survey commissioners, who successfully eluded McNair's men, reported to Governor Lucas that they deemed it "prudent" to halt their work until "some efficient preparatory measures" could be taken. (Precautions had actually been taken. On April 15, General Bell had been ordered to muster five hundred men to protect the commissioners. Bell was able to raise only 292 men, and word regarding his preparedness only reached the commissioners after Phillips Corners.)

After the skirmish at Phillips Corners, Michigan continued to enforce the Pains and Penalties Act. In early May, Major Stickney was arrested while visiting Monroe and charged with acting as a judge in the April elections. Claiming that "vindictiveness" was being carried "to such extremes," Stickney wrote Lucas from a Monroe jail that he had been treated in "a very evil manner." He said he had been dragged through the streets of Monroe and denied "refreshments of any kind" for fourteen hours. (Stickney believed the Michiganians planned to use starvation to "soften" him up). The Ohioan also contended that it was time for the federal government to chastise the "lawless desperadoes" who had "become very troublesome to the West." Other attacks upon Ohioans were also reported, including one at the office of the *Toledo Gazette,* where a mob demolished the printing press. The *Gazette* later referred to these acts as "worse than Algerine robbery or Turkish persecution." This active enforcement of the Pains and Penalties Act led some Michiganians to express apprehension about the "dark and portentous" news from the disputed territory. On May 2, the *Monroe Sentinel* declared, "It would appear that neither party thinks of receding. . . . We are informed that [Lucas] has determined to raise 10,000 men, and at all hazards run the line and establish the jurisdiction of Ohio over the southern parts of Michigan."

Lucas was not raising a large armed force, but he was convinced that if the federal government was not going to act, Ohio must. Though Ohio had disbanded its militia in early May because of a lack of provisions, Lucas called a special session of the state legislature to "adopt prompt measures" to sustain Ohio's rights. In late June, inflamed by Governor Lucas, who characterized Michigan's actions as "reckless vengeance, scarcely paralleled in the history of the civilized nations," the Ohio lawmakers passed legislation enforcing Ohio's claim to the Toledo Strip. The laws made the forcible abduction of an Ohio citizen a crime punishable by three to seven years at hard labor, formed the disputed territory into Lucas County with Toledo as its county seat, appropriated $300,000 to implement these measures, gave the governor the authority to borrow another $300,000, and, to establish—at least symbolically—jurisdiction over the strip, ordered the Court of Common Pleas to hold session at Toledo on the first Monday in September.

While Ohio prepared to defend its perceived rights, delegates to Michigan's constitutional convention labored in Detroit. In mid-June they completed their work. Besides creating a state constitution, the delegates offered a long treatise on why the Toledo Strip belonged to Michigan. They concluded by warning: "The people of this Territory will resist, by all lawful means in their power, any attempt to invade their country."

On July 11, 1835, Secretary of War Cass informed President Jackson, "I can assure you . . . that no other resistance will be made to Ohio, than an attempt to serve the ordinary judicial process." Cass also noted, "a contest will be unavoidable if Ohio does not temper both its hostile language and proceedings." But the secretary also admitted that Mason did not favor compromise with Ohio. On that same day, Mason informed President Jackson that he regretted "this unfortunate controversy." Mason added that he would "faithfully" continue to discharge his duties as a public officer of the federal government but that he could not forget that he had "the rights of a high minded and patriotic people" in his hands.

By midsummer tensions had heated up again. There were rumors of hundreds, even thousands, of Ohioans mustering to take over the Toledo Strip. On July 15, Monroe County deputy sheriff Joseph Wood arrived in Toledo to arrest Two Stickney, one of Benjamin's sons, for helping another Toledoan resist arrest. (Curiously, Major Stickney named his sons after numbers and his daughters after states.) Wood confronted Stickney at the Davis Inn, a hotbed of Ohio partisans. Stickney resisted arrest and stabbed the deputy with a small penknife. Wood was taken to a nearby inn where a local physician pronounced him mortally wounded. After the attack, the Ohioans at the Davis Inn warned Michigan officials to "keep away," for they had "their knives sharpened and rifles loaded." On the day after Wood was wounded, Monroe County district attorney J. Q. Adams observed that "all law and authority emanating from Michigan is openly trampled upon and set at defiance by a large portion of the citizens of Toledo." It was also reported that fifty to seventy-five of Toledo's leading citizens pledged to resist further Michigan arrests as long as they had "a drop of blood left."

The Ohioans soon had their chance. In retaliation for wounding Wood, who did recover and was the Toledo War's only casualty, Mason ordered the Monroe County sheriff and an armed posse of more than two hundred men to arrest Stickney. When the Michiganians reached Toledo they discovered that two Stickney and the other Ohio stalwarts had fled. (Mason later requested that Lucas extradite Stickney, but the Ohio governor refused.) The Michiganians satisfied themselves with arresting Major Stickney, who proved uncooperative and had to be tied to his horse on the way back to Monroe.

On August 17, at the urging of President Jackson, Governor Mason convened the territorial legislative council to consider the compromise measures proposed by Jackson's commissioners. In a lengthy address, Mason repeatedly attacked the actions of Ohio, while arguing that any effort at joint jurisdiction of the Toledo Strip would be impossible. Mason again agreed to suspend the Pains and Penalties Act and allow Ohio to resurvey the border, but he would not recognize equal claim over the territory. Mason offered the legislative council two options: to accept the compromise, which would "sacrifice the rights of the territory" and jeopardize the constitutional "protection afforded to the smaller states, against the unjust demands of the larger," or to reject the measure, which would probably lead to "violence and insurrection." Mason admitted that his feelings were "not disguised," but if violence were the result, then "the responsibility of that issue would rest upon others, not upon us."

Arguing that Michigan had taken "no improper step" in resisting Ohio efforts "to extend her boundaries," the legislative council queried, "Is it Michigan or Ohio which prepares to violate the public peace by a trespass upon the acknowledged territory of the other?" The legislative council noted that Ohio's complaint about the Pains and Penalties Act was no different than if the authorities of Canada took exception to its enactment. Finally, the council declared that until Congress recognized Ohio's claim to the disputed territory, the Toledo Strip would be defended as if it were a part of Michigan. Mason sent the council's rejection of the commissioners' compromise to President Jackson with a note that concluded, "The consequences attending such a state of things are deeply to be regretted, but they must rest with those who might prevent their occurrence."

For his part, Governor Lucas continued to exert Ohio's claims to the disputed territory. On July 31, Mason received word that twenty-five boxes of Ohio rifles had reached

Toledo. Mason claimed that these weapons represented only a small portion of the armaments being collected for use against Michigan officials. A few days later, General Brown informed Mason that Governor Lucas was raising an army "of some magnitude" to protect the Ohio court session to be convened at Toledo in early September. Lucas, indeed, had ordered a muster of Ohio volunteers in early August "to march at a moment's warning, to defend the rights and honor of the state." Some Ohioans eagerly responded to the call. One Chillicothe, Ohio, warrior even offered Lucas a complete plan of battle to force Mason to surrender "like a ground hog, with a dog between him and his hole." Lucas also sent a small quantity of weapons to Port Miami.

On August 29, citing Mason's overzealous defense of Michigan's rights, President Jackson fired the young governor. Political expediency dictated that the Toledo Strip controversy would be resolved by Congress, and until then Michigan would have to yield. Unaware that he had been fired, Mason, who had ordered two hundred mounted men be raised to help the Monroe County sheriff prevent Ohio's early September court session, joined the men as they marched toward Toledo.

The Michigan militiamen enjoyed themselves on their march to Toledo. J. Wilkie Moore, a twenty-one-year-old who had come to Michigan from New York in 1833, recalled that before leaving Detroit the militia paraded and drilled.

> Some of us were armed with guns, but the great majority carried long broom handles, and with these on our shoulders we went through the military evolutions. Crowds turned out to see us and the town was full of excitement. There was no sort of uniform even among our officers, and the only attempt in that direction was that some of the "invading army" stuck differently colored feathers in their hat bands.

Between Detroit and Toledo, according to Moore, the Michigan militia

> had a vast amount of fun. . . . The farming people en route generally welcomed us enthusiastically because we were "fighting for Michigan." They did a great deal for our creature comforts, giving us mush and milk and cooking us regular meals. We returned these favors by stealing pigs and chickens—of course we called it foraging. These we would carry along and get cooked at the next farm house. Sometimes we got them cooked on the very farms where we stole them. But, even if they knew this, the good-natured farmers endured it without complaint, because we were on our way to fight for Michigan.

Despite their gaiety, Moore and the other Michiganians "were all very much in earnest" in their efforts to stop the Ohioans. On the evening of September 6 the militiamen camped eight miles from Toledo; they expected "bloodshed" the next day. Late the next morning, the Michigan militia, totaling by some reports as many as twelve hundred men, entered Toledo. They discovered neither Ohio soldiers nor governmental officials. The Michiganians remained in Toledo for several days and entertained themselves by tearing up the gardens and stripping the orchards of Major Stickney. Following a public review of the troops, Mason and his men returned home confident that they had thwarted Governor Lucas' plans.

The presence of the Michigan militia had not prevented the Ohioans from "holding court." At 3:00 A.M., while the Michigan militia slept, a party of Ohio judges, court officials, and twenty armed men stealthily crept to an old schoolhouse in Toledo. There they declared court in session. The proceedings were hastily recorded on bits of paper and deposited in the clerk's bell-crowned hat. The court adjourned to a nearby tavern to celebrate. The festivities were rudely disrupted when word arrived that the Michiganians were in pursuit. The alarm proved false, and in their haste to escape the Ohioans lost the clerk's hat. It was retrieved, and by 6:00 A.M. the judicial party was back in Ohio.

The firing of Governor Mason ended the Toledo War. Mason's successor, John S. Horner, pardoned those Ohioans who had violated the Pains and Penalties Act, an action that made the new territorial governor unpopular with many Michiganians and led to threats to his safety. Later that fall, Ohio re-marked the Harris Line without incident.

On October 5, 1835, Michigan voters chose a state legislature, elected Mason governor of the state of Michigan and overwhelmingly approved the state constitution. But the controversy over the Toledo Strip delayed Michigan's official recognition as the nation's twenty-sixth state until January 1837. Before joining the Union, Michigan was forced to give up the Toledo Strip and accept the unpopulated, remote western Upper Peninsula. Given the rugged beauty and rich natural resources of the western Upper Peninsula, it is hard to conclude that Michigan really lost the Toledo War.

BIBLIOGRAPHIC NOTE

Sources used in preparing this section, or recommended for further reading, include:

Bulkley, John M. "The Toledo War." *History of Monroe County.* Chicago: Lewis Publishing Company, 1913. 1:137–61.

Burton, Clarence M. "Toledo and Patriot Wars." *The City of Detroit.* Detroit: Clarke Publishing Company, 1922. 1:1058–65.

Detroit Democratic Free Press. (Various issues during 1835.)

George, Sister Mary Karl. *Drums Along the Maumee.* Farmington, Mich., [1970s]

———. *The Rise and Fall of Toledo, Michigan: The Toledo War.* Lansing: Michigan Historical Commission, 1971.

Hemans, Lawton T. *The Life and Times of Stevens T. Mason.* Lansing: Michigan Historical Commission, 1930.

Hoyt, William D., Jr. "Benjamin C. Howard and the Toledo War." *Ohio State Archaeological and Historical Quarterly* 60 (1951): 297–307.

Hudson Post-Gazette, Mar. 10, 1931, p. 2; Mar. 13, 1931, p. 2.

McNair, William. "The Battle of Phillips Corners." *Michigan Pioneer and Historical Collections* 12 (1898): 409–14.

Michigan Legislature, Senate. *Journal of the Senate of the State of Michigan . . . in the year 1837.* Detroit: John S. Bagg, 1837. Documents 17 and 18, pp. 118–62.

Moore, J. Wilkie. "How They Fought: Personal Recollections of the Contest with Ohio Fifty Years Ago." *Michigan Pioneer and Historical Collections* 7 (1886): 69–73.

Robertson, John. "The Toledo War." *Michigan in the War.* Lansing: W. S. George & Co., 1882. 1028–32.

The Territorial Papers of the United States: The Territory of Michigan. Vol. 12. Washington: U.S. Government Printing Office, 1945.

United States Congress. *Senate Executive Documents,* vol. 286, doc. 7, 1st Session, 24th Congress.

Wanger, Eugene G. "Collecting the Toledo War." *Michigan Historical Review* 24, no. 2 (Fall 1998): 144–60.

Way, Willard. *The Fact and Historical Events of the Toledo War of 1835.* Toledo: Daily Commercial Steambook and Job Printing House, 1869.

Way, Willard V. "Ohio-Michigan War." *Settlement of Western Country.* Bowling Green, Ohio: Historical Publications Company, 1923[?]. 247–93.

Wing, Talcott E. "The Toledo War." *History of Monroe County, Michigan.* New York: Munsell and Company, 1890. 181–99.

An interesting poem describing Michigan sentiments about the Toledo War can be found in the *Michigan Pioneer and Historical Collections* 6 (1883): 60–61.

TOLEDO WAR RELATED HISTORIC SITES AND MONUMENTS IN MICHIGAN

Stevens Thomson Mason Memorial Statue, Capitol Park, Detroit, Wayne County
Toledo War Historic Marker, Seward, Ohio (Formerly Phillips Corners, Michigan)
"War" With Happy Ending County Historic Marker, Erie, Monroe County

LIST OF RELEVANT MICHIGAN ILLUSTRATIONS

Toledo War—Representative Soldiers

Atwell, Willis. *Do You Know.* [Grand Rapids]: Booth Newspapers, 1937. Pp. 1, 5, 7, 40. Representations of events that occurred during the war.

Detroit Magazine. Detroit Free Press, May 9, 1971, pp. 16–17. Cartoons illustrating "war" scenes.

George, Mary Karl. *Drums Along the Maumee.* [Farmington, Mich., 1970s] Pp. [9], [13], [15]. Humorous drawings of selected events.

———. *The Rise and Fall of Toledo, Michigan.* Lansing: Michigan Historical Commission, 1971. P. 60. Coarse rendering of hypothetical Michigan militiaman.

McConnell, David B. *Discover Michigan.* Hillsdale, Mich.: Hillsdale Educational Publishers, 1981. P. 56. Soft depiction of Michigan soldiers marching.

———. *Forging the Peninsulas.* Hillsdale, Mich.: Hillsdale Educational Publishers, 1989. P. 141. Crudely drawn depiction of altercation.

———. *Michigan's Story.* Hillsdale, Mich.: Hillsdale Educational Publishers, 1996. P. 95. Representation of episode during conflict.

MacMullan, Elna Lahti. *Michigan Since 1600.* Hillsdale, Mich.: Hillsdale Educational Publishers, 1967. P. 35. Caricatures of related happenings.

Magazine of Michigan, Feb. 1931, pp. 8–9. Michigan troops in file under march.

Michigan History Magazine, Sept.-Oct. 1985, p. 41. Picture of drum used during the "war."

Michigan History Magazine, Sept.-Oct. 1986, p. [50]. Sketch of volunteers marching in downtown Detroit.

Ohio Historical Society. *Timeline* 4, no. 5 (Oct.-Nov. 1987): 8. Representation of typical militia muster during the era.

Russell, Francis. *History of the Making of the Nation.* New York: Heritage Publishing Company, 1968. Pp. 186–87. Unflattering drawing of militia of the times.

Toledo War—Specific Soldiers

Adam, John J. In Everts and Stewart, *Combination Atlas Map of Lenawee County, Michigan.* Chicago, 1874. P. 9. Also Chapman Brothers, *Portrait and Biographical Album of Lenawee County, Michigan.* Chicago, 1888. P. [464].

Bisonette, Gabriel D. In Talcott E. Wing, *History of Monroe County, Michigan.* New York: Munsell and Company, 1890. Opposite p. 121.

Brown, Joseph W. In Willis Atwell, *Do You Know.* [Grand Rapids]: Booth Newspapers, 1937. P. 9. Also John I. Knapp, and R. I. Bonner, *Illustrated History and Biographical Record of Lenawee County, Michigan.* Adrian, Mich.: Times Printing Company, 1903. P. 66.

Carpenter, Guy. In Everts and Stewart, *Combination Atlas Map of Lenawee County, Michigan*. Chicago, 1874. P. 27.

Cone, Linus. In L. H. Everts and Company, *History of Oakland County, Michigan*. Philadelphia, 1877. P. 150.

Edwards, Asa G. In Everts and Abbott, *History of Hillsdale County, Michigan*. Philadelphia, 1879. Between pp. 216 and 217.

Felch, Alpheus. In Photograph Collection, State Archives of Michigan, Lansing. Also Charles Richard Tuttle, *General History of the State of Michigan*. Detroit: Tyler and Company, 1873. P. 727.

Whipple, Charles W. In Photograph Collection, State Archives of Michigan, Lansing.

ORGANIZATIONAL CHART OF PARTICIPATING MICHIGAN UNITS

The number of Michigan men, extracted from the rosters, is listed after each company.

Field and Staff of Major General Joseph W. Brown, Commander

1st Regiment, 1st Brigade, 1st Division (Wayne)
Major James Bucklin, commanding

Field and Staff	12
Nahum P. Thayer, 1st Company (Greenfield)	14
John F. Rupley, 2nd Company (Dearborn)	36
Jonas Goodell, 3rd Company (Ecorse)	08
Thomas Gildard, 4th Company (Redford Rifles)	14
Martin Greenman, 5th Company (Springwells? Rifles)	12
Asahel L. Bird, 6th Company (Monguagon)	12
Charles M. Bull, 7th Company (Detroit City Guards)	12
George R. Griswold, 8th Company (Detroit Rifle Corps)	19
John Wright, Independent Company of Light Dragoons (Detroit)	20

1st Regiment, 2nd Brigade, 1st Division (Washtenaw County) 190 (figures by company unavailable)
Colonel Jonathan D. Davis, commanding

Albert Stevens, 1st Company
Richard Boughton, 2nd Company (Plymouth)
Charles McCormick, 3rd Company (Dixboro? Washtenaw Rifles)
Eli Derby, 4th Company (Ypsilanti? Rifles)
Emery Richardson, 5th Company (Ann Arbor Rifles)
Alexander Crane, 6th Company (Dexter Rifles)
James M. Murray, 7th Company (Salem)
Horace Leek, 8th Company (Scio)
Sheffield B. Newton, Baggage Guard (York)

Detachment, 2nd Regiment, 2nd Brigade, 1st Division (Washtenaw)
Colonel Martin M. Davis, commanding

Field and Staff	30
Peter Slingerland, Washtenaw Horse Guards (Ann Arbor)	12
Jesse Taylor, Artillery	11
Washtenaw Militia	86

Oakland Detachment, 4th Regiment, 3rd Brigade, 2nd Division
Major Frederick A. Sprague, commanding

Field and Staff	25
George Brownell, 1st Company (Farmington)	38
Linus Conc, 2nd Company (Troy)	38
John W. Ingram, 3rd Company (Pontiac)	33
Haron Haskins, 4th Company (West Bloomfield)	43
Orange Foot, Cavalry (Rochester)	09

Shelby Volunteers, 3rd Regiment, 4th Brigade, 2nd Division
Commander Unknown

Field and Staff	05
Erastus Day (Romeo)	09
Jesse O. Ferris (Mount Clemens Rifles)	08
Orson Sheldon (Utica)	30
Alpheus White, Artillery (Detroit)	06

2nd Regiment, 5th Brigade, 3rd Division (Monroe County)
Colonel Warner Wing, commanding

Field and Staff	32
George B. Darrow, Company B (Dundee?)	25
Gabriel Bissonette, Company F (Raisinville)	06
Heman N. Spaulding, Company G (Summerfield)	29
Noyes A. Wadsworth, Company I (Frenchtown)	18
Joseph Morass, Company J (Erie)	16
John Bradford, Company K (LaSalle)	18
Joseph Wood, Independent Company of Light Horse (Monroe)	42

8th Regiment, 5th Brigade, 3rd Division (Lenawee County)
Colonel Davis Smith, commanding

Field and Staff	35
Reuben Hall, 1st Company (East Raisin)	17
John Densmore, 2nd Company (Adrian)	36
Peleg Pettis, 3rd Company (Blissfield)	24
Horatio Baldwin, 4th Company (Clinton)	35
Ebenezer Davis, 5th Company (Franklin)	30
Augustus Montgomery, 6th Company (Ridgeway)	25
Milton Hoag, 7th Company (Tecumseh Rifles)	16
Jedediah Raymond, 8th Company	23

Miscellaneous	22
Total Number of Michigan Soldiers in the Toledo War	1,181

ROSTER OF MICHIGAN MEN
IN THE TOLEDO WAR

Name	Rank	Military Unit	Service Dates	Remarks
Abbey, H.	PVT	Griswold's Company	09/03/35–09/10/35	
Abbott, E. P.	PVT	Bull's Company	09/03/35–09/10/35	
Abbott, G.	PVT	Bull's Company	09/03/35–09/10/35	
Abbott, George C.	MUS	Bucklin's Regiment	09/03/35–09/10/35	
Abell, Alexander G.	PVT	Rupley's Company	09/03/35–09/10/35	
Aber, Aaron	VOL	Martin Davis' Detachment	03/27/35–03/31/35	Washtenaw County Militia
Adair, Edmund E.	3CP	Sheldon's Company	09/03/35–09/10/35	
Adair, Samuel	PVT	Shelby Volunteers	09/03/35–09/10/35	
Adam, John J.	2LT	Davis' Company	09/03/35–09/10/35	
Adams, Alfred B.	3SG	Sheldon's Company	09/03/35–09/10/35	
Adams, Julius	PVT	Brownell's Company	09/03/35–09/10/35	
Adams, Leonard	PVT	Brownell's Company	09/03/35–09/10/35	
Adams, Vinal	PVT	Davis' Rifle Regiment	09/03/35–09/10/35	
Adams, William S.	FIF	Oakland Detachment	09/03/35–09/10/35	
Aiken, Daniel	SGT	Thayer's Company	09/03/35–09/10/35	
Alexander, J.	PVT	Bull's Company	09/03/35–09/10/35	
Allard, Joseph W.	PVT	Davis Smith's Regiment	09/03/35–09/10/35	
Allen, Henry	2SG	Ingram's Company	09/03/35–09/10/35	
Allen, Horatio	PVT	Rupley's Company	09/03/35–09/10/35	
Allen, J. T.	PVT	Davis' Rifle Regiment	09/03/35–09/10/35	

Name	Rank	Military Unit	Service Dates	Remarks
Allen, Orville S.	PVT	Bull's Company	09/03/35–09/10/35	
Alling, Alanson	PVT	Baldwin's Company	09/03/35–09/10/35	
Allisson, Samuel	PVT	Haskins' Company	09/03/35–09/10/35	
Ames, Lorenzo J.	PVT	Raymond's Company	09/03/35–09/10/35	
Andrews, Alonzo	PVT	Davis' Rifle Regiment	09/03/35–09/10/35	
Andrews, Asa	PVT	Ingram's Company	09/03/35–09/10/35	
Andrews, Frederick	PVT	Davis' Rifle Regiment	09/03/35–09/10/35	
Arnold, William	PVT	Day's Company	09/03/35–09/10/35	
Ashley, Elkanah	PVT	Haskins' Company	09/03/35–09/10/35	
Atwood, Joseph	PVT	Gildard's Company	09/03/35–09/10/35	
Auscomb, Aaron	PVT	Wright's Company	09/03/35–09/10/35	
Austin, O. B.	PVT	Hall's Company	09/03/35–09/10/35	
Ayers, Andrew	PVT	Pettis' Company	09/03/35–09/10/35	
Ayres, Nathaniel B.	VOL	Martin Davis' Detachment	03/27/35–03/31/35	Washtenaw County Militia
Ayres, Silas	PVT	Darrow's Company	09/03/35–09/10/35	
Babcock, Hiram	PVT	Spaulding's Company	09/03/35–09/10/35	
Babcock, John	PVT	Davis' Rifle Regiment	09/03/35–09/10/35	
Bachelor, Samuel W.	DMR	Oakland Detachment	09/03/35–09/10/35	
Bacon, Daniel S.	QUD	F&S 3rd Division	09/03/35–09/10/35	
Bacon, Marshall J.	GOA	Unassigned	09/03/35–09/10/35	
Bailey, Benjamin F.	3SG	Brownell's Company	09/03/35–09/10/35	
Bailey, Calvin	PVT	Gildard's Company	09/03/35–09/10/35	
Bailey, Lewis E.	CAP	Wing's Regiment	09/03/35–09/10/35	Adjutant
Baldwin, Daniel	PVT	Rupley's Company	09/03/35–09/10/35	
Baldwin, Horatio N.	CAP	Baldwin's Company	09/03/35–09/10/35	

NAME	RANK	MILITARY UNIT	SERVICE DATES	REMARKS
Ball, Joel	PVT	Montgomery's Company	09/03/35–09/10/35	
Ball?, Aug F.	VOL	Martin Davis' Detachment	03/27/35–03/31/35	Washtenaw County Militia
Ballard, Arden H.	VOL	Martin Davis' Detachment	03/27/35–03/31/35	Washtenaw County Militia
Ballard, William A.	2LT	Davis' Rifle Regiment	09/03/35–09/10/35	
Ballou, Royal	VOL	Martin Davis' Detachment	03/27/35–03/31/35	Washtenaw County Militia
Bangor, William	2SG	Spaulding's Company	09/03/35–09/10/35	
Bangs, Keeler E.	PVT	Davis Smith's Regiment	09/03/35–09/10/35	
Bangs, Lemuel L.	PVT	Hall's Company	09/03/35–09/10/35	
Banker, Henry	VOL	Martin Davis' Detachment	03/27/35–03/31/35	Washtenaw County Militia
Banker, Peter	VOL	Martin Davis' Detachment	03/27/35–03/31/35	Washtenaw County Militia
Barker, Darius	PVT	Davis' Rifle Regiment	09/03/35–09/10/35	
Barker, George	PVT	Rupley's Company	09/03/35–09/10/35	
Barker, Peleg	PVT	Rupley's Company	09/03/35–09/10/35	
Barkley, Thomas	PVT	Taylor's Company	09/03/35–09/10/35	
Barlow, Daniel	PVT	Davis' Rifle Regiment	09/03/35–09/10/35	
Barnard, James	PVT	Wadsworth's Company	09/03/35–09/10/35	
Barnes, Aurora	PVT	Brownell's Company	09/03/35–09/10/35	
Barns, William	PVT	Raymond's Company	09/03/35–09/10/35	
Barret, Israel	PVT	Pettis' Company	09/03/35–09/10/35	
Barron, Antoine	PVT	Wood's Company	09/03/35–09/10/35	
Barstow, John	PVT	Darrow's Company	09/03/35–09/10/35	
Bartlett, John H.	2CP	Wood's Company	09/03/35–09/10/35	
Bartlett, Solon	2CP	Spaulding's Company	09/03/35–09/10/35	
Barton, Harvey	2LT	Davis' Rifle Regiment	09/03/35–09/10/35	
Barton, Jacob	PVT	Darrow's Company	09/03/35–09/10/35	

NAME	RANK	MILITARY UNIT	SERVICE DATES	REMARKS
Bates, D. W.	2SG	Raymond's Company	09/03/35–09/10/35	
Bates, George C.	1LT	Bull's Company	09/03/35–09/10/35	
Batter, Nathaniel	1CP	Ingram's Company	09/03/35–09/10/35	
Bebee, Daniel	PVT	Davis' Company	09/03/35–09/10/35	
Bebee, Eldridge C.	1SG	Greenman's Company	09/03/35–09/10/35	
Bebee, Joel	PVT	Davis' Company	09/03/35–09/10/35	
Beckwith, Sheldon	1LT	Gildard's Company	09/03/35–09/10/35	
Beeden, John Jr.	MAJ	Davis' Rifle Regiment	09/03/35–09/10/35	
Beenup?, John	VOL	Martin Davis' Detachment	03/27/35–03/31/35	Washtenaw County Militia
Beers, Marcus	PVT	Taylor's Company	09/03/35–09/10/35	
Belcher, Henry	PVT	Raymond's Company	09/03/35–09/10/35	
Belcher, John	PVT	Densmore's Company	09/03/35–09/10/35	
Bell, Benjamin	PVT	Gildard's Company	09/03/35–09/10/35	
Bell, Harrison M.	PVT	Gildard's Company	09/03/35–09/10/35	
Bell, Henry Y.	PVT	Gildard's Company	09/03/35–09/10/35	
Bell, James	PVT	Davis' Company	09/03/35–09/10/35	
Bellows, Ruppis	PVT	Thayer's Company	09/03/35–09/10/35	
Bennett, Albon	MUS	Wing's Regiment	09/03/35–09/10/35	1st MUS Monroe Band
Bennett, Andrew	PVT	Cone's Company	09/03/35–09/10/35	
Bennett, Asahel	1SG	Haskins' Company	09/03/35–09/10/35	
Bennett, Levi	PVT	Densmore's Company	09/03/35–09/10/35	
Bennett, Moses T.	MUS	Raymond's Company	09/03/35–09/10/35	
Berdino, Henry D.	PVT	Morass' Company	09/03/35–09/10/35	
Bernard, Joseph	PVT	Wadsworth's Company	09/03/35–09/10/35	
Bernard, Moses	PVT	Spaulding's Company	09/03/35–09/10/35	
Betts, Peter	PVT	Montgomery's Company	09/03/35–09/10/35	

Michigan Men in the Toledo War

Name	Rank	Military Unit	Service Dates	Remarks
Bidwell, Clark	PVT	Spaulding's Company	09/03/35–09/10/35	
Bidwell, Orlando	PVT	Spaulding's Company	09/03/35–09/10/35	
Bigelow, William	1CP	Baldwin's Company	09/03/35–09/10/35	
Bigget, Alexander	PVT	Thayer's Company	09/03/35–09/10/35	
Bilbain, Benjamin	PVT	Davis Smith's Regiment	09/03/35–09/10/35	
Bird, Asahel L.	CAP	Bird's Company	09/03/35–09/10/35	
Bissonette, Gabriel David	CAP	Bissonette's Company	09/03/35–09/10/35	
Bivins, Myron	PVT	Baldwin's Company	09/03/35–09/10/35	
Bixley, Alonzo F.	PVT	Densmore's Company	09/03/35–09/10/35	
Blackman, Philetas	PVT	Davis' Rifle Regiment	09/03/35–09/10/35	
Blake, Norman	PVT	Densmore's Company	09/03/35–09/10/35	
Blanchard, Erastus	PVT	Davis' Rifle Regiment	09/03/35–09/10/35	
Blanchard, John	PVT	Brownell's Company	09/03/35–09/10/35	
Blanchard, Norman	PVT	Rupley's Company	09/03/35–09/10/35	
Blanchard, Sidney F.	1LT	Davis Smith's Regiment	09/03/35–09/10/35	Quartermaster
Bliss, William	PVT	Pettis' Company	09/03/35–09/10/35	
Blossom, Ansel Jr.	PVT	Baldwin's Company	09/03/35–09/10/35	
Boardman, William E.	ADC	Unassigned	09/03/35–09/10/35	
Bodin, Russell	SGT	Hall's Company	09/03/35–09/10/35	
Bolton, Noble	PVT	Day's Company	09/03/35–09/10/35	
Bond, Edwin	2LT	Davis' Rifle Regiment	09/03/35–09/10/35	
Bongon, Hyacinth	PVT	Morass' Company	09/03/35–09/10/35	
Booth, C. M.	2SG	Davis' Rifle Regiment	09/03/35–09/10/35	
Bordon, Joseph	PVT	Wadsworth's Company	09/03/35–09/10/35	
Borron, Gilliet	PVT	Bradford's Company	09/03/35–09/10/35	
Borron, John B.	PVT	Morass' Company	09/03/35–09/10/35	

NAME	RANK	MILITARY UNIT	SERVICE DATES	REMARKS
Borron, Joseph	PVT	Bradford's Company	09/03/35–09/10/35	
Boss, Randall	PVT	Baldwin's Company	09/03/35–09/10/35	
Boughton, Richard	CAP	Davis' Rifle Regiment	09/03/35–09/10/35	
Bourson, Anthony	PVT	Wright's Company	09/03/35–09/10/35	
Bowan, James	VOL	Martin Davis' Detachment	03/27/35–03/31/35	Washtenaw County Militia
Bowen, E. S.	PVT	Rupley's Company	09/03/35–09/10/35	
Boyce, John	VOL	Martin Davis' Detachment	03/27/35–03/31/35	Washtenaw County Militia
Boyd, James	PVT	Hall's Company	09/03/35–09/10/35	
Bradford, Alfred	PVT	Rupley's Company	09/03/35–09/10/35	
Bradford, John	CAP	Bradford's Company	09/03/35–09/10/35	
Bradner, Enos	2LT	Davis' Rifle Regiment	09/03/35–09/10/35	
Bradner, Ezra	1LT	Davis' Rifle Regiment	09/03/35–09/10/35	
Bradner, Ira G.	1SG	Davis' Rifle Regiment	09/03/35–09/10/35	
Bradnor, John	1CP	Davis' Rifle Regiment	09/03/35–09/10/35	
Brainard, R.	DMR	Davis' Rifle Regiment	09/03/35–09/10/35	
Brewer, William	2LT	Davis' Rifle Regiment	09/03/35–09/10/35	
Brewer, William	PVT	Davis' Rifle Regiment	09/03/35–09/10/35	
Brier, Thomas C.	PVT	Davis' Rifle Regiment	09/03/35–09/10/35	
Brockford, Simon	TEB	Oakland Detachment	09/03/35–09/10/35	
Broduck, M.	2SG	Wing's Regiment	09/03/35–09/10/35	
Brower, R. D.	VOL	Martin Davis' Detachment	03/27/35–03/31/35	Washtenaw County Militia
Brown, David D.	PVT	Davis' Rifle Regiment	09/03/35–09/10/35	
Brown, Elias	DMR	Oakland Detachment	09/03/35–09/10/35	
Brown, J.	PVT	Griswold's Company	09/03/35–09/10/35	
Brown, John	VOL	Martin Davis' Detachment	03/27/35–03/31/35	Washtenaw County Militia

NAME	RANK	MILITARY UNIT	SERVICE DATES	REMARKS
Brown, Joseph White	GEM	F&S MI Militia	09/03/35–09/10/35	
Brown, Simeon B.	2LT	Wright's Company	09/03/35–09/10/35	
Brownell, George	CAP	Oakland Detachment	09/03/35–09/10/35	
Brownell, John L.	1LT	Oakland Detachment	09/03/35–09/10/35	Quartermaster
Brumley, Peter	4SG	Densmore's Company	09/03/35–09/10/35	
Buck, Allen	PVT	Davis' Rifle Regiment	09/03/35–09/10/35	
Buck, John	PVT	Thayer's Company	09/03/35–09/10/35	
Bucklin, James	MAJ	Bucklin's Regiment	09/03/35–09/10/35	
Bugby, Daniel	PVT	Densmore's Company	09/03/35–09/10/35	
Bugby, Elias	PVT	Densmore's Company	09/03/35–09/10/35	
Bugrand, Alexis	WAG	Wing's Regiment	09/03/35–09/10/35	
Bull, Charles M.	CAP	Bull's Company	09/03/35–09/10/35	
Bullock, Elijah	PVT	Brownell's Company	09/03/35–09/10/35	
Bumpus, H. H.	VOL	Martin Davis' Detachment	03/27/35–03/31/35	Washtenaw County Militia
Bumpus, S. R.	VOL	Martin Davis' Detachment	03/27/35–03/31/35	Washtenaw County Militia
Bunnell, A.	PVT	Slingerland's Company	09/03/35–09/10/35	
Burdino, Augustus	1SG	Morass' Company	09/03/35–09/10/35	
Burdino, Lewis	2SG	Morass' Company	09/03/35–09/10/35	
Burgess, Nelson	4SG	Haskins' Company	09/03/35–09/10/35	
Burgess, Orrin	PVT	Ingram's Company	09/03/35–09/10/35	
Burlington, John	3CP	Montgomery's Company	09/03/35–09/10/35	
Burnett, Asa	PVT	Davis' Rifle Regiment	09/03/35–09/10/35	
Burnett, Cyrus	1LT	Davis' Rifle Regiment	09/03/35–09/10/35	
Burr, Hollister	PVT	Baldwin's Company	09/03/35–09/10/35	
Burwell, Peter R.	PVT	Davis' Company	09/03/35–09/10/35	

Name	Rank	Military Unit	Service Dates	Remarks
Bushey, Flavius	PVT	Bradford's Company	09/03/35–09/10/35	
Butler, David	PVT	Pettis' Company	09/03/35–09/10/35	
Butterfield, Ephraim	PVT	Davis' Rifle Regiment	09/03/35–09/10/35	
Butterfield, Levi B.	4SG	Davis' Rifle Regiment	09/03/35–09/10/35	
Button, Gamet	PVT	Thayer's Company	09/03/35–09/10/35	
Caldwell, John	PVT	Wood's Company	09/03/35–09/10/35	
Campau, Antoine	PVT	Wadsworth's Company	09/03/35–09/10/35	
Campau, Antoine	PVT	Wood's Company	09/03/35–09/10/35	
Campau, James	PVT	Bird's Company	09/03/35–09/10/35	
Campbell, James	PVT	Wadsworth's Company	09/03/35–09/10/35	
Campbell, William	PVT	Wright's Company	09/03/35–09/10/35	
Cane, David	PVT	Brownell's Company	09/03/35–09/10/35	
Canniff, E. C.	PVT	Bissonette's Company	09/03/35–09/10/35	
Carl, James	PVT	Davis' Rifle Regiment	09/03/35–09/10/35	
Carleton, Guy	PVT	Davis' Rifle Regiment	09/03/35–09/10/35	
Carlisle, David	PVT	Ingram's Company	09/03/35–09/10/35	
Carman, Jacob	TEB	Oakland Detachment	09/03/35–09/10/35	
Carpenter, Guy	1LT	Pettis' Company	09/03/35–09/10/35	
Carr, Elijah P.	DMR	Davis' Rifle Regiment	09/03/35–09/10/35	
Carter, G.	PVT	Baldwin's Company	09/03/35–09/10/35	
Carter, Harleigh	PVT	Sheldon's Company	09/03/35–09/10/35	
Carter, James B.	1SG	Sheldon's Company	09/03/35–09/10/35	
Carter, N. M.	PVT	Baldwin's Company	09/03/35–09/10/35	
Case, Daniel	PVT	Ingram's Company	09/03/35–09/10/35	
Caston, Ziba	VOL	Martin Davis' Detachment	03/27/35–03/31/35	Washtenaw County Militia
Caulkins, Ephraim	PVT	Sheldon's Company	09/03/35–09/10/35	

NAME	RANK	MILITARY UNIT	SERVICE DATES	REMARKS
Celladden, Ruben	PVT	Cone's Company	09/03/35–09/10/35	
Chamberlin, Joseph	PVT	Bradford's Company	09/03/35–09/10/35	
Chamberlin, Peter	PVT	Bradford's Company	09/03/35–09/10/35	
Chamberlin, Wells	VOL	Martin Davis' Detachment	03/27/35–03/31/35	Washtenaw County Militia
Chamberlin, William C.	PVT	Brownell's Company	09/03/35–09/10/35	
Chambers, Henry C.	PVT	Haskins' Company	09/03/35–09/10/35	
Champion, S	VOL	Martin Davis' Detachment	03/27/35–03/31/35	Washtenaw County Militia
Champion, Salmon Jr.	PVT	Slingerland's Company	09/03/35–09/10/35	
Chandler, George	PVT	Baldwin's Company	09/03/35–09/10/35	
Chandler, Joseph N.	2LT	Davis Smith's Regiment	09/03/35–09/10/35	
Chandler, Philander M.	PVT	Baldwin's Company	09/03/35–09/10/35	
Chapill, Calvin	2LT	Ingram's Company	09/03/35–09/10/35	
Chapin, Elom	PVT	Haskins' Company	09/03/35–09/10/35	
Chapin, Zelotus	3SG	Cone's Company	09/03/35–09/10/35	
Chapman, Stephen	PVT	Brownell's Company	09/03/35–09/10/35	
Chappell, George	PVT	Raymond's Company	09/03/35–09/10/35	
Charter, Orange	4SG	Darrow's Company	09/03/35–09/10/35	
Chatfield, Eli	1LT	Hall's Company	09/03/35–09/10/35	
Chester, John	GOS	Unassigned	09/03/35–09/10/35	
Chester, Oliver	PVT	Darrow's Company	09/03/35–09/10/35	
Chipman, Aaron B.	PVT	Taylor's Company	09/03/35–09/10/35	
Chorid, Leon	PVT	Wadsworth's Company	09/03/35–09/10/35	
Church, Sylvanus	3CP	Martin Davis' Detachment	09/03/35–09/10/35	
Cicotte, J. J.	PVT	Griswold's Company	09/03/35–09/10/35	
Cisson, William B.	PVT	Davis' Rifle Regiment	09/03/35–09/10/35	
Clark, Charles W.	PVT	Rupley's Company	09/03/35–09/10/35	

NAME	RANK	MILITARY UNIT	SERVICE DATES	REMARKS
Clarke, John B.	1SG	Rupley's Company	09/03/35–09/10/35	
Clarke, Silas	FIF	Bucklin's Regiment	09/03/35–09/10/35	
Clinton, Henry	2SG	Bradford's Company	09/03/35–09/10/35	
Clyne, Jacob	PVT	Haskins' Company	09/03/35–09/10/35	
Coates, Francis	PVT	Montgomery's Company	09/03/35–09/10/35	
Coates, William	PVT	Brownell's Company	09/03/35–09/10/35	
Cockhart, James	3CP	Ingram's Company	09/03/35–09/10/35	
Cohart, Hiram	2LT	Haskins' Company	09/03/35–09/10/35	
Colby, William S.	2LT	Martin Davis' Detachment	09/03/35–09/10/35	
Cole, Hiram	PVT	Montgomery's Company	09/03/35–09/10/35	
Cole, Joshua	PVT	Baldwin's Company	09/03/35–09/10/35	
Collar, Calvin	VOL	Martin Davis' Detachment	03/27/35–03/31/35	Washtenaw County Militia
Collar, Isaac K.	VOL	Martin Davis' Detachment	03/27/35–03/31/35	Washtenaw County Militia
Collins, Charles	VOL	Martin Davis' Detachment	03/27/35–03/31/35	Washtenaw County Militia
Collins, George	VOL	Martin Davis' Detachment	03/27/35–03/31/35	Washtenaw County Militia
Collins, William H.	4SG	Davis' Rifle Regiment	09/03/35–09/10/35	
Collum, William	PVT	Davis Smith's Regiment	09/03/35–09/10/35	
Colwin, Stephen	1SG	Densmore's Company	09/03/35–09/10/35	
Compton, Henry	VOL	Martin Davis' Detachment	03/27/35–03/31/35	Washtenaw County Militia
Compton, Ransom	PVT	Davis' Rifle Regiment	09/03/35–09/10/35	
Comstock, Edwin	PVT	Densmore's Company	09/03/35–09/10/35	
Comstock, Isaac	VOL	Martin Davis' Detachment	03/27/35–03/31/35	Washtenaw County Militia
Comstock, Joseph H.	VOL	Martin Davis' Detachment	03/27/35–03/31/35	Washtenaw County Militia
Comstock, N.	VOL	Martin Davis' Detachment	03/27/35–03/31/35	Washtenaw County Militia
Comstock, Willard	PVT	Taylor's Company	09/03/35–09/10/35	
Cone, Linus	CAP	Cone's Company	09/03/35–09/10/35	

NAME	RANK	MILITARY UNIT	SERVICE DATES	REMARKS
Conklin, Isaac N.	VOL	Martin Davis' Detachment	03/27/35–03/31/35	Washtenaw County Militia
Conklin, John	PVT	Davis' Rifle Regiment	09/03/35–09/10/35	
Conlish, Peter	PVT	Darrow's Company	09/03/35–09/10/35	
Conner, Isaac	PVT	Davis' Rifle Regiment	09/03/35–09/10/35	
Consino, Boswell	PVT	Morass' Company	09/03/35–09/10/35	
Consino, Francis	1LT	Morass' Company	09/03/35–09/10/35	
Consor, Jesse	4SG	Wood's Company	09/03/35–09/10/35	
Conturo, Dominique	PVT	Wadsworth's Company	09/03/35–09/10/35	
Cook, Ferris	2CP	Montgomery's Company	09/03/35–09/10/35	
Cook, Moses B.	PVT	Davis Smith's Regiment	09/03/35–09/10/35	
Cook, Nathan	PVT	Thayer's Company	09/03/35–09/10/35	
Cooney, Owen	PVT	Bradford's Company	09/03/35–09/10/35	
Corbey, Hiram	PVT	Bird's Company	09/03/35–09/10/35	
Corey, Cyrus H.	FIF	Davis' Rifle Regiment	09/03/35–09/10/35	
Corey, Hiram D.	FIF	Davis' Rifle Regiment	09/03/35–09/10/35	
Cornish, Jared B.	1LT	Davis' Rifle Regiment	09/03/35–09/10/35	
Corvill, James	PVT	Sheldon's Company	09/03/35–09/10/35	
Corwin, Jesse	PVT	Davis' Rifle Regiment	09/03/35–09/10/35	
Cousino, Francis	1LT	Wing's Regiment	09/03/35–09/10/35	
Covert, Abram B.	PVT	Davis' Rifle Regiment	09/03/35–09/10/35	
Cox, Robert	PVT	Hoag's Company	09/03/35–09/10/35	
Crandall, Ira D.	PVT	Wing's Regiment	09/03/35–09/10/35	
Crane, Alexander D.	CAP	Davis' Rifle Regiment	09/03/35–09/10/35	
Crane, David	PVT	Oakland Detachment	09/03/35–09/10/35	
Crawford, George	PVT	Ingram's Company	09/03/35–09/10/35	
Crawford, James	PVT	Cone's Company	09/03/35–09/10/35	

NAME	RANK	MILITARY UNIT	SERVICE DATES	REMARKS
Crawford, Riley C.	FIF	Cone's Company	09/03/35–09/10/35	SCU
Crawford, Robert S.	PVT	Ferris' Company	09/03/35–09/10/35	
Crego, Stephen	COR	Wood's Company	09/03/35–09/10/35	
Cressey, Alonzo	SUM	Davis Smith's Regiment	09/03/35–09/10/35	
Croff, John A.	2SG	Rupley's Company	09/03/35–09/10/35	
Crowfoot, Amri W.	PVT	Haskins' Company	09/03/35–09/10/35	
Crowfoot, Hiram	2LT	Haskins' Company	09/03/35–09/10/35	
Crown, Robert	VOL	Martin Davis' Detachment	03/27/35–03/31/35	Washtenaw County Militia
Crump, Edward	1CP	Wood's Company	09/03/35–09/10/35	
Cummings, Robert M.	PVT	Ingram's Company	09/03/35–09/10/35	
Cunningham, J.	PVT	Bull's Company	09/03/35–09/10/35	
Cure, Martin	PVT	Densmore's Company	09/03/35–09/10/35	
Curtiss, Josiah	PVT	Raymond's Company	09/03/35–09/10/35	
Curtiss, Perry W.	PVT	Spaulding's Company	09/03/35–09/10/35	
Curtiss, Philo	2CP	Cone's Company	09/03/35–09/10/35	
Curtiss, Samuel	PVT	Wood's Company	09/03/35–09/10/35	
Dagerman, Alexander	PVT	Davis' Rifle Regiment	09/03/35–09/10/35	
Dailey, William	PVT	Davis Smith's Regiment	09/03/35–09/10/35	
Daily, John B.	2LT	Bradford's Company	09/03/35–09/10/35	
Dan, Thomas	2LT	Griswold's Company	09/03/35–09/10/35	
Daniels, John	1SG	Davis' Company	09/03/35–09/10/35	
Daniels, Reuben	PVT	Davis' Company	09/03/35–09/10/35	
Darby, Abram	PVT	Davis' Company	09/03/35–09/10/35	
Darby, John B.	2LT	Bradford's Company	09/03/35–09/10/35	
Darby, Peter	PVT	Davis' Company	09/03/35–09/10/35	
Dare, Thomas	2LT	Griswold's Company	09/03/35–09/10/35	

Name	Rank	Military Unit	Service Dates	Remarks
Darlin, Cyrus	PVT	Raymond's Company	09/03/35–09/10/35	
Darrah, Henry B.	4CP	Wood's Company	09/03/35–09/10/35	
Darrow, George B.	CAP	Darrow's Company	09/03/35–09/10/35	AKA George M Danah
Davenport, Cornelius	PVT	Montgomery's Company	09/03/35–09/10/35	
Davidson, Simeon	3SG	Davis Smith's Regiment	09/03/35–09/10/35	
Davidson, William C.	1SG	Davis' Rifle Regiment	09/03/35–09/10/35	
Davis, Alonzo	PVT	Cone's Company	09/03/35 09/10/35	
Davis, B. B.	VOL	Martin Davis' Detachment	03/27/35–03/31/35	Washtenaw County Militia
Davis, Ebenezer	CAP	Davis' Company	09/03/35–09/10/35	
Davis, Jonathan D.	COL	Davis' Rifle Regiment	09/03/35–09/10/35	
Davis, Joseph Y.	ENS	Gildard's Company	09/03/35–09/10/35	
Davis, Martin M.	COL	Martin Davis' Detachment	09/03/35–09/10/35	Acting Brigadier General
Davis, Zenas	PVT	Davis' Rifle Regiment	09/03/35–09/10/35	
Dawson, James	PVT	Rupley's Company	09/03/35–09/10/35	
Dawson?, William	VOL	Martin Davis' Detachment	03/27/35–03/31/35	Washtenaw County Militia
Day, Erastus	CAP	Day's Company	09/03/35–09/10/35	
DeBarr, Samuel	PVT	Davis' Rifle Regiment	09/03/35–09/10/35	
Decker, William	PVT	Gildard's Company	09/03/35–09/10/35	
Densmore, John	CAP	Densmore's Company	09/03/35–09/10/35	
Densmore, Joseph	PVT	Davis' Rifle Regiment	09/03/35–09/10/35	
Deorly, Henry	PVT	Davis' Company	09/03/35–09/10/35	
Depew, Ezra N.	PVT	Sheldon's Company	09/03/35–09/10/35	
Derby, Eli	CAP	Davis' Rifle Regiment	09/03/35–09/10/35	
Derby, John B.	2LT	Bradford's Company	09/03/35–09/10/35	
Derbyshire, Sidney	PVT	Davis Smith's Regiment	09/03/35–09/10/35	
Derwin, Appollos	MAJ	Wing's Regiment	09/03/35–09/10/35	

NAME	RANK	MILITARY UNIT	SERVICE DATES	REMARKS
Deshaw, Francis	PVT	Spaulding's Company	09/03/35–09/10/35	
Deshon, Asbert G.	MUS	Shelby Volunteers	09/03/35–09/10/35	
Dickinson, M. M.	PVT	Davis' Rifle Regiment	09/03/35–09/10/35	
Dickinson, Silas	1LT	Davis' Rifle Regiment	09/03/35–09/10/35	
Dicks, Alexander	3SG	Wright's Company	09/03/35–09/10/35	
Dirbey, James	PVT	Ferris' Company	09/03/35–09/10/35	
Dodean, Gabriel	PVT	Morass' Company	09/03/35–09/10/35	
Dodge, Hiram	PVT	Baldwin's Company	09/03/35–09/10/35	
Dodge, John	PVT	Densmore's Company	09/03/35–09/10/35	
Dodge, Joshua	3SG	Spaulding's Company	09/03/35–09/10/35	
Donehan, Patrick	PVT	Thayer's Company	09/03/35–09/10/35	
Doran, Hanson	PVT	Davis' Rifle Regiment	09/03/35–09/10/35	
Douglas, Columbus C.	ENS	Ferris' Company	09/03/35–09/10/35	
Drake, Walter	1LT	Brownell's Company	09/03/35–09/10/35	
Drown, Appollos	MAJ	Wing's Regiment	09/03/35–09/10/35	
Drummond, D.	PVT	Morass' Company	09/03/35–09/10/35	
Duchene, Joseph	PVT	Wadsworth's Company	09/03/35–09/10/35	
Dunbar, Almon	MUS	Wing's Regiment	09/03/35–09/10/35	Monroe Band
Dunbar, Austin	MUS	Wing's Regiment	09/03/35–09/10/35	Monroe Band
Dunbar, William	MUS	Wing's Regiment	09/03/35–09/10/35	Monroe Band
Dunn, James	CAP	Bucklin's Regiment	09/03/35–09/10/35	Adjutant
Dunning, Daniel	2SG	Montgomery's Company	09/03/35–09/10/35	
Dunning, Jehial	PVT	Davis' Rifle Regiment	09/03/35–09/10/35	
Dunsmore, Joseph	VOL	Martin Davis' Detachment	03/27/35–03/31/35	Washtenaw County Militia
Dutton, Justin	PVT	Thayer's Company	09/03/35–09/10/35	
Duval, Stephen	3CP	Wood's Company	09/03/35–09/10/35	

NAME	RANK	MILITARY UNIT	SERVICE DATES	REMARKS
Eaton, C. C.	2SG	Hoag's Company	09/03/35–09/10/35	
Eaton, Ebenezer C.	MAJ	Martin Davis' Detachment	09/03/35–09/10/35	Brigade Major
Eddington, John B.	VOL	Martin Davis' Detachment	03/27/35–03/31/35	Washtenaw County Militia
Eddy, B.	DMR	Davis' Rifle Regiment	09/03/35–09/10/35	
Edmunds, Jacob	PVT	Slingerland's Company	09/03/35–09/10/35	
Edwards, Asa G.	1LT	Davis' Company	09/03/35–09/10/35	
Ellis, Charles	QUS	Martin Davis' Detachment	09/03/35–09/10/35	
Ellis, Elexis	PVT	Baldwin's Company	09/03/35–09/10/35	
Ellis, Elijah	PVT	Taylor's Company	09/03/35–09/10/35	
Ellison, James	PVT	Wood's Company	09/03/35–09/10/35	
Elmore, Aaron W.	PVT	Davis' Rifle Regiment	09/03/35–09/10/35	
Embury, George	PVT	Montgomery's Company	09/03/35–09/10/35	
Emerson, Gideon	PVT	Darrow's Company	09/03/35–09/10/35	
Emmons, J. B.	PVT	Bull's Company	09/03/35–09/10/35	
Enos, James	PVT	Spaulding's Company	09/03/35–09/10/35	
Ensworth, A. S.	PVT	Baldwin's Company	09/03/35–09/10/35	
Entell, Reuben	PVT	White's Company	09/03/35–09/10/35	
Entricon, William W.	PVT	Brownell's Company	09/03/35–09/10/35	
Evans, Luther	PVT	Densmore's Company	09/03/35–09/10/35	
Evans, Samuel B.	CLT	Davis Smith's Regiment	09/03/35–09/10/35	
Everett, William	PVT	Davis' Rifle Regiment	09/03/35–09/10/35	
Ewell, Libeas	2CP	Sheldon's Company	09/03/35–09/10/35	
Farnum, Joseph S.	4SG	Ingram's Company	09/03/35–09/10/35	
Farrer, George	QUS	Wing's Regiment	09/03/35–09/10/35	
Felch, Alpheus	ADC	Unassigned	09/03/35–09/10/35	AKA Alpheus Phelps
Ferris, Jesse Owen	CAP	Ferris' Company	09/03/35–09/10/35	

NAME	RANK	MILITARY UNIT	SERVICE DATES	REMARKS
Field, Jonathan E.	1LT	Martin Davis' Detachment	09/03/35–09/10/35	Brigade Quartermaster
Fisk, Hanford W.	2SG	Cone's Company	09/03/35–09/10/35	
Fisk, Joshua	PVT	Davis' Rifle Regiment	09/03/35–09/10/35	
Foot, Jacob J.	1LT	Davis' Rifle Regiment	09/03/35–09/10/35	
Foot, Orange	CAP	Oakland Detachment	09/03/35–09/10/35	
Force, Henry	PVT	Densmore's Company	09/03/35–09/10/35	
Fossett, Chauncey S.	PVT	Wood's Company	09/03/35–09/10/35	
Foster, Abolom	PVT	Baldwin's Company	09/03/35–09/10/35	
Foster, Booth C.	PVT	Davis' Rifle Regiment	09/03/35–09/10/35	
Fowler, Ira	PVT	Rupley's Company	09/03/35–09/10/35	
Fowler, Samuel	PVT	Sheldon's Company	09/03/35–09/10/35	
Fox, Zenas	3SG	Foot's Company	09/03/35–09/10/35	
Frain, George	VOL	Martin Davis' Detachment	03/27/35–03/31/35	Washtenaw County Militia
Fralick, Peter	1LT	Davis' Rifle Regiment	09/03/35–09/10/35	Paymaster
Frank, E.	PVT	Griswold's Company	09/03/35–09/10/35	
Franklin, F.	PVT	Bissonette's Company	09/03/35–09/10/35	
Frasier, Joseph	PVT	Wright's Company	09/03/35–09/10/35	
Freeland, A.	MUS	Shelby Volunteers	09/03/35–09/10/35	
Fuller, Barzilla	PVT	Greenman's Company	09/03/35–09/10/35	
Fuller, George	PVT	Davis' Company	09/03/35–09/10/35	
Fuller, John	QUS	Davis' Rifle Regiment	09/03/35–09/10/35	
Fuller, Lewis	1LT	Greenman's Company	09/03/35–09/10/35	
Fuller, S.	2SG	Greenman's Company	09/03/35–09/10/35	
Fuller, S. E.	PVT	Greenman's Company	09/03/35–09/10/35	
Fuller, William A.	PVT	Sheldon's Company	09/03/35–09/10/35	
Furgerson, Alexander	PVT	Pettis' Company	09/03/35–09/10/35	

Name	Rank	Military Unit	Service Dates	Remarks
Gambell, William	PVT	Haskins' Company	09/03/35–09/10/35	
Gamble, James	PVT	Hall's Company	09/03/35–09/10/35	
Gardner, Francis	PVT	Davis' Rifle Regiment	09/03/35–09/10/35	
Garfield, Orrin G.	PVT	Brownell's Company	09/03/35–09/10/35	
Garland, Jerome	PVT	Griswold's Company	09/03/35–09/10/35	
Garrett, John	PVT	Gildard's Company	09/03/35–09/10/35	
Gates, Samuel	1LT	Davis' Rifle Regiment	09/03/35–09/10/35	
German, Asa	PVT	Hoag's Company	09/03/35–09/10/35	
Gerton, Richard	SUM	Martin Davis' Detachment	09/03/35–09/10/35v	
Gibson, Thomas	PVT	Haskins' Company	09/03/35–09/10/35	
Gilbert, Albert	PVT	Pettis' Company	09/03/35–09/10/35	
Gilbert, Gillet	PVT	Densmore's Company	09/03/35–09/10/35	
Gilbert, M. H.	VOL	Martin Davis' Detachment	03/27/35–03/31/35	Washtenaw County Militia
Gildard, Thomas	CAP	Gildard's Company	09/03/35–09/10/35	AKA Thomas Geldred
Giles, Abil	VOL	Martin Davis' Detachment	03/27/35–03/31/35	Washtenaw County Militia
Giles, Ebinezer	VOL	Martin Davis' Detachment	03/27/35–03/31/35	Washtenaw County Militia
Gillispie, M. M.	SGM	Davis' Rifle Regiment	09/03/35–09/10/35v	
Godfrey, William	PVT	Raymond's Company	09/03/35–09/10/35	
Godfroy, Phillip S.	PVT	Wood's Company	09/03/35–09/10/35	
Goff, Hiram	PVT	Shelby Volunteers	09/03/35–09/10/35	
Goff, William	PVT	Sheldon's Company	09/03/35–09/10/35	
Golden, Harman	PVT	Davis' Rifle Regiment	09/03/35–09/10/35	
Golding, Robert	PVT	Ingram's Company	09/03/35–09/10/35	
Goodell, E. B.	DMM	Davis' Rifle Regiment	09/03/35–09/10/35	
Goodell, Jonas	CAP	Goodell's Company	09/03/35–09/10/35	AKA Jonas Godell
Goodman, Daniel	QUG	Unassigned	09/03/35–09/10/35	

NAME	RANK	MILITARY UNIT	SERVICE DATES	REMARKS
Goodrich, Alanson	2LT	Foot's Company	09/03/35–09/10/35	AKA Alonzo Goodrich
Goodrich, Chester	COR	Foot's Company	09/03/35–09/10/35	
Goodrich, David	DMR	Oakland Detachment	09/03/35–09/10/35	
Goodrich, H. P.	PVT	Davis' Rifle Regiment	09/03/35–09/10/35	
Goodrich, Horace H.	PVT	Bradford's Company	09/03/35–09/10/35	
Goodrich, Morrell	1LT	Martin Davis' Detachment	09/03/35–09/10/35	
Goodrich, Peter	TEB	Davis' Rifle Regiment	09/03/35–09/10/35	
Goodrich, Willard R.	3CP	Cone's Company	09/03/35–09/10/35	
Goodwin, Daniel	QUG	Unassigned	09/03/35–09/10/35	
Gorton, Richard	SUM	Martin Davis' Detachment	09/03/35–09/10/35	
Goulding, Zena	1SG	Ingram's Company	09/03/35–09/10/35	
Graham, Theodore H.	PVT	Densmore's Company	09/03/35–09/10/35	
Graham, Walter	PVT	Raymond's Company	09/03/35–09/10/35	
Grant, David	PVT	Wright's Company	09/03/35–09/10/35	
Grant, John	PVT	Wright's Company	09/03/35–09/10/35	
Gray, Orren	PVT	Darrow's Company	09/03/35–09/10/35	
Green, Calvin A.	1SG	Brownell's Company	09/03/35–09/10/35	
Green, Chauncey	PVT	Brownell's Company	09/03/35–09/10/35	
Green, George	PVT	Baldwin's Company	09/03/35–09/10/35	
Green, Isaac W.	3SG	Haskins' Company	09/03/35–09/10/35	
Green, William	PVT	Brownell's Company	09/03/35–09/10/35	
Greenman, Chandley	DMR	Bucklin's Regiment	09/03/35–09/10/35	
Greenman, Martin	CAP	Greenman's Company	09/03/35–09/10/35	
Greer, William	PVT	Ingram's Company	09/03/35–09/10/35	
Gridley, G. T.	VOL	Martin Davis' Detachment	03/27/35–03/31/35	Washtenaw County Militia

NAME	RANK	MILITARY UNIT	SERVICE DATES	REMARKS
Gridley, Jesse B.	PVT	Sheldon's Company	09/03/35–09/10/35	
Griswold, George R.	CAP	Griswold's Company	09/03/35–09/10/35	
Guoin, Appolon	4SG	Wright's Company	09/03/35–09/10/35	
Guoin, Francis	PVT	Wright's Company	09/03/35–09/10/35	
Hadsill, Cyrus	PVT	Haskins' Company	09/03/35–09/10/35	
Haff, Rufus K.	PVT	Cone's Company	09/03/35–09/10/35	
Haggerty, H.	PVT	Greenman's Company	09/03/35–09/10/35	
Haight, William T.	PVT	Baldwin's Company	09/03/35–09/10/35	
Hall, David	1LT	Bradford's Company	09/03/35–09/10/35	
Hall, Elihu	PVT	Darrow's Company	09/03/35–09/10/35	
Hall, Isaac	PVT	Day's Company	09/03/35–09/10/35	
Hall, Joseph E.	CAP	Davis Smith's Regiment	09/03/35–09/10/35	Adjutant
Hall, Reuben L.	CAP	Hall's Company	09/03/35–09/10/35	
Hall, Stephen	PVT	Ferris' Company	09/03/35–09/10/35	
Hall, Walton J.	PVT	Darrow's Company	09/03/35–09/10/35	
Hallack, William R.	SGT	Day's Company	09/03/35–09/10/35	
Halsted, Soloman	PVT	Raymond's Company	09/03/35–09/10/35	
Hamilton, John	VOL	Martin Davis' Detachment	03/27/35–03/31/35	Washtenaw County Militia
Hammond, A. H.	VOL	Martin Davis' Detachment	03/27/35–03/31/35	Washtenaw County Militia
Hammond, Dennis	VOL	Martin Davis' Detachment	03/27/35–03/31/35	Washtenaw County Militia
Hanmer, James	3LT	Wright's Company	09/03/35–09/10/35	
Hannard, Samuel	PVT	Haskins' Company	09/03/35–09/10/35	
Hannibal, Thomas	2SG	Wright's Company	09/03/35–09/10/35	
Hanson, John	PVT	Wood's Company	09/03/35–09/10/35	
Hardy, Stephen P.	PVT	Davis' Rifle Regiment	09/03/35–09/10/35	

NAME	RANK	MILITARY UNIT	SERVICE DATES	REMARKS
Harman, Ebenezer	PVT	Montgomery's Company	09/03/35–09/10/35	
Harmon, Caleb C.	VOL	Martin Davis' Detachment	03/27/35–03/31/35	
Harmon, D.	DMR	Davis' Rifle Regiment	09/03/35–09/10/35	
Harper, George	PVT	Davis' Rifle Regiment	09/03/35–09/10/35	
Harris, Hiram	MUS	Shelby Volunteers	09/03/35–09/10/35	
Harris, Josiah	PVT	Spaulding's Company	09/03/35–09/10/35	
Harris, Silas	PVT	Cone's Company	09/03/35–09/10/35	
Hart, Joel Abram	PVT	Spaulding's Company	09/03/35–09/10/35	
Hart, Levi	PVT	Davis' Rifle Regiment	09/03/35–09/10/35	
Hart, Lewis	PVT	Spaulding's Company	09/03/35–09/10/35	
Hart, Roswell	PVT	Davis' Rifle Regiment	09/03/35–09/10/35	
Hart, William	PVT	Davis' Rifle Regiment	09/03/35–09/10/35	
Harwell, James	PVT	Bird's Company	09/03/35–09/10/35	
Harwood, John P.	DMR	Spaulding's Company	09/03/35–09/10/35	
Hascall, Charles C.	COL	F&S MI Militia	09/03/35–09/10/35	
Hascall, Samuel	PVT	Haskins' Company	09/03/35–09/10/35	
Hascall, William	PVT	Haskins' Company	09/03/35–09/10/35	
Hase, William	FIF	Bucklin's Regiment	09/03/35–09/10/35	
Haskins, Comfort	DMR	Bucklin's Regiment	09/03/35–09/10/35	
Haskins, Haron	CAP	Haskins' Company	09/03/35–09/10/35	
Haskins, Luther	PVT	Raymond's Company	09/03/35–09/10/35	
Haskins, William	PVT	Raymond's Company	09/03/35–09/10/35	
Hawkins, Abram	PVT	Montgomery's Company	09/03/35–09/10/35	
Hawkins, John R.	VOL	Martin Davis' Detachment	03/27/35–03/31/35	
Hawkins, Levi	PVT	Rupley's Company	09/03/35–09/10/35	
Hawkins, William A.	1SG	Baldwin's Company	09/03/35–09/10/35	

NAME	RANK	MILITARY UNIT	SERVICE DATES	REMARKS
Haynes, W. A.	VOL	Martin Davis' Detachment	03/27/35–03/31/35	
Hays, Andrew L.	PHY	F & S MI Militia	??/??/35–??/??/35	SCU
Heacock, William	PVT	Davis' Rifle Regiment	09/03/35–09/10/35	
Hermans, H.	SUA	Unassigned	09/03/35–09/10/35	
Herrington, Aaron B.	PVT	Taylor's Company	09/03/35–09/10/35	
Herrington, Hiram	PVT	Ingram's Company	09/03/35–09/10/35	
Herrington, James	TEB	Davis' Rifle Regiment	09/03/35–09/10/35	
Hewson, James	PVT	Haskins' Company	09/03/35–09/10/35	
Hicklin, Thomas	PVT	Davis' Rifle Regiment	09/03/35–09/10/35	
Higby, Ezra	3LT	Martin Davis' Detachment	09/03/35–09/10/35	
Hill, Alvin	2SG	Pettis' Company	09/03/35–09/10/35	
Hill, Hiram	PVT	Pettis' Company	09/03/35–09/10/35	
Hill, Samuel B.	2LT	Davis' Rifle Regiment	09/03/35–09/10/35	
Hill, William	PVT	Goodell's Company	09/03/35–09/10/35	
Hillock, Hugh	QUA	Davis Smith's Regiment	09/03/35–09/10/35	
Hilvine, Albut	PVT	Rupley's Company	09/03/35–09/10/35	
Hinckley, Archange	PVT	Rupley's Company	09/03/35–09/10/35	
Hiscock, Isaac	1LT	Davis' Rifle Regiment	09/03/35–09/10/35	
Hiscock, John	3SG	Martin Davis' Detachment	09/03/35–09/10/35	
Hoag, Milton	CAP	Hoag's Company	09/03/35–09/10/35	
Hodge, Warren	PVT	Bissonette's Company	09/03/35–09/10/35	
Holden, Lorton	VOL	Martin Davis' Detachment	03/27/35–03/31/35	Washtenaw County Militia
Holloway, Butler	SGT	Hall's Company	09/03/35–09/10/35	
Holmes, Conrad	PVT	Davis' Rifle Regiment	09/03/35–09/10/35	
Holmes, Miranda	2SG	Sheldon's Company	09/03/35–09/10/35	
Hooney, Stephen	PVT	Densmore's Company	09/03/35–09/10/35	

NAME	RANK	MILITARY UNIT	SERVICE DATES	REMARKS
Hopkins, Samuel P.	PVT	Wood's Company	09/03/35–09/10/35	
Horness, Henry M.	PVT	Haskins' Company	09/03/35–09/10/35	
Horton, James	PVT	Davis' Rifle Regiment	09/03/35–09/10/35	
Hotchkiss, Burton	2LT	Wood's Company	09/03/35–09/10/35	
Hough, Olmsted	PVT	Baldwin's Company	09/03/35–09/10/35	
Houghton, Henry B.	PVT	Davis' Rifle Regiment	09/03/35–09/10/35	
Houghton, Nehemiah	PVT	Davis' Rifle Regiment	09/03/35–09/10/35	
Houning, Charles	PVT	Davis' Rifle Regiment	09/03/35–09/10/35	
House, Thomas A.	3CP	Davis' Rifle Regiment	09/03/35–09/10/35	
Howard, Alfred	PVT	Davis' Rifle Regiment	09/03/35–09/10/35	
Howard, Jacob M.	2LT	Bull's Company	09/03/35–09/10/35	
Howard, John D.	DMM	Hoag's Company	09/03/35–09/10/35	
Howland, H. H.	1CP	Cone's Company	09/03/35–09/10/35	
Hubbard, George	2SG	Davis' Rifle Regiment	09/03/35–09/10/35	
Hubbard, Henry G.	GOS	Unassigned	09/03/35–09/10/35	
Hubbard, Ira	1CP	Davis' Rifle Regiment	09/03/35–09/10/35	
Hull, Levi J.	VOL	Martin Davis' Detachment	03/27/35–03/31/35	Washtenaw County Militia
Hungerfield, Horace	SGM	Wing's Regiment	09/03/35–09/10/35	
Huntley, Nelson	PVT	Sheldon's Company	09/03/35–09/10/35	
Hurd, Lyman	1SG	Wood's Company	09/03/35–09/10/35	
Hutchinson, James	PVT	Bird's Company	09/03/35–09/10/35	
Ingersoll, Edward	DMR	Oakland Detachment	09/03/35–09/10/35	
Ingersoll, Riley	TEA	Wing's Regiment	09/03/35–09/10/35	
Ingraham, Nathan	PVT	Darrow's Company	09/03/35–09/10/35	
Ingram, John W.	CAP	Ingram's Company	09/03/35–09/10/35	
Jackson, Anson	PVT	Pettis' Company	09/03/35–09/10/35	

Name	Rank	Military Unit	Service Dates	Remarks
Jackson, Jabez H.	PVT	Densmore's Company	09/03/35–09/10/35	
Jackson, Jasper G.	3SG	Rupley's Company	09/03/35–09/10/35	
Jackson, Jesse	PVT	Montgomery's Company	09/03/35–09/10/35	
Jacobs, James	PVT	Davis Smith's Regiment	09/03/35–09/10/35	
Jacobs, Lewis	PVT	Morass' Company	09/03/35–09/10/35	
Jacox, William	PVT	Bird's Company	09/03/35–09/10/35	
James, Mason I.	1LT	Foot's Company	09/03/35–09/10/35	AKA Marvin J. James
Jeffries, Charles C.	SUR	Martin Davis' Detachment	09/03/35–09/10/35	
Jenkins, Lyman G.	PVT	Baldwin's Company	09/03/35–09/10/35	
Jennings, J.	PVT	Griswold's Company	09/03/35–09/10/35	
Jenny, Lyman T.	SUA	Unassigned	09/03/35–09/10/35	
Jenny, Phineas W.	1LT	Haskins' Company	09/03/35–09/10/35	
Joffers, Charles C.	SUR	Martin Davis' Detachment	09/03/35–09/10/35	
John, James L.	1LT	Sheldon's Company	09/03/35–09/10/35	
Johnson, E. H.	PVT	Davis' Rifle Regiment	09/03/35–09/10/35	
Johnson, Franklin	CSY	Wing's Regiment	09/03/35–09/10/35	
Johnson, Henry	PVT	Wright's Company	09/03/35–09/10/35	
Johnson, Hollis	4SG	Raymond's Company	09/03/35–09/10/35	
Jones, Joseph	PVT	Cone's Company	09/03/35–09/10/35	
Jones, Philander H.	PVT	Ingram's Company	09/03/35–09/10/35	
Jones, Willis C.	PVT	Cone's Company	09/03/35–09/10/35	
Joslin, Chauncey	VOL	Martin Davis' Detachment	03/27/35–03/31/35	Washtenaw County Militia
Juberville, Antoine	PVT	Goodell's Company	09/03/35–09/10/35	
Jude, Sheldon	3CP	Davis' Rifle Regiment	09/03/35–09/10/35	
Keets, Sidney	PVT	Slingerland's Company	09/03/35–09/10/35	
Kelley, Asa L.	PVT	Haskins' Company	09/03/35–09/10/35	

Name	Rank	Military Unit	Service Dates	Remarks
Kelley, James O.	4SG	Martin Davis' Detachment	09/03/35–09/10/35	
Kennedy, William	PVT	Davis' Rifle Regiment	09/03/35–09/10/35	
Kent, William	TEA	Wing's Regiment	09/03/35–09/10/35	
Ketchum, Stephen	PVT	Hoag's Company	09/03/35–09/10/35	
Keyes, John F.	TEB	Oakland Detachment	09/03/35–09/10/35	
Kidzu, James T.	1SG	Pettis' Company	09/03/35–09/10/35	
Kimball, Isaac B.	PVT	Wood's Company	09/03/35–09/10/35	
King, Alanson	PVT	Sheldon's Company	09/03/35–09/10/35	
King, Charles A.	1SG	Davis' Rifle Regiment	09/03/35–09/10/35	
King, Cyrus	PVT	Densmore's Company	09/03/35–09/10/35	
King, George	4SG	Sheldon's Company	09/03/35–09/10/35	
King, Jesse H.	PVT	Wing's Regiment	09/03/35–09/10/35	
Kirkham, Elijah	PVT	Haskins' Company	09/03/35–09/10/35	
Knaggs, Thomas	PVT	Wadsworth's Company	09/03/35–09/10/35	
Knaggs, Thomas	PVT	Wood's Company	09/03/35–09/10/35	
Knapp, Ebenezer	2SG	Davis' Company	09/03/35–09/10/35	
Knapp, John	PVT	Pettis' Company	09/03/35–09/10/35	
Knight, Benjamin	PVT	Brownell's Company	09/03/35–09/10/35	
Knight, Eli	DMR	Davis' Company	09/03/35–09/10/35	
Knight, Lyman	PVT	Davis' Rifle Regiment	09/03/35–09/10/35	
Knight, Merlin	PVT	Davis' Company	09/03/35–09/10/35	
Knight, Orson	DMR	Davis' Company	09/03/35–09/10/35	
Lackman, Edward	PVT	Bird's Company	09/03/35–09/10/35	
Lacy, John S.	1LT	Davis' Rifle Regiment	09/03/35–09/10/35	
Lacy, Lewis A.	DMR	Davis' Rifle Regiment	09/03/35–09/10/35	
Lafleur, Gabriel	PVT	Wood's Company	09/03/35–09/10/35	

NAME	RANK	MILITARY UNIT	SERVICE DATES	REMARKS
Lafontaine, Lewis	2CP	Wright's Company	09/03/35–09/10/35	
Lambert, Henry A.	PVT	Cone's Company	09/03/35–09/10/35	
Landon, Jacob	3SG	Davis' Rifle Regiment	09/03/35–09/10/35	
Landon, Jacob R.	4SG	Davis' Rifle Regiment	09/03/35–09/10/35	
Lane, Charles W.	VOL	Martin Davis' Detachment	03/27/35–03/31/35	Washtenaw County Militia
Lane, Elihu	PVT	Baldwin's Company	09/03/35–09/10/35	
Lane, M.	PVT	Martin Davis' Detachment	03/27/35–03/31/35	Drafted
Lane, Peter	DMR	Davis' Rifle Regiment	09/03/35–09/10/35	
Langdon, Henry	PVT	Davis' Company	09/03/35–09/10/35	
Lapage, Oliver	PVT	Wadsworth's Company	09/03/35–09/10/35	
Lapham, Benjamin	4SG	Greenman's Company	09/03/35–09/10/35	
Lapham, Joseph	MAJ	Martin Davis' Detachment	09/03/35–09/10/35	
Lapoint, John B.	PVT	Morass' Company	09/03/35–09/10/35	
Larabell, Alexis	PVT	Bradford's Company	09/03/35–09/10/35	
Larue, A. L.	VOL	Martin Davis' Detachment	03/27/35–03/31/35	Washtenaw County Militia
Laselle, Antoine	PVT	Wood's Company	09/03/35–09/10/35	
Law, Simeon	PVT	Brownell's Company	09/03/35–09/10/35	
Lawrence, Osmer A.	PVT	Taylor's Company	09/03/35–09/10/35	
Ledyard, Phillip	3CP	Davis' Rifle Regiment	09/03/35–09/10/35	
Lee, Horatio	4SG	Brownell's Company	09/03/35–09/10/35	
Lee, William	2LT	Brownell's Company	09/03/35–09/10/35	
Leech, Gurdon C.	ENS	Sheldon's Company	09/03/35–09/10/35	
Leech, Payne K.	PVT	Sheldon's Company	09/03/35–09/10/35	
Leek, Horace	CAP	Davis' Rifle Regiment	09/03/35–09/10/35	AKA Hiram Leeks
Legors, Isaac	PVT	Haskins' Company	09/03/35–09/10/35	
Leonard, Jacob	1SG	Bradford's Company	09/03/35–09/10/35	

NAME	RANK	MILITARY UNIT	SERVICE DATES	REMARKS
Leonard, Morris	PVT	Darrow's Company	09/03/35–09/10/35	
LeRoy, Benjamin	PVT	Davis' Rifle Regiment	09/03/35–09/10/35	
Leverman, Abner	PVT	Cone's Company	09/03/35–09/10/35	
Lewis, Daniel S.	PVT	Montgomery's Company	09/03/35–09/10/35	
Lewis, Griffith	PVT	Brownell's Company	09/03/35–09/10/35	
Lewis, H.	DMR	Davis' Rifle Regiment	09/03/35–09/10/35	
Lewis, Halsey	PVT	Hoag's Company	09/03/35–09/10/35	
Lewis, Levi	1LT	Darrow's Company	09/03/35–09/10/35	
Lewis, Philo	DMR	Davis' Rifle Regiment	09/03/35–09/10/35	
Lewitt, Benjamin	PVT	Davis' Rifle Regiment	09/03/35–09/10/35	
Little, M. A.	PVT	Greenman's Company	09/03/35–09/10/35	
Lognier, August	3SG	Bradford's Company	09/03/35–09/10/35	
Long, Henry	PVT	Bird's Company	09/03/35–09/10/35	
Long, John	PVT	Rupley's Company	09/03/35–09/10/35	
Loomis, Anson B.	PVT	Slingerland's Company	09/03/35–09/10/35	
Loreman, Joseph	PVT	Bird's Company	09/03/35–09/10/35	
Low, Elisha	PVT	Pettis' Company	09/03/35–09/10/35	
Low, Isaiah	3SG	Densmore's Company	09/03/35–09/10/35	
Low, Justice	PVT	Davis Smith's Regiment	09/03/35–09/10/35	
Lowell, Miles	1SG	Davis' Rifle Regiment	09/03/35–09/10/35	
Lowrey, Joseph	PVT	Davis' Rifle Regiment	09/03/35–09/10/35	
Lyman, Otis	PVT	Davis' Company	09/03/35–09/10/35	
Lyons, Michael	PVT	Bradford's Company	09/03/35–09/10/35	
Madison, Wilcox	PVT	Bird's Company	09/03/35–09/10/35	
Maiden, Martin	PVT	Brownell's Company	09/03/35–09/10/35	
Majors, Royal	PVT	Davis' Rifle Regiment	09/03/35–09/10/35	

NAME	RANK	MILITARY UNIT	SERVICE DATES	REMARKS
Mallett, Cyrenus	PVT	Densmore's Company	09/03/35–09/10/35	
Mann, E.	1CP	Martin Davis' Detachment	09/03/35–09/10/35	
Manore, John	PVT	Morass' Company	09/03/35–09/10/35	
Markham, F. L.	SUR	Davis' Rifle Regiment	09/03/35–09/10/35	
Markham, J.	PVT	Taylor's Company	09/03/35–09/10/35	
Markham, Silas	PVT	Baldwin's Company	09/03/35–09/10/35	
Markham, William W.	TEB	Davis' Rifle Regiment	09/03/35–09/10/35	
Martin, Calvin	PVT	Densmore's Company	09/03/35–09/10/35	
Martin, George W.	PVT	Gildard's Company	09/03/35–09/10/35	
Martin, James	VOL	Martin Davis' Detachment	03/27/35–03/31/35	Washtenaw County Militia
Marvin, Dennis	FIF	Oakland Detachment	09/03/35–09/10/35	
Marvin, Henry	3SG	Wood's Company	09/03/35–09/10/35	
Mason, Stevens Thomson	CIC	Michigan Militia	09/03/35–09/10/35	
Matthews, John	PVT	Haskins' Company	09/03/35–09/10/35	
Matthewson, Jesse A.	PVT	Brownell's Company	09/03/35–09/10/35	
Matthewson, William	PVT	Bird's Company	09/03/35–09/10/35	
Mattison, Benjamin	PVT	Rupley's Company	09/03/35–09/10/35	
McAllaster, G.	VOL	Martin Davis' Detachment	03/27/35–03/31/35	Washtenaw County Militia
McAnthon, Soloman	PVT	Davis' Rifle Regiment	09/03/35–09/10/35	
McBoody, James	3SG	Raymond's Company	09/03/35–09/10/35	
McBride, James	1LT	Wood's Company	09/03/35–09/10/35	
McCall, Elias O.	1LT	Ferris' Company	09/03/35–09/10/35	
McCauley, William	1LT	Davis' Rifle Regiment	09/03/35–09/10/35	Quartermaster
McCloskey, James	SAD	Wood's Company	09/03/35–09/10/35	
McClure, H.	PVT	Griswold's Company	09/03/35–09/10/35	
McCormick, Charles M.	CAP	Davis' Rifle Regiment	09/03/35–09/10/35	

NAME	RANK	MILITARY UNIT	SERVICE DATES	REMARKS
McCormick, Daniel	PVT	Baldwin's Company	09/03/35–09/10/35	
McCormick, John	4CP	Martin Davis' Detachment	09/03/35–09/10/35	
McCoullogh, John	VOL	Martin Davis' Detachment	03/27/35–03/31/35	Washtenaw County Militia
McCurdy, William	1LT	Davis' Rifle Regiment	09/03/35–09/10/35	
McDowell, Thomas	PVT	Wood's Company	09/03/35–09/10/35	
McEldowrey, Andrew	PVT	Darrow's Company	09/03/35–09/10/35	
McKnight, Samuel	SGT	Bird's Company	09/03/35–09/10/35	
McLane, Charles	PVT	Davis' Rifle Regiment	09/03/35–09/10/35	
McMichael, William	PVT	Haskins' Company	09/03/35–09/10/35	
McNeil, A. R.	PVT	Hoag's Company	09/03/35–09/10/35	
McNott, John	PVT	Montgomery's Company	09/03/35–09/10/35	
McRoberts, Daniel	2LT	Raymond's Company	09/03/35–09/10/35	
McRoberts, James	PVT	Ingram's Company	09/03/35–09/10/35	
McVay, James	1SG	Wright's Company	09/03/35–09/10/35	
Melley, Peter	PVT	Thayer's Company	09/03/35–09/10/35	
Merithan, William	DMM	Oakland Detachment	09/03/35–09/10/35	
Merlin, William	PVT	Sheldon's Company	09/03/35–09/10/35	
Merrill, Squire C.	VOL	Martin Davis' Detachment	03/27/35–03/31/35	Washtenaw County Militia
Mettez, Antoine	PVT	Wood's Company	09/03/35–09/10/35	
Mettez, Eli	PVT	Wadsworth's Company	09/03/35–09/10/35	
Mettez, Francis	WAG	Wing's Company	09/03/35–09/10/35	
Mettez, George	PVT	Griswold's Company	09/03/35–09/10/35	
Mettez, Peter	PVT	Griswold's Company	09/03/35–09/10/35	
Miller, Jacob	VOL	Martin Davis' Detachment	03/27/35–03/31/35	Washtenaw County Militia
Miller, James	PVT	Wing's Regiment	09/03/35–09/10/35	
Miller, John	PVT	Davis' Rifle Regiment	09/03/35–09/10/35	

NAME	RANK	MILITARY UNIT	SERVICE DATES	REMARKS
Miller, Minow	PVT	Montgomery's Company	09/03/35–09/10/35	
Miller, William	DMR	Bucklin's Regiment	09/03/35–09/10/35	
Mills, George M.	PVT	Baldwin's Company	09/03/35–09/10/35	
Minegar, William	PVT	Wright's Company	09/03/35–09/10/35	
Minnock, Daniel	PVT	Rupley's Company	09/03/35–09/10/35	
Minor, Doren	PVT	Hoag's Company	09/03/35–09/10/35	
Moffit, John	2SG	Davis Smith's Regiment	09/03/35–09/10/35	
Montgomery, Augustus	CAP	Montgomery's Company	09/03/35–09/10/35	
Montgomery, John	MAJ	Martin Davis' Detachment	09/03/35–09/10/35	
Moon, James	PVT	Griswold's Company	09/03/35–09/10/35	
Moore, Aaron	PVT	Sheldon's Company	09/03/35–09/10/35	
Moore, Charles	VOL	Martin Davis' Detachment	03/27/35–03/31/35	Washtenaw County Militia
Moore, Ira	VOL	Martin Davis' Detachment	03/27/35–03/31/35	Washtenaw County Militia
Moore, Jacob Wilkie	UNK	Fitzpatrick's Company	??/??/35–??/??/35	SCU
Moore, William	PVT	Sheldon's Company	09/03/35–09/10/35	
Moorehouse, Ezra C.	3SG	Hoag's Company	09/03/35–09/10/35	
Moran, Edward	PVT	Griswold's Company	09/03/35–09/10/35	
Moran, Peter	ENS	Morass' Company	09/03/35–09/10/35	
Morass, Joseph	CAP	Morass' Company	09/03/35–09/10/35	
Morgan, Chester	PVT	Cone's Company	09/03/35–09/10/35	
Morgan, Lewis	PVT	Hoag's Company	09/03/35–09/10/35	
Morris, James W.	FIF	Bucklin's Regiment	09/03/35–09/10/35	
Morriss, John	PVT	Ingram's Company	09/03/35–09/10/35	
Morse, Richard E.	SUR	Davis' Rifle Regiment	09/03/35–09/10/35	
Morse, Richard E.	VOL	Martin Davis' Detachment	03/27/35–03/31/35	Surgeon? Washtenaw Co Militia
Morton, Aurora D.	PVT	Davis' Company	09/03/35–09/10/35	

NAME	RANK	MILITARY UNIT	SERVICE DATES	REMARKS
Much, Harry	PVT	Davis' Rifle Regiment	09/03/35–09/10/35	
Mulhollen, John	PVT	Wood's Company	09/03/35–09/10/35	
Murdock, Fulsan	PVT	Baldwin's Company	09/03/35–09/10/35	
Murray, James M.	CAP	Davis' Rifle Regiment	09/03/35–09/10/35	AKA James McMurray
Murray, John H.	SGM	Martin Davis' Detachment	09/03/35–09/10/35	
Myers, Henry	PVT	Rupley's Company	09/03/35–09/10/35	
Navarre, Charles	PVT	Wood's Company	09/03/35–09/10/35	
Navarre, Joseph P.	PVT	Wood's Company	09/03/35–09/10/35	
Neil, J.	PVT	Bull's Company	09/03/35–09/10/35	
Nettleton, Davis	PVT	Davis' Company	09/03/35–09/10/35	
Newton, Sheffieto B.	CAP	Davis' Rifle Regiment	09/03/35–09/10/35	
Nichols, Cyrel H.	2SG	Davis' Rifle Regiment	09/03/35–09/10/35	
Nichols, Tidy T.	PVT	Davis' Rifle Regiment	09/03/35–09/10/35	
Nichols, William	PVT	White's Company	09/03/35–09/10/35	
Nixon, Thomas	PVT	Rupley's Company	09/03/35–09/10/35	
Noden, Antoine	PVT	Wadsworth's Company	09/03/35–09/10/35	
Noden, Antoine	PVT	Wood's Company	09/03/35–09/10/35	
Nolan, Andrew	TEB	Davis' Rifle Regiment	09/03/35–09/10/35	
Norcross, Aaron	PVT	Hall's Company	09/03/35–09/10/35	
Norris, Joseph Jr.	PVT	Wadsworth's Company	09/03/35–09/10/35	
North, William	PVT	Davis' Rifle Regiment	09/03/35–09/10/35	
Norton, John	PVT	Montgomery's Company	09/03/35–09/10/35	
Nowland, James	2CP	Martin Davis' Detachment	09/03/35–09/10/35	
Noyes, Horace A.	CAP	Davis' Rifle Regiment	09/03/35–09/10/35	Adjutant
Noyes, Lorenzo	CPL	Pettis' Company	09/03/35–09/10/35	
Odell, David	PVT	Thayer's Company	09/03/35–09/10/35	

NAME	RANK	MILITARY UNIT	SERVICE DATES	REMARKS
Odell, Samuel	PVT	Davis' Rifle Regiment	09/03/35–09/10/35	
Older, John S.	PVT	Densmore's Company	09/03/35–09/10/35	
Orcott, Ezra	PVT	Densmore's Company	09/03/35–09/10/35	
Osborn, Thomas	PVT	Day's Company	09/03/35–09/10/35	
Osgood, Leonard W.	PVT	Slingerland's Company	09/03/35–09/10/35	
Ousterhout, Flowers	PVT	Davis Smith's Regiment	09/03/35–09/10/35	
Ousterhout, Henry	PVT	Davis' Rifle Regiment	09/03/35–09/10/35	
Owen, Armenius	PVT	Bissonette's Company	09/03/35–09/10/35	
Owen, Samuel	PVT	Davis' Rifle Regiment	09/03/35–09/10/35	
Packhurst, Abel	1LT	Martin Davis' Detachment	09/03/35–09/10/35	Paymaster
Palmer, Cyrus	3SG	Montgomery's Company	09/03/35–09/10/35	
Palmer, James	PVT	Davis' Rifle Regiment	09/03/35–09/10/35	
Palmer, P.	PVT	Montgomery's Company	09/03/35–09/10/35	
Parker, Chauncey	PVT	Ingram's Company	09/03/35–09/10/35	
Parker, Linus	PVT	Ingram's Company	09/03/35–09/10/35	
Parker, William H.	DMR	Spaulding's Company	09/03/35–09/10/35	
Parkhurst, Abel	1LT	Martin Davis' Detachment	09/03/35–09/10/35	Paymaster
Parks, Allen N.	PVT	Foot's Company	09/03/35–09/10/35	
Parks, Austin B.	PVT	Davis' Rifle Regiment	09/03/35–09/10/35	
Parks, Calvin C.	LUT	Unassigned	09/03/35–09/10/35	
Parmington, Thomas	PVT	Darrow's Company	09/03/35–09/10/35	
Parrish, Nichols L.	MUS	Hoag's Company	09/03/35–09/10/35	
Partridge, Richard	MUS	Wing's Regiment	09/03/35–09/10/35	Monroe Band
Patchin, S. W.	VOL	Martin Davis' Detachment	03/27/35–03/31/35	Washtenaw County Militia
Patrick, Charles V.	PVT	Cone's Company	09/03/35–09/10/35	
Patterson, Caleb	PVT	Davis Smith's Regiment	09/03/35–09/10/35	

NAME	RANK	MILITARY UNIT	SERVICE DATES	REMARKS
Patterson, Elleny	1SG	Davis Smith's Regiment	09/03/35–09/10/35	
Patterson, Joseph H.	PVT	Densmore's Company	09/03/35–09/10/35	
Patterson, Michael A.	SUR	Davis Smith's Regiment	09/03/35–09/10/35	
Peacock, Thomas	PVT	Davis' Rifle Regiment	09/03/35–09/10/35	
Pearl, Lewis	PVT	Bradford's Company	09/03/35–09/10/35	
Pearsall, Henry J.	DMR	Oakland Detachment	09/03/35–09/10/35	
Peck, Edward W.	1LT	Cone's Company	09/03/35–09/10/35	
Peck, Silas	PVT	Sheldon's Company	09/03/35–09/10/35	
Peerson, James	VOL	Martin Davis' Detachment	03/27/35–03/31/35	Washtenaw County Militia
Perce, William	FIF	Davis' Rifle Regiment	09/03/35–09/10/35	
Perry, Artisson	PVT	Haskins' Company	09/03/35–09/10/35	
Perry, Samuel	PVT	Davis' Rifle Regiment	09/03/35–09/10/35	
Pettibone, Milton	1SG	Davis' Rifle Regiment	09/03/35–09/10/35	
Pettibone, Milton	PVT	Davis' Rifle Regiment	09/03/35–09/10/35	
Pettis, Peleg	CAP	Pettis' Company	09/03/35–09/10/35	
Peuse, George W.	VOL	Martin Davis' Detachment	03/27/35–03/31/35	Washtenaw County Militia
Phelps, Benjamin	1LT	Oakland Detachment	09/03/35–09/10/35	Paymaster
Phelps, John P.	PVT	Day's Company	09/03/35–09/10/35	
Phelps, Martin	PVT	Cone's Company	09/03/35–09/10/35	
Phelps, Orrin	PVT	Raymond's Company	09/03/35–09/10/35	
Philbrick, Harrison	PVT	Brownell's Company	09/03/35–09/10/35	
Philips, Benjamin	1LT	Oakland Detachment	09/03/35–09/10/35	Paymaster
Phillip, Jeremiah Jr.	PVT	Slingerland's Company	09/03/35–09/10/35	
Phillips, William	PVT	Raymond's Company	09/03/35–09/10/35	
Pierce, Melvin B.	PVT	Pettis' Company	09/03/35–09/10/35	
Pinckney, Elijah	PVT	Cone's Company	09/03/35–09/10/35	

Name	Rank	Military Unit	Service Dates	Remarks
Place, Silas H.	PVT	Rupley's Company	09/03/35–09/10/35	
Platt, Jonas H.	PVT	Davis' Rifle Regiment	09/03/35–09/10/35	
Ponjetle, Hubert	PVT	Wadsworth's Company	09/03/35–09/10/35	
Pool, Alanson	1CP	Spaulding's Company	09/03/35–09/10/35	
Porter, Willard	PVT	Haskins' Company	09/03/35–09/10/35	
Possier, Francis	1SG	Wadsworth's Company	09/03/35–09/10/35	
Post, Jacob	PVT	Montgomery's Company	09/03/35–09/10/35	
Powelson, Morris	PVT	Ingram's Company	09/03/35–09/10/35	
Powers, G. W.	PVT	Rupley's Company	09/03/35–09/10/35	
Pratt, Abiah	VOL	Martin Davis' Detachment	03/27/35–03/31/35	Washtenaw County Militia
Pratt, Isaac	2SG	Davis' Rifle Regiment	09/03/35–09/10/35	
Pratt, James S.	PVT	Brownell's Company	09/03/35–09/10/35	
Prentice, Henry	PVT	Rupley's Company	09/03/35–09/10/35	
Prentiss, Joseph C.	PVT	Cone's Company	09/03/35–09/10/35	
Prew, Charles	PVT	Wadsworth's Company	09/03/35–09/10/35	
Pritchette, Kintzing	GOS	Unassigned	09/03/35–09/10/35	
Pulty, Marcus	3SG	Greenman's Company	09/03/35–09/10/35	
Purce, James	PVT	Rupley's Company	09/03/35–09/10/35	
Purchase, Henry	PVT	Bissonette's Company	09/03/35–09/10/35	
Quick, Tunis	PVT	Rupley's Company	09/03/35–09/10/35	
Rall, Benjamin	3SG	Davis' Rifle Regiment	09/03/35–09/10/35	
Ramsey, Erastus	PVT	Davis' Rifle Regiment	09/03/35–09/10/35	
Ransdell, R.	PVT	Baldwin's Company	09/03/35–09/10/35	
Ransford, Luther	PVT	Cone's Company	09/03/35–09/10/35	
Rawley, Marcus	PVT	Raymond's Company	09/03/35–09/10/35	
Raymond, Jedediah	CAP	Raymond's Company	09/03/35–09/10/35	

NAME	RANK	MILITARY UNIT	SERVICE DATES	REMARKS
Raymond, R. W.	2SG	Davis' Rifle Regiment	09/03/35–09/10/35	
Reed, Don A.	PVT	Hoag's Company	09/03/35–09/10/35	
Reed, Ranson	PVT	Haskins' Company	09/03/35–09/10/35	
Reed, William	FIF	Davis' Rifle Regiment	09/03/35–09/10/35	
Reeves, Isaac	PVT	Davis' Rifle Regiment	09/03/35–09/10/35	
Reisted, Daniel	4SG	Davis' Rifle Regiment	09/03/35–09/10/35	
Reno, M.	PVT	Griswold's Company	09/03/35–09/10/35	
Reopel, Antoine	PVT	Morass' Company	09/03/35–09/10/35	
Retan, William	PVT	Brownell's Company	09/03/35–09/10/35	
Rexford, F. K.	VOL	Martin Davis' Detachment	03/27/35–03/31/35	Washtenaw County Militia
Reynolds, Thomas	PVT	Darrow's Company	09/03/35–09/10/35	
Reynolds, William	PVT	Ingram's Company	09/03/35–09/10/35	
Rhoades, James P.	PVT	Cone's Company	09/03/35–09/10/35	
Rhodes, Oliver	CPL	Pettis' Company	09/03/35–09/10/35	
Rice, Paul	1LT	Thayer's Company	09/03/35–09/10/35	
Richard, David W.	PVT	Cone's Company	09/03/35–09/10/35	
Richards, Richard	PVT	Ingram's Company	09/03/35–09/10/35	
Richardson, Emery	CAP	Davis' Rifle Regiment	09/03/35–09/10/35	
Richardson, Israel B.	SUM	Oakland Detachment	09/03/35–09/10/35	
Richardson, James	3SG	Ingram's Company	09/03/35–09/10/35	
Rivard, Antoine	PVT	Wood's Company	09/03/35–09/10/35	
Roach, James A.	4CP	Spaulding's Company	09/03/35–09/10/35	
Roberts, L. G.	VOL	Martin Davis' Detachment	03/27/35–03/31/35	Washtenaw County Militia
Roberts, William	PVT	Haskins' Company	09/03/35–09/10/35	
Robertson, Calvin	PVT	Davis Smith's Regiment	09/03/35–09/10/35	

NAME	RANK	MILITARY UNIT	SERVICE DATES	REMARKS
Robertson, Samuel K.	PVT	Davis Smith's Regiment	09/03/35–09/10/35	
Rogers, Moses	2SG	Martin Davis' Detachment	09/03/35–09/10/35	
Rollo, W.	VOL	Martin Davis' Detachment	03/27/35–03/31/35	Washtenaw County Militia
Ronbeck, Henry P.	PVT	Davis' Rifle Regiment	09/03/35–09/10/35	
Rood, Sidney L.	1LT	Griswold's Company	09/03/35–09/10/35	
Roof, George C.	1LT	Spaulding's Company	09/03/35–09/10/35	
Roosevelt, Cornelius	SGM	Oakland Detachment	09/03/35–09/10/35	
Roosevelt, Nelson	1LT	Ingram's Company	09/03/35–09/10/35	
Root, Charles	4CP	Davis' Rifle Regiment	09/03/35–09/10/35	
Root, George E.	1LT	Spaulding's Company	09/03/35–09/10/35	
Root, H. E.	PVT	Davis' Rifle Regiment	09/03/35–09/10/35	
Root, James W.	PVT	Davis' Rifle Regiment	09/03/35–09/10/35	
Root, Sheldon C.	PVT	Rupley's Company	09/03/35–09/10/35	
Rosin, Alexander	PVT	Foot's Company	09/03/35–09/10/35	
Rossiter, Seymour	PVT	Griswold's Company	09/03/35–09/10/35	
Rowland, Isaac S.	GOS	Unassigned	09/03/35–09/10/35	
Ruden, John Jr.	MAJ	Davis' Rifle Regiment	09/03/35–09/10/35	
Rudman, George	PVT	Greenman's Company	09/03/35–09/10/35	
Ruland, William	PVT	Wood's Company	09/03/35–09/10/35	
Rundell, Josiah	VOL	Martin Davis' Detachment	03/27/35–03/31/35	Washtenaw County Militia
Runyan, John Jr.	PVT	Brownell's Company	09/03/35–09/10/35	
Rupley, John F.	CAP	Rupley's Company	09/03/35–09/10/35	
Russell, Harvey L.	TEA	Martin Davis' Detachment	09/03/35–09/10/35	
Russell, James	1SG	Spaulding's Company	09/03/35–09/10/35	
Sadler, Joshua L.	PVT	Cone's Company	09/03/35–09/10/35	

NAME	RANK	MILITARY UNIT	SERVICE DATES	REMARKS
Salisbury, Daniel	PVT	Densmore' Company	09/03/35–09/10/35	
Salisbury, George	CPL	Raymond's Company	09/03/35–09/10/35	
Salisbury, Moses	PVT	Raymond's Company	09/03/35–09/10/35	
Sanders, James	VOL	Martin Davis' Detachment	03/27/35–03/31/35	Washtenaw County Militia
Satterlee, George	PVT	Hall's Company	09/03/35–09/10/35	
Satterlee, John	PVT	Davis' Rifle Regiment	09/03/35–09/10/35	
Savage, Eber M.	PVT	Baldwin's Company	09/03/35–09/10/35	
Savage, Harrison	PVT	Davis' Rifle Regiment	09/03/35–09/10/35	
Sawyer, Franklin	1SG	Bull's Company	09/03/35–09/10/35	
Sawyer, Leander Jr.	PVT	Davis' Rifle Regiment	09/03/35–09/10/35	
Sawyer, Leander Sr.	2SG	Davis' Rifle Regiment	09/03/35–09/10/35	
Saxton, William	PVT	Hall's Company	09/03/35–09/10/35	
Scoville, Daniel W.	PVT	Montgomery's Company	09/03/35–09/10/35	
Secord, Henry B.	2LT	Davis' Rifle Regiment	09/03/35–09/10/35	
Seeley, Charles	PVT	Davis' Rifle Regiment	09/03/35–09/10/35	
Seley, Sylvester	PVT	Day's Company	09/03/35–09/10/35	
Seymour, Isaac	PVT	Davis' Rifle Regiment	09/03/35–09/10/35	
Shaddock, Samuel D.	SGT	Ferris' Company	09/03/35–09/10/35	
Shafee, Jesse	PVT	Davis' Rifle Regiment	09/03/35–09/10/35	
Shafer, Soloman	PVT	Davis' Rifle Regiment	09/03/35–09/10/35	
Shay, A. B.	VOL	Martin Davis' Detachment	03/27/35–03/31/35	Washtenaw County Militia
Shelcock, Robert	PVT	Sheldon's Company	09/03/35–09/10/35	
Sheldon, Orson	CAP	Sheldon's Company	09/03/35–09/10/35	AKA Ason Shelby
Sheldon, William	1CP	Sheldon's Company	09/03/35–09/10/35	
Sherman, Jonathan B.	PVT	Haskins' Company	09/03/35–09/10/35	

Name	Rank	Military Unit	Service Dates	Remarks
Sherman, Samuel	2SG	Haskins' Company	09/03/35–09/10/35	
Sherman, Welcome	PVT	Hall's Company	09/03/35–09/10/35	
Shew, James	PVT	Wood's Company	09/03/35–09/10/35	
Shirts, James	4CP	Ingram's Company	09/03/35–09/10/35	
Shons, Braddock	VOL	Martin Davis' Detachment	03/27/35–03/31/35	Washtenaw County Militia
Showerman, Deloss	VOL	Martin Davis' Detachment	03/27/35–03/31/35	Washtenaw County Militia
Shuart, Elisher	VOL	Martin Davis' Detachment	03/27/35–03/31/35	Washtenaw County Militia
Shull, David	PVT	Hall's Company	09/03/35–09/10/35	
Simmons, Benjamin	PVT	Brownell's Company	09/03/35–09/10/35	
Simpson, Andrew	PVT	Ingram's Company	09/03/35–09/10/35	
Sisson, Thomas	QUA	Davis Smith's Regiment	09/03/35–09/10/35	
Skidmore, James	PVT	Foot's Company	09/03/35–09/10/35	
Skinner, B. L.	FIM	Davis Smith's Regiment	09/03/35–09/10/35	
Skinner, Benjamin F.	FIF	Baldwin's Company	09/03/35–09/10/35	
Slater, Henry	PVT	Davis' Company	09/03/35–09/10/35	
Sliger, Lewis W.	PVT	Davis' Rifle Regiment	09/03/35–09/10/35	
Slingerland, Peter	CAP	Slingerland's Company	09/03/35–09/10/35	AKA Peter Kingsland
Sloat, Albert N.	PVT	Brownell's Company	09/03/35–09/10/35	
Sloat, Henry B.	PVT	Davis' Rifle Regiment	09/03/35–09/10/35	
Sloat, William	PVT	Davis' Rifle Regiment	09/03/35–09/10/35	
Slout, George	PVT	Pettis' Company	09/03/35–09/10/35	
Smith, D. N.	UNK	Unknown	??/??/35–??/??/35	SCU Washtenaw History p. 603
Smith, Davis	COL	Davis Smith's Regiment	09/03/35–09/10/35	
Smith, Ebenezer F.	TEB	Oakland Detachment	09/03/35–09/10/35	
Smith, George	4CP	Cone's Company	09/03/35–09/10/35	

Name	Rank	Military Unit	Service Dates	Remarks
Smith, Henry	INS	Unassigned	09/03/35–09/10/35	
Smith, Isaac	PVT	Cone's Company	09/03/35–09/10/35	
Smith, Israil	VOL	Martin Davis' Detachment	03/27/35–03/31/35	Washtenaw County Militia
Smith, James	PVT	Brownell's Company	09/03/35–09/10/35	
Smith, James F.	PVT	Wing's Regiment	09/03/35–09/10/35	
Smith, Jeremiah	2SG	Densmore's Company	09/03/35–09/10/35	
Smith, John	MUS	Wing's Regiment	09/03/35–09/10/35	Monroe Band
Smith, Joshua	PVT	Gildard's Company	09/03/35–09/10/35	
Smith, Martin H.	3CP	Spaulding's Company	09/03/35–09/10/35	
Smith, Nelson	1SG	Davis' Rifle Regiment	09/03/35–09/10/35	
Smith, Simon	PVT	Brownell's Company	09/03/35–09/10/35	
Smith, William H.	PVT	Davis' Rifle Regiment	09/03/35–09/10/35	
Smith, William M.	SUR	Wing's Regiment	09/03/35–09/10/35	
Smith, William T.	PVT	Cone's Company	09/03/35–09/10/35	
Snow, Frederick	PVT	Haskins' Company	09/03/35–09/10/35	
Soden, Levi	PVT	Ingram's Company	09/03/35–09/10/35	
Solo, John	1CP	Wright's Company	09/03/35–09/10/35	
Solon, J. B.	PVT	Spaulding's Company	09/03/35–09/10/35	
Sousal, John Baptiste	PVT	Wood's Company	09/03/35–09/10/35	
Southard, S. M.	VOL	Martin Davis' Detachment	03/27/35–03/31/35	Washtenaw County Militia
Southard, Stephen	VOL	Martin Davis' Detachment	03/27/35–03/31/35	Washtenaw County Militia
Southerland, John	PVT	Davis' Rifle Regiment	09/03/35–09/10/35	
Southworth, Lorenzo	PVT	Davis Smith's Regiment	09/03/35–09/10/35	
Spaulding, Heman N.	CAP	Spaulding's Company	09/03/35–09/10/35	AKA Herman M. Spaulding
Spaulding, Sylvanus	4SG	Spaulding's Company	09/03/35–09/10/35	
Spaulding, William A.	PVT	Davis' Rifle Regiment	09/03/35–09/10/35	

NAME	RANK	MILITARY UNIT	SERVICE DATES	REMARKS
Spears, John	3CP	Davis' Rifle Regiment	09/03/35–09/10/35	
Spears, William	PVT	Davis' Rifle Regiment	09/03/35–09/10/35	
Spencer, J. C.	PVT	Foot's Company	09/03/35–09/10/35	
Spencer, Simeon	ENS	Baldwin's Company	09/03/35–09/10/35	
Sprague, Frederick A.	MAJ	Oakland Detachment	09/03/35–09/10/35	
Sprague, Henry	2LT	Cone's Company	09/03/35–09/10/35	
Sprague, Thomas S.	MUS	Raymond's Company	09/03/35–09/10/35	
Sprague, Timothy	PVT	Spaulding's Company	09/03/35–09/10/35	
Sprague, William P.	FIF	Oakland Detachment	09/03/35–09/10/35	
Squires, James	PVT	Spaulding's Company	09/03/35–09/10/35	
St. John, Henry	PVT	Davis' Company	09/03/35–09/10/35	
St. John, James	1LT	Sheldon's Company	09/03/35–09/10/35	
St. Sousal, John Baptiste	PVT	Wood's Company	09/03/35–09/10/35	
Stack, G. H.	VOL	Martin Davis' Detachment	03/27/35–03/31/35	Washtenaw County Militia
Stalstiner, J.	PVT	Davis' Rifle Regiment	09/03/35–09/10/35	
Standly, Joseph	VOL	Martin Davis' Detachment	03/27/35–03/31/35	Washtenaw County Militia
Stanley, Charles	PVT	Cone's Company	09/03/35–09/10/35	
Stark, John B.	VOL	Martin Davis' Detachment	03/27/35–03/31/35	Washtenaw County Militia
Starkwether, Alfred	PVT	Davis' Rifle Regiment	09/03/35–09/10/35	
Starkwether, John	PVT	Davis' Rifle Regiment	09/03/35–09/10/35	
Starkwether, Samuel	1CP	Davis' Rifle Regiment	09/03/35–09/10/35	
Stephens, John S.	PVT	Cone's Company	09/03/35–09/10/35	
Sterner, Gabriel	PVT	Davis' Rifle Regiment	09/03/35–09/10/35	
Stevens, Albert	CAP	Davis' Rifle Regiment	09/03/35–09/10/35	
Stevenson, John	PVT	Greenman's Company	09/03/35–09/10/35	
Stewart, John	PVT	Baldwin's Company	09/03/35–09/10/35	

NAME	RANK	MILITARY UNIT	SERVICE DATES	REMARKS
Stewart, Smith	2SG	Wood's Company	09/03/35–09/10/35	
Stewart, Willard N.	FIF	Bucklin's Regiment	09/03/35–09/10/35	
Stickney, Neland	PVT	Ingram's Company	09/03/35–09/10/35	
Stimpson, Jesse	PVT	Sheldon's Company	09/03/35–09/10/35	
Stimpson?, G. W.	VOL	Martin Davis' Detachment	03/27/35–03/31/35	Washtenaw County Militia
Stockford, George	PVT	Davis' Rifle Regiment	09/03/35–09/10/35	
Stone, A.	VOL	Martin Davis' Detachment	03/27/35–03/31/35	Washtenaw County Militia
Stone, Danford M.	PVT	Pettis' Company	09/03/35–09/10/35	
Stone, Jonathan	PVT	Rupley's Company	09/03/35–09/10/35	
Stone, Warren	PVT	Davis' Rifle Regiment	09/03/35–09/10/35	
Stone, Warren	TEB	Davis' Rifle Regiment	09/03/35–09/10/35	
Stoughton, Samuel D.	2CP	Ingram's Company	09/03/35–09/10/35	
Stout, Nathan L.	1SG	Cone's Company	09/03/35–09/10/35	
Straight, George W.	PVT	Darrow's Company	09/03/35–09/10/35	
Straight, Henry Jr.	PVT	Morass' Company	09/03/35–09/10/35	
Straight, Hiram W.	PVT	Darrow's Company	09/03/35–09/10/35	
Straight, Marvin B.	BUG	Wood's Company	09/03/35–09/10/35	
Strong, John	PVT	Thayer's Company	09/03/35–09/10/35	
Strong, Roswell Jr.	PVT	Slingerland's Company	09/03/35–09/10/35	
Stuck, Charles	VOL	Martin Davis' Detachment	03/27/35–03/31/35	Washtenaw County Militia
Sturgess, John	PVT	Haskins' Company	09/03/35–09/10/35	
Sull, Adna	PVT	Cone's Company	09/03/35–09/10/35	
Sullivan, Peter	PVT	Gildard's Company	09/03/35–09/10/35	
Sutfin, Peter B.	3SG	Baldwin's Company	09/03/35–09/10/35	
Sutfin, William	PVT	Baldwin's Company	09/03/35–09/10/35	

NAME	RANK	MILITARY UNIT	SERVICE DATES	REMARKS
Sutherland, J.	DMR	Davis' Rifle Regiment	09/03/35–09/10/35	
Sutton, Benjamin	PVT	Densmore's Company	09/03/35–09/10/35	
Sutton, George W.	PVT	Cone's Company	09/03/35–09/10/35	
Swan, John	4SG	Cone's Company	09/03/35–09/10/35	
Swartons, Nathaniel	PVT	Davis Smith's Regiment	09/03/35–09/10/35	
Sweat, David	PVT	Slingerland's Company	09/03/35–09/10/35	
Swich, John	PVT	Montgomery's Company	09/03/35–09/10/35	
Swich, M. J.	2LT	Montgomery's Company	09/03/35–09/10/35	AKA Allan J. Swich
Swift, Orrin	DMR	Bucklin's Regiment	09/03/35–09/10/35	
Tacia, Dominique	WAG	Wing's Regiment	09/03/35–09/10/35	
Tailor, John R.	3SG	Darrow's Company	09/03/35–09/10/35	
Tallman, T. E.	PVT	Griswold's Company	09/03/35–09/10/35	
Taylor, Asahel	PVT	Davis Smith's Regiment	09/03/35–09/10/35	
Taylor, Jesse W.	CAP	Taylor's Company	09/03/35–09/10/35	AKA Jesse Paxton
Taylor, John	PVT	Haskins' Company	09/03/35–09/10/35	
Taylor, William	MUS	Wing's Regiment	09/03/35–09/10/35	Monroe Band
Teal, Aseph	PVT	Darrow's Company	09/03/35–09/10/35	
Tebo, John B.	PVT	Goodell's Company	09/03/35–09/10/35	
Tebo, Richard	PVT	Goodell's Company	09/03/35–09/10/35	
Ten Eyck, Conrad A.	QUT	Unassigned	09/03/35–09/10/35	
Tendall, Noah H.	SGT	Hall's Company	09/03/35–09/10/35	
Terry, Derastus	MAJ	Davis Smith's Regiment	09/03/35–09/10/35	
Thayer, Nahum P.	CAP	Thayer's Company	09/03/35–09/10/35	
Thomas, Hiram	PVT	Sheldon's Company	09/03/35–09/10/35	
Thomas, Jasper	2LT	Rupley's Company	09/03/35–09/10/35	

NAME	RANK	MILITARY UNIT	SERVICE DATES	REMARKS
Thomas, John	1LT	Rupley's Company	09/03/35–09/10/35	
Thomas, Willard	TEB	Oakland Detachment	09/03/35–09/10/35	
Thompson, George	3SG	Davis' Rifle Regiment	09/03/35–09/10/35	
Thompson, William	SUR	Unassigned	09/03/35–09/10/35	
Throop, Ezra	PVT	Brownell's Company	09/03/35–09/10/35	
Thurston, Daniel	MUS	Raymond's Company	09/03/35–09/10/35	
Tibbetts, Benjamin	ENS	Pettis' Company	09/03/35–09/10/35	
Tooker, Ira	PVT	Pettis' Company	09/03/35–09/10/35	
Torbon, Nicholas	PVT	Densmore's Company	09/03/35–09/10/35	
Torrey, Derastus	MAJ	Davis Smith's Regiment	09/03/35–09/10/35	
Town, T. M.	VOL	Martin Davis' Detachment	03/27/35–03/31/35	Washtenaw County Militia
Townson, Zebulon	PVT	Davis' Rifle Regiment	09/03/35–09/10/35	
Tracy, Thomas	PVT	Wadsworth's Company	09/03/35–09/10/35	
Tremble, Francis	PVT	Wright's Company	09/03/35–09/10/35	
Trip, Milo	PVT	Spaulding's Company	09/03/35–09/10/35	
Tucker, Willard	PVT	Brownell's Company	09/03/35–09/10/35	
Turner, Soloman	PVT	Haskins' Company	09/03/35–09/10/35	
Tuttle, Isaac	PVT	Ingram's Company	09/03/35–09/10/35	
Tuttle, John	4CP	Baldwin's Company	09/03/35–09/10/35	
Tyler, Ira	VOL	Martin Davis' Detachment	03/27/35–03/31/35	Washtenaw County Militia
Tyler, R. O.	VOL	Martin Davis' Detachment	03/27/35–03/31/35	Washtenaw County Militia
Ullman, Isaac J.	QUB	F&S 5th Brigade	09/03/35–09/10/35	
Utley, Uriah	SGT	Thayer's Company	09/03/35–09/10/35	
Van Alstine, Abram	TEA	Wing's Regiment	09/03/35–09/10/35	
Van Alstine, Andrew	PVT	Spaulding's Company	09/03/35–09/10/35	
Van Doren, Israel	PVT	Densmore's Company	09/03/35–09/10/35	

NAME	RANK	MILITARY UNIT	SERVICE DATES	REMARKS
Van Horn, George C.	PVT	Davis Smith's Regiment	09/03/35–09/10/35	
Van Orden, Charles	PVT	Davis' Rifle Regiment	09/03/35–09/10/35	
Van Riper, John	PVT	Wright's Company	09/03/35–09/10/35	
Van Sackle, Miles	PVT	Rupley's Company	09/03/35–09/10/35	
Van Wagoner, D.	PVT	Brownell's Company	09/03/35–09/10/35	
Velod, James	PVT	Wood's Company	09/03/35–09/10/35	
Voorheis, Sebring	VOL	Martin Davis' Detachment	03/27/35–03/31/35	Washtenaw County Militia
Voorhes, Andrew D.	SUR	Oakland Detachment	09/03/35–09/10/35	
Voorhies, William	VOL	Martin Davis' Detachment	03/27/35–03/31/35	Washtenaw County Militia
Voorhis, Scott	PVT	Cone's Company	09/03/35–09/10/35	
Wadsworth, N. W.	VOL	Martin Davis' Detachment	03/27/35–03/31/35	Washtenaw County Militia
Wadsworth, Noyes M.	CAP	Wadsworth's Company	09/03/35–09/10/35	
Wadsworth, Wedworth W.	MUS	Wing's Regiment	09/03/35–09/10/35	Bandmaster, Monroe Band
Wait, Luther	PVT	Rupley's Company	09/03/35–09/10/35	
Waldron, George	PVT	Brownell's Company	09/03/35–09/10/35	
Walker, Andrew C.	PVT	Brownell's Company	09/03/35–09/10/35	
Wall, T. B.	SUR	Unassigned	09/03/35–09/10/35	Surgeon General
Wallace, John W.	VOL	Martin Davis' Detachment	03/27/35–03/31/35	Washtenaw County Militia
Wallace, William	2SG	Foot's Company	09/03/35–09/10/35	
Walworth, William	PVT	Densmore's Company	09/03/35–09/10/35	
Ward, Caleb	PVT	Montgomery's Company	09/03/35–09/10/35	
Warner, Albert	1SG	Wing's Regiment	09/03/35–09/10/35	
Warner, James M.	2SG	Brownell's Company	09/03/35–09/10/35	
Warner, Joseph W.	PVT	Davis' Company	09/03/35–09/10/35	
Warren, Reuben	PVT	Ferris' Company	09/03/35–09/10/35	
Warren, Stephen	PVT	Pettis' Company	09/03/35–09/10/35	

NAME	RANK	MILITARY UNIT	SERVICE DATES	REMARKS
Watson, Horace	PVT	Davis' Rifle Regiment	09/03/35–09/10/35	
Watson, Walter	FIM	Davis' Rifle Regiment	09/03/35–09/10/35	
Webber, Joseph	PVT	Haskins' Company	09/03/35–09/10/35	
Webster, William H.	1LT	Day's Company	09/03/35–09/10/35	
Welch, B.	PVT	Ingram's Company	09/03/35–09/10/35	
Welch, Eleazer	VOL	Martin Davis' Detachment	03/27/35–03/31/35	Washtenaw County Militia
Welch, Horace	1LT	Martin Davis' Detachment	09/03/35–09/10/35	Quartermaster
Welch, James	1SG	Martin Davis' Detachment	09/03/35–09/10/35	
Welch, Owin	VOL	Martin Davis' Detachment	03/27/35–03/31/35	Washtenaw County Militia
Wells, Lewis	PVT	White's Company	09/03/35–09/10/35	
Wells, Morris	PVT	White's Company	09/03/35–09/10/35	
Wells, Norman C.	2LT	Davis' Rifle Regiment	09/03/35–09/10/35	
Wells, Russell	PVT	White's Company	09/03/35–09/10/35	
Wells, Samuel	SGT	Goodell's Company	09/03/35–09/10/35	
West, George	3SG	Wing's Regiment	09/03/35–09/10/35	
West, James	PVT	Taylor's Company	09/03/35–09/10/35	
Westgate, Levi	PVT	Hall's Company	09/03/35–09/10/35	
Weston, Henry T.	PVT	Davis' Rifle Regiment	09/03/35–09/10/35	
Whater, William	PVT	Hoag's Company	09/03/35–09/10/35	
Wheeler, Benjamin F.	PVT	Wood's Company	09/03/35–09/10/35	
Wheeler, Calvin	CAP	Unknown	??/??/35–??/??/35	SCU Washtenaw History p. 604
Wheeler, Eli	PVT	Davis' Company	09/03/35–09/10/35	
Wheeler, Harvey G.	PVT	Haskins' Company	09/03/35–09/10/35	
Wheeler, Herbut	PVT	Davis' Company	09/03/35–09/10/35	
Wheeler, John	PVT	Davis' Company	09/03/35–09/10/35	

NAME	RANK	MILITARY UNIT	SERVICE DATES	REMARKS
Whipple, Charles W	IND	F&S 3rd Division	09/03/35–09/10/35	
Whipple, Eseck B.	2SG	Bull's Company	09/03/35–09/10/35	
White, A.	PVT	Griswold's Company	09/03/35–09/10/35	
White, Almon H.	1LT	Wing's Regiment	09/03/35–09/10/35	Quartermaster
White, Alpheus	CAP	White's Company	09/03/35–09/10/35	
White, Bart	PVT	Hoag's Company	09/03/35–09/10/35	
White, Nelson	2LT	Spaulding's Company	09/03/35–09/10/35	
Whitman, Henry	PVT	Davis' Company	09/03/35–09/10/35	
Whitmore, Alfred	3CP	Davis' Rifle Regiment	09/03/35–09/10/35	
Whitney, Jackson	PVT	Hall's Company	09/03/35–09/10/35	
Wickwire, Frederic	PVT	Hall's Company	09/03/35–09/10/35	
Wilkins, George A. Jr.	PVT	Montgomery's Company	09/03/35–09/10/35	
Willard, George	1SG	Darrow's Company	09/03/35–09/10/35	
Willcox, David B.	DMM	Bucklin's Regiment	09/03/35–09/10/35	
Willcox, James N.	PVT	Haskins' Company	09/03/35–09/10/35	
Willfair, George	PVT	Haskins' Company	09/03/35–09/10/35	
Williams, George	PVT	Davis' Rifle Regiment	09/03/35–09/10/35	
Williams, Joseph	PVT	Rupley's Company	09/03/35–09/10/35	
Williams, Orrisson	PVT	Haskins' Company	09/03/35–09/10/35	
Williamson, J.	PVT	Slingerland's Company	09/03/35–09/10/35	
Willing, William J.	DMR	Baldwin's Company	09/03/35–09/10/35	
Willington, Joseph H.	ENS	Darrow's Company	09/03/35–09/10/35	
Willitt, Alexander	PVT	Goodell's Company	09/03/35–09/10/35	
Willson, Amos	PVT	Haskins' Company	09/03/35–09/10/35	
Willson, Benjamin	PVT	Wood's Company	09/03/35–09/10/35	

Name	Rank	Military Unit	Service Dates	Remarks
Willson, Isaac	PVT	Davis' Rifle Regiment	09/03/35–09/10/35	
Willson, James	1SG	Davis' Rifle Regiment	09/03/35–09/10/35	
Winchester, Thomas D.	4SG	Rupley's Company	09/03/35–09/10/35	
Wing, Warner	COL	Wing's Regiment	09/03/35–09/10/35	
Winslow, Ansal	PVT	Hoag's Company	09/03/35–09/10/35	
Wintworth, Lyman	4CP	Sheldon's Company	09/03/35–09/10/35	
Wisner, Deby	PVT	Davis' Rifle Regiment	09/03/35–09/10/35	
Withington, Joseph H.	ENS	Darrow's Company	09/03/35–09/10/35	
Wood, Joseph	CAP	Wood's Company	09/03/35–09/10/35	
Wood, Mathew	VOL	Martin Davis' Detachment	03/27/35–03/31/35	Washtenaw County Militia
Wood, Philetus W.	PVT	Davis' Company	09/03/35–09/10/35	
Wood, Richard L.	PVT	Darrow's Company	09/03/35–09/10/35	
Wood, William H.	DMR	Davis Smith's Regiment	09/03/35–09/10/35	
Wooden, Peter	PVT	Slingerland's Company	09/03/35–09/10/35	
Woodruff, James	VOL	Martin Davis' Detachment	03/27/35–03/31/35	Washtenaw County Militia
Woodruff, S. R.	VOL	Martin Davis' Detachment	03/27/35–03/31/35	Washtenaw County Militia
Woods, Zeba	PVT	Pettis' Company	09/03/35–09/10/35	
Woodworth, W. M.	PVT	Wood's Company	09/03/35–09/10/35	
Wright, Edward	1SG	Gildard's Company	09/03/35–09/10/35	
Wright, John	1LT	Wright's Company	09/03/35–09/10/35	
Wright, Moses	3CP	Davis Smith's Company	09/03/35–09/10/35	
Wright, Samuel	PVT	Davis' Company	09/03/35–09/10/35	
Wycoff, Charles	PVT	Taylor's Company	09/03/35–09/10/35	
Yopell, Alexander	PVT	Goodell's Company	09/03/35–09/10/35	
Youd, Jacob	PVT	Davis Smith's Regiment	09/03/35–09/10/35	
Yound, Jackson C.	DMR	Oakland Detachment	09/03/35–09/10/35	

NAME	RANK	MILITARY UNIT	SERVICE DATES	REMARKS
Young, Darwin	PVT	Brownell's Company	09/03/35–09/10/35	
Young, James	PVT	Pettis' Company	09/03/35–09/10/35	
Young, Saltane	PVT	Wing's Regiment	09/03/35–09/10/35	
Young, Thomas	PVT	Davis' Rifle Regiment	09/03/35–09/10/35	
Youngs, Noah	PVT	Haskins' Company	09/03/35–09/10/35	

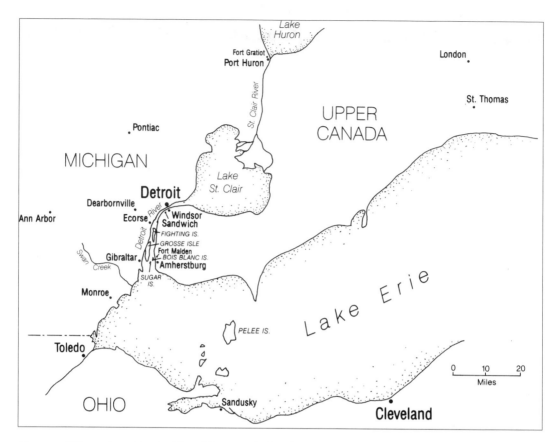

Theater of Operations, Patriot War. (*Cartography by Sherm Hollander*)

PATRIOT WAR,
1838–1839

Michigan in the Patriot War

In late 1837 Louis Joseph Papineau, a respected seigneur and lawyer, led a revolt against English-speaking colonial authorities in Lower Canada (present-day Quebec). A major cause of the uprising was the influx of non-French immigrants, who jeopardized the French-Canadian traditional way of life. At the same time, rebels in Upper Canada (present-day Ontario), led by William Lyon Mackenzie, sought to overthrow the oligarchy that had a stranglehold on the governmental system. Though Papineau's efforts garnered more popular support than those of Mackenzie, both uprisings were quickly suppressed. When their revolts failed, the Canadian rebels fled to the United States. Convinced that this was a popular uprising against British oppression and tyranny, Americans from Vermont to Michigan offered their sympathies and active support to the demoralized Canadians. These sympathies turned into armed aggression that threatened U.S.-British relations as groups of Canadian refugees and Americans, known as Patriots, repeatedly crossed the U.S.-Canadian border throughout 1838 in an attempt to liberate the Canadian provinces from their British colonial rulers.

On December 12, 1837, Detroiters gathered at the city hall to demonstrate their support for the Canadian rebels. Presided over by John Langy, a local hotel owner, the assemblage resolved that while Americans should not violate U.S. laws or jeopardize our neutrality with Great Britain, "every American citizen is free and at liberty to act for himself . . . in the cause of an injured and oppressed people." Such actions included offering their services as soldiers. On Christmas Day at the Detroit City Theatre, a meeting to ease the suffering of Canadian refugees netted $134.56 and ten rifles. According to the *Detroit Morning Post,* "the theatre was thronged to excess" as the Canadian refugees told "of their sufferings, and the murderous, blood-hound cruelty of the British soldiery." The following day, another meeting at the city hall resulted in the creation of a committee to establish a depot for provisions, arms, and munitions of war "necessary to protect the refugee patriots, who seek our protection, from insult or from the kidnapping agents of any country or power." The committee was also charged with enrolling volunteers to peaceably and quietly guard the refugees.

Michiganians outside of Detroit also sympathized with the Patriot cause. On December 21 citizens gathered at the Monroe County courthouse and unanimously adopted resolutions supporting the rebels' cause. Led by some of the community's most prominent citizens, the assemblage pledged that all people had a right to resist tyranny and cheered "the enslaved Canadians" onward in their course "to rid themselves from oppression." The Patriots also received support from the Michigan press. Proclaiming that the rebels were overthrowing a century of British persecution, the *Pontiac Courier* offered its sympathies because "Our citizens . . . always sympathize with the oppressed."

As American support for the Patriots intensified all along the border, both federal and state governmental officials took precautionary measures. In mid-November, President Martin Van Buren issued an uninspiring proclamation that ordered all Americans to obey U.S. laws. In his message to Congress in late November, Van Buren underscored the dilemma U.S. officials faced in stopping Americans from violating the existing peaceful relations between the United States and Canada. While recognizing an obligation to remain neutral and restrain American citizens, the president also admitted the propriety of an expression of sympathy for Canadians in their struggle for freedom. In late December, Michigan governor Stephens T. Mason issued a formal proclamation cautioning and enjoining residents of the state, as well as all other persons residing within its borders, "to abstain and desist from the commission of any act which may, in the least degree, violate the laws of the United States, or disturb the peace and amity now existing between the people of this Union and the government of Great Britain." Mason also ordered the arrest of all persons violating U.S. neutrality laws.

But many Michiganians—confident that the Canadian rebellions represented a widespread popular movement against oppressive British rule—rejected their government's pleas. The persistence and magnitude of this support led one public official to express great astonishment at the strong Patriot support "by a proportion" of Detroit's citizenry. Characterizing Mason's December proclamation as "humbug," the *Pontiac Courier* presaged that it would not dampen the enthusiasm for the Canadian Patriots. "People will meet in public. They will pass resolutions. And if they think proper to shoulder their rifles, go over to Canada and join the Whig cause, they will do it."

The determination expressed by the *Courier* and others was soon evident across southeastern Michigan as meetings and resolutions were transformed into semiorganized armies intent upon invading Canada. On December 31 a dozen volunteers were enlisted at a rally in Pontiac. Reports of similar meetings in Macomb County purportedly raised an additional three hundred volunteers to aid in Upper Canada's liberation. A meeting in Ann Arbor on January 6, 1838, resulted in twenty-four volunteers leaving for Detroit. Two days after the Ann Arbor gathering, the *Detroit Advertiser* affirmed Patriot volunteers were "hourly arriving from the interior." Besides Michigan residents, the Patriots' ranks were swelled with refugees fleeing Upper Canada.

By the end of the first week of January 1838, several hundred Patriots had gathered at various points along the Detroit River. They soon threatened the public peace when they raided arsenals at Monroe and Detroit and stole more than eight hundred stand of arms. Michigan officials sought to discourage the Patriots. Because of the ordnance thefts, Brigadier General Hugh Brady, commandant of the U.S. Seventh Military District, who did not have a single man in that department that he could order for guard duty, federalized the Brady Guards; the fifty-two men were divided between the Dearbornville arsenal and the Detroit magazine. Brady also sent a squad of men to remove the arms and munitions from Port Huron's Fort Gratiot and take them to Detroit.

On January 6 the rebels seized the schooner *Ann,* moored at the Detroit wharf, loaded it with the stolen ordnance, a quantity of provisions, and more than one hundred men. The vessel immediately headed downriver for Gibraltar, a hamlet of not more than twenty families. On the twenty-mile journey, the *Ann* was joined by several smaller boats carrying Patriot volunteers. That same evening Patriot general Thomas Jefferson Sutherland reached the Gibraltar encampment with a force of sixty-two men who had volunteered when he stopped in Cleveland, Ohio. Sutherland assumed command of the Patriot force and directed Edward Theller, a Detroit druggist and city water tax collector, to command the *Ann.*

On the same day that the *Ann* left Detroit, U.S. Marshall Conrad Ten Eyck organized a posse, headed downriver, confronted the Patriots, and ordered their surrender. The rebels refused and, according to one source, Ten Eyck's men were "threatened with the contents of an eighteen pounder if they approached nearer than hailing distance." Following Ten Eyck's failure, Mason, at the urging of the U.S. district attorney, Daniel Goodwin, mobilized two hundred state militia. Leaving at 1:00 A.M. on January 8, Mason's force proceeded to Dearbornville where it was armed at the U.S. arsenal. The governor and his men arrived at Gibraltar, where they discovered that the Patriots had left. Late that evening Mason and the militia returned to Detroit where they dispersed "a large body of men," who had attempted to seize the schooner *Brady* and head "to the seat of the war." The governor's troops also confiscated the Patriots' weapons following what the *Detroit Free Press* described as a "slight skirmish."

The Canadians living across the Detroit River expressed "no small degree of astonishment and righteous indignation" at the Patriots' activities in Michigan. Without any British regulars at Fort Malden, the residents of Amherstburg and Sandwich prepared for an imminent invasion by mobilizing four hundred poorly armed militiamen—men who were convinced that this emergency had little to do with Canadian liberty—but was an American invasion of conquest.

On the morning of January 9, the Patriot army occupied Bois Blanc, a Canadian island opposite Amherstburg. Hoisting the Patriot flag of two stars on a field of red, white, and blue, General Sutherland hoped to arouse sympathy among the Canadians by decreeing

> You are called upon by the Voice of your bleeding Country to join the Patriot Forces, and free your Land from Tyranny. Hordes of worthless parasites of the British Crown are quartered upon you to devour your substance, to outrage your rights, to let loose upon your defenseless Wives and Daughters a brutal soldiery. Rally then around the Standard of Liberty, and Victory and a glorious future, of independence and prosperity will be yours.

On the evening of the ninth the *Ann,* boasting one small cannon, raised anchor and "threw some round shot and grape" into Amherstburg. As the vessel neared the Canadian shore, the Canadian militia opened fire, damaging the *Ann's* rigging. The *Ann* quickly ran aground and was captured. Of the twenty-one men aboard, only one, a Canadian refugee, was killed. Several others were wounded, including Theller and Colonel W. W. Dodge of Monroe. Besides the prisoners, the Canadians captured three hundred muskets, ten kegs of powder, three cannon, and miscellaneous armaments. The prisoners, including thirteen Americans (nine of whom were Michiganians), were incarcerated in Amherstburg.

On the morning of January 10, General Sutherland offered another declaration that all Canadians who resisted the liberators would face "the horrors of War." Inexplicably, after issuing this bold pronouncement, Sutherland ordered a retreat, abandoned his troops, and returned to Detroit. On the same morning, Detroit Patriots seized another vessel, the *Erie,* to carry supplies and recruits to the Patriot camp. Although opposed by General Brady and a few militiamen, the Patriots succeeded because of the aid they received from sympathetic bystanders, as well as the refusal by American officials to open fire to stop the Patriots.

Activities along the Detroit River had reached the critical stage. Described as "the theatre of intense, almost uncontrollable excitement," Detroit was in turmoil. One Detroiter wrote, "You cannot conceive the intensity of the excitement in this city." All intercourse between the two sides of the river had ceased and the safety of both public and private property was of great concern. The Sandwich magistrates asked Governor Mason if he considered the attack upon Canada by the *Ann,* a vessel armed in Michigan, an invasion. Furthermore, they inquired if Mason would consider it an invasion "of your country" if the Canadians attacked the Patriots "wherever we can find them." Mason immediately responded that he wanted peace along the border preserved, but he could not "permit, without resistence," any invasion of the sovereign and independent state over which he presided. Realizing that the situation required more than written assurances, Mason proceeded to Sugar Island, where the Patriots had retreated when Sutherland deserted them. Mason ferried the three-hundred-man army back to Gibraltar, confiscated their weapons and dispersed them. Although a tense calm had returned to the Detroit River, pessimism and apprehensions abounded. General Brady declared that he would "not be surprised if one-third of the able bodied men of the State would join the Patriots."

The first invasion of Upper Canada had proven disastrous, but the Patriots along the Detroit River remained confident. Their cause received a boost of support following the sinking of the *Caroline,* an American vessel ferrying men and material to the Patriot government-in-exile on Navy Island, near Buffalo, New York. A Canadian raiding party burned the vessel in American waters near Schlosser, New York, in late December 1837. The action left one American dead. In its wake Canadian officials publicly praised the raiders, which left Americans furious.

Word of the sinking of the *Caroline* reached Michigan in the midst of the *Ann* fiasco. In the Michigan House of Representatives, Alexander W. Buel offered a resolution that the destruction of the *Caroline* and the "inhuman massacre of a portion of its crew [estimates ranged as high as twenty-two] . . . is an indignity to our common country, which calls loudly for reparation." The *Detroit Free Press* warned their neighbors across the river that if they undertook a similar invasion, "the yeomanry of Michigan would rise as one and avenge the outrage." The *Detroit Daily Advertiser* agreed with the *Free Press* but hoped to decrease the excitement already prevalent in the community. Pledged to remain open-minded, the *Advertiser* printed a long letter from an Upper Canadian Loyalist explaining that most Canadians had no desire to overturn their government. Referring to the newly established, American-supported Republic of Texas, the correspondent concluded by warning that "Americans should examine before they act, and ever remember that Upper Canada is not Texas; that Canadians are not Texans, and that Great Britain is not Mexico."

On January 13—the day after Governor Mason dispersed the Patriot force at Sugar Island—Detroiters gathered at city hall with Mason, Mayor Henry Howard, and U.S. district attorney Daniel Goodwin and declared support for the government's efforts to preserve neutrality. To prevent a recurrence of the seizure of the *Ann* and the raids on arsenals, Detroit officials organized a town guard, which patrolled the city and riverbank every night. If an emergency arose, an alert was sounded by ringing the bell of the Presbyterian church. At the same time, General Brady federalized six companies of Michigan militia.

The *Ann* affair also led Michigan officials to call for the stationing of more federal troops in Michigan. Given the "extraordinary state of excitement and exasperation manifested by the inhabitants, not only of Canada but of this state," the Michigan House of Representatives overwhelmingly resolved on January 11 that the governor request that no less than two regiments of U.S. troops be sent to Michigan. General Brady concurred and informed General Winfield Scott that while the two cannon stolen earlier from Fort Gratiot had been recovered, these "acts of folly" would persist until "a portion of the regular Army is within supporting distance of the Civil authority." In response to these and other pleas, U.S. secretary of war Joel R. Poinsett ordered four hundred army recruits to the border. On January 27, Colonel William J. Worth arrived in Detroit with 160 soldiers aboard the *Robert Fulton*. Brady sent small detachments of regulars to Fort Gratiot and the Dearborn Arsenal, while retaining the remainder at Detroit.

In early February Brady discharged the Michigan militia because the border had been so quiet. He even predicted that "no further effort will be made in this State to embody men for the purpose of invading her Majesty's dominions." But even as General Brady penned these words, the tranquility along the border was jeopardized. By mid-afternoon hundreds of Patriots, commanded by Donald McLeod, a native Scot who had served in both the British Navy and Army, began gathering at Gibraltar.

The Patriots were confident of their imminent success. Detroiter James L. Schoolcraft boasted on February 22 that while the queen of England might send ten thousand troops to prevent the Canadian independence movement, "these 10,000 can be cut and sliced just as were the forces of Burgoin [sic], Cornwallis and Packingham [sic]." Since the Patriots fought for liberty, Schoolcraft asserted "we can't be whiped [sic], or when they whip us, we won't stay whipped."

Both U.S. and state officials responded to the Patriots' movements. At Brady's request, Governor Mason remobilized six companies of militia. The men no sooner had been mustered than Brady discharged them because he feared that by furnishing arms and ammunition to the militia he would "sustain the cause [he] was desirous to suppress." Brady's action was motivated by several events, most notably the conduct of militia lieutenant colonel Charles Jackson. Sent to Dearbornville to transfer four hundred stands of arms to Detroit, Jackson not only declined a guard proffered by Brady but left the weapons unattended when they reached Detroit. As a result, 240 muskets were stolen. Besides this act of negligence or "connivance with those against whom [Jackson] was especially selected to act," Brady noted that some of the conscripted militia were friendly to the Patriot cause. "At least one of the Captains," Brady declared, "had openly avowed, in the event of a collision between his company and the Patriots, to give them his arms." On February 24 word of the Patriot gathering at Gibraltar prompted Brady to send his second-in-command, Major John Garland, downriver. By the time Garland reached Ecorse, nine miles south of Detroit, the Patriots had left U.S. waters. Garland then positioned his troops to intercept any Patriot retreat.

Across the Detroit River, Canadians experienced numerous problems. In addition to fears of imminent Patriot attack, they faced a shortage of provisions. Western Canadians were dependent upon imported American foodstuffs, especially from Michigan, and ridicule and abuse of Detroit merchants who sold to the Canadians made those suppliers unreliable. To make matters worse, the need to keep several hundred troops on alert placed an additional strain upon the already limited supplies. By the time Patriot leader McLeod reached Michigan, the Canadian defense consisted of approximately 200 militia along the St. Clair River and approximately 120 regulars and 400 militiamen between Sandwich and Amherstburg. These forces included a two-gun section of Royal artillery, the St. Thomas volunteer cavalry, and various Indian allies available upon call.

Tensions along the Detroit River climaxed on February 25 as the Patriots invaded Fighting Island, a swampy thin islet seven miles long in Canadian waters. The liberators raised their tricolored flag and offered cries of "God save the Republic of the Canadas" and "God save the people and equal rights." Though the Patriots, who were reported to number from one to three hundred, had ample provisions, they had invaded Canada with six rifles, one musket, and a carriageless six-pound cannon mounted on a dry-goods box. The stolen rifles entrusted to Major Jackson had been discovered by the authorities, and efforts to procure additional arms from public arsenals had failed. During the night, however, thirty-five serviceable muskets were added to their weaponry.

Notified of the Patriots' arrival on the evening of January 24, the Canadians mobilized their forces. At 3:00 the next morning, two companies of British regulars and one artillery piece left Fort Malden. They arrived opposite Fighting Island at 6:30 A.M. and were joined by Colonel H. D. Townsend, commander of the Twenty-fourth Regiment, and the St. Thomas Cavalry. At 7:00 A.M. nearly four hundred militia from Sandwich joined Townsend and the regulars. According to Robert McFarlan, a Michigan Patriot on Fighting Island, the arrival of the British regulars "with their bright muskets flashing in the morning sun" did not inspire confidence in the minds of the Patriots.

Ordered to quickly dislodge the intruders before they strengthened their position, Townsend opened a steady artillery fire on the island. According to the British colonel, the Patriots became "much discomposed by the precision and rapidity of the fire." Townsend ordered an assault. With the regulars in the center and the militia on the flanks, the British force fired several volleys, which were returned by the relatively few Patriots who possessed weapons. One firing of the Patriot cannon dislodged it from its makeshift carriage, rendering it useless. Outnumbered and outgunned, the Patriots fled back across the ice into Michigan. There they were disarmed, arrested, and transported to Detroit. During the skirmish, the British suffered no casualties. Various reports indicated that five Patriots were wounded.

Much of the Michigan press viewed Fighting Island as the Patriot's death knell. General Brady concurred. Citing disorganization and their lack of provisions and weapons, Brady concluded that "they must soon be convinced, if they are not already, of the utter futility of such an undertaking and will disperse and return to their homes."

Not all of the Patriots in the vicinity of western Lake Erie had been routed at Fighting Island. On February 25 a force of four hundred men under the command of Colonel H. C. Seward left Sandusky, Ohio, and landed on Pelee Island, a rectangular-shaped Canadian island in the middle of western Lake Erie sixty miles from Detroit. On March 1, Colonel Maitland left Fort Malden with a large force consisting mostly of British regulars. Maitland's men sleighed thirty-five miles over the frozen expanse of Lake Erie and engaged the Patriots on March 2. The ensuing battle left the British force with five killed and twenty-eight wounded (two mortally), while the Patriot losses were approximately eleven killed, forty-five wounded (one mortally), and eleven captured (of which five were wounded).

Events following the conflicts on Fighting and Pelee Islands bore a resemblance to the days after the *Ann* incident. Once again Michigan public officials, private citizens, and journalists expressed concern about events along the border. Yet, this time their concern included a greater fear of war with Great Britain, as well as a corresponding need to strengthen the state's defenses. John Anderson of Monroe wrote his brother that many in that city anticipated war with Britain. Although some citizens, including Anderson, were horrified at this prospect, he admitted that among many others "a desire for War is Manifest." The *Monroe Gazette* regretted that the frontier troubles might result in war but added, "if this is to be brought upon us by causes beyond our control, we can yield a willing sacrifice the blood and treasure it will cost. Let the honor of the nation be at stake." Others downplayed the chances of war by reporting on Patriot fiascos elsewhere along the border and ridiculing their farcical efforts to liberate Canada.

Regardless of the possibilities of war, Michiganians undertook measures to fortify their defenses. Amidst rumors that the Canadians were constructing rocket batteries opposite Detroit, the state legislature revised the state militia system. Although it is questionable whether the new system would have, in the opinion of the *Detroit Free Press*, led to Upper Canada's capture in two weeks should war break out, it did result in the state's forty thousand eligible militiamen being ordered to gather on Saturdays in March, April, and May for "martial exercise." The rumors of British rocket batteries also led a committee of prominent Detroiters to visit the Canadian shore. The visitors were well received and witnessed no offensive military preparations.

During the spring and summer of 1838, except for sporadic incidents of hostility between Michiganians and Canadians, the Michigan/Canadian border was quiet. In late May three British officers from Fort Malden were pelted with stones, eggs, and vituperatives during their visit to Detroit. There were also reports of a planned Patriot crossing of the Detroit River on July 4, but it never materialized.

Throughout the summer General Brady patrolled the border with armed vessels. But with fewer than one hundred regulars and an unreliable militia, he continually reminded his superiors that his force was too meager to guarantee that he could stop every

Patriot incursion. In July, Brady received three additional companies of regulars from the Second U.S. Artillery. The government also ordered U.S. customs agents to use vigilance to obtain witnesses and evidence to aid in prosecuting anyone violating the neutrality laws. In early July the sloop *Texas* was seized in Detroit because it was fitted out with armaments "for the purpose of committing hostilities against a foreign country." The armaments—sixteen rifles, a pair of pistols, and a sword—were seized because they also had been imported and not declared to the port collector. On August 13, Detroit customs officers discovered and commandeered three dissembled cannon in crates aboard the vessel *Bunker Hill*. The courts in Michigan were also active. As a result of the mid-February theft of ordnance entrusted to his care, Major Charles Jackson was court-martialed for negligence and conduct unbecoming an officer.

The Canadians also strengthened their defenses. By early June three thousand regulars were deployed across Upper Canada (Ontario). Canadian authorities also hired secret agents to operate in the United States and report on Patriot activities. Like the Americans, the British increased the numbers of ships patrolling the Great Lakes. Unlike the Americans, they viewed the Rush-Bagot Treaty of 1817, which limited each country to two armed vessels on the Upper Great Lakes, as a peacetime measure that was inoperative during this period of border raids. Although informing the U.S. government that their actions were defensive, the British did not ask to negotiate the matter. By early autumn the British had four vessels on Lake Erie alone and was making provisions to increase the fleet to five.

The British pressed U.S. authorities to guarantee that there would be no future Patriot incursions. On November 3, British ambassador to the United States Henry Fox informed acting U.S. secretary of state Aaron Vail that the "mischief" on the border had reached a point where the president's "immediate interference . . . can alone avert the most terrible and afflicting consequences." Fox explained that for a year the Canadian provinces had been in a state of "warlike alarm" defending themselves against "the hostile citizens of a friendly State." He added that if future Patriot invasions occurred, disastrous consequences "would ensue." The British ambassador concluded by warning that if these invasions enjoyed even "transient" success "the United States would necessarily become answerable to Great Britain for "the whole amount of the damage sustained."

In the fall of 1838 the Patriots in Michigan undertook their boldest moves to date. Following a pitched battle between Patriot and British forces near Prescott, Upper Canada, in early November, Governor George Arthur of Upper Canada believed that an attack upon western Canada was expected anytime. The governor's fears were based on reports indicating that as many as a thousand Patriots were bivouacked opposite Sandwich and Amherstburg. Arthur also learned that Patriots were training further north near Fort Gratiot. In mid-October Colonel Richard Airey, commandant at Fort Malden, received a detailed description of an attack on Fort Malden. Five steamers were to ferry men from Buffalo and Cleveland to destroy the village and fort. The report proved false, but not before the militia was mustered. In early November the militia cavalry patrolled the lake and river shores near Amherstburg. Later that month the Sandwich *Western Herald* reported that residents from Windsor to Amherstburg were "kept on the qui vive every night of last week" in anticipation of invasion. By the first of December the situation had worsened as "the old and the young, the rich and the poor," were kept "marching and countermarching, patrolling and keeping sentry."

United States authorities made numerous efforts to halt Patriot filibustering. Some of these efforts, like urging arsenals be more closely guarded and enforcing the more stringent neutrality laws that Congress had recently adopted, ignored the necessary element that might have hindered the Patriots—a large U.S. military presence. Though additional troops had been sent to the northern border throughout 1838, by autumn there were only two thousand U.S. soldiers guarding the thousand-mile frontier. Brady repeatedly informed his superiors that the few troops under his command were spread too thin to effectively stop Patriot movements. In October, Brady noted, "I have an Arsenal & Magazine to guard, a Fort to garrison and a frontier of one hundred miles to cover, with four companies averaging about eighteen men for duty to a company." In late November Brady reminded U.S. secretary of state John Forsyth that his district covered 140 miles and that every village and town along the way contained Patriot supporters.

Brady did keep his small force active exploring every report of Patriot activity, but he was unable to prevent a Patriot rendezvous in southern Michigan in late November. Detroit hotels soon became Patriot organizational centers, and Brady reported that the city was "full" of Patriots and that many more were collecting along the Detroit River between the Michigan capital and Monroe. On November 27 the *Monroe Gazette* reported that two to three hundred men were bivouacked near Swan Creek in southeastern Wayne County. Patriot William Putnam, a Canadian refugee, reported that the three hundred men at Swan Creek were "in good health and spirits." A descendant of American Revolution hero Israel Putnam added that it would be difficult to find "few more noble and sober men."

Unable to stop the rendezvous, Brady's actions, especially confiscating arms caches, did frustrate the liberators' plans and prompted some Patriots to conclude that their cause was hopeless. John H. Harmon, a Cleveland printer, later recalled that "quarrels and dissensions among the men and officers" reduced the force of four hundred Cleveland Hunters who had journeyed to Michigan to fewer than 140. Another Patriot reported that "a great many" invaders deserted after Brady's seizure of weapons, while another attributed the desertion to the failure of Patriot leaders to act forcefully in organizing the invasion.

Despite these setbacks, Patriot general Edward Bierce, an Ohio lawyer, and his second-in-command, William Putnam, were confident of victory. Reassuring his followers that they were the vanguard of fifty-thousand Patriots, half of whom were ready to cross at a moment's notice, Bierce showed his men letters from Upper Canadians indicating a willingness to overthrow the existing provincial government. Bierce even told his troops that only officeholders remained loyal to the Canadian government and that Patriots in Upper Canada had recently defeated British regulars near London. The Patriots also believed that their force was to be augmented by five hundred Poles and eight hundred Kentuckians.

Late on the afternoon of December 3, following the army's consumption of half a barrel of brandy, Bierce ordered the invasion of Upper Canada. About midnight on this cold, moonless night, the Patriots, possessing an inadequate number of weapons, stealthily marched to Detroit's wharf and boarded the steamer *Champlain*. Problems continued to plague the invaders. Some Patriots later claimed that their efforts to leave the *Champlain* had been thwarted by a guard of a dozen men. Several irresolute liberators cut the vessel's tiller ropes to sabotage the invasion, but the ropes were repaired. After a three-hour delay, the *Champlain* crossed into Canadian waters. About 4:00 A.M., four miles north of Windsor, the vessel dropped anchor. According to two participants, there was a great deal of "confusion" on the *Champlain* once it anchored. Some invaders resisted going ashore, but Bierce's threat to cut down anyone who refused convinced all to disembark. The invaders moved to the small community of Windsor where they surrounded a barracks housing two dozen Canadian militiamen. The Patriots burned the barracks and took half the militiamen prisoner; the remainder escaped. Two Canadians died in the affair: one was killed in the fighting, the other perished in the flames. To the cries of "Remember the Caroline," the Patriots also burned the steamer, *Thames,* which was docked a hundred yards from the barracks. Bierce reorganized his forces and sent one hundred men under Putnam to the orchard of François Baby south of the village to oppose any force headed from Sandwich. The general, accurately described by a subordinate as "wanting in courage," joined the rearguard and the militia captives.

Although the Canadians had dropped their vigilance when General Brady seized the Patriots' weapons a few days earlier, they responded immediately when word reached Sandwich of the invasion. As the ranking officer in Sandwich and the area's most prominent politician, Colonel John Prince notified Fort Malden. Two companies of militia, approximately fifty men, and a group of "gentlemen volunteers" soon followed. The Canadians arrived at the Baby orchard at 7:00 A.M. The outnumbered invaders fired one volley before they fled. Putnam and a Colonel Harvell, a six-foot-two-inch, two-hundred-pound Kentuckian, were killed. By 8:00 A.M. the Patriots in the orchard had been routed, and the Canadians had turned their attention to Bierce's rearguard. At this point Colonel Prince arrived on the scene and ordered the entire militia force back to Sandwich to counter a rumored Patriot threat to the village. At that time, a Patriot prisoner was brought to Prince who ordered his immediate execution. The militia reached Sandwich by 8:30 A.M. Informed that the Patriots still controlled Windsor, Prince refused to send any troops until the British regulars arrived from Fort Malden. While at Sandwich, Prince ordered two additional Patriot prisoners executed.

The British regulars, one hundred strong, with a field piece and forty or fifty Indian allies, arrived at Sandwich at 11:00 A.M. Commanded by Captain Broderick, the force headed for Windsor with Colonel Prince and the militia bringing up the rear. By noon Broderick's force occupied Windsor only to discover that the Patriots had fled upriver. According to one of Bierce's men, the fleeing Patriots returned to their morning landing place only to discover that the *Champlain* had left. A search for anything that could float produced enough canoes to transport approximately thirty Patriots to an island in American waters. From there they found a boat and crossed over to the Michigan mainland. Several were arrested by U.S. vessels patrolling the river. The Battle of Windsor decimated Bierce's army; twenty-six were killed, and at least forty-four were taken prisoner. Four Canadians died, including a prominent Sandwich physician, John J. Hume.

The days immediately following the Battle of Windsor were filled with foreboding for citizens and authorities on both sides of the Michigan-Canadian border. Although soundly defeated, the Patriots appeared stronger and better organized than at any previous time. On December 6, 1838, General Brady's informants claimed that at least four hundred Patriots were in the vicinity of Detroit waiting to renew the war. Brady despaired that his own observations indicated that the numbers were not exaggerated. The discouraged general asked what was to be done when the Patriots were "fed, lodged & cheered on by a large portion of our own citizens." Another concern among Michiganians was the prospect of British retaliation. On December 6, Michigan militia general John R. Williams informed U.S. secretary of war Joel Poinsett that reliable information indicated that the British at Fort Malden at Amherstburg were under orders to attack Michigan once Patriot disturbances had quieted down.

By mid-January 1839, General Brady admitted that excitement following the Battle of Windsor had cooled "considerably." Although Brady admitted that there were "still a few agitators at work" in Detroit, he did not expect any difficulties. A month later, one Detroit Patriot glumly observed, "Patriot news is almost gone here." Except for isolated border incidents and the continued strengthening of defenses on both sides of the Detroit River, the Patriot War in Michigan had ended.

Often overlooked during the border disturbances of 1838 are the efforts of Governor Mason, General Brady, and other Michigan officials to stop the Patriots. In early January 1838, Mason organized an expedition to Gibraltar where the Patriots were bivouacked. According to Patriot general Theller, when smoke from the governor's schooner appeared on the horizon the Patriots fled to Bois Blanc Island—an isle outside of American waters. Mason returned to Detroit where he dispersed "a large body" of Patriot reinforcements headed for Bois Blanc. Several days later, Sandwich authorities asked Mason whether he would consider an invasion "of your country" if the Canadians attacked the Patriots "wherever we can find them." Mason responded by returning downriver. After learning that the Patriots had retreated to Sugar Island, which belonged to Michigan, the governor ferried the invaders back to the mainland and disarmed and dispersed them.

In mid-February, Mason accompanied General Brady in an effort to thwart a rumored Patriot invasion force along the St. Clair River north of Detroit. Again on March 10, 1838, Mason responded promptly when several Detroiters discharged weapons toward Windsor. Accompanied by two deputy marshals, the governor stopped the shooting. Mason also issued several proclamations demanding that Michiganians obey American neutrality laws; pleaded with Washington to strengthen his hand in dealing with the Patriots; and called several public meetings to condemn the Patriots' activities.

General Brady worked tirelessly to thwart rumored Patriot filibusters. Several times Brady federalized the Michigan militia to defend arsenals and forts under his jurisdiction. In February 1838, upon receiving word that the Patriots were gathering south of Detroit, Brady sent his second-in-command, Major John Garland, downriver to intercept the Patriots. When the Patriots retreated from Fighting Island, Garland's men disarmed and arrested the would-be liberators and transported them to Detroit. Following Patriot activity on the St. Clair River in June 1838, Brady moved quickly dispatching a schooner and troops to patrol this area, which was twenty-five miles north of Detroit. In early July, Brady prevented a theft of arms from the U.S. arsenal at Dearborn and kept a schooner patrolling the Detroit

River to halt a rumored filibuster. The general also visited and worked closely with Canadian and British authorities, and shared with them information about Patriot activities.

In late November 1838, as Patriots once again gathered in southeastern Michigan, Brady increased his vigilance. A Patriot arms cache was seized on December 2. The general also commissioned all operational vessels in Detroit for official use. Brady was confident that the Patriots' plans had been thwarted. Prior to the December 3 Patriot seizure of the *Champlain* to cross the Detroit River, Brady had been assured by the vessel's owner that the *Champlain* was inoperative. Once aware of the Patriots' invasion, Brady immediately activated his flotilla. Amidst shouts of derision and threats of assassination, he arrested Patriots retreating from their setback at Windsor. Brady also intensified his patrols of the Detroit River, which prevented any additional Patriot excursions into Canada.

Michigan officials, both elected and appointed, faced three problems in restraining the Patriots: first, the sense of mission Americans felt in spreading liberty and their corresponding belief that individual rights superseded law; second, the politicization prevalent in many facets of American society; and third, the ambiguous lines of authority between state and federal government.

During the 1830s, American political thinking was still dominated by ideas popular during the American Revolution. Americans believed England to be ruled by an archaic, oppressive government that was the antithesis of American institutions and America's implacable enemy. Although the years following the War of 1812 witnessed the resolution of various disputes between the United States and Great Britain, distrust of the British still pervaded U.S. public opinion.

Americans were also confident that American democracy was a model for all the world to follow. American support for the French Revolution and later the Greek Revolution was a forerunner of the American assumption that Canadians would welcome an end to British colonial rule. The heritage of the American Revolution also induced Americans to accept the idea of rebellion as a means of obtaining this end.

The universality of American belief in revolution, in British corruption, and in the moral superiority of democracy was evident in the widespread support for the Patriots. Such support crossed political and social lines. While only a minority of Michigan residents favored an active or official American presence in supporting the liberation of Canada, most, including their leaders, sympathized with the Canadian quest for liberty. Writing to Patriot general Thomas Sutherland after the ill-fated Patriot invasion of Bois Blanc Island in January 1838, residents of Palmer, in St. Clair County, conceded that they were "bound to observe a strict neutrality" but added that "it would be deceptious [sic] . . . as citizens of this Republican Government, to conceal from you the fact that our feelings and sympathies are enlisted and excited in the revolution which is now going on in the two Canadian Provinces."

Prevailing political philosophies growing out of the American Revolution presented grave problems for authorities attempting to control the Patriots. Prime among these was the belief that law came from the people and was valid only as long as it served the needs of and was upheld by the majority. As one astute Detroiter observed at the height of the Patriots' activities, "under a Government where the law is but the embodied spirit of public opinion, it becomes, in a great degree, inoperative, where that opinion does not sustain it."

The American belief in popular sovereignty is best exemplified by the futile efforts to prosecute those Patriots who fell into the hands of American authorities. At Thomas Sutherland's trial in January 1838, U.S. district attorney Daniel Goodwin tried to prosecute the Patriot general for preparing the military expedition that left Michigan and invaded Upper Canada. Goodwin faced both uncooperative witnesses and a federal judge who repeatedly sustained defense objections to evidence that might have confirmed Sutherland's activities. U.S. District Court judge Ross Wilkins' dismissal of the case against Sutherland for lack of evidence was only the first of several similar cases. In July and December 1838 at least seven Patriots, arrested following filibusters into Upper Canada, were also released by Judge Wilkins.

In mid-1839, Goodwin tried to prosecute acknowledged Patriots Edward Theller and Donald McLeod, leaders in the Bois Blanc and Fighting Island campaigns. According to the *Detroit Daily Advertiser,* the district attorney was "met at every step, with unexpected opposition and censure." The *Advertiser* added that "the bias and sympathy of both the Court and Jury, was in favor of the accused, however imperative the law, and clear the facts might be." Indeed, the only successful prosecution of a Patriot in Michigan was that of John Vreeland, Patriot ordinance officer at the Battle of Fighting Island, in July 1838. However, his conviction may have resulted from factors other than his Patriot allegiance, including the allegation that he was a counterfeiter.

The biggest difficulty in successfully prosecuting the Patriots was the inability to gather evidence. Citizens apparently felt no obligation to incriminate people engaged in illegal actions if they did not themselves view these actions as wrong. On January 9, 1838, District Attorney Goodwin admitted "the extreme difficulty" in acquiring a correct knowledge "of facts or of the doings" of the Patriots. A year later, Judge Wilkins observed that enforcing neutrality laws was difficult because so "few are willing to give the requisite information." As late as mid-1839 a Detroit grand jury declared they were openly sympathetic toward "any nation earnestly engaged in the assertion of its liberty and independence." Finding dependable juries made the prosecutor's job even more difficult. In mid-1838 members of a Detroit grand jury, which had been convened to determine whether American neutrality laws had been violated, were charged themselves with having given money and aid to the Patriots.

To such Americans, enforcement of laws they questioned clearly took a secondary position to preservation of "rights." As the Patriots gathered near Detroit during the days before the Battle of Windsor, the *Detroit Daily Advertiser* noted how difficult it was to convince "many of our sober-minded and peace loving citizens that the appearance of so many individuals, at the present juncture, and under the peculiar circumstances, indicate something wrong, or . . . that their [sic] existed any very urgent necessity for an efficient night patrol." A few weeks later, Judge Wilkins reiterated this attitude. Deciding for the owners of the *Champlain,* which Detroit port collector John McDonell had seized on December 5, 1838, to prevent any further Patriot filibusters, Wilkins ordered the vessel released. Admitting that the fear of renewed hostilities explained McDonell's "over reaction," the federal judge declared that the guarantee of American civil liberties, even if they included violations of the peace, should outweigh efforts to enforce the laws.

Michigan residents in the 1830s claimed other real and perceived rights and liberties guaranteed them under the Constitution. Among them were the right to bear arms, freedom from a standing army, and freedom from excessive government. In mid-February 1838, at a time of extensive Patriot activity, stolen U.S. ordnance and untrustworthy Michigan militiamen, the *Detroit Daily Free Press* estimated that four-fifths of Detroit's population thought government officials had become "unnecessarily rigid" in suppressing the Patriots. Legislative efforts to order militia units to engage in "martial exercise and company drill"—a direct response to the Patriot's activities—prompted criticism of "this unconstitutional act." "If our country were in danger from threatened invasion," the *Pontiac Courier* argued, "the militia to a man would turn out to defend it. But there is no danger." The *Ann Arbor State Journal* also criticized General Brady for "tampering with the rights and feelings of our citizens" when he dismissed the militia following indications that several members sympathized with the Patriots.

More serious criticism of violations of constitutional guarantees occurred in July 1838 when U.S. authorities raided the home of Edward Heath, a well-known Patriot. Although the authorities possessed a search warrant, no Patriot weapons were discovered. Citing the constitutional right to possess firearms, one Detroiter responded to the search by querying, "Shall a Brady . . . dressed in a little brief authority, and backed by United States soldiers, trample on our rights—search our houses—and by a display of bayonets still the exhibition of every independent emotion?" Similar criticism of United States government actions occurred in December 1838 when one Michigan resident described the efforts to arrest Patriots fleeing from the aborted Windsor invasion, as "shameful conduct of a free government."

A greater U.S. military presence was essential to curtail the Patriots, yet General Brady's constant urgings for more troops went largely unheeded. In July 1838, Brady informed U.S. adjutant general R. Jones that "the conviction that military aid was at hand tended to encourage the deputy marshalls in the performance of their duties." However, six months later Brady's regular army force, which was responsible for more than one hundred miles of Michigan-Canadian border, totaled about one hundred men. Congress increased the size of the army in mid-1838, but the effort lacked the speed necessary to make it an effective deterrent to the Patriots' filibustering. After six months' rancorous debate, Congress expanded the army to 12,500 men—an official increase of a mere 5,000. The army's involvement in fighting Indians (in December 1837 nine of the army's thirteen regiments were in Florida) and the traditional aversion to a large standing army, especially in peacetime, limited the number of regular troops available for service on the northern frontier. In December 1838 a Detroit rally denounced the way the army was being used on the frontier. The Detroiters circulated a petition criticizing President Martin Van Buren for stationing a standing army "in time of peace," which endangered the lives of Americans and imprisoned others, all "on the mere pretence that a law of the Union has been or is about to be infracted." Decrying the nature of man to seize power, the petition further criticized the use of the military in a role "calculated for a Civil Police."

Civil and military authorities attempting to control the Patriots were also hampered by popular beliefs of mission and the dominance of individual rights. However, civilian leaders were also political creatures, whose success depended upon election and appointment. As a result, officeholders were forced to consider the political ramifications of their every movement. The 1830s marked the birth of mass political involvement in American society. The expansion of white male suffrage, greater voter interest, and the development of a two-party system highlighted the decade. Although both political parties had many loyal supporters, general public opinion was important since in Michigan neither party commanded a dominant majority.

Much of the domestic criticism of Governor Mason regarding his handling of the Patriots came from his political opponents. In early January 1838 the *Detroit Daily Advertiser,* the Whig's leading organ, repeatedly attacked the Democratic administration for being "spell bound with apathy" or taking actions that appeared "a good deal farcical." When the governor called a January 6, 1838, meeting to support the public officials' efforts to preserve neutrality, the *Advertiser* dismissed the rally as too little and too late.

Other Michigan officeholders also found themselves under political attack. On two separate occasions Detroit port collector McDonell, a Democratic political appointee, was forced to defend his actions against the *Advertiser's* criticism. The most serious case came after the Battle of Windsor when McDonell was accused of not discharging "the trust required in him" and allowing the Patriots to seize the *Champlain.* In a communique to Collector McDonell, however, General Brady concluded: "the activity, vigilance and anxiety, exhibited by you, at all times, since the commencement of the late patriot disturbances, and your evident desire to perform your duty to your country to the extent of your power, have been, sufficient pledges to me, that nothing but deep deception practiced upon you, could have led to the result we all so much deplore."

As the chief executive responsible for maintaining order, Governor Mason, a supporter of local rights during Michigan's quest for statehood a few years earlier, was in a particularly delicate position. His actions risked not only his career but the well-being of his entire party. Responding to the governor's December 27, 1837, pronouncement prohibiting Michigan residents from volunteering to join the Patriots' liberation of Canada, the *Pontiac Courier* argued that "when the governor's political success depended upon the admission of our state into the Union, he contended that the people had an undoubted right to act in their original capacity, without any regard to the forms of law." (In 1835, Mason, then Michigan's acting territorial governor, proved so aggressive in demanding that Michigan be admitted as a state, he threatened war with Ohio and was subsequently fired by President Andrew Jackson.) The *Pontiac Courier* concluded that the governor's recent declaration violated the people's will and added that if Michiganians thought it "proper to shoulder their rifles, go over to Canada and join the [Patriot] cause, they will do it."

Mason's position was further complicated by certain Michigan Democrats who were ardent Patriots. One notable Patriot was Benjamin Kingsbury, editor of the *Detroit Morning Post.* In early January 1838, Mason refuted a *Post* accusation that he secretly hoped that Michigan residents would violate American neutrality laws. Later that same year the *Post* mocked President Van Buren's demands that citizens obey neutrality laws by issuing a parody of his November proclamation. Besides not wanting to offend the British queen, the *Post's* version had the president issue an order enjoining "my army to kill and murder all who did not obey this proclamation."

One of the tenets of the Hunters Lodges, the societies devoted to the Patriot cause, was support for political candidates who favored the liberation of Canada. Several observers agreed with one Michiganian who predicted in December 1838, "political annihilation" to any politician that supported "the futile efforts of quelling the wild-fire of Canadian liberty." Edward Theller, the former Patriot general turned Detroit newspaper editor, reported in October 1839 that he had received requests from all across the state asking him which candidates they should support. Even as late as 1841 there were indications that Patriot sympathizers near Detroit intended to support only political candidates that favored Canada's liberation.

Both political parties did their best to curry Patriot favor. At a gathering at the Detroit City Hall on March 23, 1838, the Democrats adopted a resolution criticizing the Whigs' actions toward the Patriots. According to the Democrats, the Whigs' actions savored strongly of "the arrogance of aristocracy" and were "in perfect keeping" with the Whigs' favorite and adopted principle—"that the people are unqualified and uncapable of self-government."

The Whigs, too, had to hedge their political positions. In January 1838 the *Detroit Daily Advertiser* responded to charges that it supported British colonial rule in Canada by declaring that "we yield to none in an ardent desire that Canadians may be successful in their efforts." A year later the *Advertiser,* which had spent the entire year criticizing the Democratic authorities for incompetence and urging extreme caution in American involvement in aiding Canada's quest for liberation, still believed that the cause of Canadian freedom was "dear to every true American bosom." There are also indications that prominent Detroit Whigs George C. Bates and Edward Brooks, later appointed port collector and district attorney, were active Patriots.

A third dilemma confronting American authorities involved lines of authority in controlling the Patriots. Faced with a situation where strong measures were needed to restrain American aggressors in matters dealing with a foreign nation, the U.S. government responded sluggishly.

During the early 1820s, Americans supported the Greeks' struggle for freedom against the Turkish empire. In the Michigan Territory, editorials and rallies among Detroit's fewer than two thousand residents hailed the freedom-loving Greeks. "Greek Fever" led to funds being collected for the Greeks and several Michigan towns being named after Greek revolutionary heroes.

Unlike this outpouring of support for distant Greece, which the United States government could pass off as a private matter not requiring government involvement, the American response to the liberation of Canada presented direct, unavoidable problems for the federal government. It created international incidents that could have led to war. The situation was further complicated since controlling the Patriots required the active involvement of the states' law enforcement agencies. However, the international nature of the crisis and the unwillingness of Americans to obey the laws left the federal government in a quandary as to how to react.

That request was slow to come, as federal officials, conscious of demands for limited government and sympathy for the spread of liberty, ordered the enforcement of neutrality laws but failed to provide the means necessary to accomplish that task. Besides not providing an adequate military force, the federal government dragged its feet in passing the laws necessary to prevent violations of American neutrality. On January 5, 1838, President Van Buren asked Congress to revise the 1818 neutrality laws, which gave the government power to punish offenders only after acts had been committed. Concerned about increasing the civil powers of the executive, Congress became absorbed "in acutely recriminatory political debate" about strengthening the law.

In the meantime, authorities on the border pressed for more effective laws. In mid-February 1838, Governor Mason reminded the president that the existing laws did not allow for the seizure of arms and munitions of war, which upon "reasonable suspicion" were destined for an expedition against a foreign power at peace with the United States. Finally, in March, Congress passed a new neutrality law. However, the legislation did not strengthen the penal provisions of the existing law. Moreover, the new act was so cluttered with provisions for legal and judicial procedure to be followed before vessels and arms could be detained after seizures that the power of the civil authorities was as restricted as it had been under the former law.

The dilemma created by these lines of authority is best characterized by an episode in late 1838. Ordered "to use increased vigilance" in watching the Patriots' movements in September of that year, U.S. marshal Conrad Ten Eyck appointed at least twenty new deputies along the Michigan-Canadian border. Upon learning of the appointments, U.S. secretary of state John Forsyth expressed shock. Conceding that Ten Eyck's presence made him the best judge of how many deputies were needed, Forsyth added that at two dollars per day, plus expenses, Ten Eyck's appointees probably exceeded the number that were needed or could be afforded.

There is no doubt that Governor Mason and many other public officials in Michigan would have enjoyed seeing Canada's liberation from Great Britain. But they also were cognizant that the Patriots' activities were illegal and that they jeopardized the existing peace between the United States and Great Britain. These officials succeeded in suppressing the Patriots on numerous occasions. Considering the various emotional, institutional, and physical handicaps they worked under, they could have accomplished little more.

BIBLIOGRAPHIC NOTE

Some of the best sources of information about Michigan's involvement in the Patriot War are:

Bishop, Levi. "Recollections of the 'Patriot War' of 1838–39 on this Frontier." *Michigan Pioneer and Historical Collections* 12 (1887): 414–24.

Bulkley, John M. "The Patriot War." *History of Monroe County.* Chicago: Lewis Publishing Company, 1913. 1:162–66.

Burton, Clarence M. "Toledo and Patriot Wars." *The City of Detroit.* Detroit: Clarke Publishing Company, 1922. 1:1058–65.

Corey, Albert. *Canadian-American Relations Along the Detroit River.* Detroit: Wayne State University Press, 1957.

Douglas, R. Alan. *Uppermost Canada: The Western District and the Detroit Frontier, 1800–1850.* Detroit: Wayne State University Press, 2001. 157–76.

Hamil, Fred C. "American Recruits for the Invasion of Windsor." *Detroit Historical Society Bulletin* 15, no. 6 (Mar. 1959): 7–14.

Landon, Fred. "Trial and Punishment of the Patriots Captured at Windsor in December 1838," *Michigan History* 18, no. 1 (Spring 1934): 25–32.

McFarlan, Robert. "The Patriot War: The Battle of Fighting Island." *Michigan Pioneer and Historical Collections* 7 (1884): 89–92.

Morrison, Neil F. "The Battles of Fighting Island and Pelee Island." *Michigan History* 32, no. 3 (Fall 1948): 227–32.

Prucha, Francis, ed. "Reports of General Brady on the Patriot War." *Canadian Historical Review* 31, no. 1 (Mar. 1950): 56–58.

Rosentreter, Roger L. "To Free Upper Canada: Michigan and the Patriot War, 1837–1839." Ph.D. diss., Michigan State University, 1983.

———. "To Liberate Canada: Michigan and the Patriot War." *Michigan History* 73, no. 5 (Sept./Oct. 1989): 24–31.

Ross, Robert B. "The Patriot War." *Michigan Pioneer and Historical Collections* 21 (1892): 509–609.

Solvick, Stanley D. "The Brady Guards: Michigan Volunteers During the Patriot War 1838–1839." *Detroit Society for Genealogical Research Magazine* 45, no. 1 (Fall 1981): 15–16.

Spirit of '76. Aug. 17, 1839–Oct. 17, 1840. [This Detroit daily newspaper was published by one of the leaders of the Michigan Patriots trying to overthrow the Canadian government by invading the country from this state.]

Patriot War Related Historic Sites and Monuments in Michigan

Commandant's Quarters, DAR Bronze Tablet, Michigan and Monroe Streets, Dearborn, Wayne County
Commandant's Quarters State Historic Marker, Dearborn Arsenal, Wayne County

List of Relevant Michigan Illustrations

Patriot War—Representative Soldiers

Atwell, Willis. *Do You Know.* [Grand Rapids]: Booth Newspapers, 1937. P. 319. A drawing of the typical soldier of that era.

General Photograph Collection, Burton Historical Collections, Detroit Public Library. Image showing "the landing of the Patriots."

Michigan History Magazine. Sept./Oct. 1989, pp. 24–31. Soft depictions of activities by the Patriots.

Windrow, Martin, and Gerry Embleton. *Military Dress of North America, 1665–1970.* New York: Charles Scribner's Sons, 1973. P. 77. Image of American Army uniforms for the period.

Patriot War—Specific Soldiers

Brady, Hugh. In Frank E. Stevens, *The Black Hawk War.* Chicago: Frank E. Stevens, 1903. Opposite p. 120.
Hubbard, Bela. Reading Room File, Burton Historical Collection, Detroit Public Library.

Patriot War—Theater of Operations

General Photograph Collection, Burton Historical Collection, Detroit Public Library. Detroit in 1837.
Photograph Collection, Dearborn Historical Museum, Dearborn Michigan. Dearborn Arsenal.

Organizational Chart of Participating Michigan Units

The number of Michigan men, extracted from the rosters, is listed after each company.

1st Regiment, 1st Brigade, 1st Division (Wayne County)
Brigadier General Benjamin F. H. Witherell, commanding
  Isaac Rowland, Independent Company of Brady Guards (Detroit)   99

Levi W. Beebe, Company C (Detroit)	95
Paul Rice, Company E	45
Thomas Martin, Company F (Grosse Pointe)	(unknown)
James M. Burger (Detroit)	45
William P. Patrick (Detroit)	110

3rd Regiment, 3rd Brigade, 3rd Division (Macomb County)
Major General John Stockton, commanding

William G. Page, Clinton Guards (Mt. Clemens)	(unknown)

2nd Regiment, 5th Brigade, 3rd Division
Colonel Henry Smith, commanding

Joseph Wood (Gibralter)	33

Unidentified Companies From the Michigan Militia
Commander Unknown

Captain Hunter (Oakland County)	(unknown)
Captain Rockwell (Oakland County)	(unknown)

Miscellaneous units	10
Total Number of Michigan Soldiers in the Patriot War	437

ROSTER OF MICHIGAN MEN
IN THE PATRIOT WAR

Name	Rank	Military Unit	Service Dates	Remarks
Abbott, John S.	PVT	Rowland's Company	01/05/38–02/04/38	ASD 03/01/39–05/31/39
Abel, Alexander G.	PVT	Rowland's Company	03/01/39–05/31/39	
Adams, Charles S.	PVT	Rowland's Company	12/06/38–02/22/39	ASD 03/01/39–05/31/39
Adams, Orville S.	PVT	Rowland's Company	12/06/38–02/22/39	ASD 03/01/39–05/31/39
Alexander, A.	PVT	Patrick's Company	02/08/38–03/01/38	
Allen, Orville S.	PVT	Rowland's Company	12/06/38–02/22/39	ASD 03/01/39–05/31/39
Andrews, Robert	PVT	Burger's Company	01/06/38–01/31/38	
Andrews, Thomas B.	PVT	Rowland's Company	01/05/38–02/04/38	
Armstrong, James A.	2SG	Rowland's Company	01/05/38–02/04/38	ASD 12/06/38–02/22/39 as 2LT
Ashley, John I.	2LT	Rowland's Company	01/05/38–02/04/38	ASD 12/06/38–02/22/39; 03/01/39–05/31/39
Ashley, Peter	PVT	Rice's Company	01/06/38–01/31/38	
Atherton, Amasa G.	PVT	Rowland's Company	12/06/38–02/22/39	ASD 03/01/39–05/31/39
Atterbury, John G.	PVT	Rowland's Company	01/05/38–02/04/38	ASD 12/06/38–02/22/39; 03/01/39–05/31/39
Bacon, Marshall I.	1SG	Rowland's Company	01/05/38–02/04/38	
Banks, A. T.	PVT	Beebe's Company	01/06/38–01/31/38	
Barrett, W. H.	PVT	Patrick's Company	01/06/38–01/31/38	
Bates, George C.	PVT	Rowland's Company	01/05/38–02/04/38	ASD 12/06/38–02/22/39; 03/01/39–05/31/39
Batten, John	PVT	Wood's Company	02/13/38–02/16/38	
Beard, George	PVT	Bebee's Company	01/06/38–01/31/38	ASD 02/08/38–02/28/38
Beaufait, F.	PVT	Rice's Company	01/06/38–01/31/38	

314

NAME	RANK	MILITARY UNIT	SERVICE DATES	REMARKS
Beaufait, Vital	3SG	Rice's Company	01/06/38–01/31/38	
Beebe, Levi W.	CAP	Beebe's Company	01/06/38–01/31/38	ASD 02/08/38–02/28/38
Bement, R. B.	PVT	Burger's Company	01/06/38–01/31/38	
Benham, E.	PVT	Beebe's Company	02/08/38–02/28/38	
Benley, Francis	PVT	Rice's Company	01/06/38–01/31/38	
Bennett, S. W.	3CP	Wood's Company	02/13/38–02/16/38	
Berrien, John M.	COL	F&S 1st MI Regiment	01/06/38–03/01/38	
Bishop, George A.	PVT	Burger's Company	01/06/38–01/31/38	
Bishop, George W.	PVT	Burger's Company	01/06/38–01/31/38	
Bishop, Levi	MUS	Patrick's Company	01/06/38–01/31/38	ASD 02/08/38–03/01/38
Bissell, C. B.	PVT	Patrick's Company	01/06/38–01/31/38	
Boden, William	PVT	Patrick's Company	02/08/38–03/01/38	
Botton, Joseph	PVT	Patrick's Company	01/06/38–01/31/38	ASD 02/08/38–03/01/38
Brady, Hugh	GEB	F&S 2nd US Infantry	??/??/38–??/??/39	
Brainard, F.	PVT	Patrick's Company	01/06/38–01/31/38	
Brakeman, J.	PVT	Beebe's Company	01/06/38–01/31/38	ASD 02/08/38–02/28/38
Branaby, T. B.	PVT	Beebe's Company	01/06/38–01/31/38	
Brennan, John	PVT	Patrick's Company	02/08/38–03/01/38	
Brink, Nicholas	PVT	Beebe's Company	01/06/38–01/31/38	
Bristol, Charles L.	SGT	Burger's Company	01/06/38–01/31/38	
Brooks, Edward	MAJ	F&S 1st MI Regiment	01/06/38–01/31/38	ASD 02/08/38–02/28/38
Brown, Ezra	PVT	Patrick's Company	01/06/38–01/31/38	
Brown, Morris S.	4SG	Patrick's Company	01/06/38–01/31/38	ASD 02/08/38–03/01/38
Buck, Simpson	PVT	Rowland's Company	03/01/39–05/31/39	
Buel, A. T.	PVT	Beebe's Company	01/06/38–01/31/38	ASD 02/08/38–02/28/38
Buhl, Christian H.	CPL	Rowland's Company	01/05/38–02/04/38	ASD 03/01/39–05/31/39 as 4SG

Michigan Men in the Patriot War

Name	Rank	Military Unit	Service Dates	Remarks
Bull, Charles M.	PVT	Rowland's Company	01/05/38–02/04/38	ASD 03/01/39–05/31/39
Bull, George C.	PVT	Rowland's Company	01/05/38–02/04/38	
Bull, James	PVT	Burger's Company	01/06/38–01/31/38	
Burger, James M.	CAP	Burger's Company	01/06/38–01/31/38	
Burnett, W.	PVT	Beebe's Company	01/06/38–01/31/38	ASD 02/08/38–02/28/38
Burnham, C.	PVT	Patrick's Company	01/06/38–01/31/38	ASD 02/08/38–03/01/38
Burnham, Thomas M.	PVT	Rowland's Company	01/05/38–02/04/38	ASD 12/06/38–02/22/39; 03/01/39–05/31/39
Burrows, Gates	PVT	Patrick's Company	01/06/38–01/31/38	
Calahan, D.	PVT	Patrick's Company	01/06/38–01/31/38	ASD 02/08/38–03/01/38
Campau, Antony	PVT	Rice's Company	01/06/38–01/31/38	
Campau, Henry	PVT	Rice's Company	01/06/38–01/31/38	
Caniff, James H.	PVT	Beebe's Company	02/08/38–02/28/38	
Cann, Robert	PVT	Patrick's Company	01/06/38–01/31/38	
Card, William	PVT	Burger's Company	01/06/38–01/31/38	
Carland, Michael	PVT	Patrick's Company	02/08/38–03/01/38	
Carpenter, Nathan B.	PVT	Beebe's Company	02/08/38–02/28/38	
Champ, William	4CP	Beebe's Company	01/06/38–01/31/38	ASD 02/08/38–02/28/38 as 4SG
Chapman, James	PVT	Rowland's Company	12/06/38–02/22/39	ASD 03/01/39–05/31/39
Chase, J. M.	PVT	Patrick's Company	01/06/38–01/31/38	ASD 02/08/38–03/01/38
Chase, R. C.	PVT	Patrick's Company	01/06/38–01/31/38	
Chester, John	PVT	Rowland's Company	01/05/38–02/04/38	ASD 12/06/38–02/22/39; 03/01/39–05/31/39
Chittenden, William F.	2LT	Patrick's Company	01/06/38–01/31/38	ASD 02/08/38–03/01/38
Churchill, Marcellus C.	PVT	Rowland's Company	12/06/38–02/22/39	ASD 03/01/39–05/31/39
Clark, G. S.	PVT	Wood's Company	02/13/38–02/16/38	
Clark, W. L.	PVT	Patrick's Company	01/06/38–01/31/38	
Clark, Z. M.	PVT	Rowland's Company	03/01/39–05/31/39	

NAME	RANK	MILITARY UNIT	SERVICE DATES	REMARKS
Clayton, William	PVT	Patrick's Company	01/06/38–01/31/38	
Clements, Samuel	1CP	Patrick's Company	01/06/38–01/31/38	ASD 02/08/38–03/01/38
Clinton, H.	PVT	Beebe's Company	01/06/38–01/31/38	
Cochuway, Glory	PVT	Rice's Company	01/06/38–01/31/38	
Cockburn, Peter R.	PVT	Wood's Company		Enrolled but not present
Codnall, H.	PVT	Rice's Company	01/06/38–01/31/38	
Cole, D.	MUS	Beebe's Company	01/06/38–01/31/38	ASD 02/08/38–02/28/38
Cole, James	PVT	Patrick's Company	02/08/38–03/01/38	
Cole, William	PVT	Beebe's Company	01/06/38–01/31/38	ASD 02/08/38–02/28/38
Compeau, Joseph	PVT	Beebe's Company	01/06/38–01/31/38	ASD 02/08/38–02/28/38
Comstock, Horace H.	QUT	F&S MI Militia	01/06/38–01/31/38	ASD 02/08/38–02/28/38
Condy, John	PVT	Rice's Company	01/06/38–01/31/38	
Conner, James I.	CPL	Burger's Company	01/06/38–01/31/38	
Conner, Richard	1SG	Rice's Company	01/06/38–01/31/38	
Conney, Chris	PVT	Patrick's Company	02/08/38–03/01/38	
Connor, James S.	PVT	Rowland's Company	01/05/38–02/04/38	ASD 12/06/38–02/22/39; 03/01/39–05/31/39
Cook, Otis	3CP	Patrick's Company	01/06/38–01/31/38	ASD 02/08/38–03/01/38
Corland, Daniel	PVT	Patrick's Company	02/08/38–03/01/38	
Coster, William	PVT	Burger's Company	01/06/38–01/31/38	
Coultier, Israel	PVT	Rowland's Company	12/06/38–02/22/39	ASD 03/01/39–05/31/39
Covert, William H.	PVT	Rowland's Company	12/06/38–02/22/39	ASD 03/01/39–05/31/39
Cowen, F. A.	PVT	Patrick's Company	01/06/38–01/31/38	
Cowles, Noah	PVT	Beebe's Company	02/08/38–02/28/38	
Cowles, Zalman J.	PVT	Rowland's Company	12/06/38–02/22/39	ASD 03/01/39–05/31/39
Coyl, W. R.	PVT	Patrick's Company	02/08/38–03/01/38	
Craig, Alexander	PVT	Wood's Company		Enrolled but not present

317

NAME	RANK	MILITARY UNIT	SERVICE DATES	REMARKS
Crane, James G.	PVT	Rowland's Company	01/05/38–02/04/38	PEN
Crockett, G. D.	PVT	Beebe's Company	01/06/38–01/31/38	
Daniels,	MUS	Beebe's Company	02/08/38–02/28/38	Forename unknown
Davis, Caleb F.	PVT	Rowland's Company	01/05/38–02/04/38	ASD 12/06/38–02/22/39; 03/01/39–05/31/39
Davis, Charles	PVT	Patrick's Company	02/08/38–03/01/38	
Davis, George	PVT	Rowland's Company	01/05/38–02/04/38	
Davis, Marvin	PVT	Wood's Company	02/13/38–02/16/38	
Dayley, John	PVT	Burger's Company	01/06/38–01/31/38	
Delong, Charles E.	2LT	Beebe's Company	01/06/38–01/31/38	ASD 02/08/38–02/28/38
Demill, Peter E.	PVT	Rowland's Company	01/05/38–02/04/38	
Denno, Peter	PVT	Wood's Company	02/13/38–02/16/38	
Dewry, George M.	PVT	Beebe's Company	01/06/38–01/31/38	ASD 02/08/38–02/28/38
Dickinson, W. L.	PVT	Beebe's Company	01/06/38–01/31/38	
Dixon, Samuel	3CP	Beebe's Company	02/08/38–02/28/38	
Dixon, Winslow	PVT	Beebe's Company	02/08/38–02/28/38	
Dolson, Levi F.	PVT	Rice's Company	01/06/38–01/31/38	
Donolly, David	PVT	Patrick's Company	02/08/38–03/01/38	
Donolly, Peter	PVT	Patrick's Company	02/08/38–03/01/38	
Dorherty, C.	PVT	Beebe's Company	02/08/38–02/28/38	
Doty, George	PVT	Rowland's Company	01/05/38–02/04/38	ASD 03/01/39–05/31/39
Doty, Henry	PVT	Rowland's Company	01/05/38–02/04/38	ASD 12/06/38–02/22/39; 03/01/39–05/31/39
Doty, John	PVT	Patrick's Company	01/06/38–01/31/38	
Dow, Amos	PVT	Burger's Company	01/06/38–01/31/38	
Doyle, Edward	PVT	Patrick's Company	02/08/38–03/01/38	
Doyle, Michael	PVT	Patrick's Company	02/08/38–03/01/38	
Drake, E. or T. G.	PVT	Rowland's Company	03/01/39–05/31/39	

NAME	RANK	MILITARY UNIT	SERVICE DATES	REMARKS
Dune, James	PVT	Rice's Company	01/06/38–01/31/38	
Dune, John	PVT	Rice's Company	01/06/38–01/31/38	
Dune, Justice	PVT	Rice's Company	01/06/38–01/31/38	
Durett, Gabriel	PVT	Rice's Company	01/06/38–01/31/38	
Dygert, H.	PVT	Beebe's Company	01/06/38–01/31/38	ASD 02/08/38–02/28/38
Eastbrook, Ethor	PVT	Burger's Company	01/06/38–01/31/38	
Easterbrook, E.	PVT	Patrick's Company	01/06/38–01/31/38	
Eastman, George B.	CPL	Burger's Company	01/06/38–01/31/38	
Eaton, Ward	PVT	Burger's Company	01/06/38–01/31/38	
Eldridge, Charles	PVT	Burger's Company	01/06/38–01/31/38	
Eldridge, James	PVT	Burger's Company	01/06/38–01/31/38	
Emerson, Curtiss	PVT	Burger's Company	01/06/38–01/31/38	
Emerson, E.	PVT	Patrick's Company	01/06/38–01/31/38	
Ensign, L. H.	PVT	Beebe's Company	01/06/38–01/31/38	ASD 02/08/38–02/28/38
Farnsworth, Benjamin S.	PVT	Patrick's Company	01/06/38–01/31/38	ASD 02/08/38–03/01/38
Farnsworth, James H.	PVT	Rowland's Company	01/05/38–02/04/38	ASD 12/06/38–02/22/39; 03/01/39–05/31/39
Ferdell, Edward	PVT	Wood's Company		Enrolled but not present
Ferguson, Eralsy	1LT	Beebe's Company	01/06/38–01/31/38	ASD 02/08/38–02/28/38
Field, Orus	PVT	Beebe's Company	02/08/38–02/28/38	
Fish, D. D.	PVT	Patrick's Company	01/06/38–01/31/38	ASD 02/08/38–03/01/38
Fisher, Merritt	PVT	Rowland's Company	01/05/38–02/04/38	
Fitzpatrick, D.	PVT	Patrick's Company	02/08/38–03/01/38	
Flatley, William	PVT	Patrick's Company	02/08/38–03/01/38	
Flattery, John	1LT	Patrick's Company	01/06/38–01/31/38	ASD 02/08/38–03/01/38
Foot, George	3CP	Beebe's Company	01/06/38–01/31/38	ASD 02/08/38–02/28/38 as 3SG
Frost, C. K.	3SG	Beebe's Company	01/06/38–01/31/38	

NAME	RANK	MILITARY UNIT	SERVICE DATES	REMARKS
Furguson, John	PVT	Wood's Company	02/13/38–02/16/38	
Gage, M. L.	PVT	Beebe's Company	02/08/38–02/28/38	
Gallagher, Domnick	PVT	Patrick's Company	02/08/38–03/01/38	
Galliger, J. B.	PVT	Beebe's Company	01/06/38–01/31/38	
Galpin, Horace Jr.	SGT	Burger's Company	01/06/38–01/31/38	
Gant, Samuel	PVT	Rice's Company	01/06/38–01/31/38	
Garrison, Henry D.	LUT	Burger's Company	01/06/38–01/31/38	
Gault, W. A.	1SG	Beebe's Company	01/06/38–01/31/38	
Getty, James	PVT	Patrick's Company	01/06/38–01/31/38	ASD 02/08/38–03/01/38
Gibson, James	PVT	Patrick's Company	02/08/38–03/01/38	
Gillett, Reynolds	PVT	Beebe's Company	01/06/38–01/31/38	ASD 02/08/38–02/28/38
Godban, Henry	PVT	Beebe's Company	02/08/38–02/28/38	
Godfrey, George	PVT	Patrick's Company	01/06/38–01/31/38	ASD 02/08/38–03/01/38
Green, William	PVT	Patrick's Company	01/06/38–01/31/38	ASD 02/08/38–03/01/38
Griffin, P.	PVT	Patrick's Company	01/06/38–01/31/38	ASD 02/08/38–03/01/38
Grifford, Charles	PVT	Rice's Company	01/06/38–01/31/38	
Griswold, Charles R.	PVT	Rowland's Company	01/05/38–02/04/38	ASD 03/01/39–05/31/39
Gubby, Charles	PVT	Beebe's Company	01/06/38–01/31/38	ASD 02/08/38–02/28/38
Haight, R.	PVT	Patrick's Company	01/06/38–01/31/38	ASD 02/08/38–03/01/38
Hall, William	PVT	Patrick's Company	01/06/38–01/31/38	
Hall, William	PVT	Rowland's Company	12/06/38–02/22/39	ASD 03/01/39–05/31/39
Halloway, Jerome	PVT	Burger's Company	01/06/38–01/31/38	
Halsted, E. O.	PVT	Beebe's Company	01/06/38–01/31/38	
Hand, George E.	PVT	Rowland's Company	01/05/38–02/04/38	ASD 12/06/38–02/22/39
Hanmor, James	PVT	Beebe's Company	01/06/38–01/31/38	

NAME	RANK	MILITARY UNIT	SERVICE DATES	REMARKS
Hanson, John	2SG	Wood's Company	02/13/38–02/16/38	
Harbaugh, David E.	CPL	Rowland's Company	01/05/38–02/04/38	
Harrington, Charles	PVT	Rowland's Company	01/05/38–02/04/38	
Harris, William	PVT	Burger's Company	01/06/38–01/31/38	
Hart, Stephen	PVT	Wood's Company		Enrolled but not present
Hartimer, Christian	PVT	Beebe's Company	02/08/38–02/28/38	
Haufman, F.	PVT	Beebe's Company	02/08/38–02/28/38	
Hayden, H.	PVT	Patrick's Company	02/08/38–03/01/38	
Heacock, Th.	PVT	Beebe's Company	01/06/38–01/31/38	
Henry, James C.	PVT	Rowland's Company	12/06/38–02/22/39	ASD 03/01/39–05/31/39
Hickcon, D. S.	PVT	Beebe's Company	01/06/38–01/31/38	ASD 02/08/38–02/28/38
Hickcox, George S.	2CP	Beebe's Company	01/06/38–01/31/38	
Hickox, David S.	PVT	Rowland's Company	12/06/38–02/22/39	ASD 03/01/39–05/31/39
Hide, M. D.	PVT	Beebe's Company	01/06/38–01/31/38	ASD 02/08/38–02/28/38
Higgins, H.	PVT	Patrick's Company	02/08/38–03/01/38	
Higgins, John	PVT	Patrick's Company	01/06/38–01/31/38	ASD 02/08/38–03/01/38
Highriter, William	2LT	Wood's Company	02/13/38–02/16/38	
Hill, Frederick C.	PVT	Wood's Company	02/13/38–02/16/38	
Hill, Joseph G.	PVT	Rowland's Company	12/06/38–02/22/39	ASD 03/01/39–05/31/39
Hinchman, J. T.	PVT	Beebe's Company	01/06/38–01/31/38	
Hines, Michael	PVT	Rice's Company	01/06/38–01/31/38	
Hinman, B. F.	PVT	Beebe's Company	01/06/38–01/31/38	ASD 02/08/38–02/28/38
Holbrook, Dewitt C.	PVT	Rowland's Company	03/01/39–05/31/39	
Hooker, Casper H.	PVT	Rowland's Company	01/05/38–02/04/38	ASD 12/06/38–02/22/39; 03/01/39–05/31/39
Hovey, A. W.	PVT	Beebe's Company	01/06/38–01/31/38	ASD 02/08/38–02/28/38

Name	Rank	Military Unit	Service Dates	Remarks
Howard, Manly D.	PVT	Beebe's Company	01/06/38–01/31/38	ASD 02/08/38–02/28/38
Howland, William W.	MUS	Beebe's Company	01/06/38–01/31/38	ASD 02/08/38–02/28/38
Howland, William W.	MUS	Rowland's Company	12/06/38–02/22/39	ASD 03/01/39–05/31/39
Hubbard, Bela	LUT	Burger's Company	01/06/38–01/31/38	
Hubbard, Henry G.	PVT	Rowland's Company	01/05/38–02/04/38	
Hughs, P.	PVT	Patrick's Company	01/06/38–01/31/38	ASD 02/08/38–03/01/38
Hyat, H.	PVT	Beebe's Company	01/06/38–01/31/38	
Hyette, Henry	PVT	Burger's Company	01/06/38–01/31/38	
Ingersoll, Walter D.	PVT	Rowland's Company	01/05/38–02/04/38	ASD 12/06/38–02/22/39; 03/01/39–05/31/39
Isdale, D.	PVT	Beebe's Company	01/06/38–01/31/38	ASD 02/08/38–02/28/38
Jackson, Charles	CLT	F&S 1st MI Regiment	01/06/38–01/31/38	ASD 02/08/38–02/28/38. Adjutant
Jarorski, McKotay	PVT	Wood's Company	02/13/38–02/16/38	
Jerome, Edwin	PVT	Burger's Company	01/06/38–01/31/38	
Jones, Griffith H.	PVT	Rowland's Company	01/05/38–02/04/38	ASD 12/06/38–02/22/39; 03/01/39–05/31/39
Jones, Thomas	PVT	Wood's Company	02/13/38–02/16/38	
Joslin, N.	PVT	Beebe's Company	01/06/38–01/31/38	
Joslin, N.	PVT	Patrick's Company	01/06/38–01/31/38	
Kearsley, Edmond R.	1LT	Rowland's Company	01/05/38–02/04/38	ASD 12/06/38–02/22/39; 03/01/39–05/31/39
Kelly, Michael	PVT	Beebe's Company	02/08/38–02/28/38	
Kendrick, S. N.	PVT	Beebe's Company	02/08/38–02/28/38	
Kenedey, A.	PVT	Patrick's Company	01/06/38–01/31/38	
Kerchefes, J. F.	PVT	Beebe's Company	01/06/38–01/31/38	
Killans, P. E.	PVT	Patrick's Company	01/06/38–01/31/38	
King, J. E.	PVT	Beebe's Company	01/06/38–01/31/38	ASD 02/08/38–02/28/38
Kingsbury, Benjamin Jr.	PVT	Burger's Company	01/06/38–01/31/38	
Kingsley, I. or J.	PVT	Patrick's Company	01/06/38–1/31/38	ASD 02/08/38–03/01/38

NAME	RANK	MILITARY UNIT	SERVICE DATES	REMARKS
Kinsbury, Benjamin	PVT	Beebe's Company	01/06/38–01/31/38	
Knapp, Benjamin E.	2CP	Patrick's Company	01/06/38–01/31/38	ASD 02/08/38–03/01/38
Knapp, Lucius H.	1SG	Wood's Company	02/13/38–02/16/38	
Laderoot, Eli	PVT	Rice's Company	01/06/38–01/31/38	
Laderoot, J. P.	PVT	Rice's Company	01/06/38–01/31/38	
Laderoot, Lambert	2SG	Rice's Company	01/06/38–01/31/38	
Laderoot, P.	PVT	Rice's Company	01/06/38–01/31/38	
Laderoot, William	PVT	Rice's Company	01/06/38–01/31/38	
Laurent, John	PVT	Wood's Company	02/13/38–02/16/38	
Lawrence, Daniel	PVT	Wood's Company		Enrolled but not present
Lawson, Thaddius	PVT	Wood's Company		Enrolled but not present
LeBreton, Benjamin	SGT	Burger's Company	01/06/38–01/31/38	
Leval, A.	PVT	Patrick's Company	01/06/38–01/31/38	
Long, John	PVT	Patrick's Company	02/08/38–03/01/38	
Lowe, Tobias	PVT	Rowland's Company	12/06/38–02/22/39	ASD 03/01/39–05/31/39
Lowry, I. or J.	PVT	Patrick's Company	01/06/38–01/31/38	
Lyon, Anson E.	PVT	Rowland's Company	03/01/39–05/31/39	
Lyster, John	PVT	Patrick's Company	02/08/38–03/01/38	
Mack, Charles A	PVT	Rowland's Company	01/05/38–02/04/38	ASD 12/06/38–02/22/39; 03/01/39–05/31/39
Mack, William	PVT	Patrick's Company	02/08/38–03/01/38	
Malomey, John	PVT	Patrick's Company	02/08/38–03/01/38	
Maloy, J.	PVT	Beebe's Company	01/06/38–01/31/38	ASD 02/08/38–02/28/38
Mansell, James R.	PVT	Patrick's Company	01/06/38–01/31/38	
Marsac, F.	PVT	Rice's Company	01/06/38–01/31/38	
Marsack, Charles	PVT	Rice's Company	01/06/38–01/31/38	
Marshall, Anthony	PVT	Beebe's Company	02/08/38–02/28/38	

NAME	RANK	MILITARY UNIT	SERVICE DATES	REMARKS
McCarthy, John	PVT	Rowland's Company	12/06/38–02/22/39	ASD 03/01/39–05/31/39
McDonall, B.	PVT	Beebe's Company	01/06/38–01/31/38	ASD 02/08/38–02/28/38
McDonell, D. D.	4SG	Beebe's Company	01/06/38–01/31/38	ASD 02/08/38–02/28/38 as 2SG
McDonell, E.	PVT	Beebe's Company	01/06/38–01/31/38	
McFarlin, A.	PVT	Patrick's Company	01/06/38–01/31/38	
McGilvery, Robert	PVT	Wood's Company	02/13/38–02/16/38	
McHugh, William	PVT	Beebe's Company	02/08/38–02/28/38	
McIntyre, Daniel	PVT	Beebe's Company	01/06/38–01/31/38	ASD 02/08/38–02/28/38
McMillan, Jesse	PVT	Rowland's Company	01/05/38–02/04/38	ASD 12/06/38–02/22/39; 03/01/39–05/31/39
McNair, David A.	PVT	Burger's Company	01/06/38–01/31/38	
McNillen, J.	PVT	Patrick's Company	02/08/38–03/01/38	
McPharlin, J.	PVT	Beebe's Company	01/06/38–01/31/38	ASD 02/08/38–02/28/38
McReynolds, Andrew T.	3SG	Rowland's Company	01/05/38–02/04/38	MNI Thomas
McReynolds, John	PVT	Rowland's Company	01/05/38–02/04/38	ASD 12/06/38–02/22/39; 03/01/39–05/31/39
McWilliams, Ed	PVT	Patrick's Company	02/08/38–03/01/38	
Mead, I.	PVT	Patrick's Company	01/06/38–01/31/38	
Menigan, Thomas	PVT	Patrick's Company	02/08/38–03/01/38	
Metcalf, Elijah H.	PVT	Rowland's Company	01/05/38–02/04/38	ASD 12/06/38–02/22/39; 03/01/39–05/31/39
Miller, George	PVT	Beebe's Company	02/08/38–02/28/38	
Mills, John	PVT	Patrick's Company	02/08/38–03/01/38	
Moon, George C.	PVT	Rowland's Company	01/05/38–02/04/38	ASD 12/06/38–02/22/39; 03/01/39–05/31/39
Moon, Milton	PVT	Beebe's Company	01/06/38–01/31/38	ASD 02/08/38–02/28/38
Moore, Benjamin B.	PVT	Rowland's Company	01/05/38–02/04/38	ASD 12/06/38–02/22/39; 03/01/39–05/31/39
Moore, Jacob Wilkie	UNK	Michigan Militia	??/??/??–??/??/??	SCU Also claimed to be spi
Moran, Edward	3CP	Rice's Company	01/06/38–01/31/38	
Moran, Isadore	1CP	Rice's Company	01/06/38–01/31/38	

NAME	RANK	MILITARY UNIT	SERVICE DATES	REMARKS
Morsac, F.	PVT	Rice's Company	01/06/38–01/31/38	
Morsack, G. F.	PVT	Rice's Company	01/06/38–01/31/38	
Morse, C. P.	1CP	Beebe's Company	01/06/38–01/31/38	
Morse, S. R.	PVT	Rice's Company	01/06/38–01/31/38	
Morse, Stephen B.	PVT	Burger's Company	01/06/38–01/31/38	
Morting, George	1LT	Rice's Company	01/06/38–01/31/38	
Mose, Joseph	PVT	Rice's Company	01/06/38–01/31/38	
Mullet, James H.	PVT	Rowland's Company	12/06/38–02/22/39	ASD 03/01/39–05/31/39
Murphy, William W.	1LT	F&S 2nd MI Regiment	02/11/38–02/16/38	Adjutant
Nagles, Henry A.	PVT	Rowland's Company	01/05/38–02/04/38	ASD 03/01/39–05/31/39
Nichols, Robert	PVT	Patrick's Company	01/06/38–01/31/38	ASD 02/08/38–03/01/38
Nims, Rodolphus	MUS	Wood's Company	02/13/38–02/16/38	
Norvell, Spencer	PVT	Rowland's Company	01/05/38–02/04/38	ASD 03/01/39–05/31/39
Nugent, George	PVT	Beebe's Company	01/06/38–01/31/38	
O'Brien, John	PVT	Patrick's Company	02/08/38–03/01/38	
O'Callahan, William	PVT	Patrick's Company	02/08/38–03/01/38	
O'Neil, Brien	PVT	Patrick's Company	02/08/38–03/01/38	
Olmsted, William B.	1LT	Wood's Company	02/13/38–02/16/38	
Owings, Rodolphus	PVT	Wood's Company		Enrolled but not present
Page, William G.	CAP	Clinton Guards	??/??/38–??/??/38	
Parsons, Samuel	PVT	Patrick's Company	01/06/38–01/31/38	
Patrick, William P.	CAP	Patrick's Company	01/06/38–01/31/38	ASD 02/08/38–03/01/38
Patterson, S.	PVT	Rice's Company	01/06/38–01/31/38	
Paye, A.	PVT	Rice's Company	01/06/38–01/31/38	
Peckham, Robert	PVT	Patrick's Company	01/06/38–01/31/38	
Pelak, Alexander	PVT	Wood's Company	02/13/38–02/16/38	

NAME	RANK	MILITARY UNIT	SERVICE DATES	REMARKS
Peltier, Charles	PVT	Rowland's Company	01/05/38–02/04/38	ASD 03/01/39–05/31/39
Penney, Charles W.	CPL	Rowland's Company	01/05/38–02/04/38	ASD 12/06/38–02/22/39; 03/01/39–05/31/39
Peran, Globe	PVT	Rice's Company	01/06/38–01/31/38	
Perham, Victor	PVT	Wood's Company		Enrolled but not present
Petty, John G.	PVT	Rowland's Company	01/05/38–02/04/38	ASD 12/06/38–02/22/39; 03/01/39–05/31/39
Phelps, R.	PVT	Patrick's Company	01/06/38–01/31/38	ASD 02/08/38–03/01/38
Phillips, A. M.	PVT	Patrick's Company	01/06/38–01/31/38	ASD 02/08/38–03/01/38
Phillips, Joseph	PVT	Wood's Company	02/13/38–02/16/38	
Phillips, William	PVT	Patrick's Company	01/06/38–01/31/38	
Piche, E.	PVT	Rice's Company	01/06/38–01/31/38	
Piche, Louis	PVT	Rice's Company	01/06/38–01/31/38	
Pierson, John	PVT	Rowland's Company	01/05/38–02/04/38	
Piquette, John B.	CPL	Burger's Company	01/06/38–01/31/38	
Pool, Jasper	PVT	Patrick's Company	01/06/38–01/31/38	
Potts, Charles	PVT	Burger's Company	01/06/38–01/31/38	
Pratt, Peter N.	4CP	Patrick's Company	01/06/38–01/31/38	ASD 02/08/38–03/01/38
Proby, Edward	PVT	Beebe's Company	01/06/38–01/31/38	
Proby, Edward	PVT	Rowland's Company	03/01/39–05/31/39	
Proby, W.	PVT	Beebe's Company	02/08/38–02/28/38	
Protenas, P.	PVT	Patrick's Company	01/06/38–01/31/38	
Quackenbush, Christian M.	PVT	Rowland's Company	12/06/38–02/22/39	ASD 03/01/39–05/31/39 as MUS
Radford, Robert	PVT	Patrick's Company	02/08/38–03/01/38	
Ramsey, H. K.	PVT	Beebe's Company	01/06/38–01/31/38	ASD 02/08/38–02/28/38
Rankin, Lewis	PVT	Beebe's Company	02/08/38–02/28/38	
Rawson, Norman	PVT	Rowland's Company	12/06/38–02/22/39	ASD 03/01/39–05/31/39

NAME	RANK	MILITARY UNIT	SERVICE DATES	REMARKS
Readry, Morris	PVT	Beebe's Company	01/06/38–01/31/38	ASD 02/08/38–02/28/38
Reardon, I. I.	PVT	Patrick's Company	01/06/38–01/31/38	ASD 02/08/38–03/01/38
Redmon, William I.	1SG	Patrick's Company	01/06/38–01/31/38	ASD 02/08/38–03/01/38
Rees, Thomas J.	PVT	Rowland's Company	12/06/38–02/22/39	ASD 03/01/39–05/31/39
Renwick, L. N.	PVT	Beebe's Company	01/06/38–01/31/38	
Rice, Paul	CAP	Rice's Company	01/06/38–01/31/38	
Rich, G. M.	PVT	Beebe's Company	02/08/38–02/28/38	
Rich, J. G.	PVT	Beebe's Company	01/06/38–01/31/38	
Robinson, Elisha	PVT	Burger's Company	01/06/38–01/31/38	
Robinson, W.	PVT	Beebe's Company	01/06/38–01/31/38	ASD 02/08/38–02/28/38
Rood, G. F.	PVT	Patrick's Company	01/06/38–01/31/38	ASD 02/08/38–03/01/38
Rood, Jerry G.	PVT	Beebe's Company	02/08/38–02/28/38	
Rowland, Isaac S.	CAP	Rowland's Company	01/05/38–02/04/38	ASD 12/06/38–02/22/39; 03/01/39–05/31/39
Ruthoan, John	PVT	Patrick's Company	01/06/38–01/31/38	ASD 02/08/38–03/01/38
Ryan, Michael	2SG	Patrick's Company	01/06/38–01/31/38	ASD 02/08/38–03/01/38
Rysden, C. H.	PVT	Beebe's Company	01/06/38–01/31/38	ASD 02/08/38–02/28/38
Sawyer, Franklin Jr.	PVT	Rowland's Company	01/05/38–02/04/38	ASD 12/06/38–02/22/39; 03/01/39–05/31/39
Scruby, Charles	PVT	Patrick's Company	02/08/38–03/01/38	
Sergent, David	3SG	Wood's Company	02/13/38–02/16/38	
Seymour, E. P.	PVT	Beebe's Company	01/06/38–01/31/38	ASD 02/08/38–02/28/38
Seymour, Elisha P.	4CP	Rowland's Company	12/06/38–02/22/39	ASD 03/01/39–05/31/39
Shane, Boby	PVT	Rice's Company	01/06/38–01/31/38	
Shane, George	PVT	Rice's Company	01/06/38–01/31/38	
Shavain, Joseph	2CP	Rice's Company	01/06/38–01/31/38	
Shoemaker, I. or J.	PVT	Patrick's Company	01/06/38–01/31/38	

NAME	RANK	MILITARY UNIT	SERVICE DATES	REMARKS
Short, I. or J.	PVT	Patrick's Company	01/06/38–01/31/38	
Sibley, Alexander H.	PVT	Rowland's Company	01/05/38–02/04/38	ASD 12/06/38–02/22/39; 03/01/39–05/31/39
Sill, Francis	PVT	Burger's Company	01/06/38–01/31/38	
Sims, F.	PVT	Patrick's Company	01/06/38–01/31/38	
Slooper, John	PVT	Rice's Company	01/06/38–01/31/38	
Smith, A.	PVT	Patrick's Company	01/06/38–01/31/38	
Smith, Addison	PVT	Burger's Company	01/06/38–01/31/38	
Smith, George	PVT	Patrick's Company	01/06/38–01/31/38	ASD 02/08/38–03/01/38
Smith, Henry	COL	F&S 2nd MI Regiment	02/11/38–02/16/38	
Smith, James S.	PVT	Rowland's Company	12/06/38–02/22/39	ASD 03/01/39–05/31/39
Smith, Patrick	PVT	Patrick's Company	02/08/38–03/01/38	
Smith, Samuel C.	3SG	Patrick's Company	01/06/38–01/31/38	ASD 02/08/38–03/01/38
Smolk, A.	PVT	Patrick's Company	01/06/38–01/31/38	
Smolk, Myron A.	PVT	Rowland's Company	01/05/38–02/04/38	ASD 03/01/39–05/31/39
Snow, Josiah	PVT	Beebe's Company	01/06/38–01/31/38	
Sparling, Benjamin	PVT	Burger's Company	01/06/38–01/31/38	
Spencer, Garry	PVT	Beebe's Company	01/06/38–01/31/38	ASD 02/08/38–02/28/38
Sprague, M.	MUS	Patrick's Company	01/06/38–01/31/38	ASD 02/08/38–03/01/38
Starks, A.	PVT	Beebe's Company	01/06/38–01/31/38	
Stevens, Marcus	PVT	Rowland's Company	12/06/38–02/22/39	ASD 03/01/39–05/31/39
Stimson, Benjamin G.	PVT	Rowland's Company	03/01/39–05/31/39	
Storms, C.	PVT	Beebe's Company	01/06/38–01/31/38	ASD 02/08/38–02/28/38
Strickland, G.	PVT	Patrick's Company	01/06/38–01/31/38	ASD 02/08/38–03/01/38
Strong, Herman N.	PVT	Rowland's Company	01/05/38–02/04/38	ASD 12/06/38–02/22/39; 03/01/39–05/31/39
Stuart, David	PVT	Rowland's Company	01/05/38–02/04/38	
Swan, Israel	PVT	Wood's Company	02/13/38–02/16/38	

NAME	RANK	MILITARY UNIT	SERVICE DATES	REMARKS
Sweeny, Daniel	PVT	Patrick's Company	01/06/38–01/31/38	
Sweeny, James	PVT	Patrick's Company	01/06/38–01/31/38	
Swift, Jason	SGT	Burger's Company	01/06/38–01/31/38	
Swift, William	PVT	Burger's Company	01/06/38–01/31/38	
Taylor, Robert	1CP	Wood's Company	02/13/38–02/16/38	
Thomas, Augustus	2CP	Wood's Company	02/13/38–02/16/38	
Thorn, John	4CP	Wood's Company	02/13/38–02/16/38	
Titus, P. S.	PVT	Patrick's Company	01/06/38–01/31/38	
Titus, Silas	PVT	Rowland's Company	01/05/38–02/04/38	
Town, D. H.	PVT	Burger's Company	01/06/38–01/31/38	
Trowbridge, Charles A.	PVT	Rowland's Company	01/05/38–02/04/38	ASD 12/06/38–2/22/39; 03/01/39–05/31/39
Tryon, Charles	PVT	Burger's Company	01/06/38–01/31/38	
Turner, Albion	PVT	Burger's Company	01/06/38–01/31/38	
Tuttle, A.	MUS	Patrick's Company	01/06/38–01/31/38	ASD 02/08/38–03/01/38
Updyke, Scott W.	PVT	Rowland's Company	12/06/38–02/22/39	ASD 03/01/39–05/31/39
Vance, Samuel	PVT	Wood's Company		Enrolled but not present
Vanderhoof, Silas	PVT	Burger's Company	01/06/38–01/31/38	
VanMaeter, Joseph G.	PVT	Patrick's Company	01/06/38–01/31/38	ASD 02/08/38–03/01/38
Wadsworth, Noyes W.	MUS	F&S 2nd MI Regiment	02/13/38–02/16/38	
Wagstaff, Robert	PVT	Rowland's Company	01/05/38–02/04/38	ASD 12/06/38–02/22/39; 03/01/39–05/31/39
Wales, Chauncey	PVT	Rowland's Company	12/06/38–02/22/39	ASD 03/01/39–05/31/39
Wales, Chauncy	PVT	Beebe's Company	01/06/38–01/31/38	ASD 02/08/38–02/28/38
Walker, John	PVT	Burger's Company	01/06/38–01/31/38	
Warren, Isaac	PVT	Patrick's Company	01/06/38–01/31/38	ASD 02/08/38–03/01/38
Warren, John T.	PVT	Rowland's Company	12/06/38–02/22/39	ASD 03/01/39–05/31/39
Watkins, Washington	PVT	Rowland's Company	01/05/38–02/04/38	ASD 12/06/38–02/22/39; 03/01/39–05/31/39

NAME	RANK	MILITARY UNIT	SERVICE DATES	REMARKS
Watson, E. W.	PVT	Burger's Company	01/06/38–01/31/38	
Watson, George C.	PVT	Beebe's Company	02/08/38–02/28/38	
Watson, George C.	PVT	Rowland's Company	12/06/38–02/22/39	ASD 03/01/39–05/31/39
Watson, James	PVT	Rowland's Company	01/05/38–02/04/38	
Webster, Matthew Howard	PVT	Rowland's Company	12/06/38–02/22/39	ASD 03/01/39–05/31/39
Weeks, W. H.	PVT	Beebe's Company	01/06/38–01/31/38	ASD 02/08/38–02/28/38
Wells, John	PVT	Rowland's Company	01/05/38–02/04/38	
Wells, William H.	PVT	Rowland's Company	12/06/38–02/22/39	ASD 03/01/39–05/31/39
Whaling, Nicholas	2SG	Beebe's Company	01/06/38–01/31/38	ASD 02/08/38–02/28/38 as 1SG
Wheaton, George	PVT	Beebe's Company	02/08/38–02/28/38	
Wheelock, David S.	PVT	Rowland's Company	12/06/38–02/22/39	ASD 03/01/39–05/31/39
Whipple, Eseck B.	PVT	Rowland's Company	01/05/38–02/04/38	ASD 03/01/39–05/31/39
Wight, D.	PVT	Beebe's Company	01/06/38–01/31/38	
Wight, James D.	PVT	Burger's Company	01/06/38–01/31/38	
Wilcox, David B.	PVT	Rowland's Company	12/06/38–02/22/39	ASD 03/01/39–05/31/39
Williams, Alpheus Starkey	PVT	Rowland's Company	01/05/38–02/04/38	ASD 03/01/39–05/31/39
Williams, Charles W.	PVT	Patrick's Company	02/08/38–03/01/38	
Williams, H. W.	CPL	Burger's Company	01/06/38–01/31/38	
Williams, H. W.	PVT	Patrick's Company	01/06/38–01/31/38	ASD 02/08/38–03/01/38
Williams, James M.	PVT	Beebe's Company	02/08/38–02/28/38	
Williams, Morris M.	PVT	Rowland's Company	12/06/38–02/22/39	ASD 03/01/39–05/31/39
Winder, John	PVT	Rowland's Company	01/05/38–02/04/38	ASD 12/06/38–02/22/39; 03/01/39–05/31/39
Wingert, William	PVT	Rowland's Company	01/05/38–02/04/38	ASD 12/06/38–02/22/39
Wood, Joseph	CAP	Wood's Company	02/13/38–02/16/38	
Wright, A.	PVT	Beebe's Company	02/08/38–02/28/38	
Wright, J. L.	PVT	Beebe's Company	02/08/38–02/28/38	

NAME	RANK	MILITARY UNIT	SERVICE DATES	REMARKS
Wycott, D.	PVT	Patrick's Company	01/06/38–01/31/38	
Wynecoop, James	DMR	Rice's Company	01/06/38–01/31/38	
Wynecoop, Lenery	DMR	Rice's Company	01/06/38–01/31/38	
Wynecoop, William	PVT	Rice's Company	01/06/38–01/31/38	
Young, Anson	PVT	Patrick's Company	01/06/38–01/31/38	ASD 02/08/38–03/01/38

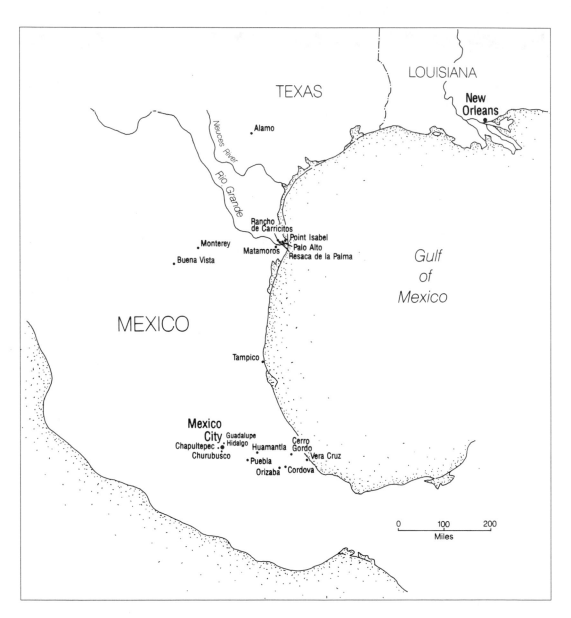

Theater of Operations, Mexican War. (*Cartography by Sherm Hollander*)

MEXICAN WAR, 1846–1848

Michigan in the Mexican War

On May 11, 1846, President James Polk sent a message to Congress that concluded, "The cup of forbearance [has] been exhausted. . . . Now, after reiterated menaces, Mexico has passed the boundary of the United States, has invaded our territory and shed American blood on American soil." Polk decreed that war existed between the United States and Mexico despite "all our efforts to avoid it." Two days later, Congress concurred by a vote of 40 to 2 in the Senate and 174 to 14 in the House of Representatives. Ten million dollars was appropriated for war materiel and the recruitment of fifty thousand volunteers.

The causes of the Mexican War included the inability of U.S. citizens to obtain compensation for claims against the Mexican government; Mexican anger over the U.S. annexation of Texas; disagreement over the southern boundary of Texas; the instability of Mexico's government, which made negotiation difficult; and the determination of U.S. expansionists, notably President Polk, to obtain the Mexican provinces of California and New Mexico with money if possible, by force if necessary. When Congress recommended the annexation of Texas in March 1845, Mexico broke off diplomatic relations. Yet, there existed a need for negotiation. The traditional southern boundary of Texas had been the Neuces River; however, the Texans now claimed the Rio Grande River. In the summer of 1845, U.S. major general Zachary Taylor, under orders from President Polk, established a force of 1,500 men on the Neuces River. By mid-October that body had been expanded to 3,500 men—half the standing U.S. Army. In March 1846, Polk ordered Taylor to advance to the Rio Grande River, where he constructed Fort Texas at Point Isabel.

In late 1845, President Polk sent John Slidell of Louisiana to Mexico to discuss the various disputes between the two countries. Slidell's mission ended in failure, and in early 1846 the frustrated emissary wrote Polk, "Be assured that nothing is to be done with these people until they have been chastised." Polk agreed, and on May 9, while the president informed the cabinet that Mexico's actions justified war, news arrived in Washington that Mexican troops had crossed the Rio Grande and ambushed an American patrol, leaving eleven U.S. soldiers dead.

The April 25 attack on Captain Seth B. Thornton's dragoons at Rancho de Corricitos was one of the few U.S. setbacks in the war. On May 3 a numerically superior Mexican force under the command of General Mariano Arista laid siege to Fort Texas. Several days later, Taylor's army defeated the Mexicans at Palo Alto. Taylor's regulars pursued Arista and, though outnumbered three to one, routed the Mexicans two days later at the Battle of Resaca de la Palma. On May 18, Taylor crossed the Rio Grande and occupied Matamoros.

Michiganians watched the events that led to war with Mexico with great interest. In January 1845 the Democratic-controlled state legislature passed resolutions urging the annexation of Texas. However, the transfer of garrison troops to Taylor's force in Texas before the outbreak of hostilities led some Michiganians to worry that such actions might subject the frontier to attacks by the "barbarous" Indians and the "covetous" British. Most Michiganians responded enthusiastically when war was declared. On June 3, 1846, Detroiters gathered at city hall in "unprecedented" numbers to show their support for the war effort. Amidst cheers and applause, the Detroiters resolved that the "insults and injuries" perpetrated by the Mexicans against this country left the United States no recourse but to "resort to arms." Declaring their "country right in this contest," the residents of the state capital noted: "That whether right or wrong when the constituted authorities of the country enact and proclaim the existence of a war, we deem it the duty of every good citizen to suspend the censorship of individual opinion until the restoration of peace, and unitedly support the government in the exercise of its constitutional functions." The assemblage also promised to "cheerfully" fill Michigan's quota of men "to defend the honor and soil of our common country."

To aid the war effort Michigan was ordered to enlist one regiment of infantry, which was to be held in readiness until called. Michigan's quota was rapidly filled as thirteen companies (eleven infantry and two cavalry) came forward. Most of the companies came from the southeastern Lower Peninsula: Detroit (4) and the counties of Wayne (1), Lenawee (3), Monroe (2), and St. Clair (1); Berrien and Hillsdale Counties also forwarded one company each.

Not all Michiganians, especially not all the Whigs, gave their unqualified support to the war against the Mexicans. The *Kalamazoo Michigan Telegraph* warned that the war would damage "the honor of the republic, which aspires to be the model of the world," while the *Marshall Statesman* denounced the declaration of war as an "injustice." The paper professed: "We may be traitors, but if so, it is because we desire to preserve inviolate the honor of the Republic, to extricate her from the difficulties into which unprincipled men have plunged her, and as speedily as possible to stop the shedding of our countrymen's blood." Much of Michigan's opposition to the war came from abolitionists. As Stephen F. Brown, a Schoolcraft farmer, succinctly explained, the war had been started by "the base minions of slavery . . . for the purpose of strengthening an institution which stifles the energies and blunts the nobler faculties of the human soul."

Despite Whig and abolitionist opposition, which was at best a vocal minority, the U.S. war effort moved ahead rapidly. In September 1846, General Taylor defeated the Mexicans at Monterrey. During the winter of 1846–47, U.S. forces enjoyed battlefield successes in northern Mexico and California. In February 1847, General Taylor countered a Mexican offensive and destroyed a larger enemy army near Buena Vista.

At the same time Taylor was engaging the Mexicans at Buena Vista, Major General Winfield Scott established his headquarters at Tampico in preparation for a campaign to capture Mexico City. On March 9, Scott's force of more than 8,600 men made an unprecedented amphibious landing south of the Mexican stronghold of Vera Cruz. Vera Cruz was besieged and fell on March 29. In early April, Scott's army began the over-250-mile journey inland toward the Mexican capital. On April 18 the Americans routed a Mexican force led by General Santa Anna at the mountain pass of Cerro Gordo. (Santa Anna, with U.S. assistance, had returned from exile in Cuba in August 1846 to regain control of the Mexican government and negotiate a settlement favorable to the United States. Once back in his country, the captor of the Alamo vowed to continue to fight against the United States.) In May, Scott halted his advance at Puebla. It was not the Mexicans that stopped Scott but the end of the twelve-month enlistment of many of his volunteer regiments. Since only 10 percent of his volunteers reenlisted, Scott had to wait for reinforcements.

By the spring of 1847, Michigan had made only a minor contribution to the war effort. The volunteers who had come forward a year earlier had not been called into federal service. A few Michigan men had joined the regular army, but the five-year term of service discouraged enlistment. (Volunteers only served for the war's duration.) Though Michigan had few men in arms, the war was still of interest. The proprietor of a Detroit hotel changed the name of his establishment to the Buena Vista Hotel to honor General Taylor's victory, and the legislature resolved that "wisdom, patriotism and humanity" required the United States "to prosecute with vigor" a war "that had been . . . forced upon us."

Nevertheless, opponents remained vocal. The Reverends George Duffield of Detroit and John Montieth of Monroe led a small group of Protestants opposed to the war. In March 1847 abolitionist James Birney of Saginaw described the war as "unjust" and "unconstitutional." The Michigan State Anti-Slavery Society characterized the war as "unjust, unchristian, uncalled for, and an act more in accordance with the days of savage ignorance than those of an (so-called) enlightened and Christian republic." In the late spring of 1847, the state's Liberty Party resolved: "We regard the supporters of Slavery and the Slave Power and the Mexican War, as traitors to the best interests of the nation."

Despite such vocal opposition, many Michiganians wanted the state to play a more active role in the war. In February 1847 the Michigan legislature appropriated ten thousand dollars to outfit a regiment of volunteers. However, the federal government had not yet requested the troops. Michigan's opportunity finally came that spring when Congress authorized the recruitment of ten regiments of regulars. The Fifteenth U.S. Infantry was to be composed of companies from Ohio (5), Michigan (3), Iowa (1) and Wisconsin (1). Michigan and Wisconsin were also ordered to raise a company of dragoons or cavalry.

Under the guidance of Captain Andrew T. McReynolds, a thirty-eight-year-old Detroit state legislator, Company K, Third U.S. Dragoons, was easily recruited. (The desire to see action in Mexico and the fear that a volunteer regiment might never be requested from Michigan overrode the concern of enlisting for five years.) Company K also included Lieutenants John T. Brown and J. C. D. Williams, sons of Michigan militia generals Joseph W. Brown and John R. Williams. (Senator Lewis Cass' son, Lewis Jr., served in the Third Dragoons as a major.) During the last week of April, Company K, composed entirely of men all over six feet tall, left Detroit via steamboat to Toledo. From Toledo, Company K traveled by canalboat to Cincinnati and by river steamer to New Orleans—the debarkation point for U.S. troops headed to Mexico. Company K arrived at Vera Cruz in mid-May. Escorting a convoy to General Scott's army at Puebla, Company K came under fire and became the first Michigan men to engage the Mexicans. The June 6 attack was repulsed, but Private Cornelius R. Combs of Tecumseh became the state's first war fatality. McReynold's company and Company F, First Dragoons, served as Scott's personal escort, and from these two companies the general selected Private James N. A. L. Simonds of Lenawee County and nine others as his bodyguard.

Also recruited in Michigan were Companies A, E, and G, Fifteenth U.S. Infantry. Since Michigan had the second largest number of men in the Fifteenth, it received the honor of having the unit's second-in-command. Lieutenant Colonel Joshua Howard, a fifty-four-year-old Detroiter, had entered the regular army during the War of 1812 and remained in service until 1835. A Whig in politics, Howard's many accomplishments included superintending the construction of the U.S. arsenal at Dearborn, Michigan. (The regiment's colonel was George W. Morgan of Ohio). Company A, commanded by Captain Eugene Vandeventer of Flint, and Company E, commanded by Captain Isaac D. Toll of Centreville, left Detroit in late April. Company G, commanded by Captain Frazey M. Winans of Monroe, was sent north to relieve members of the Second Infantry stationed at Fort Mackinac and Fort Brady.

After arriving at Vera Cruz, the Fifteenth Infantry moved to Puebla. Unprepared for the climate and topography, the men suffered greatly. Captain Toll, a twenty-nine-year-old New York native, later recalled that the failure to march during the early hours to avoid the midsummer heat was devastating for the Americans. On a day when ten men in the regiment died of heat prostration, Toll recalled that Corporal Napoleon B. Perkins carried "two large, extra rubber bags" with water that he "judiciously" distributed, which "saved the entire company from loss." Toll noted that many men, "overcome with the heat," discarded their knapsacks, blankets, and coats, "which were afterwards sorely needed . . . in the mountain bivouac." Less than two months after arriving in Mexico, Captain Toll observed that the varieties in climate, combined with diseases like diarrhea, dysentery, and yellow fever, had reduced his company to less than half its original number.

On August 7, 1847, General Scott renewed his advance to Mexico City. Two weeks later, at Churubusco, the Fifteenth Infantry, mustering only 282 men fit for service, helped rout the strongly entrenched Mexican defenders. Companies A and E suffered at least two killed and twenty-two wounded (four mortally). Colonel Morgan was also wounded, and Lieutenant Colonel Howard assumed command of the regiment. The Michigan dragoons in Company K also played a major role at Churubusco. Until then the horsemen had been engaged primarily in picket duty and reconnaissance. At Churubusco they pursued the fleeing Mexican infantry until stopped by a devastating cannon fire from the fortified positions around Mexico City. For gallant and meritorious duty, Captain McReynolds, who was wounded, was breveted major.

On August 21 the Mexicans requested an armistice to consider U.S. peace proposals. Two weeks later, the fighting resumed when Santa Anna rejected U.S. offers to end the war. For the assault on the Mexican capital Scott had approximately seven thousand men; Santa Anna defended the city with twice that number.

One key position that lay between the Americans and the capture of the city was the Castle of Chapultepec, the Mexican military academy that stood on a hill defending the city's western approaches. On September 13 the Americans opened a bombardment of Chapultepec. Under heavy enemy fire, U.S. infantrymen, including the Fifteenth, then charged up the two-hundred-foot hill. At the base of the castle the men had to wait for the scaling ladders to be positioned. Once they scaled the walls, the fighting was hand to hand. According to Lieutenant Colonel Howard, within thirty minutes of the beginning of the attack, the colors of the Fifteenth were waving from the top of a fortress that the Mexicans had thought to be impregnable. Upon seeing the U.S. flag, Santa Anna remarked, "I believe if we were to plant our batteries in Hell the damned Yankees would take them from us." On September 14, Scott's victorious army entered Mexico City. With fewer than eleven thousand troops and cut off from reinforcements and his supply base, Scott had defeated an enemy three times larger. The Duke of Wellington, the conqueror of Napoleon, later commented that the march to Mexico City was "unsurpassed in military annals."

While Scott's army occupied Mexico City, another U.S. force commanded by Brigadier General Joseph Lane left Vera Cruz to relieve the besieged U.S. garrison at Puebla. The American force included Company G, Fifteenth Infantry, which had been freed from its garrison duty in northern Michigan by the Brady Guards, a company of Detroiters commanded by Captain Morgan L. Gage.

Two days from Puebla, General Lane learned that Santa Anna, who had escaped Mexico City when it was captured, was at Humantla. Without waiting for Lane's main body to join him, Major S. H. Walker and four companies of cavalry moved into Humantla and dispersed two thousand Mexican lancers. Walker believed the fighting was over, and his men scattered into the city. The Mexican lancers returned and surprised Walker's men, killing several, including the Texas major. Lane's main body of troops reached the city and sent the Mexicans fleeing. However, the death of Walker, a popular cavalryman, shocked the Americans. The events immediately following Walker's death are unclear. According to Lieutenant William Wilkins, son of prominent Detroit judge Ross Wilkins and a second lieutenant in Company G, General Lane ordered his men to avenge Walker's death by pillaging the city. Other sources fail to substantiate this claim. What is clear is that Humantla became the victim of some of the worst atrocities caused by American soldiers in Mexico. According to Wilkins:

> Grog shops were broken open first, and then, maddened with liquor every species of outrage was committed [by the soldiers.] Old women and girls were stripped of the[ir] clothing—and many suffered still greater outrages. Men were shot by [the] dozens, while concealing their property[.] [C]hurches, stores and dwelling houses [were] ransacked. The town rung with shouts, screams[,] reports of fire arms and the crash of timber and glass as the troops battered down the doors and windows. Even the streets were strewn with different articles which had been thrown away to make room for more valuable plunder. . . . Dead horses and men lay about pretty thick, while drunken soldiers, yelling and screeching, were breaking open houses or chasing some poor Mexicans who had abandoned their houses and fled for life.

Wilkins noted that the plunder taken by the Americans "was very large" and included hundreds of dollars of gold, silks, and jewelry. Lane's command left Humantla that evening, but hundreds of U.S. soldiers stopped along the roadside and rejoined their command the following day. Lane reached Puebla on October 12 and proceeded to Mexico City, where Company G finally joined the Fifteenth Infantry.

In mid-October 1847 the War Department requested that a volunteer regiment be raised in Michigan. Governor William L. Greenley appointed Thomas B. W. Stockton of Flint as colonel of the First Regiment Michigan Volunteers and Alpheus S. Williams of Detroit as the regiment's second in command. Greenley also appointed the company commanders, who were responsible for filling their companies.

With enthusiasm ebbing for a war that appeared over, recruiting went slowly. Captain Nicholas Greusel Jr. of Company D ("Rough and Ready Guards") used patriotic newspaper advertisements to induce enlistments. Describing General Scott's army—then occupying Mexico City—as in a "critical" condition and surrounded by "a hostile and vindictive population," Captain Greusel urged anyone seeking to experience "the glorious successes and trying perils" of those fighting men in Mexico to join his company. Greusel, a prominent Detroit German immigrant, even offered monetary inducements to anyone who even brought in recruits (up to five dollars per recruit). He also reminded potential enlistees that they would receive 160 acres or one hundred dollars when they were discharged. The recruitment of the First Michigan suffered from two additional problems. Imperfect state militia laws allowed men to receive enlistment bonds, while not compelling them to be mustered into federal service. As a result, captains reported that their companies were full only to discover that their forces had dwindled by as much as two-thirds when the men reported to camp. Moreover, camp discipline was so lax that desertion was a major problem. Rewards were posted, but there are few accounts of deserters being captured or returned.

Despite slow recruiting, public support for the First Michigan was high. In accepting a sword at a public ceremony in Detroit, Captain Greusel described his men as a "determined and gallant band," and promised Detroiters that the First Michigan would demonstrate the same "skill and bravery" that had been repeatedly exhibited by the nation's volunteer soldiers in Mexico. On December 24–25, 1847, Companies A, B, C, D, E, and F of the First Michigan, led by Colonel Stockton, left Detroit. Dressed in dark blue jackets, sky blue pants, and caps with buttons embossed with the Michigan coat of arms, the Michigan men traveled by rail to Cincinnati and by boat to New Orleans. They arrived in Vera Cruz in late January. On February 9, 1848, Companies H, I, and K, commanded by Lieutenant Colonel Williams, left Detroit for Mexico. They arrived in Vera Cruz on March 11, the day after the U.S. Senate ratified the Treaty of Guadalupe Hidalgo ending the Mexican War.

Once in Mexico the Michigan men escorted supply and specie trains between Vera Cruz and inland posts. (Army policy dictated that all local supplies be purchased with gold). The convoys usually were shadowed by Mexican guerrillas. After one such trip, Second Lieutenant Elisha Wright of Clinton noted that the reconnaissance patrol had been fired upon. According to Wright, "Our men returned the fire and wounded one of the enemies' horses. Both parties ran, our men for the camp [train] and the Mexicans for the chaparral." The guerrillas offered little further resistance during the five-day trip to Cordova. According to Wright, that was probably because the Mexicans saw the imprint "Michigan Volunteers" on the men's knapsacks. Located in a fertile valley at the base of Mount Orizaba, Cordova, a city of several thousand people, became the home of the First Michigan (except for Company G, which had not yet arrived in Mexico). From Cordova the First Michigan escorted supply trains between Vera Cruz and Orizaba.

The experiences of the First Michigan varied. Second Lieutenant Paul W. H. Rawles claimed that two-thirds of the local citizens supported the guerrillas and would take "the first opportunity of ridding themselves" of the American occupation troops. However, Captain Jonathan Whittenmeyer, the forty-eight-year-old commander of Company F, offered a different opinion. While describing the Mexicans as "the most insignificant looking people on earth," the St. Joseph resident noted that "few" Americans were "willing to leave this country abandoned to robbers and other nations, after effectually conquering and getting the good will of the large portions of the Mexicans." Lieutenant Wright also noted that:

> The Americans are great favorites of the Mexicans here, and are in return treated well by our troops. When we arrived here, we were very much fatigued, warm, and dry, and while we were standing to be reviewed on the plaza, the senoritas (girls) and boys passed along the ranks with pitchers of cool and fresh water for the tired and almost fainting soldiers; and for that kind act, received the everlasting gratitude of the troops.

At Cordova the First Michigan drilled twice during the morning and once in the evening. When not drilling, escorting a wagon train or suffering the boredom of garrison duty, the Michigan men seemed to enjoy being an army of occupation. Lieutenant Wright found bullfights "a terrible spectacle," but Wright offered his fiancée a different opinion of a fandango that he and Second Lieutenant Lorin L. Comstock of Adrian attended.

> Comstock and I were out one evening and happened to drop in to a Mexican tavern; a young Mexican invited us to go with him to a fandango and we concluded to go. Several of his friends also went along [and] . . . after walking about a mile we began to hear music and were soon in a crowd of both sexes, going it on the loud. We were introduced around as Americanos Captains and were received very cordially and soon found ourselves on very familiar terms and were invited to dance. I excused myself but Comstock went ahead. The music was excellent, consisting of a harp and guitar accompanied with the voice of all present that could sing. The gentlemen and ladies were dressed with great propriety, the gentlemen mostly in white linen but some with velvet pants. The ladies were dressed in white.

Comstock and Wright asked senoritas to join them for coffee, and he continued: "Don't we look pretty, Comstock and I, sitting at the table and drinking whiskey out of a bottle with two very dark complexioned young ladies. The ladies by this time had become quite sociable and complimented the Americanos quite beyond our ability to reciprocate."

Though the Michigan men were ready to leave, "the girls insisted" they stay and dance, which they did. Wright noted that when Comstock and he left the dance they were "shaking . . . with laughter at the novelty and fun of the scene we had witnessed and participated in." There is no record as to whether Wright's fiancée saw any humor in his fandango experiences.

Despite the gaiety of bullfights and fandangos, the First Michigan also experienced hardships at Cordova. In early April, Captain Whittenmeyer wrote home that Mexico was an "extremely healthy" country. However, diseases, especially diarrhea and yellow fever, soon took their toll on the Michigan men. During its last month at Cordova the First Michigan had between 100 and 170 men in the regimental hospital at any one time. When the regiment left Cordova for home, about 30 percent of the men were unable to walk and had to ride in its wagons.

In late May 1848 the Mexican government ratified the Treaty of Guadalupe Hidalgo, which gave the United States the land that comprises the present-day states of California, Utah, and Nevada, and parts of Arizona, New Mexico, and Colorado. The treaty also established the Rio Grande River as the U.S.-Mexican border and obligated the United States to pay $15 million in claims held by American citizens against Mexico.

On June 5 the First Michigan formally received its colors in a ceremony at Cordova. A week later, it left Cordova. In order to protect the health of the men, U.S. troops were held at Japala and moved to the coast only when vessels were available to take them to New Orleans. At Vera Cruz, Company G, which had arrived in Mexico in early May, joined the First Michigan Regiment.

In late June 1848 the First Michigan arrived in New Orleans. Companies A, E, G, and I were sent by steamer to Cincinnati and by rail and boat to Detroit. The remaining companies were sent by boat to Chicago and then to Detroit. By July 10 the men passing through Cincinnati, some of whom had to escape from a canal boat that sank, had arrived in Michigan. The six other companies reached Detroit on July 16. There they were greeted by "an immense throng," which according to the *Detroit Free Press,* "gave the brave Wolverine volunteers such cheers as seemed to revive their drooped spirits."

Those "drooped spirits" existed in part because many of the Michigan men had sold their extra clothing in Cordova before heading home. Confident of receiving several months' back pay and being mustered out at New Orleans, these men planned to buy civilian clothes and take private passage back to Michigan. However, to ensure that the veterans reached home, the government changed its policy and returned the soldiers to their original muster location before discharging them. Wearing their last uniform, which was often in tatters, the Michigan volunteers reached Detroit in a pitiful state. According to several regimental officers, the situation was worsened by "a few disaffected spirits" whose disdain for military discipline had made the return trip even more "discomforting."

Although the piecemeal return of the Michigan veterans apparently prevented a local celebration to welcome them home, a meeting was held at the U.S. courthouse in Detroit on July 17 to alleviate the men's sufferings. The Michigan Central Railroad offered free transportation home to all volunteers. Pledges of money and food were also collected, as well as offers of assistance in legal and business matters. The latter were intended to help veterans avoid being swindled out of the land warrants they received upon being discharged from the service.

On July 31, Company K, Third U.S. Dragoons, which had left Vera Cruz on July 2, was discharged at Jefferson Barracks in Missouri. The Fifteenth U.S. Infantry also left Mexico in early July, and by mid-August, Companies A, E, and G had been mustered out of service. The Michigan men in the Fifteenth U.S. Infantry suffered 13 battle-related deaths and 65 disease-related deaths. These three companies experienced only 17 desertions. Since the muster rolls for Company K, Third Dragoons, are missing, casualties are harder to determine. Deaths in company K were 4 killed-in-action and 14 dead from disease. However, since only 17 of the original 104 men who left Detroit in April 1847 returned fifteen months later, it is certain that Company K's losses were greater than this.

The First Michigan, which never participated in heavy fighting, suffered no fatalities killed in action, but at least 206 volunteers died of disease. (This toll includes Lieutenant Wright, who returned to Clinton in July in a "weak, debilitated, and emaciated condition." He died on July 27, 1848.) The First also suffered 157 desertions. Of the original 973 men on the muster rolls, 599 were mustered out in July 1848. Stationed at Forts Mackinac and Brady, the Brady Guards suffered no deaths and only 13 desertions.

The Mexican War was unlike any previous war experienced by Michiganians. Though the war was fought in a distant land, inventions like the telegraph and the penny press exposed state residents to the conflict on a daily basis for the first time. News of the Battle of Churubusco appeared in the Detroit newspapers only two days after it occurred. The number of Michigan men on active duty in the Mexican War exceeded its commitment in previous wars. With approximately 350,000 citizens, Michigan sent over 1,500 to war—more than many other states, including New York, which had nine times more people than Michigan. The war also left more Michiganians dead than in all previous wars combined. (Most of the soldiers who died in Michigan during the War of 1812 were Kentuckians.) More important, the Mexican War generated more opposition in Michigan than any other previous war. This opposition continued to grow after the war ended and—coupled with the concern over the extension of slavery into newly acquired territory—precipitated the sectional conflict that in 1854 led to the formation of the Republican party in Jackson, Michigan. In the 1860s, however, Michigan's involvement in the Mexican War would be dwarfed by its response to an even greater crisis—the Civil War.

BIBLIOGRAPHIC NOTE

Sources used in preparing this section, or recommended for further reading, include:

"American Gallantry and Daring in the Mexican War." *Lansing Republican,* Oct. 8, 1879, p. 3.
"Annual Report of the Adjutant and Quarter Master General of the State of Michigan." Joint Documents of the Legislature of the State of Michigan. Detroit, 1848, and Lansing, 1849.
Bauer, K. Jack. *The Mexican War.* New York: Macmillan and Company, 1974.
Bonner, Richard I. "Military History." *Memoirs of Lenawee County, Michigan.* Madison: Western Historical Association, 1909. 639–43.
Bulkley, John M. "In the Mexican War." *History of Monroe County.* Chicago: Lewis Publishing Company, 1913. 1:170–74.
Burton, Clarence. "The War With Mexico." *The City of Detroit Michigan.* Detroit: S. J. Clarke Publishing Company, 1922. 2:1066–70.

Charnley, Jeffrey G. "Swords into Plowshares: A Hope Unfulfilled: Michigan Opposition to the Mexican War, 1846–1848." *The Old Northwest,* 8, no. 3 (Fall 1982): 199–222.

Cutler, Harry G. "Mexican War and Hon. Isaac D. Toll." *History of St. Joseph County, Michigan.* Chicago: Lewis Publishing Company, 1911. 238–40.

Durant, Samuel. "Mexican War." *History of Kalamazoo County, Michigan.* Philadelphia: Everts & Abbott, 1880. 174–76.

Fuller, George N. "The Mexican War." *Historic Michigan.* Dayton: National Historical Association, 1924. 1:486–92.

———. "The Mexican War." *Michigan: A Centennial History of the State.* Chicago: Lewis Publishing Company, 1939. 321–25.

Leake, Paul. "Mexican War." *History of Detroit.* Chicago: Lewis Publishing Company, 1912. 146–48.

"Michigan Aided in Mexican War," *Detroit Free Press,* July 2, 1916, p. 15.

Michigan Legislature. *Joint Documents of the Senate and House of Representatives at the Annual Session of 1848.* Detroit: Bagg & Harmon, 1848. Document 7, pp. 25–43.

"Only Mexican War Veteran Living in Detroit," *Detroit Tribune* 26 April 1914, p. 7.

Palmer, Friend. "Colonel Joshua Howard a Man of Note." *Early Days in Detroit.* Detroit: Richmond & Backus, 1906. 594–600.

Robertson, John. "The Mexican War." *Michigan in the War.* Lansing: W. S. George & Co., 1882. 1033–36.

Scott, Craig Roberts. "Descriptive Book of Company G. 15th U.S. Infantry. 1847–1848." *Detroit Society for Genealogical Research Magazine* 56, no. 1 (Fall 1992): 3–7; 56, no. 2 (Winter 1993): 61–63.

Seeley, Thaddeus D. "The Mexican War." *History of Oakland County, Michigan.* Chicago: Lewis Publishing Company, 1912. 273–74.

Shapiro, Madeleine S. "Michigan Public Opinion, the Mexican War, and the Wilmot Proviso." M.A. thesis, Wayne State University, 1964.

Smith, Kenneth A. "Michigan's Military Participation in the Mexican War." M.A. thesis, Wayne State University, 1951.

Toll, Isaac. "Michigan Soldiers in Mexico," *Michigan Pioneer and Historical Collections* 7 (1884).

Toll, Isaac D. "A Mexican War Veteran's Reminiscences." *Lansing [Weekly] Journal,* June 20–27, 1884.

———. "Michigan's Record in the War with Mexico," *Michigan Pioneer and Historical Collections* 2 (1877–78): 171–77.

Welch, Richard W. *Michigan in the Mexican War.* Durand: The Author, 1967.

Wing, Talcott E. "The Mexican War," *History of Monroe County, Michigan.* New York: Munsell & Company, 1890. 343–46.

Wittenmyer, John. "Letter From Capt. Wittenmyer," *Niles Republican,* May 20, 1848, pp. 2–3.

Wright, Elisha. Papers. Bentley Historical Library, University of Michigan, Ann Arbor.

A potentially valuable source of information, the records of the Mexican War Veterans Association (Michigan chapter), was destroyed by fire in Ludington in July 1882. The printed Proceedings of this group can be found in various major libraries around the State.

MEXICAN WAR RELATED HISTORIC SITES AND MONUMENTS IN MICHIGAN

Alpheus S. Williams Statue, Belle Isle, Detroit, Wayne County

Centreville Prairie River Cemetery, Company E, 15th U.S. Infantry Monument, Centerville, St. Joseph County

Colonel Brodhead's Office State Historic Marker, Wayne County

Fort Brady City Historic Marker, Sault Ste. Marie, Chippewa County

Fort Brady Federal Historic Monument, Sault Ste. Marie, Chippewa County

Fort Brady State Historic Marker, Chippewa County

Fort Wayne State Historic Marker, Wayne County

Fort Wilkins State Historic Marker, Keweenaw County

General John R. Williams Bronze Tablet, Grand River and Woodward Aves., Detroit

Mexican-American War Memorial Bronze Tablet, Caledonia, Kent County
Mexican-American War Memorial Bronze Tablet, Clinton, Lenawee County
Mexican-American War Memorial Bronze Tablet, U of M, Washtenaw County

LIST OF RELEVANT MICHIGAN ILLUSTRATIONS

Mexican War—Representative Soldiers

Company of Military Historians. *Military Uniforms in America. Vol. 2, Years of Growth, 1796–1851.* San Rafael, Calif.: Presidio Press, 1977. Pp. [125], [127]. Color images of various uniforms.

Detroit Evening News, Sept. 25, 1895, p. 5. Rough sketch of Mexican War veterans meeting in Detroit.

Downey, Fairfax. *Indian Wars of the U.S. Army, 1776–1865.* Garden City, N.Y.: Doubleday & Company, 1963. Pp. 150, 154. Sample uniforms of selected branches of the service.

Kannik, Preben. *Military Uniforms in Color.* New York: Macmillan Company, 1968. P. [89], items 289–92. Period figures posing in military garb.

Lawford, James, ed. *The Cavalry.* New York: Bobbs-Merrill Company, 1976. Pp. 158–59. Color painting of U.S. Dragoons in action.

Nelson, Henry Loomis. *Uniforms of the United States Army.* New York: Sagamore Press, 1959. Plate 19. Color depiction of the four basic uniforms worn during the War.

State Archives of Michigan. Group photograph of "Reunion of Veterans of the Mexican War, Lansing, Oct. 1st, 1879."

Steffen, Randy. *The Horse Soldier, 1776–1943,* vol. 1. Norman: University of Oklahoma Press, 1977. Pp. 101, 106, 110, 112, 114, 121, 123, 128, 157, 162–64, 175, 176, color plate 2. Realistic portrayals of attire for all branches of the military.

Todd, Frederick P. *Soldiers of the American Army, 1775–1954.* Chicago: Henry Regnery Company, 1954. Plate 13. Good color rendition of 3rd Artillery soldiers.

Windrow, Martin, and Gerry Embleton. *Military Dress of North America, 1665–1970.* New York: Charles Scribner's Sons, 1973. Pp. 77, 79. A series of action figures showing a broad gamut of military dress.

Mexican War—Specific Soldiers

Beach, Samuel E. In Photograph Collection, Oakland County Pioneer and Historical Society, Pontiac. Also L. H. Everts and Company, *History of Oakland County, Michigan.* Philadelphia, 1877. P. 113.

Brodhead, Thornton F. In Robert B. Ross and George B. Catlin, *Landmarks of Wayne County and Detroit.* Detroit: Evening News Association, 1898. Opposite p. 216. Also Isabella E. Swan, *The Deep Roots.* Grosse Ile, Mich., 1976. P. 249.

Cass, Lewis, Jr. In Amon Carter Museum, *Eyewitness to War.* Washington, D.C.: Smithsonian Institution Press, 1989. Pp. 220–22.

Comstock, Loren L. In Photograph Collection, State Archives of Michigan, Lansing.

Curtenius, Frederick W. In Photograph Collection, State Archives of Michigan, Lansing.

Flanders, Francis. In *History of St. Joseph County, Michigan.* Philadelphia: L. H. Everts and Company, 1877. Opposite p. 209.

Gage, Morgan L. In Photograph Collection, State Archives of Michigan, Lansing.

McReynolds, Andrew T. In Photograph Collection, State Archives of Michigan, Lansing. Also Charles Richard Tuttle, *General History of the State of Michigan.* Detroit: Tyler and Company, 1873. P. 577.

Marble, Ephraim. In Chapman Brothers, *Portrait and Biographical Album of Calhoun County, Michigan.* Chicago, 1891. P. 396.

Orcutt, Benjamin F. In Photograph Collection, State Archives of Michigan, Lansing. Also Everts and Abbott, *History of Kalamazoo County, Michigan.* Philadelphia, 1880. P. 281. Also Chapman Brothers, *Portrait and Biographical Record of Kalamazoo, Allegan, and Van Buren Counties, Michigan.* Chicago, 1892. Opposite p. 1012.

Pittman, James E. In Photograph Collection, State Archives of Michigan, Lansing. Also Silas Farmer, *The History of Detroit and Michigan.* Detroit: Silas Farmer and Company, 1889. After p. 1166.

Richardson, Israel B. In Photograph Collection, State Archives of Michigan, Lansing. Also Frank B. Woodford, *Father Abraham's Children*. Detroit: Wayne State University Press, 1961. Opposite p. 84. Also Michigan Adjutant General, *Record of Service of Michigan Volunteers in the Civil War*, vol. 2. Kalamazoo: Ihling Brothers, 1906[?]. P. 143.

Rowland, Isaac S. In Stanley D. Solvick, *Let the Drum Beat*. Detroit: Wayne State University Press, 1988. P. [50].

Schwarz, John E. In Photograph Collection, State Archives of Michigan, Lansing.

Smith, Henry. In Talcott E. Wing, *History of Monroe County, Michigan*. New York: Munsell and Company, 1890. Opposite p. 297.

Stockton, Thomas B. In Photograph Collection, State Archives of Michigan, Lansing.

Toll, Isaac D. In L. H. Everts and Company, *History of St. Joseph County, Michigan*. Philadelphia, 1877. P. 207.

Wilkins, William D. In Photograph Collections, Bentley Historical Library, University of Michigan, Ann Arbor.

Willcox, Orlando B. In Photograph Collection, State Archives of Michigan, Lansing. Also Frank B. Woodford, *Father Abraham's Children*. Detroit: Wayne State University Press, 1961. Opposite p. 21. Also Silas Farmer, *The History of Detroit and Michigan*. Detroit: Silas Farmer and Company, 1889. After p. 1106.

Williams, Alpheus S. In Western Biographical Publishing Company, *American Biographical History of Eminent and Self Made Men*. Michigan Volume. Cincinnati, 1878. Opposite p. 163. Also Stanley D. Solvick, *Let the Drum Beat*. Detroit: Wayne State University Press, 1988. P. [50].

Williams, Thomas. In Willis Atwell, *Do You Know*. [Grand Rapids]: Booth Newspapers, 1937. P. 216.

The only Michigan uniform believed to have survived from the Mexican-American War is in the possession of the Lake Erie Marshlands Museum near Gibraltar in southeastern Wayne County. The flag of the First Michigan Infantry is in the holdings of the Detroit Historical Museum.

Mexican War—Theater of Operations

There are numerous images of this conflict, and since it is the only military action included in this book that did not take place on Michigan soil, no pictures have been cited in this category.

ORGANIZATIONAL CHART OF PARTICIPATING MICHIGAN UNITS

The number of Michigan men, extracted from the rosters, is listed after each company.

1st Regiment, Michigan Volunteer Infantry, Colonel Thomas Stockton, commanding

1st Battalion, Major John Ruehle, commanding

Company A, Frederick W. Curtenius (Kalamazoo County)	99
Company B, Grover N. Buel (Jackson and St. Clair Counties)	107
Company C, Alfred H. Hanscom (Oakland and Shiawassee Cos.)	101
Company D, Nicholas Greusel (Wayne County)	100
Company E, Isaac S. Rowland (Southeastern Michigan)	100
Company F, John Whittenmeyer (Berrien County)	94

2nd Battalion, Lt. Colonel Alpheus S. Williams, commanding

Company G, Daniel Hicks (Southern Michigan)	110
Company H, Walter W. Dean (Southeastern Michigan)	107
Company I, John Van Arman (Southern Michigan)	108
Company K, James M. Williams (Southeastern Michigan)	107

Independent Companies of Michigan Militia

Adrian Guards, Daniel Hicks (Lenawee County, Not Activated)	66
Brady Guards, Morgan L. Gage (Wayne County, Activated)	87
Montgomery Guards, William O'Callaghan (Detroit, Not Activated)	96
North Lenawee Volunteers, Joseph W. Brown (Tecumseh, Not Activated)	13
Scott Guards, Nicholas Greusel Jr. (Detroit, Not Activated)	44

Federal Units with Significant Michigan Militia

Company K, 3rd U.S. Dragoons, Andrew McReynolds (Southeastern Michigan)	111
Company B, 3rd U.S. Infantry, Nathaniel Macrae	48
Company B, 5th U.S. Infantry, Ephraim K. Smith	28
Company A, 6th U.S. Infantry, George Hutter	42
Company K, 6th U.S. Infantry, Charles S. Lovell	18
Company A, 15th U.S. Infantry, Eugene Vandeventer (Southwestern Michigan)	92
Company E, 15th U.S. Infantry, Isaac D. Toll (Southwestern Michigan	96
Company G, 15th U.S. Infantry, Frazey M. Winans (Southeastern Michigan)	103
Company H, U.S. Mounted Rifles, Charles F. Ruff	12
United States Navy	12

Soldiers in Miscellaneous State and Federal Units   401

Total Number of Michigan Men in the Mexican War   2,096

ROSTER OF MICHIGAN MEN
IN THE MEXICAN WAR

Name	Age	Hgt	Eye	Hair	Cpx	Trade	Born	Home	Rank	Unit
Abernathy, Silas S.	23	6.02	GRY	DRK	LGT	Carpenter	Monroe Co NY		PVT	COM A 15th US INF
Ackerly, William	23	5.10	BLU	BWN	LGT	Farmer	Orleans Co NY		PVT	COM I 1st MI INF
Ackerman, Thomas C.	33	5.05	BLK	BLK	DRK	Carpenter	Cortland Co NY	Pontiac MI	PVT	COM C 1st MI INF
Ackerman, Thomas F.	18	5.09	HZL	BWN	FIR	Farmer	Bloomfield MI	Detroit MI	PVT	COM I 1st MI INF
Adair, William	28	5.10	GRY	BWN	FIR	Farmer	Queen Co IRE		PVT	COM H US MTD RIF
Adams, David	21	5.07	BLU	LGT	FIR	Farmer	Aurora NY		PVT	COM E 15th US INF
Adams, Joseph	27	5.06	BLK	BLK	SWR	Laborer	Brackingham ENG	Monroe MI	PVT	COM G 15th US INF
Agin, Daniel	35	5.06	HZL	DRK	DRK	Laborer	Turlee IRE		PVT	COM B 5th US INF
Aicken, Samuel	25	5.08	BLU	BWN	LGT	Blacksmith	Ballymoney IRE		PVT	COM E 1st MI INF
Aims, John	18	5.05	BWN	LGT	FIR	Clerk	Germany	Detroit MI	MUS	COM E 1st MI INF
Ainsley, Thomas	24	5.08	BLU	BWN	LGT	Laborer	Onondaga Co NY		PVT	COM A 15th US INF
Alband, Gottfried	27	5.07	GRY	BWN	LGT	Laborer	Obermiller GER	Detroit MI	PVT	Brady Guards
Albers, Edward	31	5.04	GRY	BWN	DRK	Rainmaker	Germany	Detroit MI	PVT	COM E 1st MI INF
Albro, Andrew	21	5.07	HZL	FIR	RUD	Blacksmith	Onondaga Co NY		PVT	COM K 3rd US DRG
Aldrich, Amos								Adrian MI	PVT	Adrian Guards
Aldrich, Ervin								Adrian MI	PVT	Adrian Guards
Aldrich, Jacob	19	5.06	BLK	BWN	DRK	Farmer	Madison Co NY	Adrian MI	PVT	COM H 1st MI INF
Aldrich, Samuel	22	5.05	BLK	BWN	DRK	Farmer	Madison Co NY	Adrian MI	PVT	COM H 1st MI INF
Aldrich, Wiley								Adrian MI	PVT	Adrian Guards
Alexander, Sidney P.	22	5.07	BLU	BWN	LGT	Clothier	Essex Co NY		PVT	COM A 15th US INF
Alexander, William H.	21	5.10	BLU	BWN	LGT	Carpenter	Oswego Co NY	Marshall MI	4CP	COM I 1st MI INF

ENROLLED	MUSTERED	DISCHARGED	REMARKS
04/14/47 Utica, MI	04/27/47 Detroit, MI	05/14/47 Camp Washington	Discharged near Cincinnati OH
11/15/47 Marshall, MI	12/01/47 Detroit, MI		Died at Detroit MI 01/01/48
11/30/47 Pontiac MI	12/01/47 Detroit MI	07/26/48 Detroit MI	Received Pension
01/24/48 Detroit MI	02/01/48 Detroit MI	07/18/48 Detroit MI	Received pension
07/16/47 Kalamazoo MI	07/16/47 Kalamazoo MI	07/31/48 Jefferson BKS MO	
04/27/47 Grand Rapids MI	04/29/47 Detroit MI		Deserted from hospital at New Orleans LA 01/13/48
04/22/47 Monroe MI	04/30/47 Detroit MI		Died of diarrhea at Jalapa MEX 09/02/47
07/15/47 Detroit MI	Detroit MI	08/01/48 East Pascagoula MS	
11/20/47 Monroe MI	12/04/47 Detroit MI	07/09/48 Jefferson BKS MO	Left sick at Detroit 12/25/47, then at New Orleans
11/20/47 Detroit MI	12/04/47 Detroit MI	07/18/48 Detroit MI	
04/21/47 Detroit MI	04/27/47 Detroit MI		Died of disease at Vera Cruz MEX 07/02/47
06/18/47 Detroit MI	06/18/47 Detroit MI	06/30/48 Detroit MI	Received pension. Also known as Gottfried Erbin.
11/20/47 Perrysburg OH	12/04/47 Detroit MI	07/18/48 Detroit MI	Received Pension
03/29/47 Detroit MI	04/22/47 Detroit MI	07/20/48	Left sick in hospital at Puebla MEX 08/07/47
06/01/46 Adrian MI			VTS WNA
06/01/46 Adrian MI			VTS WNA
11/20/47 Adrian MI	12/01/47 Detroit MI		Died at Cordova MEX 04/16/48 of spine disease
11/20/47 Adrian MI	12/01/47 Detroit MI		Died of diarrhea at Cordova MEX 05/07/48
06/01/46 Adrian MI			VTS WNA
04/16/47 Pontiac MI	04/27/47 Detroit MI		Deserted at New Orleans LA 10/30/47
11/15/47 Marshall MI	12/01/47 Detroit MI	07/18/48 Detroit MI	

Name	Age	Hgt	Eye	Hair	Cpx	Trade	Born	Home	Rank	Unit
Alger, Henry L.	27	5.10	DRK	DRK	DRK	Farmer	Oxford, Canada	Thornville MI	PVT	COM G 1st MI INF
Alger, Sylvester P.	18	6.00	BLU	DRK	LGT	Joiner	Oneida Co NY		MUS	COM G 1st MI INF
Allan, Gabriel	32	5.08	BLK	BLK	DRK	Brickmaker	Detroit MI		PVT	COM H 16th US INF
Allen, Benjamin S.	22					Farmer	Seneca Co NY	Adrian MI	PVT	Adrain Guards
Allen, Charles	23	5.08	BWN	BWN	DRK	Barber	Lynn, MA		PVT	COM K 3rd US DRG
Allen, Daniel	30	5.07	BLK	BWN	DRK	Carpenter	Cunoya? County		PVT	COM K 3rd US DRG
Allen, Ephriam	21	5.08	BLU	BLK	FLD	Farmer	Washington NY		PVT	COM G 15th US INF
Allen, George	19	5.05	GRY	BLK	RUD	Blacksmith	Pontiac MI	Pontiac MI	PVT	COM A 15th US INF
Allen, John W.	24	5.10	BLU	BRN	FLD	Farmer	Niagara Co NY		PVT	COM G 15th US INF
Allen, Levi J.	20	5.09	BWN	LGT	LGT	Farmer	Onondaga Co NY	Pontiac MI	PVT	COM C 1st MI INF
Allen, Reuben	21	5.03	BLU	LGT	LGT	Laborer	Dutchess Co NY		PVT	COM A 15th US INF
Allois, Gustof								Detroit MI	PVT	Scott Guards
Almy, Frederick	20	5.05	BLU	LGT	LGT	Teamster	Monroe Co NY		PVT	COM A 1st MI INF
Almy, James	24	5.06	BLU	BWN	LGT	Farmer	Monroe Co NY		PVT	COM A 1st MI INF
Alport, Phineas L.	21	5.10	GRY	BWN	FIR	Farmer	Orleans Co NY	Marshall MI	PVT	COM I 1st MI INF
Alvord, William A.	21	6.00	HZL	BWN	DRK	Farmer	Leroy NY		PVT	COM H US MTD RIF
Ames, Benajah	32	5.07	BLU	BWN	LGT	Carpenter	Byron NY	Battle Creek MI	PVT	COM G 1st MI INF
Ames, Jeremiah B.	19	5.09	BLU	LGT	LGT	Laborer	Livingston NY		PVT	US MTD RIF
Amidon, George S.	22	5.10	HZL	DRK	DRK	Farmer	Erie PA		PVT	COM E 15th US INF
Amidon, George P.	21	5.08	BLU	FIR	FIR	Farmer	Stockton NY		PVT	COM G 15th US INF
Amsden, Jared R.	18	5.11	BLU	LGT	LGT	Farmer	Orleans Co NY		PVT	COM G 1st MI INF
Anderson, Robert	34	5.10	BLU	BWN	FIR	Laborer	Donn IRE	Pontiac MI	PVT	COM A 15th US INF
Andrews, William H.	28								PVT	COM D 1st MI INF
Andrus, James	19	5.11	BWN	DRK	DRK	Mason	Broome Co NY		PVT	COM G 1st MI INF
Armbruster, Ignas						Laborer		Detroit MI	PVT	Scott Guards
Armstrong, Daniel G.	21	5.07	GRY	BWN	LGT	Laborer	Penfield NY		PVT	COM A 15th US INF

ENROLLED	MUSTERED	DISCHARGED	REMARKS
02/20/48 Canandaigua MI	03/01/48 Detroit MI		Died 07/21/48
01/25/48 Monroe MI	02/01/48 Detroit MI	07/18/48 Detroit MI	Sent to hospital at New Orleans from Vera Cruz 06/05/48
04/12/47		06/14/48 Monterey MEX	DFD. AKA Gabriel Allard
06/01/46 Adrian MI			VTS WNA
03/31/47 Detroit MI	04/22/47 Detroit MI		ASG COM C 3rd US DRG 01/04/48. DES 06/28/48.
04/08/47 Tecumseh MI	04/22/47 Detroit MI		Deserted at New Orleans LA 05/15/47
04/30/47 Detroit MI	04/30/47 Detroit MI	08/04/48 Covington KY	Received pension
04/19/47 Pontiac MI	04/27/47 Detroit MI	08/04/48 Covington KY	Transferred to COM K 15th US INF 12/26/47
04/15/47 Detroit MI	04/30/47 Detroit MI		Deserted at Detroit MI 04/30/47
11/30/47 Pontiac MI	12/01/47 Detroit MI	07/26/48 Detroit MI	Received pension
04/06/47 Utica MI	04/27/47 Detroit MI	08/21/48	TRA COM B 15th US INF 12/26/47
06/03/46 Detroit MI			VTS WNA
11/05/47 Grand Rapids MI	11/19/47 Detroit MI		Deserted at New Orleans LA 06/14/48. PEN
11/05/47 Kalamazoo MI	11/19/47 Detroit MI		Deserted at Detroit MI 12/24/47
12/20/47 Marshall MI	01/01/48 Detroit MI	07/18/48 Detroit MI	Received pension. AKA Leonard P. Alport.
07/17/47 Battle Creek MI	07/17/47 Battle Creek MI	07/31/48 Jefferson BKS MO	Received pension
02/20/48 Battle Creek MI	03/01/48 Detroit MI	07/18/48 Detroit MI	Received pension
07/23/47 Otsego MI	07/23/47 Otsego MI		Died at Jefferson Barracks MO 09/26/47
04/24/47 Fawn River MI	04/27/47 Detroit MI	08/06/48 Cincinnati OH	
04/17/47 Adrian MI	04/30/47 Detroit MI	08/21/48	Received pension
02/20/48 Battle Creek MI	03/01/48 Detroit MI	07/18/48 Detroit MI	STH at New Orleans from Vera Cruz 06/05/48. PEN
03/29/47 Pontiac MI	04/27/47 Detroit MI	02/20/48	Transferred to COM E 15th US INF 12/26/47. PEN
11/14/47 Manchester MI	11/14/47 Detroit MI		Died at Vera Cruz MEX 05/14/48
02/20/48 Battle Creek MI	03/01/48 Detroit MI	07/18/48 Detroit MI	Sent to New Orleans hospital from Vera Cruz 06/05/48
06/03/46 Detroit MI			VTS WNA
04/15/47 Ann Arbor MI	04/27/47 Detroit MI		Deserted at Cincinnati OH 05/18/47

Name	Age	Hgt	Eye	Hair	Cpx	Trade	Born	Home	Rank	Unit
Armstrong, John L.		6.00	HZL	DRK	DRK			Guerney OH	PVT	COM B 3rd US INF
Armstrong, Stephen	21	5.06	BLU	FIR	FIR	Blacksmith	Batavia NY		PVT	COM K 3rd US DRG
Arnold, Charles C.	19	5.06	GRY	LGT	FIR	Farmer	New York State		PVT	COM D US MTD RIF
Arnold, Stephen	22	5.06	HZL	BWN	DRK	Farmer	Toronto, Canada		PVT	COM K 3rd US DRG
Arnold, William	30	5.10	BLU	BWN	FLD	Farmer	St. Lawrence NY	Clinton MI	PVT	COM H 1st MI INF
Arnole, William A.	18	5.07	DRK	FIR	DRK	Farmer	Virginia		PVT	COM A US MTD RIF
Arnot, Francis	32	6.01	BLU	LGT	LGT	Lumberman	Bavaria GER	Detroit MI	PVT	COM D 1st MI INF
Aseltine, John Jr.	24	5.10	BLU	BWN	FIR	Cooper	Falkirk, Canada		PVT	COM A 15th US INF
Ashby, James	27	5.09	HZL	DRK	FIR			Leroy NY	PVT	COM B 3rd US INF
Atkinson, John	31	5.07	BLU	BWN	DRK	Laborer	England		PVT	COM A 1st MI INF
Augur, Cristopher C.	26	5.09				Soldier		Kendall NY	1LT	COM G 4th US INF
Austin, Curtis	20	5.10	BLU	BWN	DRK	Farmer	Wayne Co NY	Schoolcraft MI	PVT	COM A 1st MI INF
Austin, George N.	22	6.02	BLU	BWN	LGT	Farmer	Wayne Co NY	Ionia MI	PVT	COM I 1st MI INF
Austin, Jesse E.	21	5.10	DRK	BWN	DRK	Farmer	England	Almont MI	PVT	COM K 1st MI INF
Austin, Joseph								Detroit MI	PVT	Montgomery Guards
Axford, Daniel	29	5.09	HZL	BLK	RUD	Farmer	Upper Canada		PVT	COM K 3rd US DRG
Axford, Ross D.	26	6.00	BLU	DRK	LGT	Farmer	Trenton NJ	Lake Orion MI	PVT	COM C 1st MI INF
Axtell, Octavius A.	26	5.11	HZL	BLK	LGT	Farmer	Berkshire MA	Kalamazoo MI	PVT	COM A 1st MI INF
Ayers, Riley	22	5.08	BLU	BWN	FLD	Farmer	Wolcott NY	Blissfield MI	PVT	COM H 1st MI INF
Ayers, Russell	20	5.07	BLU	BWN	FLD	Farmer	Wolcott NY	Blissfield MI	PVT	COM H 1st MI INF
Aylward, James	37	5.07	BWN	BWN	LGT	Stonecutter	St. Johns CAN	Flint MI	PVT	COM E 1st MI INF
Ayres, William C.	21	5.09	BWN	LGT	SDY	Farmer	Rochester NY		PVT	COM K 3rd US DRG
Babbit, Samuel T.	27	6.00	BLK	BLK	FIR	Farmer	Ontario Co NY		PVT	COM I 1st MI INF
Babcock, Delos	21	5.08	BLU	LGT	LGT	Farmer	Royalton NY		PVT	COM C 1st MI INF
Babe, Christofer	32	6.01	BLU	LGT	DRK	Surveyor	Montreal Canada	Detroit MI	CPL	COM D 1st MI INF
Bacon, Soloman	18	5.10	BLU	LGT	LGT	Farmer	Wayne Co NY		PVT	COM E 15th US INF

Enrolled	Mustered	Discharged	Remarks
03/01/47 Detroit MI	03/01/47 Detroit MI	07/25/48 East Pascagoula MS	Taken prisoner 09/07/47
04/06/47 Detroit MI	04/22/47 Detroit MI	11/05/47 Puebla MEX	Left sick in hospital at Puebla MEX 08/07/47
08/16/47 Kalamazoo MI	08/16/47 Kalamazoo MI	08/01/48 Jefferson BKS MO	
04/07/47 Tecumseh MI	04/22/47 Detroit MI	07/31/48 St. Louis MO	ASG COM D 3rd DRG 01/04/48. AKA Stephen H. Johnson?
11/20/47 Clinton MI	12/01/47 Detroit MI	07/27/48 Detroit MI	
09/22/46		08/28/48 Jefferson BKS MO	Wounded at Cerro Gordo MEX 04/18/47
11/14/47 Detroit MI	11/14/47 Detroit MI		Died of diarrhea at Cordova MEX 05/20/48
04/20/47 Ann Arbor MI	04/27/47 Detroit MI		Died of disease at Chapultepec MEX 12/01/47
03/01/47 Detroit MI	03/01/47 Detroit MI	07/25/48	
11/05/47 Kalamazoo MI	11/19/47 Detroit MI		Deserted at Detroit MI 12/22/47
02/16/47			Received pension. MNI Columbus
11/05/47 Schoolcraft MI	11/19/47 Detroit MI	07/18/48 Detroit MI	In hospital at Cordova MEX. Received pension.
12/20/47 Ionia MI	01/01/48 Detroit MI	07/18/48 Detroit MI	Received pension
11/15/47 Dryden MI	12/01/47 Detroit MI	07/28/48 Detroit MI	Received pension
??/??/46 Detroit MI			VTS WNA
04/08/47 Detroit MI	04/22/47 Detroit MI	07/20/48	Left sick in hospital at Puebla MEX 08/07/47
11/30/47 Pontiac MI	12/01/47 Detroit MI	07/26/48 Detroit MI	Transferred to COM B 1st MI INF 01/01/48
11/05/47 Kalamazoo MI	11/19/47 Detroit MI	07/18/48 Detroit MI	In hospital at Cordova MEX
11/20/47 Blissfield MI	12/01/47 Detroit MI	07/27/48 Detroit MI	Received pension
11/20/47 Blissfield MI	12/01/47 Detroit MI	07/27/48 Detroit MI	Received pension
11/20/47 Detroit MI	12/04/47 Detroit MI	07/18/48 Detroit MI	
04/14/47 Detroit MI	04/22/47 Detroit MI	10/30/47 Mexico City MEX	Discharged for disability. Received pension.
01/01/48 Detroit MI	01/01/48 Detroit MI		DES at Trenton on the march 02/12/48
11/30/47 Southfield MI	12/01/47 Detroit MI		Died 06/27/48 at Vicksburg MS en route to Detroit MI
11/14/47 Detroit MI	11/14/47 Detroit MI	07/26/48 Detroit MI	Appointed 3rd SGT 01/01/48
04/23/47 Jackson MI	04/27/47 Detroit MI	08/06/48 Cincinnati OH	Received Pension

Name	Age	Hgt	Eye	Hair	Cpx	Trade	Born	Home	Rank	Unit
Bahre, Louis	40	5.08	HZL	BWN	DRK	Cabinet-maker	Celle, Hanover	Detroit MI	PVT	Brady Guards
Baird, Artimus D.	22	5.10	BLU	LGT	FIR	Farmer	Morgan Co OH	Monroe MI	PVT	COM G 15th US INF
Baker, Charles	22	5.09	BLU	BLK	LGT	Blacksmith	Lafayette NY		PVT	COM C 1st MI INF
Baker, Charles C.	22	5.09	BLU	DRK	DRK	Blacksmith	Seneca Co NY		PVT	COM C 1st MI INF
Baker, George W.	20	5.11	BLU	BWN	FIR	Farmer	Stark Co OH	Marshall MI	PVT	COM I 1st MI INF
Baker, Ira	28	6.02	GRY	BLK	DRK	Farmer	Wayne Co NY		PVT	COM F 2nd US INF
Baker, Thomas S.								Adrian MI	PVT	Adrian Guards
Balcom, Joseph E.	28	5.07	BLU	BWN	LGT	Farmer	Livingston Co NY	Kalamazoo MI	PVT	COM A 1st MI INF
Baldwin, Isaac	25	5.10	BLU	BWN	FIR	Farmer	Chemung Co NY	Hartland MI	2SG	COM C 1st MI INF
Baldwin, John	33	5.05	BLU	LGT	FIR	Sailor	Providence RI		RCT	US Army
Baldwin, Samuel T.	33	5.08	BLU	DRK	LGT	Farmer	Yates Co NY		PVT	COM G 1st MI INF
Ball, Alden	21	5.10	BLU	SDY	FIR	Farmer	Essex VT		PVT	COM K 3rd US DRG
Ball, Davis J.	32	5.06	BLU	BWN	FIR	Barber	Ontario Co NY		PVT	COM F 1st MI INF
Ball, Gilbert	21	5.10	BLU	BWN	DRK	Farmer	Essex VT		PVT	COM K 3rd US DRG
Ball, Myron C.	30	6.00	BLK	BWN	LGT	Farmer	Oswego Co NY		PVT	BAT ? 1st US ART
Bamford, Robert	22	5.08	GRY	SDY	SDY	Shoemaker	Prescott, CAN		PVT	COM E 15th US INF
Banghart, Theodore	18	5.09	HZL	BWN	DRK	Farmer	Axeford NJ	Almont MI	PVT	COM K 1st MI INF
Banks, Matthew	24	6.01	BLU	DRK	FIR	Laborer	New Foundland	Detroit MI	PVT	COM B 1st MI INF
Barber, James T.	20	5.11	BLU	SDY	LGT	Mechanic		Dundee MI	PVT	COM H 1st MI INF
Barclay, John	21	5.10	GRY	DRK	FIR	Carpenter	Prescott CAN	Detroit MI	CPL	COM K 3rd US DRG
Barden, Marshall	22	6.00	GRY	DRK	DRK	Cooper	Southwick MA		PVT	COM D 2nd US INF
Bardwell, Jonathon W.	24	5.05	GRY	LGT	DRK	Blacksmith	Madison Co NY		PVT	COM G 15th US INF
Barker, Bleeker L.	26	5.07	BLU	LGT	LGT	Painter	Oneida Co NY	Grand Rapids MI	PVT	COM A 1st MI INF
Barlow, Ira W.	20	6.00	GRY	FIR	FIR	Miller	Livingston Co NY		PVT	COM K 3rd US DRG
Barnes, Albert	25	5.09	BLU	BWN	FIR	Farmer	Genesee Co NY		RCT	US Army
Barnes, James	22	5.08	BLU	BWN	DRK	Blacksmith	Monroe Co NY	Union City MI	PVT	COM I 1st MI INF

ENROLLED	MUSTERED	DISCHARGED	REMARKS
06/18/47 Detroit MI	06/18/47 Detroit MI	06/30/48 Detroit MI	
04/23/47 Monroe MI	04/30/47 Detroit MI		Died of diarrhea at Puebla MEX 01/16/48
11/30/47 Corunna MI	12/01/47 Detroit MI		Deserted at Detroit MI 12/17/47
02/20/48 Ypsilanti MI	03/01/48 Detroit MI	07/18/48 Detroit MI	STH at New Orleans from Vera Cruz 06/05/48
11/15/47 Marshall MI	12/01/47 Detroit MI	07/18/48 Detroit MI	
06/24/46 Detroit MI			Died at Matamora MEX 04/21/47
06/01/46 Adrian MI			VTS WNA
11/05/47 Kalamazoo MI	11/19/47 Detroit MI	07/18/48 Detroit MI	In hospital at Cordova. Died at Detroit MI 07/25/48
11/30/47 Pontiac MI	12/01/47 Detroit MI	07/26/48 Detroit MI	
05/31/48 Detroit MI	Detroit MI	06/20/48 Newport KY	PEN
04/01/48 Detroit MI	04/01/48 Detroit MI		Died of yellow fever at Vera Cruz 05/31/48
04/01/47 Detroit MI	04/22/47 Detroit MI	10/30/47 Mexico City MEX	Discharged for disability
11/15/47 Adrian MI	12/02/47 Detroit MI		Deserted at Detroit MI 12/24/47
04/01/47 Detroit MI	04/22/47 Detroit MI		DET teamster 06/01/47. DOD at Perote 08/06/47
05/14/47 Detroit MI	Detroit MI	08/30/48 Ft Columbus NY	DES 06/24/47 and apprehended 07/02/47
04/07/47 Jackson MI	04/27/47 Detroit MI		Deserted 05/17/47 at Cincinnati OH
12/24/47 Kalamazoo MI	01/20/48 Detroit MI	07/28/48 Detroit MI	Received pension
11/02/47 Port Huron MI	11/12/47 Detroit MI	07/26/48 Detroit MI	
11/20/47 Monroe MI	12/01/47 Detroit MI		Deserted at Detroit MI 12/28/47
03/25/47 Detroit MI	04/22/47 Detroit MI	07/31/48 Jefferson BKS MO	ASG COM C 3rd US DRG 01/04/48
06/22/46 Monroe MI		01/03/48 New Orleans LA	Discharged on surgeon's certificate
04/02/47 Detroit MI	04/30/47 Detroit MI	08/04/48 Covington KY	
11/05/47 Grand Rapids MI	11/19/47 Detroit MI	07/18/48 Detroit MI	
04/16/47 Detroit MI	04/22/47 Detroit MI	11/05/47 Puebla MEX	LIH sick at Puebla 08/07/47. DSC. PEN
05/27/48 Detroit MI	Detroit MI	06/20/48 Newport KY	
11/15/47 Union City MI	12/01/47 Detroit MI	07/18/48 Detroit MI	

Name	Age	Hgt	Eye	Hair	Cpx	Trade	Born	Home	Rank	Unit
Barnes, William A.	22	5.10	BLU	BWN	FLD	Laborer	Canada		PVT	COM G US MTD RIF
Barney, Amos	32	5.09	GRY	BWN	FIR	Farmer	Hanover NY	Battle Creek MI	1SG	COM I 1st MI INF
Barney, Daniel	22	6.02	BLK	LGT	LGT	Landlord	Wayne Co NY	Detroit MI	PVT	COM C 1st MI INF
Barnhart, John I.	19	5.06	GRY	BWN	FLD				PVT	COM I 1st MI INF
Barrett, James W.	21	5.08	HZL	BWN	DRK	Farmer	Oswego Co NY		PVT	COM E 15th US INF
Barrett, John	45	5.10	BLU	AUB	SDY	Carpenter	France	Detroit MI	PVT	COM D 1st MI INF
Barrett, Jonathon G.	23	5.06	BLU	BWN	FIR	Laborer	Oswego Co NY		PVT	COM E 15th US INF
Barrett, Milo	20	5.08	BWN	DRK	LGT	Laborer	Ontario Co NY		PVT	COM G 1st MI INF
Barron, Y. E.								St. Clair MI	2LT	St. Clair Guards
Barrone, Simon	25	5.10	BLK	BWN	FLD	Farmer	Stack OH	Monroe MI	PVT	COM H 1st MI INF
Barry, Garret								Detroit MI	PVT	Montgomery Guards
Bartholomew, Hiram M.	20	5.11	GRY	DRK	FIR	Farmer	Ohio		PVT	COM G 15th US INF
Bartholomew, Horace	30	5.10	BLU	LGT	LGT	Farmer	Geneva OH	Fawn River MI	PVT	COM E 15th US INF
Bartholomew, Levi	20	5.07	BWN	AUB	FIR	Laborer	Geneva OH	Fawn River MI	PVT	COM E 15th US INF
Bartholomew, Theron	25	5.08	BLK	DRK	DRK	Blacksmith	Geneva OH	Fawn River MI	PVT	COM E 15th US INF
Bartlett, Joseph	20	5.11	BLU	BWN	FIR	Blacksmith	Lower Canada	Niles MI	PVT	COM F 1st MI INF
Bartlett, Norman								Adrian MI	PVT	Adrian Guards
Bartlett, Ransom								Adrian MI	PVT	Adrian Guards
Barton, Charles E.	18	5.05	BLU	LGT	LGT	Tailor	Onondaga Co NY		PVT	COM G 1st MI INF
Bartram, Ezra	21	5.07	DRK	BWN	DRK	Farmer	Newbury NY	Adrian MI	PVT	COM H 1st MI INF
Bartram, Walter B.	24	5.11	GRY	BWN	FIR	Farmer			PVT	COM I 1st MI INF
Bascom, Elliott Milo	20	5.10	GRY	DRK	LGT	Farmer	Bergen NY		PVT	COM F 2nd US INF
Bassett, Elias	18	5.08	BLU	DRK	DRK	Laborer	Monroe Co NY		PVT	COM K 1st MI INF
Bassett, Michael	20					Painter	Amherstburg CAN		PVT	COM H 1st MI INF
Bastard, Harvey	26	6.00	GRY	BLK	DRK	Painter	Devonshire ENG		PVT	COM G 15th US INF
Bates, Franklin	22	5.10	GRY	BLK	LGT	Farmer	Tioga? Co NY		FAR	COM K 3rd US DRG

ENROLLED	MUSTERED	DISCHARGED	REMARKS
07/17/47 Otsego MI	07/17/47 Otsego MI		Died 03/30/48 at Mexico City
11/15/47 Battle Creek MI	12/01/47 Detroit MI	07/18/48 Detroit MI	PEN
11/30/47 Detroit MI	12/01/47 Detroit MI	07/26/48 Detroit MI	
11/15/47 Adrian MI	12/01/47 Detroit MI	02/02/48 Detroit MI	Discharged by legal process
04/12/47 Grand Rapids MI	04/27/47 Detroit MI	08/06/48 Cincinnati OH	
11/14/47 Detroit MI	11/14/47 Detroit MI	07/26/48 Detroit MI	Left sick at Vera Cruz MEX 02/06/48
04/12/47 Grand Rapids MI	04/27/47 Detroit MI	08/06/48 Cincinnati OH	
02/20/48 Jackson MI	03/01/48 Detroit MI		Died at Vera Cruz MEX 05/31/48
??/??/46 St. Clair MI			VTS WNA
11/20/47 Monroe MI	12/01/47 Detroit MI		Deserted at Vienna MI 02/14/48
??/??/46 Detroit MI			VTS WNA
04/17/47 Monroe MI	04/30/47 Detroit MI	08/04/48 Covington KY	
04/07/47 Fawn River MI	04/27/47 Detroit MI		PMT CPL 08/06/47. Died at Chapultepec 09/25/47. PEN
04/21/47 Fawn River MI	04/27/47 Detroit MI	07/20/48 Baton Rouge LA	Left sick at Vera Cruz 06/18/47. Received pension
04/27/47 Fawn River MI	04/27/47 Detroit MI	08/21/48	PMT CPL 05/17/47. RTR 08/20/47. LIH New Orleans 1848
11/15/47 Niles MI	12/02/47 Detroit MI		Died due to inflamation of lungs at Cordova 04/01/48
06/01/46 Adrian MI			VTS WNA
06/01/46 Adrian MI			VTS WNA
02/20/48 Battle Creek MI	03/01/48 Detroit MI		Deserted at Detroit MI 04/10/48
11/20/47 Adrian MI	12/01/47 Detroit MI		Deserted at Detroit MI 01/14/48
11/15/47 Marshall MI	12/01/47 Detroit MI		Died at Detroit MI 12/31/47
06/25/46 Detroit MI		06/25/51 Camp Far West CA	In MI Soldiers' Home (#4261). PEN
11/15/47 Dryden MI	12/01/47 Detroit MI	01/08/48 Detroit MI	Discharged by civil authority
10/14/47 Monroe MI	12/01/47 Detroit MI	07/27/48 Detroit MI	Received pension
04/14/47 Adrian MI	04/30/47 Detroit MI		Died at Puebla MEX of typhoid fever 03/11/48
04/08/47 Tecumseh MI	04/22/47 Detroit MI	10/30/47 Mexico City MEX	Discharged for disability

Name	Age	Hgt	Eye	Hair	Cpx	Trade	Born	Home	Rank	Unit
Bates, Richard	25	5.10	BLU	LGT	FIR	Brickmaker	Genesee Co NY	Adrian MI	PVT	COM F 1st MI INF
Baum, Frederick	21	5.09	BLU	DRK	LGT	Shoemaker	Baden GER	Monroe MI	PVT	COM G 15th US INF
Baxter, Charles	22	5.06	BLU	BWN	FIR	Farmer	Dunham, Quebec		PVT	COM I 1st MI INF
Beach, Clark R.	22	6.01	BLK	BLK	LGT	Shoemaker	Niagara Co NY	Adrian MI	1SG	COM G 1st MI INF
Beach, Marshall	18	5.05	HZL	BWN	LGT	Farmer	Bronson OH		PVT	COM K 1st MI INF
Beach, Samuel Elmore	22	5.10	BLK	BWN	LGT	Clerk	Lewiston NY	Pontiac MI	2LT	COM A 15th US INF
Beagle, James	22	6.02	HZL	BWN	FIR	Painter	New York State	Detroit MI	CPL	COM K 3rd US DRG
Beals, Manly W.	18	5.05	DRK	BLK	DRK	Laborer	Kalamazoo MI	Kalamazoo MI	PVT	COM A 1st MI INF
Beaman, Joshua	25	5.08	BLU	BWN	FIR	Farmer	Franklin Co NY		PVT	COM K 3rd US DRG
Beatty, Joseph	24	5.08	DRK	DRK	DRK	Laborer	Wayne, Ireland		PVT	COM B 3rd US INF
Beck, Adam	32	5.08	GRY	BWN	DRK	Joiner	Dumfries, SCO		RCT	US Army
Becker, Henry W.	29	5.06	GRY	BLK	DRK	Farmer	Locke NY	Ann Arbor MI	PVT	COM K 1st MI INF
Beckwith, Augustus S.									PVT	COM D 1st MI INF
Bedell, Tobias W.	24	5.06	HZL	BWN	LGT	Laborer	Saratoga Co NY		PVT	COM K 1st MI INF
Bedford, John	23	5.10	BLU	BWN	LGT	Laborer	Ireland		PVT	COM A 15th US IN
Beebe, Henry A.	19	5.10	BLU	BWN	DRK	Farmer	Ontario Co NY		PVT	COM E 15th US INF
Beecher, Sherman C.	28	5.11	GRY	LGT	LGT	Seaman	Orleans Co NY	Grand Rapids MI	3CP	COM A 1st MI INF
Beir, John	26	5.07	BLU	LGT	LGT	Laborer	Biean GER	Detroit MI	PVT	Brady Guards
Belford, John	23	5.10	BLU	BWN	LGT	Laborer	Ireland		PVT	COM A 15th US INF
Belknap, James A.	21	5.05	HZL	DRK	LGT	Farmer	Monroe Co NY		PVT	COM G 1st MI INF
Bellinger, William L.	45	5.09	BLK	BWN	FLD	Tradesman	Newburg NY	Perrysburg OH	PVT	COM H 1st MI INF
Bement, Roswell	21	5.06	BLU	DRK	LGT	Laborer	Victory NY		PVT	COM A 15th US INF
Bemus, Cyrus C.	19	5.06	GRY	BWN	FIR	Painter	New York State		PVT	COM I 1st MI INF
Benedict, Edward H.	26	5.11	BWN	BWN	DRK	Farmer	Trumbull Co OH	Detroit MI	SGT	COM K 3rd US DRG
Beniteau, Clement	26	5.08	BLK	BLK	FIR	Clerk	Detroit or CAN	Detroit MI	PVT	COM K 3rd US DRG
Benjamin, Daniel	26	5.08	GRY	LGT	FLD	Farmer	Rockland NY		RCT	US Army

ENROLLED	MUSTERED	DISCHARGED	REMARKS
11/15/47 Adrian MI	12/02/47 Detroit MI	07/28/48 Detroit MI	
04/13/47 Monroe MI	04/30/47 Detroit MI	08/04/48 Covington KY	
01/24/48 Tallmadge MI	02/01/48 Detroit MI		Died at Toledo OH 07/10/48
11/10/47 Adrian MI	12/01/47 Detroit MI	07/18/48 Detroit MI	Received pension
11/15/47 Dryden MI	12/01/47 Detroit MI		Deserted at Detroit MI 12/28/47
03/23/47	04/09/47 Detroit MI	08/04/48 Covington KY	PMT 1LT 05/31/47. TRA COM G 12/26/47. PEN
03/26/17 Detroit MI	04/22/17 Detroit MI	07/31/18 Jefferson BKS MO	TRA COM D 01/04/18
11/05/47 Kalamazoo MI	11/19/47 Detroit MI	07/18/48 Detroit MI	In hospital at Cordova MEX
04/09/47 Tecumseh MI	04/22/47 Detroit MI	08/01/48 Jefferson BKS MO	LIH at Puebla 08/07/47. AKA Bedman PEN
03/23/47 Detroit MI	03/23/47 Detroit MI		Deserted 01/24/48
05/03/48 Detroit MI	Detroit MI		Died en route to Newport KY 05/29/48
11/15/47 Ann Arbor MI	12/01/47 Detroit MI	07/28/48 Detroit MI	Buried Oak Hill Cemetery, Clermont FL. PEN
11/14/47 Ypsilanti MI	11/14/47 Detroit MI	11/20/47 Detroit MI	Discharged by writ of habeas corpus as minor
11/15/47 Ypsilanti MI	12/01/47 Detroit MI		DES at Detroit 12/16/47. VTS COM D 2nd US INF. PEN
03/29/47 Pontiac MI			TRA COM G. Left sick at Mexico City 02/01/48
04/26/47 Niles MI	04/27/47 Detroit MI		LIH New Orleans 06/20/47. Died at Vera Cruz 07/19/47
11/05/47 Grand Rapids MI	11/19/47 Detroit MI	07/18/48 Detroit MI	PMT 2CP 12/01/47. PMT 1CP 03/01/48
06/18/47 Detroit MI	06/18/47 Detroit MI	06/30/48 Detroit MI	
03/29/47 Pontiac MI	04/27/47 Detroit MI	07/27/48 Baton Rouge LA	TRA COM G 12/26/47. LIH Mexico City 02/01/48. PEN
01/25/48 Detroit MI	02/01/48 Detroit MI		Died at Detroit MI 04/10/48
11/20/47 Perrysburg OH	12/01/47 Detroit MI		TRA COM G. LIH New Orleans 02/09/48. Died 07/20/48
04/15/47 Utica MI	04/27/47 Detroit MI	08/04/48 Covington KY	TRA COM H 12/26/47. PEN
11/15/47 Grand Rapids MI	12/01/47 Detroit MI		Deserted at Detroit MI 02/09/48
04/05/47 Detroit MI	04/22/47 Detroit MI	07/31/48 Jefferson BKS MO	TRA COM E 01/04/48. Received Pension
04/22/47 Detroit MI	04/22/47 Detroit MI	08/01/48 Jefferson BKS MO	LIH Puebla MEX 08/07/47. PEN. AKA Clement Boniteau
05/30/48 Detroit MI	Detroit MI	06/28/48 Newport KY	

Name	Age	Hgt	Eye	Hair	Cpx	Trade	Born	Home	Rank	Unit
Bennett, Egbert	45	6.00	BLU	LGT	LGT	Hatter	Greene Co NY		PVT	COM E 1st MI INF
Bennett, Harvey	22	5.06	GRY	BWN	LGT	Farmer	Niagara Co NY		PVT	COM E 15th US INF
Bennett, James H.	40	5.07	BLK	DRK	LGT	Clerk	Philadelphia PA	Detroit MI	PVT	COM B 1st MI INF
Bennett, John I.	43	5.10	BLU	BWN	LGT	Farmer	Hartford CT		PVT	COM K 1st MI INF
Berger, John	35	5.05	GRY	DRK	DRK	Laborer	Switzerland		PVT	COM B 1st MI INF
Berkley, William	21	5.09	BLU	BWN	FIR	Laborer	Orange Co NY		PVT	COM A 6th US INF
Bertram, Joel	18	5.04	BLK	BWN	DRK	Laborer	Genesee Co NY	Adrian MI	PVT	COM F 1st MI INF
Biers, Abraham	25	5.10	BLU	BWN	FLD	Laborer	Syracuse NY		PVT	COM E 15th US INF
Bietry, John A.	21	5.11	GRY	BLK	DRK	Cooper	France	Battle Creek MI	PVT	COM G 1st MI INF
Bigelow, Alexander C.	19	6.00	BLK	BWN	FLD	Farmer	St. Lawrence Co	Adrian MI	PVT	COM H 1st MI INF
Bigelow, Alonzo								Adrian MI	PVT	Adrian Guards
Bigelow, Charles								Adrian MI	PVT	Adrian Guards
Bigler, Jacob	45	5.10	GRY	BWN	LGT	Farmer	Sussex NJ		PVT	COM C 1st MI INF
Bigler, William	18	5.10	BLU	BWN	FLD	Brassman	Hamburg GER	Cincinnati OH	PVT	COM H 1st MI INF
Billings, Daniel E.	22	5.05	BLU	LGT	LGT	Sailor	Portsmouth NH	Detroit MI	PVT	COM B 1st MI INF
Billsby, Charles	27	5.07	BLU	SDY	LGT	Laborer	Monroe Co NY		PVT	COM A 15th US INF
Birch, Philetus P.	23	5.08	DRK	DRK	LGT	Laborer	Palmyra NY		PVT	COM A 15th US INF
Birch, William	31	6.00	BLU	BWN	FLD	Butcher	Farmsden ENG		PVT	COM K US MTD RIF
Bird, George								Adrian MI	PVT	Adrian Guards
Bissel, Andrew J.	18	5.08	DRK	BWN	LGT	Laborer	Richmond Co NY	Holly MI	PVT	COM A 15th US INF
Bissinett, Alexander	19	5.08	GRY	DRK	DRK	Farmer	Monroe Co NY		PVT	COM G 15th US INF
Bissinett, Battraw	23	5.07	BLK	BLK	DRK	Farmer	Monroe Co MI		PVT	COM G 15th US INF
Bittke, Christian	30	5.06	GRY	BWN	DRK	Farmer	Prussia	Detroit MI	PVT	COM H 1st MI INF
Bixby, William L.	24	5.09	BLU	SDY	LGT	Farmer	Ellisburg NY	Cassopolis MI	PVT	COM K 1st MI INF
Black, Benjamin A.	28	6.00	GRY	BLK	FIR	Laborer	Brown NY		PVT	COM I 1st MI INF
Blackmer, John	34	5.08	BLU	FIR	FIR	Farmer	Lanesborough VT		RCT	COM ? 3rd US DRG

ENROLLED	MUSTERED	DISCHARGED	REMARKS
11/20/47 Detroit MI	12/04/47 Detroit MI		Deserted at Detroit MI 12/24/47
04/20/47 Jackson MI	04/27/47 Detroit MI	08/21/48	
11/02/47 Port Huron MI	11/12/47 Detroit MI	07/26/48 Detroit MI	
11/15/47 Ypsilanti MI	12/01/47 Detroit MI	07/28/48 Detroit MI	
11/02/47 Port Huron MI	11/12/47 Detroit MI		Died at Cordova MEX 06/12/48
09/07/46 Detroit MI	09/07/46 Detroit MI		Died at Anton Sisardo MEX 03/08/47
11/15/47 Adrian MI	12/02/47 Detroit MI		Died at Cordova MEX 06/04/48. AKA Joel Bartram
04/10/47 Fawn River MI	04/27/47 Detroit MI		Died at Perote MEX 08/20/47
02/20/48 Battle Creek MI	03/01/48 Detroit MI	07/18/48 Detroit MI	Received pension
11/20/47 Adrian MI	12/01/47 Detroit MI		Died at Ash's Landing IN 07/05/48
06/01/46 Adrian MI			VTS WNA
06/01/46 Adrian MI			VTS WNA
11/30/47 Pontiac MI	12/01/47 Detroit MI		Died at New Orleans LA 05/06/48. PEN
11/20/47 Toledo OH	12/01/47 Detroit MI		Deserted at Cincinnati OH 02/21/48
11/02/47 Port Huron MI	11/12/47 Detroit MI	07/26/48 Detroit MI	Alias Edward Billings. Received pension
04/07/47 Pontiac MI	04/27/47 Detroit MI	07/24/48 Baton Rouge LA	TRA COM B 12/26/47. PEN
04/13/47 Pontiac MI	04/27/47 Detroit MI	11/10/47 Puebla MEX	Discharged for disability. PEN
07/17/47 Kalamazoo MI	07/17/47 Kalamazoo MI	07/31/48 Jefferson BKS MO	DOD incurred in Mexico 02/28/49. AKA William Burch
06/01/46 Adrian MI			VTS WNA
04/02/47 Pontiac MI	04/27/47 Detroit MI	08/04/48 Cincinnati OH	TRA COM I 12/26/47. PEN
04/15/47 Monroe MI	04/30/47 Detroit MI		LIH New Orleans 07/12/48. Died 07/20/48
04/14/47 Monroe MI	04/30/47 Detroit MI		Died of diarrhea at Camp Ferguson 07/02/48
11/20/47 Adrian MI	12/01/47 Detroit MI	07/27/48 Detroit MI	Received pension
12/24/47 Jackson MI	01/20/48 Detroit MI	07/28/48 Detroit MI	PEN
11/15/47 Adrian MI	12/01/47 Detroit MI		Died at Cordova MEX 06/13/48
04/23/48 Detroit MI	Detroit MI	07/16/48 Jefferson BKS MO	

Name	Age	Hgt	Eye	Hair	Cpx	Trade	Born	Home	Rank	Unit
Blair, Charles	44					Farmer	Otsego Co NY	Franklin TWP MI	2SG	NTH Lenawee VOL
Blake, Michael	19	5.07	BLU	BLK	DRK	Laborer	Toronto CAN		PVT	COM F 1st MI INF
Blanchard, Reuben M.	25	5.05	BLU	LGT	FLD	Blacksmith	Wayne Co NY	Coldwater MI	PVT	COM I 1st MI INF
Blanchard, Stillman									1LT	NTH Lenawee VOL
Blennis, Uriah	21	5.07	BLU	LGT	LGT	Farmer	New York State	Detroit MI	PVT	COM E 1st MI INF
Bletter, John	28	5.07	HZL	SDY	SDY	Physician	Baden GER		PVT	COM K 3rd US DRG
Bliss, Abraham	36	5.07	BLU	LGT	LGT	Cooper	New York State	Jackson Co MI	PVT	COM B 1st MI INF
Bloye, John	30	5.08	BLU	BWN	FIR	Tanner	England		PVT	COM K 6th US INF
Blum, George								Detroit MI	PVT	Scott Guards
Bock, John						Laborer		Detroit MI	3SG	Scott Guards
Bodine, Barton	18	5.06	HZL	FIR	FIR	Farmer	Block Dist. CAN		RCT	COM K 3rd US DRG
Bohl, Jacob	37	5.06	HZL	BWN	LGT		Bavaria GER		PVT	COM D 1st MI INF
Bonnell, Simeon	26	5.09	BLU	BWN	FIR	Farmer	Seneca Co NY		PVT	COM E 15th US INF
Booker, Alonzo	20	5.07	BLU	BWN	DRK	Farmer	Coos NH	Pontiac MI	PVT	COM C 1st MI INF
Booram, William	44	6.02	BLU	BWN	DRK	Farmer	New Jersey		PVT	COM I 1st MI INF
Booth, Jacob	18	5.06	BLK	AUB	LGT	Bookbinder	New York NY		PVT	COM A 15th US INF
Botsford, Edward	18	5.08	GRY	BWN	LGT	Laborer	Monroe Co NY		PVT	COM A 15th US INF
Botsford, Horace	20	5.08	GRY	BWN	LGT	Laborer	Monroe Co NY		PVT	COM A 15th US INF
Bouchard, Stephen						Blacksmith		Detroit MI	1LT	Lafayette Guards
Bouin, Andrew K.	21	5.09	BLU	DRK	LGT	Shoemaker	Baden GER		PVT	COM G 15th US INF
Boule, Eusebe								Detroit MI	3LT	Lafayette Guards
Bourns, John	30	5.07	BLU	BWN	LGT	Laborer	Ireland	Adrian MI	PVT	COM F 1st MI INF
Bovee, George W.	20	5.06	BLU	BWN	LGT	Sailor	Ontario Co NY		PVT	COM G 1st MI INF
Bowen, Oliver H. P.	23	5.10	BLU	BWN	FLD	Farmer	Cattaraugus NY		PVT	COM K 1st MI INF
Bower, William	26	5.09	GRY	BWN	DRK	Farmer	Germany	St. Louis MO	PVT	COM H 1st MI INF
Bowers, Thomas H.	32	5.09	HZL	BWN	DRK	Laborer	England	Adrian MI	PVT	COM F 1st MI INF

ENROLLED	MUSTERED	DISCHARGED	REMARKS
06/06/46 Tecumseh MI			VTS WNA
11/15/47 Niles MI	12/02/47 Detroit MI		Deserted at New Orleans LA 01/18/48
11/15/47 Coldwater MI	12/01/47 Detroit MI		Died at Detroit MI 07/27/48
06/06/46 Tecumseh MI			VTS WNA
11/20/47 Saginaw MI	12/04/47 Detroit MI	07/18/48 Detroit MI	Received pension
03/27/47 Detroit MI	04/22/47 Detroit MI	07/31/48 Jefferson BKS MO	TRA COM D 01/04/48
11/02/47 Port Huron MI	11/12/47 Detroit MI	07/26/48 Detroit MI	
02/19/48 Detroit MI	Detroit MI	07/31/48 Jefferson BKS MO	
06/03/46 Detroit MI			VTS WNA
06/03/46 Detroit MI			VTS WNA
04/21/48 Detroit MI	Detroit MI	07/14/48 Jefferson BKS MO	PEN
10/30/47 Woodville OH	01/01/48 Springfield	04/25/48 Cordova MEX	DFD. Died on board ship in Gulf of Mexico 06/10/48
04/22/47 Grand Rapids MI	04/27/47 Detroit MI		Died at Rio Ledens MEX 06/14/48
11/30/47 Pontiac MI	12/01/47 Detroit MI	07/26/48 Detroit MI	
11/15/47 Hastings MI	12/01/47 Detroit MI		Died near New Orleans on boat to Detroit 06/29/48. PEN
04/15/47 Ann Arbor MI	04/27/47 Detroit MI	11/06/47 Chapultepec MEX	Discharged for disability
04/13/47 Pontiac MI	04/27/47 Detroit MI	05/01/47 Detroit MI	Discharged by civil authority
04/13/47 Pontiac MI	04/27/47 Detroit MI	05/01/47 Detroit MI	Discharged by civil authority
??/??/46 Detroit MI			VTS WNA
04/13/47 Monroe MI	04/30/47 Detroit MI	08/21/48	
??/??/46 Detroit MI			VTS WNA
11/15/47 Adrian MI	12/02/47 Detroit MI	07/28/48 Detroit MI	
02/20/48 Toledo OH	03/01/48 Detroit MI		Died at Detroit MI 07/15/48
12/24/47 Jackson MI	01/01/48 Detroit MI		Deserted at Detroit MI 02/12/48
11/20/47 Adrian MI	12/01/47 Detroit MI	07/27/48 Detroit MI	
11/15/47 Adrian MI	12/02/47 Detroit MI		Died at Vera Cruz MEX 05/07/48

Michigan Men in the Mexican War

Name	Age	Hgt	Eye	Hair	Cpx	Trade	Born	Home	Rank	Unit
Bowles, William	33	5.07	BLU	SDY	FLD	Laborer	Dunstable ENG		PVT	COM A 6th US INF
Bowman, William	25	5.08	BLU	SDY	FIR	Carpenter	Green Bay WI		PVT	BTY K 1st US ART
Boyd, Robert	25	5.06	BLU	SDY	FIR	Laborer	Galway IRE	Detroit MI	PVT	COM D 1st MI INF
Boyington, William D.	26	5.11	DRK	BWN	DRK	Sailor	New York NY		PVT	COM A 1st MI INF
Boyt, Louis C.	27	5.10	HZL	BLK	DRK	Gentleman	Monroe MI	Detroit MI	3CP	Brady Guards
Brackelbank, Joseph	21	5.09	BLU	BWN	FIR	Farmer	Ontario Co NY	Canandagua MI	PVT	COM F 1st MI INF
Braden, Barnard	26	5.05	GRY	SDY	SDY	Laborer	Addison VT		PVT	COM E 15th US INF
Braden, John	21	5.10	GRY	LGT	RUD	Laborer	New York NY		PVT	COM A 15th US INF
Braden, Kasbur								Detroit MI	PVT	Scott Guards
Bradley, James	28	5.10	DRK	BLK	DRK	Laborer	Port Huron MI		PVT	COM A 6th US INF
Bradock, George I.	19	5.05	DRK	DRK	DRK	Lawyer	New York State		PVT	COM I 1st MI INF
Brady, Hugh						Grocer		Detroit MI	PVT	Montgomery Guards
Brady, William	22	5.10	DRK	BWN	DRK	Farmer	Virginia		PVT	COM I 1st MI INF
Brainard, Franklin D.	21	6.00	HZL	BWN	DRK	Laborer	Sandusky OH	Detroit MI	PVT	COM G 15th US INF
Brandard, Frank D.	21	5.11	HZL	BWN	DRK	Laborer	Sandusky OH		PVT	COM G 15th US INF
Brandon, Manassah	18	5.06	BLU	LGT	LGT	Stonecutter	Otsego Co NY		PVT	COM F 1st MI INF
Branguin, William C.	24	5.07	BLU	LGT	LGT	Farmer	England	Silver Lake MI	PVT	COM H 1st MI INF
Brannock, Henry L.	21	5.06	BLU	BLK	DRK	Farmer	Elbe NY		PVT	COM A 15th US INF
Bray, Richard	24	5.10	BLU	DRK	FIR	Laborer	Oxford ENG		PVT	COM G 15th US INF
Brazell, James	24	5.08	BWN	DRK	FIR	Tailor	Kings Co IRE	Detroit MI	PVT	COM B 3rd US INF
Breckbill, Henry									2CP	NTH Lenawee VOL
Brenan, John								Detroit MI	PVT	Montgomery Guards
Brent, Levi	38	6.00	BLK	BLK	LGT			Jackson MI	PVT	COM E 1st MI INF
Brickell, Zebulon M.	23	5.09	BLK	BLK	DRK	Farmer	Greenbrier VA		PVT	COM E 15th US INF
Briezenderfer, Michael	32	5.08	GRY	LGT	FIR	Blacksmith	Witzberg GER		RCT	Montgomery Guards
Briggs, Ashley	41	5.03	BLU	BWN	FIR	Cooper	Cayuga Co NY	Ypsilanti MI	PVT	COM H 1st MI INF

362

ENROLLED	MUSTERED	DISCHARGED	REMARKS
11/18/46 Detroit MI	11/18/46 Detroit MI		Slightly wounded in the battle of Mexico 08/27/47
09/07/47 Detroit MI	Detroit MI	08/20/48 Fort Columbus NY	
01/13/48 New Orleans LA	01/13/48 New Orleans LA	07/26/48 Detroit MI	
11/05/47 Grand Rapids MI	11/19/47 Detroit MI		HOA at Cordova 04/09/48. Buried at Detroit 07/31/48
06/18/47 Detroit MI	06/18/47 Detroit MI	06/30/48 Detroit MI	
11/15/47 Niles MI	12/02/47 Detroit MI	07/28/48 Detroit MI	
04/06/47 Jackson MI	04/27/47 Detroit MI	08/06/48 Cincinnati OH	
04/15/47 Pontiac MI	04/27/47 Detroit MI	08/04/48 Covington KY	TRA COM K 12/26/47. Received pension
06/03/46 Detroit MI			VTS WNA
10/13/46 Detroit MI	10/13/46 Detroit MI		Wounded at battle of Molino del Rey MEX 09/08/47
11/15/47 Grand Rapids MI	12/01/47 Detroit MI		Died at Detroit MI 12/29/47
05/28/46 Detroit MI			VTS WNA
11/15/47 Hillsdale MI	12/01/47 Detroit MI		Deserted at Detroit MI 01/15/48
03/29/47 Detroit MI	04/30/47 Detroit MI		Died on ship Lapland of diarrhea 07/08/48. AKA Branard
03//29/47 Detroit			Died on board ship Lapland of chronic diarrhea 07/07/48
11/15/47 Niles MI	12/02/47 Detroit MI	07/28/48 Detroit MI	LIH Vera Cruz MEX 02/04/48. Received pension
11/20/47 Freedom MI	12/01/47 Detroit MI	07/27/48 Detroit MI	Received Pension
04/05/47 Utica MI	04/27/47 Detroit MI	08/04/48 Covington KY	TRA COM K 12/26/47
04/13/47 Monroe MI	04/30/47 Detroit MI	08/21/48	Left sick at New Orleans LA 07/12/47
03/02/47 Detroit MI	03/02/47 Detroit MI	07/25/48 East Pascagoula MS	
06/06/46 Tecumseh MI			VTS WNA
05/28/46 Detroit MI			VTS WNA
11/20/47 Jackson MI	12/04/47 Detroit MI		Died of diarrhea at New Orleans 03/05/48. AKA Bunt
04/08/47 Niles MI	04/27/47 Detroit MI		Died at Chapultepec MEX 11/22/47. MNI Montgomery Pike
10/26/47 Detroit MI			Company disbanded before muster
12/20/47 Ypsilanti MI	01/01/48 Detroit MI	02/28/48 Detroit MI	Discharged on surgeon's certificate. PEN

Name	Age	Hgt	Eye	Hair	Cpx	Trade	Born	Home	Rank	Unit
Briggs, Porter	21	5.07	HZL	BWN	RUD	Blacksmith	Wayne Co NY		RCT	COM ? 3rd US DRG
Brightman, David J.	25	6.00	BLU	DRK	LGT	Laborer	Marcellus NY		PVT	COM B 1st MI INF
Brinick, Edward								Detroit MI	PVT	Montgomery Guards
Briskby, Thomas	21	5.09	HZL	BWN	LGT	Laborer	Yorkshire ENG	Detroit MI	PVT	COM D 1st MI INF
Brodhead, Thornton F.	25					Lawyer	S New Market NH	Pontiac MI	1LT	COM A 15th US INF
Brooks, Joseph	32	5.08	GRY	BLK	DRK	Farmer	Phelps NY		PVT	BTY K 1st US ART
Brown, Charles R.	28	5.09	BLU	BWN	FLD	Clerk	Newburg NY	Hillsdale MI	PVT	COM H 1st MI INF
Brown, Frederick	21	5.09	BLU	DRK	LGT	Shoemaker	Baden GER		PVT	COM G 15th US INF
Brown, Hiram	21	5.07	GRY	LGT	FIR	Farmer	Chautauqua NY		PVT	COM A 15th US INF
Brown, John P.	30	5.10	HZL	BWN	DRK	Farmer	Redslenger GER		PVT	COM B 5th US INF
Brown, John M.	18	5.10	HZL	DRK	FIR	Farmer	Madison Co NY		PVT	COM D 1st MI INF
Brown, John T.	28						New York State	Tecumseh MI	1LT	COM K 3rd US DRG
Brown, Joseph White	52				DRK	Businessman	Bucks Co PA	Tecumseh MI	CAP	NTH Lenawee VOL
Brown, Samuel Jr.	37	5.09	BLK	DRK	DRK		Fairlee VT		PVT	COM A 1st MI INF
Brown, Simeon B.	34					Businessman	Bridgewater NH	St. Clair MI	CAP	St. Clair Guards
Brown, Timothy W.	24	6.04	GRY	BWN	DRK	Farmer	Lansing NY		PVT	COM C 1st MI INF
Brown, William Scott	25						Lyons NY	Ann Arbor MI	CAP	F&S 1st MI INF
Brownell, Benjamin Jr.	24							Adrian MI	2LT	COM K 1st MI INF
Brownyard, Sebastian	21	5.10	HZL	DRK	LGT	Cooper	France		PVT	COM G 1st MI INF
Bruak, Jacob	20	5.09	BLK	BWN	FLD	Farmer	Walcott NY	Hillsdale MI	PVT	COM H 1st MI INF
Bruette, Thomas	26	5.07	BLK	BLK	DRK	Tinsmith	Canada	Detroit MI	PVT	COM K 3rd US DRG
Brumfield, John B.	22	5.10	GRY	BWN	FIR	Lawyer	Greene Co NY	Grand Rapids MI	PVT	COM I 1st MI INF
Bryant, Charles B.	25	5.10	GRY	BWN	FIR	Carpenter	Shoreheim VT		PVT	COM E 15th US INF
Buchanan, James	22	5.06	GRY	BWN	FLD	Farmer	Shelby OH	Elkhart IN	PVT	COM H 1st MI INF
Buck, Henry	19	5.08	BLU	LGT	LGT	Farmer	New York State	Hudson MI	PVT	COM H 1st MI INF
Buck, Nathan W.	38	5.10	GRY	BWN	DRK	Shoemaker	Essex Co NY	Marshall MI	PVT	COM I 1st MI INF

ENROLLED	MUSTERED	DISCHARGED	REMARKS
06/03/48 Detroit MI	Detroit MI	07/16/48 Jefferson BKS MO	
11/02/47 Port Huron MI	11/12/47 Detroit MI		Died at Cordova MEX 06/02/48
??/??/46 Detroit MI			VTS WNA
11/04/47 Detroit MI	11/14/47 Detroit MI	07/26/48 Detroit MI	Admitted to MI Veterans' Facility (#3278). PEN
04/09/47 Detroit MI	04/20/47 Detroit MI	07/31/48 Cincinnati OH	PMT Adjutant 03/25/47. PMT CAP 12/02/47. TRA COM G
06/28/47 Detroit MI	Detroit MI	08/20/48 Fort Columbus NY	Received pension
11/20/47 Hillsdale MI	12/01/47 Detroit MI		Deserted at Detroit MI 01/08/48
04/13/47 Monroe MI			
04/10/47 Utica MI	04/27/47 Detroit MI		Died of wounds received at Mexico City 10/26/47
10/05/47 Detroit MI	Detroit MI		Died at Tacubaya MEX of diarrhea 02/22/48. MNI Peter
11/14/47 Ypsilanti MI	11/14/47 Detroit MI		Died at Vera Cruz MEX 05/25/48
03/09/47 Tecumseh MI	04/09/47	07/20/48	Died 10/05/49 from illness caught at Puebla MEX. PEN
06/06/46 Tecumseh MI			VTS WNA
11/05/47 Allegan MI	11/09/47 Detroit MI		LIH New Orleans 06/24/48. DOD at New Orleans 07/26/48
??/??/46 St. Clair MI			VTS WNA
11/30/47 Corunna MI	12/01/47 Detroit MI		LIH Jefferson BKS 07/07/48. Died 08/05/48
02/14/48 Ann Arbor MI	04/12/48 Cordova MEX	07/29/48 Detroit MI	Appointed by the President. PMT CSA. PEN
10/30/47 Adrian MI	12/01/47 Detroit MI	07/28/48 Detroit MI	Had harelip
02/20/48 Battle Creek MI	03/01/48 Detroit MI	07/18/48 Detroit MI	Sent to New Orleans hospital from Vera Cruz 06/05/48
11/20/47 Hillsdale MI	12/01/47 Detroit MI		Deserted at Detroit MI 01/14/48
04/22/47 Detroit MI	04/22/47 Detroit MI		DOD at Mixcoac MEX 09/12/47. AKA Thomas Brunet
01/24/48 Grand Rapids MI	02/01/48 Detroit MI	07/18/48 Detroit MI	MNI Benjamin. PEN. AKA John B. Bromfield
04/14/47 Grand Rapids MI	04/27/47 Detroit MI	08/06/48 Cincinnati OH	
11/20/47 Adrian MI	12/01/47 Detroit MI		Died at Toledo OH 07/10/48
11/20/47 Hudson MI	12/01/47 Detroit MI	07/27/48 Detroit MI	Received Pension
11/15/47 Marshall MI	12/01/47 Detroit MI		Died at Detroit MI 08/15/48. PEN

Name	Age	Hgt	Eye	Hair	Cpx	Trade	Born	Home	Rank	Unit
Buckholder, John	34	5.07	GRY	BWN	FIR	Farmer	West Canada	Grand Rapids MI	PVT	COM I 1st MI INF
Buel, David E.	24	6.04	DRK	DRK	DRK	Sailor	Wisdom NY	Port Huron MI	3SG	COM B 1st MI INF
Buel, Grover N.	31	6.00	BLK	BWN	FIR	Merchant	Northumberland	Port Huron MI	CAP	COM B 1st MI INF
Bugbee, John								Adrian MI	2CP	Adrian Guards
Bullard, John	26	5.08	BLU	BWN	LGT	Tavernkeep	Wayne Co NY		PVT	COM E 1st MI INF
Bullen, Alphanso H.	21	5.04	GRY	LGT	LGT	Carpenter	Genesee Co NY		PVT	COM B US MTD RIF
Bunker, Cyreno R.	19	5.10	BWN	DRK	DRK	Farmer	Kent Co MI		PVT	COM G 1st MI INF
Bunnell, Bennajah J.	26					Clothier	Tioga Co NY		RCT	Montgomery Guards
Bunnell, Lafayette H.	23	5.11	DRK	DRK	LGT	Druggist	Rochester NY		PVT	COM B 1st MI INF
Bunnell, William	24	5.09	BLK	BWN	DRK	Farmer	Genesee Co NY		PVT	COM F 1st MI INF
Burch, Nicholas	25	5.10	BLU	BWN	LGT	Laborer	Chautauqua Co NY	Kalamazoo MI	PVT	COM A 1st MI INF
Burchard, John	18	5.05	DRK	BLK	LGT	Blacksmith	Montreal CAN		PVT	Brady Guards
Burdeno, Augustus D.	35	5.09	BLK	BLK	DRK	Carpenter	Wayne Co MI		2SG	COM A 15th US INF
Burger, William	23	5.08	BLU	BLK	LGT	Farmer	Adams OH		PVT	COM F 1st MI INF
Burgess, Philo	28	6.04	BLU	BWN	LGT	Farmer	Grafton VT		PVT	COM E 15th US INF
Burke, Alexander	27	5.08	BLU	SDY	LGT	Farmer	Wayne Co MI		PVT	COM C 1st MI INF
Burke, Peter	32	5.09	GRY	DRK	SAL	Laborer	Ireland		PVT	COM A 15th US INF
Burlingham, Thomas	18	5.07	BWN	BWN	FIR	Teamster	Nicolet? CAN		PVT	COM E 15th US INF
Burnett, Wellington C.	18	5.10	GRY	BWN	FIR	Farmer	Hampton CT	Highland MI	PVT	COM D 15th US INF
Burnham, Charles	22	5.11	BWN	BWN	FIR	Printer	Burlington VT	Detroit MI	PVT	COM K 3rd US DRG
Burnham, Eben	18	5.06	HZL	BWN	LGT	Blacksmith	Washtenaw Co MI	Saline MI	PVT	COM D 1st MI INF
Burns, Asder	23	5.10	DRK	DRK	FIR	Laborer	Erie PA		PVT	COM B 3rd US INF
Burns, Edward								Detroit MI	PVT	Montgomery Guards
Burns, John								Detroit MI	PVT	Montgomery Guards
Burns, John	35	5.06	GRY	BWN	DRK	Soldier	Dublin IRE		PVT	COM B 5th US INF
Burns, William								Detroit MI	2CP	Montgomery Guards

ENROLLED	MUSTERED	DISCHARGED	REMARKS
01/24/48 Grand Rapids MI	02/01/48 Detroit MI	07/18/48 Detroit MI	
11/02/47 Port Huron MI	11/12/47 Detroit MI	07/26/48 Detroit MI	PEN
10/30/47 Port Huron MI	11/12/47 Detroit MI		Died at Cordova MEX of vomito 06/07/48
06/01/46 Adrian MI			VTS WNA
11/20/47 Hillsdale MI	12/04/47 Detroit MI		Died at Cordova MEX 06/04/48. PEN
08/25/47 Kalamazoo MI	08/25/47 Kalamazoo MI	07/31/48 Jefferson BKS MO	
02/20/48 Grand Rapids MI	03/01/48 Detroit MI	07/18/48 Detroit MI	STH at New Orleans LA from Vera Cruz 06/05/48. PEN
11/08/47 Battle Creek MI			Company disbanded before muster
11/02/47 Port Huron MI	11/12/47 Detroit MI	07/26/48 Detroit MI	HOS from date of muster. PEN
11/15/47 Battle Creek MI	12/02/47 Detroit MI		Deserted at Detroit MI 12/25/47
11/05/47 Kalamazoo MI	11/19/47 Detroit MI	07/18/48 Detroit MI	AKA Nicholas Birch
06/14/47 Detroit MI	06/18/47 Detroit MI	06/30/48 Detroit MI	
04/01/47 Detroit MI	04/22/47 Detroit MI	03/26/48 Cuernavaca MEX	TRA COM G 12/26/47. Discharged for disability
11/15/47 Niles MI	12/02/47 Detroit MI		Deserted at New Orleans LA 01/18/48
04/26/47 Niles MI	04/27/47 Detroit MI		Died at Chapultepec MEX 01/31/48
11/30/47 Corunna MI	12/01/47 Detroit MI	07/26/48 Detroit MI	Sent to hospital at Vera Cruz MEX 02/07/48
04/27/47 Pontiac MI	04/27/47 Detroit MI	08/06/48 Cincinnati OH	TRA COM G 12/26/47. PMT CPL 07/18/48
04/09/47 Grand Rapids MI	04/27/47 Detroit MI		Deserted near Baton Rouge LA 05/27/47
04/19/47 Dayton OH		08/03/48 Covington KY	TRA COM E 12/??/47. PMT 2LT 06/18/48. PEN
04/16/47 Detroit MI	04/22/47 Detroit MI	07/31/48 Jefferson BKS MO	TRA COM D 01/04/48
11/14/47 Ypsilanti MI	11/14/47 Detroit MI	07/26/48 Detroit MI	
03/24/47 Detroit MI	03/24/47 Detroit MI	07/25/48 East Pascagoula MS	
05/28/46 Detroit MI			VTS WNA
05/28/46 Detroit MI			VTS WNA
08/24/47 Detroit MI	Detroit MI	08/01/48 East Pascagoula MS	
05/28/46 Detroit MI			VTS WNA

Name	Age	Hgt	Eye	Hair	Cpx	Trade	Born	Home	Rank	Unit
Buschar, Frederick	31	5.04	BLU	FIR	FIR	Laborer	Germany		PVT	COM K 3rd US INF
Bush, Andrew	18	5.06	BLU	LGT	LGT	Laborer	Kalamazoo MI		PVT	COM A 1st MI INF
Bush, Meredith	42							Laningfield OH	PVT	COM H 1st MI INF
Bushy, Francis	21	5.07	DRK	DRK	DRK	Laborer	Beauharnois CAN		PVT	COM B 3rd US INF
Buswell, Bray W.	18	5.07	BLU	LGT	LGT	Laborer	Rockingham NH	Detroit MI	PVT	COM A 1st MI INF
Butler, Elnathan	26	5.07	BLU	SDY	LGT	Farmer	Ireland	Clinton MI	PVT	COM H 1st MI INF
Butler, Henry	24	5.08	BLU	BWN	LGT	Farmer	Schodack NY		PVT	COM K 1st MI INF
Butler, Martin	34	5.10	BLU	BWN	FIR	Laborer	Waterford IRE		RCT	Montgomery Guards
Butler, Patrick	25	5.05	GRY	BWN	FIR	Engineer	Tipperary IRE		PVT	COM B 5th US INF
Butler, Stephen	34	5.10	GRY	BWN	LGT	Farmer	Providence MA		PVT	COM C 5th US INF
Buyer, George	25	5.06	GRY	BWN	LGT	Shoemaker	Baden GER		PVT	COM D 1st MI INF
Buzzell, William R.	18	5.08	BLU	DRK	LGT	Laborer	Westmaden NY		PVT	COM A 15th US INF
Cabicha, Charles	24	5.05	GRY	BLK	SAL	Laborer	Wayne Co MI		PVT	COM G 15th US INF
Cadwell, Cornelius	18	5.08	BLK	BWN	DRK	Laborer	Wayne Co MI	Waterloo MI	PVT	COM A 1st MI INF
Cady, Elisha	21	5.08	BLU	SDY	FIR	Farmer	Ontario Co NY		PVT	COM K 3rd US DRG
Cahoon, Hugh	27	5.09	GRY	BWN	FLD	Tanner	Antrim IRE		PVT	COM B 3rd US INF
Cain, Alanson	24	5.10	BLU	LGT	FIR	Distiller	Berkshire Co MA		PVT	COM K 3rd US DRG
Caldrich, William								Adrian MI	4CP	Adrian Guards
Caleb, William H.	19	5.08	GRY	BWN	DRK	Farmer	Delaware Co NY		PVT	COM K 3rd US DRG
Calicot, Benjamin	22	5.04	BLU	BWN	FIR	Farmer	Wolcott NY		PVT	COM K 6th US INF
Calkins, Charles	21	5.09	GRY	BLK	DRK	Cooper	Cayuga Co NY		PVT	COM A 15th US INF
Calliton, Richard	32	5.05	BLU	BWN	LGT	Laborer	Alburg VT		PVT	COM B 3rd US INF
Camp, Henry C.	34	5.08	HZL	GRY	DRK	Laborer	Durham? CT	Ypsilanti MI	PVT	COM K 1st MI INF
Campbell, John	29	5.08	HZL	LGT	LGT	Painter	Niagara CAN		PVT	COM B 1st MI INF
Campbell, John	35	5.09	BLU	BWN	DRK	Carpenter	Livingston NY		PVT	COM E 15th US INF
Campbell, William	28	5.09	BLU	DRK	LGT	Laborer	Monaghan? IRE		PVT	COM B 1st MI INF

Enrolled	Mustered	Discharged	Remarks
12/20/46 Mackinac MI			Died of diarrhea at camp on Seona River 06/17/49
11/05/47 Kalamazoo MI	11/19/47 Detroit MI		Deserted from Detroit MI 12/15/47
02/21/48 Springfield	02/28/48 New Orleans LA		Died on Mississippi River 07/06/48
03/05/47 Detroit MI	03/05/47 Detroit MI		Died at Mexico City MEX 12/13/47
11/05/47 Kalamazoo MI	11/19/47 Detroit MI	07/18/48 Detroit MI	AKA Bray W. Boswell
11/20/47 Clinton MI	12/01/47 Detroit MI	07/27/48 Detroit MI	Alias Michael Butler. Received pension
11/15/47 Howell MI	12/01/47 Detroit MI		Died at Detroit MI 02/12/48
11/01/47 Detroit MI			Company disbanded before muster
09/18/47 Detroit MI	Detroit MI		At post on Clear Fork of Brazos River TX
05/14/47 Detroit MI	Detroit MI	08/31/48 East Pascagoula MS	Transferred to COM G
11/14/47 Detroit MI	11/14/47 Detroit MI	07/26/48 Detroit MI	Received pension
04/02/47 Pontiac MI	04/27/47 Detroit MI		Died at Mexico City MEX of disease 10/29/47
04/09/47 Detroit MI	04/30/47 Detroit MI	04/20/48 Baton Rouge LA	Discharged for disability
11/05/47 Kalamazoo MI	11/19/47 Detroit MI	07/18/48 Detroit MI	Received pension
04/07/47 Detroit MI			Deserted at Detroit MI 04/14/47
04/10/47 Port Huron MI	04/10/47 Port Huron MI		Died at Mexico City 11/26/47
04/08/47 Tecumseh MI	04/22/47 Detroit MI	10/29/47 Mexico City MEX	Discharged for disability. Received Pension
06/01/46 Adrian MI			VTS WNA
04/08/47 Tecumseh MI	04/22/47 Detroit MI	07/20/48	LIH Puebla MEX 08/07/47
11/24/47 Detroit MI	11/24/47 Detroit MI	07/28/48 Jefferson BKS MO	PEN
04/05/47 Ann Arbor MI	04/27/47 Detroit MI		Died of disease at Puebla MEX 07/17/47
04/15/47 Detroit MI	04/15/47 Detroit MI	07/25/48 East Pascagoula MS	
11/15/47 Ypsilanti MI	12/01/47 Detroit MI	07/28/48 Detroit MI	
11/02/47 Port Huron MI	11/12/47 Detroit MI		Deserted at Detroit MI 11/26/47
04/13/47 Niles MI	04/27/47 Detroit MI		ODS Vera Cruz with QUT Dept. Died 11/30/47?
11/02/47 Port Huron MI	11/12/47 Detroit MI		Died 07/26/48. PEN

Name	Age	Hgt	Eye	Hair	Cpx	Trade	Born	Home	Rank	Unit
Campion, William	27	5.08	BLU	LGT	LGT	Tailor	Queen Co IRE	Ann Arbor MI	PVT	COM E 1st MI INF
Canfield, Albert B.	19	5.09	BLU	BWN	FIR	Farmer	Auburn NY	Hillsdale MI	PVT	COM H 1st MI INF
Canfield, John	27	5.08	BLK	BLK	DRK	Farmer	Ontario Co NY		PVT	COM F 1st MI INF
Cannan, James						Teamster		Detroit MI	PVT	Montgomery Guards
Capper, Aaron M.	25	5.08	DRK	DRK	DRK	Cabinet-maker	Winchester VA	Detroit MI	4SG	COM F 1st MI INF
Carberry, John	20	6.01	BLU	BWN	FIR	Boatman	Brown Co OH	Niles MI	3SG	COM F 1st MI INF
Carby, William	28	5.07	HZL	SDY	SDY	Laborer	Utica NY		PVT	COM K 3rd US DRG
Carey, Isaac	26	5.11	HZL	SDY	FIR	Farmer	Genesee Co NY		PVT	COM K 3rd US DRG
Cargill, Samuel P.	22	5.06	GRY	SDY	FIR	Clerk	Ontario Co NY	Detroit MI	PVT	COM K 3rd US DRG
Carl, William	40	5.11	BLK	LGT	DRK	Laborer	Ireland	Detroit MI	PVT	COM E 1st MI INF
Carland, Richard	22	5.06	HZL	BWN	LGT	Shoemaker	Cork IRE	Detroit MI	PVT	Brady Guards
Carleton, Israel E.	26						New Hampshire	St. Clair MI	1LT	St. Clair Guards
Carney, James	18	5.04	BLK	BWN	LGT	Blacksmith	Maine? NY	Dexter MI	PVT	COM H 1st MI INF
Carney, Samuel	35	5.05	BLU	LGT	LGT	Laborer	Ontario Co NY		PVT	COM A 15th US INF
Carpenter, Hiram W.	21	6.00	GRY	DRK	FIR	Blacksmith	Bangor NY		PVT	COM B 1st MI INF
Carpenter, Jerome	19	5.00	BLU	BWN	LGT	Shoemaker	Macomb Co MI		PVT	COM H 16th US INF
Carpenter, Nathaniel	33	6.01	BWN	DRK	DRK	Soldier	Waterboro ME		PVT	COM B 1st MI INF
Carr, Daniel	40	6.01	BLU	BLK	DRK	Painter	Cayuga Co NY	Constantine MI	PVT	COM G 1st MI INF
Carr, John	18	5.03	BLK	DRK	DRK	Farmer	Livingston NY	Detroit MI	PVT	COM K 1st MI INF
Carr, John	18	5.05	GRY	BWN	LGT	Farmer	Sussex NJ		PVT	COM C 1st MI INF
Carr, Robert	19	5.07	BLU	LGT	FIR	Farmer	NJ or NY	Pontiac MI	PVT	COM C 1st MI INF
Carrigan, Hugh	45	5.07	BLU	BWN	DRK	Laborer	Fermanagh IRE		PVT	Brady Guards
Carroll, William	25	5.11	BLU	BWN	FLD	Farmer	Buffalo NY		PVT	COM E 15th US INF
Carruthers, Walter	27	6.03	BLU	SDY	LGT	Carpenter	Glasgow SCO		PVT	COM K 6th US INF
Cartwright, Franklin	21	5.09	BLU	LGT	LGT	Laborer	Livingston NY		PVT	COM A 15th US INF
Cartwright, Horace C.	20	5.08	GRY	DRK	FIR	Laborer	Avon NY	Mt. Clemens MI	1CP	COM B 1st MI INF

ENROLLED	MUSTERED	DISCHARGED	REMARKS
11/20/47 Detroit MI	12/04/47 Detroit MI	07/18/48 Detroit MI	
11/20/47 Hillsdale MI	12/01/47 Detroit MI	01/18/48	Discharged by writ of habeas corpus. PEN
11/15/47 Niles MI	12/02/47 Detroit MI		Deserted at New Orleans LA 01/18/48
05/28/46 Detroit MI			VTS WNA
11/15/47 Niles MI	12/02/47 Detroit MI	07/28/48 Detroit MI	PMT 3SG 12/31/47. LIH Vera Cruz MEX 02/05/48
11/15/47 Niles MI	12/02/47 Detroit MI	07/28/48 Detroit MI	PMT 2SG 12/31/47. PMT 1SG 04/01/48. PEN
03/27/47 Detroit MI	04/22/47 Detroit MI	07/31/48 Jefferson BKS MO	TRA COM E 01/04/48. Died Sacramento CA 06/16/84
04/03/47 Detroit MI	04/22/47 Detroit MI		LIH Puebla MEX 08/07/47. Died 12/12/48
04/06/47 Detroit MI	04/22/47 Detroit MI	02/15/48 Mexico City MEX	TRA COM D 01/04/48. DFD. PEN. MNI Pidesco
11/20/47 Detroit MI	12/04/47 Detroit MI		DES 12/24/47. Rejoined COM 03/19/48. DUC 03/20/48
06/18/47 Detroit MI	06/18/47 Detroit MI	06/30/48 Detroit MI	PEN
??/??/46 St. Clair MI			VTS WNA
12/20/47 Dexter MI	01/01/48 Detroit MI		LIH New Orleans 06/24/48. Died 06/25/48. AKA Camey
04/09/47 Ann Arbor MI	04/27/47 Detroit MI		KIA at Churubusco MEX 08/20/47
11/02/47 Port Huron MI	11/12/47 Detroit MI	01/31/48 Vera Cruz MEX	Discharged on surgeon's certificate. PEN
04/19/47 Michigan City			Deserted at Michigan City IN 04/25/47
11/02/47 Port Huron MI	11/12/47 Detroit MI		Died at Detroit MI 11/26/47. PEN
02/20/48 Centreville MI	03/01/48 Detroit MI	07/18/48 Detroit MI	Made musician 05/09/48
01/20/48 Kalamazoo MI	02/01/48 Detroit MI	07/28/48 Detroit MI	
11/30/47 Pontiac MI	12/01/47 Detroit MI		Died at New Orleans LA 06/25/48 en route from Mexico
11/30/47 Pontiac MI	12/01/47 Detroit MI	07/26/48 Detroit MI	
06/14/47 Detroit MI	06/18/47 Detroit MI		Deserted at Detroit MI 06/21/47
04/26/47 Niles MI	04/27/47 Detroit MI		Died at Puebla MEX 09/20/47. PEN
11/25/47 Detroit MI	11/25/47 Detroit MI	05/01/48 Newport KY	
04/15/47 Utica MI	04/27/47 Detroit MI	07/20/48	TRA COM C 12/26/47. PEN
11/02/47 Port Huron MI	11/12/47 Detroit MI	07/26/48 Detroit MI	PEN

Name	Age	Hgt	Eye	Hair	Cpx	Trade	Born	Home	Rank	Unit
Cary, Daniel	24	5.07	BLU	DRK	LGT	Shoemaker	Galway Co IRE	Detroit MI	1SG	Brady Guards
Case, Horace	35	6.00	BLU	BWN	FIR	Cooper	Oneida Co NY	Grand Rapids MI	MUS	COM I 1st MI INF
Case, Orrin S.	34	5.08	BLU	BLK	DRK	Printer	Ontario Co NY	Kalamazoo MI	PVT	COM A 1st MI INF
Case, Seymour	22	5.07	BWN	LGT	LGT	Farmer	Canandaigua NY		PVT	COM G 1st MI INF
Cass, Lewis Jr.	31						Ohio	Detroit MI	MAJ	F&S 3rd US DRG
Cassad, Samuel	28	5.09	BLU	DRK	FLD	Lawyer	Sussex NJ		RCT	US Army
Castle, Thomas	21	5.06	HZL	SDY	SDY	Waiter	New York NY		PVT	COM K 3rd US DRG
Caswell, Horace	22	5.08	GRY	BWN	FLD	Carpenter	Orleans Co NY	Ionia MI	PVT	COM I 1st MI INF
Caswell, James	20	5.11	GRY	BWN	FLD	Farmer	Orleans Co NY		PVT	COM I 1st MI INF
Caswell, John	18	5.04	GRY	BWN	FLD	Farmer	Orleans Co NY	Ionia MI	PVT	COM I 1st MI INF
Caswell, Samuel H.	22	5.08	HZL	BWN	FIR	Farmer	New York State		PVT	COM H US MTD RIF
Cavenaugh, Moses H.	31	6.00	BLU	BLK	LGT	Laborer	Livingston NY	Kalamazoo MI	PVT	COM A 1st MI INF
Cavis, Charles								Adrian MI	PVT	Adrian Guards
Ceady, Chandler	18	5.09	BLU	LGT	LGT	Farmer	Monroe MI		PVT	COM K 3rd US DRG
Chadwick, Samuel Jr.	29						Ohio	Three Rivers MI	1LT	COM E 1st MI INF
Chaffee, Jerome								Adrian MI	PVT	Adrian Guards
Chamberlain, Daniel	45	5.08	HZL	BWN	FIR	Farmer	Berkshire MA		PVT	COM C 1st MI INF
Chamberlain, Luther	22	5.06	BLU	BWN	LGT	Machinist	Allegany Co NY		RCT	US Army
Chaple, Joshua B.	24	5.10	BLU	LGT	FIR	Carpenter	Malden CAN	Pontiac MI	PVT	COM C 1st MI INF
Chapman, Curt								Detroit MI	PVT	Montgomery Guards
Chapman, Edmund A.	21	5.07	BLU	LGT	LGT	Farmer	Madison Co NY	Schoolcraft MI	PVT	COM A 1st MI INF
Chapman, William R.	24	5.07	BLU	BWN	LGT	Farmer	Malone NY		PVT	COM C 1st MI INF
Chappell, Granville D.	21	5.05	HZL	BWN	LGT	Laborer	Palmyra NY		PVT	COM B 3rd US INF
Charles, Andrew	23	5.04	HZL	BLK	LGT	Cigarmaker	Ireland		PVT	Brady Guards
Charlesworth, James F.	20	5.08	BLU	LGT	RUD	Tailor	Belmont Co OH		PVT	COM H US MTD RIF
Charlesworth, Richard W	18	5.05	GRY	LGT	FLD	Farmer	St. Clairville OH		PVT	COM H US MTD RIF

ENROLLED	MUSTERED	DISCHARGED	REMARKS
06/18/47 Detroit MI	06/18/47 Detroit MI	06/30/48 Detroit MI	
11/15/47 Grand Rapids MI	12/01/47 Detroit MI	07/18/48 Detroit MI	Drummer
11/05/47 Kalamazoo MI	11/19/47 Detroit MI	07/18/48 Detroit MI	PMT 4SG 05/25/48 at Cordova. Received pension
02/20/48 Ypsilanti MI	03/01/48 Detroit MI	07/18/48 Detroit MI	STH at New Orleans LA from Vera Cruz 06/05/48
03/03/47	04/09/47	07/20/48	
05/04/48 Detroit MI	Detroit MI	06/20/48 Newport KY	
03/26/47 Detroit MI	04/22/47 Detroit MI	07/31/48 Jefferson BKS MO	TRA COM C 01/04/48
12/20/47 Otisco MI	01/01/48 Detroit MI	07/18/48 Detroit MI	PEN
12/20/47 Otisco MI	01/01/48 Detroit MI		Died in Detroit MI hospital
12/20/47 Otisco MI	01/01/48 Detroit MI	07/18/48 Detroit MI	PEN
07/29/47 Kalamazoo MI	07/29/47 Kalamazoo MI		Died at Baton Rouge LA 07/17/48
11/05/47 Kalamazoo MI	11/19/47 Detroit MI	07/18/48 Detroit MI	
06/01/16 Adrian MI			VTS WNA
04/07/47 Tecumseh MI	04/22/47 Detroit MI		Died from disease at Mexico City 09/23/47
10/30/47 Jackson MI	12/04/47 Detroit MI	06/30/48 Washington DC	On FUR 30 days from 03/28/48. Leave renewed 30 days
06/01/46 Adrian MI			VTS WNA
11/30/47 Pontiac MI	12/01/47 Detroit MI		Died at Chicago 07/02/48 en route from Mexico. PEN
04/05/47 Detroit MI	04/05/47 Detroit MI		Deserted at Detroit MI 04/05/47
11/30/47 Pontiac MI	12/01/47 Detroit MI	05/17/48 Cordova MEX	Died in service of apoplexy. AKA John Chapel. PEN
??/??/46 Detroit MI			VTS WNA
11/05/47 Schoolcraft MI	11/09/47 Detroit MI	07/18/48 Detroit MI	
11/30/47 Owosso MI	12/01/47 Detroit MI	01/28/48 Vera Cruz MEX	Discharged for crime in service
04/06/47 Detroit MI	04/06/47 Detroit MI		LIH New Orleans LA 06/19/47. DES 01/23/48
06/18/47 Detroit MI	06/18/47 Detroit MI	06/30/48 Detroit MI	
07/24/47 Kalamazoo MI	07/24/47 Kalamazoo MI	07/31/48 Jefferson BKS MO	PEN
07/09/47 Kalamazoo MI	07/09/47 Kalamazoo MI	07/31/48 Jefferson BKS MO	

373

Name	Age	Hgt	Eye	Hair	Cpx	Trade	Born	Home	Rank	Unit
Chase, Charles	28	6.04	GRY	BWN	DRK	Farmer	New York State		PVT	COM I 1st MI INF
Chase, Ichabod	23	5.11	BLU	BWN	LGT	Farmer	Novi MI	Iosco MI	PVT	COM K 1st MI INF
Chase, Levi	40	5.11	GRY	BWN	FLD	Farmer	New York State		PVT	COM I 1st MI INF
Chatfield, Robert E.	18	5.07	BLU	LGT	LGT	Farmer	Onondaga Co NY		PVT	COM E 15th US INF
Childs, Edwin	23	5.06	BLK	BLK	DRK	Mason	Middlesex CT	Kalamazoo MI	PVT	COM A 1st MI INF
Chittenden, William F.	35	6.00	HZL	DRK	FLD	Blacksmith	Kent ENG	Detroit MI	2LT	Brady Guards
Church, Abner H.	23	5.06	BLU	LGT	LGT	Farmer	Montgomery NY		PVT	COM E 15th US INF
Church, Albert H.	19	5.05	HZL	BWN	LGT	Farmer	Avon NY	Ann Arbor MI	PVT	COM K 1st MI INF
Church, Alvin H.	30	5.09	GRY	BWN	LGT	Printer	Amsterdam NY		PVT	COM K 1st MI INF
Church, Henry C.	22	5.04	GRY	BWN	LGT	Laborer	Avon NY	Washtenaw Co	PVT	COM K 1st MI INF
Church, Hudson A.	19	5.09	GRY	BWN	LGT	Farmer	Covington NY		PVT	COM E 15th US INF
Cicotte, James J.						Constable	Detroit MI	Detroit MI	2LT	Lafayette Guards
Clairoux, Louis D.	31	5.10	DRK	BLK	DRK	Grocer	St Benoit CAN	Detroit MI	2LT	COM E 1st MI INF
Clare, Harman	26	5.06	BWN	DRK	LGT	Cooper	Montreal CAN	Pontiac MI	PVT	COM C 1st MI INF
Clarey, James	29	5.08	GRY	SDY	LGT	Laborer	Waterford IRE		PVT	COM A 6th US INF
Clark, Asa Jr.	26	5.10	BLU	BWN	FIR	Farmer	Wayne Co NY		PVT	COM C 1st MI INF
Clark, John								Detroit MI	PVT	Montgomery Guards
Clark, John R.	23					Merchant	Ontario Co NY	Adrian MI	2SG	Adrian Guards
Clark, Lemuel	25	5.06	BLU	LGT	LGT	Soldier	East Union OH		PVT	COM B 5th US INF
Clark, Lewis G.	22	5.05	GRY	LGT	LGT	Laborer	Cochecton NY		PVT	COM A 15th US INF
Clark, Michael								Detroit MI	PVT	Montgomery Guards
Clark, Nelson	24	6.00	BLK	DRK	DRK	Laborer			PVT	COM B 1st MI INF
Clark, Thomas									3SG	NTH Lenawee VOL
Clarke, Charles	21	5.08	HZL	BWN	SDY	Blacksmith	Oakland Co MI		PVT	COM K 3rd US DRG
Clarke, John	27	6.00	BLU	BWN	FLD	Carpenter	Vermont		PVT	COM K 1st MI INF
Cleveland, Nathan M.	18	5.10	BLU	LGT	LGT	Laborer	Polly NY		PVT	COM D 1st MI INF

ENROLLED	MUSTERED	DISCHARGED	REMARKS
11/15/47 Hastings MI	12/01/47 Detroit MI		Died in Detroit MI hospital 12/29/47
11/15/47 Howell MI	12/01/47 Detroit MI	07/28/48 Detroit MI	Received pension
11/15/47 Hastings MI	12/01/47 Detroit MI		Died in Detroit MI hospital 12/28/47. PEN
04/26/47 Jackson MI	04/27/47 Detroit MI	08/06/48 Cincinnati OH	
11/05/47 Kalamazoo MI	11/19/47 Detroit MI	07/18/48 Detroit MI	PMT 4CP 02/01/48. PMT 3CP 03/01/48. PEN
06/18/47 Detroit MI	06/18/47 Detroit MI	06/30/48 Detroit MI	
04/15/47 Jackson MI	04/27/47 Detroit MI		Died at Puebla MEX 09/17/47
11/15/47 Ann Arbor MI	12/01/47 Detroit MI	07/28/48 Detroit MI	Received pension
12/24/47 Ann Arbor MI	01/01/48 Detroit MI	07/28/48 Detroit MI	Left at New Orleans LA by mistake 06/26/48
11/15/47 Ann Arbor MI	12/01/47 Detroit MI		Died of fever at Cordova MEX 04/20/48
04/06/47 Niles MI	04/27/47 Detroit MI	08/06/48 Cincinnati OH	
??/??/46 Detroit MI			VTS WNA
10/30/47 Detroit MI	12/04/47 Detroit MI	07/18/48 Detroit MI	Received pension
11/30/47 Pontiac MI	12/01/47 Detroit MI	07/26/48 Detroit MI	AKA Harman Clair
11/30/46 Detroit MI	11/30/46 Detroit MI		DES Jefferson BKS 09/16/48, apprehended 09/22/18. PEN
11/30/47 Utica MI	12/01/47 Detroit MI	07/26/48 Detroit MI	Sent to hospital at Vera Cruz MEX 02/02/48
??/??/46 Detroit MI			VTS WNA
06/01/46 Adrian MI			VTS WNA
07/05/47 Detroit MI	Detroit MI	08/01/48 East Pascagoula MS	
03/29/47 Pontiac MI	04/27/47 Detroit MI	08/04/48 Cincinnati OH	TRA COM H 12/26/47. TRA COM I 05/10/48. PEN
05/28/46 Detroit MI			VTS WNA
11/02/47 Port Huron MI	11/12/47 Detroit MI		Deserted at Detroit MI 11/25/47
06/06/46 Tecumseh MI			VTS WNA
04/07/47 Detroit MI	Detroit MI		Deserted at Detroit MI 04/14/47
11/15/47 Ypsilanti MI	12/01/47 Detroit MI		Deserted at Detroit MI 12/10/47
11/14/47 Marshall MI	11/14/47 Detroit MI		TRA COM A 01/01/48. Died at Cordova MEX 02/18/48

375

Name	Age	Hgt	Eye	Hair	Cpx	Trade	Born	Home	Rank	Unit
Cleveland, Silas P.	18	5.09	HZL	BWN	FIR	Carpenter	Wayne Co NY		PVT	COM I 1st MI INF
Cline, Edward C.	18	5.03	GRY	SDY	LGT	Farmer	Rochester NY	Newport MI	PVT	COM E 1st MI INF
Cline, Henry	37	5.08	BLK	BLK	DRK	Shoemaker	Germany		PVT	COM F 1st MI INF
Clitz, Henry B.	23					Soldier	Sacketts Harbor		2LT	COM ? 3rd US INF
Clitz, John M.	25					Mariner	Sacketts Harbor		MID	US Navy
Cobb, Joseph G.	28	5.08	BWN	BWN	LGT	Shoemaker	Paris NY	Detroit MI	PVT	COM B 1st MI INF
Coberly, Isaac	19	5.10	BLK	BLK	FLD	Laborer	Virginia		PVT	COM F 1st MI INF
Coghlan, Daniel						Butcher		Detroit MI	1LT	Montgomery Guards
Cogswell, Henry	21	5.08	BLU	LGT	FIR	Cooper	Halifax CAN		PVT	COM K 6th US INF
Cole, Benjamin	20	5.11	BLU	LGT	FLD	Farmer	Wyoming Co NY	Niles MI	MUS	COM F 1st MI INF
Cole, Daniel	42	5.05	GRY	DRK	DRK	Farmer	Otsego Co NY	Adrian MI	PVT	COM F 1st MI INF
Cole, Niles	19	6.01	DRK	DRK	DRK	Farmer	Wyoming Co NY	Niles MI	PVT	COM F 1st MI INF
Coleman, Alexander B.	31	5.05	BLU	RED	RUD	Mason	Sussex Co NJ		PVT	COM G 15th US INF
Coleman, Harry B.	20								3CP	COM K 1st MI INF
Coleman, John M.	19	5.05	BLU	BWN	SDY	Laborer	Wayne Co NY	Kalamazoo MI	PVT	COM A 1st MI INF
Coleman, Oscar F.	20	5.05	BLU	BWN	DRK	Farmer	Wayne Co NY	Kalamazoo MI	PVT	COM A 1st MI INF
Collins, James	19	5.06	BLU	LGT	LGT	Gunsmith	New York State		MUS	Brady Guards
Collins, Jeddediah A.	32	4.09	GRY	BWN	FIR	Carpenter	Washington RI		PVT	COM B 3rd US INF
Collins, John	21	5.05	GRY	LGT	FIR	Laborer	Epsom ENG		PVT	COM B 3rd US INF
Combs, Cornelius R.	23	5.10	BLU	BWN	DRK	Farmer	Seneca Co NY		PVT	COM K 3rd US DRG
Comstock, Edwin	21	5.09	BWN	DRK	DRK	Farmer	Townfield NY		PVT	COM E 15th US INF
Comstock, Horace W.	20					Clerk	Lockport NY	Adrian MI	3CP	Adrian Guards
Comstock, Lorin L.	23	5.07	BLU	BWN	FLD	Merchant	Orleans Co NY	Adrian MI	2LT	COM K 1st MI INF
Conant, Charles O.	25	5.08	BLU	LGT	LGT		Pontiac MI	Pontiac MI	2LT	COM C 1st MI INF
Condon, Gustavus F.	20	6.03	GRY	BWN	LGT	Teamster	Jefferson Co NY	Kalamazoo MI	PVT	COM A 1st MI INF
Condon, Robert	29	5.07	BLK	BWN	DRK	Furnaceman	Detroit MI	Detroit MI	PVT	Brady Guards

ENROLLED	MUSTERED	DISCHARGED	REMARKS
11/15/47 Marshall MI	12/01/47 Detroit MI		Left sick at Detroit MI 02/08/48. Died 02/12/48
11/20/47 Toledo OH	12/04/47 Detroit MI	07/18/48 Detroit MI	
11/15/47 Niles MI	12/02/47 Detroit MI		Deserted at Detroit MI 12/16/47
			PMT 1LT 04/18/47 for gallantry. MNI Boynton
			Master on Brig Hecla from 02/22/47. PEN. MNI Mellen
11/02/47 Port Huron MI	11/12/47 Detroit MI	07/26/48 Detroit MI	Died at Detroit MI 08/27/48
11/15/47 Blissfield MI	12/02/47 Detroit MI		Deserted at Detroit MI 12/23/47
05/28/46 Detroit MI			VTS WNA
01/07/48 Detroit MI	Detroit MI		Deserted 05/24/48
11/15/47 Niles MI	12/02/48 Detroit MI	07/28/48 Detroit MI	Fifer. LIH at Vera Cruz MEX 02/01/48
11/15/47 Adrian MI	12/02/47 Detroit MI	02/04/48 Vera Cruz MEX	Discharged for disability. Received pension
11/15/47 Niles MI	12/02/47 Detroit MI	07/28/48 Detroit MI	Received pension
04/15/47 Detroit MI	04/30/47 Detroit MI	08/04/48 Covington KY	Received pension
01/20/48 West Unity OH	02/01/48 Detroit MI		DES at Sandusky OH 02/16/48. Forename may be Henry
11/05/47 Kalamazoo MI	11/19/47 Detroit MI	07/18/48 Detroit MI	Received pension
11/05/47 Kalamazoo MI	11/19/47 Detroit MI	07/18/48 Detroit MI	Received pension
06/07/47 Detroit MI	06/18/47 Detroit MI		Drummer. Deserted at Fort Mackinac MI 11/16/47
03/27/47 Detroit MI	03/27/47 Detroit MI		Died at Mexico City MEX 01/09/48. PEN
03/25/47 Detroit MI	03/25/47 Detroit MI		PMT CPL 10/01/47. Deserted 12/15/47
04/07/47 Tecumseh MI	04/22/47 Detroit MI		KIA in fight with guerillas near Papa Vegas 06/06/47
04/29/47 Detroit MI	04/29/47 Detroit MI	08/06/48 Cincinnati OH	Received pension
06/01/46 Adrian MI			VTS WNA
10/30/47 Adrian MI	01/20/47 Detroit MI	07/28/48 Detroit MI	PEN
12/01/47 Pontiac MI	12/01/47 Detroit MI	07/26/48 Detroit MI	
11/05/47 Kalamazoo MI	11/19/47 Detroit MI	07/18/48 Detroit MI	Received pension
06/18/47 Detroit MI	06/18/47 Detroit MI	06/30/48 Detroit MI	

Michigan Men in the Mexican War

Name	Age	Hgt	Eye	Hair	Cpx	Trade	Born	Home	Rank	Unit
Cone, Harmon	18	5.06	BLU	FLX	FIR	Laborer	Orville VT	Southfield MI	PVT	COM G 15th US INF
Conklin, Oakley	21	5.09	BLU	BWN	DRK	Blacksmith	Sussex Co NJ		PVT	COM G 1st MI INF
Conklin, Richard	21	5.08	BLK	BWN	DRK	Farmer	Onondaga Co NY		PVT	COM K 3rd US DRG
Conkwright, James	38	5.10	BLU	BWN	DRK	Farmer	Rutland VT	Hastings MI	PVT	COM I 1st MI INF
Conley, Harvey	19	5.08	DRK	DRK	LGT	Farmer	Cayuga Co NY	Adamsville MI	PVT	COM F 1st MI INF
Conner, James	33	5.04	BLU	BWN	LGT	Laborer	Londonderry IRE		PVT	US Army
Connor, Peter	38	5.06	BLU	LGT	FIR	Soldier	Carlon IRE		PVT	COM A 6th US INF
Cook, Almond	21	5.09	LGT	LGT	LGT	Farmer	Madison OH		PVT	COM ? US MTD RIF
Cook, Darwin D.	24	5.08	DRK	BLK	DRK	Farmer	Hebron		3SG	COM K 1st MI INF
Cook, David L.	25	5.10	BLU	LGT	LGT	Cooper	Seneca Co NY		2CP	COM G 1st MI INF
Cook, Henry Jr.	23	5.10	DRK	DRK	DRK	Farmer	Westminster CAN	China TWP St. Clair Co	3SG	COM B 1st MI INF
Cook, James M.	21	5.09	BLU	AUB	LGT	Farmer	Guilderland NY		PVT	COM B 1st MI INF
Cook, John B.	21	5.07	HZL	SDY	LGT	Farmer	Orleans Co NY		PVT	COM F US MTD RIF
Cook, John H.	23	5.06	BLU	LGT	FLD	Farmer	Plattsburgh NY	Niles MI	PVT	COM E 15th US INF
Cook, Lorenzo D.	23	5.05	GRY	DRK	DRK	Farmer	Washington Co NY	Summit MI	PVT	COM G 1st MI INF
Cooley, Thomas M.	22			BLK		Lawyer	Attica NY	Tecumseh MI	1LT	NTH Lenawee VOL
Cools, Charles L.	30	5.09	GRY	BWN	LGT	Laborer	Brush BEL		PVT	COM A 6th US INF
Coon, Henry	20	6.00	GRY	BWN	FIR	Laborer	Neversink NY		PVT	COM E 15th US INF
Coon, William A.	22	6.03	GRY	BWN	FIR	Shoemaker	Sullivan Co NY	Coldwater MI	3SG	COM I 1st MI INF
Coon, William L.	20	5.06	BLU	SDY	FLD	Distiller	Oakland Co MI	Mottville MI	PVT	COM F 1st MI INF
Cooper, Caleb	23	5.04	BLU	BWN	FIR	Cooper		Pontiac MI	PVT	COM C 1st MI INF
Cooper, George A.	20	5.10	GRY	BWN	LGT	Farmer	Oneida Co NY		PVT	COM E 15th US INF
Cooper, Horace	18	5.08	BLU	BWN	LGT	Farmer	Chazy? NY	Hillsdale MI	PVT	COM H 1st MI INF
Cooper, Ira A.	22	6.00	BLU	AUB	FIR	Farmer	Sharon VT		PVT	BTY I 1st US ART
Cooper, John D.	26	5.07	BLK	BLK	FIR	Blacksmith	Onondaga Co NY	Milford MI	PVT	COM C 1st MI INF
Cooper, Joseph	21	5.08	BLU	LGT	LGT	Laborer	Cayuga Co NY	Detroit MI	PVT	COM E 1st MI INF

ENROLLED	MUSTERED	DISCHARGED	REMARKS
04/21/47 Detroit MI	04/30/47 Detroit MI	08/04/48 Covington KY	
02/20/48 Centreville MI	03/01/48 Detroit MI	07/18/48 Detroit MI	STH at New Orleans LA from Vera Cruz 06/05/48. PEN
04/06/47 Tecumseh MI	04/22/47 Detroit MI	06/31/48 Jefferson BKS MO	TRA COM C 01/04/48. PEN
11/15/47 Hastings MI	12/01/47 Detroit MI	07/18/48 Detroit MI	
11/15/47 Niles MI	12/02/47 Detroit MI	07/28/48 Detroit MI	Received pension
05/14/47 Detroit MI	Detroit MI		Deserted 06/15/47
08/18/46 Detroit MI	08/18/46 Detroit MI	06/27/48 New Orleans LA	WIA battle of Mexico City 08/27/47. DFD
06/23/47 Kalamazoo MI	06/23/47 Kalamazoo MI		Deserted at Kalamazoo MI 07/04/47
11/15/47 Ann Arbor MI	01/20/48 Detroit MI	07/28/48 Detroit MI	Received pension
01/25/48 Battle Creek MI	02/01/48 Detroit MI		Lost overboard in the Gulf of Mexico 06/19/48
11/02/47 Port Huron MI	11/12/47 Detroit MI		Died at Cordova MEX of diarrhea 04/29/48
11/02/47 Port Huron MI	11/12/47 Detroit MI	07/26/48 Detroit MI	Received pension
07/24/47 Kalamazoo MI	07/24/47 Kalamazoo MI	07/29/48 Jefferson BKS MO	Received pension
04/06/47 Niles MI	04/27/47 Detroit MI	08/06/48 Cincinnati OH	WIA battle of Churubusco MEX 08/20/47
01/20/48 Ann Arbor MI	02/01/48 Detroit MI	07/18/48 Detroit MI	Received pension
??/??/46 Tecumseh MI			VTS WNA. MNI McIntyre
08/07/46 Detroit MI	08/07/46 Detroit MI		Died at Puebla MEX 07/08/47
04/09/47 Fawn River MI	04/27/47 Detroit MI	08/06/48 Cincinnati OH	PMT 2CP 05/09/47. Reduced to ranks 12/26/47
11/15/47 Coldwater MI	12/01/47 Detroit MI	07/18/48 Detroit MI	
11/15/47 Niles MI	12/02/47 Detroit MI	07/28/48 Detroit MI	Received pension
01/01/48 Bellevue OH	01/01/48 Bellevue OH	07/26/48 Detroit MI	Received pension
04/09/47 Jackson MI	04/27/47 Detroit MI	08/06/48 Cincinnati OH	WIA 08/20/47. Received pension
11/20/47 Blissfield MI	12/01/47 Detroit MI	07/27/48 Detroit MI	Appointed musician 04/01/48
09/29/47 Detroit MI	Detroit MI	08/30/48 Governor's Isl. NY	
11/30/47 Milford MI	12/01/47 Detroit MI	07/26/48 Detroit MI	PEN
11/20/47 Ypsilanti MI	12/04/47 Detroit MI	07/18/48 Detroit MI	Received pension

Name	Age	Hgt	Eye	Hair	Cpx	Trade	Born	Home	Rank	Unit
Cooper, Joseph L.								Adrian MI	PVT	Adrian Guards
Copley, John J.	21	5.09	BLU	BWN	DRK	Farmer	Otsego Co NY		PVT	COM E 15th US INF
Corbus, James G.	21	5.09	GRY	BWN	DRK	Carpenter	Wayne Co MI		4CP	COM E 15th US INF
Corbus, Richard W.	21	5.05	BLU	LGT	LGT	Cooper	Wayne Co NY		PVT	COM E 15th US INF
Corbus, Samuel B.	18	5.06	BLU	SDY	FIR	Carpenter	Wayne Co MI		MUS	COM E 15th US INF
Corby, Wilson	23							Jackson MI	PVT	COM H 1st MI INF
Corey, Vincent P.	20	5.10	BLU	LGT	FLD	Laborer	Seneca Co NY	Detroit MI	PVT	COM E 1st MI INF
Cornell, Fitch	21	5.08	GRY	BWN	FIR	Farmer	Montgomery Co NY	Bronson MI	PVT	COM E 15th US INF
Cornwell, Henry B.	22	5.09	BLU	BWN	DRK	Clerk	Yates Co NY		PVT	COM K 3rd US DRG
Cortney, Henry	22	5.08	GRY	BWN	FLD	Farmer	Kilkenny IRE	Grand Rapids MI	PVT	COM E 1st MI INF
Cortright, Robert F.	26	5.11	BLU	DRK	DRK	Farmer	Orange Co NY		PVT	COM G 1st MI INF
Cottle, Simon	35	5.07	BLU	BWN	FIR	Farmer	England	Detroit MI	PVT	COM D 1st MI INF
Coughlan, Thomas								Detroit MI	PVT	Montgomery Guards
Covel, Emerson G.	38							Detroit MI	ENA	USS Mississippi
Cox, Francis A.	18	5.05	BLU	DRK	LGT	Farmer	Kingston CAN		PVT	COM G 1st MI INF
Cox, Ludlow	20	5.10	BLK	DRK	DRK	Farmer	Oakland Co MI		PVT	COM E 15th US INF
Craig, Robert	27	5.10	BLU	BWN	FIR	Farmer	Ireland		PVT	COM K 1st MI INF
Cramer, Walter	21	5.10	BLU	BLK	DRK	Farmer	Canada	Kalamazoo MI	PVT	COM A 1st MI INF
Crandall, Alanson W.	21	5.11	BLU	BWN	FIR	Cooper	Madison Co NY	Adrian MI	PVT	COM G 15th US INF
Crandall, Elisha D.	21	5.08	DRK	BWN	DRK	Clerk	New York State		PVT	COM K 6th US INF
Crane, Peter	27	5.09	GRY	DRK	LGT	Teamster	Sligo IRE	Port Huron MI	PVT	COM B 1st MI INF
Crane, Thomas D.	22	5.08	BLU	BWN	FIR	Farmer	Ohio		PVT	COM I 1st MI INF
Cress, Thompson H.	18	5.05	BLU	AUB	DRK	Farmer	Seneca Co NY	Liberty MI	PVT	COM B 1st MI INF
Cressy, Justus I.	18	5.06	GRY	RED	LGT	Printer	Livingston Co NY	Hillsdale MI	PVT	COM K 1st MI INF
Crider, Joseph C.	21	5.07	BLU	LGT	LGT	Laborer	Prattsburg NY		PVT	COM C 5th US INF
Cronk, James W.	45	6.00	BLU	BWN	LGT	Farmer	Livingston Co NY	Genesee Co MI	4SG	COM E 1st MI INF

Michigan Men in the Mexican War

Enrolled	Mustered	Discharged	Remarks
06/01/46 Adrian MI			VTS WNA
04/09/47 Niles MI	04/27/47 Detroit MI	08/03/48 Washington DC	Left sick at Cincinnati OH 05/18/47. PEN
04/19/47 Fawn River MI	04/27/47 Detroit MI	08/06/48 Cincinnati OH	PMT CPL 07/09/47. Received pension
04/26/47 Marshall MI	04/27/47 Detroit MI		WIA 08/20/47. Died at Mexico City 10/07/47
04/19/47 Fawn River MI	04/27/47 Detroit MI	08/06/48 Cincinnati OH	Received pension
11/20/47 Jackson MI	12/01/47 Detroit MI		Died of diarrhea at Cordova MEX 05/23/48
11/20/47 York MI	12/04/47 Detroit MI	07/18/48 Detroit MI	Received pension
04/19/47 Fawn River MI	04/27/47 Detroit MI	10/27/47 Chapultepec MEX	WIA 08/20/47. Discharged for disability. PEN
04/06/47 Detroit MI	04/22/47 Detroit MI	07/20/48	LIH Puebla MEX 08/07/47
11/20/47 Grand Rapids MI	12/04/47 Detroit MI	07/18/48 Detroit MI	Received pension
02/20/48 Sturgis MI	03/01/48 Detroit MI	07/18/48 Jefferson BKS MO	STH at New Orleans from Vera Cruz MEX 06/05/48. PEN
11/14/47 Detroit MI	11/14/47 Detroit MI	07/26/48 Detroit MI	PMT CPL 02/01/48
05/28/46 Detroit MI			VTS WNA
			Died at sea of yellow fever 12/28/47. PEN
01/20/48 Detroit MI	02/01/48 Detroit MI	07/18/48 Detroit MI	STH New Orleans LA from Vera Cruz MEX 06/05/48
04/17/47 Fawn River MI	04/27/47 Detroit MI		Died at Covington KY 07/23/48
11/15/47 Ypsilanti MI	12/01/47 Detroit MI		Deserted at Detroit MI 12/10/47
11/05/47 Kalamazoo MI	11/19/47 Detroit MI		Died at Cordova MEX 06/09/48
04/15/47 Adrian MI	04/30/47 Detroit MI		WIA 08/12/47. Died at Jalapa MEX 08/25/47
03/08/48 Detroit MI	Detroit MI	07/31/48 Jefferson BKS MO	
11/02/47 Port Huron MI	11/12/47 Detroit MI	07/26/48 Detroit MI	
01/24/48 Grand Rapids MI	02/01/48 Detroit MI		Died at Cordova MEX 06/12/48
11/02/47 Jackson MI	11/12/47 Detroit MI	07/26/48 Detroit MI	MNI Huey. PEN. AKA Thompson Kress
01/20/48 Adrian MI	02/01/48 Detroit MI	07/28/48 Detroit MI	PEN. AKA Justin S. Cressy
06/15/47 Detroit MI	Detroit MI	11/18/47 Perote MEX	PEN
11/20/47 Flint MI	12/04/47 Detroit MI		Died of diarrhea at Cordova 05/11/48. MNI Warner. PEN

Name	Age	Hgt	Eye	Hair	Cpx	Trade	Born	Home	Rank	Unit
Cronk, Norton	18	5.08	BLU	LGT	LGT	Farmer	Genesee Co MI		PVT	COM E 1st MI INF MI
Crosby, Derias	24	5.10	BLU	BWN	FIR	Farmer	Monroe Co NY	Pontiac MI	PVT	COM C 1st MI INF
Crosby, William	22	5.10	BLU	BWN	LGT	Cooper	Oswego Co NY		PVT	COM H 1st MI INF
Cross, Jonathan								Adrian MI	PVT	Adrian Guards
Crosswell, Charles M.	20					Carpenter	Newburg NY	Adrian MI	PVT	Adrian Guards
Crowe, Thomas	33	5.09	HZL	BWN	DRK	Laborer	Clare Co IRE		PVT	COM E 15th US INF
Crowfoot, Nathaniel L.	28	5.06	BLU	BWN	LGT	Cooper	Bristol NY		PVT	COM E 15th US INF
Crowley, Timothy Jr.	20	5.04	BLU	DRK	FIR	Laborer	Cork IRE		PVT	COM E 15th US INF
Cruice, Daniel	18	5.08	GRY	BWN	SDY	Printer	Ireland	Detroit MI	PVT	COM K 3rd US DRG
Crum, William	26	5.11	BLU	RED	LGT	Cooper	Manchester Co NY	Hillsdale MI	PVT	COM G 15th US INF
Crumpler, Thomas	26	5.06	BLU	LGT	LGT	Laborer	England		PVT	COM A 15th US INF
Cubichu, Charles	34	5.05	GRY	BLK	SAL	Laborer	Wayne Co MI		PVT	COM G 15th US INF
Culbrett, James	20	5.07	BLU	BWN	LGT	Miller	Madison Co NY		PVT	COM C 1st MI INF
Cumings, Hiram	19	5.08	BLK	BLK	FLD	Laborer	New York NY		RCT	COM K 6th US INF
Cumming, Thomas B.	19	5.07	BLK	BLK	DRK	Law Study	Monroe Co NY	Ann Arbor MI	2SG	COM A 1st MI INF
Cummings, Charles W.	25								2LT	COM F 1st MI INF
Cunningham, John	30	5.08	HZL	SDY	FIR	Painter	Cayuga Co NY	Detroit MI	1SG	COM E 15th US INF
Curl, Charles S.	21	5.07	GRY	BLK	LGT	Farmer	Brockport NY	Corunna MI	PVT	COM C 1st MI INF
Currant, William	28	5.06	BLU	LGT	FIR	Sailor	Falmouth ENG		PVT	COM B 5th US INF
Curtenius, Frederick W.	40	6.00	GRY	BWN	LGT	Farmer	New York NY	Kalamazoo MI	CAP	COM A 1st MI INF
Curtin, Joseph	24	5.05	BLU	BWN	LGT	Shoemaker	Ireland	Monroe MI	PVT	COM H 1st MI INF
Curtis, Sylvester	40	6.00	BLU	BWN	LGT	Hatter	Ontario Co NY	Detroit MI	MUS	Brady Guards
Cushing, Thomas	19	5.10	BLU	LGT	LGT	Farmer	Irondequoit NY		PVT	COM B 1st MI INF
Cuthbert, Elijah M.	22	5.05	BLU	LGT	LGT	Farmer	Vermont	Monroe MI	PVT	COM H 1st MI INF
Daily, George C.	28	5.10	BLU	BWN	FIR	Shoemaker	Lower Canada		PVT	COM K 3rd US DRG
Damm, John A.						Tavernkeep		Detroit MI	PVT	Scott Guards

Enrolled	Mustered	Discharged	Remarks
11/20/47 Saginaw MI	12/04/47 Detroit MI	04/26/48 Cordova MEX	Discharged on surgeon's certificate
11/30/47 Pontiac MI	12/01/47 Detroit MI	07/26/48 Detroit MI	
11/20/47	12/01/47 Detroit MI	07/27/48 Detroit MI	
06/01/46 Adrian MI			VTS WNA
06/01/46 Adrian MI			VTS WNA
04/26/47 Niles MI	04/27/47 Detroit MI	08/06/48 Cincinnati OH	
04/07/47 Fawn River MI	04/27/47 Detroit MI		Died at Cuernavaca MEX 05/17/48
04/14/47 Grand Rapids MI	04/27/47 Detroit MI	08/06/48 Cincinnati OH	
04/01/47 Detroit MI	04/22/47 Detroit MI		Died of disease at Mexico City 11/12/47
04/13/47 Adrian MI	04/30/47 Detroit MI	08/04/48 Covington KY	PEN
04/06/47 Pontiac MI	04/27/47 Detroit MI		TRA COM H 12/26/47. ODS Vera Cruz MEX 06/16/47
04/07/47 Detroit MI		04/20/48 Baton Rouge LA	DIS on surgeon's certificate of disability
11/30/47 Pontiac MI	12/01/47 Detroit MI	07/26/48 Detroit MI	
03/15/48 Detroit MI	03/15/48 Detroit MI		Deserted at Detroit MI 04/09/48
11/05/47 Grand Rapids MI	11/19/47 Detroit MI	04/26/48	DIS on being PMT LUT in 15th US INF. MNI Barnes
10/30/47 Niles MI	12/02/47 Detroit MI		Died of fever at New Orleans LA 01/25/48
04/02/47 Detroit MI	04/27/47 Detroit MI		Died of wounds at Churubusco MEX 08/24/47. PEN
11/30/47 Corunna MI	12/01/47 Detroit MI	07/26/48 Detroit MI	Received pension
11/01/47 Detroit MI	Detroit MI	08/01/48 East Pascagoula MS	DES at Vera Cruz 05/11/48. Rejoined COM 06/24/48
10/30/47 Kalamazoo MI	11/19/47 Detroit MI	07/18/48 Detroit MI	MNI William
11/20/47 Adrian MI	12/01/47 Detroit MI	07/27/48 Detroit MI	
06/18/47 Detroit MI	06/18/47 Detroit MI	06/30/48 Detroit MI	Fifer
11/02/47 Port Huron MI	11/12/47 Detroit MI		Deserted at Detroit MI 12/26/47
11/20/47 Monroe MI	12/01/47 Detroit MI		Deserted at Detroit MI 12/28/47
04/06/47 Tecumseh MI	04/22/47 Detroit MI	07/20/48	LIH Puebla MEX 08/07/47
06/03/46 Detroit MI			VTS WNA

Name	Age	Hgt	Eye	Hair	Cpx	Trade	Born	Home	Rank	Unit
Dance, Joseph	35	5.05	BLU	BWN	FLD	Farmer	Schenectady NY		PVT	COM K 1st MI INF
Danforth, Samuel	28	5.09	BLU	DRK	DRK	Sailor	Milo NY	Detroit MI	PVT	COM D 1st MI INF
Darby, James B.	21	5.11	GRY	FIR	FIR	Farmer	St Catherines		RCT	COM ? 3rd US DRG
Darindinger, Dorres	24	5.07	HZL	BWN	LGT	Farmer	Switzerland		PVT	COM K 1st MI INF
Darling, James M.	26	5.08	BLU	RED	RUD	Teacher	Orleans Co NY	Detroit MI	PVT	COM G 15th US INF
Darling, William	22	5.05	GRY	BWN	LGT	Farmer	Virginia	Detroit MI	PVT	COM E 1st MI INF
Davenport, John	20	5.09	BLK	LGT	LGT	Printer	Manchester NY		PVT	COM E 15th US INF
Davidson, Joseph B.	24	5.11	BWN	BWN	DRK	Farmer	Ridgebury PA		RCT	COM ? 3rd US DRG
Davidson, Simeon	41					Farmer	Lodi NY	Macon MI	4SG	NTH Lenawee VOL
Davis, Alexander W.	22	5.08	GRY	DRK	LGT	Laborer	Waterloo NY	Grand Blanc MI	PVT	COM A 15th US INF
Davis, Caleb F.	36	5.05	GRY	LGT	LGT	Painter	Roxbury MA	Detroit MI	2LT	Brady Guards
Davis, Charles H.	31								UNK	US Navy
Davis, David	34	5.10	HZL	BWN	DRK	Hosteler	Genesee Co NY		4SG	COM K 3rd US DRG
Davis, Delos									1LT	COM B 1st MI INF
Davis, Franklin	35	5.07	BLU	BWN	FIR	Stonecutter	Massachusetts		PVT	COM K 6th US INF
Davis, Franklin F.	38	5.08	BLU	DRK	RED	Engineer	Massachusetts		PVT	COM E 1st MI INF
Davis, Frederick S.	18	5.06	DRK	BWN	FLD	Farmer	Wayne Co NY	Adrian MI	PVT	COM H 1st MI INF
Davis, George								Adrian MI	PVT	Adrian Guards
Davis, Harry W.	22	5.11	BLK	BLK	FIR	Moulder	Oneida Co NY	Pontiac MI	3SG	COM C 1st MI INF
Davis, James H.	20	5.09	BLU	BWN	LGT	Farmer	Ontario Co NY		PVT	COM E 15th US INF
Davis, James J.									2LT	Truago Guards
Davis, Lewis	21	5.07	HZL	BWN	FIR	Butcher	Erie Co NY		PVT	COM A 6th US INF
Davis, Michael	22	5.08	BLK	BWN	LGT	Blacksmith	Canada	Buffalo NY?	PVT	COM H 1st MI INF
Davis, Samuel	28	6.00	BLU	BLK	DRK	Brickmaker	Ashtabula OH	Niles MI	PVT	COM F 1st MI INF
Davis, William	22	5.05	GRY	BWN	DRK	Farmer	Canada	Detroit MI	PVT	COM K 1st MI INF
Davison, Joseph H.	20	5.11	GRY	LGT	LGT	Farmer	Geneva NY		PVT	COM H US MTD RIF

Enrolled	Mustered	Discharged	Remarks
11/15/47 Saline MI	12/01/47 Detroit MI		Died at Cordova MEX 06/12/48. PEN
11/14/47 Detroit MI	11/14/47 Detroit MI	07/26/48 Detroit MI	
05/09/48 Detroit MI	Detroit MI		Died at Newport KY 07/17/48
11/15/47 Saline MI	12/01/47 Detroit MI	07/28/48 Detroit MI	Left sick at New Orleans LA 06/24/48
04/15/47 Detroit MI	04/30/47 Detroit MI	08/21/48	PEN
11/20/47 Saginaw MI	12/04/47 Detroit MI	07/18/48 Detroit MI	Received pension
04/08/47 Fawn River MI	04/27/47 Detroit MI	01/12/48 Chapultepec MEX	Discharged for disability
05/12/48 Detroit MI	Detroit MI	07/16/48 Jefferson BKS MO	Received pension
06/06/46 Tecumseh MI			VTS WNA
04/13/47 Pontiac MI	04/27/47 Detroit MI	11/25/47 Chapultepec MEX	WIA battle of Mexico City. DFD. PEN
06/18/47 Detroit MI	06/18/47 Detroit MI	06/30/48 Detroit MI	
01/28/47 Detroit MI	Norfolk VA		Served on USS Bainbridge
04/12/47 Detroit MI	04/22/47 Detroit MI	08/08/48 Jefferson BKS MO	TRA COM G 01/07/48
11/12/47 Detroit MI			RES at Detroit 12/47. SCU
03/07/48 Detroit MI	Detroit MI	07/28/48 Jefferson BKS MO	
11/20/47 Detroit MI	12/04/47 Detroit MI	12/24/47 Detroit MI	
11/20/47 Adrian MI	12/01/47 Detroit MI	12/28/47 Detroit MI	Discharged by writ of habeas corpus
06/01/46 Adrian MI			VTS WNA
11/30/47 Pontiac MI	12/01/47 Detroit MI	07/26/48 Detroit MI	PEN
04/16/47 Jackson MI	04/27/47 Detroit MI	08/06/48 Cincinnati OH	Received pension
??/??/46 Truago MI			VTS WNA
09/07/46 Detroit MI	09/07/46 Detroit MI		Died at Perote MEX 12/14/47
11/20/47 Monroe MI	12/01/47 Detroit MI	07/27/48 Detroit MI	
11/15/47 Niles MI	12/02/47 Detroit MI	07/28/48 Detroit MI	Left sick at Vera Cruz MEX 02/04/48
11/15/47 Detroit MI	12/01/47 Detroit MI	07/28/48 Detroit MI	
08/23/47 Kalamazoo MI	08/23/47 Kalamazoo MI	07/31/48 Jefferson BKS MO	PEN. AKA James S. Davidson

Name	Age	Hgt	Eye	Hair	Cpx	Trade	Born	Home	Rank	Unit
Davison, Richard	27	5.10	HZL	BWN	DRK	Lawyer	Cavan Co IRE		RCT	US Army
Dawson, Robert	24	5.09	GRY	BWN	DRK	Harness-maker	Cavan Co IRE		RCT	US Army
Day, James S.	18	6.00	DRK	BLK	DRK	Farmer	Genesee Co NY	Kalamazoo MI	PVT	COM A 1st MI INF
Day, Patrick	31	5.06	BLU	FIR	FIR	Soldier	Limerick Co IRE		PVT	COM A 6th US INF
Dayton, Orson	20	6.01	BWN	BWN	LGT	Farmer	Orange Co NY		PVT	COM G 1st MI INF
Dean, Alonzo	20	5.08	BLU	LGT	LGT	Mason	Brown NY		PVT	COM I 1st MI INF
Dean, Edwin D.	24	5.11	BWN	DRK	DRK	Farmer	Auburn NY		PVT	COM K 1st MI INF
Dean, Samuel C.	22	5.08	BLU	BWN	FIR	Mason	Brown NY	Bellevue OH	PVT	COM I 1st MI INF
Dean, Walter W.	30		BLK	DRK	DRK			Monroe MI	CAP	COM H 1st MI INF
Decker, George W.								Adrian MI	PVT	Adrian Guards
DeGrey, John	35	5.05	HZL	BLK	FIR	Cooper	Montreal CAN		PVT	COM B 3rd US INF
Deits, Martin L.	23	5.11	BLU	BWN	FIR	Farmer	Wayne Co NY		PVT	COM ? US MTD RIF
Deitz, Albert	22	5.04	BLU	AUB	DRK	Farmer	Webster NY		PVT	COM B 1st MI INF
Delong, Chandler	22	5.08	HZL	BWN	DRK	Laborer	Wayne Co NY		PVT	COM A 15th US INF
Delong, Charles	25	5.07	BLK	BWN	DRK	Laborer	Wayne Co NY		PVT	COM A 15th US INF
Deming, William C.	21	5.08	BLU	FLX	FIR	Farmer	Chautauqua Co NY		PVT	COM G 15th US INF
Dempsey, John	26	5.04	HZL	BWN	FIR	Laborer	Dublin IRE		PVT	COM B 3rd US INF
Deneke, Frederick								Detroit MI	PVT	Scott Guards
Denio, Erastus M.	22	5.07	BWN	DRK	RUD	Clerk	Monroe Co NY		4CP	COM K 3rd US DRG
Dennison, James P.	26	6.01	BLU	AUB	LGT	Miller	Chenango Co NY	Sturgis MI	3CP	COM G 1st MI INF
Densmore, Joseph	36	5.11	BLU	LGT	LGT	Laborer	Canada		PVT	COM K 1st MI INF
Depung, William H.	18	5.04	BLU	LGT	LGT	Blacksmith	Rochester NY	Howell MI	MUS	COM E 1st MI INF
DeShane, Francis	19	5.09	BWN	BLK	DRK	Painter	Detroit MI		PVT	COM A 1st MI INF
DeShriver, Joseph	43	5.09	BWN	GRY	LGT	Laborer	Belgium	Detroit MI	PVT	COM E 1st MI INF
DeSteirns, Joseph	19	5.09	DRK	LGT	FIR	Farmer	Erie Co OH		RCT	Montgomery Guards
Deuel, John C.	25	5.09	BLU	BWN	FIR	Lawyer	Saratoga NY	Marshall MI	1LT	COM G 1st MI INF

ENROLLED	MUSTERED	DISCHARGED	REMARKS
04/29/48 Detroit MI	Detroit MI		Deserted 05/04/48
04/29/48 Detroit MI	Detroit MI		Deserted 05/04/48
11/05/47 Kalamazoo MI	11/19/47 Detroit MI	07/18/48 Detroit MI	Received pension
10/24/46 Detroit MI	10/24/46 Detroit MI	10/24/51 Fort Ripley MN	PMT CPL 06/17/47. PMT SGT 09/01/48. PEN
02/20/48 Centreville MI	03/01/48 Detroit MI	07/18/48 Detroit MI	STH New Orleans LA from Vera Cruz MEX 06/05/48
11/15/47 Marshall MI	12/01/47 Detroit MI		Deserted at Detroit MI 01/01/48
10/10/47		05/20/48	LIH New Orleans. SCU by pension 21770. MNI David
02/16/48 Bellevue OH	02/29/48 New Orleans LA		DES Detroit. PEN for service with COM I 3rd OH INF
10/30/47 Monroe MI	12/01/47 Detroit MI	07/27/48 Detroit MI	
06/01/46 Adrian MI			VTS WNA
05/07/47 Detroit MI	Detroit MI	07/25/48 East Pascagoula MS	Received Pension
08/17/47 Kalamazoo MI	08/17/47 Kalamazoo MI		Died at Vera Cruz MEX 12/20/47. Duncan's COM. AKA Martin L. Deets
11/02/47 Jackson MI	11/12/47 Detroit MI	07/26/48 Detroit MI	Received pension. AKA Albert Diets
04/12/47 Ann Arbor MI	04/27/47 Detroit MI		Died of disease at Puebla MEX 07/28/47
04/14/47 Ann Arbor MI	04/27/47 Detroit MI	08/21/48	TRA COM B 12/26/47
04/15/47 Adrian MI	04/30/47 Detroit MI		PMT CPL 04/21/47. RTR 12/26/47. LIH Perote MEX
04/01/47 Detroit MI	04/01/47 Detroit MI		Died at Mexico City 09/25/47
06/03/46 Detroit MI			VTS WNA
04/22/47 Detroit MI	04/22/47 Detroit MI	08/08/48 Jefferson BKS MO	TRA COM G 01/04/48
02/20/48 Sturgis MI	03/01/48 Detroit MI	07/18/48 Detroit MI	
12/24/47 Ann Arbor MI	01/01/48 Detroit MI		Left sick at New Orleans LA 06/24/48
11/20/47 Howell MI	12/04/47 Detroit MI	07/18/48 Detroit MI	
11/05/47 Kalamazoo MI	11/19/47 Detroit MI	07/18/48 Detroit MI	AKA Francis O'Shane
11/20/47 Detroit MI	12/04/47 Detroit MI	01/07/48 New Orleans LA	Discharged on surgeon's certificate. PEN
10/27/47 Detroit MI			Company disbanded before muster
10/30/47 Marshall MI	12/01/47 Detroit MI	07/18/48 Detroit MI	Also lists occupation as EGN. PEN. AKA John C. Duel

Michigan Men in the Mexican War

Name	Age	Hgt	Eye	Hair	Cpx	Trade	Born	Home	Rank	Unit
Devally, Thomas	28	5.05	BLU	DRK	DRK	Laborer	Ireland		PVT	COM E 15th US INF
Devereaw, John								Adrian MI	PVT	Adrian Guards
Deville, George	23	5.05	HZL	BLK	LGT	Carpenter	Loraine FRA	Detroit MI	PVT	Brady Guards
Deville, John						Tailor		Detroit MI	PVT	Scott Guards
Dewey, Hiram	21	5.06	HZL	BWN	DRK	Farmer	Otsego Co? NY		RCT	US Army
Dickerson, Thomas	24	5.04	BLU	SDY	FLD	Farmer	Trumbull Co OH		PVT	COM H US MTD RIF
Dickinson, Clark	22		HZL	BWN	FIR	Distiller	Broome Co NY		PVT	COM G 15th US INF
Dickinson, Hiram Jr.	18	5.08	DRK	BLK	DRK	Laborer	Williamsburg MA	Detroit MI	PVT	COM K 1st MI INF
Dickinson, Hiram Sr.	44	5.08	BLU	GRY	LGT	Miller	Williamsburg MA	Detroit MI	2SG	COM K 1st MI INF
Diltz, Charles	23	5.07	BLU	FIR	FIR	Coachman	Delaware Co NY		PVT	COM K 3rd US DRG
Dimock, John A.	35	5.07	GRY	BWN	RUD	Laborer	Canada		PVT	COM K US MTD RIF
Dingman, Felix	23	5.11	BLU	AUB	DRK	Laborer	Montgomery Co NY		PVT	COM A 15th US INF
Dinnen, Richard	23	5.10	HZL	BWN	DRK	Farmer	Limerick IRE		PVT	COM E 1st MI INF
Disbrow, James Q.						Teacher		Adrian MI	PVT	Adrian Guards
Disbrow, Loren E.	18	5.06	BLK	BWN	FIR	Cooper	Waterford CAN	Elyria OH	PVT	COM I 1st MI INF
Disman, John	19	5.11	BLU	DRK	LGT	Laborer	Canada	Howard Co CAN	PVT	COM E 1st MI INF
Dix, James A.	20	5.06	HZL	BWN	DRK	Porter	Springwells MI	Detroit MI	PVT	Brady Guards
Dixon, John	32	5.08	BLU	BWN	FIR	Laborer	Monaghan IRE		PVT	COM A 6th US INF
Dodge, Charles G.	24	5.07	BLK	BLK	DRK	Carpenter	Madison Co NY		4CP	COM A 1st MI INF
Dodge, Nathaniel	20	5.10	GRY	LGT	LGT	Farmer	Broome Co NY		PVT	COM E 15th US INF
Donaldson, Jonathan	29	5.11	BLU	LGT	LGT	Joiner	Seneca Co NY		PVT	COM G 1st MI INF
Dooley, Patrick	32	5.09	HZL	BLK	LGT	Laborer	Ringsend IRE		PVT	COM I 5th US INF
Doremus, Peter	36	6.00	BLK	BWN	DRK	Blacksmith	Romulus NY		PVT	COM K 6th US INF
Dorrance, David P.	27	5.09	BLK	DRK	DRK	Carpenter	Bristol NY		PVT	COM K 1st MI INF
Dorrel, Charles	25	5.08	BLU	BLK	DRK	Sailor	Monroe MI	Dundee MI	PVT	COM H 1st MI INF
Dorrel, Stephen	20	5.08	BLU	BWN	LGT	Farmer	Monroe MI	Dundee MI	PVT	COM H 1st MI INF

Michigan Men in the Mexican War

ENROLLED	MUSTERED	DISCHARGED	REMARKS
04/06/47 Niles MI	04/27/47 Detroit MI		Died at Puebla MEX 07/27/47
06/01/46 Adrian MI			VTS WNA
06/18/47 Detroit MI	06/18/47 Detroit MI	06/30/48 Detroit MI	Received pension
06/03/46 Detroit MI			VTS WNA
02/02/48 Detroit MI	Detroit MI		
08/18/47 Kalamazoo MI	08/18/47 Kalamazoo MI	07/31/48 Jefferson BKS MO	AKA Thomas Dickinson
04/16/47 Adrian MI	04/30/47 Detroit MI		Died at Vera Cruz MEX of diarrhea 08/27/47
11/15/47 Detroit MI	12/01/47 Detroit MI	07/28/48 Detroit MI	
12/01/47 Detroit MI	01/20/48 Detroit MI	07/28/48 Detroit MI	Received pension
04/05/47 Detroit MI	04/22/47 Detroit MI	10/30/47	WIA Molino del Rey MEX 09/08/47. DFD. PEN
07/21/47 Otsego MI	07/21/47 Otsego MI	07/31/48 Jefferson BKS MO	
04/12/47 Ann Arbor MI	04/27/47 Detroit MI	08/04/48 Covington KY	TRA COM G 12/26/47. Received pension
11/20/47 Detroit MI	12/04/47 Detroit MI	12/24/47 Detroit MI	
06/01/46 Adrian MI			VTS WNA
02/16/48 Lower Sandusky	02/29/48 New Orleans LA	07/18/48 Detroit MI	Received bounty land
01/16/48 New Orleans LA	01/16/48 New Orleans LA	07/18/48 Detroit MI	
06/18/47 Detroit MI	06/18/47 Detroit MI	06/30/48 Detroit MI	Received pension
08/18/46 Detroit MI	08/18/46 Detroit MI		
11/05/47 Kalamazoo MI	11/19/47 Detroit MI	04/26/48 Cordova MEX	DSC for disability. Received pension
04/10/47 Jackson MI	04/27/47 Detroit MI	08/06/48 Cincinnati OH	
02/20/48 Saline MI	03/01/48 Detroit MI		Deserted at Detroit MI 04/12/48
05/18/47 Detroit MI	Detroit MI	08/01/48 East Pascagoula MS	
03/28/48 Detroit MI	Detroit MI	05/01/48 Newport KY	Rejected from service
11/15/47 Howell MI	12/01/47 Detroit MI		Deserted at Detroit MI 01/31/48
11/20/47 Monroe MI	12/01/47 Detroit MI		Died at Cordova MEX 05/25/48
11/20/47 Monroe MI	12/01/47 Detroit MI		Died at Jefferson BKS 07/25/48

NAME	AGE	HGT	EYE	HAIR	CPX	TRADE	BORN	HOME	RANK	UNIT
Dorris, Isaac G.	21	5.11	BLU	BWN	FIR	Farmer	Wayne Co NY	Blissfield MI	PVT	COM H 1st MI INF
Douglass, Eugene	18	5.11	DRK	BWN	DRK	Farmer	Orleans Co NY	Adrian MI	PVT	COM H 1st MI INF
Douglass, Thomas W.	21	5.08	BLU	SDY	FIR	Carpenter	Buffalo NY		RCT	US Army
Dow, James	23	5.10	BLU	BWN	FIR	Miller	Scotland		PVT	COM K 6th US INF
Dowells, George	22	5.10	BLK	BLK	DRK	Cabinet-maker	Wayne Co NY	Pontiac MI	PVT	COM C 1st MI INF
Dowlan, William								Detroit MI	PVT	Montgomery Guards
Downey, William J.	19	5.06	BLU	BWN	DRK	Seaman	Cork IRE	Detroit MI	PVT	COM A 1st MI INF
Downing, Richard	22	5.09	BLU	BWN	FIR	Laborer	Devonshire ENG		PVT	US Army Ordnance
Doyle, John	25	5.08	GRY	DRK	LGT	Laborer	Dublin IRE	Port Huron MI	PVT	COM B 1st MI INF
Doyle, Michael P.	19					Tailor?	Ireland	Detroit MI	2LT	COM G 15th US INF
Doyle, William H.	27	5.07	BLU	BWN	LGT	Printer	Detroit MI		PVT	COM A 15th US INF
Drake, Bronson	21	5.09	GRY	LGT	LGT				PVT	COM A 15th US INF
Drew, Delos	18						Cooperstown NY	Adrian MI	PVT	Adrian Guards
Drew, Israel	21	5.07	BLU	DRK	LGT	Farmer	Cattaraugus NY		PVT	COM G 15th US INF
Drew, Joshua C.	18	5.11	BLU	BWN	LGT	Stonecutter	Dundee MI	Dundee MI	PVT	COM H 1st MI INF
Driggs, Samuel E. Jr.	20	5.08	BLU	BWN	LGT	Butcher	Chenango? Co NY	Hillsdale MI	2CP	COM H 1st MI INF
Drown, Alfred H.	42	5.10	BLK	GRY	LGT	Cooper	Ontario Co NY		PVT	COM F 1st MI INF
Drum, James M.	21	5.11	BLK	BLK	FIR	Moulder	Oneida Co NY	Romeo MI	PVT	COM C 1st MI INF
Drum, Patrick	24	5.07	BLU	BWN	SDY	Farmer	Dublin IRE		PVT	COM K 3rd US DRG
Drummey, Michael								Detroit MI	PVT	Montgomery Guards
Duchane, Francis	19	5.07	BLK	BLK	DRK	Painter	Detroit MI	Detroit MI	PVT	Brady Guards
Duchane, John	18	5.07	BLK	BLK	DRK	Painter	Detroit MI	Detroit MI	PVT	Brady Guards
Dudley, William	33	5.06	BLU	SDY	SDY	Mason	New London CT		PVT	COM K 3rd US DRG
Duerr, Gotlieb						Tailor		Detroit MI	PVT	Scott Guards
Duffy, Thomas	32	5.09	BLU	SDY	LGT	Carpenter	Dover ENG		PVT	COM B 5th US INF
Duke, Michael	25	5.11	GRY	BWN	DRK	Laborer	Westmeath IRE		RCT	COM ? 3rd US DRG

ENROLLED	MUSTERED	DISCHARGED	REMARKS
11/20/47 Blissfield MI	12/01/47 Detroit MI		Died at Detroit MI 03/11/48. AKA Isaac G. Dorais
11/20/47 Adrian MI	12/01/47 Detroit MI		Deserted at Detroit MI 12/29/47
10/01/46 Detroit MI	10/01/46 Detroit MI		Deserted at Detroit MI 10/05/46
02/02/48 Detroit MI	Detroit MI		Died at Newport KY 04/28/48
11/30/47 Pontiac MI	12/01/47 Detroit MI	07/26/48 Detroit MI	
05/28/46 Detroit MI			VTS WNA
01/02/48 New Orleans LA	01/02/48 New Orleans LA	07/18/48 Detroit MI	MNI James
12/08/46 Detroit MI	Detroit MI		Artificer
11/02/47 Port Huron MI	11/12/47 Detroit MI	07/26/48 Detroit MI	
04/09/47 Detroit MI	04/09/47 Detroit MI		Died at Perote MEX of typhus 10/23/47. MNI Patrick
04/14/47 Pontiac MI	04/27/47 Detroit MI	05/01/47 Cincinnati OH	Discharged by board of inspectors
04/17/47 Utica MI	04/27/47 Detroit MI	05/01/47 Detroit MI	Discharged by civil authority
06/01/46 Adrian MI			VTS WNA
04/14/47 Monroe MI	04/30/47 Detroit MI	08/04/47 Covington KY	
11/20/47 Monroe MI	12/01/47 Detroit MI		Deserted at Detroit MI 01/12/48
11/20/47 Hillsdale MI	12/01/47 Detroit MI	07/27/48 Detroit MI	
11/15/47 Niles MI	12/02/47 Detroit MI	04/26/48 Cordova MEX	Discharged for disability. PEN
11/30/47 Romeo MI	12/01/47 Detroit MI	07/26/48 Detroit MI	
04/14/47 Detroit MI	04/22/47 Detroit MI	07/31/48 Jefferson BKS MO	TRA COM D 01/04/48
05/28/46 Detroit MI			VTS WNA
06/18/47 Detroit MI	06/18/47 Detroit MI	06/30/48 Detroit MI	
06/10/47 Detroit MI	06/18/47 Detroit MI	06/30/48 Detroit MI	
03/25/47 Detroit MI	04/22/47 Detroit MI	07/31/48 Jefferson BKS MO	TRA COM D 01/04/48. Received pension
06/03/46 Detroit MI			VTS WNA
09/23/47 Detroit MI	Detroit MI		DES 10/09/47. Apprehended 11/10/47. DES 03/27/48
05/14/48 Detroit MI	Detroit MI		Deserted 07/??/48

Name	Age	Hgt	Eye	Hair	Cpx	Trade	Born	Home	Rank	Unit
Dulin, James	18	5.06	BLU	BWN	LGT	Laborer	Ireland	Kalamazoo MI	PVT	COM A 1st MI INF
Duncan, Henry		6.00	HZL	DRK	DRK	Harness-maker	Sault Ste Marie MI	Detroit MI	4CP	COM G 1st MI INF
Duncomb, William	18	5.05	BLU	BWN	LGT	Farmer	Saratoga Co NY		PVT	COM H 1st MI INF
Dunham, Sylvanus	31	5.08	GRY	BWN	LGT	Miller	Bradford PA		PVT	COM E 1st MI INF
Dunlap, Alexander	35	5.11	BLU	SDY	FIR	Farmer	Chittenden VT		PVT	COM H 1st MI INF
Dunlavy, James	24	5.06	DRK	BWN	DRK	Farmer	Ireland	Palmyra MI	PVT	COM H 1st MI INF
Dunn, John	30	5.08	GRY	BLK	RUD	Fifer	Kildare IRE		PVT	COM B 3rd US INF
Dunning, John	35	5.06	GRY	BWN	LGT	Musician	Miorllwek ENG		MUS	US Army
Durell, Charles	21	5.07	DRK	BLK	LGT	Chairmaker	Detroit MI	Sault Ste Marie MI	PVT	Brady Guards
Dutton, David R.	22	5.06	BLU	BWN	FLD	Farmer	Madison Co NY	Marshall MI	PVT	COM I 1st MI INF
Duvalier, John	38	5.06	BLK	GRY	DRK	Painter	Paris FRA	Niles MI	PVT	COM F 1st MI INF
Eagan, William	22	5.10	HZL	BWN	DRK	Farmer	Ireland		PVT	COM K 3rd US DRG
Eames, William L.	18	5.09	BLU	BLK	DRK	Farmer	Jefferson Co NY		PVT	COM A 1st MI INF
Earl, Enoch T.	35	5.08	HZL	BLK	DRK	Painter	Romulus NY	Oakland MI	PVT	COM F 1st MI INF
Earl, John G.	41	5.08	BLU	LGT	DRK	Laborer	Montgomery Co NY	Niles MI	3CP	COM F 1st MI INF
Eastman, Ahira G.	41					Lawyer	Vermont	Adrian MI	2LT	COM G 15th US INF
Eaton, Dan	18	5.10	GRY	RED	LGT	Shoemaker	Howland OH		PVT	COM K 1st MI INF
Eaton, Orrin D.	18	5.11	BLU	BWN	LGT	Farmer	Monroe MI	Monroe MI	PVT	COM H 1st MI INF
Ebenbeck, Louis	22	5.06	BWN	BLK	DRK	Shoemaker	Germany	Maumee OH	PVT	COM E 1st MI INF
Eberling, Joseph	36	5.06	BLU	SDY	LGT	Papermaker	Germany	Milwaukee WI	PVT	COM F 1st MI INF
Eberstein, George						Shoemaker		Detroit MI	4SG	Scott Guards
Eddy, Charles	22	5.10	BLU	BWN	LGT	Shoemaker	Wayne Co NY		PVT	COM E 15th US INF
Eddy, Oliver	30	5.10	BLU	BWN	SDY	Farmer	Tyrone IRE	Kalamazoo MI	PVT	COM A 1st MI INF
Edgarton, Charles E.	21	5.11	BLK	LGT	LGT	Clerk	Madison Co NY		1SG	COM B 1st MI INF
Edmunds, Andrew	18	5.07	GRY	BWN	FIR	Farmer	Upper Canada		PVT	COM I 1st MI INF
Edmunds, Ansel W.	22	6.03	BLK	BWN	DRK	Blacksmith	Essex NY	Coldwater MI	PVT	COM I 1st MI INF

Enrolled	Mustered	Discharged	Remarks
11/05/47 Detroit MI	11/19/47 Detroit MI	07/18/48 Detroit MI	
02/20/48 Canandaigua MI	03/01/48 Detroit MI	07/18/48 Detroit MI	PEN
11/20/47 Tecumseh MI	12/01/47 Detroit MI	07/27/48 Detroit MI	Received pension
11/20/47 Jackson MI	12/04/47 Detroit MI	07/18/48 Detroit MI	PEN
11/20/47 Adrian MI	12/01/47 Detroit MI		Died on canal boat 07/12/48
11/20/47 Palmyra MI	12/01/47 Detroit MI		Deserted at Detroit MI 01/14/48
03/24/47 Detroit MI	03/24/47 Detroit MI	07/25/48 East Pascagoula MS	
03/25/47 Detroit MI	03/25/47 Detroit MI	06/26/48 Newport BKS KY	
06/18/47 Detroit MI	06/18/47 Detroit MI	06/30/48 Detroit MI	
11/15/47 Marshall MI	12/01/47 Detroit MI	07/18/48 Detroit MI	PEN
11/15/47 Niles MI	12/02/47 Detroit MI		Left sick at Jefferson Barracks MO 07/07/48
04/07/47 Detroit MI	04/22/47 Detroit MI	07/31/48 Jefferson BKS MO	TRA COM C 01/04/48
11/05/47 Kalamazoo MI	11/19/47 Detroit MI	03/10/48 Vera Cruz MEX	Discharged on surgeon's certificate of disability
11/15/47 Niles MI	12/02/47 Detroit MI		Died at Cordova MEX 06/05/48
11/15/47 Niles MI	12/02/47 Detroit MI	07/28/48 Detroit MI	PEN
03/02/47 Adrian MI	04/09/47 Detroit MI	05/31/47	Resigned 05/31/47. Received pension
01/20/48 West Unity OH	02/01/48 Detroit MI	07/28/48 Detroit MI	
11/20/47 Monroe MI	12/01/47 Detroit MI	07/27/48 Detroit MI	PEN
11/20/47 Perrysburg OH	12/04/47 Detroit MI	07/18/48 Detroit MI	STH Vera Cruz 02/06/48. Joined COM at Cordova 02/22/48
11/15/47 Niles MI	12/02/47 Detroit MI	07/28/48 Detroit MI	Received pension. AKA Joseph Ebling
06/03/46 Detroit MI			VTS WNA
04/07/47 Jackson MI	04/27/47 Detroit MI		PMT 4CP 05/09/47. DES at Cincinnati OH 05/17/47
11/05/47 Kalamazoo MI	11/19/47 Detroit MI	07/18/48 Detroit MI	
11/02/47 Port Huron MI	11/12/47 Detroit MI	07/26/48 Detroit MI	
11/15/47 Marshall MI	12/01/47 Detroit MI		Deserted at Detroit MI 12/21/47
11/15/47 Marshall MI	12/01/47 Detroit MI	07/18/48 Detroit MI	

Name	Age	Hgt	Eye	Hair	Cpx	Trade	Born	Home	Rank	Unit
Edmunds, Oliver P.	19	5.09	BLK	BWN	DRK	Blacksmith	Norfolk CAN	Marshall MI	PVT	COM I 1st MI INF
Ellis, Avery	25	5.08	BLU	BLK	DRK	Blacksmith	Yates Co NY		PVT	COM K 3rd US DRG
Ellis, Commodore D.	21	5.09	BLU	BWN	WHT	Farmer	Yates Co NY		PVT	COM K 3rd US DRG
Ellis, William	23	5.07	BLU	BWN	DRK	Farmer	Yates Co NY		PVT	COM K 3rd US DRG
Ellis, William	26	5.10	BLK	DRK	DRK	Laborer	Cambridge VT	Detroit MI	PVT	COM D 1st MI INF
Ellsworth, George W.	23	5.08	BLU	DRK	FIR	Farmer	Rensselaer Co NY		PVT	COM E 15th US INF
Elmer, Elliot	18	5.05	HZL	BWN	LGT	Laborer	Bainbridge NY		PVT	COM B 3rd US INF
Else, Henry						Tailor		Detroit MI	PVT	Scott Guards
Elsworth, Joseph	45	5.07	GRY	GRY	FIR	Bootmaker	Sussex Co NJ		RCT	Montgomery Guards
Elwell, Isaac N.	21	5.10	BLU	LGT	RUD	Farmer	Genesee Co NY		PVT	COM ? US MTD RIF
Enders, Casper	34	5.08	BLU	LGT	LGT	Cabinet-maker	Liebenstein GER	Detroit MI	PVT	Brady Guards
Englehardt, Peter	34	5.05	GRY	GRY	FIR	Laborer	Bavaria GER	Detroit MI	PVT	COM G 15th US INF
Engler, Louis	44	5.08	BLU	DRK	DRK	Laborer	England	Detroit MI	PVT	COM B 1st MI INF
Erd, John								Detroit MI	1CP	Scott Guards
Erwin, William P.	25	5.05	GRY	DRK	FIR	Wheel-wright	Ontario Co NY		PVT	COM E 15th US INF
Esty, George	22	5.09	BLU	BWN	FIR	Laborer	Chautauqua Co NY	Grand Rapids MI	PVT	COM I 1st MI INF
Eton, Henry E.	25	5.09	BLU	BWN	FIR	Clerk	Clare IRE		RCT	US Army
Evans, Charles	23	5.10	HZL	BWN	FIR	Farmer	Franklin Co NY	Marshall MI	PVT	COM I 1st MI INF
Eveland, John H.	30	5.07	BLU	BWN	LGT	Joiner	London CAN		PVT	COM D 1st MI INF
Everard, Francis	34	5.07	GRY	BWN	FLD	Miller	Suffolk ENG	Detroit MI	PVT	Brady Guards
Everett, Hiram	24	5.10	BLU	BLK	DRK	Farmer	Hunterdon Co NJ	Kalamazoo MI	CPL	COM A 1st MI INF
Fargo, John	23	5.09	BLU	LGT	FIR	Lawyer	Madison Co NY		PVT	COM I 1st MI INF
Fargo, Richard M.	24	5.10	BLU	BWN	FIR	Carpenter	Madison Co NY		PVT	COM I 1st MI INF
Fay, Nicholas	26	5.06	GRY	SDY	SDY	Barber	Bavaria GER	Detroit MI	PVT	COM D 1st MI INF
Feeter, John	20	5.04	HZL	DRK	LGT	Tailor	Hesse GER	Detroit MI	PVT	COM C 1st MI INF
Feldburgh, John F.	19	5.08	BLU	LGT	FIR	Clerk	New York NY		PVT	COM E 1st MI INF

ENROLLED	MUSTERED	DISCHARGED	REMARKS
11/15/47 Marshall MI	12/01/47 Detroit MI	07/18/48 Detroit MI	
04/05/47 Tecumseh MI	04/22/47 Detroit MI		Died of disease at Mexico City 09/24/47
04/05/47 Tecumseh MI	04/22/47 Detroit MI		Left sick in hospital at Vera Cruz MEX 06/03/47
04/06/47 Tecumseh MI	04/22/47 Detroit MI	07/31/48 Jefferson BKS MO	TRA COM C 01/04/48. Received pension
11/14/47 Detroit MI	11/14/47 Detroit MI	07/26/48 Detroit MI	Received pension
04/22/47 Grand Rapids MI	04/27/47 Detroit MI	08/06/48 Cincinnati OH	
03/09/47 Detroit MI	03/09/47 Detroit MI	07/25/48 East Pascagoula MS	AKA Elmer Elliot
06/03/46 Detroit MI			VTS WNA
11/04/47 Detroit MI			Company disbanded before muster
07/18/47 Kalamazoo MI	07/18/47 Kalamazoo MI	02/19/48 Vera Cruz MEX	Discharged for disability
06/18/47 Detroit MI	06/18/47 Detroit MI	06/30/48 Detroit MI	
04/21/47 Detroit MI	04/30/47 Detroit MI	08/04/48 Covington KY	
12/23/47 Detroit MI	12/31/47 Detroit MI	07/26/48 Detroit MI	
06/03/46 Detroit MI			VTS WNA
04/19/47 Fawn River MI	04/27/47 Detroit MI	08/06/48 Cincinnati OH	Served as waiter to CAP Toll 09/26/47–10/27/47
01/24/48 Tallmadge MI	02/01/48 Detroit MI	07/18/48 Detroit MI	
06/03/48 Detroit MI	Detroit MI	06/26/48 Newport KY	
11/15/47 Marshall MI	12/01/47 Detroit MI		STH at New Orleans LA 06/24/48. Died 06/26/48
11/14/47 Ypsilanti MI	11/14/47 Detroit MI		Died at Detroit MI 07/17/48. PEN
06/18/47 Detroit MI	06/18/47 Detroit MI	06/30/48 Detroit MI	
11/05/47 Kalamazoo MI	11/19/47 Detroit MI	07/18/48 Detroit MI	PMT 3SG 01/01/48. PMT 2SG 02/02/48. PEN
11/15/47 Grand Rapids MI	12/01/47 Detroit MI		Deserted at Detroit MI 02/06/48
11/15/47 Grand Rapids MI	12/01/47 Detroit MI		Deserted at Detroit MI 02/06/48
11/14/47 Detroit MI	11/14/47 Detroit MI	07/26/48 Detroit MI	
10/30/47 Detroit MI	10/30/47 Detroit MI	07/26/48 Detroit MI	STH at Vera Cruz 02/05/48 with wife as laundress
11/20/47 Detroit MI	12/04/47 Detroit MI	07/18/48 Detroit MI	Left sick in hospital at Vera Cruz MEX 05/05/48

Name	Age	Hgt	Eye	Hair	Cpx	Trade	Born	Home	Rank	Unit
Fentre, John	20	5.05	HZL	DRK	LGT		Germany		PVT	COM B 1st MI INF
Ferier, Nelson	31	5.08	GRY	BWN	DRK	Laborer	Orange Co NY		RCT	US Army
Ferris, Lewis	34	6.00	BLU	BWN	LGT	Laborer	Dutchess Co NY		RCT	US Army
Field, Christopher	36	6.00	BLU	GRY	LGT	Farmer	Monroe Co NY	Clinton MI	PVT	COM H 1st MI INF
Fields, William D.								Adrian MI	PVT	Adrian Guards
Finch, Samuel	40	5.10	BLU	BLK	LGT	Farmer	Cayuga Co NY		PVT	COM E 1st MI INF
Fineughty, John	27	5.08	GRY	BLK	FIR	Tailor	Galway IRE		PVT	COM A 6th US INF
Fink, Valentine	23	5.05	GRY	LGT	LGT	Carpenter	Germany	Perrysburg OH	PVT	COM E 1st MI INF
Fish, Hiram	22	5.07	BLU	LGT	LGT	Farmer	Cattaraugus NY		PVT	COM A 1st MI INF
Fish, Isaac J.	26	5.08	GRY	BWN	LGT	Teamster	Wayne Co OH	Toledo OH	PVT	COM H 1st MI INF
Fisher, Adam	21								PVT	COM D 1st MI INF
Fisher, Daniel	31	5.08	BLK	BLK	DRK	Tailor	Northampton PA	Kalamazoo MI	PVT	COM A 1st MI INF
Fisher, James	26	5.06				Laborer	Ireland		PVT	COM F 1st MI INF
Fisk, David J.	20	5.08	BLU	BWN	LGT	Farmer	Allegany Co NY		PVT	COM ? 15th US INF
Fisk, Leander	27	5.07	BLU	BWN	DRK	Clerk	Windham Co CT	Clinton MI	PVT	COM H 1st MI INF
Fitch, James	28	5.05	GRY	SDY	FIR	Farmer	Loud IRE	Monroe MI	PVT	COM G 15th US INF
Fitsimmons, Michael	23	5.07	HZL	BWN	DRK	Sailor	South IRE		RCT	COM ? 3rd US DRG
Fitzgerald, Leonard O.	19	5.00	HZL	BWN	SDY	Farmer	Ontario Co NY		PVT	COM A 1st MI INF
Fitzgerald, Michael	27	5.07	BLU	BWN	SDY	Cooper	Ireland		PVT	COM K 3rd US DRG
Fitzgerald, Patrick	25	5.07	BLU	BWN	LGT	Laborer	Limerick IRE		PVT	US Army
Fitzmorris, Patrick								Detroit MI	PVT	Montgomery Guards
Fitzpatrick, Thomas								Detroit MI	PVT	Montgomery Guards
Fitzpatrick, William								Detroit MI	PVT	Montgomery Guards
Flanagan, Hugh						Shoemaker		Detroit MI	1CP	Montgomery Guards
Flanders, Francis Jr.	27	5.04	BLK	BWN	DRK	Student	Coos NH		2SG	COM E 15th US INF
Fleming, Thomas T.	27	5.08	BLU	LGT	LGT	Farmer	Monmouth NJ	Edwardsburg MI	PVT	COM F 1st MI INF

Michigan Men in the Mexican War

Enrolled	Mustered	Discharged	Remarks
11/02/47 Port Huron MI	11/12/47 Detroit MI	07/26/48 Detroit MI	AKA Fenter. In hospital at Vera Cruz 02/48. PEN
04/12/48 Detroit MI	Detroit MI	06/20/48 Newport KY	
04/12/48 Detroit MI	Detroit MI		Died at Detroit MI 05/15/48. PEN. RBL
11/20/47 Clinton MI	12/01/47 Detroit MI	07/27/48 Detroit MI	PEN
06/01/46 Adrian MI			VTS WNA
11/20/47 Detroit MI	12/04/47 Detroit MI		Died at Detroit MI 02/07/48
07/29/46 Detroit MI	07/29/46 Detroit MI		WIA at Molino del Rey MEX 09/08/47
11/20/47 Perrysburg OH	12/04/47 Detroit MI	07/18/48 Detroit MI	Received pension
11/05/47 Kalamazoo MI	11/19/47 Detroit MI		Deserted at Detroit MI 12/10/47
11/20/47 Toledo OH	12/01/47 Detroit MI	07/27/48 Detroit MI	Received pension
11/14/47 Detroit MI	11/14/47 Detroit MI		Deserted at New Orleans LA 01/18/48
11/05/47 Kalamazoo MI	11/19/47 Detroit MI	07/18/48 Detroit MI	Home on FUR 03/11/48. Rejoined COM 07/08/48. PEN
11/15/47 Niles MI	12/02/47 Detroit MI		Deserted at Detroit MI 02/05/48
04/19/47 Jackson MI			
11/20/47 Clinton MI	12/01/47 Detroit MI	07/27/48 Detroit MI	PMT QUS 04/01/48. Received pension
04/14/47 Monroe MI	04/30/47 Detroit MI	08/04/48 Covington KY	Received pension
05/10/48 Detroit MI	Detroit MI	07/16/48 Jefferson BKS MO	
11/05/47 Kalamazoo MI	11/19/47 Detroit MI	12/17/47 Detroit MI	Discharged by Judge Wilkins on account of his minority
04/14/47 Detroit MI	04/22/47 Detroit MI	07/31/48 Jefferson BKS MO	TRA COM D 01/04/48
05/24/47 Detroit MI	Detroit MI	08/02/47 Newport KY	Discharge by surgeon's certificate of disability
??/??/46 Detroit MI			VTS WNA
05/28/46 Detroit MI			VTS WNA
05/28/46 Detroit MI			VTS WNA
05/28/46 Detroit MI			VTS WNA
04/06/47 Fawn River MI	04/27/47 Detroit MI	08/21/48	PMT 1SG 05/09/47. PMT DMM 05/17/47
11/15/47 Niles MI	12/02/47 Detroit MI	07/07/48 New Orleans LA	Discharged for disability

Name	Age	Hgt	Eye	Hair	Cpx	Trade	Born	Home	Rank	Unit
Flint, George H.	36	5.07	BLU	GRY	LGT	Cooper	Ontario Co NY	Milford MI	PVT	COM C 1st MI INF
Flower, Cecil A.	21	6.01	BLU	SDY	LGT	Farmer	Erie PA		PVT	COM G US MTD RIF
Foley, Thomas	25	5.05	BLU	BWN	FIR	Laborer	Leatrim IRE		PVT	COM A 6th US INF
Foot, Charles D.	18	5.06	BLU	DRK	FLD	Cooper	Livingston Co NY		PVT	Brady Guards
Foot, Foster	22	5.11	BLU	BWN	LGT	Cooper	Livingston Co NY	Battle Creek MI	4SG	COM G 1st MI INF
Foot, Josiah	20	5.05	BLU	DRK	LGT	Laborer	Shelby NY		PVT	COM A 15th US INF
Forbes, Nicholas J.	23	5.06	GRY	BWN	FIR	Laborer	Madison Co NY		PVT	COM B 3rd US INF
Ford, John	19	5.08	BLU	LGT	LGT	Laborer	Byron NY		PVT	COM B 5th US INF
Ford, John	28	5.07	BLU	BWN	PAL	Laborer	Co May ENG	Detroit MI	PVT	COM G 15th US INF
Ford, John H.	28	5.09	GRY	BWN	FIR	Cooper	St. Clair NY	Detroit MI	4CP	COM C 1st MI INF
Ford, John T.	38	5.09	GRY	BWN	LGT	Mason	Jefferson Co NY		PVT	COM G 1st MI INF
Fordham, William	30	5.06	GRY	BWN	LGT	Carpenter	Batavia NY	Battle Creek MI	PVT	COM B 3rd US INF
Fordham, William	31	5.06	BLU	BWN	LGT	Carpenter	Batavia NY	Battle Creek MI	PVT	COM G 1st MI INF
Forseman, Joseph	31	6.01	BLU	SDY	FIR	Blacksmith	Lycoming Co PA	Cassopolis MI	PVT	COM F 1st MI INF
Forsyth, Russell	40	5.05	BLK	DRK	DRK	Farmer	Rensselaer Co NY	Pontiac MI	PVT	COM C 1st MI INF
Foster, John F.	32	6.00	BLU	LGT	LGT	Gardner	Rothaum IRE		PVT	COM G 15th US INF
Foster, John W.	21	5.07	GRY	BWN	FIR	Laborer	Madison Co NY		PVT	COM I 1st US ART
Foster, William F.	22	5.11	BLU	LGT	LGT	Boatman	Vergennes VT	Niles MI	PVT	COM F 1st MI INF
Fowler, John	19	5.09	BLU	DRK	LGT	Blacksmith	Boston MA		PVT	COM G 1st MI INF
Foy, Edward R.									RCT	COM ? 3rd US DRG
Frank, Nicholas								Adrian MI	PVT	Adrian Guards
Franklin, Benjamin	21	6.00	BLU	LGT	LGT	Laborer	Cheshire Co NH	White Pigeon MI	PVT	COM G 1st MI INF
Freeland, John P.	23	5.08	BLU	BWN	DRK	Joiner	Passaic NJ		4CP	COM E 1st MI INF
Freelon, Thomas W. Jr.	23	5.08	GRY	BWN	LGT	Lawyer	Norwich VT	Kalamazoo MI	1LT	COM E 15th US INF
Freeman, Edmund	18	5.06	HZL	BWN	DRK	Farmer	Livingston Co NY	Manchester MI	PVT	COM K 1st MI INF
Freeman, Warren	21	5.09	BLU	BWN	LGT	Farmer	Franklin Co VT		PVT	COM E 15th US INF

ENROLLED	MUSTERED	DISCHARGED	REMARKS
11/30/47 Milford MI	12/01/47 Detroit MI	07/26/48 Detroit MI	
08/24/47 Kalamazoo MI	08/24/47 Kalamazoo MI	07/31/48 Jefferson BKS MO	Received pension
08/24/46 Detroit MI	08/24/46 Detroit MI	08/28/48 Jefferson BKS MO	
06/18/47 Detroit MI	06/18/47 Detroit MI		Deserted at Detroit MI 06/21/47
01/25/48 Battle Creek MI	02/01/48 Detroit MI	07/18/48 Detroit MI	
04/12/47 Pontiac MI	04/27/47 Detroit MI	08/06/48 Cincinnati OH	TRA COM E 12/26/47
03/23/47 Detroit MI	03/23/47 Detroit MI		Died at Mexico City 11/23/47
03/12/47 Detroit MI	03/12/47 Detroit MI		LIH New Orleans LA 06/19/47. Died 10/20/47
04/08/47 Detroit MI	04/30/47 Detroit MI	07/28/48 Baton Rouge LA	Left sick in Mexico 02/01/48. RBL
11/30/47 Pontiac MI	12/01/47 Detroit MI	07/26/48 Detroit MI	Removed 12/23/47. Reappointed 01/01/48
02/20/48 Adrian MI	03/01/48 Detroit MI	07/18/48 Detroit MI	STH at New Orleans LA from Vera Cruz MEX 06/05/48
03/08/47 Detroit MI	03/08/47 Detroit MI	05/17/47 Newport KY	Rejected from US service. Joined COM G 1st MI INF
02/20/48 Jackson MI	03/01/48 Detroit MI	07/18/48 Detroit MI	
11/15/47 Niles MI	12/02/47 Detroit MI	07/28/48 Detroit MI	PMT CPL 01/19/48. Received pension
11/30/47 Pontiac MI	12/01/47 Detroit MI	07/26/48 Detroit MI	Received pension
04/06/47 Monroe MI	04/30/47 Detroit MI		Left sick at Perote MEX 10/06/47
08/23/47 Detroit MI	Detroit MI	08/30/48 Gov's Island NY	Received pension
11/15/47 Niles MI	12/02/47 Detroit MI	07/28/48 Detroit MI	
01/25/48 Battle Creek MI	02/01/48 Detroit MI		Died at Detroit MI 04/13/48
05/12/48 Detroit MI	Detroit MI	07/16/48 Jefferson BKS MO	
06/01/46 Adrian MI			VTS WNA
02/20/48 Constantine MI	03/01/48 Detroit MI	07/18/48 Detroit MI	AKA Benjamin F. Reed. Received pension
11/20/47 Detroit MI	12/04/47 Detroit MI	07/18/48 Detroit MI	LIH Vera Cruz MEX 05/05/48
03/02/47	04/09/47 Detroit MI	07/31/48	PMT CAP 09/13/47 for gallantry at Chapultepec. PEN
01/20/48 Grass Lake MI	02/01/48 Detroit MI	07/28/48 Detroit MI	
04/27/47 Jackson MI	04/27/47 Detroit MI		Died at Perote MEX 09/11/47

Name	Age	Hgt	Eye	Hair	Cpx	Trade	Born	Home	Rank	Unit
Freer, Allen J.	18	5.08	BLU	LGT	LGT	Farmer	Burlington VT		PVT	COM K 1st MI INF
French, Normon T.	18	5.07	HZL	BWN	DRK	Farmer	Bloomfield NY		RCT	US Army
French, Rensalaer H.	18	5.05	BLK	BWN	LGT	Farmer	Summit Co OH		PVT	COM E 15th US INF
Friend, John	36	5.10	HZL	DRK	DRK	Farmer	Kent Co ENG		PVT	COM G 1st MI INF
Fuler, John	21	5.05	HZL	DRK	LGT	Sailor	Germany		PVT	COM B 1st MI INF
Fuller, Dorr K.	21	5.11	BLU	DRK	LGT	Carpenter	Cayuga Co NY		PVT	COM A 15th US INF
Fuller, Isaac	19	5.08	HZL	DRK	LGT	Laborer	Ohio	Goshen IN	PVT	COM F 1st MI INF
Fuller, Joseph K.	44	5.08	BLU	BLK	DRK	Farmer	Broome Co NY	Kalamazoo MI	PVT	COM A 1st MI INF
Fuller, Timothy L.	21	5.08	BLU	RED	FLD	Farmer	Genesee Co NY		RCT	US Army
Fuller, William	30	5.10	HZL	DRK	DRK	Brewer	Devonshire ENG		PVT	COM G 1st MI INF
Fullerton, Cephas	18	5.10	BLU	LGT	LGT	Farmer	Yates Co NY	Dearborn MI	PVT	COM D 1st MI INF
Fullerton, Charles K.	18	5.07	GRY	SDY	LGT	Laborer	Bedford MI		PVT	COM G 15th US INF
Fullerton, Almonid	33	5.08	BLU	BWN	DRK	Bricklayer	Seneca Co NY		PVT	COM C 5th US INF
Fulson, John K.	18	5.07	BLU	LGT	LGT	Farmer	Brooklyn NY		PVT	COM A 1st MI INF
Funston, Lewis R.	18	5.06	BLU	BWN	LGT	Farmer	Detroit MI		PVT	COM C 1st MI INF
Gage, Morgan L.	40	5.09	GRY	LGT	LGT	Saddler	Troy NY	Detroit MI	CAP	Brady Guards
Gage, Nathan	19								PVT	COM E 1st MI INF
Galvin, Martin	30	5.09	GRY	BWN	LGT	Laborer	Kings Co IRE		PVT	COM A 6th US INF
Galway, John	24	5.07	BLU	LGT	LGT	Soldier	Cork IRE	Detroit MI	4CP	COM D 1st MI INF
Gardiner, Oliver P.	27	5.10	BLU	BWN	FIR	Mason	New York State	Grand Rapids MI	PVT	COM I 1st MI INF
Gardner, Job	27	5.10	BLK	DRK	DRK	Laborer	England		PVT	COM K 6th US INF
Gardner, Henry J.	23	5.05	BLU	DRK	LGT		Hampshire ENG	Detroit MI	PVT	COM B 1st MI INF
Garland, John S.	24	5.04	BLU	LGT	LGT	Soldier	Detroit MI		2LT	COM E 4th US ART
Garvick, John F.	22	5.09	HZL	FIR	LGT	Laborer	Baden GER		PVT	COM A 6th US INF
Gates, Elijah M.	23	5.07	GRY	BWN	FIR	Millwright	Berks Co PA	Adrian MI	PVT	COM G 15th US INF
Gates, Lucius	22	5.05	BLU	SDY	LGT	Farmer	Orleans Co NY	Clinton MI	PVT	COM H 1st MI INF

Enrolled	Mustered	Discharged	Remarks
12/24/47 Dryden MI	01/01/48 Detroit MI		Died at Detroit MI 01/17/48
05/13/48 Detroit MI	Detroit MI	06/30/48 Newport KY	Received pension
04/07/47 Jackson MI	04/27/47 Detroit MI		Died at Perote MEX 10/20/47. AKA Van Rensalaer
01/25/48 Grand Rapids MI	02/01/48 Detroit MI		Died at Vera Cruz MEX 06/07/48. PEN
11/02/47	11/12/47 Detroit MI	07/26/48 Detroit MI	
04/12/47 Pontiac MI	04/27/47 Detroit MI	08/03/48 Covington KY	WIA Mexico City 08/20/47. PMT CPL 11/08/47. PEN
11/15/47 Niles MI	12/02/47 Detroit MI		Died at Cordova MEX 06/19/48
11/05/47 Kalamazoo MI	11/19/47 Detroit MI		LIH New Orleans 06/24/48. Died 06/26/48. PEN
05/13/48 Detroit MI	Detroit MI	06/20/48 Newport KY	Received pension
02/20/48 Toledo OH	03/01/48 Detroit MI		Deserted at Detroit MI 04/10/48
11/14/47 Pontiac MI	11/14/47 Detroit MI	07/26/48 Detroit MI	
03/29/47 Detroit MI	04/30/47 Detroit MI	07/06/48 Vera Cruz MEX	Discharged for disability. PEN
05/20/47 Detroit MI	Detroit MI	Vera Cruz MEX	DES 05/22/47. Found 05/29/47. Died 09/21/47. PEN
11/05/47 Kalamazoo MI	11/19/47 Detroit MI		Deserted at New Orleans LA 06/24/48
11/30/47 Pontiac MI	12/01/47 Detroit MI		DES at Detroit MI 12/23/47. AKA Lewis R. Fenston
06/18/47 Detroit MI	06/18/47 Detroit MI	06/30/48 Detroit MI	Commanding at Fort Mackinac from 06/25/47. PEN
11/20/47 Coldwater MI	12/04/47 Detroit MI		Deserted at Detroit MI 12/24/47
11/30/46 Detroit MI	11/30/46 Detroit MI		
11/14/47 Detroit MI	11/14/47 Detroit MI	07/26/48 Detroit MI	Received pension
01/24/48 Plainfield MI	02/01/48 Detroit MI	07/18/48 Detroit MI	
02/26/48 Detroit MI	Detroit MI	07/28/48 Jefferson BKS MO	
11/02/47 Port Huron MI	11/12/47 Detroit MI	07/26/48 Detroit MI	
03/08/47 Philadelphia PA		11/29/61	PMT 1LT 05/20/49. PEN. MNI Spotswood
01/13/47 Detroit MI	Detroit MI		
04/13/47 Adrian MI	04/30/47 Detroit MI		Died of wounds at Jalapa MEX 09/04/47
11/20/47 Clinton MI	12/01/47 Detroit MI	07/27/48 Detroit MI	Received pension

Michigan Men in the Mexican War

Name	Age	Hgt	Eye	Hair	Cpx	Trade	Born	Home	Rank	Unit
Gaudry, Joseph	40	5.08	GRY	DRK	DRK	Carpenter	Montreal CAN	Detroit MI	PVT	COM D 1st MI INF
Geffels, Peter	21	5.05	BLU	BWN	LGT	Farmer	New York State		PVT	COM E 1st MI INF
George, Thomas	22	5.05	BLU	RED	LGT	Farmer	Ayrshire SCO		RCT	COM K 6th US INF
George, William	27	5.07	BLK	BLK	DRK	Laborer	Scotland		PVT	COM E 1st MI INF
Getzendaner, Gabriel	25	6.02	GRY	BLK	LGT	Joiner	Fayette Co PA	Pontiac MI	PVT	COM C 1st MI INF
Gibbs, John	30	5.09	BLU	BLK	LGT	Saddler	Schoharie Co NY		PVT	COM E 15th US INF
Giblin, Timothy	31	5.06	BLU	SDY	SDY	Laborer	Ireland	Detroit MI	PVT	COM F 1st MI INF
Gibson, Isaac	21	5.06	BLU	BWN	FIR	Wagon-maker	Ireland	Detroit MI	PVT	COM K 3rd US DRG
Gibson, William	27	5.06	BLU	BWN	FIR	Carpenter	Monaghan IRE	Detroit MI	PVT	COM K 3rd US DRG
Gies, Conrad								Detroit MI	PVT	Scott Guards
Gies, Paul								Detroit MI	PVT	Scott Guards
Gilbert, George								Detroit MI	PVT	Montgomery Guards
Gilbert, William	18	5.00	GRY	DRK	SDY	Farmer	Orleans Co NY	Pontiac MI	PVT	COM C 1st MI INF
Gilger, John	44	5.08	BLU	LGT	LGT	Farmer	Germany	Lower Sandusky OH	PVT	COM K 1st MI INF
Gillett, Eugene N. B.	18	5.05	GRY	BWN	FIR	Laborer	Springwater NY		RCT	US Army
Gillett, Hosea E.	19	5.09	DRK	BLK	DRK	Laborer	Sullivan Co NY		PVT	COM E 15th US INF
Gillman, Darwin	18	5.06	BLU	LGT	LGT	Farmer	Canada		PVT	COM D 1st MI INF
Gillman, Thomas P.	23								CPL	COM B 1st MI INF
Gillmore, Soloman	24	5.05	BLU	BWN	FIR	Farmer	Auburn NY	Branch Co MI	PVT	COM E 15th US INF
Gimple, Simon	34	5.09	BLU	BWN	SAL	Miller	Bavaria GER		PVT	COM G 15th US INF
Girand, Daniel Jr.	20	5.10	BLU	BWN	FIR	Professor	Stratford CT		PVT	COM C 1st MI INF
Gleason, James	21	5.08	HZL	LGT	LGT	Moulder	Yates Co NY	Mt Clemens MI	MUS	COM B 1st MI INF
Gleason, Moses	21	5.09	HZL	BWN	DRK	Laborer	Ft Covington VT		PVT	COM B 3rd US INF
Glevanz, Joseph	22	5.07	BLU	DRK	DRK	Laborer	Baden GER		PVT	COM G 15th US INF
Goetchius, Thomas C.	27							Almont MI	2LT	COM G 1st MI INF
Goetz, Joseph	32	5.07	GRY	DRK	DRK	Soldier	Bavaria GER		1SG	COM A 15th US INF

Enrolled	Mustered	Discharged	Remarks
11/14/47 Detroit MI	11/14/47 Detroit MI	07/26/48 Detroit MI	
11/20/47 Detroit MI	12/04/47 Detroit MI	12/24/47 Detroit MI	Discharged by civil authority for being a minor
11/17/47 Detroit MI	11/19/47 Detroit MI	07/23/48 East Pascagoula MS	Received pension
11/20/47 Detroit MI	12/04/47 Detroit MI	07/18/48 Detroit MI	
11/30/47 Pontiac MI	12/01/47 Detroit MI	07/26/48 Detroit MI	
04/08/47 Niles MI	04/27/47 Detroit MI	08/06/48 Cincinnati OH	
11/15/47 Detroit MI	12/02/47 Detroit MI	07/28/18 Detroit MI	AKA Timothy Gitelin
04/05/47 Detroit MI	04/22/47 Detroit MI	07/31/48 Jefferson BKS MO	TRA COM D 01/04/48. Received pension
04/10/47 Detroit MI	04/22/47 Detroit MI		KIA with guerillas at Neutin Nueva MEX 08/10/47. PEN
06/03/46 Detroit MI			VTS WNA
06/03/46 Detroit MI			VTS WNA
05/28/46 Detroit MI			VTS WNA
11/30/47 Pontiac MI	12/01/47 Detroit MI	07/26/48 Detroit MI	
02/29/48 New Orleans LA	02/29/48 New Orleans LA	07/28/48 Detroit MI	
05/01/48 Detroit MI	Detroit MI	06/17/48 Newport KY	Rejected from service
04/06/47 Fawn River MI	04/27/47 Detroit MI	08/06/48 Cincinnati OH	ODS in QUT Department at Vera Cruz 06/18/47–10/05/47
11/14/47 Detroit MI	11/14/47 Detroit MI		Deserted at Detroit MI 12/19/47
11/02/47 Port Huron MI	11/12/47 Detroit MI	02/25/48 Cordova MEX	Discharged on surgeon's certificate. PEN
04/07/47 Fawn River MI	04/27/47 Detroit MI		Died at Nopoluca MEX 06/08/48
04/08/47 Monroe MI	04/30/47 Detroit MI	08/04/48 Covington KY	Received pension
11/30/47 Pontiac MI	12/01/47 Detroit MI	07/26/48 Detroit MI	Left sick at Detroit MI 12/24/47
11/02/47 Port Huron MI	11/12/47 Detroit MI	07/26/48 Detroit MI	Received pension
03/19/47 Detroit MI	03/19/47 Detroit MI	07/31/48 East Pascagoula MS	
04/14/47 Monroe MI	04/30/47 Detroit MI	08/04/48 Covington KY	
10/30/47 Almont MI	12/01/47 Detroit MI	07/18/48 Detroit MI	
04/01/47 Detroit MI	04/22/47 Detroit MI	08/04/48 Cincinnati OH	TRA COM C 12/26/47

Name	Age	Hgt	Eye	Hair	Cpx	Trade	Born	Home	Rank	Unit
Goneirer, Conrad	28	5.05	GRY	BLK	LGT	Carpenter	Austria		PVT	COM D 1st MI INF
Goodman, John B.	25	5.11	BLU	BWN	DRK	Clerk	Philadelphia PA	Niles MI	2LT	COM E 15th US INF
Goodwin, Wheeler B.	22	5.10	BLU	BWN	LGT	Carpenter	Bloomfield NY	Pontiac MI	PVT	COM C 1st MI INF
Gooley, John L.	18								SEA	US Navy
Gordon, Michael	27	5.05	BLU	BLK	LGT	Harness-maker	London ENG		PVT	COM A 15th US INF
Gordon, Robert	18	5.09	GRY	BWN	DRK	Farmer	St. Johns SCO		RCT	COM ? 3rd US DRG
Gordon, Wesley	21	5.09	HZL	LGT	DRK	Farmer	Murray NY		PVT	COM E 15th US INF
Gore, Jacob								Detroit MI	PVT	Scott Guards
Gorton, Richard L.	33	5.05	HZL	DRK	DRK	Physician	Onondaga Co NY		PVT	COM B 3rd US INF
Gould, John G.	18	5.05	BLU	LGT	FIR	Laborer	New York State		PVT	COM B 1st MI INF
Gracel, Christian	27								PVT	COM E 1st MI INF
Graden, Benedict	25	5.04	BWN	BWN	FIR	Farmer	Sislam SWT		PVT	COM B 5th US INF
Graham, John	29	5.08	GRY	LGT	FIR	Farmer	Tyrone IRE		CPL	COM G 15th US INF
Granger, Gordon	25					Soldier	Joy NY	Detroit MI	2LT	COM ? US MTD RIF
Granger, Samuel	37	5.08	BLU	BWN	LGT	Farmer	Hadley MA		RCT	COM K 6th US INF
Grant, Daniel	19	5.08	BLU	YEL	FIR	Farmer	Glasgow SCO	Pittsfield MI	PVT	COM G 15th US INF
Graves, Benjamin T.	43	5.11	BLU	DRK	LGT	Farmer	Bennington Co VT		MUS	COM G 1st MI INF
Graves, William	20	5.05	BWN	GRY	LGT	Painter	Auburn NY	Detroit MI	PVT	Brady Guards
Gray, Edward	25	5.08	GRY	BWN	RUD	Farmer	Mayo Co IRE		CPL	COM K 3rd US DRG
Gray, James	19	6.00	BLU	DRK	DRK	Cooper	Erie PA		PVT	COM A 1st MI INF
Gray, William B.	27						Fairfield VA	Niles MI	2LT	COM F 1st MI INF
Green, Ira H.	18	5.02	BLU	BWN	FLD	Farmer	Canada	Detroit MI	PVT	COM K 1st MI INF
Green, Minord	23	5.06	BLU	LGT	LGT	Clerk	Westerlo NY		RCT	US Army
Gregory, Charles	35						Danbury CT	Jonesville MI	1LT	Governor's Guard
Greusel, Joseph						Shoemaker		Detroit MI	SGM	Scott Guards
Greusel, Nicholas Jr.	30	6.02	BLU	LGT	FIR	Clerk	Blieskastel GER	Detroit MI	CAP	COM D 1st MI INF

Enrolled	Mustered	Discharged	Remarks
11/14/47 Detroit MI	11/14/47 Detroit MI	07/26/48 Detroit MI	Received pension
03/02/47	04/09/47 Detroit MI		PMT 1LT 05/31/47. KIA at Churubusco 08/20/47
11/30/47 Pontiac MI	12/01/47 Detroit MI	07/26/48 Detroit MI	Received pension. AKA Wheeler B. Govwin
09/18/47 Detroit MI	New York		Served on USS Cumberland
04/12/47 Pontiac MI	04/27/47 Detroit MI	08/04/48 Covington KY	TRA COM H 12/26/47. PEN
04/21/48 Detroit MI	Detroit MI	07/16/48 Jefferson BKS MO	
04/21/47 Coldwater MI	04/27/47 Detroit MI	08/06/48 Cincinnati OH	WIA 08/20/47. Received pension
06/03/46 Detroit MI			VTS WNA
03/01/47 Detroit MI	03/01/47 Detroit MI	07/25/48 East Pascagoula MS	PEN. AKA Richard L. Gatens
11/02/47 Port Huron MI	11/12/47 Detroit MI		Deserted at Detroit MI 12/01/47
11/20/47 Monroe MI	12/04/47 Detroit MI		Deserted at Detroit MI 12/24/47
08/16/47 Detroit MI	Detroit MI	08/01/48 East Pascagoula MS	Received pension
04/15/47 Monroe MI	04/30/47 Detroit MI	07/24/48 Baton Rouge LA	Left sick at Mexico City 02/01/48
			PMT 1LT 08/20/47. PMT CAP 09/13/47 for gallantry
09/23/47 Detroit MI	09/23/47 Detroit MI	06/20/48 Newport KY	
04/27/47 Detroit MI	04/30/47 Detroit MI	08/04/48 Covington KY	
02/20/48 Flint MI	03/01/48 Detroit MI	07/18/48 Detroit MI	Left sick at New Orleans LA 05/02/48
06/18/47 Detroit MI	06/18/47 Detroit MI		Deserted at Detroit MI 06/21/47
04/01/47 Detroit MI	04/22/47 Detroit MI	07/31/48 Jefferson BKS MO	TRA COM D 01/04/48
11/05/47 Schoolcraft MI	11/19/47 Detroit MI	07/18/48 Detroit MI	
10/19/47 Niles MI	12/02/47 Detroit MI	06/20/48 Niles MI	Sick with yellow fever at Vera Cruz. MNI Bartley. PEN
11/15/47 Ypsilanti MI	12/01/47 Detroit MI	07/28/48 Detroit MI	PEN
06/29/47 Detroit MI	Detroit MI		Deserted 07/28/47
??/??/46 Hillsdale MI			VTS WNA
06/03/46 Detroit MI			VTS WNA. AKA Joseph Gruesel
10/30/47 Detroit MI	11/14/47 Detroit MI	07/23/48 Detroit MI	Received pension. AKA Nicholas Gruesel

405

Name	Age	Hgt	Eye	Hair	Cpx	Trade	Born	Home	Rank	Unit
Grey, Edward	25	5.08	GRY	BWN	RUD	Farmer	Mayo Co IRE		1SG	COM K 3rd US DRG
Gribby, Charles	40	5.07	CST	BLK	LGT	Packer	Detroit MI	Detroit MI	PVT	COM B 1st MI INF
Griffin, Andrew J.	18	5.09	DRK	DRK	LGT	Laborer	Wilmington NY		PVT	COM A 15th US INF
Griffin, Antoine	26	5.07	BLU	SDY	LGT	Laborer	Detroit MI	Detroit MI	PVT	COM B 1st MI INF
Griffin, John	31	5.10	BLU	BWN	LGT	Laborer	Detroit MI	Detroit MI	PVT	COM B 1st MI INF
Griffin, John W.	20	5.06	BLU	BWN	LGT	Farmer	Canada		PVT	COM D 1st MI INF
Griffin, Jonas A.	18	5.05	BLU	BWN	LGT	Farmer	Canada		PVT	COM D 1st MI INF
Grinnell, Samuel W.	24	6.00	GRY	SDY	FIR	Farmer	Hillsdale NY		PVT	BAT K 1st US ART
Groat, Robert B. Sr.	44	5.07	GRY	GRY	DRK	Farmer	Canada	Niles MI	PVT	COM F 1st MI INF
Groat, Robert Y. Jr.	18	5.04	BWN	DRK	DRK	Laborer	Lower Canada	Niles MI	PVT	COM F 1st MI INF
Grove, Harrison D.	23	6.03	BLK	BLK	LGT	Boatman	Otsego Co NY		1CP	COM G 1st MI INF
Grow, Chauncey	18	5.05	BLU	BWN	LGT	Farmer	Orleans Co NY	Silver Lake MI	PVT	COM H 1st MI INF
Gubby, Charles	31	5.07	BWN	BLK	LGT	Packer	Detroit MI		PVT	COM B 1st MI INF
Guild, George	28	5.08	GRY	LGT	LGT	Laborer	Sterlingshire		PVT	COM G 1st MI INF
Guilliams, Richard S.	40	6.03	HZL	BWN	FLD	Farmer	Franklin VA	LaPorte IN	PVT	COM F 1st MI INF
Guisler, John	20	5.08	BLU	BWN	LGT	Laborer	Metz FRA	Detroit MI	PVT	Brady Guards
Gurney, Charles Miller	18	5.07	BLU	LGT	LGT	Farmer	Prattsburg NY		PVT	COM G 1st MI INF
Guthrie, Frederick S.	18								4CP	COM K 1st MI INF
Hacket, Orlando A.	22	5.07	HZL	BWN	FLD	Carpenter	Livingston Co NY		PVT	COM F 1st US MTD RIF
Haddiman, Isaiah	19	5.08	BWN	BWN	LGT	Farmer	Livingston Co NY	White Pigeon MI	PVT	COM G 1st MI INF
Haggerty, Barton	23	5.06	BLK	BWN	DRK	Farmer	Oneida Co NY	Cassopolis MI	PVT	COM A 1st MI INF
Haight, John	21	5.10	BLU	LGT	FIR	Carpenter	Chataugua Co NY		RCT	COM ? 3rd US DRG
Haines, Aaron B.	28	5.02	BLU	BWN	FIR	Farmer	Sherman NY	Pontiac MI	PVT	COM C 1st MI INF
Haines, Nathan D.	22	5.08	BLU	LGT	LGT	Laborer	Montgomery Co NY		PVT	COM A 15th US INF
Hajker, Conrad	21	5.11	GRY	LGT	FIR	Shoemaker	Germany		RCT	COM ? 3rd US DRG
Halbert, Jasper G.	24	5.08	BLK	DRK	LGT	Farmer	Genesee Co NY		PVT	COM G 1st MI INF

ENROLLED	MUSTERED	DISCHARGED	REMARKS
04/01/47 Detroit MI	04/22/47 Detroit MI	07/31/48 Jefferson BKS MO	TRA COM D 01/07/48
11/02/47 Jackson MI	11/12/47 Detroit MI	07/26/48 Detroit MI	
04/05/47 Pontiac MI	04/27/47 Detroit MI		Died of disease at Perote MEX 08/20/47
11/02/47 Port Huron MI	11/12/47 Detroit MI	07/26/48 Detroit MI	
11/02/47 Port Huron MI	11/12/47 Detroit MI	07/26/48 Detroit MI	
11/14/47 Detroit MI	11/14/47 Detroit MI		Deserted at Detroit MI 12/09/47
11/14/49 Detroit MI	11/14/49 Detroit MI		Deserted at Detroit MI 12/19/47
08/25/47 Detroit MI	Detroit MI	08/20/48 Fort Columbus NY	
11/15/47 Niles MI	12/02/47 Detroit MI	07/22/48 New Orleans LA	Discharged for disability. PEN
11/15/47 Niles MI	12/02/47 Detroit MI	07/22/48 Detroit MI	Discharged for disability. PEN
02/20/48 Adrian MI	03/01/48 Detroit MI	07/18/48 Detroit MI	
11/20/47 Freedom MI	12/01/47 Detroit MI	07/27/48 Detroit MI	
11/12/47 Detroit MI	Detroit MI	07/26/48 Detroit MI	Served as cook in US hospital since 02/21/48
02/20/48 Jackson MI	03/01/48 Detroit MI	07/18/48 Detroit MI	STH at New Orleans LA from Vera Cruz MEX 06/05/48
11/15/47 Niles MI	12/02/47 Detroit MI		Died at Woodville OH 12/29/47
06/18/47 Detroit MI	06/18/47 Detroit MI	06/30/48 Detroit MI	AKA John Greisler
02/20/48 Jackson MI	03/01/48 Detroit MI	07/18/48 Detroit MI	STH at New Orleans from Vera Cruz 06/05/48. PEN
11/15/47 Almont MI	01/20/48 Detroit MI	07/28/48 Detroit MI	
06/21/47 Kalamazoo MI	06/21/47 Kalamazoo MI	07/29/48 Jefferson BKS MO	Received pension. MNI Allen
02/20/48 White Pigeon MI	03/01/48 Detroit MI	07/18/48 Detroit MI	Received pension
11/05/47 Kalamazoo MI	11/19/47 Detroit MI	07/18/48 Detroit MI	PMT 4CP 03/01/48. Received pension
05/02/48 Detroit MI	Detroit MI		Deserted 05/24/48
11/30/47 Pontiac MI	12/01/47 Detroit MI	07/26/48 Detroit MI	AKA Aaron B. Hayner
04/03/47 Pontiac MI	04/27/47 Detroit MI		Died of disease at Perote MEX 07/15/47
04/20/48 Detroit MI	Detroit MI	07/16/48 Jefferson BKS MO	
02/20/48 Battle Creek MI	03/01/48 Detroit MI	07/18/48 Detroit MI	STH at New Orleans LA from Vera Cruz MEX 06/05/48

Name	Age	Hgt	Eye	Hair	Cpx	Trade	Born	Home	Rank	Unit
Hale, William	22	5.07	HZL	BWN	DRK	Clerk	Logan OH		RCT	US Army
Haley, Reuben	26	5.04	HZL	DRK	DRK	Farmer	Covington KY		PVT	COM E 15th US INF
Hall, Abraham B.	23	6.01	HZL	DRK	DRK	Merchant	Steuben Co NY		3SG	COM G 1st MI INF
Hall, Amos	19	5.09	BLU	LGT	LGT	Laborer	Ireland CAN	Port Huron MI	PVT	COM B 1st MI INF
Hall, Hiram	25	5.09	GRY	DRK	DRK	Farmer	Orleans Co NY	Detroit MI	PVT	COM B 1st MI INF
Hall, Nathaniel B.	23	6.00	HZL	BLK	DRK	Farmer	Ontario Co NY		PVT	COM K 3rd US DRG
Hall, Samuel	22	5.08	BLK	BLK	DRK				PVT	COM E 1st MI INF
Hall, Thomas	25	5.04	BLU	BWN	FIR	Carpenter	Yates Co NY	Detroit MI	PVT	COM E 1st MI INF
Hall, William	22	5.07	BLU	BWN	FIR	Farmer	Erie PA	Pontiac MI	PVT	COM C 1st MI INF
Halligan, John	27	5.06	BWN	BLK	DRK	Laborer	Ireland		PVT	COM F 1st MI INF
Hamblin, Chandler	21	5.07	GRY	BWN	LGT	Farmer	Onondaga Co NY	Paw Paw MI	PVT	COM A 1st MI INF
Hamblin, David W.	23	5.04	BLK	BLK	FLD	Farmer	Howard NY		PVT	COM E 15th US INF
Hames, Charles	19	5.04	BWN	BWN	LGT	Cooper	Seneca Co NY	Detroit MI	PVT	COM E 1st MI INF
Hames, William	22	5.07	BLK	BLK	DRK	Mason	Monroe Co NY		PVT	COM G 1st MI INF
Hamilton, Edwin J.	21	5.09	BLU	BWN	LGT	Teacher	Lenawee Co MI	Cassopolis MI	2CP	COM F 1st MI INF
Hammond, Milton D.	18	5.07	HZL	SDY	LGT	Farmer	Chautauqua Co NY	Hillsdale MI	PVT	COM H 1st MI INF
Hanchett, George W.	23	5.04	BLK	BLK	DRK	Laborer	Avon TWP NY		PVT	COM A 15th US INF
Hancock, Samuel M.	21	5.07	GRY	FIR	FIR	Farmer	Orleans Co NY		RCT	COM ? 3rd US DRG
Hand, James								Detroit MI	PVT	Montgomery Guards
Hand, John								Detroit MI	PVT	Montgomery Guards
Handa, Robert	32	5.04	BLU	BWN	LGT	Farmer	Reading NY		PVT	COM A 15th US INF
Hanks, Daniel P.	22	5.04	GRY	SDY	FIR	Carpenter	Perry OH	Bronson MI	PVT	COM E 15th US INF
Hanley, Michael	25	5.06	BLU	BWN	DRK	Laborer	Roscommon Co IRE	Detroit MI	PVT	COM A 6th US INF
Hannahs, Nathaniel	25	5.06	BLU	BWN	FIR	Farmer	Madison Co OH		PVT	COM E 15th US INF
Hanscom, Alfred H.	29	5.10	BLU	BWN	LGT		Pontiac MI	Pontiac MI	CAP	COM C 1st MI INF
Hanscom, Andrew J.	21	5.11	BLU	LGT	LGT		Detroit MI	Pontiac MI	2LT	COM C 1st MI INF

ENROLLED	MUSTERED	DISCHARGED	REMARKS
07/02/47 Detroit MI	Detroit MI		Deserted 07/05/47
04/26/47 Niles MI	04/27/47 Detroit MI		Died at Puebla MEX 10/05/47
01/25/48 Lansing MI	02/01/48 Detroit MI	07/18/48 Detroit MI	
11/02/47 Port Huron MI	11/12/47 Detroit MI		Died en route to Vera Cruz MEX 06/14/48
11/02/47 Port Huron MI	11/12/47 Detroit MI	07/26/48 Detroit MI	AKA Hiram Hull
04/03/47 Detroit MI	04/22/47 Detroit MI		LIH at Puebla MEX 06/07/47
11/20/47 Detroit MI	12/04/47 Detroit MI		Deserted at Detroit MI 12/24/47
11/20/47 Detroit MI	12/04/47 Detroit MI	07/18/48 Detroit MI	PEN
11/30/47 Romeo MI	12/01/47 Detroit MI	07/26/48 Detroit MI	
11/15/47 Niles MI	12/02/47 Detroit MI		Deserted at Detroit MI 12/23/47
11/05/47 Paw Paw MI	11/19/47 Detroit MI	07/18/48 Detroit MI	AKA Chandler Hamlin
04/06/47 Niles MI	04/27/47 Detroit MI	08/06/48 Cincinnati OH	Received pension
11/20/47 Battle Creek MI	12/04/47 Detroit MI	07/18/48 Detroit MI	
02/20/48 Battle Creek MI	03/01/48 Detroit MI	07/18/48 Detroit MI	PEN
11/15/47 Niles MI	12/02/47 Detroit MI		Died at Detroit MI 02/07/48
11/20/47 Hillsdale MI	12/01/47 Detroit MI	07/27/48 Detroit MI	Received pension
04/12/47 Utica MI	04/27/47 Detroit MI	08/21/48	TRA COM B 12/26/47. Received pension
05/20/48 Detroit MI	Detroit MI	07/16/48 Jefferson BKS MO	
05/28/46 Detroit MI			VTS WNA
??/??/46 Detroit MI			VTS WNA
03/21/47 Pontiac MI	04/27/47 Detroit MI		TRA COM H 12/26/47. ODS Vera Cruz MEX
04/13/47 Fawn River MI	04/27/47 Detroit MI		Died at Churubusco MEX from wounds 08/31/47
09/16/46 Detroit MI	09/16/46 Detroit MI		
04/24/47 Yankee Springs	04/27/47 Detroit MI		Deserted near Baton Rouge LA 05/27/47
12/01/47 Pontiac MI	12/01/47 Detroit MI	07/26/48 Detroit MI	PEN
12/01/47 Pontiac MI	12/01/47 Detroit MI	07/26/48 Detroit MI	Received pension

NAME	AGE	HGT	EYE	HAIR	CPX	TRADE	BORN	HOME	RANK	UNIT
Hare, Levi V.	24	5.07	HZL	BWN	FIR	Farmer	Dutchess Co NY	Lansing MI	PVT	COM I 1st MI INF
Harmon, Edwin	22							Delhi MI	PVT	COM H 1st MI INF
Harney, Sylvester	20	5.08	BLU	BLK	DRK	Farmer	Clarence NY		PVT	COM K 1st MI INF
Harper, Charles	22	5.06	BLK	BLK	DRK	Farmer	Philadelphia PA	Pontiac MI	PVT	COM C 1st MI INF
Harrington, Elisha	20	5.06	GRY	DRK	FLD	Farmer	Seneca Co NY		PVT	COM K 1st MI INF
Harrington, George W.	21	5.09	BLK	BWN	FIR	Farmer	Rensselaer NY	Lansing MI	PVT	COM C 1st MI INF
Harris, George R.	37	5.05	GRY	DRK	DRK	Sailor	Lime TWP NY	Troy MI	PVT	COM G 1st MI INF
Harris, Herman	21	5.06	HZL	BWN	LGT	Farmer	Cattaraugus NY		PVT	COM K 3rd US DRG
Harris, Lemuel W.	18	5.06	BWN	BWN	DRK	Cabinet-maker	Cayuga Co NY	Paw Paw MI	PVT	COM A 1st MI INF
Harris, Stephen M.	23	5.05	GRY	BWN	DRK	Farmer	Cayuga Co NY	Paw Paw MI	PVT	COM A 1st MI INF
Harrison, William H.	28	5.08	GRY	LGT	LGT	Farmer	New York NY	Paw Paw MI	2CP	COM A 1st MI INF
Hart, Frederick	18					Business-man	Albany NY	Adrian MI	PVT	Adrian Guards
Hart, Hiram	23	5.08	BLK	BLK	DRK	Farmer	Somerset Co PA		PVT	COM G 1st MI INF
Hart, Thomas	29	5.04	GRY	LGT	LGT	Laborer	Tipperary IRE		PVT	COM B 3rd US INF
Hartgrove, Charles G.	22	5.09	BLK	BLK	DRK	Farmer	Woodford? Co KY	Detroit MI	3CP	COM E 1st MI INF
Hartiveg, Charles	29	5.07	BLU	DRK	LGT	Butcher	Hanover GER	Detroit MI	PVT	COM D 1st MI INF
Hartwell, Albert	18	5.06	HZL	BLK	LGT	Laborer	Sodas NY		PVT	COM A 4th US INF
Hartwell, Rufus G.	19	5.09	GRY	BWN	FIR	Farmer	Clinton Co NY		PVT	COM I 1st MI INF
Harvie, John	28	5.05	BLU	SDY	FIR	Clerk	Glasgow SCO		PVT	COM A 6th US INF
Harwood, Washington								Adrian MI	PVT	Adrian Guards
Hasenfleur, Peter	25	5.07	FIR	AUB	LGT	Farmer	New York State	Brighton MI	PVT	COM C 1st MI INF
Haskell, Rufus	26	5.08	GRY	RED	FIR	Laborer	Hammond NY	St. Clair MI	PVT	COM B 1st MI INF
Haskins, William	36	5.11	BLU	DRK	DRK	Farmer	New York State	Grand Haven MI	PVT	COM G 1st MI INF
Hath, Henry S.	23	5.05	BLU	RED	FIR	Farmer	Bridgewater VT	Monroe MI	PVT	COM G 15th US INF
Haurican, Thomas								Detroit MI	PVT	Montgomery Guards
Haviland, John	18	5.05	BLU	SDY	LGT	Laborer	Ireland	Pontiac MI	PVT	COM A 15th US INF

ENROLLED	MUSTERED	DISCHARGED	REMARKS
01/24/48 Grand Rapids MI	02/01/48 Detroit MI	07/18/48 Detroit MI	Received pension
12/20/47 Delhi MI	01/01/48 Detroit MI		Died at Detroit MI 01/31/48
11/15/47 Almont MI	12/01/47 Detroit MI		Deserted at Detroit MI 02/05/48
11/30/47 Corunna MI	12/01/47 Detroit MI	07/26/48 Detroit MI	
12/24/47 Toledo OH	01/01/48 Detroit MI		Deserted at Sandusky OH 02/16/48
11/30/47 Pontiac MI	12/01/47 Detroit MI	07/26/48 Detroit MI	AKA George W. Herrington
02/20/48 Canandaigua MI	03/01/48 Detroit MI	07/18/48 Detroit MI	PEN
04/05/47 Tecumseh MI	04/22/47 Detroit MI		LIH at Perote MEX 07/03/47
11/05/47 Paw Paw MI	11/19/47 Detroit MI	07/18/48 Detroit MI	In hospital at Cordova MEX. PEN. AKA Hawes
11/05/47 Paw Paw MI	11/19/47 Detroit MI	07/18/48 Detroit MI	In hospital at Cordova MEX. PEN. AKA Hawes
11/05/47 Paw Paw MI	11/19/47 Detroit MI	07/18/48 Detroit MI	PMT 1CP 12/01/47. PMT 4SG 03/01/48. PEN. MNI Henry
06/01/46 Adrian MI			VTS WNA
02/20/48 Toledo OH	03/01/48 Detroit MI		Died of yellow fever at Vera Cruz MEX 06/10/48
04/05/47 Detroit MI	04/05/47 Detroit MI		Died at Sante Fe 07/02/48
11/20/47 Detroit MI	12/04/47 Detroit MI	07/18/48 Detroit MI	
11/14/47 Detroit MI	11/14/47 Detroit MI	07/26/48 Detroit MI	
03/04/47 Detroit MI	03/04/47 Detroit MI	07/27/48 Camp Jeff Davis MS	
11/15/47 Marshall MI	12/01/47 Detroit MI	02/28/48 Detroit MI	Discharged by legal process
12/21/46 Detroit MI	12/21/46 Detroit MI		
06/01/46 Adrian MI			VTS WNA
11/30/47 Pontiac MI	12/01/47 Detroit MI	07/26/48 Detroit MI	PEN. AKA Peter Hasenplug/Hasselflein
11/02/47 Port Huron MI	11/12/47 Detroit MI	07/26/48 Detroit MI	PEN
01/25/48 Grand Haven MI	02/01/48 Detroit MI	07/18/48 Detroit MI	
04/07/47 Detroit MI	04/30/47 Detroit MI	08/04/48 Covington KY	
05/28/46 Detroit MI			VTS WNA
04/08/47 Pontiac MI	04/27/47 Detroit MI		Killed at battle of Chapultepec MEX 09/13/47

Name	Age	Hgt	Eye	Hair	Cpx	Trade	Born	Home	Rank	Unit
Hawes, Ebenezer	33	5.09	BWN	DRK	LGT	Broker	Genesee Co NY	Detroit MI	2LT	COM B 1st MI INF
Hawkins, Samuel	30	5.10	DRK	BLK	DRK	Wagon-maker	Gloucestershire	Kalamazoo MI	PVT	COM A 1st MI INF
Hawley, Sanford	45	5.08	GRY	GRY	LGT	Hatter			PVT	COM A 1st MI INF
Hayes, Cornelius	31	5.07	DRK	DRK	DRK	Shoemaker	Tipperary? IRE		PVT	COM G 1st MI INF
Hayes, John	22	5.07	BLU	BWN	LGT	Laborer	Kentucky		PVT	COM A 6th US INF
Haylock, William	35	5.08	BLU	DRK	DRK	Laborer	Cambridge ENG		PVT	COM B 3rd US INF
Head, William	30	5.08	BLU	BWN	LGT	Miller	Fairfax VA		PVT	Brady Guards
Healey, Henry S.	20	5.09	HZL	BLK	DRK	Farmer	Yates Co NY	Flint MI	PVT	COM G 1st MI INF
Healey, James B.	23	5.10	BLU	BWN	LGT	Cooper	Constable NY		PVT	COM A 15th US INF
Heath, Franklin H.	20	6.00	BLU	BWN	LGT	Farmer	Allegany Co NY		PVT	COM A 1st MI INF
Heath, Sylvester	19	5.08	BLU	LGT	LGT			Ypsilanti MI	PVT	COM E 1st MI INF
Hecox, Horace C.	18	5.07	BLU	LGT	FIR	Farmer	Richland OH	Adrian MI	PVT	COM I 1st MI INF
Hefferman, John						Laborer		Detroit MI	PVT	Montgomery Guards
Hefferman, Patrick								Detroit MI	PVT	Montgomery Guards
Heidlauf, John	29	5.07	BWN	BLK	DRK	Farmer	Germany		PVT	COM K 3rd US DRG
Heinzman, Frederick	23	5.10	BLU	BLK	DRK	Farmer	Wittenberg GER	Ann Arbor MI	PVT	COM A 1st MI INF
Heinzman, Lewis	24	5.11	BLU	BLK	DRK	Farmer	Wittenberg GER	Ann Arbor MI	PVT	COM A 1st MI INF
Helfer, William S.	18	5.05	GRY	LGT	DRK	Farmer	Richland Co OH	Lagrange IN	PVT	COM G 1st MI INF
Helmes, James W.								Adrian MI	2LT	Adrian Guards
Helms, Victor H.	34	5.09	GRY	DRK	LGT	Baker	Monroe Co NY	Adrian MI	2SG	COM G 1st MI INF
Hemstret, Jacob	18	5.07	GRY	RED	DRK	Mariner	Yorktown CAN	Detroit MI	PVT	COM G 15th US INF
Henderson, Daniel S.	31	5.08	GRY	LGT	LGT	Painter	Leeds CAN	Buffalo NY	PVT	COM E 1st MI INF
Hendrick, Cyrus	37	6.00	DRK	GRY	LGT	Sailor	Hartford Co CT		PVT	COM B 1st MI INF
Henkel, John	29	5.05	GRY	GRY	FLD	Laborer	Speckswinkle GER	Detroit MI	4CP	Brady Guards
Henry, Patrick	40	5.09	BLU	BLK	DRK	Laborer	Ireland	Niles MI	PVT	COM F 1st MI INF
Hersh, Adam						Cigarmaker		Detroit MI	PVT	Scott Guards

ENROLLED	MUSTERED	DISCHARGED	REMARKS
10/30/47 Port Huron MI	11/12/47 Detroit MI	07/26/48 Detroit MI	
11/05/47 Kalamazoo MI	11/19/47 Detroit MI	07/18/48 Detroit MI	Born in England
11/05/47 Paw Paw MI	11/19/47 Detroit MI		LIH Vera Cruz MEX 03/13/48. DSC
02/20/48 Toledo OH	03/01/48 Detroit MI	07/18/48 Detroit MI	STH at New Orleans LA from Vera Cruz MEX 06/05/48
12/05/46 Detroit MI	12/05/46 Detroit MI		Died at Vera Cruz MEX 05/04/47
03/09/47 Detroit MI	03/09/47 Detroit MI		Left sick at Perote Castle 08/02/47. Died 09/23/47
06/18/47 Detroit MI	06/18/47 Detroit MI	06/30/48 Detroit MI	
04/01/48 Detroit MI	04/01/48 Detroit MI	07/18/48 Detroit MI	
04/05/47 Ann Arbor MI	Detroit MI	07/25/47 Baton Rouge LA	WIA at Mexico City 08/20/47. TRA COM I 12/26/47
11/05/47 Allegan MI	11/19/47 Detroit MI	04/26/48 Cordova MEX	Discharged on surgeon's certificate of disability
11/20/47 Saginaw MI	12/04/47 Detroit MI	07/18/48 Detroit MI	LIH at Urbana OH 01/02/48. Joined at Cordova 03/19/48
11/15/47 Adrian MI	12/01/47 Detroit MI		Left sick at New Orleans LA 07/28/48
05/28/46 Detroit MI			VTS WNA
05/28/46 Detroit MI			VTS WNA
04/10/47 Detroit MI	04/22/47 Detroit MI	07/31/48 Jefferson BKS MO	TRA COM D 01/04/48. AKA John Headlauf
11/19/47 Kalamazoo MI	11/19/47 Detroit MI	07/26/48 Detroit MI	TRA COM D 01/01/48
11/19/47 Kalamazoo MI	11/19/47 Detroit MI	07/26/48 Detroit MI	TRA COM D 01/01/48
02/20/48 White Pigeon MI	03/01/48 Detroit MI	07/18/48 Detroit MI	
06/01/46 Adrian MI			VTS WNA
11/10/47 Adrian MI	12/01/47 Detroit MI		Died in the Gulf of Mexico 06/10/48. PEN
03/27/47 Detroit MI	04/30/47 Detroit MI		Died of diarrhea at Jalapa 08/28/47. AKA Jacob Hemsted
01/16/48 New Orleans LA	01/16/48 New Orleans LA	07/18/48 Detroit MI	AKA David S. Henderson
11/02/47 Port Huron MI	11/12/47 Detroit MI		Deserted at Detroit MI 12/07/47
06/18/47 Detroit MI	06/18/47 Detroit MI	06/30/48 Detroit MI	Reduced to the ranks 04/02/48
11/15/47 Niles MI	12/02/47 Detroit MI		Died of dropsy at New Orleans LA 03/05/48
06/03/46 Detroit MI			VTS WNA

Name	Age	Hgt	Eye	Hair	Cpx	Trade	Born	Home	Rank	Unit
Hess, Charles								Detroit MI	PVT	Scott Guards
Hess, Wilhelm	22	5.07	BLU	SDY	LGT	Wagon-maker	Obermiller GER	Detroit MI	PVT	Brady Guards
Hesslop, Vincent	34	5.10	GRY	BWN	DRK	Farmer	Cumberland ENG		PVT	COM D 1st MI INF
Hetherington, Isaac	19	5.06	BLU	BLK	DRK	Farmer	New York NY		PVT	COM D 1st MI INF
Hewitt, George W.	18	5.05	BLU	LGT	LGT	Laborer	Wyoming Co NY	Macomb Co MI	MUS	COM A 15th US INF
Hewitt, Isaac	19	5.07	BLU	BWN	LGT	Farmer	Orleans Co NY	Schoolcraft MI	4SG	COM A 1st MI INF
Hewitt, Marble	21	5.07	BLU	BWN	FIR	Farmer	Wayne Co NY		PVT	COM D 1st MI INF
Hickcox, Ambrose								Ann Arbor MI	PVT	COM K 3rd US DRG
Hickey, John	22	5.10	BLU	BWN	FIR	Laborer	Carlow IRE		RCT	COM ? 3rd US DRG
Hickox, Luman	25	5.09	BLU	DRK	DRK	Hostler	Allegheny Co PA		PVT	COM G 1st MI INF
Hickox, Marshall	38	5.08	BLK	DRK	LGT	Carpenter	New Haven CT	Detroit MI	PVT	COM B 1st MI INF
Hicks, Daniel	35					Clerk	Newburgh NY	Adrian MI	CAP	COM G 1st MI INF
Hicks, George W.	21						Watertown MY	Adrian MI	PVT	Adrian Guards
Hicks, Nelson A.	21	5.05	GRY	LGT	LGT	Painter	Oswego Co NY		PVT	COM H US MTD RIF
Hidloff, Christian F.	26	5.08	HZL	BWN	DRK	Laborer	Germany		PVT	COM E 1st MI INF
Higbee, Edward S.	24	5.09	HZL	BLK	DRK	Physician	Ogdenburg NY		PVT	Brady Guards
Higby, Austin	18	5.11	DRK	BLK	DRK	Farmer	Cayuga Co NY	Deerlick OH	PVT	COM K 1st MI INF
Hildreth, Hiram	31	5.11	HZL	BWN	FIR	Laborer	Ontario Co NY		PVT	COM I 1st MI INF
Hill, George								Detroit MI	PVT	Montgomery Guards
Hill, William	26	5.06	BLU	BWN	LGT	Laborer	England	Chicago IL	PVT	COM F 1st MI INF
Hill, John	35	5.11	HZL	BLK	DRK	Farmer	Cumberland ME		PVT	COM K 3rd US DRG
Hills, Frederick C.	23	5.10	BLU	LGT	FIR	Lawyer	Oswego Co NY	Grandville MI	PVT	COM I 1st MI INF
Hilman, Thomas S.	23	5.09	BLU	DRK	LGT	Tradesman	Troy VT		PVT	COM B 1st MI INF
Himes, Adam I.	21	5.08	GRY	BWN	LGT	Laborer	Stuttgart GER	Detroit MI	PVT	COM D 1st MI INF
Hinks, John C.	36	6.01	BLU	BWN	LGT	Farmer	Onondaga Co NY	Almont MI	1SG	COM K 1st MI INF
Hinman, Ranseller H	21	5.08	BLU	FIR	FIR	Farmer	Genesee Co NY		PVT	COM K 3rd US DRG

Enrolled	Mustered	Discharged	Remarks
06/03/46 Detroit MI			VTS WNA
06/18/47 Detroit MI	06/18/47 Detroit MI	06/30/48 Detroit MI	Received pension
11/14/47 Ann Arbor MI	11/14/47 Detroit MI	07/26/48 Detroit MI	AKA Vincent Hyslop
11/14/47 Port Huron MI	11/14/47 Detroit MI	07/26/48 Detroit MI	
04/13/47 Utica MI	04/27/47 Detroit MI	08/21/48	TRA COM G 12/26/47
11/05/47 Schoolcraft MI	11/19/47 Detroit MI	02/01/48	Resigned from service
11/14/47 Wayne MI	11/14/47 Detroit MI		Died on the Mississippi River 07/05/48
04/20/47 Ann Arbor MI	04/22/47 Detroit MI		LIH at Puebla MEX 08/07/47. AKA Heacock
05/22/48 Detroit MI	Detroit MI	07/16/48 Jefferson BKS MO	
02/20/48 Flint MI	03/01/48 Detroit MI	07/18/48 Detroit MI	STH at New Orleans LA from Vera Cruz MEX 06/05/48
11/02/47 Port Huron MI	11/12/47 Detroit MI	07/26/48 Detroit MI	
10/30/47 Adrian MI	12/01/47 Detroit MI	07/18/48 Detroit MI	PEN
06/01/46 Adrian MI			VTS WNA
06/28/47 Kalamazoo MI	06/28/47 Kalamazoo MI	07/31/48 Jefferson BKS MO	Received pension. MNI Arnold
11/20/47 Ann Arbor MI	12/04/47 Detroit MI	07/18/48 Detroit MI	LIH at Vera Cruz 05/05/48. PEN. MNI Francis
06/18/47 Detroit MI	06/18/47 Detroit MI	06/30/48 Detroit MI	
01/20/48 Grass Lake MI	02/01/48 Detroit MI	07/28/48 Detroit MI	
11/15/47 Palmyra MI	12/01/47 Detroit MI		Died at Cordova MEX 06/13/48
??/??/46 Detroit MI			VTS WNA
11/15/47 St. Joseph MI	12/02/47 Detroit MI	07/28/48 Detroit MI	
04/06/47 Tecumseh MI	04/22/47 Detroit MI		LIH at Perote MEX 07/03/47
11/15/47 Grandville MI	12/01/47 Detroit MI	07/18/48 Detroit MI	
11/02/47 Port Huron MI	11/12/47 Detroit MI	07/26/48 Detroit MI	
11/14/47 Detroit MI	11/14/47 Detroit MI	07/26/48 Detroit MI	
11/15/47 Almont MI	01/20/48 Detroit MI	07/28/48 Detroit MI	Received pension. AKA John Henks
04/02/47 Detroit MI	04/22/47 Detroit MI	07/31/48 Jefferson BKS MO	TRA COM C 01/04/48. Received pension

Name	Age	Hgt	Eye	Hair	Cpx	Trade	Born	Home	Rank	Unit
Hirea, William W.								Adrian MI	PVT	Adrian Guards
Hodges, Herman M.	18	6.00	BLU	BLK	LGT	Farmer	Erie Co NY	Almont MI	PVT	COM H 1st MI NF
Hodges, Samuel	21	5.11	BLU	LGT	LGT	Farmer	South Bend IN		PVT	COM ? 15th US INF
Hodges, Samuel	22	5.11	GRY	BWN	FIR	Farmer	South Bend IN		PVT	COM B 5th US INF
Hoffman, Satterlee	21						Michigan	Niles MI	2LT	BAT ? 1st US ART
Hofmyer, Frederick								Detroit MI	PVT	Scott Guards
Hollaway, Alpheus S.	29	5.09	BLU	BWN	FIR	Carpenter	Ontario Co NY		PVT	COM K 3rd US DRG
Holliday, Jonathan C.	20	5.07	GRY	FLX	LGT	Farmer	Allegany Co NY		PVT	COM G 15th US INF
Holliday, Sylvester	21	5.07	BLU	BWN	FIR	Shoemaker	Erie Co NY		PVT	COM E 15th US INF
Hollister, Samuel E.	22	5.08	BLU	LGT	LGT	Farmer	Mansfield NY		PVT	COM B 1st MI INF
Holmes, Abiram O.									1SG	NTH Lenawee VOL
Holmes, David	21	5.11	GRY	SDY	LGT	Clerk	Ireland	Detroit MI	PVT	COM E 1st MI INF
Holmes, Julius J. A.	24	5.08	HZL	BWN	DRK	Farmer	Stockbridge NY	Tecumseh MI	1SG	COM K 3rd US DRG
Holmes, Lucius B.	18	5.07	BLU	LGT	FIR	Laborer	Orleans Co NY	Marshall MI	PVT	COM F 1st MI INF
Holmes, Luman	25	5.02	GRY	BWN	FLD	Farmer	Burlington VT	York MI	PVT	COM K 1st MI INF
Holmes, Myron R.	18	5.04	BLU	LGT	FLD	Laborer	Washtenaw Co MI		PVT	COM K 1st MI INF
Holt, Darius	19	5.06	GRY	LGT	LGT	Laborer	Fairfield OH	Lyons OH	PVT	COM A 1st MI INF
Holt, Frederick	25	5.10	BLU	LGT	FIR	Farmer	Prussia		PVT	COM H 1st MI INF
Hooker, John	20	5.08	BLU	LGT	LGT	Mason	Steuben Co NY		PVT	COM G 1st MI INF
Hopkins, Daniel								Adrian MI	PVT	Adrian Guards
Hopkins, George W.	36	5.01	BLU	LGT	LGT	Shoemaker	Hopkinton NY		PVT	COM B 1st MI INF
Hopkins, Reuben	32	5.07	BLU	BLK	RUD	Laborer	Prebble NY		PVT	COM A 15th US INF
Hopkinson, William B.	34	6.00	GRY	BLK	DRK	Laborer	Brooklyn NY		PVT	COM A 15th US INF
Horregan, Michael								Detroit MI	PVT	Montgomery Guards
Horton, James H.	37	5.06	GRY	BWN	FIR	Farmer	New York State		PVT	COM I 1st MI INF
Hough, Olmsted	49					Sheriff	Columbia Co NY		4CP	NTH Lenawee VOL

Enrolled	Mustered	Discharged	Remarks
06/01/46 Adrian MI			VTS WNA
12/20/47 Okama MI	01/01/48 Detroit MI	07/18/48 Detroit MI	TRA COM G at New Orleans LA. Received pension
04/24/47 Niles MI			
09/30/47 Detroit MI	Detroit MI	08/01/48 East Pascagoula MS	
03/08/47			KIA at battle of Churubusco 08/20/47
06/03/46 Detroit MI			VTS WNA
04/09/47 Tecumseh MI	04/22/47 Detroit MI		LIH at Puebla MEX 08/07/47
04/02/47 Detroit MI	04/30/47 Detroit MI	08/04/48 Covington KY	PEN
04/21/47 Fawn River MI	04/27/47 Detroit MI	08/03/48 Cincinnati OH	Received pension
11/02/47 Port Huron MI	11/12/47 Detroit MI		Died 06/15/48 en route to Vera Cruz MEX
06/06/46 Tecumseh MI			VTS WNA
11/20/47 Detroit MI	12/04/47 Detroit MI	07/18/48 Detroit MI	
04/05/47 Tecumseh MI	04/22/47 Detroit MI	10/27/47 Mexico City MEX	
11/15/47 Marshall MI	12/02/47 Detroit MI	07/28/48 Detroit MI	DES at Detroit 12/27/47. Rejoined 04/21/48. PEN
11/15/47 York MI	12/01/47 Detroit MI	07/28/48 Detroit MI	
11/15/47 Ypsilanti MI	12/01/47 Detroit MI	07/08/48 New Orleans LA	Discharged on account of disability
11/05/47 Kalamazoo MI	11/19/47 Detroit MI		DES at Detroit MI 12/25/47. AKA Darius Molt
11/20/47 Adrian MI	12/01/47 Detroit MI	07/27/48 Detroit MI	Received pension
02/20/48 Jackson MI	03/01/48 Detroit MI	07/18/48 Detroit MI	STH at New Orleans LA from Vera Cruz MEX 06/05/48
06/01/46 Adrian MI			VTS WNA
11/02/47 Port Huron MI	11/12/47 Detroit MI		Deserted at Detroit MI 12/05/47
04/19/47 Pontiac MI	04/27/47 Detroit MI	08/04/48 Cincinnati OH	TRA COM F 12/26/47. Received pension
04/23/47 Detroit MI	04/27/47 Detroit MI	08/04/48 Cincinnati OH	WIA at Mexico City 08/20/47. TRA COM I 12/26/47. PEN
??/??/46 Detroit MI			VTS WNA
11/15/47 Hastings MI	12/01/47 Detroit MI		Deserted at Detroit MI 01/27/48
06/06/46 Tecumseh MI			VTS WNA

Name	Age	Hgt	Eye	Hair	Cpx	Trade	Born	Home	Rank	Unit
Houghtelin, John B.	18	6.00	BLU	LGT	LGT	Miller	Cayuga Co NY		PVT	COM D 1st MI INF
Howard, Alexander K.	27	5.08	DRK	DRK	DRK	Merchant	Easton MA	Detroit MI	1LT	Brady Guards
Howard, Joshua A.	54						Eaton MA	Dearborn MI	CLT	F&S 15th US INF
Howard, Oliver D.	25	5.08	BLU	BWN	LGT	Farmer	Bornford VT		PVT	COM I 5th US INF
Howe, Emery	18	5.07	GRY	LGT	FLD	Farmer	Stafford NY		PVT	COM K 1st MI INF
Howe, John A.	23	6.02	BLU	BLK	DRK	Distiller	Cortland Co NY	Niles MI	PVT	COM F 1st MI INF
Howell, Edwin	24	5.09	HZL	FIR	FIR	Farmer	Monroe Co NY		PVT	COM K 3rd US DRG
Howell, William T.	35					Lawyer	New York State	Hillsdale MI	CAP	Governor's Guard
Howes, Aaron M.	24	5.10	BLU	BLK	LGT	Farmer	Putnam Co NY	Lansing MI	PVT	COM H 1st MI INF
Howlet, John R.								Adrian MI	PVT	Adrian Guards
Howser, John W.	38								MUS	COM K 1st MI INF
Hubbard, David Jr.	26	5.05	BLU	BWN	LGT	Lawyer	Rutland VT	Schoolcraft MI	PVT	COM A 1st MI INF
Hubert, John	22	5.04	BLU	BWN	DRK	Laborer	Germany		PVT	COM D 1st MI INF
Huff, Levi	21	5.06	BWN	BLK	FIR	Laborer	Port Washington		PVT	COM B 5th US INF
Hughes, Edward	21	5.08	BLU	BWN	FIR	Laborer	Ireland		RCT	COM ? 3rd US DRG
Hughs, Peter	45	5.09	BLU	LGT	LGT	Laborer	Ireland	Detroit MI	PVT	COM K 1st MI INF
Hungerford, Charles B.	25	5.11	BLU	FIR	SDY	Porter	Dansville NY	Detroit MI	PVT	COM K 3rd US DRG
Hunt, Charles B.	18	5.07	BLK	BLK	DRK	Farmer	Middlebury VT	Pontiac MI	PVT	COM C 1st MI INF
Hunt, Edward	21	5.06	BLU	SDY	SDY	Laborer	Buffalo NY		PVT	COM G 15th US INF
Hunt, Henry J.	27					Soldier	Detroit MI	Detroit MI	1LT	BAT ? 2nd US ART
Hunt, Thomas H.	24	5.09	BLK	BLK	LGT		Pontiac MI	Pontiac MI	1LT	COM C 1st MI INF
Hunt, William C.								Adrian MI	PVT	Adrian Guards
Hunter, Randall	23	5.08	BLU	LGT	FIR	Farmer	Onondaga Co NY	Hillsdale MI	PVT	COM H 1st MI INF
Hurd, David	21	6.03	BLK	BWN	LGT	Farmer	Tompkins Co NY	Monroe MI	PVT	COM H 1st MI INF
Hurlburt, Simeon	18	5.10	BLK	BWN	LGT	Farmer	Mayand NY	Clinton MI	PVT	COM H 1st MI INF
Hurst, William	33	5.09	BLU	DRK	LGT	Stonecutter	Lancastershire		PVT	COM G 1st MI INF

ENROLLED	MUSTERED	DISCHARGED	REMARKS
11/14/47 Detroit MI	11/14/47 Detroit MI	07/26/48 Detroit MI	
06/18/47 Detroit MI	06/18/47 Detroit MI	06/30/48 Detroit MI	CMD at Fort Brady MI beginning 06/24/47. PEN
04/09/47 Detroit MI	Detroit MI	08/07/48 Cincinnati OH	PMT to BVT COL 09/13/47 for gallantry at Chapultepec
05/18/47 Detroit MI	Detroit MI	08/01/48 East Pascagoula MS	
11/15/47 Phelps MI	12/01/47 Detroit MI		Deserted at Sandusky OH 02/16/48
11/15/47 Niles MI	12/02/47 Detroit MI		Died at Detroit MI 07/27/48
04/01/47 Detroit MI	04/22/47 Detroit MI	07/31/48 Jefferson BKS MO	LIH at Puebla MEX 06/07/47
??/??/46 Hillsdale MI			VTS WNA
01/18/48 Lansing MI	02/01/48 Detroit MI	07/27/48 Detroit MI	Received pension
06/01/46 Adrian MI			VTS WNA
12/24/47 Hudson MI	01/20/48 Detroit MI	07/28/48 Detroit MI	PEN
11/05/47 Schoolcraft MI	11/19/47 Detroit MI	07/18/48 Detroit MI	PMT SGM 12/10/47
11/14/47 Detroit MI	11/14/47 Detroit MI		Died at Cordova MEX 06/07/48. AKA Herbert/Hulbert
08/03/47 Detroit MI	Detroit MI	07/01/48 Jalapa MEX	Born in Ohio
04/19/48 Detroit MI	Detroit MI	07/16/48 Jefferson BKS MO	
12/24/47 Detroit MI	01/01/48 Detroit MI		Died at Detroit MI 02/03/48
04/05/47 Detroit MI	04/22/47 Detroit MI	07/31/48 Jefferson BKS MO	TRA COM D 01/04/48. Received pension
11/30/47 Pontiac MI	12/01/47 Detroit MI	07/26/48 Detroit MI	PEN: MNI AKA H. Died at Cincinnati OH April 1919
04/08/47 Monroe MI	04/30/47 Detroit MI	08/04/48 Covington KY	
			PMT CAP 08/20/47, MAJ 09/13/47. PEN. MNI Jackson
12/01/47 Pontiac MI	12/01/47 Detroit MI	07/26/48 Detroit MI	PEN
06/01/46 Adrian MI			VTS WNA
11/20/47 Hillsdale MI	12/01/47 Detroit MI		Deserted at Detroit MI 12/26/47
11/20/47 Monroe MI	12/01/47 Detroit MI	07/27/48 Detroit MI	Received pension
11/20/47 Clinton MI	12/01/47 Detroit MI		Left at Joliet 07/12/48. Arrived at Clinton 11/14/48
01/25/48 Detroit MI	02/01/48 Detroit MI		Deserted at Detroit MI 04/12/48. Born in ENG

Name	Age	Hgt	Eye	Hair	Cpx	Trade	Born	Home	Rank	Unit
Husted, Henry	23	5.06	BLU	SDY	LGT	Farmer	Manchester NY		PVT	COM B 5th US INF
Hutton, Elery	22	5.08	BLU	BWN	LGT	Laborer	Steuben Co NY		PVT	COM B 3rd US INF
Hutton, Lewis W.	19	5.05	BLU	BWN	LGT	Blacksmith	Barrington NY		RCT	COM A 15th US INF
Hyatt, John B.	33	5.10	BLU	BWN	FLD	Moulder	New Brunswick		RCT	COM ? 3rd US DRG
Ide, Charles	21	5.08	GRY	DRK	DRK	Farmer	Orleans Co NY		PVT	COM G 1st MI INF
Iness, William P.	26								PVT	COM B 1st MI INF
Ingle, James	28	5.07	BLU	LGT	LGT	Clothier	England	Corunna MI	PVT	COM C 1st MI INF
Inglis, William	28	5.07	BLU	DRK	FIR	Laborer	Reufenshire SCO		PVT	COM G 15th US INF
Irish, Albert D.	18	5.10	GRY	DRK	LGT	Cabinet-maker	Madison Co NY	Grand Rapids MI	PVT	COM G 1st MI INF
Irvine, George	30	6.00	BWN	LGT	FIR	Laborer	Ireland	Detroit MI	PVT	COM E 1st MI INF
Irwin, David	32	5.07	BLK	BWN	DRK	Laborer	Newberry NY	Grand Rapids MI	PVT	COM E 1st MI INF
Irwin, Stephen	18	6.00	BLU	LGT	LGT	Cooper	Yates Co NY		PVT	COM A 1st MI INF
Ives, Cyrus B.	33	6.01	BLU	BWN	LGT	Farmer	Oneida Co NY	Madison MI	PVT	COM H 1st MI INF
Ives, James	18	5.06	BLU	LGT	FIR	Farmer	Chattaraugus NY		MUS	COM E 15th US INF
Jackson, Francis	20	5.08	BLK	DRK	DRK	Farmer	New Jersey	Monroe MI	PVT	COM G 15th US INF
Jackson, Joel M.	21	5.08	GRY	BLK	DRK	Farmer	Erie NY		PVT	COM K 3rd US DRG
Jackson, John	37	5.07	BWN	BLK	DRK	Laborer	Tunbridge VT	Kalamazoo MI	PVT	COM A 1st MI INF
Jackson, William J. S.	29	5.11	BLU	DRK	DRK	Lawyer	Lebanon OH		PVT	COM B 5th US INF
Jacobs, Philip	35							Dexter MI	PVT	COM H 1st MI INF
Jamieson, John	18	5.06	BLU	BWN	FIR	Laborer	Lower Canada	Detroit MI	PVT	COM I 1st MI INF
Jarvis, Ralph	25	5.10	BLK	BWN	FIR	Carpenter	Parishville NY	Adrian MI	2SG	COM I 1st MI INF
Jenkinson, David	23	5.07	BLU	BWN	DRK	Laborer	Armagh IRE		PVT	COM B 3rd US INF
Jenks, Ambrose K.	19	5.08	BLU	DRK	DRK	Blacksmith	Marcellus NY		PVT	COM K 1st MI INF
Jerolomon, Jordon	18	5.07	BLU	BWN	FIR	Farmer	New York State	Marshall MI	PVT	COM I 1st MI INF
Jerome, Tompkins D.								Adrian MI	3SG	Adrian Guards
Jewitt, John	44	5.06	BLU	GRY	LGT	Shoemaker	Philadelphia PA	Detroit MI	PVT	COM B 1st MI INF

ENROLLED	MUSTERED	DISCHARGED	REMARKS
10/30/47 Detroit MI	Detroit MI	08/01/48 East Pascagoula MS	
04/01/47 Detroit MI	04/01/47 Detroit MI	04/13/47 Detroit MI	Discharged by civil authority as a minor
04/09/47 Pontiac MI	Detroit MI	04/15/47 Detroit MI	Discharged as a minor
05/16/48 Detroit MI	Detroit MI	07/16/48 Jefferson BKS MO	Born in Nova Scotia
02/20/48 Detroit MI	03/01/48 Detroit MI		Died at Vera Cruz MEX 06/05/48
01/24/48 Vera Cruz MEX	01/31/48 Vera Cruz MEX	03/05/48	
11/30/47 Corunna MI	12/01/47 Detroit MI	07/26/48 Detroit MI	AKA James Jingall
04/09/47 Monroe MI	04/30/47 Detroit MI	11/24/47 Perote MEX	PMT SGT 04/21/47. DFD. Born in Scotland
01/25/48 Grand Rapids MI	02/01/48 Detroit MI	07/18/48 Detroit MI	
11/20/47 Detroit MI	12/04/47 Detroit MI		Deserted at New Orleans LA 01/17/48
11/20/47 Grandville MI	12/04/47 Detroit MI	07/18/48 Detroit MI	Received pension
11/05/47 Paw Paw MI	11/19/47 Detroit MI	07/18/48 Detroit MI	
11/29/47 Adrian MI	12/01/47 Detroit MI	07/27/48 Detroit MI	PEN
04/26/47 Niles MI	04/27/47 Detroit MI	08/06/48 Cincinnati OH	
04/16/47 Monroe MI	04/30/47 Detroit MI	08/04/48 Covington KY	Received pension
04/01/47 Detroit MI	04/22/47 Detroit MI		LIH at Puebla MEX 08/07/47
01/02/48 New Orleans LA	01/02/48 New Orleans LA		Died at Detroit MI 07/23/48
10/11/47 Detroit MI	Detroit MI	08/01/48 East Pascagoula MS	
01/18/48 Dexter MI	02/01/48 Detroit MI		Died on Lake Erie aboard the steamboat Albany 02/10/48
12/20/47 Detroit MI	01/01/48 Detroit MI	07/18/48 Detroit MI	
11/15/47 Adrian MI	12/01/47 Detroit MI	07/18/48 Detroit MI	
03/13/47 Detroit MI	03/13/47 Detroit MI	07/25/48 East Pascagoula MS	
11/15/47 Saline MI	12/01/47 Detroit MI		Died at Detroit MI 01/01/48
11/15/47 Marshall MI	12/01/47 Detroit MI	07/18/48 Detroit MI	PEN. AKA Jerdan Jerelaman
06/01/46 Adrian MI			VTS WNA
11/02/47 Jackson MI	11/12/47 Detroit MI	07/26/48 Detroit MI	

NAME	AGE	HGT	EYE	HAIR	CPX	TRADE	BORN	HOME	RANK	UNIT
Jirault, Antonio	21	5.08	HZL	BWN	DRK	Drummer	Detroit MI		RCT	US Army
Johnson, Abraham	25	5.05	GRY	SDY	FIR	Shoemaker	New Lisbon OH		PVT	COM A 6th US INF
Johnson, Anthony						Clothier		Detroit MI	2LT	Montgomery Guards
Johnson, Clark	21	5.09	HZL	BWN	DRK	Millwright	Nickel CAN		RCT	US Army
Johnson, David	29	5.07	BLU	BWN	RUD	Laborer	Richmond NY		PVT	COM A 15th US INF
Johnson, George M.	22	5.11	BLU	BWN	LGT	Farmer	Knox OH	Frederickton OH	PVT	COM H 1st MI INF
Johnson, Jerome H.	18	5.08	GRY	DRK	LGT	Laborer	Pontiac MI		PVT	COM A 15th US INF
Johnson, John B.	22	5.09	GRY	FIR	FIR	Blacksmith	Trenton NJ		CPL	COM A 6th US INF
Johnson, John H.	26	5.06	GRY	LGT	LGT	Farmer	New Paltz NY		PVT	COM K 1st MI INF
Johnson, Otis	35	5.09	BLU	SDY	SAL	Cooper	Chepachet RI	Northfield MI	PVT	COM G 15th US INF
Johnson, Robert	18	5.06	BLU	SDY	FIR	Farmer	Genesee Co NY	Northfield MI	PVT	COM G 15th US INF
Johnson, William T.	18	5.03	BLK	BWN	FIR	Miller	Oakland Co MI		PVT	COM C 1st MI INF
Johnston, Alexander W.	33	6.01	BLU	BWN	LGT	Farmer	Scotland	New York NY	PVT	COM H 1st MI INF
Johnston, Anthony						Clothier		Detroit MI	2LT	Montgomery Guards
Johnston, James	34	5.04	HZL	BWN	SDY	Carpenter	Halifax CAN		MUS	COM K 3rd US DRG
Johnston, Robert	31	5.10	HZL	BLK	DRK	Laborer	Argyle SCO	Detroit MI	PVT	Brady Guards
Joles, George H.	19							Delhi MI	PVT	COM H 1st MI INF
Jones, Enoch H.	19	5.08	GRY	DRK	LGT	Laborer	Orangeville NY		PVT	COM B 1st MI INF
Jones, Francis A. S.	18	5.10	BLU	DRK	DRK	Boatman	Tuscarawas Co OH		PVT	COM H US MTD RIF
Jones, Henry B.								Adrian MI	PVT	Adrian Guards
Jones, Hugh	27	5.07	HZL	BWN	DRK	Blacksmith	Moranshire ENG	Detroit MI	PVT	Brady Guards
Jones, James	34	5.06	BLK	BLK	DRK	Farmer	Kent Co ENG		PVT	COM G 1st MI INF
Jones, Lyman	18		GRY	DRK	DRK				PVT	COM G 1st MI INF
Jones, Morgan	26	5.10	HZL	BLK	DRK	Farmer	Cayuga Co NY	Flint MI	PVT	COM K 1st MI INF
Jones, Oliver L.	24	5.09	BLU	DRK	DRK	Farmer	Vermont		PVT	COM D 1st MI INF
Jones, Orlando	21	5.07	BLU	BWN	DRK	Farmer	Genesee Co NY		RCT	US Army

ENROLLED	MUSTERED	DISCHARGED	REMARKS
11/29/47 Detroit MI	Detroit MI		Deserted at Detroit MI 12/03/47
08/10/46 Detroit MI	08/10/46 Detroit MI		Died at Puebla MEX 07/16/47
05/28/46 Detroit MI			VTS WNA
09/23/47 Detroit MI	Detroit MI		Deserted at Detroit MI 09/28/47
04/16/47 Pontiac MI	04/27/47 Detroit MI	08/04/48 Covington KY	TRA COM K 12/26/47
11/20/47 Hillsdale MI	12/01/47 Detroit MI	07/27/48 Detroit MI	
04/03/47 Pontiac MI	04/27/47 Detroit MI	08/04/48 Cincinnati OH	TRA COM I 12/26/47
10/02/46 Detroit MI	10/02/46 Detroit MI		
12/24/47 Jackson MI	01/01/48 Detroit MI	07/28/48 Detroit MI	PMT CPL 03/05/48. LIH at Memphis TN 07/08/48
04/27/47 Detroit MI	04/30/47 Detroit MI	08/04/48 Covington KY	
04/27/47 Detroit MI	04/30/47 Detroit MI	08/04/48 Covington KY	Received pension
11/30/47 Southfield MI	12/01/47 Detroit MI		Deserted at Detroit MI 12/13/48
11/20/47 Toledo OH	12/01/47 Detroit MI	07/27/48 Detroit MI	
??/??/46 Detroit MI			VTS WNA
04/01/47 Detroit MI	04/22/47 Detroit MI		DOD Puebla MEX 07/25/47. Born in Nova Scotia
06/18/47 Detroit MI	06/18/47 Detroit MI	06/30/48 Detroit MI	PMT 4SG 09/23/47
12/20/47 Delhi MI	01/01/48 Detroit MI		Deserted at Detroit MI 01/29/48
11/02/47 Port Huron MI	11/12/47 Detroit MI		Died at Cordova MEX 05/09/48
08/01/47 Otsego MI	08/01/47 Otsego MI	07/31/48 Jefferson BKS MO	Received pension
06/01/46 Adrian MI			VTS WNA
06/18/47 Detroit MI	06/18/47 Detroit MI	06/30/48 Detroit MI	
02/20/48 Battle Creek MI	03/01/48 Detroit MI		Deserted at New Orleans LA 05/01/48
02/20/48 Adrian MI	03/01/48 Detroit MI		Died at Detroit MI 04/02/48
11/15/47 Flushing MI	12/01/47 Detroit MI	07/28/48 Detroit MI	Received pension
11/14/47 Detroit MI	11/14/47 Detroit MI		Deserted at Detroit MI 11/19/47
04/25/48 Detroit MI	Detroit MI		Deserted 05/24/48

Name	Age	Hgt	Eye	Hair	Cpx	Trade	Born	Home	Rank	Unit
Jordon, Frederick	19								PVT	COM I 1st MI INF
Jordon, James	32								PVT	COM I 1st MI INF
Joyce, Daniel M.	25	5.10	GRY	BLK	FIR	Laborer	Niagara Co NY	Marshall MI	PVT	COM I 1st MI INF
Joyce, Justus	18	5.07	GRY	BWN	FIR	Farmer	Niagara Co NY		PVT	COM I 1st MI INF
Judson, Lucius L.	25	6.00	BLU	BWN	LGT	Butcher	Hiram OH	Detroit MI	1CP	COM H 1st MI INF
Juetten, John J.	25	5.06	BLU	BWN	FIR	Cooper	Prussia	Milwaukee WI	PVT	COM F 1st MI INF
Juilerrat, George U.	33	5.07	DRK	BLK	DRK	Tailor	Switzerland	West Unity OH	PVT	COM K 1st MI INF
Justus, Edward	30	5.04	HZL	BWN	FLD	Laborer	Cork IRE		RCT	US Army
Kailey, Chandler	18	5.09	BLU	LGT	LGT	Farmer	Monroe Co NY		PVT	COM K 3rd US DRG
Kaminsky, Andrew						Printer		Detroit MI	PVT	Scott Guards
Katus, Allois						Blacksmith		Detroit MI	1SG	Scott Guards
Kaufman, Frederick						Tailor		Detroit MI	2LT	Scott Guards
Kaufman, John F.								Detroit MI	2LT	Scott Guards
Kavaney, John	29	5.05	HZL	GRY	LGT	Laborer	Slidel IRE		PVT	COM B 3rd US INF
Keele, Isaac M.								Adrian MI	PVT	Adrian Guards
Keeler, Coleman	20		BLU	SDY	LGT	Clerk	Ohio	Toledo OH	PVT	COM H 1st MI INF
Keenan, William	32	6.00	HZL	BWN	FIR	Clerk	Dogherty IRE	Detroit MI	PVT	COM E 1st MI INF
Kelleher, Eugene	30	5.08	BLU	LGT	FIR	Soldier	Cork IRE		PVT	COM B 5th US INF
Keller, Daniel	29	5.07	BLU	BWN	RUD	Carpenter	Kerry IRE		RCT	US Army
Kelley, Edward	28	5.09	BLK	BWN	LGT	Laborer	Ireland		PVT	COM A 15th US INF
Kelliket, Benjamin	22	5.05	BLU	BWN	FIR	Farmer	Wayne Co NY		RCT	Montgomery Guards
Kellogg, Benjamin	24	5.02	BLU	BWN	LGT	Teamster	Ira NY		PVT	COM E 1st MI INF
Kellogg, Charles	24	5.08	BLK	BLK	DRK	Tinner	Trenton NJ		PVT	COM A 6th US INF
Kelly, James	49	5.06	BLU	BWN	LGT	Blacksmith	Montreal CAN		PVT	COM B 3rd US INF
Kelly, James	27	5.06	BLU	BWN	LGT	Cooper	Cumberland ME	Manchester MI	PVT	COM E 1st MI INF
Kelly, Robert	23	5.08	BLU	RED	SDY	Carpenter	Cahir IRE	Grand Rapids MI	PVT	COM D 1st MI INF

Enrolled	Mustered	Discharged	Remarks
11/15/47 Adrian MI	12/01/47 Detroit MI	02/08/48 Detroit MI	Discharged by legal process as minor
11/15/47 Adrian MI	12/01/47 Detroit MI		Deserted at Detroit MI 02/01/48
01/24/48 Marshall MI	02/01/48 Detroit MI	07/18/48 Detroit MI	Received pension
11/15/47 Marshall MI	12/01/47 Detroit MI		Deserted at Detroit MI 12/21/47
11/20/47 Hillsdale MI	12/01/47 Detroit MI	07/27/48 Detroit MI	Received pension
11/15/47 St. Joseph MI	12/02/47 Detroit MI	07/28/48 Detroit MI	PEN. MNI Joseph. AKA John J. Justin
01/20/48 Grass Lake MI	02/01/48 Detroit MI	07/28/48 Detroit MI	PEN
10/11/47 Detroit MI	Detroit MI		Deserted 10/26/47
04/06/47 Tecumseh MI			Died at Mexico City 09/23/47
06/03/46 Detroit MI			VTS WNA
06/03/46 Detroit MI			VTS WNA
06/03/46 Detroit MI			VTS WNA
06/03/46 Detroit MI			VTS WNA
03/01/47 Detroit MI	03/01/47 Detroit MI		Died by drowning at New Orleans LA 06/14/47
06/01/46 Adrian MI			VTS WNA
11/20/47 Toledo OH	12/01/47 Detroit MI		Deserted at expiration of furlough 12/26/47
11/20/47 Detroit MI	12/04/47 Detroit MI		Died of intemperance at Newport KY 12/27/47
09/11/47 Detroit MI	Detroit MI	08/21/48 East Pascagoula MS	
05/02/48 Detroit MI	Detroit MI		Deserted 05/20/48
04/17/47 Utica MI	04/27/47 Detroit MI		Died of sun stroke at Camp Rio San Juan 06/19/47
10/27/47 Detroit MI			Company disbanded before muster
11/20/47 Battle Creek MI	12/04/47 Detroit MI	07/18/48 Detroit MI	
10/05/46 Kalamazoo MI	10/05/46 Kalamazoo MI		Deserted at Detroit MI 10/06/46
03/11/47 Detroit MI	03/11/47 Detroit MI	07/25/48 East Pascagoula MS	AKA James Keely. PEN
11/20/47 Coldwater MI	12/04/47 Detroit MI	07/18/48 Detroit MI	PEN. AKA Kelley
11/14/47 Detroit MI	11/14/47 Detroit MI	07/26/48 Detroit MI	Received pension under true name, Robert Henderson

Name	Age	Hgt	Eye	Hair	Cpx	Trade	Born	Home	Rank	Unit
Kemp, John	45	5.07	BLU	LGT	LGT	Soldier	Norfolk ENG	Port Huron MI	PVT	COM E 1st MI INF
Kendall, Nelson	23	5.07	BLU	SDY	FIR	Porter	Philadelphia PA		PVT	COM G 15th US INF
Kennedy, Frederick A.	35					Farmer	Brighton ENG	Hanover MI	2LT	NTH Lenawee VOL
Kennedy, John	28	5.05	GRY	DRK	DRK	Farmer	Dublin IRE	Detroit MI	PVT	COM B 1st MI INF
Kennedy, John	34	6.00	BLU	BWN	FLD	Farmer	Meath Co IRE		PVT	COM K 3rd US DRG
Kennicat, James	19	5.10	HZL	SDY	LGT	Cabinet-maker	Allegany Co NY	Greenbush MI	PVT	Brady Guards
Kenny, Stephen D.								Detroit MI	PVT	Montgomery Guards
Kent, Andrew J.	21	5.10	GRY	BWN	LGT	Farmer	Steuben Co NY		PVT	COM A 1st MI INF
Kent, Jacob	22	5.09	BLK	BLK	DRK	Laborer	London CAN		PVT	COM A 15th US INF
Keyes, Benjamin P.	28	5.05	GRY	SDY	FIR	Harness-maker	Albany NY		PVT	COM A 6th US INF
Keyes, George	21	5.08	HZL	BWN	FIR	Farmer	Crawford NY	Marshall MI	PVT	COM I 1st MI INF
Keys, Samuel	30	5.09	GRY	BWN	FIR	Carpenter	Onondaga Co NY	Marshall MI	4SG	COM I 1st MI INF
Kick, John	26	5.08	HZL	RED	FLD	Brewer	Baum GER	Monroe MI	PVT	COM G 15th US INF
Kidder, Addison N.	21	5.04	BLU	BLK	LGT	Farmer	Ontario Co NY	Hudson MI	3SG	COM H 1st MI INF
Kidder, Erastus	23	5.05	BLU	BWN	FIR	Farmer	Pennsylvania		PVT	COM F US MTD RIF
Kiles, James C.	22	6.03	GRY	BWN	LGT	Tailor	Toronto CAN	Adrian MI	PVT	COM G 1st MI INF
Kimball, Elanson	22	5.05	HZL	DRK	DRK	Laborer	Cattaraugus NY	Detroit MI	PVT	Brady Guards
Kimball, Nelson H.	25					Carpenter	Martinsburg NY	Adrian MI	PVT	Adrian Guards
Kimball, Truman P.								Adrian MI	PVT	Adrian Guards
King, Augustus	32	5.00	HZL	BLK	DRK	Carpenter	Windsor CAN	Detroit MI	PVT	Brady Guards
King, Herman	30								PVT	COM D 1st MI INF
King, Jesse	37	5.09	BLU	BWN	FIR	Laborer	Germany	Lower Sandusky OH	PVT	COM I 1st MI INF
King, John	21	5.06	HZL	BLK	DRK	Laborer	Aplebern GER	Detroit MI	PVT	Brady Guards
King, John E.	28	5.08	BLU	BWN	LGT	Clerk	North Hamton NH	Detroit MI	1LT	COM B 1st MI INF
King, John H.	27					Soldier	Michigan		CAP	COM F 1st US INF
Kingsland, James S.	42					Moulder	New York State		1LT	COM I 1st MI INF

Enrolled	Mustered	Discharged	Remarks
11/20/47 Detroit MI	12/04/47 Detroit MI	07/18/48 Detroit MI	
04/12/47 Monroe MI	04/30/47 Detroit MI	08/04/48 Covington KY	Received pension
06/06/46 Tecumseh MI			VTS WNA
11/02/47 Port Huron MI	11/12/47 Detroit MI	07/26/48 Detroit MI	
03/26/47 Detroit MI	04/22/47 Detroit MI	07/31/48 Jefferson BKS MO	PMT SGT 03/26/47. RTR 09/11/47 and TRA COM C
06/18/47 Detroit MI	06/18/47 Detroit MI	06/30/48 Detroit MI	AKA James Kinnecat
05/28/46 Detroit MI			VTS WNA
11/05/47 Kalamazoo MI	11/19/47 Detroit MI	05/09/48 New Orleans LA	DSC. Left at New Orleans LA 06/16/48. PEN
04/10/47 Ann Arbor MI	04/27/47 Detroit MI	07/24/48 Baton Rouge LA	TRA COM K 12/26/47
11/24/46 Detroit MI	11/24/46 Detroit MI		Died at Puebla MEX 08/15/47
11/15/47 Marshall MI	12/01/47 Detroit MI	07/18/48 Detroit MI	Received pension. AKA George Kyes
11/15/47 Marshall MI	12/01/47 Detroit MI	07/18/48 Detroit MI	Received pension. AKA Samuel Kies
04/06/47 Detroit MI	04/30/47 Detroit MI	08/04/48 Covington KY	
11/20/47 Hudson MI	12/01/47 Detroit MI	07/27/48 Detroit MI	TRA COM G from Detroit MI hospital. PEN
06/28/47 Kalamazoo MI	06/28/47 Kalamazoo MI	07/26/48 Jefferson BKS MO	
01/25/48 Lexington MI	02/01/48 Detroit MI	07/18/48 Detroit MI	
06/18/47 Detroit MI	06/18/47 Detroit MI	06/30/48 Detroit MI	
06/01/46 Adrian MI			VTS WNA
06/01/46 Adrian MI			VTS WNA
06/18/47 Detroit MI	06/18/47 Detroit MI	06/30/48 Detroit MI	
11/14/47 Detroit MI	11/14/47 Detroit MI		Deserted at Detroit MI 11/19/47
02/15/48 Lower Sandusky	02/29/48 New Orleans LA	.	Died of diarrhea at Cordova MEX 05/19/48
06/18/47 Detroit MI	06/18/47 Detroit MI	06/30/48 Detroit MI	Born in Prussia. AKA John Kaenig. PEN
10/30/47 Port Huron MI	11/12/47 Detroit MI	07/26/48 Detroit MI	Commanding officer. MNI Edward. PEN
			MNI Haskell
10/30/47 Adrian MI	12/01/47 Detroit MI	07/18/48 Detroit MI	On recruiting duty in Detroit MI. PEN

Name	Age	Hgt	Eye	Hair	Cpx	Trade	Born	Home	Rank	Unit
Kinsey, James D.	27	6.00	BLU	BLK	LGT	Blacksmith	Middlesex NY		PVT	COM E 15th US INF
Kirby, Frederick L.	18	5.08	GRY	DRK	DRK	Cooper	Sackets Harbor	Leslie MI	PVT	COM B 1st MI INF
Kirchner, Frederick	26	5.09	BLU	LGT	LGT	Blacksmith	Hesse GER	Monroe MI	PVT	COM G 15th US INF
Kirk, Isaac H.	23	5.06	BLK	BWN	LGT	Farmer	Montgomery VA	St. Joseph MI	PVT	COM F 1st MI INF
Kirkner, Thomas	31	5.06	BLU	FIR	LGT	Soldier	Loudenback AUS		PVT	COM A 6th US INF
Kirsch, John	25	5.04	BLU	LGT	FIR	Laborer	Strasburg FRA		PVT	COM B 3rd US INF
Klevanz, Ignatius	25	5.04	BLU	LGT	LGT	Laborer	Baden GER	Monroe MI	PVT	COM G 15th US INF
Kline, Joshua	20	5.06	HZL	BWN	FLD	Farmer	Oakland Co MI	Detroit MI	PVT	COM G 15th US INF
Klotz, Bartel	25	5.06	BLU	DRK	LGT	Laborer	Baden GER	Monroe MI	PVT	COM G 15th US INF
Knapp, Abram								Adrian MI	PVT	Adrian Guards
Knapp, Bartolomew	21	5.11	BLU	LGT	FIR	Farmer	Cattaraugus NY		RCT	US Army
Knapp, Stephen	22	5.07	BLU	LGT	FLD	Farmer	New York State		PVT	COM I 1st MI INF
Knecht, Caspar	25	5.05	HZL	BLK	SAL	Farmer	Wirtemberg GER		PVT	COM G 15th US INF
Knecht, George	23	5.04	HZL	BWN	SAL	Farmer	Wirtemberg GER		PVT	COM G 15th US INF
Knecht, Louis	30	5.05	LGT	BWN	RUD	Farmer	Wirtemberg GER		PVT	COM G 15th US INF
Knox, Philetus P.	29	5.08	BLK	DRK	DRK	Laborer	Montreal CAN	Detroit MI	PVT	COM D 1st MI INF
Koch, Frederick						Butcher		Detroit MI	PVT	Scott Guards
Koch, William R.	28	5.11	DRK	BWN	RUD	Miller	Richmond Co PA	Pontiac MI	PVT	COM A 15th US INF
Kochler, Augustus	35	5.08	BLU	BWN	FIR	Steward	Saxony GER		PVT	COM C 2nd US INF
Kohland, Matthias	38	5.10	BLU	LGT	DRK	Carpenter	Bavaria		PVT	COM D 1st MI INF
Kunze, George						Clerk		Detroit MI	3CP	Scott Guards
Kunze, Louis						Shoemaker		Detroit MI	2LT	Scott Guards
Labrach, Charles	20	5.10	BLK	BLK	DRK	Carpenter	Montreal CAN	Marshall MI	PVT	COM I 1st MI INF
Ladd, Daniel								Detroit MI	PVT	Montgomery Guards
Ladd, George W.	23	5.10	GRY	DRK	DRK	Blacksmith	Wake Co NC		PVT	COM G 1st MI INF
Ladd, John	22	5.08	BLU	BWN	FIR	Laborer	Bovina NY		PVT	COM E 15th US INF

Enrolled	Mustered	Discharged	Remarks
04/06/47 Jackson MI			Died at Chapultepec MEX 12/13/47
11/02/47 Port Huron MI	11/12/47 Detroit MI	07/26/48 Detroit MI	
04/19/47 Monroe MI	04/30/47 Detroit MI		Died of diarrhea at Jalapa MEX 08/26/47
11/15/47 Niles MI	12/02/47 Detroit MI		Died at Detroit MI 07/24/48
12/21/46 Detroit MI	12/21/46 Detroit MI		
03/04/47 Detroit MI	04/04/47 Detroit MI	07/25/48 East Pascagoula MS	
04/19/47 Monroe MI	04/30/47 Detroit MI	08/04/48 Covington KY	Received pension. AKA Ignatz Klevens
04/06/47 Detroit MI	04/30/47 Detroit MI		Died of sun stroke at Jalapa MEX 09/27/47
04/14/47 Monroe MI	04/30/47 Detroit MI	08/04/48 Covington KY	Received pension
06/01/46 Adrian MI			VTS WNA
10/21/47 Detroit MI	Detroit MI		Deserted 10/30/47
11/15/47 Marshall MI	12/01/47 Detroit MI		Died at Detroit MI 12/10/47
04/26/47 Detroit MI	04/30/47 Detroit MI		Deserted at Detroit MI 06/26/47
04/27/47 Detroit MI	04/30/47 Detroit MI	08/04/48 Covington KY	
04/26/47 Detroit MI	04/30/47 Detroit MI	11/27/47 Perote MEX	Discharged for disability. Received pension
11/14/47 Detroit MI	11/14/47 Detroit MI		Died at Detroit MI 09/20/48
06/03/46 Detroit MI			VTS WNA
04/09/47 Pontiac MI	04/27/47 Detroit MI		WIA at battle of Chapultepec. Died 09/07/47
10/15/46 Fort Mackinac		06/05/48 Mexico City MEX	
11/14/47 Ypsilanti MI	11/14/47 Detroit MI	01/28/48	Discharged on account of disability
06/03/46 Detroit MI			VTS WNA
06/03/46 Detroit MI			VTS WNA
11/15/47 Marshall MI	12/01/47 Detroit MI	07/18/48 Detroit MI	AKA Louis LaBrash. PEN
??/??/46 Detroit MI			VTS WNA
04/15/48 Cincinnati OH	04/15/48 Cincinnati OH	06/29/48 New Orleans LA	Discharged on surgeon's certificate
04/09/47 Fawn River MI	04/27/47 Detroit MI		Died at Puebla MEX 09/24/47

Name	Age	Hgt	Eye	Hair	Cpx	Trade	Born	Home	Rank	Unit
Ladd, John J. R.	43	5.05	BLU	BWN	LGT	Farmer	Franklin Co VT	Clinton MI	PVT	COM H 1st MI INF
Laforge, Matthew	19	5.08	HZL	BLK	DRK	Farmer	Hamtramck MI	Detroit MI	PVT	Brady Guards
Lahan, John	28	5.09	BLU	GRY	FIR	Laborer	Ireland	Chicago IL	PVT	COM F 1st MI INF
Laib, Lewis	28	5.09	HZL	BLK	DRK	Butcher	Burgstadt GER	Detroit MI	PVT	COM D 1st MI INF
Laible, Eugene	22					Clerk	Ettenheim GER	Detroit MI	PVT	Scott Guards
Laisdiell, Luther	24	5.07	GRY	DRK	DRK	Moulder	St. Albans VT		PVT	COM K 1st MI INF
Lake, Charles C.	19	5.05	BLU	BWN	LGT	Laborer	Seneca Co NY	Kalamazoo MI	PVT	COM A 1st MI INF
Laker, George	30	5.04	BLU	LGT	FLD	Farmer	England	Adrian MI	PVT	COM F 1st MI INF
Laker, John	22	5.08	BLU	LGT	FLD	Farmer	England	Adrian MI	PVT	COM F 1st MI INF
Lamb, Caleb A.	21	5.08	GRY	BWN	LGT	Shoemaker	Waterloo NY		RCT	US Army
Lamb, Mahon H.	20	5.10	GRY	DRK	LGT	Laborer	Rome NY		PVT	COM B 1st MI INF
LaMotte, Charles	44	5.02	GRY	BWN	DRK	Laborer	Canada	St. Joseph MI	PVT	COM F 1st MI INF
Lamour, John	18	5.07	HZL	DRK	DRK	Laborer	Canada		PVT	COM A 15th US INF
Lanagan, Dennis								Detroit MI	PVT	Montgomery Guards
Lane, Abraham	27	5.10	BLU	DRK	LGT	Accountant	Cork IRE		PVT	COM G 1st MI INF
Lapier, Charles	27								PVT	COM D 1st MI INF
Lapier, John B.	20	5.06	BLU	BWN	LGT	Baker	Detroit MI	Detroit MI	PVT	Brady Guards
Larkin, William	28	5.07	BLU	BLK	FIR	Sailor	Ireland	Buffalo NY	PVT	COM F 1st MI INF
Larned, Frank H.	20					Soldier	Detroit MI	Detroit MI	2LT	COM ? US VTG
Latham, Benjamin W.								Monroe MI	1LT	Monroe Guards
Lavalette, John B.	44	5.07	BLK	BLK	DRK	Carpenter	Montreal CAN	Detroit MI	PVT	COM D 1st MI INF
Lawrence, Alexander	20	5.07	DRK	SDY	FIR	Cabinet-maker	Saratoga Co NY	Monroe MI	PVT	COM G 15th US INF
Lawrence, Ralph	43	5.08	BLU	DRK	LGT	Farmer	Berkshire MA	Mottville MI	PVT	COM F 1st MI INF
Lawrence, Wellington	19	5.09	BLK	DRK	DRK	Farmer	Middletown NY	Almont MI	PVT	COM K 1st MI INF
Lawson, John F.	21	5.03	DRK	BWN	LGT	Farmer	Lincolnshire ENG		PVT	COM G 1st MI INF
Lawyer, Samuel E.	21	5.06	BLK	SDY	LGT	Butcher	Richmond VA	Detroit MI	3CP	COM B 1st MI INF

ENROLLED	MUSTERED	DISCHARGED	REMARKS
12/20/47 Clinton MI	01/01/47 Detroit MI		Died of diarrhea at Cordova MEX 05/17/48
06/18/47 Detroit MI	06/18/47 Detroit MI		Deserted at Detroit MI 06/21/47. PEN
11/15/47 Niles MI	12/02/47 Detroit MI	07/28/48 Detroit MI	
11/14/47 Detroit MI	11/14/47 Detroit MI	07/26/48 Detroit MI	
06/03/46 Detroit MI			VTS WNA
12/24/47 Richmond MI	01/01/48 Detroit MI		Fell overboard from steamboat near St. Louis MO
11/05/47 Kalamazoo MI	11/19/47 Detroit MI	07/??/48 Detroit MI	PEN. Died on board transport 06/22/48?
11/15/47 Adrian MI	12/02/47 Detroit MI		LIH at New Orleans LA 06/24/48. Died 07/??/48. PEN
11/15/47 Adrian MI	12/02/47 Detroit MI	07/28/48 Detroit MI	AKA John Larken
06/01/48 Detroit MI	Detroit MI	06/20/48 Newport KY	
11/02/47 Port Huron MI	11/12/47 Detroit MI		Died en route to Vera Cruz MEX 06/15/48
11/15/47 Niles MI	12/02/47 Detroit MI	07/28/48 Detroit MI	PEN
04/13/47 Ann Arbor MI	04/27/47 Detroit MI	07/25/48 Baton Rouge LA	LIH at Vera Cruz 06/16/47. TRA COM F 12/26/47. PEN
05/28/46 Detroit MI			VTS WNA
01/25/48 Detroit MI	03/01/48 Detroit MI		Deserted at Detroit MI 04/09/48
11/14/47 Detroit MI	11/14/47 Detroit MI		Deserted at Detroit MI 12/22/47
06/18/47 Detroit MI	06/18/47 Detroit MI	06/30/48 Detroit MI	
11/15/47 Niles MI	12/02/47 Detroit MI	07/28/48 Detroit MI	
03/08/47	04/09/47		TRA COM ? 2nd US ART 06/27/48. PEN. MNI Hunt
??/??/46 Monroe MI			VTS WNA
11/14/47 Detroit MI	11/14/47 Detroit MI	07/26/48 Detroit MI	
11/14/47 Monroe MI	04/30/47 Detroit MI	08/04/48 Covington KY	Received pension
11/15/47 Niles MI	12/02/47 Detroit MI		Died at Detroit MI 12/26/47
11/15/47 Almont MI	12/01/47 Detroit MI	07/28/48 Detroit MI	Received pension
02/20/48 Hillsdale MI	03/01/48 Detroit MI	07/18/48 Detroit MI	STH at New Orleans LA from Vera Cruz MEX 06/05/48
11/02/47 Detroit MI	11/12/47 Detroit MI	07/26/48 Detroit MI	Received pension

Name	Age	Hgt	Eye	Hair	Cpx	Trade	Born	Home	Rank	Unit
Lay, Rodney H.	30	5.11	GRY	DRK	LGT	Farmer	Niagara Co NY		PVT	COM C 1st MI INF
Leake, John W.	28	5.06	GRY	BWN	DRK	Merchant	Erie Co NY		CPL	COM K 3rd US DRG
Leavenworth, John L.	22	5.07	HZL	BWN	FIR	Farmer	Columbia Co NY		PVT	COM K 3rd US DRG
Lee, John	26	5.11	HZL	BLK	DRK	Farmer	New York NY		PVT	COM G 5th US INF
Lee, John H.	28	5.08	BLU	LGT	LGT	Farmer	Ireland		PVT	COM I 5th US INF
Leeson, William M.	28	5.08	GRY	BWN	FIR	Soldier	Belfast IRE		RCT	Montgomery Guards
Leggett, Peter	33	5.08	BLU	DRK	DRK	Laborer		Detroit MI	PVT	COM B 1st MI INF
Legro, Ebenezer	24	5.10	HZL	BLK	DRK	Soldier	St. Lawrence NY		1SG	COM G 15th US INF
Leith, David	34	5.11	HZL	BWN	FIR	Merchant	Caithness SCO		PVT	COM B 5th US INF
Lemaine, Louis	26	5.07	BLU	SDY	LGT	Merchant	Minster GER	Detroit MI	PVT	Brady Guards
Lemcke, Henry C.	34					Physician	Germany	Detroit MI	SUA	F&S 1st MI INF
Lemon, George	25	5.09	BLK	BWN	DRK	Cooper	Orleans Co NY		PVT	COM I 1st MI INF
Leonard, James	34	5.08	BLU	DRK	DRK	Laborer	Scotland		PVT	COM A 15th US INF
Letts, Andrew	19	5.04	BLU	BWN	FIR	Farmer	Oswego Co NY	Corunna MI	PVT	COM C 1st MI INF
Lewis, David H.	33	5.10	BLU	LGT	LGT	Lumber-man	Drydon NY		PVT	COM B 1st MI INF
Lewis, James O.	28	5.08	DRK	BLK	DRK	Farmer	Ontario Co NY	Kalamazoo MI	PVT	COM A 1st MI INF
Lewis, Lyman	35	5.08	BLU	BWN	DRK	Carpenter	Tompkins Co NY	Detroit MI	FIF	COM D 1st MI INF
Lewis, William								Adrian MI	PVT	Adrian Guards
Lillie, Charles B.	25	5.11	BLU	BWN	DRK	Cooper	Springfield CT		PVT	COM E 15th US INF
Linn, Hugh	23	5.08	BLU	LGT	LGT	Farmer	Concord PA	Detroit MI	PVT	COM B 1st MI INF
Linson, Henry								Detroit MI	MUS	Montgomery Guards
Litchfield, William								Adrian MI	PVT	Adrian Guards
Little, Edward	25	5.05	GRY	BWN	FLD	Laborer	Ireland	Grand Rapids MI	PVT	COM E 1st MI INF
Livingston, James	22	5.06	BLU	BWN	FIR	Laborer	Albany NY	Palmer MI	PVT	COM B 1st MI INF
Lochman, Carle	28	5.09	BLU	FIR	LGT	Farmer	Darmstadt GER		PVT	COM A 6th US INF
Logan, Hugh	22	5.08	GRY	LGT	FIR	Farmer	Derry Co IRE		RCT	Montgomery Guards

Enrolled	Mustered	Discharged	Remarks
11/30/47 Pontiac MI	12/01/47 Detroit MI		STH at Vera Cruz MEX 02/02/48. Died 03/16/48
04/18/47 Tecumseh MI	04/22/47 Detroit MI		Died from diesase at Puebla MEX 08/07/47
04/05/47 Detroit MI	04/22/47 Detroit MI		LIH at Perote MEX 07/02/47. Died 09/22/47
05/14/47 Detroit MI	Detroit MI		Died of typhus at Puebla MEX 01/06/48
05/24/47 Detroit MI	Detroit MI		Deserted 04/01/48
10/22/47 Detroit MI			Company disbanded before muster
11/02/47 Port Huron MI	11/12/47 Detroit MI	07/26/48 Detroit MI	
07/21/47 Ft. Mackinac MI		08/21/48 Newport KY	TRA COM C. PEN
11/16/47 Detroit MI	Detroit MI	08/01/48 East Pascagoula MS	PMT CPL 04/02/48. Received pension
06/18/47 Detroit MI	06/18/47 Detroit MI	06/30/48 Detroit MI	Born in Prussia
10/30/47 Detroit MI	12/31/47 Detroit MI	07/29/48 Detroit MI	DOD from war at Monroe 02/27/49. MNI Charles. PEN
11/15/47 Marshall MI	12/01/47 Detroit MI		LIH at Detroit 02/08/48. DFD from broken leg
04/15/47 Detroit MI	04/27/47 Detroit MI	02/24/48 Vera Cruz MEX	TRA COM B 12/26/47. Discharged for disability
11/30/47 Corunna MI	12/01/47 Detroit MI	07/26/48 Detroit MI	
11/02/47 Port Huron MI	11/12/47 Detroit MI		Died of diarrhea at Cordova MEX 05/01/48
11/05/47 Kalamazoo MI	11/19/47 Detroit MI		Died on SS Palmetto en route to New Orleans 06/22/48
11/14/47 Perrysburg OH	11/14/47 Detroit MI	07/26/48 Detroit MI	
06/01/46 Adrian MI			VTS WNA
04/10/47 Niles MI	04/27/47 Detroit MI	03/18/48 Baton Rouge LA	LIH at Vera Cruz MEX 06/18/47. DFD PEN
11/02/47 Port Huron MI	11/12/47 Detroit MI	07/26/48 Detroit MI	
05/28/46 Detroit MI			VTS WNA
06/01/46 Adrian MI			VTS WNA
11/20/47 Grand Rapids MI	12/04/47 Detroit MI	07/18/48 Detroit MI	
11/02/47 Port Huron MI	11/12/47 Detroit MI	07/26/48 Detroit MI	
12/23/46 Detroit MI	12/23/46 Detroit MI		TRA COM D 2nd US INF 08/10/48. Deserted 04/23/49
10/18/47 Detroit MI			Company disbanded before muster

Name	Age	Hgt	Eye	Hair	Cpx	Trade	Born	Home	Rank	Unit
Logan, William B.	23	5.10	BLK	BWN	DRK	Carpenter	Windsor VT	Wakeshma MI	PVT	COM A 1st MI INF
Long, Isaac	21	5.07	BLU	BLK	LGT	Cooper	New Haven NY	Corunna MI	PVT	COM C 1st MI INF
Longstreet, Robert R.	30	5.10	BLU	FIR	FIR	Teacher	Trenton NJ		PVT	COM K 3rd US DRG
Loomis, John	21	5.07	HZL	DRK	DRK	Laborer	Montgomery PA		PVT	COM B 3rd US INF
Loomis, Samuel	21	5.10	BWN	BWN	DRK	Farmer	Rochester NY		RCT	COM ? 3rd US DRG
Loomis, William	29	5.10	BLU	BWN	DRK	Farmer	Onondaga Co NY		PVT	COM A 6th US INF
Loranger, Joseph Jr.	35							Monroe MI	CAP	Monroe Dragoons
Lorenz, Henry J.	23	5.05	HZL	BWN	LGT	Weaver	Munich GER	Detroit MI	PVT	COM G 15th US INF
Losey, Jesse B.	18	5.06	BLU	BWN	LGT	Farmer	Cayuga Co NY	Tecumseh MI	PVT	COM H 1st MI INF
Louden, Amos G.	18	5.05	BLU	SDY	FIR	Laborer	New York State	Jackson MI	PVT	COM E 1st MI INF
Louison, John B.	40	5.07	BWN	DRK	DRK	Carpenter	Montreal CAN	Grand Rapids MI	PVT	COM D 1st MI INF
Lovejoy, William H.	26	5.07	GRY	LGT	LGT	Cooper	Columbia Co NY	Corunna MI	PVT	COM C 1st MI INF
Low, Edward	33	5.09	GRY	LGT	LGT	Blacksmith	Edinburgh SCO		PVT	COM G 1st MI INF
Lowell, Hudson R.	24	5.06	BLU	DRK	DRK	Laborer	Allegany Co NY		PVT	COM G 1st MI INF
Lower, John	30	5.10	HZL	BWN	LGT	Soldier	Washington Co MD	Detroit MI	PVT	COM B 1st MI INF
Lowing, Isaac W.	25	6.04	BLU	BWN	LGT	Lawyer	Genesee Co NY	Grandville MI	3CP	COM I 1st MI INF
Loyd, James	25	5.05	BLK	BLK	LGT	Chairmaker	Dublin IRE	Detroit MI	PVT	COM B 1st MI INF
Lozier, Samuel	25	5.07	BLU	BWN	DRK	Sailor	Chatham CAN		PVT	Brady Guards
Lucas, William H.	36	5.06	BLU	BWN	LGT	Farmer	Columbus NY	Adrian MI	PVT	COM H 1st MI INF
Luce, Benjamin F.	22							Monroe MI	2LT	COM H 1st MI INF
Ludwig, John J. C.	25	5.08	HZL	BLK	DRK	Laborer	Schwarzburg GER		PVT	COM D 1st MI INF
Lull, Franklin R.	20	5.11	HZL	BWN	FIR	Farmer	Rutland VT	Lockport IL	PVT	COM I 1st MI INF
Lurvey, Alonzo	21	5.10	BLU	BWN	FIR	Cooper	Genesee Co NY		PVT	COM K 3rd US DRG
Luther, Isaac S.	24	5.08	BLU	DRK	DRK	Potter	Jefferson Co NY		PVT	COM G 1st MI INF
Lyman, Charles	37	5.04	BLU	BWN	LGT	Farmer	Orange Co NY		PVT	COM D 1st MI INF
Lynch, Dennis R.	24	5.08	BLU	FIR	FIR	Blacksmith	Ireland		PVT	COM K 3rd US DRG

ENROLLED	MUSTERED	DISCHARGED	REMARKS
11/05/47 Kalamazoo MI	11/19/47 Detroit MI	07/13/48 Detroit MI	DSC for ordinary disability. Died 08/15/48
11/30/47 Detroit MI	12/01/47 Detroit MI	07/26/48 Detroit MI	Also known as Isaac DeLong. Received pension
04/12/47 Detroit MI	04/22/47 Detroit MI		Lost on march between Puebla and St. Martine 08/08/47
04/08/47 Detroit MI	04/08/47 Detroit MI	07/25/48 East Pascagoula MS	
06/05/48 Detroit MI	Detroit MI	07/10/48 East Pascagoula MS	
08/14/46 Detroit MI	08/14/46 Detroit MI	04/12/48 Tacubaya MEX	WIA 08/27/47. Discharged for disability
??/??/46 Monroe MI			VIS WNA
03/27/47 Detroit MI	04/30/47 Detroit MI	08/04/48 Covington KY	PMT CPL 04/21/47. RTR 02/27/48. MNI Jacob
11/20/47 Clinton MI	12/01/47 Detroit MI		Died at Cordova MEX 06/11/48
11/20/47 Battle Creek MI	12/04/47 Detroit MI		Died at New Orleans LA of lung inflamation 01/17/48
11/14/47 Detroit MI	11/14/47 Detroit MI	07/26/48 Detroit MI	PEN
11/30/47 Corunna MI	12/01/47 Detroit MI	07/26/48 Detroit MI	PEN
01/25/48 Grand Rapids MI	02/01/48 Detroit MI	07/18/48 Detroit MI	
02/20/48 Battle Creek MI	03/01/48 Detroit MI		Deserted at New Orleans LA 05/01/48
11/02/47 Port Huron MI	11/12/47 Detroit MI	07/26/48 Detroit MI	PMT Musician 01/22/48
11/15/47 Grandville MI	12/01/47 Detroit MI	07/18/48 Detroit MI	Received pension
11/02/47 Port Huron MI	11/12/47 Detroit MI	07/26/48 Detroit MI	
06/18/47 Detroit MI	06/18/47 Detroit MI		Deserted at Fort Mackinac MI 07/16/47
11/20/47 Adrian MI	12/01/47 Detroit MI		LIH at Jefferson Barracks MO 07/06/48
10/30/47 Monroe MI	12/01/47 Detroit MI	07/27/48 Detroit MI	Acting Adjutant
11/14/47 Detroit MI	11/14/47 Detroit MI		Deserted at Detroit MI 11/20/47
11/15/47 Marshall MI	12/01/47 Detroit MI	07/18/48 Detroit MI	
04/14/47 Detroit MI	04/22/47 Detroit MI		LIH at Puebla MEX 08/07/47. AKA Alonzo Linvey
02/20/48 Centreville MI	03/01/48 Detroit MI	07/18/48 Detroit MI	STH at New Orleans LA from Vera Cruz MEX 06/05/48
11/14/47 Detroit MI	11/14/47 Detroit MI		Deserted at Detroit MI 11/19/47
04/03/47 Detroit MI	04/22/47 Detroit MI	08/08/48 Jefferson BKS MO	TRA COM G as blacksmith 01/04/48

NAME	AGE	HGT	EYE	HAIR	CPX	TRADE	BORN	HOME	RANK	UNIT
Lynch, John	27	5.07	BLU	SDY	FIR	Laborer	Kerry Co IRE	Ann Arbor MI	PVT	COM E 1st MI INF
Lynson, Henry R.	45								MUS	COM K 1st MI INF
Lyon, Oscar O.	18	5.09	BLU	DRK	LGT	Carpenter	Pontiac MI		PVT	COM A 15th US INF
Lyon, Perry	23	5.07	BLK	BLK	DRK	Miller	Oakland Co MI	Pontiac MI	4SG	COM C 1st MI INF
Lyon, William	21	5.08	HZL	BWN	DRK	Farmer	Jefferson Co NY		PVT	COM D 1st MI INF
Lyons, Lewis	18	5.06	BLU	LGT	LGT	Farmer	Ithaca NY	Pontiac MI	PVT	COM C 1st MI INF
Mabee, Harvey W.	21	5.07	DRK	BWN	FIR	Farmer	York MI		RCT	Montgomery Guards
Mackey, Michael	25	5.08	GRY	BWN	DRK	Farmer	Orleans Co NY	Pontiac MI	PVT	COM C 1st MI INF
Magill, Charles H.	21	5.06	HZL	BWN	LGT	Laborer	Newbery NY		PVT	US Army
Magoin, John	26	5.06	HZL	DRK	DRK	Laborer	Orange Co NY		PVT	COM ? 5th US INF
Magoon, William J.	24							Silver Lake MI	2SG	COM H 1st MI INF
Mahoney, Daniel								Detroit MI	PVT	Montgomery Guards
Mahoney, Dennis	33	5.07	GRY	DRK	LGT	Wheel-wright	Ireland		RCT	US Army
Mallard, John H.	44	5.08	GRY	BWN	FIR	Farmer	Nottingham ENG	Marshall MI	PVT	COM I 1st MI INF
Malloy, Terrence	35	5.05	GRY	BWN	LGT	Soldier	Kings Co IRE		PVT	COM A 6th US INF
Manhardt, John	34	5.03	BLU	GRY	FLD	Farmer	Baden GER		PVT	COM G 15th US INF
Manitius, Charles P.	21	5.09	BLU	LGT	FIR	Soldier	Germany	Detroit MI	PVT	COM H 1st MI INF
Mann, Lewis	29	5.07	GRY	DRK	DRK	Laborer	Worms GER	Detroit MI	PVT	COM D 1st MI INF
Manning, John H.	22	6.00	BLK	BLK	DRK	Tailor	Wayne Co MI		PVT	COM G 1st MI INF
Manning, Rockwell								Hillsdale MI	2LT	Governor's Guards
Mansfield, Richard	22	5.05	BLK	BWN	FIR	Soldier	Germany	Detroit MI	PVT	COM H 1st MI INF
Manter, Daniel E.	23	5.10	BLU	DRK	FLD	Carpenter	Somerset Co ME		PVT	US Army Ordnance
Manton, William H.	23	5.07	BLU	DRK	LGT	Shoemaker	Kent Co DE		PVT	COM E 15th US INF
Manvell, John	34	5.09	DRK	BWN	FIR	Painter	Hackney ENG		RCT	Montgomery Guards
Marble, Ephraim	21	5.09	GRY	LGT	LGT	Farmer	Somerset NY	Marshall MI	PVT	COM G 15th US INF
Marks, John	33	5.10	BLU	BWN	DRK	Soldier	Washington Co PA		PVT	COM K 3rd US DRG

ENROLLED	MUSTERED	DISCHARGED	REMARKS
11/20/47 Detroit MI	12/04/47 Detroit MI	07/18/48 Detroit MI	
12/24/47 Detroit MI	01/20/48 Detroit MI		Died on board ship 07/15/48
04/05/47 Pontiac MI	04/27/47 Detroit MI	08/03/48 Covington KY	TRA COM C 12/26/47
11/30/47 Pontiac MI	12/01/47 Detroit MI	07/26/48 Detroit MI	
11/14/47 Albion MI	11/14/47 Detroit MI		Died on the Ohio River? 05/01/48
11/30/47 Corunna MI	12/01/47 Detroit MI	07/26/48 Detroit MI	Received pension
10/23/47 Detroit MI			Company disbanded before muster
11/30/47 Pontiac MI	12/01/47 Detroit MI	07/26/48 Detroit MI	PMT 4CP 12/23/47
03/09/47 Detroit MI	03/09/47 Detroit MI		Deserted at Detroit MI 04/23/47
11/18/46 Detroit MI	Detroit MI		Deserted 08/??/46?
11/20/47 Freedom MI	12/01/47 Detroit MI	07/27/48 Detroit MI	AKA William J. Morgan
??/??/46 Detroit MI			VTS WNA
10/11/47 Detroit MI	Detroit MI		Deserted 10/24/47
01/24/48 Marshall MI	02/01/48 Detroit MI		Died at New Orleans LA 06/25/48
11/30/46 Detroit MI	11/30/46 Detroit MI		Died in hospital at Jefferson BKS MO 09/23/48
03/29/47 Detroit MI	04/30/47 Detroit MI	08/04/48 Covington KY	AKA John Mainhardt
11/20/47 Adrian MI	12/01/47 Detroit MI	07/27/48 Detroit MI	
11/14/47 Detroit MI	11/14/47 Detroit MI	07/26/48 Detroit MI	
02/20/48 Saline MI	03/01/48 Detroit MI	07/18/48 Detroit MI	STH at New Orleans LA from Vera Cruz MEX 05/31/48
??/??/46 Hillsdale MI			VTS WNA
11/20/47 Adrian MI	12/01/47 Detroit MI	07/27/48 Detroit MI	
04/01/47 Detroit MI	Detroit MI	05/31/48 Detroit MI	Discharged for disability. Received pension
04/09/47 Niles MI	04/27/47 Detroit MI	08/06/48 Cincinnati OH	PMT CPL 06/16/47. AKA Marston/Maston/Morrison
10/25/47 Detroit MI			Company disbanded before muster
04/09/47 Detroit MI	04/30/47 Detroit MI	08/04/48 Covington KY	PMT CPL 03/01/48. Received pension
03/20/47 Detroit MI			Died of disease at Detroit MI 04/23/47

Name	Age	Hgt	Eye	Hair	Cpx	Trade	Born	Home	Rank	Unit
Marr, Dustin	20	5.02	GRY	LGT	DRK	Farmer	Markam	Canada	PVT	COM K 1st MI INF
Marsden, James	34	5.05	BLU	GRY	SAL	Tailor	Bristol ENG	Sault Ste Marie MI	PVT	Brady Guards
Marshall, John	33	5.05	BLU	BWN	FLD	Farmer	Hanover GER		PVT	COM G 15th US INF
Martin, Francis T.	18	5.08	HZL	BWN	FIR	Laborer	Poughkeepsie NY	Ionia MI	PVT	COM I 1st MI INF
Martin, John	44	5.10	BLU	GRY	LGT	Mason	Sunbury PA		PVT	COM K 1st MI INF
Martin, William	23	5.09	GRY	BWN	FIR	Farmer	Dutchess Co NY		SGT	COM A 6th US INF
Martin, William	37	5.08	BLK	BLK	DRK	Tailor	Ireland	Detroit MI	PVT	COM C 1st MI INF
Marvin, Alexander								Adrian MI	PVT	Adrian Guards
Marun, James								Detroit MI	PVT	Montgomery Guards
Mason, Edwin D.	24	5.11	BLK	BLK	DRK	Farmer	Monroe Co NY	Coldwater MI	PVT	COM G 1st MI INF
Mason, James	20	6.01	LGT	DRK	LGT	Blacksmith	Elba TWP NY		PVT	COM G 1st MI INF
Mason, Orson	18	5.06	BLU	BLK	DRK	Wheel-wright	Wayne Co MI		PVT	COM G 1st MI INF
Mathews, Alonzo	22	5.07	BLU	BWN	DRK	Shoemaker	Herkimer Co NY	Kalamazoo MI	PVT	COM A 1st MI INF
Mattison, Bryton	26	5.06	BLU	RED	LGT	Cigar-maker	Manchester VT	Pontiac MI	PVT	Brady Guards
May, Charles S.	18	5.06	BLU	BLK	DRK	Farmer	Berkshire MA	Richland MI	PVT	COM A 1st MI INF
Maynes, Edward	26	6.00	GRY	FIR	RUD	Carpenter	Tyrone IRE		RCT	US Army
Mayo, Lyman	44	6.02	BLU	BWN	FIR	Farmer	Augusta NY		RCT	Montgomery Guards
McAlaster, Cornelius	26	5.10	GRY	BWN	SDY	Soldier	Ireland		PVT	COM B 5th US INF
McAllister, Joseph	24	5.09	BLU	SDY	FIR	Mason	Glasgow SCO		PVT	COM K 6th US INF
McAuliff, Bartolemew	40	5.08	GRY	BWN	FIR	Laborer	Limerick Co IRE		RCT	Montgomery Guards
McCall, James	30	5.09	BLU	BWN	LGT	Cooper	Hartford CT		PVT	COM B 3rd US INF
McCamley, William M.	19	5.09	BLK	BWN	LGT	Farmer	Onondaga Co NY	Battle Creek MI	PVT	COM G 1st MI INF
McCann, John	34	5.11	BLU	DRK	RUD	Laborer	Onslow Co IRE		PVT	COM A 15th US INF
McCleary, John	25	5.07	BLU	DRK	FIR	Wagon-maker	Salem NY		PVT	COM E 15th US INF
McClellin, James	32	6.01	GRY	BWN	DRK	Farmer	Montgomery Co NY		RCT	COM ? 3rd US DRG
McCloskey, Daniel	27	5.10	GRY	BWN	FIR	Farmer	Orange Co NY		PVT	COM K 6th US INF

ENROLLED	MUSTERED	DISCHARGED	REMARKS
12/15/47 Howell MI	01/01/48 Detroit MI	07/28/48 Detroit MI	Received pension. AKA Dustin Mann
06/18/47 Detroit MI	06/18/47 Detroit MI	06/30/48 Detroit MI	
04/16/47 Detroit MI	04/30/47 Detroit MI	04/30/48 New Orleans LA	DFD. Proper name was Johannes Marschat
12/20/47 Portland MI	01/01/48 Detroit MI		Died of consumption at New Orleans LA 03/05/10
12/15/47 Ypsilanti MI	01/01/48 Detroit MI	07/15/48 Jefferson BKS MO	LIH Detroit MI 02/09/48. TRA COM G. PEN
01/08/47 Detroit MI	Detroit MI		PEN
11/30/47 Detroit MI	12/01/47 Detroit MI	07/26/48 Detroit MI	PEN
06/01/46 Adrian MI			VTS WNA
??/??/46 Detroit MI			VTS WNA
02/20/48 Battle Creek MI	03/01/48 Detroit MI		STH New Orleans 06/05/48. DUC Jefferson BKS 07/07/48
02/20/48 Jackson MI	03/01/48 Detroit MI		Died at Detroit MI 04/05/48
02/20/48 Jackson MI	03/01/48 Detroit MI		LIH at New Orleans LA 06/24/48. Died 06/26/48
11/05/47 Kalamazoo MI	11/19/47 Detroit MI	07/18/48 Detroit MI	
06/18/47 Detroit MI	06/18/47 Detroit MI	06/30/48 Detroit MI	
11/05/47 Kalamazoo MI	11/19/47 Detroit MI	12/02/47 Detroit MI	Discharged by Wayne CTY MI Circuit Court as minor
05/24/48 Detroit MI	Detroit MI	07/16/48 Jefferson BKS MO	
11/08/47 Detroit MI			Company disbanded before muster
09/29/47 Detroit MI	Detroit MI	08/01/48 East Pascagoula MS	
11/24/47 Detroit MI	11/24/47 Detroit MI	07/31/48 Jefferson BKS MO	
10/25/47 Detroit MI			Company disbanded before muster
04/03/47 Detroit MI	04/03/47 Detroit MI		
02/20/48 Lima OH	03/01/48 Detroit MI	07/18/48 Detroit MI	Received pension
04/05/47 Pontiac MI	04/27/47 Detroit MI	08/06/48 Cincinnati OH	WIA Mexico City 08/20/47. TRA COM E 08/26/47. PEN
04/20/47 Grand Rapids MI	04/27/47 Detroit MI		Died at Puebla MEX 11/23/47
05/31/48 Detroit MI	Detroit MI	07/16/48 Jefferson BKS MO	
02/01/48 Detroit MI	Detroit MI	07/31/48 Jefferson BKS MO	

439

Name	Age	Hgt	Eye	Hair	Cpx	Trade	Born	Home	Rank	Unit
McCormick, Virgil	21	5.09	DRK	BWN	LGT	Farmer	Seneca Co NY	Ypsilanti MI	PVT	COM G 15th US INF
McCormick, William	19								PVT	COM E 1st MI INF
McCoy, William H.	32	5.06	GRY	DRK	LGT	Farmer	Caton NY	Port Huron MI	PVT	COM B 1st MI INF
McCune, Philip	33	5.10	BLU	BLK	DRK	Blacksmith	Washington Co PA		PVT	COM G 1st MI INF
McDavit, John	43	5.05	BLU	BWN	LGT	Sailor	Ireland		PVT	COM E 1st MI INF
McDermot, Andrew F.	28								LAN	US Navy
McDermott, Owen						Carpenter		Detroit MI	PVT	Montgomery Guards
McDivitt, Patrick	28	6.00	HZL	BLK	DRK	Tailor	Derry IRE		PVT	COM K 3rd US DRG
McDonald, Donald	27	6.00	BLU	LGT	LGT	Farmer	Scotland	Detroit MI	PVT	COM F 1st MI INF
McDonald, Estes	20	5.08	GRY	BLK	DRK	Carpenter	Schenectady NY	Adrian MI	1CP	COM I 1st MI INF
McDonald, James	42	5.06	BLU	DRK	LGT	Soldier	Dublin IRE	Detroit MI	PVT	COM G 15th US INF
McDonald, John	24	5.10	BLU	RED	FLD	Blacksmith	Ireland	Jackson MI	PVT	COM I 1st MI INF
McDonald, William	21	5.05	BLU	BWN	DRK	Blacksmith	Oswego Co NY		PVT	COM G 15th US INF
McDonough, Patrick	35	5.10	BLU	BWN	FIR	Soldier	Sligo IRE		RCT	Montgomery Guards
McDonough, William	33	5.08	BLU	BWN	LGT	Laborer	Ireland		PVT	COM E 15th US INF
McElvain, George W.	24	5.04	HZL	BWN	FIR	Farmer	Marion OH		PVT	COM H US MTD RIF
McFaden, James	21	5.09	GRY	DRK	DRK	Sailor	Kingston CAN		PVT	COM I 5th US INF
McFarlan, James H.	24	5.10	BLU	LGT	FIR	Cooper	Saratoga Co NY		RCT	COM ? 3rd US DRG
McGaffey, David	21	5.10	BLK	BLK	DRK	Carpenter	Champaign Co OH	White Pigeon MI	PVT	COM G 1st MI INF
McGhee, Barney	28	5.10	GRY	DRK	FIR	Laborer	Athlone IRE		PVT	COM A 6th US INF
McGinnis, Isaac	35	5.05	GRY	LGT	FIR	Tailor	Ulster Co NY		PVT	COM B 5th US INF
McHardy, Samuel	18	5.08	BLU	LGT	LGT	Laborer	London CAN	Port Huron MI	PVT	COM B 1st MI INF
McHenry, George R.	27	5.08	BLU	BWN	LGT	Blacksmith	Warren TN or PA	Kalamazoo MI	PVT	COM A 1st MI INF
McIntire, Robert G.	23	6.00	BLU	BWN	FIR	Mason	Canada		PVT	COM K 3rd US DRG
McIntosh, Edward W.	24	5.10	HZL	BWN	FIR	Farmer	Madison Co NY		PVT	COM K 3rd US DRG
McIntyre, Samuel	38	6.00	BLU	DRK	LGT	Shoemaker	Biddeford? ME	Dexter MI	PVT	COM B 1st MI INF

ENROLLED	MUSTERED	DISCHARGED	REMARKS
04/13/47 Detroit MI	04/30/47 Detroit MI	08/04/48 Covington KY	PEN
11/20/47 Toledo OH	12/04/47 Detroit MI		Deserted at Detroit MI 12/24/47
11/02/47 Port Huron MI	11/12/47 Detroit MI	07/26/48 Detroit MI	
02/20/48 Battle Creek MI	03/01/48 Detroit MI	07/18/48 Detroit MI	STH at New Orleans LA from Vera Cruz MEX 05/31/48
11/20/47 Detroit MI	12/04/47 Detroit MI	07/18/48 Detroit MI	LIH at Vera Cruz MEX 05/05/48
01/19/47 Detroit MI	New Orleans LA		Deserted. MNI Francis
05/28/46 Detroit MI			VTS WNA
03/26/47 Detroit MI	04/22/47 Detroit MI	07/31/48 Jefferson BKS MO	TRA COM C 01/07/48
11/15/47 Niles MI	12/02/47 Detroit MI	07/28/48 Detroit MI	AKA Daniel McDonald
11/15/47 Jackson MI	12/01/47 Detroit MI	07/18/48 Detroit MI	Received pension
04/26/47 Detroit MI	04/30/47 Detroit MI		Died of diarrhea at Perote MEX 11/03/47. PEN
11/15/47 Jackson MI	12/01/47 Detroit MI	07/18/48 Detroit MI	LIH at New Orleans LA en route to Mexico 03/05/48
04/02/47 Detroit MI	04/30/47 Detroit MI	08/04/48 Covington KY	
11/08/47 Detroit MI			Company disbanded before muster
04/05/47 Niles MI	04/27/47 Detroit MI		Died at Puebla MEX 10/14/47
08/17/47 Kalamazoo MI	08/17/47 Kalamazoo MI	07/31/48 Jefferson BKS MO	Received pension
03/01/47 Detroit MI	03/01/47 Detroit MI	08/01/48 Camp Jeff Davis MS	Received pension
05/20/48 Detroit MI	Detroit MI	07/16/48 Jefferson BKS MO	
02/20/48 Constantine MI	03/01/48 Detroit MI	07/18/48 Detroit MI	Received pension
11/10/46 Detroit MI	11/10/46 Detroit MI	06/15/48 Jalapa MEX	Discharged for disability
11/16/48 Detroit MI	Detroit MI	08/01/48 East Pascagoula MS	Received pension
11/02/47 Port Huron MI	11/12/47 Detroit MI	07/26/48 Detroit MI	
11/05/47 Kalamazoo MI	11/19/47 Detroit MI	07/18/48 Detroit MI	Received pension
04/06/47 Detroit MI	04/22/47 Detroit MI		LIH at Puebla MEX 08/07/47
04/16/47 Detroit MI	04/22/47 Detroit MI	01/09/48 Vera Cruz MEX	LIH at Puebla MEX 08/07/47. DFD. PEN
11/02/47 Port Huron MI	11/12/47 Detroit MI	07/26/48 Detroit MI	

Name	Age	Hgt	Eye	Hair	Cpx	Trade	Born	Home	Rank	Unit
McKeann, Joshua L.	25	5.09	BLU	BWN	RUD	Carpenter	Ayr SCO		PVT	F&S US MTD RIF
McKeeby, Lemuel C.	22	5.06	BLU	LGT	LGT	Shoemaker	New York NY		PVT	Brady Guards
McKenzie, Alexander	39	5.10	HZL	DRK	DRK	Cook	Ireland	Detroit MI	PVT	COM K 1st MI INF
McKenzie, Duncan	21	5.07	BLU	SDY	FIR	Sailor	Glengarry SCO?		PVT	COM A 15th US INF
McKenzie, James D.	27	6.00	BLU	BLK	LGT	Laborer	Middlesex Co NY	Jackson MI	PVT	COM E 15th US INF
McKindrick, William								Detroit MI	MUS	Montgomery Guards
McKinney, Barney	32	5.06	BLU	GRY	LGT	Laborer	Ireland	Hillsdale MI	PVT	COM F 1st MI INF
McKinstry, James P.	42					Mariner	Hudson NY	Detroit MI	LUT	US Navy
McKnowen, Michael	28	5.08	BLU	BWN	FIR	Laborer	Ireland		PVT	COM F 1st MI INF
McKnugent, John	21	5.08	BWN	BWN	DRK	Teacher	Amherst Isl CAN		RCT	COM ? 3rd US DRG
McLallen, Horatio	26	5.07	BLU	DRK	DRK	Laborer	Meridian? NY		PVT	COM A 15th US INF
McLane, Chester L.	24	5.09	GRY	BWN	FLD	Student	New York State		PVT	COM K 1st MI INF
McLaughlin, Cornelius	32	5.07	DRK	DRK	DRK	Shoemaker	Ireland	Ypsilanti MI	PVT	COM K 1st MI INF
McLaughlin, John								Detroit MI	PVT	Montgomery Guards
McLaughlin, William	28	5.05	BLU	BWN	FIR	Teamster	Ireland		PVT	COM G 15th US INF
McLean, George H.	32	6.00	GRY	BLK	DRK	Lawyer	Yates Co NY	Saline MI	PVT	COM G 1st MI INF
McLin, Curtis	28	5.08	HZL	BWN	LGT	Farmer	Clinton OH	Kalamazoo MI	PVT	COM A 1st MI INF
McLin, William H.	27	5.07	DRK	BWN	LGT	Tailor	Ohio	Kalamazoo MI	PVT	COM A 1st MI INF
McLouth, Nathan P.	33	5.08	GRY	BLK	DRK	Farmer	Wayne Co NY		PVT	COM I 1st MI INF
McManman, John								Detroit MI	3LT	Montgomery Guards
McMannis, Philip	32	5.06	HZL	BLK	DRK	Weaver	Ireland	Niles MI	PVT	COM F 1st MI INF
McManus, Thomas	18	5.04	DRK	BWN	DRK	Laborer	Orange Co VT		PVT	COM A 1st MI INF
McManus, Thomas	21	5.05	LGT	AUB	RUD	Musician	Fermanagh Co IRE	Detroit MI	PVT	COM G 15th US INF
McMillin, Archibald						Shoemaker		Detroit MI	MUS	Montgomery Guards
McMullen, Aaron	22	5.05	HZL	BWN	DRK	Farmer	Gore CAN	Grandville MI	MUS	COM I 1st MI INF
McNair, Clement D.	24					Clerk		Detroit MI	2LT	COM E 1st MI INF

Michigan Men in the Mexican War

ENROLLED	MUSTERED	DISCHARGED	REMARKS
08/01/47 Kalamazoo MI	08/01/47 Kalamazoo MI	08/01/48 Jefferson BKS MO	Received pension
06/18/47 Detroit MI	06/18/47 Detroit MI	06/30/48 Detroit MI	Received pension. MNI Clarke
12/15/47 Northfield MI	01/01/48 Detroit MI	07/28/48 Detroit MI	
04/21/47 Detroit MI	04/27/47 Detroit MI	08/04/48 Covington KY	TRA COM K 12/26/47. PEN
04/06/47 Jackson MI	04/27/47 Detroit MI		Killed at Chapultepec MEX 09/13/47. AKA Kenzie
05/28/46 Detroit MI			VTS WNA
11/15/47 Hillsdale MI	12/02/47 Detroit MI	07/28/48 Detroit MI	
02/01/26			Serving on board steamer Michigan 1845–1846
11/15/47 Niles MI	12/02/47 Detroit MI		Deserted at New Orleans LA 01/16/48
05/09/48 Detroit MI	Detroit MI	07/16/48 Jefferson BKS MO	
04/14/47 Utica MI	04/27/47 Detroit MI	08/21/48	TRA COM K 12/26/47. Received pension
12/15/47 Northfield MI	01/01/48 Detroit MI		Deserted at New Orleans LA 03/04/48
12/15/47 Ypsilanti MI	01/01/48 Detroit MI	07/28/48 Detroit MI	
05/28/46 Detroit MI			VTS WNA
04/05/47 Monroe MI	04/30/47 Detroit MI	08/04/48 Covington KY	Received pension
02/20/48 Saline MI	03/01/48 Detroit MI	07/18/48 Detroit MI	
11/05/47 Kalamazoo MI	11/19/47 Detroit MI	07/18/48 Detroit MI	
11/05/47 Kalamazoo MI	11/19/47 Detroit MI	07/18/48 Detroit MI	Received pension
11/15/47 Jackson MI	12/01/47 Detroit MI		Died at Soledad River going to Vera Cruz 06/16/48. PEN
05/28/46 Detroit MI			VTS WNA
11/15/47 Niles MI	12/02/47 Detroit MI		LIH New Orleans 01/16/48. LIH St. Louis 07/07/48. PEN
11/05/47 Detroit MI	11/19/47 Detroit MI		Deserted at New Orleans LA 01/18/48
04/20/47 Detroit MI	04/30/47 Detroit MI	08/04/48 Covington KY	
05/28/46 Detroit MI			VTS WNA
11/15/47 Grandville MI	12/01/47 Detroit MI	07/18/48 Detroit MI	Fifer. Received pension
10/30/47 Detroit MI	12/04/47 Detroit MI	07/18/48 Detroit MI	

Name	Age	Hgt	Eye	Hair	Cpx	Trade	Born	Home	Rank	Unit
McNair, Eaton	26	5.11	BWN	BWN	LGT	Farmer	Livingston Co NY	Adrian MI	PVT	COM G 15th US INF
McNamara, James	37	5.08	BLU	BWN	DRK	Farmer	Ireland	Niles MI	PVT	COM F 1st MI INF
McNett, Jackson	21	5.09	GRY	BWN	FIR				PVT	COM I 1st MI INF
McNulty, James	36	5.08	BLU	DRK	LGT	Laborer	Tyrone IRE		PVT	COM B 3rd US INF
McOmber, William A.								Adrian MI	PVT	Adrian Guards
McPee, John	29								4SG	COM K 1st MI INF
McQuicken, John	18	4.05	GRY	BLK	FLD	Farmer	Albany NY	Niles MI	MUS	COM F 1st MI INF
McReynolds, Andrew T.	39	5.09			FLD	Lawyer	Dungarvan IRE	Detroit MI	CAP	COM K 3rd US DRG
McSweeney, Nathaniel						Grocer	Detroit MI		PVT	Montgomery Guards
McWilliams, Andrew S.	28	5.11	BLK	BLK	LGT	Clerk	Orange Co NY		4SG	COM E 15th US INF
McWilliams, William	27	5.07	GRY	BWN	LGT	Farmer	New York State	Caledonia MI	PVT	COM K 1st MI INF
Meacham, Charles T.	18	5.01	BLU	BWN	FIR	Farmer	Franklin OH	Pontiac MI	MUS	COM C 1st MI INF
Meacham, Edward	21	5.05	BLU	BWN	FIR	Laborer	Erie Co PA		PVT	COM E 15th US INF
Meacham, Milton	29	5.09	GRY	BWN	LGT	Farmer	Chenango Co NY		PVT	COM E 15th US INF
Meeker, George B.	30	5.10	BLU	BWN	LGT	Laborer	Hillbough VT		PVT	COM B 1st MI INF
Meeker, Warren E.	27	5.08	GRY	BWN	DRK	Farmer	Chittenden? VT		PVT	COM D 1st MI INF
Meigs, Benjamin	18	5.05	GRY	BWN	DRK	Laborer	Orleans Co VT	Monroe MI	PVT	COM G 15th US INF
Melzien, Frederick	27	5.10	BLU	LGT	LGT	Carpenter	Germany		PVT	COM G 1st MI INF
Mensing, William F.	34	5.10	HZL	BWN	DRK	Surveyor	Hanover GER		PVT	COM B 3rd US INF
Merker, George F.	24	5.05	HZL	BLK	DRK	Baker	Hanault GER	Detroit MI	PVT	Brady Guards
Merker, Jacob								Detroit MI	PVT	Scott Guards
Merker, John J.						Blacksmith		Detroit MI	PVT	Scott Guards
Merrifield, Edwin R.	23					Clerk	Catskill NY	Lansing MI	2LT	COM A 15th US INF
Merritt, Adra								Detroit MI	PVT	Montgomery Guards
Merritt, Zeba W.	24	5.09	BLK	BLK	DRK	Tinner	Montpelier VT		SGT	COM K 3rd US DRG
Mertz, Michael								Detroit MI	PVT	Scott Guards

ENROLLED	MUSTERED	DISCHARGED	REMARKS
04/13/47 Adrian MI	04/30/47 Detroit MI	08/04/48 Covington KY	Received pension
11/15/47 Niles MI	12/02/47 Detroit MI		Drowned 2 miles below St. Louis MO 07/06/48. PEN
11/15/47 Adrian MI	12/01/47 Detroit MI		Deserted at Detroit MI 01/01/48
03/08/47 Detroit MI	03/08/47 Detroit MI		
06/01/46 Adrian MI			VTS WNA
11/15/47 Ann Arbor MI	01/20/48 Detroit MI		Deserted at Detroit MI 02/01/48
11/15/47 Niles MI	12/02/47 Detroit MI	07/28/48 Detroit MI	Drummer
03/09/47	04/09/47	07/31/48	WIA Mexico City and PMT MAJ 08/20/47. MNI Thomas. PEN
05/28/46 Detroit MI			VTS WNA
04/07/47 Niles MI	04/27/47 Detroit MI		PMT SGT 08/26/47. LIH at New Orleans LA 07/07/48
12/24/47 Howell MI	01/01/47 Detroit MI	07/28/48 Detroit MI	
11/30/47 Pontiac MI	12/01/47 Detroit MI	07/26/48 Detroit MI	Received pension
04/26/47 Fawn River MI	04/27/47 Detroit MI		Died at Puebla MEX 02/09/48
04/06/47 Jackson MI	04/27/47 Detroit MI		ODS Vera Cruz MEX as teamster since 06/12/47
11/02/47 Port Huron MI	11/12/47 Detroit MI		Died en route to Detroit MI 07/03/48
11/14/47 Detroit MI	11/14/47 Detroit MI		Deserted at Detroit MI 11/22/47
04/12/47 Monroe MI	04/30/47 Detroit MI	08/04/48 Covington KY	
04/15/48 Cincinnati OH	04/15/48 Cincinnati OH	07/18/48 Detroit MI	STH at New Orleans LA from Vera Cruz MEX 06/05/48
03/18/47 Detroit MI	03/18/47 Detroit MI		PMT CPL 08/06/47. Resigned 08/19/47
06/18/47 Detroit MI	06/18/47 Detroit MI	06/30/47 Detroit MI	AKA Frederick Merker. PEN
06/03/46 Detroit MI			VTS WNA
06/03/46 Detroit MI			VTS WNA
03/09/47	04/09/47 Detroit MI	02/17/48	LIH Puebla 08/10/47. Resigned. PEN. MNI Randolph
??/??/46 Detroit MI			VTS WNA
03/24/47 Detroit MI	04/22/47 Detroit MI	07/31/48 Jefferson BKS MO	TRA COM C 01/04/48. Received pension
06/03/46 Detroit MI			VTS WNA

Name	Age	Hgt	Eye	Hair	Cpx	Trade	Born	Home	Rank	Unit
Metcalf, Norman	22	6.03	GRY	BWN	DRK	Farmer	Bedford OH		PVT	COM E 15th US INF
Metty, Peter	29	5.04	BLU	BWN	DRK	Painter	Detroit MI	Detroit MI	PVT	Brady Guards
Meyer, William	30	5.11	BLU	DRK	LGT	Clerk	Germany		PVT	COM E 1st MI INF
Milleo, Soloman	26	6.02	HZL	BWN	FIR	Soldier	Middletown MD		SGT	COM C 5th US INF
Miller, Henry	36	5.07	BLU	BWN	DRK	Farmer	Floyd Co KY	Kalamazoo MI	PVT	COM A 1st MI INF
Miller, Isaac	18	5.06	GRY	LGT	LGT	Farmer	New Jersey	Pontiac MI	PVT	COM D 1st MI INF
Miller, Jacob	37	5.08	BLU	BWN	DRK	Farmer	Saratoga Co NY	Hadley MI	PVT	COM C 1st MI INF
Miller, James B.	21	5.08	GRY	DRK	LGT	Farmer	Pittsford NY	Detroit MI	PVT	COM B 1st MI INF
Miller, James C.	24	5.05	BLU	DRK	LGT	Cooper	Baltimore MD		1CP	COM G 1st MI INF
Miller, John									1CP	NTH Lenawee VOL
Miller, John	20	5.06	BLU	DRK	LGT	Laborer			PVT	COM B 1st MI INF
Miller, John	29						Prussia		PVT	COM I 1st MI INF
Miller, John	30	5.07	GRY	BWN	FIR	Farmer	Germany	Ionia MI	PVT	COM I 1st MI INF
Miller, Rufus								Detroit MI	PVT	Montgomery Guards
Miller, William	33	5.05	GRY	DRK		Laborer	Germany	Detroit MI	PVT	Brady Guards
Miller, William	34	5.08	GRY	BWN	FIR	Weaver	Cavan Co IRE		PVT	COM B 5th US INF
Milligan, Abel	26	5.10	BLU	FLX	FIR	Farmer	New Jersey	Monroe MI	PVT	COM G 15th US INF
Milligan, Moses	22	6.00	GRY	LGT	FIR	Farmer	Seneca Co NY	Monroe MI	PVT	COM G 15th US INF
Milotta, Benjamin	38	5.06	HZL	BLK	DRK	Shoemaker	Canada	Detroit MI	PVT	COM D 1st MI INF
Mils, Oromel E.	20	5.08	BLU	LGT	LGT	Sailor	Bragin NY		PVT	COM B 1st MI INF
Miron, Antoine	29	5.06	LGT	BLK	RUD	Voyageur	Montreal CAN	Detroit MI	PVT	COM G 15th US INF
Mitchell, Alexander	27								PVT	COM E 1st MI INF
Mitchell, Patrick	33	6.00	BLU	BLK	DRK	Mason	Roscommon IRE		PVT	COM G 1st MI INF
Mitchell, William	28	5.10	GRY	BWN	FLD	Laborer	Grand Island NY		PVT	COM E 1st MI INF
Mock, Max	27	5.08	GRY	RED	FLD	Blacksmith	Wartzburg GER		PVT	Brady Guards
Mockmoer, William	18	5.07	GRY	SDY	LGT	Laborer	Rushville NY		PVT	COM A 15th US INF

ENROLLED	MUSTERED	DISCHARGED	REMARKS
04/19/47 Niles MI	04/27/47 Detroit MI	01/18/48 Puebla MEX	LIH Puebla MEX 08/10/47. DFD. PEN
06/18/47 Detroit MI	06/18/47 Detroit MI	06/30/48 Detroit MI	Received pension. AKA Peter Mitty
12/04/47 Detroit MI	12/04/47 Detroit MI	07/18/48 Detroit MI	Serving as wardmaster in Army hospital since 12/31/47
04/14/47 Detroit MI	Detroit MI	06/26/48 Jalapa MEX	
11/05/47 Kalamazoo MI	11/19/47 Detroit MI	07/18/48 Detroit MI	
11/14/47 Pontiac MI	11/14/47 Detroit MI	07/26/48 Detroit MI	
11/30/47 Lapeer MI	12/01/47 Detroit MI		STII Vera Cruz MEX 01/25/48. Died at Detroit 07/21/48
11/02/47 Port Huron MI	11/12/47 Detroit MI	07/26/48 Detroit MI	PEN
11/10/47 Adrian MI	12/01/47 Detroit MI		Deserted at New Orleans LA 05/02/48
06/06/46 Tecumseh MI			VTS WNA
11/02/47 Port Huron MI	11/12/47 Detroit MI		Deserted at Detroit MI 11/14/47
12/20/47 Ionia MI	01/01/48 Detroit MI	07/18/48 Detroit MI	RBL PEN
12/20/47 Ionia MI	01/01/48 Detroit MI	07/18/48 Detroit MI	
??/??/46 Detroit MI			VTS WNA
06/18/47 Detroit MI	06/18/47 Detroit MI	06/30/48 Detroit MI	
08/31/47 Detroit MI	Detroit MI	03/22/48	PMT CPL 03/04/48. Resigned
04/10/47 Monroe MI	04/30/47 Detroit MI	08/04/48 Covington KY	
04/12/47 Monroe MI	04/30/47 Detroit MI	08/04/48 Covington KY	PEN
11/14/47 Detroit MI	11/14/47 Detroit MI	07/26/48 Detroit MI	
11/02/47 Port Huron MI	11/12/47 Detroit MI	07/26/48 Detroit MI	
04/12/47 Detroit MI	04/30/47 Detroit MI		DOW at Jalapa MEX 08/27/47. AKA Antoine Merion
11/20/47 Monroe MI	12/04/47 Detroit MI		Deserted at Detroit MI 12/24/47
02/20/48 Detroit MI	03/01/48 Detroit MI		Died 07/25/48. PEN
11/20/47 Union City MI	12/04/47 Detroit MI		Deserted at Detroit MI 12/24/47
06/18/47 Detroit MI	06/18/47 Detroit MI		DES at Detroit MI 06/21/47. PEN. AKA Max Man
04/27/47 Detroit MI	04/27/47 Detroit MI	08/04/48 Cincinnati OH	TRA COM I 12/26/47

Name	Age	Hgt	Eye	Hair	Cpx	Trade	Born	Home	Rank	Unit
Moffitt, James	28	6.00	BLU	BWN	FIR	Clothier	Montgomery Co NY		PVT	COM E 15th US INF
Mogg, John	32	5.06	BLK	BWN	FLD	Blacksmith	Germany	Detroit MI	PVT	COM H 1st MI INF
Mollison, John	28	5.10	HZL	BWN	DRK	Soldier	Glasgow SCO		PVT	COM A 6th US INF
Monroe, Morgan	25	5.09	BLU	BWN	FIR	Carpenter	Washington Co ME		RCT	US Army
Montreuil, John	32					Carpenter		Detroit MI	1SG	Lafayette Guards
Moodie, John	22								DMR	COM D 1st MI INF
Moody, Robert	26	5.10	GRY	BWN	SAL	Laborer	Sandwich CAN		PVT	COM G 15th US INF
Moon, Samuel	21	5.09	GRY	DRK	FIR	Farmer	Chautauqua Co NY		PVT	COM A 6th US INF
Moore, Alphonso D.	19	5.11	LGT	LGT	LGT	Clerk	Lewis Co NY		PVT	COM K 1st MI INF
Moore, Jacob	21	6.00	BLU	BWN	LGT	Farmer	Vermilion Co IL		PVT	COM F 15th US INF
Moore, John	39	6.00	BLK	BLK	DRK	Teamster	Columbiana Co OH		PVT	COM K 1st MI INF
Moore, Nicholas	22	5.06	BLK	BLK	DRK	Miller	Mier GER	Paw Paw MI	PVT	COM A 1st MI INF
Moore, Samuel H.	21	6.01	BLU	BWN	LGT	Farmer	Monroe Co NY	Paw Paw MI	PVT	COM A 1st MI INF
Moore, Thomas	22	5.09	GRY	BWN	DRK	Laborer	Lincolnshire		RCT	US Army
Morahan, William								Detroit MI	PVT	Montgomery Guards
Moran, Edward	28	5.07	HZL	BWN	FLD	Painter	Detroit MI	Detroit MI	PVT	Brady Guards
More, Joseph M. C.	23	5.05	GRY	DRK	LGT	Farmer	Trenton NJ		PVT	COM A 15th US INF
Morell, William	31	5.08	BWN	SDY	FIR	Laborer	Antrim Co IRE		PVT	COM A 6th US INF
Morey, Benjamin F.	20	5.10	BLU	BWN	LGT	Carpenter	Genesee Co NY	Paw Paw MI	PVT	COM A 1st MI INF
Morey, Hezekiah	31	6.02	GRY	BWN	RUD	Shoemaker	Rutland VT		RCT	US Army
Morgan, Eleazer A.	25	5.06	GRY	SDY	LGT	Shoemaker	Cayuga Co NY	Corunna MI	PVT	COM C 1st MI INF
Morgan, George	18	5.05	BLU	LGT	LGT	Laborer			PVT	COM B 1st MI INF
Morris, John	22	5.08	BLK	BLK	DRK	Brickmaker	New York State		PVT	COM G 15th US INF
Morris, Melville E.	24	5.09	BLU	SDY	LGT	Printer	Steuben Co NY	Goshen IN	PVT	COM F 1st MI INF
Morrison, William	29	5.10	GRY	BWN	LGT	Laborer	Antrim Co IRE		PVT	COM E 15th US INF
Morse, Curtis L.	18	5.08	BLU	LGT	LGT	Boatman	Delaware Co NY		PVT	COM G 1st MI INF

ENROLLED	MUSTERED	DISCHARGED	REMARKS
04/12/47 Grand Rapids MI	04/27/47 Detroit MI		Died at Puebla MEX 12/08/47
11/20/47 Detroit MI	12/01/47 Detroit MI	07/27/48 Detroit MI	
01/02/47 Detroit MI	Detroit MI		Died at New Orleans LA 03/12/47. PEN
05/12/48 Detroit MI	Detroit MI	06/20/48 Newport KY	
??/??/46 Detroit MI			VTS WNA
11/14/47 Detroit MI	11/14/47 Detroit MI		Deserted at Detroit MI 11/22/47
04/07/47 Detroit MI	04/30/47 Detroit MI	08/04/48 Covington KY	
08/17/46 Kalamazoo MI	08/17/46 Kalamazoo MI		Died at Anton Lizards MEX 03/12/47
12/15/47 Ypsilanti MI	01/01/48 Detroit MI	01/31/48 Detroit MI	Discharged by civil authority
05/07/47 Detroit MI	Detroit MI	08/04/48 Camp Butler IL	
12/15/47 Ypsilanti MI	01/01/48 Detroit MI		TRA COM G. Died at New Orleans LA
11/05/47 Paw Paw MI	11/19/47 Detroit MI	07/18/48 Detroit MI	
11/05/47 Paw Paw MI	11/19/47 Detroit MI		Died at Palo Verde MEX 06/15/48 en route from Cordova
05/26/48 Detroit MI	Detroit MI		Deserted at Detroit MI 05/27/48. Born in England
05/28/46 Detroit MI			VTS WNA
06/18/47 Detroit MI	06/18/47 Detroit MI	06/30/48 Detroit MI	PEN
03/26/47 Pontiac MI	04/27/47 Detroit MI	08/03/48 Covington KY	PMT CPL 09/17/47. TRA COM C 12/26/47. PEN
01/12/47 Detroit MI	Detroit MI		Died at Puebla MEX 08/15/47
11/05/47 Paw Paw MI	11/19/47 Detroit MI	07/18/48 Detroit MI	
05/29/48 Detroit MI	Detroit MI	06/20/48 Newport KY	
11/30/47 Corunna MI	12/01/47 Detroit MI	07/26/48 Detroit MI	Received pension
12/24/47 Lower Sandusky	12/31/47 Lower Sandusky	07/26/48 Detroit MI	
04/14/47 Detroit MI	04/30/47 Detroit MI		Died at New Orleans LA of diarrhea 07/15/48
11/15/47 Niles MI	12/02/47 Detroit MI	07/28/48 Detroit MI	PMT 4SG 12/31/47. PEN. AKA Melvin Morris
04/07/47 Jackson MI	04/27/47 Detroit MI	08/06/48 Cincinnati OH	
02/20/48 Adrian MI	03/01/48 Detroit MI	04/15/48 Napoleon OH	Discharged on writ of habeas corpus

Name	Age	Hgt	Eye	Hair	Cpx	Trade	Born	Home	Rank	Unit
Morse, Hall A.	18	5.08	BLU	LGT	LGT	Cooper	Wayne Co NY	Detroit MI	PVT	COM E 1st MI INF
Morse, Manly	18	5.08	BLU	BWN	DRK	Blacksmith	Seneca Co NY		PVT	COM A 1st MI INF
Morse, Robert B.	18	5.08	GRY	LGT	DRK	Laborer	Tompkins Co NY		PVT	COM F 1st MI INF
Morton, Dillis	20	5.08	BLU	BWN	LGT		Royalton NY	Corunna MI	PVT	COM C 1st MI INF
Mory, Ira	18	5.06	BLU	BWN	FIR	Wagon-maker	New York State		PVT	COM F US MTD RIF
Mosher, Stephen	22	5.06	HZL	BWN	DRK	Miller	Warren Co NY		PVT	COM K 3rd US DRG
Mott, Gardner A.	21	5.09	BLU	SDY	FIR	Laborer	Leeds CAN	Detroit MI	PVT	COM E 1st MI INF
Mott, Sylvanus	44	5.07	HZL	RED	FIR	Carpenter	Litchfield CT	Detroit MI	PVT	COM I 1st MI INF
Moynahan, Jeremiah								Detroit MI	PVT	Montgomery Guards
Muil, Rhinehart	19	5.05	DRK	RED	LGT	Brewer	Schonau GER	Toledo OH	PVT	COM G 1st MI INF
Muir, Edward F.	19	5.08	BLU	SDY	LGT	Farmer	Jefferson Co NY	Clinton MI	PVT	COM H 1st MI INF
Mullane, Dennis								Detroit MI	SGT	Montgomery Guards
Mullen, Thomas H.	35	5.08	HZL	BWN	FIR	Tailor	Caroline Co VA	Ionia MI	PVT	COM I 1st MI INF
Muma, Ebenezer G.	23		GRY	BWN	FIR	Farmer	Canada		PVT	COM K US MTD RIF
Muma, Henry	25	5.09	BLU	SDY	FIR	Farmer	Cleveland OH		RCT	COM K 6th US INF
Munger, Jason	25	5.07	BLK	LGT	LGT	Farmer	Livingston Co NY	Corunna MI	PVT	COM C 1st MI INF
Munger, Thomas	22	5.08	GRY	BLK	DRK	Farmer	Livingston Co NY	Corunna MI	PVT	COM C 1st MI INF
Munson, Clarke	22	5.09	BLU	BWN	FIR	Laborer	New London OH	Branch Co MI	PVT	COM E 15th US INF
Munson, George W.	35	5.08	BLU	DRK	LGT	Blacksmith	New Haven CT		PVT	COM B 3rd US INF
Munson, Jonathan	23	5.08	GRY	AUB	LGT	Gunsmith	Chenango Co NY		PVT	COM K 1st MI INF
Murdock, George	27	5.07	BLU	BWN	LGT	Carpenter	Scotland	Port Huron MI	PVT	COM B 1st MI INF
Murlin, Charles W.	22	5.10	BLK	BLK	FIR	Farmer	Oakland Co MI	Ionia MI	PVT	COM I 1st MI INF
Murphy, Thomas	28	5.08	BLU	BLK	FIR	Laborer	Wexford Co IRE		RCT	Montgomery Guards
Murray, Edward	30	5.08	BLU	LGT	LGT	Tailor	Scotland	Detroit MI	PVT	COM H 1st MI INF
Murray, Horace P.	19	5.04	GRY	BWN	LGT	Moulder	Monroe Co NY	Owosso MI	PVT	COM C 1st MI INF
Murray, Josiah	20	5.06	GRY	BLK	DRK	Laborer	Cleveland OH	Kalamazoo MI	PVT	COM A 1st MI INF

ENROLLED	MUSTERED	DISCHARGED	REMARKS
11/20/47 Ypsilanti MI	12/04/47 Detroit MI	07/18/48 Detroit MI	
11/05/47 Kalamazoo MI	11/19/47 Detroit MI		Deserted at Detroit MI 12/14/47
11/15/47 Adrian MI	12/02/47 Detroit MI		Deserted at Detroit MI 12/25/47
12/22/47 Corunna MI		02/01/48 Detroit MI	DIS for sickness. PEN
08/10/47 Centreville MI	08/10/47 Centreville MI	07/29/48 Jefferson BKS MO	Received pension
04/08/47 Tecumseh MI	04/22/47 Detroit MI	07/20/48	TRA COM E 01/04/48
11/20/47 Saginaw MI	12/04/47 Detroit MI	07/18/48 Detroit MI	AKA Moot
12/20/47 Detroit MI	01/01/48 Detroit MI	07/18/48 Detroit MI	
??/??/46 Detroit MI			VTS WNA
02/20/48 Toledo OH	03/01/48 Detroit MI	07/18/48 Detroit MI	
11/20/47 Clinton MI	12/01/47 Detroit MI	07/27/48 Detroit MI	Received pension
05/28/46 Detroit MI			VTS WNA
12/20/47 Ionia MI	01/01/48 Detroit MI	07/18/48 Detroit MI	
07/21/47 Otsego MI	07/21/47 Otsego MI	07/31/48 Jefferson BKS MO	PEN. AKA Ebenezer G. Mums
12/28/47 Detroit MI	12/28/47 Detroit MI	06/20/48 Newport KY	
11/30/47 Corunna MI	12/01/47 Detroit MI	07/26/48 Detroit MI	
11/30/47 Corunna MI	12/01/47 Detroit MI	07/26/48 Detroit MI	
04/07/47 Fawn River MI	04/27/47 Detroit MI		Died of wounds at Mexico City 10/04/47
03/05/47 Detroit MI	03/05/47 Detroit MI	03/17/47 Newport KY	Rejected from service
01/20/48 Grass Lake MI	02/01/48 Detroit MI		Deserted at Perrysburg OH 02/12/48
11/02/47 Port Huron MI	11/12/47 Detroit MI	07/26/48 Detroit MI	
12/20/47 Ionia MI	01/01/47 Detroit MI		Died at New Orleans LA 06/25/48
11/18/47 Detroit MI			Was never mustered into service
12/20/47 Detroit MI	01/01/48 Detroit MI		Deserted at Detroit MI 01/21/48
11/30/47 Corunna MI	12/01/47 Detroit MI		Died at Cordova MEX from inflamed lungs 04/20/48
11/05/47 Kalamazoo MI	11/19/47 Detroit MI		Died at Cordova MEX from heart affliction 05/14/48

Name	Age	Hgt	Eye	Hair	Cpx	Trade	Born	Home	Rank	Unit
Murray, Michael	23	5.08	BLU	BWN	LGT	Sailor	Ireland		PVT	COM F 1st MI INF
Murray, Milton C.	22	5.05	BLU	BWN	LGT	Printer	Steuben Co NY		3CP	COM C 1st MI INF
Myer, John	40	5.06	GRY	GRY	DRK	Blacksmith	Montpellier FRA	Detroit MI	PVT	COM D 1st MI INF
Myer, William	21	5.10	BLU	LGT	LGT	Cooper	Wayne Co NY		PVT	COM D 1st MI INF
Myer, William	29	5.11	BLU	DRK	LGT	Clerk	Germany	Detroit MI	PVT	COM E 1st MI INF
Myers, George W.	22	5.05	BLU	BWN	LGT	Farmer	New York State	Romeo MI	PVT	COM C 1st MI INF
Myers, Jesse	30	5.06	BLU	LGT	FIR	Lawyer	Sullivan Co NY	Detroit MI	CPL	COM K 3rd US DRG
Myers, John	26	5.09	BLU	BWN	FIR	Shoemaker	Orange Co NY		PVT	COM A 15th US INF
Myers, William	21	5.05	BLK	BWN	LGT	Farmer	Summit Co OH	Toledo OH	PVT	COM H 1st MI INF
Naphey, John	31	5.05	BLK	BLK	DRK	Shoemaker	Orange Co NY		PVT	COM A 6th US INF
Nash, Hollis	41	5.07	GRY	BWN	LGT	Wagon-maker	Chittenden VT		PVT	COM F 1st MI INF
Nederstatt, George						Shoemaker		Detroit MI	PVT	Scott Guards
Needles, John	28								PVT	COM D 1st MI INF
Neff, Calvin C.	26	5.08	BLU	DRK	FIR	Farmer	Braintree VT	Almont MI	PVT	COM K 1st MI INF
Nelson, Henry B.	24	5.08	HZL	BWN	DRK	Actor	New York NY		PVT	Brady Guards
Nelson, Peter	31	5.06	BLU	BLK	DRK	Painter	North Stonington		MUS	COM K 3rd US DRG
Nesbit, Archibald	26	5.06	BLU	LGT	FIR	Farmer	Scotland		PVT	COM B 5th US INF
Netz, Jacob	22	5.05	GRY	LGT	LGT	Bartender	Germany		PVT	COM D 1st MI INF
Newell, Minor S.	24	5.08	BLK	BLK	DRK	Farmer	Bennington NY	Flushing MI	PVT	COM K 1st MI INF
Newkirk, John	21	5.05	HZL	DRK	DRK	Laborer	Mason NY		RCT	US Army
Newman, Micah	32	5.08	BLU	BWN	FIR	Engraver	Norwich ENG		RCT	Montgomery Guards
Newton, Harris G.	18	5.05	BLK	BWN	LGT	Laborer	New York NY		PVT	COM A 1st MI INF
Newton, James A.	22	5.08	HZL	BWN	FLD	Blacksmith	Trumbull Co OH	Detroit MI	PVT	COM E 1st MI INF
Newton, John	25	5.04	BLU	BWN	FIR	Shoemaker	Lincolnshire		RCT	Montgomery Guards
Nicar, George H.	21	5.08	GRY	BLK	CLR	Blacksmith	Lynchburg VA		PVT	COM E 15th US INF
Nicholas, Leonard	27	5.06	BWN	BLK	DRK	Blacksmith	Germany		PVT	COM F 1st MI INF

ENROLLED	MUSTERED	DISCHARGED	REMARKS
11/15/47 Niles MI	12/02/47 Detroit MI		Deserted at New Orleans LA 01/16/48
11/30/47 Pontiac MI	12/01/47 Detroit MI		LIH at Jefferson BKS MO 07/07/48. Died 07/10/48
11/14/47 Detroit MI	11/14/47 Detroit MI		Died at Detroit MI 09/18/48
11/14/47 Detroit MI	11/14/47 Detroit MI		Deserted at New Orleans LA 01/25/48
11/20/47 Perrysburg OH	12/04/47 Detroit MI	07/18/48 Detroit MI	Hospital attendant since 03/01/48
11/30/47 Romeo MI	12/01/47 Detroit MI	07/26/48 Detroit MI	Received pension
04/10/47 Detroit MI	04/22/47 Detroit MI	07/31/48 Jefferson BKS MO	TRA COM D 01/04/48
04/15/47 Ann Arbor MI	Detroit MI		TRA COM G 12/26/47. LIH at Perote MEX 07/01/48
11/20/47 Toledo OH	12/01/47 Detroit MI		Died at Cordova MEX 05/03/48
10/21/46 Detroit MI	10/21/46 Detroit MI		
11/15/47 Ypsilanti MI	12/02/47 Detroit MI		Died of debility at Cordova MEX 04/20/48
06/03/46 Detroit MI			VTS WNA
11/14/47 Springfield OH	01/01/48 Springfield OH		Died at Vera Cruz MEX 05/24/48. PEN
12/15/47 Almont MI	01/01/48 Detroit MI	07/28/48 Detroit MI	PEN. AKA James Calvin Neff
06/18/47 Detroit MI	06/18/47 Detroit MI	06/30/48 Detroit MI	PMT 4CP 04/02/48
04/10/47 Detroit MI	04/22/47 Detroit MI		LIH at Puebla MEX 08/07/47. Born in CT. PEN
10/02/47 Detroit MI	Detroit MI	08/01/48 East Pascagoula MS	
11/14/47 Detroit MI	11/14/47 Detroit MI		Deserted at Detroit MI 11/23/47
12/15/47 Flushing MI	01/01/48 Detroit MI	07/28/48 Detroit MI	PEN
03/09/47 Detroit MI	03/09/47 Detroit MI		Deserted at Detroit MI 03/29/47
11/10/47 Detroit MI			Company disbanded before muster
11/05/47 Kalamazoo MI	11/19/47 Detroit MI		Deserted at Detroit MI 12/12/47
11/20/47 Ypsilanti MI	12/04/47 Detroit MI	07/18/48 Detroit MI	
11/02/47 Detroit MI			Company disbanded before muster. Born in ENG
04/09/47 Grand Rapids MI	04/27/47		Died at Puebla MEX 09/26/47. AKA George H. Nickar
11/15/47 Niles MI	12/01/47 Detroit MI	07/28/48 Detroit MI	

Name	Age	Hgt	Eye	Hair	Cpx	Trade	Born	Home	Rank	Unit
Nichols, Daniel G.	21	5.09	HZL	DRK	DRK	Farmer	Ontario Co NY		PVT	COM E 15th US INF
Nichols, John	32	5.09	BLU	BWN	LGT	Laborer	Ireland	Detroit MI	PVT	COM B 1st MI INF
Nickerson, William	19	5.08	GRY	BWN	FIR	Farmer	Orleans Co NY	Marshall MI	PVT	COM I 1st MI INF
Nitzel, Charles	27	5.08	GRY	BWN	FLD	Miller	Prussia	Milwaukee WI	PVT	COM F 1st MI INF
Norris, Henry H.	20	5.06	HZL	BWN	LGT	Carpenter	Erie Co NY	Niles MI	PVT	COM F 1st MI INF
Norris, John	22	5.08	BLU	SDY	SDY	Farmer	England	South Bend IN	4CP	COM F 1st MI INF
Northrop, Horace	18	5.04	BLK	BWN	DRK	Farmer	Monroe MI		PVT	COM E 1st MI INF
Norton, David	22	5.06	BLU	DRK	LGT	Cabinet-man	Lockport NY		PVT	COM B 1st MI INF
Norton, Ransom	39	5.11	GRY	GRY	DRK	Laborer	Newport NY	Ypsilanti MI	PVT	COM K 1st MI INF
Norton, William J.	21	6.00	BLK	LGT	LGT	Farmer	Niagara Co NY		PVT	COM E 15th US INF
Noyes, Albert G.	19	5.05	BLU	LGT	LGT	Wagon-maker	Washington Co NY		PVT	COM C 1st MI INF
Nugent, John M.	21	5.08	BWN	BWN	DRK	Teacher	Amherst Isl CAN		RCT	COM ? 3rd US DRG
O'Brien, James	28	5.04	BLU	BLK	PAL	Tailor	Meath Co IRE	Detroit MI	PVT	COM G 15th US INF
O'Brien, William	21	6.00		SDY	LGT	Butcher	Richmond		PVT	COM B 1st MI INF
O'Brien, William	29								PVT	COM E 1st MI INF
O'Callaghan, Daniel								Detroit MI	PVT	Montgomery Guards
O'Callaghan, William						Grocer		Detroit MI	CAP	Montgomery Guards
O'Conner, Richard	25	5.10	BLU	BWN	FLD	Farmer	Sunaria IRE	Detroit MI	PVT	COM H 1st MI INF
O'Hare, John	39	5.10	BLU	LGT	LGT	Mason	Limerick IRE		PVT	COM E 1st MI INF
O'Keefe, Patrick								Detroit MI	PVT	Montgomery Guards
O'Leary, John	44	5.06	BLU	LGT	FIR	Cooper	Ireland	Detroit MI	PVT	COM E 1st MI INF
O'Neal, Owen	29	5.04	BLU	DRK	FIR	Laborer	Sowit IRE		PVT	COM G US MTD RIF
O'Neil, Cornelius	35	5.07	GRY	BWN	FIR	Tailor	Donegal Co IRE		PVT	COM A 6th US INF
O'Neil, James								Detroit MI	PVT	Montgomery Guards
O'Neil, James	20	5.06	GRY	BWN	RUD	Laborer	Nova Scotia CAN		PVT	COM A 15th US INF
O'Neil, Morris	31	5.07	BLU	RED	FIR	Laborer	Cork Co IRE		RCT	Montgomery Guards

Enrolled	Mustered	Discharged	Remarks
04/26/47 Niles MI	04/27/47 Detroit MI	07/20/48 Baton Rouge LA	LIH at Vera Cruz MEX 06/18/47. Received pension
11/02/47 Port Huron MI	11/12/47 Detroit MI	07/26/48 Detroit MI	
11/15/47 Marshall MI	12/01/47 Detroit MI	07/18/48 Detroit MI	PEN
11/15/47 Niles MI	12/02/47 Detroit MI	07/28/48 Detroit MI	
11/15/47 Niles MI	12/02/47 Detroit MI		Died at Cordova of typhoid fever 05/28/48. AKA H.M. Morris
11/15/47 South Bend IN	12/02/47 Detroit MI	07/28/48 Detroit MI	PEN
11/20/47 LeRoncha	12/04/47 Detroit MI		Deserted at Detroit MI 12/24/47
11/02/47 Port Huron MI	11/12/47 Detroit MI		Deserted at Detroit MI 11/24/47. AKA Daniel Norton
12/15/47 Ypsilanti MI	01/01/48 Detroit MI		Died at New Orleans LA 07/01/48. PEN
04/09/47 Jackson MI	04/27/47 Detroit MI	01/16/48 New Orleans LA	Discharged for disability
11/30/47 Romeo MI	12/01/47 Detroit MI	12/17/47 Detroit MI	Discharged by civil authority on writ of habeas corpus
05/09/48 Detroit MI	Detroit MI	07/16/48 Jefferson BKS MO	
03/29/47 Detroit MI	04/30/47 Detroit MI		Died of diarrhea at Vera Cruz MEX 09/29/47
01/31/48 Vera Cruz MEX	02/01/48 Vera Cruz MEX	07/26/48	PMT DMM 02/02/48
11/20/47 Monroe MI	12/04/47 Detroit MI		LIH at New Orleans LA 06/24/48. Died 07/05/48. PEN
05/28/46 Detroit MI			VTS WNA
05/28/46 Detroit MI			VTS WNA
11/20/47 Detroit MI	12/01/47 Detroit MI	07/27/48 Detroit MI	Received pension
11/20/47 Detroit MI	12/04/47 Detroit MI	03/16/48 Vera Cruz MEX	Discharged on surgeon's certificate of disability
05/28/48 Detroit MI			VTS WNA
11/20/47 Detroit MI	12/04/47 Detroit MI	07/18/48 Detroit MI	
07/09/47 Kalamazoo MI	07/09/47 Kalamazoo MI	07/31/48 Jefferson BKS MO	Received pension
08/25/46 Detroit MI	08/25/46 Detroit MI		Deserted at Detroit MI 09/05/46
??/??/46 Detroit MI			VTS WNA
04/07/47 Ann Arbor MI	Detroit MI	08/04/48 Covington KY	TRA COM K 12/26/47
11/09/47 Detroit MI			COM disbanded before muster. AKA Maurice O'Neil

Name	Age	Hgt	Eye	Hair	Cpx	Trade	Born	Home	Rank	Unit
O'Sullivan, Dennis	29	5.04	BLU	BLK	PAL	Watch-maker	Kerry Co IRE		PVT	COM G 15th US INF
Oakley, Frank	21	5.04	GRY	BLK	LGT	Soldier	Poughkeepsie NY		PVT	Brady Guards
Oaks, Peter								Detroit MI	PVT	Montgomery Guards
Oaks, Preston D.	22	5.10	BLU	BWN	LGT	Farmer	Cayuga Co NY	Clinton MI	PVT	COM H 1st MI INF
Obala, Barnhardt	23	5.05	BLU	BWN	FIR	Collier	Laverque FRA	Adrian MI	PVT	COM G 15th US INF
Oberle, Joseph	30	5.05	BWN	BLK	FIR	Carpenter	Celle GER	Monroe MI	1CP	COM D 1st MI INF
Olds, Levi Theodore	24	5.07	BLU	BWN	FIR	Carpenter	Ontario Co NY		PVT	COM D US MTD RIF
Olin, Hiram W.	21	5.10	GRY	BWN	FIR	Laborer	Genesee Co NY	Bellevue MI	PVT	COM I 1st MI INF
Oliver, James	26	5.05	GRY	BWN	RUD	Laborer	England		PVT	COM A 15th US INF
Oliver, Thomas	32	5.07	BLU	BLK	LGT	Farmer	McKean Co PA		PVT	COM K 1st MI INF
Olmstead, Ephriam S.	31	6.02	HZL	BWN	LGT	Laborer	Saratoga Co NY		PVT	COM A 15th US INF
Omen, Peter	34	5.07	GRY	BLK	DRK	Laborer	Albany NY		PVT	COM I 5th US INF
Opperman, Charles A.	35	5.08	GRY	BWN	LGT	Soldier	Hanover GER		PVT	COM G 15th US INF
Orange, John	24	5.10	BWN	BWN	FIR	Tailor	Tipperary Co IRE		RCT	Montgomery Guards
Orcutt, Benjamin F.	29	5.07	BLU	BLK	DRK	Joiner	Roxbury VT	Kalamazoo MI	1SG	COM A 1st MI INF
Ormsbee, George W.	23	5.06	BLU	BWN	LGT	Chair-maker	Essex Co NY	Romeo MI	PVT	COM C 1st MI INF
Ormsby, William								Detroit MI	1SG	Montgomery Guards
Orr, George W.	24	5.11	GRY	BWN	DRK	Farmer	New York State	Plymouth MI	PVT	Brady Guards
Ort, Casper	34	5.10	GRY	DRK	DRK	Mason	Carbon? Co PA		PVT	COM C 2nd US INF
Orth, Frank	24	5.06	HZL	BWN	LGT	Shoemaker	Lardan GER	Detroit MI	PVT	Brady Guards
Osborn, Ard	26	6.00	HZL	DRK	DRK				PVT	COM G 1st MI INF
Osburn, William M.	25	5.04	HZL	DRK	FIR	Farmer	Sussex Co NJ		PVT	COM G 15th US INF
Osterhout, David B.	21	5.10	HZL	BWN	DRK	Farmer	Seneca Co NY		PVT	COM K 3rd US DRG
Owen, Ira	25	5.06	BLU	LGT	LGT	Farmer	Wayne Co NY		PVT	COM E 1st MI INF
Owen, Jonathan B.	23	5.06	BLU	DRK	DRK	Printer	Westfield CT	Romeo MI	PVT	COM C 1st MI INF
Owen, Joshua M.	27	5.09	HZL	BWN	LGT	Laborer	Wayne Co NY		PVT	COM K 1st MI INF

Michigan Men in the Mexican War

ENROLLED	MUSTERED	DISCHARGED	REMARKS
04/06/47 Detroit MI	04/30/47 Detroit MI		Deserted at Detroit MI 06/26/47
06/18/47 Detroit MI	06/18/47 Detroit MI	06/30/48 Detroit MI	Received pension
05/28/46 Detroit MI			VTS WNA
11/20/47 Clinton MI	12/01/47 Detroit MI		Died at Cordova MEX 06/16/48. PEN
04/15/47 Adrian MI	04/30/47 Detroit MI	08/04/48 Covington KY	PEN. AKA Barnhart Obarla/Oberla
11/14/47 Monroe MI	11/14/47 Detroit MI	07/26/48 Detroit MI	Received pension
06/21/47 Kalamazoo MI	06/21/47 Kalamazoo MI	08/01/48 Jefferson BKS MO	PEN. RBI
11/15/47 Bellevue MI	12/01/47 Detroit MI		Died at Detroit MI 07/27/48
04/14/47 Pontiac MI	04/27/47 Detroit MI	08/03/48 Covington KY	TRA COM C 12/26/47
12/24/47 Kalamazoo MI	01/01/48 Detroit MI		Died at Detroit MI 02/11/48
04/06/47 Pontiac MI	04/27/47 Detroit MI		TRA COM E 12/26/47. Died at Cuernavaca MEX 05/22/48
05/17/47 Detroit MI	Detroit MI	08/01/48 East Pascagoula MS	Deserted 05/22/47, apprehended 05/29/47
10/25/47 Fort Mackinac			TRA COM C 2nd INF. TRA Newport BKS KY 07/26/48
11/10/47 Detroit MI			Company disbanded before muster
11/05/47 Kalamazoo MI	11/19/47 Detroit MI	07/18/48 Detroit MI	PEN. MNI Franklin. AKA Benjamin Olcutt
11/20/47 Romeo MI	12/01/47 Detroit MI	07/26/48 Detroit MI	
05/28/46 Detroit MI			VTS WNA
06/18/47 Detroit MI	06/18/47 Detroit MI	06/30/48 Detroit MI	
10/05/46 Mackinac MI		05/07/47 Fort Mackinac MI	Discharged for disability. PEN
06/18/47 Detroit MI	06/18/47 Detroit MI	06/30/48 Detroit MI	PMT MUS (drummer) 04/01/48. Born in Bavaria
02/20/48 Ypsilanti MI	03/01/48 Detroit MI		Deserted at Detroit MI 04/12/48
03/20/47 Detroit MI	04/30/47 Detroit MI		Died at Puebla MEX of typhoid fever 03/15/48
04/09/47 Tecumseh MI	04/22/47 Detroit MI	07/31/48 Jefferson BKS MO	LIH at Vera Cruz MEX 06/03/47. PEN
11/20/47 Detroit MI	12/04/47 Detroit MI		Deserted at Detroit MI 12/24/47
11/30/47 Romeo MI	12/01/47 Detroit MI	07/26/48 Detroit MI	
11/15/47 Ypsilanti MI	12/01/47 Detroit MI		Deserted at Detroit MI 12/15/47

Name	Age	Hgt	Eye	Hair	Cpx	Trade	Born	Home	Rank	Unit
Owen, Richard	20	5.06	BLU	BLK	LGT	Brewer	Wittshire ENG	Detroit MI	PVT	COM B 1st MI INF
Packard, James M.	29	5.04	HZL	BWN	FIR	Carpenter	North Bridgewater		PVT	COM ? US MTD RIF
Packenham, Robert								Detroit MI	PVT	Montgomery Guards
Palmiter, James	29	5.08	BLU	BWN	DRK	Clerk	Ontario Co NY		4SG	COM D 1st MI INF
Papineau, Joseph M.	34	5.06	BLU	LGT	LGT	Laborer	Canada	Cleveland OH	PVT	COM B 1st MI INF
Parish, Cyrus	22	5.10	GRY	BWN	FLD	Farmer	Ontario Co NY		PVT	Brady Guards
Parish, Elisha	30	6.00	BLU	RED	LGT	Farmer	Genesee Co NY		PVT	COM K 1st MI INF
Parish, Enos	21	5.11	BLU	BWN	FIR	Farmer	Ontario Co NY		PVT	COM K 3rd US DRG
Parish, Jasper	41	6.01	GRY	BWN	DRK	Carpenter	Randolph VT	Grand Rapids MI	2SG	COM G 1st MI INF
Parish, Joel	27	5.10	BLU	BWN	FIR	Lawyer	Ontario Co NY		PVT	COM K 3rd US DRG
Parker, Augustus	27	5.10	BLU	BWN	DRK	Laborer	Cayuga Co NY		PVT	COM B 3rd US INF
Parker, Robert								Adrian MI	1CP	Adrian Guards
Parker, William	24	6.00	GRY	DRK	DRK	Butcher	Lindenshire ENG	Detroit MI	PVT	COM D 1st MI INF
Parks, Melvin	22	5.04	HZL	BWN	RUD	Farmer	Troy MI		RCT	US Army
Parsons, James D.	21	5.10	BLU	LGT	LGT	Carpenter	Germany	Bucyrus OH	PVT	COM G 1st MI INF
Parsons, Lorenzo	24	5.09	HZL	BWN	SDY	Carpenter	Hartford CT		PVT	COM K 3rd US DRG
Parsons, Sterling	22	5.05	HZL	DRK	LGT	Carpenter	Bennington NY		PVT	COM B 3rd US INF
Partelow, William	25	5.08	BLU	DRK	FIR	Butcher	Detroit MI		PVT	COM B 3rd US INF
Patton, William H.	21	5.08	HZL	BWN	FIR	Printer	Addison Co VT	Ann Arbor MI	PVT	COM K 3rd US DRG
Payne, Lyman A.	21	5.09	BLK	BLK	LGT	Farmer	Monroe Co NY		PVT	COM G 1st MI INF
Payne, William C.	22	5.07	BLU	BWN	DRK	Farmer	Cleveland OH		PVT	COM K 3rd US DRG
Pearce, William S.	35	5.06	BLU	DRK	LGT	Farmer	Monroe Co NY	Adrian MI	PVT	COM F 1st MI INF
Pearson, Thomas D.	27	5.08	BLU	BWN	FIR	Lawyer	Geneva NY		PVT	COM I 1st MI INF
Pearsons, David H.	18	5.11	GRY	LGT	LGT	Farmer	Livingston Co NY		PVT	COM D 1st MI INF
Peck, Joshua	33	5.10	BLU	GRY	LGT	Farmer	Lyme CT		RCT	US Army
Pelham, Abraham	18	5.03	BLU	LGT	FIR	Farmer	New York State		PVT	COM E 1st MI INF

Enrolled	Mustered	Discharged	Remarks
11/02/47 Port Huron MI	11/12/47 Detroit MI	07/26/48 Detroit MI	
07/13/47 Otsego MI	07/13/47 Otsego MI		Died at Vera Cruz MEX 02/08/48. Born in MA
05/28/46 Detroit MI			VTS WNA
11/14/47 Marshall MI	11/14/47 Detroit MI	07/18/48 Detroit MI	TRA COM A at Vera Cruz 02/01/48. RTR 03/01/48
11/02/47 Jackson MI	11/12/47 Detroit MI	07/23/48 Detroit MI	AKA Joseph M. Pakineau
06/15/47 Detroit MI	06/18/47 Detroit MI		Deserted at Fort Mackinac MI 10/18/47
12/15/47 Detroit MI	01/01/48 Detroit MI		Deserted at Detroit MI 02/05/48
04/12/47 Detroit MI	04/22/47 Detroit MI	07/31/48 Detroit MI	TRA COM C 01/04/48
01/25/48 Grand Rapids MI	02/01/48 Detroit MI	07/18/48 Detroit MI	
04/12/47 Detroit MI	04/22/47 Detroit MI	01/14/48 Mexico City MEX	TRA COM C 01/04/48. Discharged for disability. PEN
03/08/47 Detroit MI	03/08/47 Detroit MI	05/17/47 Newport KY	Rejected from service
06/01/46 Adrian MI			VTS WNA
11/14/47 Albion MI	11/14/47 Detroit MI	07/26/48 Detroit MI	
05/26/48 Detroit MI	Detroit MI	06/20/48 Newport KY	
04/15/48 Cincinnati OH	04/15/48 Cincinnati OH	07/18/48	Received pension
04/01/47 Detroit MI	04/22/47 Detroit MI	07/31/48 Jefferson BKS MO	TRA COM D 01/04/48
03/05/47 Detroit MI	03/05/47 Detroit MI		LIH at Vera Cruz MEX 07/15/47
04/14/47 Detroit MI	04/14/47 Detroit MI		Died in battle near Mexico City 09/13/47
04/05/47 Detroit MI	04/22/47 Detroit MI	10/30/47 Mexico City MEX	Discharged for disability
02/20/48 Toledo OH	03/01/48 Detroit MI		Died at Vera Cruz MEX 06/05/48
04/14/47 Detroit MI	04/22/47 Detroit MI		LIH at Puebla MEX 08/07/47
11/15/47 Adrian MI	12/02/47 Detroit MI	07/28/48 Detroit MI	
11/15/57 Grandville MI	12/01/47 Detroit MI		Deserted at Detroit MI 01/28/48
11/14/47 Howell MI	11/14/47 Detroit MI	07/26/48 Detroit MI	
05/11/48 Detroit MI	Detroit MI	06/20/48 Newport KY	
11/20/47 Clinton MI	12/04/47 Detroit MI	12/22/47 Detroit MI	Discharged by civil authority for being a minor

Name	Age	Hgt	Eye	Hair	Cpx	Trade	Born	Home	Rank	Unit
Peltier, Henry		5.08	GRY	FLX	FIR	Laborer	Detroit MI	Detroit MI	PVT	COM G 15th US INF
Peltier, Isadore T.	40	5.10	BLK	BLK	DRK	Carpenter	Wayne Co MI	Detroit MI	PVT	COM E 1st MI INF
Peltier, Sylvester	19	5.08	BLK	BLK	DRK	Clerk	Fort Wayne IN		CPL	COM K 3rd US DRG
Peltone, Albert	38	5.10	BLU	BWN	DRK	Cooper	Trumbull Co OH		PVT	COM C 1st MI INF
Pender, William								Detroit MI	PVT	Montgomery Guards
Perkins, Alanson	20	6.02	BLU	LGT	LGT	Farmer	Vermont		PVT	COM D 1st MI INF
Perkins, Myron								Adrian MI	PVT	Adrian Guards
Perkins, Napoleon B.	28	6.00	BWN	BWN	LGT	Carpenter	Cayuga Co NY	Niles MI	PVT	COM E 15th US INF
Perrin, Christopher	30	5.07	BLK	BLK	DRK	Farmer	Wade OH	Perrysburg OH	4CP	COM H 1st MI INF
Perry, Peter	23								SEA	US Navy
Persons, George	18	5.07	BLU	BWN	DRK	Farmer	Sandusky Co OH		PVT	COM G 1st MI INF
Peter, Egloff	23	5.07	HZL	BLK	DRK	Blacksmith	Metz FRA	Detroit MI	PVT	Brady Guards
Peternell, Charles	32						Baden GER	Cleveland OH	2LT	COM A 15th US INF
Phelps, Daniel	35	5.07	BLU	LGT	LGT	Farmer	Lansbury CT		PVT	COM C 1st MI INF
Phetteplace, Elhanen	23	5.10	BLU	BWN	FIR	Farmer	New Berlin NY		PVT	COM A 6th US INF
Phillip, Thomas	22	5.05	BLU	BLK	DRK	Miller	Wales ENG		PVT	COM A 1st MI INF
Phillips, Benjamin W.	44	5.10	BLU	GRY	LGT	Mason	Grafton CT		PVT	COM H 1st MI INF
Phillips, Edwin D.								Detroit MI	PVT	Montgomery Guards
Phillips, Franklin	24	6.00	BLU	BWN	SAL	Mechanic	Rutland VT	Brest MI	PVT	Brady Guards
Phillips, James	22	5.09	BLU	LGT	FIR	Farmer	Carlisle ENG	Adrian MI	PVT	COM H 1st MI INF
Phillips, James H.	18	5.07	GRY	LGT	LGT	Farmer	Kingston NY		PVT	COM B 1st MI INF
Phillips, John								Detroit MI	PVT	Scott Guards
Phillips, Luther H.	20	5.08	BLU	LGT	DRK	Farmer	Wayne Co NY		PVT	COM G 1st MI INF
Phillips, Nehamiah	19	5.09	BLK	BLK	LGT	Musician	Bennington NY		PVT	COM A 15th US INF
Picket, Burr	37	5.06	BLU	DRK	DRK	Shoemaker	Litchfield CT	Detroit MI	PVT	COM E 1st MI INF
Pier, Hiram H.	21	5.03	GRY	BWN	LGT	Farmer	Ontario Co NY	Chelsea MI	PVT	COM E 15th US INF

ENROLLED	MUSTERED	DISCHARGED	REMARKS
04/30/47 Detroit MI	04/30/47 Detroit MI		Died of diarrhea at Jalapa MEX 09/02/47
11/20/47 Detroit MI	12/04/47 Detroit MI		Deserted at Detroit MI 12/24/47
03/30/47 Detroit MI	04/22/47 Detroit MI	07/31/48 Jefferson BKS MO	TRA COM E 01/04/48
11/30/47 Pontiac MI	12/01/47 Detroit MI	07/26/48 Detroit MI	AKA Albert Pellone
??/??/46 Detroit MI			VTS WNA
11/14/47 Detroit MI	11/14/47 Detroit MI		Deserted at Detroit MI 11/20/47
06/01/46 Adrian MI			VTS WNA
04/08/47 Niles MI	04/27/47 Detroit MI	08/03/48 Cincinnati OH	WIA 08/20/47. PEN. MNI Bonaparte
11/20/47 Toledo OH	12/01/47 Detroit MI	07/27/48 Detroit MI	Received pension
12/22/46 Detroit MI			Deserted
02/20/48 Jackson MI	03/01/48 Detroit MI	07/18/48 Detroit MI	STH at New Orleans LA from Vera Cruz MEX 06/05/48
06/18/47 Detroit MI	06/18/47 Detroit MI	06/30/48 Detroit MI	
03/08/47	04/09/47 Detroit MI	08/04/48	PMT 1LT 08/20/47. PMT CAP 09/13/47. TRA COM H. PEN
11/30/47 Caledonia MI	12/01/47 Detroit MI		Deserted at New Orleans LA 01/18/48
08/17/46 Kalamazoo MI	08/17/46 Kalamazoo MI		PMT CPL
11/05/47 Kalamazoo MI	11/19/47 Detroit MI		Deserted at Detroit MI 12/22/47
12/20/47 Jackson MI	01/01/48 Detroit MI		Died at Cordova MEX 06/13/48. PEN
??/??/46 Detroit MI			VTS WNA
06/18/47 Detroit MI	06/18/47 Detroit MI	06/30/48 Detroit MI	
11/20/47 Adrian MI	12/01/47 Detroit MI	07/27/48 Detroit MI	Also served in COM G. PEN
11/02/47 Port Huron MI	11/12/47 Detroit MI		Died at Cordova MEX 06/09/48
06/03/46 Detroit MI			VTS WNA
02/20/48 Detroit MI	03/01/48 Detroit MI		Deserted from New Orleans LA 05/01/48
04/09/47 Pontiac MI	Detroit MI	05/15/47 Detroit MI	Discharged for being a minor
11/20/47 Flint MI	12/04/47 Detroit MI	07/18/48 Detroit MI	
04/19/47 Jackson MI	04/27/47 Detroit MI		Died at Chapultepec MEX 11/28/47. MNI Henry

Name	Age	Hgt	Eye	Hair	Cpx	Trade	Born	Home	Rank	Unit
Pierce, Benjamin A.	32							.	2CP	COM K 1st MI INF
Pierce, James D.	18							Marshall MI	2LT	COM I 1st MI INF
Pierce, Stephen V.	44	5.10	BLU	DRK	LGT	Farmer	Plainfield MA	Detroit MI	PVT	COM B 1st MI INF
Piesnecker, Henry	19	5.04	DRK	LGT	LGT	Clerk	Bavaria GER	Detroit MI	PVT	COM E 1st MI INF
Pippinger, John S.	21	5.11	BLK	BWN	FIR	Farmer	Montgomery Co OH	Goshen IN	PVT	COM F 1st MI INF
Pitcher, Edward M.	23					Merchant		Detroit MI	1LT	COM D 1st MI INF
Pitcher, Mathias	25	5.08	GRY	LGT	LGT	Laborer	Prussia	Detroit MI	PVT	COM B 1st MI INF
Pittman, James E.	21	5.09	HZL	BWN	DRK	Bookkeeper	Tecumseh MI	Detroit MI	2LT	COM D 1st MI INF
Place, Roswell B.	40	5.08	BWN	BWN	DRK	Cooper	Trumbull Co OH	Farmington MI	PVT	COM C 1st MI INF
Platt, William T.	21	5.10	BLU	BWN	FIR	Laborer	Franklin Co NY		PVT	COM ? US MTD RIF
Poland, Thomas	18	5.03	BLU	LGT	LGT	Laborer	Franklin Co VT	Toledo OH	PVT	COM E 1st MI INF
Pool, Azariah	23	5.11	BLU	SDY	SDY	Farmer	Ontario Co NY	Blissfield MI	PVT	COM H 1st MI INF
Pope, William A.	30	5.07	BLU	LGT	LGT	Cigarmaker	Frederickton VA	Detroit MI	1CP	COM E 1st MI INF
Porter, Jacob	33	6.01	BLU	BWN	FIR	Farmer	Stonington RI		PVT	COM B 5th US INF
Poss, Daniel	30	6.00	GRY	BWN	FIR	Farmer	Jefferson Co NY	Lapeer MI	2CP	COM C 1st MI INF
Poss, David	20	5.07	BWN	BWN	LGT	Farmer	Saratoga Co NY		PVT	COM C 1st MI INF
Potter, George F.	22	5.10	BLU	RED	LGT	Laborer	St Lawrence NY		PVT	COM K 1st MI INF
Potter, Henry	19	5.10	GRY	LGT	LGT	Miller	Lyons NY	Rose NY	PVT	COM B 1st MI INF
Potter, John R.	19	5.04	GRY	BWN	FLD	Farmer	Genesee Co NY		PVT	COM E 1st MI INF
Potter, Spencer	19	5.11	GRY	DRK	LGT	Cooper	Wayne Co NY	Bloomfield MI	PVT	COM K 1st MI INF
Powers, Massena W.	26	5.08	BLU	BWN	FIR	Farmer	Genesee Co NY	Adrian MI	PVT	COM G 15th US INF
Powers, Thomas	27								UNK	US Navy
Poyton, Michael	25	5.11	GRY	SDY	LGT	Laborer	Dublin IRE		PVT	COM A 6th US INF
Prangley, Levi	28	5.09	BLK	BLK	DRK	Farmer	England	Corunna MI	PVT	COM C 1st MI INF
Prater, Zephaniah	20	6.00	BLU	LGT	FIR	Cooper	Fleming Co KY	Goshen IN	PVT	COM F 1st MI INF
Pratt, Ambrose	28	5.09	BLU	BWN	LGT	Farmer	Worcester Co MA	Detroit MI	PVT	COM D 1st MI INF

462

ENROLLED	MUSTERED	DISCHARGED	REMARKS
11/15/47 Blissfield MI	12/01/47 Detroit MI		Died at New Orleans LA 06/09?/48
10/30/47 Marshall MI	12/01/47 Detroit MI	07/18/48 Detroit MI	
11/02/47 Jackson MI	11/12/47 Detroit MI	07/26/48 Detroit MI	MNI Van Rensselaer. AKA S.V.R. Price
11/20/47 Detroit MI	12/04/47 Detroit MI	07/18/48 Detroit MI	HOS 12/24/47. HOA 03/19/48. PEN
11/15/47 Niles MI	12/02/47 Detroit MI		Died of typhoid fever at New Orleans LA 01/25/48
10/30/47 Detroit MI	11/14/47 Detroit MI	07/26/48 Detroit MI	
11/02/47 Port Huron MI	11/14/47 Detroit MI	07/26/48 Detroit MI	
10/30/47 Detroit MI	11/14/47 Detroit MI	07/26/48 Detroit MI	Made Adjutant 12/09/47. Received pension
11/30/47 Detroit MI	12/01/47 Detroit MI		Died of dropsy at Cordova MEX 02/28/48. PEN
08/26/47 Kalamazoo MI	08/26/47 Kalamazoo MI	11/09/47 Jefferson BKS MO	
11/20/47 Toledo OH	12/04/47 Detroit MI	07/18/48 Detroit MI	
11/20/47 Blissfield MI	12/01/47 Detroit MI		TRA COM G. Died at San Diego MEX 06/17/48
11/20/47 Detroit MI	12/04/47 Detroit MI	07/18/48 Detroit MI	
09/23/47 Detroit MI	Detroit MI	08/01/48 East Pascagoula MS	
11/30/47 Pontiac MI	12/01/47 Detroit MI	07/26/48 Detroit MI	Received pension
11/30/47 Lapeer MI	12/01/47 Detroit MI		Deserted at Detroit MI 12/25/47
12/24/47 Ann Arbor MI	01/01/48 Detroit MI		Died at Vicksburg?
11/02/47 Jackson MI	11/12/47 Detroit MI	07/26/48 Detroit MI	
11/20/47 Grand Rapids MI	12/04/47 Detroit MI	07/18/48 Detroit MI	LIH at Vera Cruz MEX 05/05/48. PEN
12/15/47 Ann Arbor MI	01/01/48 Detroit MI	07/28/48 Detroit MI	Received pension
04/15/47 Adrian MI	04/30/47 Detroit MI	08/04/48 Covington KY	
01/27/47 Detroit MI	New Orleans LA		Deserted
11/21/46 Detroit MI	11/21/46 Detroit MI		Died at Vera Cruz MEX 05/02/47
11/30/47 Corunna MI	12/01/47 Detroit MI	07/26/48 Detroit MI	
11/15/47 Niles MI	12/02/47 Detroit MI	07/28/48 Detroit MI	
11/14/47 Ann Arbor MI	11/14/47 Detroit MI	07/26/48 Detroit MI	

NAME	AGE	HGT	EYE	HAIR	CPX	TRADE	BORN	HOME	RANK	UNIT
Pratt, Lyman K.	34	5.09	GRY	BWN	FIR	Laborer	St Lawrence NY		PVT	COM K US MTD RIF
Preston, James	34	5.07	GRY	GRY	FIR	Tailor	Loughrea Co IRE		RCT	COM ? 3rd US DRG
Preston, James	36	5.06	BLU	LGT	FIR	Tailor	Loughrea Co IRE		RCT	Montgomery Guards
Preston, Thomas Jr.	22	6.00	GRY	BWN	FIR	Farmer	England	Edwardsburg MI	PVT	COM F 1st MI INF
Price, Silas S.	19	5.10	BLK	BWN	DRK	Farmer	New York State	Allegan MI	PVT	COM A 1st MI INF
Priest, Melancton	43	5.10	BLK	BLK	DRK	Carpenter	Rutland Co NY	Detroit MI	PVT	COM D 1st MI INF
Prindle, Charles	20	5.10	GRY	DRK	LGT	Engineer	New York NY		MUS	COM B 1st MI INF
Proper, James M.	18	5.08	GRY	BWN	DRK	Laborer	Riga NY		PVT	COM A 15th US INF
Pygall, John S.	15	5.00	GRY	RED	LGT	Laborer	England	Detroit MI	MUS	COM G 1st MI INF
Pygall, Thomas	39	5.09	BLU	BWN	LGT	Tailor	Norfolk ENG		PVT	COM G 1st MI INF
Quinlan, Thomas	28	5.10	GRY	BWN	FIR	Laborer	Ireland		PVT	US Army
Rambo, William	20	5.09	HZL	DRK	LGT	Farmer	Wayne Co NY		PVT	COM E 1st MI INF
Ramos, Joseph	18								MUS	COM C 1st MI INF
Raney, Benjamin	19	5.08	BWN	BWN	DRK	Blacksmith	Atlantic Ocean		PVT	COM K 3rd US DRG
Rankin, William	27	5.03	HZL	BWN	DRK	Laborer	Newry IRE		PVT	Brady Guards
Rankin, William	27	5.05	HZL	BWN	DRK	Clerk	Erie? Co NY	Pontiac MI	PVT	COM D 1st MI INF
Rawles, Paul W.	26	6.00	BLU	BWN	LGT	Lawyer	Herkimer Co NY	Kalamazoo MI	2LT	COM A 1st MI INF
Rawson, Washington	26	5.10	BLU	BWN	FIR	Shoemaker	Tompkins Co NY		PVT	COM I 1st MI INF
Raymond, Benjamin F.	21	5.06	GRY	SDY	SDY	Shoemaker	Ontario Co NY		PVT	COM D 1st MI INF
Raymond, Eloy	19	5.07	BLK	DRK	DRK	Farmer	Sandwich CAN	Detroit MI	PVT	COM B 1st MI INF
Realy, George	18	5.01	BLU	LGT	LGT	Laborer	Germany		PVT	COM B 1st MI INF
Reason, Samuel	21	5.09	BLU	LGT	LGT	Farmer	England		RCT	US Army
Reasoner, Peter								Adrian MI	PVT	Adrian Guards
Reaume, James	36	5.06	BLK	BLK	DRK	Carpenter	Sandwich CAN		PVT	Brady Guards
Rector, William								Adrian MI	PVT	Adrian Guards
Reed, Lucius	18	5.03	GRY	BWN	LGT	Laborer	Batavia NY		PVT	Brady Guards

ENROLLED	MUSTERED	DISCHARGED	REMARKS
07/28/47 Otsego MI	09/01/47 Kalamazoo MI	07/31/48 Jefferson BKS MO	Received pension
05/16/48 Detroit MI	Detroit MI	07/16/48 Jefferson BKS MO	
10/18/47 Detroit MI			Company disbanded before muster
11/15/47 Niles MI	12/02/47 Detroit MI	07/28/48 Detroit MI	
11/05/47 Allegan MI	11/19/47 Detroit MI		Died en route home 07/03/48
11/14/47 Detroit MI	11/14/47 Detroit MI		Died at Detroit MI 09/15/48. PEN
11/02/47 Port Huron MI	11/12/47 Detroit MI		Deserted at New Orleans LA 01/17/48
03/31/47 Pontiac MI	04/27/47 Detroit MI		Died of disease at Chapultepec MEX 12/09/47
05/01/48 New Orleans LA	05/01/48 New Orleans LA	07/18/48	Received pension
02/20/48 Detroit MI	03/01/48 Detroit MI		Died at Vera Cruz MEX 06/06/48. PEN
08/30/47 Detroit MI	Detroit MI		Died at Newport BKS KY 11/23/47
11/20/47 Saline MI	12/04/47 Detroit MI	05/28/48 New Orleans LA	Discharged on surgeon's certificate of disability
02/01/48 Vera Cruz MEX	02/01/48 Vera Cruz MEX		DES at Cordova MEX 05/18/48. AKA Joseph Raymo
04/10/47 Detroit MI	04/22/47 Detroit MI	07/31/48 Jefferson BKS MO	TRA COM D 01/04/48. AKA Benjamin Rainey
06/17/47 Detroit MI	06/18/47 Detroit MI		Deserted at Fort Mackinac MI 11/15/47
12/24/47 Springwells MI	01/01/48 Springfield	07/26/48 Detroit MI	
10/30/47 Kalamazoo MI	11/19/47 Detroit MI	07/18/48 Detroit MI	Died 07/19/49 from ills of war. MNI Wideman Huntington
11/15/47 Grand Rapids MI	12/01/47 Detroit MI		Died at Detroit MI 01/01/48
11/14/47 Jackson MI	11/14/47 Detroit MI		Died at Detroit MI 12/26/47
11/02/47 Port Huron MI	11/12/47 Detroit MI	07/26/48 Detroit MI	Received pension. AKA Eli Toulouse
11/02/47 Port Huron MI	11/12/47 Detroit MI	07/26/48 Detroit MI	Received pension. AKA George Ruhle
02/02/48 Detroit MI	Detroit MI		Deserted 02/10/48
06/01/46 Adrian MI			VTS WNA
06/15/47 Detroit MI	06/18/47 Detroit MI		Deserted at Detroit MI 06/21/47
06/01/46 Adrian MI			VTS WNA
06/18/47 Detroit MI	06/18/47 Detroit MI	06/30/48 Detroit MI	

Name	Age	Hgt	Eye	Hair	Cpx	Trade	Born	Home	Rank	Unit
Reed, William	22	5.07	BLU	BLK	DRK	Shoemaker	Detroit MI	Detroit MI	PVT	Brady Guards
Reese, Bennett	34	5.05	BLK	BLK	DRK	Soldier	Philadelphia PA		PVT	COM A 6th US INF
Reeves, Stephen	44	5.08	GRY	DRK	DRK	Laborer	Cooksakin NY	Port Huron MI	PVT	COM B 1st MI INF
Regal, Isaac	33	5.08	BLU	DRK	LGT	Tailor	Northumberland	Monroe MI	PVT	COM G 15th US INF
Reily, James G.	42	5.08	GRY	BWN	FIR	Soldier	Cavan IRE		RCT	Montgomery Guards
Remington, John	24	5.11	GRY	BWN	LGT	Machinist	Pembroke NH		PVT	Brady Guards
Remington, Justin N.	22	5.08	HZL	BWN	DRK	Farmer	Niagara Co NY		PVT	COM K 3rd US DRG
Reno, Francis S.	20	5.08	HZL	BLK	DRK	Sailor	Monroe MI	Detroit MI	MUS	COM K 3rd US DRG
Reno, John								Detroit MI	PVT	Scott Guards
Renz, John G.	30	5.06	LGT	BWN	RUD	Farmer	Wirtemberg GER	Monroe MI	PVT	COM G 15th US INF
Reopell, Thomas	18	5.05	GRY	BLK	LGT	Turner	Wayne Co MI	Detroit MI	PVT	Brady Guards
Reuhle, Frederick						Grocer		Detroit MI	1LT	Scott Guards
Revell, Henry								Detroit MI	PVT	Montgomery Guards
Reynolds, Alfred	23	5.03	BLU	BWN	LGT	Carpenter	Wayne Co NY	Bronson MI	PVT	COM G 1st MI INF
Reynolds, Barney	38								PVT	COM E 1st MI INF
Reynolds, Ira	33	5.09	BLU	BWN	DRK	Farmer	Chenango Co NY		PVT	COM K 3rd US DRG
Reynolds, Oliver A. H.	19	5.09	BLU	LGT	LGT	Clerk	New York NY	Cleveland OH	4SG	COM D 1st MI INF
Reynolds, Silas	21	5.09	HZL	AUB	LGT	Laborer	Schoharie Co NY		PVT	COM A 15th US INF
Rhoades, James M.	18	5.06	BLU	LGT	LGT	Moulder	Hamburg NY		PVT	COM A 15th US INF
Rhodes, Valentine	24	5.08	GRY	BWN	FIR	Laborer	Madison Co NY	Detroit MI	PVT	COM I 1st MI INF
Ribbel, Charles	19	5.06	BLK	BWN	SDY	Farmer	Canada		PVT	COM D 1st MI INF
Rice, Edmund A.	28	6.00	BWN	BWN	LGT	Lawyer	Waitsfield VT	Kalamazoo MI	1LT	COM A 1st MI INF
Rice, Henry C.	18	5.06	HZL	SDY	FIR	Laborer	Genesee Co NY		PVT	COM A 15th US INF
Rice, Jonathan	34	5.05	BLU	BLK	DRK	Carpenter	Genesee Co NY		PVT	COM G 15th US INF
Rice, Lanchton	18	5.06	GRY	LGT	LGT	Shoemaker	Batavia NY		PVT	COM E 1st MI INF
Rice, Samuel A.	25	6.00	BLK	BWN	DRK	Lawyer	Waitsfield VT	Kalamazoo MI	2LT	COM A 1st MI INF

ENROLLED	MUSTERED	DISCHARGED	REMARKS
06/18/47 Detroit MI	06/18/47 Detroit MI	06/30/48 Detroit MI	
09/25/46 Detroit MI	09/25/46 Detroit MI		WIA at Molino del Rey MEX 09/08/47
11/02/47 Port Huron MI	11/12/47 Detroit MI	07/26/48 Detroit MI	
04/07/47 Monroe MI	04/30/47 Detroit MI	08/04/48 Covington KY	PEN. Born in PA. AKA Isaac Reagle/Ragle
11/02/47 Detroit MI			Company disbanded before muster
06/18/47 Detroit MI	06/18/47 Detroit MI	06/30/48 Detroit MI	Received pension
03/25/47 Detroit MI	04/22/47 Detroit MI	07/31/48 Jefferson BKS MO	TRA COM C 01/04/48
03/31/47 Detroit MI	04/22/47 Detroit MI	07/31/48 Jefferson BKS MO	TRA COM D 01/04/48
06/03/46 Detroit MI			VTS WNA
04/21/47 Detroit MI	04/30/47 Detroit MI	01/21/48	Died of hydrocele at Puebla MEX. MNI George. PEN
06/18/47 Detroit MI	06/18/47 Detroit MI	06/30/48 Detroit MI	AKA Thomas Raepell. PEN
06/03/46 Detroit MI			VTS WNA
05/28/46 Detroit MI			VTS WNA
02/20/48 Bronson MI	03/01/48 Detroit MI	07/18/48 Detroit MI	Appears to have received pension
11/20/47 Canandaigua MI	12/04/47 Detroit MI		Deserted at Detroit MI 12/24/47
04/09/47 Tecumseh MI	04/22/47 Detroit MI	07/31/48 Jefferson BKS MO	TRA COM C 01/04/48. PEN
11/14/47 Cleveland OH	11/14/47 Detroit MI	07/26/48 Detroit MI	
04/12/47 Pontiac MI	04/27/47 Detroit MI		LIH at Perote MEX 07/03/47. TRA COM F 12/26/47
04/12/47 Pontiac MI	04/27/47 Detroit MI	08/04/48	TRA COM F 12/26/47
01/24/48 Grand Rapids MI	02/01/48 Detroit MI	07/18/48 Detroit MI	Received pension
11/14/47 Detroit MI	11/14/47 Detroit MI		Deserted at Detroit MI 12/19/47
10/30/47 Kalamazoo MI	11/19/47 Detroit MI	07/18/48 Detroit MI	Made regimental QUT 12/22/47. PEN
04/23/47 Detroit MI	04/27/47 Detroit MI		DOD at Vera Cruz MEX 07/02/47. MNI Clay
04/07/47 Detroit MI	04/30/47 Detroit MI	Baton Rouge LA	LIH at Perote MEX 10/06/47
11/20/47 Shelby MI	12/04/47 Detroit MI		Deserted at Detroit MI 12/24/47. PEN
10/30/47 Kalamazoo MI	11/19/47 Detroit MI	07/18/48 Detroit MI	MNI Austin

Name	Age	Hgt	Eye	Hair	Cpx	Trade	Born	Home	Rank	Unit
Richard, Harris	23							Toledo OH	MUS	COM H 1st MI INF
.Richards, John	27	6.00	HZL	FIR	RUD	Carpenter	New Brunswick		RCT	US Army
Richardson, David I.	25	5.10	GRY	BWN	FIR	Lawyer	New York State		PVT	COM I 1st MI INF
Richardson, Edward								Adrian MI	PVT	Adrian Guards
Richardson, Israel B.	28					Soldier	Fairfax VT	Pontiac MI	1LT	COM ? 3rd US INF
Richardson, Nathaniel	23	5.09	GRY	DRK	DRK	Laborer	Essex Co NY		PVT	COM E 1st MI INF
Richardson, William	22	5.06	GRY	BLK	FIR	Farmer	Yorkshire ENG	Monroe MI	PVT	COM G 15th US INF
Richmond, Lyman M.	26	5.09	BLU	LGT	LGT	Teacher	Genesee Co NY		PVT	COM G 1st MI INF
Riddle, John	28	5.06	GRY	BWN	LGT	Farmer	Germany		PVT	COM K 3rd US DRG
Riggs, Claudius H.	19	5.06	GRY	BWN	LGT	Moulder	Genesee Co NY	Grand Blanc MI	PVT	COM A 15th US INF
Riggs, Loran P.	40	5.05	BLU	LGT	LGT	Farmer	Fenton MI	Fenton MI	PVT	Brady Guards
Riley, Charles	39	5.09	GRY	GRY	LGT		Ireland		PVT	COM K 1st MI INF
Risdon, James A.	28	5.10	BLU	LGT	LGT	Carpenter	Saratoga Co NY	Pontiac MI	PVT	COM C 1st MI INF
Riter, Edward	21	5.05	GRY	SDY	FIR	Laborer	Newark NJ		PVT	COM A 6th US INF
Riter, Lewis	28	5.10	BLU	BWN	FLD	Laborer	Germany	Ypsilanti MI	PVT	COM K 1st MI INF
Rittel, George								Detroit MI	DMM	Scott Guards
Roatch, Henry	19	5.11	BLU	SDY	LGT	Laborer	Johnstown NY		PVT	COM B 3rd US INF
Robb, Hugh	21	5.09	GRY	DRK	FIR	Farmer	Agreshire SCO		CPL	COM B 3rd US INF
Roberts, Horace S.	20						Rochester NY	Detroit MI	2LT	COM D 1st MI INF
Roberts, John	28	5.07	DRK	DRK	LGT	Soldier	New Haven CT	Detroit MI	4CP	COM B 1st MI INF
Roberts, Lory	31	6.00	GRY	DRK	DRK	Cooper	Cranston RI	Detroit MI	PVT	COM C 1st MI INF
Roberts, Marvin	20	5.08	GRY	BWN	LGT	Joiner	Houston Co CT		PVT	COM D 1st MI INF
Roberts, Thomas	20	5.08	GRY	BWN	LGT	Baker	Raleigh NC		PVT	COM G 5th US INF
Roberts, William	26	5.08	GRY	DRK	LGT	Laborer	Genesee Co NY	Detroit MI	PVT	COM K 1st MI INF
Robertson, Hiram T.	37	5.08	BLU	DRK	DRK	Carpenter	Midland CAN		PVT	COM G 1st MI INF
Robinson, Benjamin F.	18	5.06	BLK	LGT	LGT	Boatman	Auburn NY		PVT	COM G 1st MI INF

ENROLLED	MUSTERED	DISCHARGED	REMARKS
11/20/47 Toledo OH	12/01/47 Detroit MI	07/27/48 Detroit MI	
05/25/48 Detroit MI	Detroit MI		Born in Nova Scotia CAN
11/15/47 Grandville MI	12/01/47 Detroit MI		Died at Detroit MI 01/01/48
06/01/46 Adrian MI	.		VTS WNA
			PMT CAP 08/20/47. PMT MAJ 09/13/47. MNI Bush
11/20/47 Perrysburg OH	12/04/47 Detroit MI		Died at Cordova MEX 06/09/48
04/12/47 Monroe MI	04/30/47 Detroit MI	08/04/48 Covington KY	
02/20/48 Detroit MI	03/01/48 Detroit MI	07/18/48 Detroit MI	STH at New Orleans from Vera Cruz MEX 05/29/48. PEN
04/07/47 Tecumseh MI	04/22/47 Detroit MI		LIH at Puebla MEX 08/07/47. AKA John Rittle
04/17/47 Pontiac MI	04/27/47 Detroit MI		Died of disease at Vera Cruz 07/12/47
06/18/47 Detroit MI	06/18/47 Detroit MI	06/30/48 Detroit MI	
02/29/48 New Orleans LA	02/29/48 New Orleans LA	09/10/48	
11/30/47 Pontiac MI	12/01/47 Detroit MI	07/26/48 Detroit MI	AKA James A. Readon
12/02/46 Detroit MI	12/02/46 Detroit MI		
12/15/47 Ypsilanti MI	01/01/48 Detroit MI		LIH at New Orleans LA 06/24/48. Died 08/27/48
06/03/46 Detroit MI			VTS WNA
04/05/47 Detroit MI	04/05/47 Detroit MI	07/25/48 East Pascagoula MS	
04/06/47 Port Huron MI	04/06/47 Port Huron MI		Died at Mexico City 01/29/48
10/30/47 Detroit MI	11/14/47 Detroit MI	07/26/48 Detroit MI	
11/02/47 Port Huron MI	11/12/47 Detroit MI	07/26/48 Detroit MI	PMT CPL 05/01/48
11/30/47 Detroit MI	12/01/47 Detroit MI		STH at New Orleans 01/15/48. Died of fever 02/01/48
11/14/47 Ypsilanti MI	11/14/47 Detroit MI		Died at Cordova MEX 06/06/48
03/05/47 Detroit MI	03/05/47 Detroit MI	06/24/48 Jalapa MEX	TRA COM C
12/15/47 Howell MI	01/01/48 Detroit MI	07/28/48 Detroit MI	AKA William Rabull
02/20/48 Toledo OH	03/01/48 Detroit MI	07/18/48 Detroit MI	STH at New Orleans LA 05/02/48
02/20/48 Adrian MI	03/01/48 Detroit MI	07/18/48 Detroit MI	Received pension

Name	Age	Hgt	Eye	Hair	Cpx	Trade	Born	Home	Rank	Unit
Robinson, James								Detroit MI	PVT	Montgomery Guards
Robinson, James	21	5.04	GRY	LGT	LGT	Carpenter	Middlebury MA	Pontiac MI	PVT	COM C 1st MI INF
Robinson, James	21	5.10	GRY	BLK	DRK	Blacksmith	Niagara Co NY		PVT	COM A 1st MI INF
Robinson, John	36	5.09	BLU	BLK	FLD	Soldier	Suffolk Co ENG	Detroit MI	PVT	COM G 15th US INF
Robinson, Ruel	21	5.04	BLU	LGT	FLD	Farmer	Genesee Co NY		PVT	COM F 1st MI INF
Rockfellow, Cornelius A.	21	5.08	BLU	BWN	LGT	Farmer	Livingston Co NY		PVT	COM E 15th US INF
Rockwell, Joseph	19	5.09	BLU	BWN	LGT	Farmer	Lake Co OH	Kalamazoo MI	PVT	COM A 1st MI INF
Rodd, Timothy	20	5.08	BLK	BLK	DRK	Moulder	Monroe Co MI	Monroe MI	PVT	COM G 15th US INF
Rodgers, Franklin	18	5.05	BLU	LGT	DRK	Farmer	Lockport NY		PVT	COM G 1st MI INF
Rodwell, Justus H.								Adrian MI	PVT	Adrian Guards
Roe, Terence	32	5.05	BWN	BWN	FLD	Weaver	Ireland	Green Oak MI	PVT	COM F 1st MI INF
Rogers, Darius J.	27	5.07	BLU	LGT	LGT	Glover	Saratoga Co NY	Birmingham MI	PVT	Brady Guards
Rolfe, David	28	5.10	HZL	AUB	LGT	Farmer	Warren Co OH		PVT	COM G 1st MI INF
Rollin, Onizama	33							New Orleans LA	PVT	COM H 1st MI INF
Rollo, John	31	5.06	HZL	BLK	DRK	Farmer	Otsego Co NY		PVT	COM D 1st MI INF
Romans, Archibald	27	5.09	HZL	BWN	SAL	Laborer	Eastport ME	Detroit MI	PVT	Brady Guards
Rood, Erasmus	36	5.08	GRY	BWN	LGT	Carpenter	Preston CT	Grand Rapids MI	PVT	Brady Guards
Root, Edwin	21	5.04	BLU	BWN	RUD	Laborer	Genesee Co NY		PVT	US Army Ordnance
Root, Ira F.	30	6.00	GRY	SDY	FIR	Joiner	Steuben Co NY		PVT	COM E 1st MI INF
Rose, Benjamin	34	5.11	BLU	SDY	FIR	Sailor	Philadelphia PA		RCT	COM K 3rd US DRG
Rose, Stephen	30	5.10	HZL	BLK	DRK	Farmer	New York State	Otisco MI	PVT	COM I 1st MI INF
Rose, William	34	5.08	GRY	SDY	FIR	Carpenter	Bennington VT		RCT	COM ? 3rd US DRG
Rosecrants, Harrison	19	6.00	LGT	DRK	FIR	Farmer	Wayne Co NY	Utica MI	PVT	COM E 1st MI INF
Rosecrants, Mortimer						Soldier	New York State	Ypsilanti MI	1LT	COM ? 5th US INF
Ross, Chester	18	5.07	BLK	BWN	DRK	Farmer	Franklin Co NY	Allegan MI	PVT	COM A 1st MI INF
Ross, John	23	5.09	GRY	LGT	FIR	Farmer	Mendon NY		RCT	US Army

470

ENROLLED	MUSTERED	DISCHARGED	REMARKS
05/28/46 Detroit MI			VTS WNA
11/30/47 Pontiac MI	12/01/47 Detroit MI	07/26/48 Detroit MI	
11/05/47 Kalamazoo MI	11/19/47 Detroit MI		Deserted at Detroit MI 12/14/47
04/02/47 Detroit MI	04/30/47 Detroit MI	08/04/48 Covington KY	
11/15/47 Coldwater MI	12/02/47 Detroit MI	02/24/48 Detroit MI	DES at Detroit MI 12/25/47. Charge dropped 11/15/50
04/09/47 Jackson MI	04/27/47 Detroit MI	08/06/48 Cincinnati OH	Served as waiter to LUT Titus since 10/28/47
11/05/47 Kalamazoo MI	11/19/47 Detroit MI	07/18/48 Detroit MI	PEN
04/15/47 Monroe MI	04/30/47 Detroit MI	08/04/48 Covington KY	PEN. AKA Timothy Rood
02/20/48 Battle Creek MI	03/01/48 Detroit MI		Deserted at Detroit MI 04/10/48
06/01/46 Adrian MI			VTS WNA
11/15/47 Niles MI	12/02/47 Detroit MI	07/28/48 Detroit MI	
06/18/47 Detroit MI	06/18/47 Detroit MI	06/30/47 Detroit MI	AKA Rodgers. Received pension
04/15/48 Cincinnati OH	04/15/48 Cincinnati OH		Received pension
03/04/48 New Orleans LA	03/04/48 New Orleans LA		Died at Cordova MEX 05/26/48
11/14/47 Ypsilanti MI	11/14/47 Detroit MI	07/26/48 Detroit MI	
06/18/47 Detroit MI	06/18/47 Detroit MI	06/30/48 Detroit MI	
06/18/47 Detroit MI	06/18/47 Detroit MI	06/30/48 Detroit MI	
10/01/47 Detroit MI	Detroit MI		
11/20/47 Hillsdale MI	12/04/47 Detroit MI	07/18/48 Detroit MI	LIH at Vera Cruz MEX 05/05/48
04/26/48 Detroit MI	Detroit MI	07/16/48 Jefferson BKS MO	PEN
12/20/47 Otisco MI	01/01/48 Detroit MI		Died of diarrhea at Cordova MEX 05/07/48
04/27/48 Detroit MI	Detroit MI	07/16/48 Jefferson BKS MO	
11/20/47 Shelby MI	12/04/47 Detroit MI	07/18/48 Detroit MI	LIH at Vera Cruz MEX 05/05/48
			PMT CAP 08/20/47. Died at Ypsilanti MI 10/07/48
11/05/47 Allegan MI	11/19/47 Detroit MI		Died at Detroit MI of typhoid pneumonia 02/14/48
08/23/47 Detroit MI	Detroit MI		Deserted 09/02/47

Name	Age	Hgt	Eye	Hair	Cpx	Trade	Born	Home	Rank	Unit
Rowland, Isaac S.	36					Lawyer	New Lisbon OH	Detroit MI	CAP	COM E 1st MI INF
Rowley, Joseph A.	22								UNK	US Navy
Rowley, Norton B.	32	5.11	BLU	BWN	LGT	Carpenter	Ogden NY	Ypsilanti MI	1CP	COM K 1st MI INF
Royce, Orville	26	5.06	BLU	BWN	DRK	Farmer	Seneca Co NY		PVT	COM K 3rd US DRG
Ruby, Charles	18	5.09	GRY	BWN	LGT		Warren Co CT		PVT	COM A 15th US INF
Rucker, Daniel H.	30					Soldier	Belleville NJ	Grosse Isle MI	CAP	COM ? 1st US DRG
Ruehle, Frederick						Grocer		Detroit MI	1LT	Scott Guards
Ruehle, John V.	36	5.09	GRY	GRY	DRK	Grocer	Langensteinbach	Detroit MI	MAJ	F&S 1st MI INF
Russell, Edmund	33	5.11	GRY	LGT	FIR	Farmer	Canandaigua NY		PVT	COM I 1st MI INF
Russell, Francis S.	21					Soldier	Fort Niagara NY		2LT	COM ? US MTD RIF
Russell, Stephen	18	5.05	HZL	LGT	LGT	Farmer	England	Detroit MI	PVT	Brady Guards
Ruve, Henry								Detroit MI	PVT	Scott Guards
Ryan, James M.	29	5.09	BLU	LGT	LGT	Sailor	Detroit MI	Detroit MI	PVT	COM B 1st MI INF
Ryan, John E.						Stonecutter		Detroit MI	PVT	Montgomery Guards
Ryno, John	21	5.05	GRY	BWN	FIR	Mason	Yates Co NY		PVT	COM B 3rd US INF
Sabin, Anson	18	5.07	GRY	BWN	LGT	Blacksmith	Dansville NY	Ann Arbor MI	PVT	COM K 1st MI INF
Salisbury, Lawrence J.	23	5.09	GRY	LGT	SDY	Joiner	Aurora NY	Niles MI	CPL	COM E 15th US INF
Salter, Julius C.	21	5.08	BLU	BWN	FIR	Carpenter	St Lawrence NY	Marshall MI	PVT	COM I 1st MI INF
Salter, Orange N.	19	5.10	BLU	BWN	FIR	Laborer	St. Lawrence NY	Marshall MI	PVT	COM I 1st MI INF
Salter, Robert	22	5.07	HZL	DRK	FLD	Clerk	Niagara Co NY	Detroit MI	PVT	Brady Guards
Salute, Francis	25	5.07	HZL	FIR	RUD	Laborer	Germany		RCT	COM ? 3rd US DRG
Samuel, Thomas	37	6.00	DRK	BWN	FIR	Carpenter	Delaware Co NY		RCT	Montgomery Guards
Sanborn, John A.	22	5.08	GRY	DRK	FIR	Carpenter	N. Haverhill NH	St. Clair MI	2SG	COM B 1st MI INF
Sanderson, John	24	5.07	BLU	DRK	LGT	Boatman	Cumberland Co PA	Seville OH	PVT	COM G 1st MI INF
Sanford, Charles W.	22	5.11	BLK	BWN	DRK	Farmer	New Jersey	Silver Lake MI	PVT	COM H 1st MI INF
Saunders, Harry	44					Farmer	Whitehall NY	Truago MI	CAP	Truago Guards

Michigan Men in the Mexican War

Enrolled	Mustered	Discharged	Remarks
10/30/47 Detroit MI	12/04/47 Detroit MI	07/18/48 Detroit MI	MNI Springer
10/17/47 Detroit MI	New York NY		Served on board Cumberland and North Carolina
11/15/47 Ypsilanti MI	01/20/48 Detroit MI	07/28/48 Detroit MI	Received pension
04/08/47 Tecumseh MI	04/22/47 Detroit MI		Died of disease at Mexico City 10/09/47
04/10/47 Utica MI	04/27/47 Detroit MI	08/21/48	TRA COM K 12/26/47. Received pension
			PMT MAJ 02/23/47. PEN. MNI Henry
??/??/46 Detroit MI			VTS WNA
10/18/47 Detroit MI	12/08/47 Detroit MI	07/29/48 Detroit MI	Born in Germany. PEN
11/15/47 Marshall MI	12/01/47 Detroit MI		Died on the march from Cordova MEX 06/17/48
05/27/46			PMT 1LT 03/15/48. MNI Stephen Keyes
06/18/47 Detroit MI	06/18/47 Detroit MI	06/30/48 Detroit MI	
06/03/46 Detroit MI			VTS WNA
11/02/47 Port Huron MI	11/12/17 Detroit MI	07/26/48 Detroit MI	AKA James M. Rogan
05/28/46 Detroit MI			VTS WNA
03/31/47 Detroit MI	03/03/47 Detroit MI		Died at Mexico City 11/27/47
12/15/47 Ann Arbor MI	01/01/48 Detroit MI	07/28/48 Detroit MI	Received pension
04/06/47 Niles MI	04/27/47 Detroit MI		PMT SGT 05/17/47. DOD at Puebla MEX 07/30/47
11/15/47 Marshall MI	12/01/47 Detroit MI	07/18/48 Detroit MI	
01/24/48 Grand Rapids MI	02/01/48 Detroit MI	07/18/48 Detroit MI	
06/18/47 Detroit MI	06/18/47 Detroit MI	06/30/48 Detroit MI	
05/29/18 Detroit MI	Detroit MI	07/16/48 Jefferson BKS MO	
11/03/47 Detroit MI			Company disbanded before muster
11/02/47 Port Huron MI	11/12/47 Detroit MI	07/26/48 Detroit MI	PEN
02/20/48 Toledo OH	03/01/48 Detroit MI	07/18/48 Detroit MI	
11/20/47 Freedom MI	12/01/47 Detroit MI	07/27/48 Detroit MI	Received pension
??/??/46 Truago MI			VTS WNA

Name	Age	Hgt	Eye	Hair	Cpx	Trade	Born	Home	Rank	Unit
Sayles, John E.	18	5.04	BLK	BLK	DRK	Laborer	Upper Canada	Niles MI	PVT	COM F 1st MI INF
Schaffer, Stephen								Detroit MI	PVT	Scott Guards
Schermerhorn, Mathias	24	5.07	BLU	BWN	LGT	Farmer	Cuyahoga Co OH	Corunna MI	PVT	COM C 1st MI INF
Schlimnie, Charles	25	5.08	DRK	DRK	DRK	Soldier	Dresden GER	Detroit MI	PVT	COM K 1st MI INF
Schmidt, Henry	29	5.09	BLU	BLK	LGT	Farmer	Germany	Detroit MI	PVT	COM H 1st MI INF
Schmidt, Ludwig F.	24	5.08	HZL	BWN	DRK	Blacksmith	Germany	Ann Arbor MI	PVT	Brady Guards
Schmitdiel, John B.						Grocer		Detroit MI	PVT	Scott Guards
Schnider, Peter								Detroit MI	PVT	Scott Guards
Schnuphase, Henry	32	5.06	HZL	BWN	LGT	Cabinet-maker	Golletta GER	Detroit MI	PVT	Brady Guards
Schratz, Peter								Detroit MI	PVT	Scott Guards
Schrempf, Henry	21	5.07	GRY	DRK	DRK	Butcher	France		PVT	COM K 1st MI INF
Schuster, Jacob	27	5.06	GRY	LGT	LGT	Cooper	Prussia		PVT	COM D 1st MI INF
Schwarz, John E. Jr.	21	5.05	GRY	LGT	LGT	Broker	Philadelphia PA	Detroit MI	2LT	COM B 1st MI INF
Scofield, Daniel T.	25	5.06	HZL	AUB	FLD	Carpenter	Orleans Co NY		PVT	COM E 15th US INF
Scott, Jediah	44	5.09	GRY	BLK	FIR	Farmer	Luzerne Co PA	Volina MI	PVT	COM F 1st MI INF
Scott, John H.	20	5.04	HZL	BWN	LGT	Blacksmith	Greene Co NY		PVT	COM G 1st MI INF
Scott, Justin	22	5.09	HZL	BWN	FIR	Laborer	Monroe Co NY		PVT	COM B US MTD RIF
Scott, Nicholas	24	5.03	BLU	BWN	LGT	Farmer	Connecticut		PVT	COM D 1st MI INF
Scott, Quincy A.	22	5.08	GRY	DRK	LGT	Carpenter	Washington Co VT		PVT	COM A 15th US INF
Scrambling, Warren	18	5.04	HZL	BWN	LGT	Blacksmith	London CAN		PVT	COM A 1st MI INF
Scudder, George	21	5.10	HZL	DRK	LGT	Laborer	Hebron NY		PVT	COM A 15th US INF
Seagle, Bartley	20	5.05	BLK	BWN	DRK	Farmer	Germany	Corunna MI	PVT	COM C 1st MI INF
Seal, James A.	19	5.08	BLU	BWN	FIR	Carpenter	Onondaga Co NY	Corunna MI	PVT	COM C 1st MI INF
Seams, Henry	26	6.00	BLU	LGT	LGT	Laborer	Harwick CAN	St. Clair MI	PVT	COM B 1st MI INF
Sebring, James	20	5.08	LGT	LGT	LGT	Farmer	Orleans Co NY		PVT	COM K 1st MI INF
Seeley, William M. C.	25	5.05	BLU	SDY	LGT	Farmer	Pittsburgh PA		PVT	COM G 15th US INF

ENROLLED	MUSTERED	DISCHARGED	REMARKS
11/15/47 Niles MI	12/02/47 Detroit MI		Died of measles at Cordova MEX 05/19/48
06/03/46 Detroit MI			VTS WNA
11/30/47 Corunna MI	12/01/47 Detroit MI	07/26/48 Detroit MI	AKA Schirmerhorn, Schimerhorn
12/15/47 Toledo OH	01/01/48 Detroit MI	07/28/48 Detroit MI	
01/18/48 Detroit MI	02/01/48 Detroit MI	07/27/48 Detroit MI	PEN
06/18/47 Detroit MI	06/18/47 Detroit MI	06/30/48 Detroit MI	Received pension
06/03/46 Detroit MI			VTS WNA
06/03/46 Detroit MI			VTS WNA
06/18/47 Detroit MI	06/18/47 Detroit MI	06/30/48 Detroit MI	
06/03/46 Detroit MI			VTS WNA
12/24/47 Lexington MI	01/01/48 Detroit MI		Died at New Orleans LA 06/24/48
11/14/47 Detroit MI	11/14/47 Detroit MI		Deserted at Detroit MI 11/22/47
10/30/47 Port Huron MI	11/12/47 Detroit MI	07/26/48 Detroit MI	
04/21/47 Coldwater MI	04/27/47 Detroit MI		Deserted at Detroit MI 04/27/47
11/15/47 Volina MI	12/02/47 Detroit MI		LIH at New Orleans LA 06/24/48
02/20/48 Albion MI	03/01/48 Detroit MI		STH at New Orleans LA 06/05/48
07/13/47 Otsego MI	07/13/47 Otsego MI	07/31/48 Jefferson BKS MO	
11/14/47 Ann Arbor MI	11/14/47 Detroit MI		Died at Detroit MI 07/15/48
04/03/47 Utica MI	04/27/47 Detroit MI	08/21/48	PMT CPL 04/22/47. TRA COM I 12/26/47. PEN
11/05/47 Kalamazoo MI	11/19/47 Detroit MI		Deserted 12/08/47
04/07/47 Pontiac MI	04/27/47 Detroit MI		Died of disease at Chapultepec MEX 12/08/47
11/30/47 Corunna MI	12/01/47 Detroit MI	07/26/48 Detroit MI	AKA Bartley Seigle
11/30/47 Corunna MI	12/01/47 Detroit MI	07/26/48 Detroit MI	AKA Seil & Sill. RBL
11/02/47 Port Huron MI	11/12/47 Detroit MI	07/26/48 Detroit MI	AKA Henry Serens. PEN
12/15/47 Adrian MI	01/01/48 Detroit MI		Deserted at Detroit MI 02/02/48
04/02/47 Detroit MI	04/30/47 Detroit MI	08/04/48 Covington KY	

Name	Age	Hgt	Eye	Hair	Cpx	Trade	Born	Home	Rank	Unit
Seely, Alonzo	22	5.07	BLU	FIR	FIR	Cooper	Dutchess Co NY		PVT	COM K 3rd US DRG
Segar, Samuel	20	5.08	BLU	LGT	LGT	Clerk		Toledo OH	PVT	COM H 1st MI INF
Seger, Lafayette	22	6.00	HZL	LGT	FIR	Tanner	Steuben Co NY		PVT	COM G 15th US INF
Sellers, Michael								Adrian MI	PVT	Adrian Guards
Severy, Edward Jr.	23	5.05	DRK	BLK	DRK	Farmer	Cato NY		PVT	COM K 1st MI INF
Severy, William	23	5.06	GRY	LGT	FIR	Farmer	St Lawrence NY		PVT	COM I 1st MI INF
Seward, Daniel S.	34	5.04	BLU	BWN	FIR	Carpenter	New York State		PVT	COM K 6th US INF
Seymour, William B.	22	6.02	HZL	LGT	LGT	Farmer	Ontario Co NY		PVT	COM K 3rd US DRG
Shaler, Brainard	44	5.08	BLK	BLK	FIR	Farmer	Middlesex Co CT		PVT	COM F 1st MI INF
Shane, William H.								Adrian MI	PVT	Adrian Guards
Shanessy, Patrick						Blacksmith		Detroit MI	PVT	Montgomery Guards
Sharp, Almyron L.	33	5.10	GRY	AUB	LGT	Carpenter	Seneca Co NY		PVT	COM K 1st MI INF
Shaver, Joseph D.	22	5.11	BLU	BWN	FIR	Farmer	Orleans Co NY		PVT	COM I 1st MI INF
Shay, John	36	6.00	BWN	BWN	DRK	Laborer	Ireland		PVT	COM E 1st MI INF
Shay, Michael	24	5.06	BLU	BWN	LGT	Laborer	Cork IRE		PVT	COM D 1st MI INF
Shedtler, Abraham	41	5.09	GRY	LGT	LGT	Farmer	Onondaga Co NY	Pontiac MI	PVT	COM D 1st MI INF
Sheffield, Charles W.	22	5.11	DRK	DRK	DRK	Farmer	Bridgewater NY	Adrian MI	PVT	COM K 1st MI INF
Sheft, Owel								Detroit MI	PVT	Montgomery Guards
Sheldon, Alonzo L.								Adrian MI	PVT	Adrian Guards
Shell, Henry A.	22	6.00	BLU	SDY	LGT	Clerk	Cayuga Co NY	Milan MI	1SG	COM H 1st MI INF
Shenefelt, Henry C.	18	5.05	BLK	LGT	LGT	Farmer	Cleveland OH	Edwardsburg MI	PVT	COM F 1st MI INF
Shepard, John E.	25								4SG	COM H 1st MI INF
Shepard, Samuel	32	5.04	GRY	DRK	FLD	Farmer	Philadelphia PA		PVT	COM G 15th US INF
Sherlock, James								Detroit MI	PVT	Montgomery Guards
Sherman, John F.	18	5.04	BLK	BWN	LGT	Tailor	Saratoga Co NY	Moscow MI	PVT	COM H 1st MI INF
Sherrer, Frederick	25	5.04	BLU	SDY	DRK	Butcher	Boyer GER	Detroit MI	PVT	Brady Guards

Enrolled	Mustered	Discharged	Remarks
04/02/47 Detroit MI	04/22/47 Detroit MI		LIH at Puebla MEX 08/07/47. PEN
11/20/47 Toledo OH	12/01/47 Detroit MI		Deserted at end of furlough 12/26/47
04/26/47 Detroit MI	04/30/47 Detroit MI		Died of debility at Covington KY 07/23/48
06/01/46 Adrian MI			VTS WNA
11/15/47 Almont MI	12/01/47 Detroit MI		Died at Detroit MI 12/27/47
11/15/47 Hastings MI	12/01/47 Detroit MI	07/18/48 Detroit MI	AKA William C. Sevey. PEN
02/10/48 Detroit MI	Detroit MI	05/01/48 Newport KY	Rejected from service
04/07/47 Tecumseh MI	04/22/47	07/31/48 Jefferson BKS MO	LIH at Puebla MEX 08/07/47. PEN
11/15/47 Niles MI	12/02/47 Detroit MI	07/28/48 Detroit MI	
06/01/46 Adrian MI			VTS WNA
05/28/46 Detroit MI			VTS WNA. AKA Patrick O'Shanessy
01/20/48 Hillsdale MI	02/01/48 Detroit MI	07/28/48 Detroit MI	
11/15/47 Union City MI	12/01/47 Detroit MI		Deserted at Bellevue OH 02/18/48
11/20/47 Detroit MI	12/04/47 Detroit MI		Deserted at Perrysburg OH 12/29/47
11/14/47 Detroit MI	11/14/47 Detroit MI		DES at Santiago MEX 06/17/48. AKA Michael Shea
11/14/47 Pontiac MI	11/14/47 Detroit MI	07/26/48 Detroit MI	
12/15/47 Adrian MI	01/01/48 Detroit MI	07/28/48 Detroit MI	Received pension
??/??/46 Detroit MI			VTS WNA
06/01/46 Adrian MI			VTS WNA
11/20/47 Monroe MI	12/01/47 Detroit MI	07/27/48 Detroit MI	PEN
11/15/47 Niles MI	12/02/47 Detroit MI	07/28/48 Detroit MI	Received pension
11/20/47 Hillsdale MI	12/01/47 Detroit MI		RTR 06/01/48. LIH Memphis TN 07/03/48. Died 07/04/48
04/07/47 Detroit MI	04/30/47 Detroit MI	08/04/48 Covington KY	
05/28/46 Detroit MI			VTS WNA
11/20/47 Moscow MI	12/01/47 Detroit MI	07/27/48 Detroit MI	MNI possibly T. PEN
06/18/47 Detroit MI	06/18/47 Detroit MI	06/30/48 Detroit MI	In Michigan Veterans Facility (#2162). AKA Shearer. PEN

Name	Age	Hgt	Eye	Hair	Cpx	Trade	Born	Home	Rank	Unit
Sherwood, Hubbard	23	5.09	GRY	BWN	FIR	Carpenter	Franklin Co VT		PVT	COM H US MTD RIF
Sherwood, William B.	29	5.11	BLK	BLK	DRK	Farmer	Delaware Co NY		3SG	COM A 1st MI INF
Shew, Aaron	20	5.11	BLK	BLK	DRK	Farmer	Monroe Co MI		PVT	COM G 15th US INF
Shines, Gilbert	18	5.09	DRK	DRK	DRK	Farmer	Pennsylvania	Livingston Co MI	PVT	COM K 1st MI INF
Shortal, Thomas	22	5.07	GRY	DRK	LGT	Chair-maker	Ireland		PVT	COM A 15th US INF
Shortley, Benjamin	22	5.06	BLU	BLK	DRK	Baker	Washington Co NY		PVT	COM D 1st MI INF
Shotwell, William	32	5.06	BLU	DRK	DRK	Farmer	Roxbury NJ		RCT	US Army
Showers, Michael	25	5.08	GRY	BWN	FIR	Seaman	Oxford CAN		PVT	COM B 5th US INF
Shurtliff, Galen								Adrian MI	PVT	Adrian Guards
Shutes, John	25	6.01	HZL	BWN	DRK	Saddler	Cumberland Co NJ		PVT	COM D 1st MI INF
Sibley, Ebenezer S.	41	6.00	DRK	DRK	DRK	Soldier	Marietta OH	Detroit MI	1LT	COM ? 1st US ART
Signer, Walter	18	6.00	BLK	LGT	FIR	Farmer	Delaware Co NY		PVT	COM E 1st MI INF
Silvers, Hartwell	22	5.10	DRK	DRK	DRK	Blacksmith	Vermont	Detroit MI	PVT	COM K 1st MI INF
Simeon, Cotell	35								3CP	COM D 1st MI INF
Simmons, Alfred S.	38	5.09	BLU	BLK	FIR	Blacksmith	Chenango Co NY		PVT	COM C 1st MI INF
Simonds, James N.A.S.	21	5.08	BLU	BWN	LGT	Farmer	Wheatland NY		PVT	COM K 3rd US DRG
Simons, William	19	6.01	BLU	BWN	LGT	Laborer	Scriba NY		PVT	COM K 1st MI INF
Sines, John S.	22	5.07	GRY	LGT	LGT	Farmer	Ypsilanti MI		PVT	COM B 5th US INF
Sines, Timothy S.	18	5.06	GRY	BWN	LGT	Farmer	Superior MI	Plymouth MI	PVT	Brady Guards
Sinkey, Luke P.	20						Licking Co OH		PVT	COM C 1st MI INF
Skank, Albert	19	5.11	DRK	DRK	LGT	Farmer	Bennington NY		PVT	COM K 1st MI INF
Skank, William	33	5.08	DRK	SDY	SDY	Laborer	Rutland VT		PVT	COM B 1st MI INF
Skeely, John	24	6.00	BLU	LGT	LGT	Blacksmith	Monroe Co NY		PVT	COM G 1st MI INF
Skelton, James A.	21	5.10	GRY	LGT	SAL	Student	Plainfield NY		PVT	Brady Guards
Skinner, Timothy	20	5.07	DRK	DRK	FIR	Farmer	Plattsburgh NY	Lapeer Co MI	PVT	COM K 1st MI INF
Skinner, William J.	19	5.08	BLU	SDY	LGT	Farmer	Liester NY		PVT	Brady Guards

ENROLLED	MUSTERED	DISCHARGED	REMARKS
08/24/47 Kalamazoo MI	08/24/47 Kalamazoo MI	07/31/48 Jefferson BKS MO	
11/05/47 Kalamazoo MI	11/19/47 Detroit MI	03/20/48 Cordova MEX	Discharged for disability
04/19/47 Monroe MI	04/30/47 Detroit MI	08/04/48 Covington KY	Received pension. AKA Aaron Shoes
12/15/47 Blissfield MI	01/01/48 Detroit MI		Died of diarrhea at Cordova MEX 05/18/48
04/13/47 Pontiac MI	04/27/47 Detroit MI	04/02/48 Mexico City MEX	WIA at Mexico City 08/20/47. TRA COM K 12/26/47. PEN
11/14/47 Detroit MI	11/14/47 Detroit MI		DES at Detroit MI 11/19/47. AKA Benjamin Shirly
04/06/48 Pontiac MI	04/30/48 Detroit MI	06/23/48 Newport KY	PEN
09/20/47 Detroit MI	Detroit MI	08/01/48 East Pascagoula MS	
06/01/46 Adrian MI			VTS WNA
11/14/47 Detroit MI	11/14/47 Detroit MI	07/26/48 Detroit MI	
			PMT CAP & QUA 07/07/48. PEN. MNI Sprote
11/20/47 Jackson MI	12/04/47 Detroit MI		Died of fever at Cordova MEX 05/08/48
12/15/47 Adrian MI	01/01/48 Detroit MI	07/28/48 Detroit MI	Received pension
11/14/47 Detroit MI	11/14/47 Detroit MI	07/26/48 Detroit MI	
11/30/47 Detroit MI	12/01/47 Detroit MI		PMT FIM 12/16/47. DES at New Orleans LA 01/18/48
04/05/47 Tecumseh MI	04/22/47 Detroit MI	07/31/48 Jefferson BKS MO	TRA COM D 01/04/48. Received pension
12/15/47 Howell MI	01/01/48 Detroit MI		Died at New Orleans LA 05/06/48.
07/15/47 Detroit MI	Detroit MI	08/01/48 East Pascagoula MS	PEN
06/18/47 Detroit MI	06/18/47 Detroit MI	06/30/48 Detroit MI	PEN. AKA Timothy S. Sines
	05/10/47 Adrian MI	08/??/48 Carrolton LA	Not listed on Company rolls. PEN
12/15/47 Almont MI	01/01/48 Detroit MI		Died at Cordova MEX 05/28/48. AKA Albert Shank
11/02/47 Port Huron MI	11/12/47 Detroit MI		Deserted at Detroit MI 12/10/47. AKA William Scank
02/20/48 Ypsilanti MI	03/01/48 Detroit MI		Deserted at Detroit MI 04/12/48
06/07/47 Detroit MI	06/18/47 Detroit MI		Deserted at Fort Mackinac MI 10/27/47
12/15/47 Almont MI	01/01/48 Detroit MI		Died of fever at Cordova MEX 05/19/48
06/16/47 Detroit MI	06/18/47 Detroit MI		Deserted at Fort Mackinac MI 10/30/47

Name	Age	Hgt	Eye	Hair	Cpx	Trade	Born	Home	Rank	Unit
Sly, Asa M.	23	5.08	GRY	BWN	DRK	Farmer	Canada		PVT	COM K 1st MI INF
Sly, John	23	5.06	BLU	LGT	FIR	Waiter	England		PVT	COM K 3rd US DRG
Small, Elias	39	5.02	BLU	LGT	FIR	Carpenter	Onondaga Co NY	Pontiac MI	PVT	COM C 1st MI INF
Smart, Andrew								Detroit MI	PVT	Montgomery Guards
Smith, Albert A.	40	5.10	BLU	BWN	LGT	Miller	Dutchess Co NY	Kalamazoo MI	PVT	COM A 1st MI INF
Smith, Allen A.	23	5.06	GRY	BWN	FIR	Shoemaker	Washington Co NY	Marshall MI	PVT	COM I 1st MI INF
Smith, Asa B.	24	5.05	BLU	BLK	LGT	Wheel-wright	Canada West		PVT	COM E 15th US INF
Smith, Carlton	25	5.10	BLU	DRK	FIR	Millwright	Saratoga Co NY	Hillsdale MI	PVT	COM F 1st MI INF
Smith, Cyrus W.	18	6.00	BLU	LGT	LGT	Laborer	Garnith CAN	Port Huron MI	PVT	COM B 1st MI INF
Smith, Daniel	28	5.04	BLU	DRK	DRK	Sailor	Dutchess ME		PVT	COM B 3rd US INF
Smith, Dewitt C.								Adrian MI	PVT	Adrian Guards
Smith, Erastus J.	39	5.07	BLU	BWN	FIR	Farmer	Orleans Co NY		PVT	COM C 1st MI INF
Smith, Frank D.	23	5.08	BLU	LGT	LGT	Sailor	Erie PA	Detroit MI	2CP	COM B 1st MI INF
Smith, George								Detroit MI	PVT	Scott Guards
Smith, Harvey	21	5.07	GRY	SDY	DRK	Farmer	Niagara Co NY	Pontiac MI	PVT	COM G 15th US INF
Smith, Henry	48					Soldier	New York State	Monroe MI	MAJ	US Army
Smith, Henry A.	21	5.04	GRY	BWN	DRK	Laborer	New York NY	Detroit MI	PVT	COM E 1st MI INF
Smith, Horris A.								Detroit MI	PVT	Montgomery Guards
Smith, Isaac A.	21	5.09	BLK	DRK	DRK	Farmer	Ontario Co NY		PVT	COM E 15th US INF
Smith, Jacob	38	5.05	HZL	BWN	LGT	Laborer	Wurtemberg GER	Detroit MI	PVT	Brady Guards
Smith, James	25	5.06	BLU	LGT	LGT	Farmer	Herkimer Co NY	Detroit MI	PVT	COM D 1st MI INF
Smith, James	44	5.09	GRY	DRK	DRK	Weaver	England		PVT	COM K 1st MI INF
Smith, James B.								Adrian MI	PVT	Adrian Guards
Smith, James H.	18	5.07	GRY	LGT	DRK	Painter	Orange Co NJ	Port Huron MI	PVT	COM G 1st MI INF
Smith, Joel T. P.	26	5.07	GRY	BWN	LGT	Laborer	Dutchess Co NY		RCT	US Army
Smith, John	18	5.07	BLK	BWN	FIR	Laborer	Colburn PA		PVT	COM C 2nd US INF

ENROLLED	MUSTERED	DISCHARGED	REMARKS
12/15/47 Howell MI	01/01/48 Detroit MI		Deserted at Detroit MI 01/31/48
04/10/47 Detroit MI	04/22/47 Detroit MI		Died of disease at Perote MEX 07/04/47
11/30/47 Pontiac MI	12/01/47 Detroit MI	07/26/48 Detroit MI	
??/??/46 Detroit MI			VTS WNA
11/05/47 Kalamazoo MI	11/19/47 Detroit MI	07/18/48 Detroit MI	Hospitalized at Cordova MEX. PEN
12/20/47 Bellevue MI	01/01/48 Detroit MI	07/18/48 Detroit MI	Received pension
04/08/47 Niles MI	04/27/47 Detroit MI		Deserted near Baton Rouge LA 05/27/47
11/15/47 Hillsdale MI	12/02/47 Detroit MI		Died at Newport KY 03/??/48
11/02/47 Port Huron MI	11/12/47 Detroit MI	07/26/48 Detroit MI	PEN
04/05/47 Detroit MI	04/05/47 Detroit MI	07/25/48 East Pascagoula MS	PEN
06/01/46 Adrian MI			VTS WNA
11/30/47 Milford MI	12/01/47 Detroit MI	07/26/48 Detroit MI	Received pension
11/02/47 Port Huron MI	11/12/47 Detroit MI	07/26/48 Detroit MI	RBL
06/03/46 Detroit MI			VTS WNA
04/03/47 Detroit MI	04/30/47 Detroit MI	08/04/48 Covington KY	
03/03/47		07/24/47	QUT Dept. Died of yellow fever at Vera Cruz. PEN
11/20/47 Battle Creek MI	12/04/47 Detroit MI	07/18/48 Detroit MI	
??/??/46 Detroit MI			VTS WNA
04/21/47 Fawn River MI	04/27/47 Detroit MI	08/06/48 Cincinnati OH	DES at Detroit MI 04/27/47. WIA 08/20/47
06/18/47 Detroit MI	06/18/47 Detroit MI	06/30/48 Detroit MI	
11/14/47 Detroit MI	11/14/47 Detroit MI	07/26/48 Detroit MI	
12/24/47 Kalamazoo MI	01/01/48 Detroit MI		Died of diarrhea at Cordova MEX 05/01/48
06/01/46 Adrian MI			VTS WNA
02/20/48 Pontiac MI	03/01/48 Detroit MI	07/18/48 Detroit MI	
03/23/47 Detroit MI	03/23/47 Detroit MI		Deserted at Detroit MI 04/04/47
10/12/46 Mackinac MI			Deserted 05/09/47

Name	Age	Hgt	Eye	Hair	Cpx	Trade	Born	Home	Rank	Unit
Smith, John	44								PVT	COM B 1st MI INF
Smith, John	44	5.11	BLU	SDY	SDY	Farmer	Montgomery Co NY		PVT	COM F 1st MI INF
Smith, John H.	22								UNK	US Navy
Smith, Nathan M.	20	5.05	BLK	BWN	LGT	Clothier	Pontiac MI	Corunna MI	PVT	COM C 1st MI INF
Smith, Ray P.	34	5.04	GRY	DRK	DRK	Tailor	Dutchess Co NY		RCT	US Army
Smith, Richard	21	5.04	GRY	LGT	FIR	Cooper	Oakland Co MI		PVT	COM B 3rd US INF
Smith, Roswell	43	5.09	BLU	BWN	DRK	Farmer	Plymouth MA	Elgin IL	PVT	COM E 1st MI INF
Smith, Samuel R.	28	5.05	GRY	LGT	LGT	Farmer	Clark Co OH		PVT	COM K 1st MI INF
Smith, Stephen	26	5.05	BWN	FIR	FIR	Sailor	Hampshire ENG		PVT	COM K 3rd US DRG
Smith, Theodore B.	19	5.07	BLU	DRK	LGT	Laborer	LeRoy NY	Battle Creek MI	PVT	COM B 1st MI INF
Smith, Thomas	21	5.11	DRK	LGT	LGT	Laborer	Friendship NY		PVT	COM A 15th US INF
Smith, Thomas R.	24	5.09	BLU	LGT	LGT	Laborer	Victor NY	St. Clair Co MI	PVT	COM B 1st MI INF
Smith, William	20	5.10	HZL	RED	FIR	Laborer	England	Bridgewater MI	PVT	COM I 1st MI INF
Smith, William	24	5.03	GRY	SDY	SDY	Laborer	Clinton Co NY	Detroit MI	PVT	COM D 1st MI INF
Smith, William S.	24	5.06	GRY	BLK	DRK	Carpenter	Franklin Co PA	Fawn River MI	CPL	COM E 15th US INF
Smith, William W.	18	5.04	GRY	BWN	LGT	Laborer	Kalamazoo MI	Kalamazoo MI	PVT	COM A 1st MI INF
Smoke, Anthony	24	5.10	HZL	LGT	LGT	Farmer	Prussia	Milwaukee WI	PVT	COM F 1st MI INF
Snow, Edwin R.	27								PVT	COM B 1st MI INF
Snow, Lyman B.	21	5.07	BLU	LGT	FIR	Laborer	Strafford VT	Detroit MI	PVT	COM B 1st MI INF
Snyder, Eli	30	6.00			DRK			Ann Arbor MI	1LT	COM K 1st MI INF
Soddy, Emery	24	5.08	BLU	BWN	LGT	Farmer	Wayne Co NY	Kalamazoo MI	PVT	COM A 1st MI INF
Soddy, John W.	18	5.07	BLU	BWN	LGT	Farmer	Wayne Co NY	Kalamazoo MI	PVT	COM A 1st MI INF
Somerset, Thomas	22	5.09	BWN	BWN	FIR	Laborer	Westmead IRE		PVT	COM B 5th US INF
Soper, Carlisle B.	22	5.10	BLU	BWN	DRK	Farmer	Clinton Co NY		PVT	COM K 3rd US DRG
Spalding, George L.								Adrian MI	PVT	Adrian Guards
Spangenbergh, Charles	31	5.10	BLU	LGT	LGT	Shoemaker	Noxten GER	Detroit MI	1SG	COM D 1st MI INF

Enrolled	Mustered	Discharged	Remarks
11/02/47 Port Huron MI	11/12/47 Detroit MI	07/26/48 Detroit MI	
11/15/47 St Joseph MI	12/02/47 Detroit MI		Deserted at Perrysburg OH 12/29/47
04/08/46 Detroit MI	Baltimore MD		
11/30/47 Corunna MI	12/01/47 Detroit MI	07/26/48 Detroit MI	Received pension
04/05/47 Detroit MI	04/05/47 Detroit MI		Deserted at Detroit MI 04/27/47
03/25/47 Detroit MI	03/25/47 Detroit MI	07/25/48 East Pascagoula MS	PEN
11/20/47 Grand Rapids MI	12/04/47 Detroit MI	07/18/48 Detroit MI	
01/20/48 Grass Lake MI	02/01/48 Detroit MI	07/28/48 Detroit MI	Left by accident 20 miles above Memphis TN. PEN
04/05/47 Detroit MI	04/22/47 Detroit MI		LIH at Puebla MEX 08/07/47
11/02/47 Jackson MI	11/12/47 Detroit MI	07/26/48 Detroit MI	PEN
04/06/47 Pontiac MI	04/27/47 Detroit MI	08/04/48 Covington KY	TRA COM K 12/26/47. PEN
11/02/47 Port Huron MI	11/12/47 Detroit MI		Died at Detroit MI 07/25/48
12/20/47 Ionia MI	01/01/48 Detroit MI	07/18/48 Detroit MI	PEN
11/14/47 Albion MI	11/14/47 Detroit MI	07/26/48 Detroit MI	
04/20/47 Fawn River MI	04/27/47 Detroit MI		PMT 2SG 08/06/47. Died of diarrhea at New Orleans LA 07/09/48
11/05/47 Kalamazoo MI	11/19/47 Detroit MI	07/18/48 Detroit MI	PEN
11/15/47 Niles MI	12/02/47 Detroit MI	07/28/48 Detroit MI	
11/02/47 Port Huron MI	11/12/47 Detroit MI		Died at Cordova MEX 05/24/48
11/02/47 Port Huron MI	11/12/47 Detroit MI	08/01/48 Detroit MI	PEN
10/30/47 Ann Arbor MI	01/20/48 Detroit MI	07/28/48 Detroit MI	PEN
11/05/47 Kalamazoo MI	11/19/47 Detroit MI	07/18/48 Detroit MI	
11/05/47 Kalamazoo MI	11/19/47 Detroit MI		Died at New Orleans LA en route to Detroit MI 06/24/48
09/20/47 Detroit MI	Detroit MI	08/01/48 East Pascagoula MS	
04/08/47 Tecumseh MI	04/22/47 Detroit MI	07/31/48 Jefferson BKS MO	TRA COM D 01/04/48. Received pension
06/01/46 Adrian MI			VTS WNA
11/14/47 Detroit MI	11/14/47 Detroit MI	07/26/48 Detroit MI	Born in Westphalia

Name	Age	Hgt	Eye	Hair	Cpx	Trade	Born	Home	Rank	Unit
Sparling, Manville	21	5.06	BLU	BWN	LGT	Joiner	Genesee Co NY	Grand Rapids MI	PVT	COM A 1st MI INF
Sparrow, Michael	22	5.09	GRY	DRK	LGT	Clerk	Dublin IRE	Detroit MI	1CP	Brady Guards
Spaulding, David E.	22	5.09	DRK	BWN	FIR	Musician	Massachusetts		PVT	COM K 6th US INF
Spear, Jacob	21	5.07	GRY	BWN	DRK	Laborer	Essex Co NJ		PVT	COM B 3rd US INF
Spears, Carmi	21	6.02	BLU	LGT	RUD	Farmer	Ohio		PVT	COM E 15th US INF
Spears, Edward	24	5.09	GRY	BWN	DRK	Farmer	Clinton Co NY		RCT	US Army
Spears, William	21	6.00	GRY	FIR	FIR	Laborer	Seneca Co NY		PVT	COM A 6th US INF
Spencer, Abel H.	45	6.01	GRY	BLK	LGT	Carpenter	Rutland VT	Albion MI	PVT	COM C 1st MI INF
Spencer, Hiram	21	5.09	BLU	BLK	LGT	Blacksmith	Steuben Co NY		PVT	COM G 1st MI INF
Spencer, James	18	5.06	GRY	BWN	LGT	Farmer	Kingston CAN		PVT	COM B 3rd US INF
Spencer, Joseph	23	5.07	BLU	LGT	FIR	Farmer	Kingston CAN		PVT	COM B 3rd US INF
Sperry, Willis	36	5.05	GRY	DRK	DRK	Laborer	Locke NY	Ypsilanti MI	PVT	COM K 1st MI INF
Spicer, Nathaniel	23	5.07	HZL	BWN	FIR		Livingston Co NY		PVT	COM B US MTD RIF
Spicer, Solomon	26	5.08	BLU	LGT	LGT	Student	Essex Co NY		PVT	Brady Guards
Spikerman, Jacob	28	5.11	BLU	BWN	LGT	Laborer	Saratoga Co NY		PVT	COM B 1st MI INF
Sprague, Almus C.	26	5.11	BLU	DRK	LGT	Farmer	New York State	Clinton MI	MUS	COM H 1st MI INF
Sprague, Ara W.	24	5.09	HZL	DRK	LGT	Merchant	Dekalb? NY	Detroit MI	2SG	Brady Guards
Sprague, George	28	5.05	HZL	LGT	LGT	Shoemaker	Middlesex Co CT		RCT	US Army
Sprague, Soloman	18	5.05	BLU	BLK	DRK	Farmer	New York NY	Detroit MI	PVT	COM D 1st MI INF
Squires, Norman	21	5.11	GRY	BWN	DRK	Farmer	Lewiston NY	Detroit MI	PVT	COM D 1st MI INF
St. Dezier, Joseph	38	5.05	GRY	DRK	DRK	Laborer	France		PVT	COM B 1st MI INF
Stadtler, Christian	20	5.03	GRY	LGT	LGT	Waiter	Pattsburgh FRA	Detroit MI	PVT	COM D 1st MI INF
Stafford, William	18	5.09	LGT	LGT	LGT	Boatman	Plainfield CT	Litchfield OH	PVT	COM H 1st MI INF
Staring, Henry	44	5.10	BLU	BWN	LGT	Farmer	Herkimer Co NY	Allegan MI	PVT	COM A 1st MI INF
Starkey, Henry	19	5.09	HZL	BWN	FIR	Painter	Bainbridge NY		PVT	COM G US MTD RIF
Starkey, Lewis C.	18	5.07	BLU	LGT	LGT	Painter	Binghamton NY		PVT	COM G US MTD RIF

Michigan Men in the Mexican War

Enrolled	Mustered	Discharged	Remarks
11/05/47 Grand Rapids MI	11/19/47 Detroit MI	07/18/48 Detroit MI	LIH at Cordova MEX
06/18/47 Detroit MI	06/18/47 Detroit MI	06/30/48 Detroit MI	
02/28/48 Detroit MI	Detroit MI	07/31/48 Jefferson BKS MO	AKA David C. RBL
03/19/47 Detroit MI	03/19/47 Detroit MI	07/25/48 East Pascagoula MS	
04/12/47 Grand Rapids MI	04/27/47 Detroit MI	03/20/48 Cuernavaca MEX	DIS for disability. PEN. AKA Carmi Shear
05/15/48 Detroit MI	Detroit MI	06/20/48 Newport KY	Received pension
10/21/46 Detroit MI	10/21/46 Detroit MI		Died of wounds at Molina del Rey MEX 09/08/47
11/30/47 Detroit MI	12/01/47 Detroit MI	07/26/48 Detroit MI	
02/20/48 Jackson MI	03/01/48 Detroit MI	07/18/48 Detroit MI	Sent to hospital at New Orleans LA 05/02/48
05/06/47 Detroit MI	Detroit MI	07/25/48 East Pascagoula MS	PEN
05/06/47 Detroit MI	Detroit MI	07/25/48 East Pascagoula MS	PEN
12/15/47 Ypsilanti MI	01/01/48 Detroit MI	07/28/48 Detroit MI	
08/16/47 Kalamazoo MI	08/16/47 Kalamazoo MI	07/31/48 Jefferson BKS MO	Received pension
06/17/47 Detroit MI	06/18/47 Detroit MI		Deserted at Detroit MI 06/21/47
11/02/47 Port Huron MI	11/12/47 Detroit MI		AKA Spickerman. DUC at Detroit MI 07/25/48
11/20/47 Clinton MI	12/02/47 Detroit MI	07/27/48 Detroit MI	Received pension
06/18/47 Detroit MI	06/18/47 Detroit MI	06/30/48 Detroit MI	PEN
04/03/47 Detroit MI	04/03/47 Detroit MI		Deserted at Detroit MI 04/04/47
11/14/47 Albion MI	11/14/47 Detroit MI	07/26/48 Detroit MI	
11/14/47 Albion MI	11/14/47 Detroit MI	07/26/48 Detroit MI	
11/02/47 Port Huron MI	11/12/47 Detroit MI		Drowned on the Mississippi River 07/08/48
11/14/47 Detroit MI	11/14/47 Detroit MI	07/26/48 Detroit MI	PEN
11/20/47 Monroe MI	12/01/47 Detroit MI	07/27/48 Detroit MI	PEN
11/05/47 Allegan MI	11/19/47 Detroit MI	07/18/48 Detroit MI	
07/24/47 Kalamazoo MI	09/01/47 Kalamazoo MI	07/31/48 Jefferson BKS MO	
07/24/47 Kalamazoo MI	07/24/47 Kalamazoo MI	07/31/48 Jefferson BKS MO	Received pension. MNI Cass

485

Name	Age	Hgt	Eye	Hair	Cpx	Trade	Born	Home	Rank	Unit
Starks, William A.								Detroit MI	PVT	Montgomery Guards
Stearns, Joseph D.	19	6.00	BWN	LGT	LGT	Farmer	Erie Co OH	Rosetown MI	PVT	COM E 1st MI INF
Stebbins, Gustavus	18	5.05	GRY	RED	LGT	Laborer	Franklin Co NY		PVT	COM A 15th US INF
Steckhan, Henry	30	5.06	GRY	LGT	FLD	Merchant	Denmark	Detroit MI	3CP	COM H 1st MI INF
Steenenberg, Barnardus	23	5.08	GRY	FIR	FIR	Farmer	Holland	Milwaukee WI	PVT	COM F 1st MI INF
Stephens, William D.	21	5.09	DRK	DRK	DRK	Farmer	Adrian MI		PVT	COM K 1st MI INF
Stevens, Amasa	26								PVT	COM G 1st MI INF
Stevens, Daniel	31	5.08	HZL	BWN	DRK	Soldier	Madison Co NY	Detroit MI	2CP	COM D 1st MI INF
Stevens, John J.	22					Builder	Cleveland OH	Monroe MI	2LT	Monroe Guards
Steward, James	22	5.06	GRY	BWN	LGT	Farmer	Ontario Co NY		PVT	COM E 15th US INF
Stewart, Joseph	21	5.11	BLU	SDY	FIR	Farmer	Trenton IRE		PVT	COM G 15th US INF
Stewart, Lewis C.	20	6.01	BLU	DRK	LGT	Farmer	Washtenaw Co MI		2CP	COM G 1st MI INF
Stillman, Henry P.	20	5.10	BLK	BWN	LGT	Farmer	Cattaraugus NY	Lansing MI	PVT	COM H 1st MI INF
Stocking, Robert Q.	18	5.06	GRY	BWN	FIR	Sailor	New York State	Long Island NY	PVT	COM I 1st MI INF
Stockton, Thomas B.	42	5.08	HZL	AUB	FIR	Engineer	Walton NY	Flint MI	COL	F&S 1st MI INF
Stoddard, Chandler	20	6.00	BLU	LGT	FIR	Carpenter	Pennsylvania NY		RCT	Montgomery Guards
Stoddard, Milton	20	5.08	BLU	LGT	LGT	Farmer	George Co OH		PVT	COM K 3rd US DRG
Stone, Joseph B.	19	5.07	BLU	LGT	LGT	Farmer	Orleans Co NY	Pontiac MI	PVT	COM C 1st MI INF
Stone, Myron H.	25	5.07	BLU	BWN	LGT	Student	Warren Co NY		1CP	COM A 1st MI INF
Stone, Oliver	23	5.07	BLK	BWN	DRK	Cabinet-maker	St Lawrence CAN		PVT	COM G 15th US INF
Stone, Silas	21	5.04	BLK	BLK	FIR	Teamster	Vermont	Pontiac MI	PVT	COM C 1st MI INF
Stoner, John	18	5.08	BLU	BLK	DRK	Farmer	Onondaga Co NY	Clinton MI	PVT	COM H 1st MI INF
Stout, James W. Jr.	33	5.07	BLU	BWN	FIR	Blacksmith	Livingston Co NY	Adrian MI	PVT	COM G 15th US INF
Stowell, John	23	5.06	GRY	LGT	FIR	Soldier	New York NY		PVT	COM C 2nd US INF
Streeter, Senge									PVT	COM K 3rd US DRG
Strinbeck, Joseph								Adrian MI	PVT	Adrian Guards

Michigan Men in the Mexican War

ENROLLED	MUSTERED	DISCHARGED	REMARKS
??/??/46 Detroit MI			VTS WNA
11/20/47 Detroit MI	12/04/47 Detroit MI	07/18/48 Detroit MI	Received pension
04/07/47 Utica MI	04/27/47 Detroit MI	08/21/48	TRA COM K 12/26/47
11/20/47 Adrian MI	12/01/47 Detroit MI	07/27/48 Detroit MI	
11/15/47 Niles MI	12/02/47 Detroit MI	07/28/48 Detroit MI	AKA Bernard Steinenberg. PEN
12/15/47 Adrian MI	01/01/48 Detroit MI		Died at Passo Ancho MEX 06/13/48
02/20/48 Battle Creek MI	03/01/48 Detroit MI		Deserted at Detroit MI 04/11/48
11/14/47 Port Huron MI	11/14/47 Detroit MI	07/26/48 Detroit MI	
??/??/46 Monroe MI			VTS WNA
04/16/47 Jackson MI	04/27/47 Detroit MI	08/21/48	
04/07/47 Detroit MI	04/30/47 Detroit MI	07/25/47 New Orleans LA	DIS on writ of habeas corpus. AKA Joseph Stuart
02/20/48 Battle Creek MI	03/01/48 Detroit MI	07/18/48 Detroit MI	STH at New Orleans LA from Vera Cruz MEX
12/20/47 Lansing MI	01/01/48 Detroit MI	07/27/48 Detroit MI	AKA Henry P. Stitman
12/20/47 Otisco MI	01/01/48 Detroit MI	07/18/48 Detroit MI	Received pension
10/18/47 Detroit MI	12/08/47 Detroit MI	07/29/48 Detroit MI	Commander of regiment. MNI Baylies Whitmarsh
11/01/47 Detroit MI			Company disbanded before muster
04/08/47 Tecumseh MI	04/22/47 Detroit MI	07/31/48 Jefferson BKS MO	TRA COM D 01/04/48
11/30/47 Pontiac MI	12/01/47 Detroit MI		Buried 07/29/48
11/05/47 Kalamazoo MI	11/19/47 Detroit MI	07/18/48 Detroit MI	PMT 3SG 12/01/47. PMT 2SG 04/25/48. MNI Holly
04/15/47 Adrian MI	04/30/47 Detroit MI	08/04/48 Covington KY	Received pension
11/30/47 Pontiac MI	12/01/47 Detroit MI	07/26/48 Detroit MI	Received pension
11/20/47 Clinton MI	12/01/47 Detroit MI	07/27/48 Detroit MI	
04/15/47 Adrian MI	04/30/47 Detroit MI		Died of typhoid fever at Puebla MEX 12/20/47. PEN
07/15/46 Detroit MI			Detroit MI
04/07/47 Tecumseh MI	04/22/47 Detroit MI		LIH at Puebla MEX 08/07/47
06/01/46 Adrian MI			VTS WNA

Name	Age	Hgt	Eye	Hair	Cpx	Trade	Born	Home	Rank	Unit
Strobe, Jacob	21	5.06	GRY	DRK	LGT	Laborer	Cayuga Co NY		PVT	COM A 15th US INF
Strong, Melgar B.	22	5.11	HZL	LGT	SAL	Farmer	Monroe Co NY	Plymouth MI	PVT	Brady Guards
Stuart, David D.	22	5.09	BLK	AUB	DRK	Painter	Salem MA		BUG	COM K 6th US INF
Stuart, James M.	32					Editor	Pennsylvania ?	Niles MI	1LT	COM F 1st MI INF
Sturges, Lyman	18	5.05	BLU	SDY	LGT	Farmer	Window NY	Lyons MI	PVT	COM B 1st MI INF
Sturges, Norman	26	5.05	HZL	BWN	DRK	Farmer	Greene Co NY		PVT	COM G 1st MI INF
Sulavan, Timothy								Detroit MI	PVT	Montgomery Guards
Sullivan, Daniel								Detroit MI	PVT	Montgomery Guards
Sullivan, Jeremiah								Detroit MI	PVT	Montgomery Guards
Sumner, William	27	5.10	HZL	BWN	RUD	Shoemaker	Yorkshire ENG	Detroit MI	PVT	COM G 15th US INF
Surgeson, William	18	5.06	GRY	BWN	FIR	Laborer	Lancaster PA		PVT	COM I 1st MI INF
Sutfin, William B.	39	5.09	BLU	BLK	FLD	Farmer	Yates Co NY	Clinton MI	PVT	COM H 1st MI INF
Sutton, Michael	23	5.10	GRY	LGT	FIR	Laborer	London CAN		PVT	COM B 5th US INF
Swald, John B.	31	5.09	BLU	BLK	LGT	Cigar-maker	France		3SG	COM E 1st MI INF
Swan, David	27	5.10	BLK	BLK	FIR	Teamster	Cayuga Co NY	Pontiac MI	1SG	COM C 1st MI INF
Swartwood, Deloss	21	5.10	BLU	DRK	LGT	Shoemaker	Burton NY	Detroit MI	PVT	COM B 1st MI INF
Sweeting, Almond	27	6.00	GRY	LGT	FIR	Farmer	Oneida Co NY		PVT	COM I 1st MI INF
Swift, Loren R.	19	5.06	DRK	BWN	LGT	Farmer	Cayuga Co NY	Ada MI	MUS	COM A 1st MI INF
Swyheart, Simon	18	5.08	BLK	BWN	LGT	Laborer	Ohio	Elkhart IN	PVT	COM F 1st MI INF
Taber, John	23	5.06	BLU	BWN	FIR	Laborer	Berkshire Co ENG		PVT	COM K 3rd US DRG
Tabor, James A.	37	5.10	BLK	BLK	FIR	Farmer	Canaga NY		PVT	COM I 1st MI INF
Tabor, John	21	5.06	BLU	FIR	FIR	Laborer	East Hundra ENG		PVT	COM K 3rd US DRG
Talbort, William F.	41	6.02	BLK	BLK	DRK	Laborer	Tipperary IRE		PVT	COM E 1st MI INF
Tanner, James S.	27	5.11	BLU	BLK	LGT	Farmer	Tompkins Co NY	Niles MI	PVT	COM F 1st MI INF
Tanner, John A.	28	5.09	BLU	LGT	DRK	Farmer	Herkimer Co NY	Cedar MI	2SG	COM E 1st MI INF
Tapping, Stephen B.	28	5.06	BLU	LGT	LGT	Miller	Onondaga Co NY		PVT	COM H US MTD RIF

Enrolled	Mustered	Discharged	Remarks
04/16/47 Utica MI	Detroit MI		Died of disease at Perote MEX 09/20/47
06/18/47 Detroit MI	06/18/47 Detroit MI	06/30/48 Detroit MI	Received pension
09/??/46 Detroit		07/03/48 New Orleans LA	PEN
10/30/47 Niles MI	12/02/47 Detroit MI		Died of dysentery near Baton Rouge 06/25/48. PEN
11/02/47 Jackson MI	11/12/47 Detroit MI	07/26/48 Detroit MI	
02/20/48 Battle Creek MI	03/01/48 Detroit MI		Deserted at New Orlenas LA 05/01/48
??/??/46 Detroit MI			VTS WNA
05/28/46 Detroit MI			VTS WNA
05/28/46 Detroit MI			VTS WNA
04/09/47 Detroit MI	04/30/47 Detroit MI	08/04/48 Covington KY	
02/19/48 Urbana OH	02/29/48 New Orlenas LA		Left sick at New Orleans LA 06/25/48
01/18/48 Mason MI	02/01/48 Detroit MI	07/27/48 Detroit MI	PEN
08/26/47 Detroit MI	Detroit MI	07/20/48 New Orleans LA	LIH at Mexico City MEX 01/22/48. DFD
11/20/47 Detroit MI	12/16/47 Detroit MI	07/18/48 Detroit MI	
11/30/47 Pontiac MI	12/01/47 Detroit MI	07/26/48 Detroit MI	Received pension
11/02/47 Jackson MI	11/12/47 Detroit MI	07/26/48 Detroit MI	
11/15/47 Ypsilanti MI	12/01/47 Detroit MI		Died at Soledad River MEX 06/16/48
11/05/47 Grand Rapids MI	11/19/47 Detroit MI	07/18/48 Detroit MI	Fifer. Received pension
11/15/47 Niles MI	12/02/47 Detroit MI	07/28/48 Detroit MI	
04/01/47 Detroit MI	04/01/47 Detroit MI	07/31/48 Jefferson BKS MO	AKA Tabor. TRA COM D 01/04/48. PEN
11/15/47 Hastings MI	12/01/47 Detroit MI		AKA James A. Fabor. Died at Detroit MI 12/05/47. PEN
03/31/47 Detroit MI	04/22/47 Detroit MI	07/31/48 Washington DC	TRA COM D 01/04/48
11/20/47 Detroit MI	12/04/47 Detroit MI	07/18/48 Detroit MI	
11/15/47 Niles MI	12/02/47 Detroit MI	07/28/48 Detroit MI	PEN
11/20/47 Howell MI	12/16/47 Detroit MI	07/18/48 Detroit MI	Received pension
07/23/47 Battle Creek MI	07/23/47 Battle Creek MI	07/31/48 Jefferson BKS MO	

Name	Age	Hgt	Eye	Hair	Cpx	Trade	Born	Home	Rank	Unit
Taylor, Alva	23	5.08	BLU	LGT	LGT	Blacksmith	Wheatland NY		PVT	COM A 15th US INF
Taylor, Charles	21	5.08	GRY	DRK	DRK	Laborer	Norfolk ENG		PVT	COM B 3rd US INF
Taylor, George W.	24	5.10	BLU	BWN	DRK	Farmer	Warren Co NJ		PVT	COM G 1st MI INF
Taylor, Jerome	22	5.04	GRY	LGT	FLD	Cooper	Wayne Co NY	Marshall MI	PVT	COM F 1st MI INF
Taylor, Josiah	21	5.07	HZL	BWN	FLD	Farmer	Homer NY		PVT	COM ? US MTD RIF
Taylor, Morse K.	30	5.10	BLU	DRK	DRK		Leroy NY	Ann Arbor MI	2LT	COM I 1st MI INF
Taylor, Robert B.	30	5.05	HZL	BWN	LGT	Miller	Wyegett VT	Corunna MI	PVT	COM C 1st MI INF
Teal, Henry I.	19	6.02	GRY	LGT	LGT	Gentleman	Richmond VA	Detroit MI	PVT	COM E 1st MI INF
Tebodo, Stephen	21	5.10	BLU	LGT	LGT	Farmer	Uxbridge CAN		PVT	COM G US MTD RIF
Tennant, John E.	34	5.04	BLU	BWN	LGT	Farmer	Bruling NJ		PVT	COM H 1st MI INF
Terrell, William	34	5.07	HZL	BWN	DRK		Longford IRE		PVT	COM B 5th US INF
Terrill, Sherman	28	5.09	GRY	BLK	DRK	Laborer	Vermont		PVT	COM A 15th US INF
Terry, Adrian R.	39					Physician	Connecticut	Detroit MI	SUR	F&S 1st MI INF
Tesdale, Edward	26	5.10	BWN	RED	LGT	Farmer	Lancashire ENG	Constantine MI	PVT	COM A 1st MI INF
Thom, Alexander	22	5.06	BLU	LGT	FIR	Cooper	Great Britian	Pontiac MI	1CP	COM C 1st MI INF
Thomas, Chauncey	21	5.08	HZL	DRK	DRK	Farmer	Orleans Co NY	Saline MI	PVT	COM G 1st MI INF
Thomas, Samuel	37	6.00	GRY	LGT	LGT	Carpenter	Wayne Co MI		PVT	COM D 1st MI INF
Thomas, William	35	5.06	BLU	GRY	LGT	Laborer	Ireland	Niles MI	PVT	COM F 1st MI INF
Thompson, George W.	28	5.06	BLU	BLK	FIR	Printer	New York NY	Pontiac MI	PVT	COM C 1st MI INF
Thompson, Jacob C.	18	5.09	DRK	DRK	DRK	Farmer	Allegany Co NY		PVT	COM K 1st MI INF
Thompson, John	21	5.10	BLU	BWN	FIR	Laborer	Rush Co IN	Detroit MI	1SG	COM F 1st MI INF
Thompson, Mark	18	5.10	BLU	BWN	LGT	Farmer	Washington Co VT	Galesburg MI	PVT	COM A 1st MI INF
Thompson, William	26								SEA	US Navy
Thorne, Henry	33	5.10	BLK	BLK	DRK	Tailor	Detroit MI		4SG	Brady Guards
Thorpe, Samuel W.	25	5.07	BLU	BWN	DRK	Farmer	Jefferson Co NY		PVT	COM K 3rd US DRG
Thorpe, Theodore	21								UNK	US Navy

ENROLLED	MUSTERED	DISCHARGED	REMARKS
04/03/47 Pontiac MI	04/27/47 Detroit MI		WIA 08/20/47. TRA COM K 12/26/47. Died 07/13/48
04/08/47 Detroit MI	04/08/47 Detroit MI		LIH at Perote MEX 08/02/47. Died 08/11/47
02/20/48 Pontiac MI	03/01/48 Detroit MI		LIH at New Orleans LA 06/20/48. PEN
11/15/47 Marshall MI	12/02/47 Detroit MI	07/28/48 Detroit MI	
06/17/47 Kalamazoo MI	06/17/47 Kalamazoo MI		Deserted 10/11/47
10/30/47 Marshall MI	12/01/47 Detroit MI	07/18/48 Detroit MI	Received pension. MNI Kent
11/30/47 Corunna MI	12/01/47 Detroit MI	07/26/48 Detroit MI	
01/16/48 New Orleans LA	01/16/48 New Orleans LA		PMT 4SG 05/12/48. AKA Henry J. Teel. PEN
08/09/47 Kalamazoo MI	08/09/47 Kalamazoo MI	07/31/48 Jefferson BKS MO	AKA Tebode & Thibodo. PEN
12/20/47 Lansing MI	01/01/48 Detroit MI	07/27/48 Detroit MI	
05/20/47 Detroit MI	Detroit MI		Missing since 10/09/47 at Huamantia MEX
04/07/47 Utica MI	04/27/47 Detroit MI		LIH at Puebla MEX 08/10/47. TRA COM K 12/26/47
10/30/47 Detroit MI	11/07/47 Detroit MI	07/29/48 Detroit MI	Appointed by the President 10/30/47. PEN
11/05/47 Kalamazoo MI	11/19/47 Detroit MI	07/18/48 Detroit MI	AKA Teesdale. In hospital at Cordova MEX. PEN
11/30/47 Pontiac MI	12/01/47 Detroit MI	07/26/48 Detroit MI	
02/20/48 Adrian MI	03/01/48 Detroit MI	07/18/48 Detroit MI	
11/14/47 Detroit MI	11/14/47 Detroit MI	12/24/47 Springwells MI	Discharged by writ of habeas corpus
11/15/47 Niles MI	12/02/47 Detroit MI		Died at Cordova MEX 05/12/48 from effects of liquor
11/30/47 Pontiac MI	12/01/47 Detroit MI	07/26/48 Detroit MI	
12/15/47 Adrian MI	01/01/48 Detroit MI	01/15/48 Detroit MI	Discharged by civil authority
11/15/47 St. Joseph MI	12/02/47 Detroit MI		Resigned 12/02/47
11/05/47 Kalamazoo MI	11/19/47 Detroit MI	07/18/48 Detroit MI	
12/08/46 Detroit MI	01/04/47 New York NY	01/04/50	Served on USS Scorpion beginning 02/24/47
06/11/47 Detroit MI	06/18/47 Detroit MI	06/30/48 Detroit MI	
04/08/47 Tecumseh MI	04/22/47 Detroit MI		LIH at Puebla MEX 08/07/47
09/12/46 Detroit MI	Baltimore MD	12/??/46	Received bad discharge

Name	Age	Hgt	Eye	Hair	Cpx	Trade	Born	Home	Rank	Unit
Thrall, Norman	26	5.10	BLU	BWN	LGT	Farmer	Yates Co NY		PVT	COM A 1st MI INF
Thurston, Joseph	20	5.11	BLU	LGT	FIR	Farmer	Coos? Co NH	Dexter MI	PVT	COM E 1st MI INF
Thurston, Thomas	21	5.04	GRY	BWN	LGT	Farmer	Lycoming Co PA		PVT	COM E 15th US INF
Tiffany, William W.	18	5.10	BLU	BWN	FIR	Farmer	New York State		PVT	COM I 1st MI INF
Tift, Morris C.	20	5.11	BLK	BLK	LGT	Farmer	Washington Co RI		PVT	COM E 1st MI INF
Tilford, William	23	5.10	BLU	LGT	LGT	Carpenter	Onondaga Co NY		PVT	COM G 1st MI INF
Tingley, Reuben R.	19	5.10	BLU	SDY	LGT	Farmer	Oakland Co MI	Jackson MI	PVT	COM H 1st MI INF
Titus, Platt S.	28	5.09	GRY	BLK	DRK	Student	Cayuga Co NY	Jackson MI	2LT	COM E 15th US INF
Tobin, Nicholas	33	5.04	BLU	BWN	LGT		Cahir IRE	Detroit MI	PVT	COM D 1st MI INF
Todd, William H.	18	5.03	BLU	LGT	LGT	Miller	Onondaga Co NY	Pontiac MI	PVT	COM C 1st MI INF
Toll, Isaac D.	28	6.01	BLK	BWN	CLR	Merchant	Schenectady NY	Fawn River MI	CAP	COM E 15th US INF
Toomey, Michael								Detroit MI	PVT	Montgomery Guards
Tower, Charles H.	29	5.08	BLK	BWN	FIR	Clerk	Genesee Co NY		PVT	COM K 3rd US DRG
Townsend, Richard	28	5.08	BLK	BLK	DRK	Farmer	New York State	Monroe MI	PVT	COM E 1st MI INF
Treadwell, Semour								Adrian MI	PVT	Adrian Guards
Trim, Jerome B.	19	5.07	HZL	BWN	LGT	Laborer	Oswego Co NY	Springfield MI	PVT	Brady Guards
Trim, Pembroke	21	5.09	BLU	AUB	FIR	Farmer	Volney NY		PVT	COM B 5th US INF
Trimmer, James Y.	21	5.05	HZL	BWN	DRK	Farmer	Rochester NY	Corunna MI	PVT	COM C 1st MI INF
Trout, Laton	24	5.10	GRY	LGT	DRK	Cooper	Brown Co OH		PVT	COM G 1st MI INF
Truare, Andrew J.	18	5.06	BLK	BLK	DRK	Farmer	Jefferson Co NY	Pontiac MI	PVT	COM C 1st MI INF
Truman, John	21	5.07	DRK	DRK	DRK	Farmer	Geauga Co OH		PVT	COM K 1st MI INF
Truman, Josiah	22	5.08	DRK	DRK	DRK	Farmer	Geauga Co OH		PVT	COM K 1st MI INF
Tufts, Samuel P.	19	5.07	BLU	BLK	LGT	Carpenter	Fitchburg MA		PVT	COM F 15th US INF
Tyler, Elisha Jr.	26	5.07	BLU	BLK	LGT	Farmer	Grafton Co NH	Paw Paw MI	PVT	COM A 1st MI INF
Tyler, Matther M.	23	5.08	BLU	BWN	LGT	Boatman	Onondaga Co NY	Niles MI	2SG	COM F 1st MI INF
Tymis, Andrew	21	5.06	HZL	BLK	DRK	Laborer	Chatham CAN		PVT	COM B 3rd US INF

ENROLLED	MUSTERED	DISCHARGED	REMARKS
11/05/47 Kalamazoo MI	11/19/47 Detroit MI		Died at Cincinnati OH 07/04/48 en route to Detroit MI
11/20/47 Dexter MI	12/04/47 Detroit MI		Died at Cordova MEX of diarrhea 04/03/48
04/26/47 Niles MI	04/27/47 Detroit MI		Died at Vera Cruz MEX 07/02/48
11/15/47 Grand Rapids MI	12/01/47 Detroit MI		Died at Detroit MI 01/02/48
11/20/47 Flint MI	12/04/47 Detroit MI		Died at Cordova MEX 06/25/48
02/20/48 Sturgis MI	03/01/48 Detroit MI		Deserted at Detroit MI 04/12/48
01/18/48 Clinton MI	02/01/48 Detroit MI	07/27/48 Detroit MI	PEN. AKA Reuben R. Taigley
03/09/47 Detroit MI	04/09/47 Detroit MI	08/06/48	PMT 1LT 09/13/47 at Chapultepec MEX for gallantry
11/14/47 Detroit MI	11/14/47 Detroit MI	07/26/48 Detroit MI	Received pension
11/30/47 Detroit MI	12/01/47 Detroit MI	07/26/48 Detroit MI	
03/02/47 Fawn River MI	04/09/47 Detroit MI		Resigned 10/25/47. PEN. MNI DeGraff
05/28/46 Detroit MI			VTS WNA
04/22/47 Detroit MI	04/22/47 Detroit MI		LIH at Puebla MEX 08/07/47
11/20/47 Albion MI	12/04/47 Detroit MI		Died of pleurisy at New Orleans LA 01/11/48
06/01/46 Adrian MI			VTS WNA
06/18/47 Detroit MI	06/18/47 Detroit MI	06/30/48 Detroit MI	Received pension
09/29/47 Detroit MI	Detroit MI	08/01/48 East Pascagoula MS	
11/30/47 Corunna MI	12/01/47 Detroit MI	07/26/48 Detroit MI	PEN
04/15/48 Cincinnati OH	04/15/48 Cincinnati OH		STH at New Orleans LA 06/05/48
11/30/47 Pontiac MI	12/01/47 Detroit MI	07/26/48 Detroit MI	PEN
12/15/47 Hillsdale MI	01/01/48 Detroit MI		Died at New Orleans LA 04/29/48
11/15/47 Hillsdale MI	12/01/47 Detroit MI		Deserted at Detroit MI 12/27/47
05/07/47 Detroit MI	Detroit MI	08/04/48 Camp Butler IL	Received pension
11/05/47 Paw Paw MI	11/19/47 Detroit MI	07/18/48 Detroit MI	
11/15/47 Niles MI	12/02/47 Detroit MI		PMT 1SG 12/30/47. Died of vomito at Vera Cruz 02/11/48
03/08/47 Detroit MI	03/08/47 Detroit MI	07/25/48 East Pascagoula MS	LIH at New Orleans LA 06/19/47

Name	Age	Hgt	Eye	Hair	Cpx	Trade	Born	Home	Rank	Unit
Tyrrell, Miles	23	5.07	BLU	BWN	LGT	Laborer	Harwick CAN	Detroit MI	PVT	COM B 1st MI INF
Urban, Joseph	20	5.03	HZL	BWN	FIR	Pinepicker	Germany	Detroit MI	PVT	COM D 1st MI INF
Valentine, James A.	34	5.05	GRY	DRK	LGT	Farmer	Orange Co NY	Detroit MI	PVT	COM D 1st MI INF
Van Arman, John	28	5.08	DRK	BWN	DRK	Lawyer	Plattsburgh NY	Marshall MI	CAP	COM I 1st MI INF
Van Buren, Egbert J.	41	5.08	GRY	GRY	LGT	Merchant	Baltimore MD	Pontiac MI	2LT	COM G 1st MI INF
Van Buren, Michael E.	26	5.10	BLK	BLK	DRK	Soldier	Maryland	Pontiac MI	1LT	COM K US MTD RIF
Van Kleek, John	18	5.06	BLU	DRK	FIR	Farmer	Niagara Co NY	Almont MI	PVT	COM K 1st MI INF
Van Liende, Eugene	28	5.07	DRK	BWN	DRK	Laborer	Alaellert BEL	Detroit MI	PVT	COM K 1st MI INF
Van Liew, James	29	5.11	BLU	BWN	LGT	Footman	Seneca Co NY	Monroe MI	PVT	COM H 1st MI INF
Van Meer, Robert	18	5.09	GRY	DRK	DRK	Miller	Monroe Co NY		PVT	COM C 1st MI INF
Van Necker, Asahel G.	18	5.09	GRY	BWN	DRK	Farmer	Genesee Co NY	Marshall MI	PVT	COM I 1st MI INF
Van Riper, Cornelius G.	40	5.11	BLU	BLK	LGT	Shoemaker	Essex Co NJ	Tecumseh MI	PVT	COM H 1st MI INF
Van Skoik, William	22	5.10	GRY	AUB	SDY	Cigar-maker	Sackets Harbor		PVT	COM K 3rd US DRG
Van Vleet, Peter P.									3CP	NTH Lenawee VOL
Vanderbilt, Henry	27	5.08	BLU	BWN	LGT	Laborer	Bergen Co NJ		PVT	COM G 1st MI INF
VandeVenter, Eugene W.	32						New York State	Flint MI	CAP	COM A 15th US INF
Varner, Henry	22	6.00	GRY	SDY	LGT	Laborer	Detroit MI		PVT	COM B 3rd US INF
Varnham, Robert C.	18	5.06	BLU	LGT	LGT	Farmer	St. Joseph MI		PVT	COM D 1st MI INF
Varnham, Robert C.	19	5.07	BLU	LGT	FIR	Sailor	Brutus NY		RCT	US Army
Verlender, Angel	26	5.08	BWN	BWN	DRK	Laborer	Belgium	Detroit MI	PVT	COM B 1st MI INF
Vetor, John	30	5.04	HZL	DRK	LGT	Sailor	Germany		PVT	COM C 1st MI INF
Vincent, Jacob	42	5.05	BLU	GRY	DRK	Farmer	Saratoga Co NY	Detroit MI	PVT	COM D 1st MI INF
Voss, John	25	5.10	BLU	BWN	FIR	Clerk	Bremen GER		PVT	COM A 6th US INF
Vreeland, Isaac	42	5.11	BLU	BLK	FLD	Farmer	Bergen Co NJ	Hillsdale MI	PVT	COM H 1st MI INF
Vreeland, Jacob	22	6.00	GRY	DRK	LGT	Blacksmith	Pequannock NJ	Cincinnati OH	PVT	COM B 1st MI INF
Wadkins, Richard	20	5.09	GRY	LGT	FIR	Farmer	Ontario Co NY		PVT	COM F 1st MI INF

ENROLLED	MUSTERED	DISCHARGED	REMARKS
11/02/47 Port Huron MI	11/12/47 Detroit MI		Died of dysentery at Cordova MEX 04/24/48
11/14/47 Detroit MI	11/14/47 Detroit MI	07/26/48 Detroit MI	
11/14/47 Detroit MI	11/14/47 Detroit MI	07/26/48 Detroit MI	
10/30/47 Marshall MI	12/01/47 Detroit MI	07/18/48 Detroit MI	Received pension
10/30/47 Corunna MI	12/01/47 Detroit MI	07/18/48 Detroit MI	
05/27/46			Wounded at Churubusco. PMT CAP 09/20/47 for gallantry
12/15/47 Almont MI	01/01/48 Detroit MI	01/15/48 Detroit MI	
12/15/47 Detroit MI	01/01/48 Detroit MI	07/28/48 Detroit MI	
11/20/47 Monroe MI	12/01/47 Detroit MI	07/27/48 Detroit MI	
11/30/47 Detroit MI	12/01/47 Detroit MI		Deserted at Detroit MI 12/18/47
11/15/47 Marshall MI	12/01/47 Detroit MI	07/18/48 Detroit MI	Received pension
12/20/47 Tecumseh MI	01/01/48 Detroit MI		TRA COM G. Died at Vera Cruz MEX 05/27/48
04/16/47 Detroit MI	04/22/47 Detroit MI	01/14/48 Mexico City MEX	TRA COM C 01/04/48. Discharged for disability
06/06/46 Tecumseh MI			VTS WNA
02/20/48 Detroit MI	03/01/48 Detroit MI		Deserted at Detroit MI 04/10/48
03/09/47	Detroit MI	07/19/48 Mobile AL	PMT MAJ in 13th INF 12/22/47. MNI Winfield Scott. PEN
03/01/47 Detroit MI	03/01/47 Detroit MI	01/13/48 Mexico City MEX	Discharged for disability. PEN
11/14/47 Detroit MI	11/14/47 Detroit MI		Deserted at Detroit MI 11/22/47
01/03/48 Detroit MI	Detroit MI		Deserted 01/23/48
11/02/47 Port Huron MI	11/12/47 Detroit MI	07/26/48 Detroit MI	AKA Angel Valaud
10/30/47 Detroit MI	12/01/47 Detroit MI	08/01/48 Detroit MI	
11/14/47 Detroit MI	11/14/47 Detroit MI		Died at Detroit MI 08/22/48
12/22/46 Detroit MI	12/22/46 Detroit MI		Deserted 12/08/47
11/20/47 Hillsdale MI	12/01/47 Detroit MI		Died on canal boat 07/10/48
11/02/47 Jackson MI	11/12/47 Detroit MI	07/26/48 Detroit MI	PEN. AKA Jacob Vulaud
11/15/47 Union City MI	12/02/47 Detroit MI		Deserted at Detroit MI 12/25/47

Name	Age	Hgt	Eye	Hair	Cpx	Trade	Born	Home	Rank	Unit
Wagner, John	40	5.08	GRY	DRK	DRK	Baker	Bondolph GER	Detroit MI	2CP	Brady Guards
Wagoner, Charles L.	24	5.11	BLU	BWN	SDY	Sailor	Seneca Co NY		PVT	COM K 3rd US DRG
Waible, Jacob						Carpenter		Detroit MI	PVT	Scott Guards
Waide, John M.	28	5.06	BLU	BWN	LGT	Farmer	Ireland	Port Huron MI	PVT	COM B 1st MI INF
Waiman, John	25	5.10	BLK	BLK	DRK	Laborer	Kent ENG		PVT	COM C 1st MI INF
Waldfogel, Conrad	20	5.09	BLU	LGT	LGT	Clerk	Switzerland	Perrysburg OH	PVT	COM E 1st MI INF
Walker, George	22	5.05	HZL	BWN	FIR	Carpenter	Yorkshire ENG	Detroit MI	PVT	COM B 1st MI INF
Wall, William	20	5.08	GRY	BWN	FLD	Sailor	Ireland	Marshall MI	PVT	COM I 1st MI INF
Wallace, John B.	36	5.10	BLU	BWN	FIR	Stonecutter	Kilkenny IRE		1SG	COM E 1st MI INF
Walsh, James								Detroit MI	PVT	Montgomery Guards
Walsh, Patrick								Detroit MI	PVT	Montgomery Guards
Walsh, William	22	5.06	HZL	BWN	FIR	Baker	Limerick IRE		PVT	COM B 7th US INF
Ward, David S.								Adrian MI	PVT	Adrian Guards
Ward, Robert E.	37	5.08	BLK	BLK	DRK	Engineer	Ireland	Detroit MI	PVT	COM E 1st MI INF
Ward, Upton	26	5.04	GRY	AUB	LGT	Laborer	Bedford Co MD		PVT	COM A 6th US INF
Warner, George	21	5.05	BLU	SDY	LGT	Laborer	England		PVT	COM A 15th US INF
Warner, William	19	5.05	GRY	BWN	FLD	Laborer	Rochester NY		PVT	COM G 15th US INF
Warren, Ira S.	22	5.11	BLU	BLK	LGT	Farmer	Rutland VT	Lansing MI	PVT	COM H 1st MI INF
Warren, Isaac	25	5.05	LGT	LGT	LGT	Saddler	Lancaster Co PA	Detroit MI	PVT	COM D 1st MI INF
Warrener, Alfred	21	5.09	HZL	BWN	DRK	Cabinet-maker	Jefferson Co NY		PVT	COM K 3rd US DRG
Washington, John N.	26	5.08	BLU	BWN	LGT	Farmer	New York NY	Hillsdale MI	PVT	COM H 1st MI INF
Watenberg, John	22	5.08	BLU	LGT	LGT	Laborer	Herkimer Co NY		RCT	US Army
Watkins, Allen D.	25	5.05	GRY	BWN	DRK	Laborer	Frankfort KY		PVT	COM A 6th US INF
Watson, Joseph	23	5.07	BLK	BLK	DRK	Sailor		Detroit MI	PVT	COM D 1st MI INF
Wattels, David C.	26	5.07	HZL	BWN	LGT	Farmer	Troy PA		PVT	BAT I 1st US ART
Watters, John	15					Sailor	Detroit MI	Detroit MI	MID	US Navy

Enrolled	Mustered	Discharged	Remarks
06/18/47 Detroit MI	06/18/47 Detroit MI	06/30/48 Detroit MI	Born in Wurtemburg
04/05/47 Detroit MI	04/22/47 Detroit MI	07/31/48 Jefferson BKS MO	LIH Vera Cruz MEX 06/03/47. AKA Chauncy Wagner
06/03/46 Detroit MI			VTS WNA. AKA Jacob Wybel
11/02/47 Port Huron MI	11/12/47 Detroit MI	07/26/48 Detroit MI	
01/04/48 Cincinnati OH	01/04/48 Cincinnati OH		Taken up as deserter from the US Army
11/20/47 Perrysburg OH	12/04/47 Detroit MI	07/18/48 Detroit MI	
11/02/47 Port Huron MI	11/12/47 Detroit MI	07/26/48 Detroit MI	PEN
01/24/48 Grand Haven MI	02/01/48 Detroit MI	07/18/48 Detroit MI	
11/20/47 Detroit MI	12/16/47 Detroit MI		LIH at New Orleans LA 06/24/48
05/28/46 Detroit MI			VTS WNA
05/28/46 Detroit MI			VTS WNA
03/19/47 Detroit MI	03/19/47 Detroit MI	07/31/48 Jefferson BKS MO	
06/01/46 Adrian MI			VTS WNA
11/20/47 Detroit MI	12/04/47 Detroit MI	07/18/48 Detroit MI	Left at Vera Cruz MEX for 3 months 02/06/48
12/18/46 Detroit MI	12/18/46 Detroit MI		Died at Puebla MEX 09/13/47. PEN
04/06/47 Ann Arbor MI	04/27/47 Detroit MI	08/21/48	TRA COM C 12/26/47
03/26/47 Detroit MI	04/30/47 Detroit MI		Died at Covington KY 08/04/48
12/20/47 Lansing MI	01/01/48 Detroit MI		Died at Memphis TN 07/04/48
11/14/47 Detroit MI	11/14/47 Detroit MI	07/28/48 Detroit MI	PMT QUS 12/10/47. PMT 2LT & TRA COM F 04/01/48
04/08/47 Tecumseh MI	04/22/47 Detroit	MI	LIH at Puebla 04/07/47. PEN. AKA Alfred Warner
11/20/47 Hillsdale MI	12/01/47 Detroit MI		Died at Memphis TN 07/07/48
04/05/47 Detroit MI	04/05/47 Detroit	MI	Deserted at Detroit MI 04/13/47
08/10/46 Detroit MI	08/10/46 Detroit MI		Deserted 01/10/47
11/14/47 Detroit MI	11/14/47 Detroit MI	07/26/48 Detroit MI	
06/28/47 Detroit MI	Detroit MI	08/30/48 Governor's Isle NY	PEN. RBL. AKA Wattles
02/12/46	02/12/46		Served on board USS Saratoga

NAME	AGE	HGT	EYE	HAIR	CPX	TRADE	BORN	HOME	RANK	UNIT
Watts, John	39	5.08	GRY	BWN	LGT	Painter	Woustache ENG	Detroit MI	PVT	Brady Guards
Weaver, Peter	37	5.08	BLU	DRK	DRK	Weaver	France	Detroit MI	PVT	COM E 1st MI INF
Webb, James	19	5.06	BLU	BWN	DRK	Laborer	Herkimer Co NY		PVT	COM G US MTD RIF
Webb, Joseph	18	5.11	BLU	LGT	LGT	Farmer	Union Co IN	Niles MI	PVT	COM F 1st MI INF
Webber, William	40	5.10	BLU	BLK	LGT	Jeweler	Massachusetts	Kalamazoo MI	PVT	COM A 1st MI INF
Webber, William H.	20	5.06	BLK	BLK	DRK	Farmer	Lycoming Co PA		PVT	COM E 15th US INF
Webster, William	25	6.00	BLU	LGT	LGT	Carpenter	Westford NY	Detroit MI	PVT	COM D 1st MI INF
Weese, John	21	5.03	BLK	BWN	DRK	Sailor	Detroit MI		PVT	Brady Guards
Weideman, Henry	33	5.10	BLU	BWN	LGT	Farmer	Germany		PVT	COM H 1st MI INF
Weis, George	33	5.06	GRY	LGT	LGT	Clerk	Strasbourg FRA	Detroit MI	3SG	Brady Guards
Welch, Allen T.	22	5.08	BLU	SDY	FLD	Printer	Harrisonburg VA	Detroit MI	CPL	COM K 3rd US DRG
Welch, John	24	5.08	BLU	LGT	LGT	Laborer	Danberry NH		PVT	COM D 5th US INF
Welling, George R.	24	5.04	BLK	BLK	DRK	Merchant	Baltimore MD		PVT	COM E 15th US INF
Wellman, Neil	19	5.03	BLK	BLK	FIR	Farmer	New York State		PVT	COM I 1st MI INF
Wells, Chester	20	5.06	BLU	DRK	LGT	Carpenter	Wheatland NY		PVT	COM K 1st MI INF
Wells, George	23	5.08	GRY	BWN	LGT	Cooper	Sussex ENG		PVT	COM K 1st MI INF
Wells, Hiram A.	18	5.06	BLU	DRK	LGT	Carpenter	Wheatland NY	Armada MI	PVT	COM K 1st MI INF
Wells, James H.	27	5.07	BLU	LGT	FIR	Printer	Wyoming Co NY	Michigan Centre MI	2CP	COM E 1st MI INF
Welsh, Allen F.	22	5.08	BLU	SDY	FLD	Printer	Harrisonburg VA	Detroit MI	PVT	COM K 3rd US DRG
Welton, Uriah	18	6.01	GRY	BWN	DRK	Farmer	Genesee Co NY	Calhoun Co MI	PVT	COM I 1st MI INF
West, John	24	5.05	BLU	SDY	LGT	Laborer	England		PVT	COM A 15th US INF
West, John D.	21	5.09	BLU	FIR	FIR	Clerk	Oneida Co NY	Detroit MI	PVT	COM K 3rd US DRG
Westerfield, Cornelius	25	5.04	BLU	BWN	LGT	Carpenter	New York NY		PVT	COM A 15th US INF
Wheaton, Lemuel N.	20	5.08	BLU	BWN	DRK	Laborer	Ashtabula OH		PVT	COM A 6th US INF
Wheeler, Curtis G.	22	5.10	GRY	SDY	LGT	Farmer	Onondaga Co NY		PVT	COM K 1st MI INF
Wheeler, Gardner	18							Mason MI	PVT	COM H 1st MI INF

ENROLLED	MUSTERED	DISCHARGED	REMARKS
06/18/47 Detroit MI	06/18/47 Detroit MI	06/30/48 Detroit MI	
11/20/47 Detroit MI	12/04/47 Detroit MI	07/18/48 Detroit MI	
08/31/47 Kalamazoo MI	08/31/47 Kalamazoo MI	07/31/48 Jefferson BKS MO	AKA James Weber
11/15/47 Niles MI	12/02/47 Detroit MI	07/28/48 Detroit MI	
11/05/47 Kalamazoo MI	11/19/47 Detroit MI		Died on board ship en route to Detroit MI 07/02/48. PEN
04/26/47 Niles MI	04/27/47 Detroit MI	08/06/48 Cincinnati OH	
11/14/47 Albion MI	11/14/47 Detroit MI	07/26/48 Detroit MI	PEN
06/18/47 Detroit MI	06/18/47 Detroit MI	06/30/48 Detroit MI	
11/20/47 Toledo OH	12/01/47 Detroit MI		Died at San Diego MEX 06/17/48
06/18/47 Detroit MI	06/18/47 Detroit MI	06/30/48 Detroit MI	
04/16/47 Detroit MI	Detroit MI	10/26/47 Mexico City MEX	Discharged for disability. PEN
06/09/47 Detroit MI	Detroit MI	08/01/48 East Pascagoula MS	
04/19/47 Fawn River MI	04/27/47 Detroit MI	08/21/48	PMT 3SG 05/09/47. RTR 12/26/47
11/15/47 Hastings MI	12/01/47 Detroit MI		Deserted at Detroit MI 01/01/48
12/15/47 Armada MI	01/01/48 Detroit MI		Died at Detroit MI 07/14/48
12/24/47 Ann Arbor MI	01/01/48 Detroit MI	07/28/48 Detroit MI	PEN Left by accident at New Orleans LA 06/26/48
12/15/47 Armada MI	01/01/48 Detroit MI	07/28/48 Detroit MI	PEN
11/20/47 Jackson MI	12/04/47 Detroit MI	07/18/48 Detroit MI	
04/16/47 Detroit MI	04/22/47 Detroit MI	10/29/47 Mexico City MEX	Discharged for disability
11/15/47 Marshall MI	12/01/47 Detroit MI		Died of diarrhea at Cordova MEX 05/23/48. PEN
04/24/47 Detroit MI	04/27/47 Detroit MI	08/21/48	PEN. TRA COM K 12/26/47
04/08/47 Detroit MI	04/22/47 Detroit MI	07/31/48 Jefferson BKS MO	TRA COM D 01/04/48
04/05/47 Ann Arbor MI	04/27/47 Detroit MI		WIA at Mexico City 08/20/47. TRA COM K 12/26/47. PEN
09/12/46 Detroit MI	09/12/46 Detroit MI		Executed as deserter at Meseuague MEX 09/13/47
12/15/47 Adrian MI	01/01/48 Detroit MI		Deserted at Detroit MI 12/25/47
12/20/47 Mason MI	01/01/48 Detroit MI		Deserted at Detroit MI 01/22/48

Name	Age	Hgt	Eye	Hair	Cpx	Trade	Born	Home	Rank	Unit
Wheeler, John	21	5.07	DRK	LGT	LGT	Farmer	Monroe Co NY	Farmington MI	PVT	Brady Guards
Wheeler, William C.	24	5.07	BLU	BWN	LGT	Farmer	Chenango Co NY		PVT	COM B 5th US INF
Wheelock, Hiram	26	5.10	BLU	BWN	FLD	Laborer	Windham Co VT	Blissfield MI	PVT	COM F 1st MI INF
Whipple, William L.	23							Detroit MI	1LT	COM H 1st MI INF
Whitbeck, Milo	22	5.04	DRK	DRK	LGT	Laborer	Wayne Co NY		PVT	COM A 15th US INF
White, Charles M.	22	5.11	HZL	BWN	DRK	Farmer	Upper Canada	Grand Rapids MI	PVT	COM I 1st MI INF
White, Jerome	24	5.06	DRK	BWN	LGT	Blacksmith	Windsor CAN	Detroit MI	PVT	Brady Guards
White, Martin	23	5.09	HZL	BLK	RUD	Farmer	Canada		PVT	COM G 15th US INF
Whitehead, Asa A.								Tecumseh MI	2LT	NTH Lenawee VOL
Whitford, Norman S.	23	5.10	BLK	BLK	LGT	Farmer	Albany NY	Mason MI	PVT	COM H 1st MI INF
Whitney, Charles B.	18	5.08	BLU	LGT	LGT	Farmer	Genesee Co NY	Pontiac MI	PVT	COM C 1st MI INF
Whitney, Thomas W.	25	5.04	BLU	BWN	DRK	Farmer	Livingston Co NY	Lenawee Co MI	PVT	COM E 1st MI INF
Whitney, William A.	26					Clerk	Shelby NY	Adrian MI	2LT	Adrian Guards
Whitney, William W.	23	5.07	BLU	LGT	LGT	Farmer	New York State	Lima IN	MUS	COM A 1st MI INF
Wichterman, Joseph	22	5.07	GRY	BWN	FIR	Tanner	Stark Co OH		RCT	US Army
Wickwire, Elisur D.	29	5.09	BWN	DRK	DRK	Cooper	Shoreham VT		PVT	COM E 15th US INF
Wilcox, Somers W.	37	5.11	BWN	BLK	BWN	Farmer	Madison Co NY	Cassopolis MI	PVT	COM F 1st MI INF
Wilder, Melford C.	18	5.09	DRK	SDY	LGT	Gunsmith	Genesee Co NY		PVT	COM K 1st MI INF
Wilder, Oscar A.								Adrian MI	4SG	Adrian Guards
Wilkins, William D.	20					Law Clerk	Pittsburgh PA	Detroit MI	2LT	COM G 15th US INF
Wilkinson, David D.	23	5.09	HZL	DRK	LGT	Blacksmith	Ontario Co NY	White Pigeon MI	PVT	COM G 1st MI INF
Wilkinson, Perry	23	5.09	BLU	BWN	SDY	Farmer	Erie Co NY		PVT	COM A 1st MI INF
Wilkinson, Richard	28	5.06	BLU	BWN	DRK	Carpenter	Donegal IRE		PVT	COM A 6th US INF
Willard, Beriah	24	5.07	HZL	SDY	LGT	Laborer	Clinton Co NY	Niles MI	PVT	COM E 1st MI INF
Willcox, Orlando B.	21	6.00	BLU	BWN	FIR	Soldier	Detroit MI	Detroit MI	2LT	BAT G 4th US ART
William, James	28								UNK	US Navy

ENROLLED	MUSTERED	DISCHARGED	REMARKS
06/18/47 Detroit MI	06/18/47 Detroit MI	06/30/48 Detroit MI	PEN
10/20/47 Detroit MI	Detroit MI	06/24/48 Jalapa MEX	
11/15/47 Blissfield MI	12/02/47 Detroit MI		Died at Detroit MI 07/27/48
10/30/47 Monroe MI	12/01/47 Detroit MI	07/27/48 Detroit MI	Acting assistant commissary
04/08/47 Pontiac MI	04/27/47 Detroit MI		TRA COM B 12/26/47. Died 07/05/48
01/24/48 Grand Rapids MI	02/01/48 Detroit MI	07/18/48 Detroit MI	
06/18/47 Detroit MI	06/18/47 Detroit MI	06/30/48 Detroit MI	
04/17/47 Detroit MI	04/30/47 Detroit MI		Deserted at Detroit MI 04/30/47
??/??/46 Tecumseh MI			VTS WNA
12/20/47 Mason MI	01/01/48 Detroit MI		Died at New Orleans LA 06/24/48. PEN
11/30/47 Detroit MI	12/01/47 Detroit MI	07/26/48 Detroit MI	Admitted to MI Veterans Facility (#3840). PEN
11/20/47 Clinton MI	12/04/47 Detroit MI		Died of diarrhea at Cordova 05/21/48. MNI Ward
06/01/46 Adrian MI			VTS WNA. MNI Augustus
11/05/47 Schoolcraft MI	11/19/47 Detroit MI	07/18/48 Detroit MI	Drummer
05/11/48 Detroit MI	Detroit MI	06/20/48 Newport KY	
04/10/47 Grand Rapids MI	04/27/47 Detroit MI		LIH at Vera Cruz MEX since 07/02/48. PEN
11/15/47 Niles MI	12/02/47 Detroit MI	07/28/48 Detroit MI	PEN
12/15/47 Adrian MI	01/01/48 Detroit MI	02/01/48 Detroit MI	Discharged by civil authority
06/01/46 Adrian MI			VTS WNA
03/02/47	04/09/47 Detroit MI	08/07/48 Cincinnati OH	TRA COM F PMT 1LT 08/20/47. QUT. MNI Duncan. PEN
02/20/48 Sturgis MI	03/01/48 Detroit MI	07/18/48 Detroit MI	
11/05/47 Kalamazoo MI	11/19/47 Detroit MI		Died at New Orleans LA of typhoid 01/20/48
08/01/46 Detroit MI	08/01/46 Detroit MI		PEN
11/20/47 Ypsilanti MI	12/04/47 Detroit MI	07/18/48 Detroit MI	
07/01/47			Received pension. MNI Bolivar
08/26/46 Detroit MI	New Orleans LA		

Name	Age	Hgt	Eye	Hair	Cpx	Trade	Born	Home	Rank	Unit
Williams, Alpheus S.	37	5.08	GRY	BWN	LGT	Publisher	Saybrook CT	Detroit MI	CLT	F&S 1st MI INF
Williams, Benjamin F.	21	5.09	BLU	BWN	DRK	Laborer	Potsdam NY		PVT	COM E 15th US INF
Williams, Cornelius	35	5.06	BLK	BWN	DRK	Farmer	Chittenden Co VT	St. Joseph MI	1CP	COM F 1st MI INF
Williams, Elisha	28	5.10	BLU	BWN	FIR	Farmer	Madison Co NY		PVT	COM D 1st MI INF
Williams, George	19	5.06	BLK	BWN	LGT	Shoemaker	Genesee Co NY		PVT	COM E 15th US INF
Williams, James	25	5.08	DRK	BLK	DRK	Farmer	Devonshire ENG		RCT	Montgomery Guards
Williams, James C. D.	26	5.08					Michigan	Detroit MI	2LT	COM K 3rd US DRG
Williams, James M.	28						Detroit MI	Detroit MI	CAP	COM K 1st MI INF
Williams, John	28	5.06	GRY	BLK	LGT	Sailor	Middletown NY		RCT	US Army
Williams, Thomas	32					Soldier	Albany NY	Detroit MI	1LT	BAT ? 4th US ART
Williams, Thomas W.	25	5.06	GRY	BWN	FLD	Laborer	Liverpool ENG		PVT	COM A 6th US INF
Williams, William G.	45					Soldier	Philadelphia PA		CAP	COM ? US EGN
Williamson, Edward	21	5.11	HZL	BWN	FIR	Tailor	Perry Co PA		PVT	COM ? US MTD RIF
Wilmarth, Wilson C.	20	5.07	GRY	LGT	FIR	Laborer	Rochester NY		PVT	BAT I 1st US ART
Wilsey, Abraham	23	5.07	BLK	BLK	DRK	Cooper	Schenectady NY	Grand Rapids MI	PVT	COM A 1st MI INF
Wilson, Benjamin F.	24	5.06	DRK	DRK	DRK	Tailor	Richland Co OH	Maumee OH	PVT	COM G 1st MI INF
Wilson, Charles J.	25	5.09	BLK	BLK	DRK	Laborer	Staffordshire		PVT	COM D 1st MI INF
Wilson, Henry R.	34	5.09	HZL	BWN	RUD	Cooper	Ashtabula Co OH		RCT	COM ? 3rd US DRG
Wilson, John	18	5.06	BLU	BWN	LGT	Blacksmith	England	Kalamazoo MI	PVT	COM A 1st MI INF
Wilson, John	25	5.07	BLK	BWN	LGT	Farmer	Manchester ENG	Detroit MI	PVT	COM K 1st MI INF
Winans, Frazey M.	33					Saddler	New York State	Monroe MI	CAP	COM G 15th US INF
Winans, Philip	20	5.05	GRY	LGT	FIR	Blacksmith	Trumbull Co OH		1CP	COM I 1st MI INF
Winchell, Bachus T.	26	5.07	GRY	BWN	FIR	Shoemaker	Oneida Co NY	Monroe MI	PVT	COM G 15th US INF
Winchell, James D.	21	5.10	GRY	BWN	FIR	Carpenter	Vermont	Marshall MI	PVT	COM I 1st MI INF
Winchell, Rush	29	5.11	BLU	DRK	FIR	Shoemaker	Oneida Co NY	Monroe MI	CPL	COM G 15th US INF
Winn, Edmund	20	5.07	BLU	BLK	LGT	Cooper	Oneida Co NY		PVT	COM G 1st MI INF

ENROLLED	MUSTERED	DISCHARGED	REMARKS
10/18/47 Detroit MI	12/08/47 Detroit MI	07/29/48 Detroit MI	Received pension. MNI Starkey
04/20/47 Grand Rapids MI	04/27/47 Detroit MI		Died at Covington KY 07/27/48
11/15/47 St. Joseph MI	12/02/47 Detroit MI		PMT SGT 04/01/48. LIH at Jefferson BKS 07/06/48. PEN
11/14/47 Detroit MI	11/14/47 Detroit MI		Deserted at Detroit MI 11/18/47
04/09/47 Jackson MI	04/27/47 Detroit MI		LIH at Vera Cruz MEX 06/18/47
11/01/47 Detroit MI			Company disbanded before muster
04/09/47		07/31/48	WIA at Molino del Rey MEX 09/08/47. PMT 1LT 01/08/48
10/30/47 Detroit MI	01/20/48 Detroit MI	07/28/48 Detroit MI	Received pension. MNI Mott
08/31/47 Detroit MI	Detroit MI		Deserted 09/10/47
			PMT BVT CAP 08/20/47. PMT BVT MAJ 09/13/47
01/07/47 Detroit MI	Detroit MI	05/06/48 Jalapa MEX	Discharged for disability
			DOW at Monterey MEX 09/21/46. MNI George
07/23/47 Otsego MI	07/23/47 Otsego MI		Deserted 10/20/47
08/04/47 Detroit MI	Detroit MI	08/30/48 Governor's Isle NY	
11/05/47 Grand Rapids MI	11/19/47 Detroit MI	07/18/48 Detroit MI	
02/20/48 Toledo OH	03/01/48 Detroit MI	07/18/48 Detroit MI	PEN
11/14/47 Detroit MI	11/14/47 Detroit MI		DES at Detroit MI 11/24/47. Born in England
05/30/48 Detroit MI	Detroit MI	07/16/48 Jefferson BKS MO	
11/05/47 Kalamazoo MI	11/19/47 Detroit MI	07/18/48 Detroit MI	
12/15/47 Almont MI	01/01/48 Detroit MI	07/28/48 Detroit MI	PEN
03/02/47	04/09/47 Detroit MI	07/26/48	PMT MAJ for gallantry 08/15/47. MNI Marsh
11/15/47 Marshall MI	12/01/47 Detroit MI		Died of fever at New Orleans LA 03/05/48
04/10/47 Monroe MI	04/30/47 Detroit MI		PMT SGT 04/21/47. PEN
11/15/47 Jackson MI	12/01/47 Detroit MI	07/18/48 Detroit MI	PEN
04/05/47 Monroe MI	04/30/47 Detroit MI		Died of diarrhea at Vera Cruz MEX 09/29/47
02/20/48 Battle Creek MI	03/01/48 Detroit MI		STH at New Orleans LA 06/05/48

Name	Age	Hgt	Eye	Hair	Cpx	Trade	Born	Home	Rank	Unit
Winsor, Mortimer D.	34	5.05	BLU	LGT	FIR	Carpenter	Herkimer Co NY		PVT	COM ? US ORD
Winterhalter, John	24	5.08	BLK	BWN	LGT	Barkeeper	Friedberg GER	Detroit MI	2SG	COM D 1st MI INF
Winterhalter, Michael								Detroit MI	PVT	Scott Guards
Winters, Lewis	23	5.06	BLU	BLK	LGT	Farmer	Allegany Co NY	Monroe MI	PVT	COM H 1st MI INF
Winters, William H.	22	6.00	HZL	FIR	FIR	Farmer	Charlotte Co VT		PVT	COM K 3rd US DRG
Wise, David	23	5.09	HZL	BWN	FIR	Miller	Cumberland Co PA		PVT	COM B 3rd US INF
Wittenmeyer, John W.	48					Sheriff		Niles MI	CAP	COM F 1st MI INF
Wohleben, Godfried	19	5.06	HZL	LGT	LGT	Laborer	Bamberg GER	Detroit MI	PVT	COM D 1st MI INF
Wolf, Elisha	21	5.08	GRY	BWN	FLD	Laborer	Columbia Co NY		PVT	COM I 1st MI INF
Wood, Henry	35	5.09	BLU	LGT	FIR	Farmer	Deephold GER		PVT	COM ? 5th US INF
Wood, James M.	19	5.09	BLU	BWN	FIR	Farmer	Big Flats NY	Adrian MI	PVT	COM B 1st MI INF
Wood, Jay	28	5.08	GRY	SDY	SDY	Laborer	Onondaga Co NY		PVT	COM E 15th US INF
Wood, Milton A.	19	5.09	BLU	BWN	DRK	Farmer	Madison Co NY		PVT	COM K 3rd US DRG
Wood, Wallis W.	24	6.02	GRY	SDY	LGT	Laborer	Patterson NY		PVT	COM A 15th US INF
Woodbury, Dwight A.								Adrian MI	1SG	Adrian Guards
Woodbury, George								Adrian MI	MUS	Adrian Guards
Wooden, Samuel	21	5.06	GRY	AUB	RUD	Farmer	Seneca Co NY		PVT	COM G 15th US INF
Woodruff, John A.	20	5.07	BLK	BWN	LGT	Laborer	Walthamstow ENG	Detroit MI	PVT	COM B 1st MI INF
Woodruff, Samuel	25	5.07	GRY	BWN	FIR	Cooper	Bath NY	Marshall MI	PVT	COM I 1st MI INF
Woodruff, Timothy M.	19	5.06	GRY	AUB	LGT	Farmer	Lanesville OH	Washtenaw Co MI	PVT	COM K 1st MI INF
Woods, John	32	5.07	HZL	BWN	DRK	Painter	Hull ENG		RCT	US Army
Woods, Mathew								Detroit MI	PVT	Montgomery Guards
Woodward, William A.	22	5.11	BLU	DRK	FIR	Blacksmith	Candor NY	St. Clair MI	CPL	COM B 1st MI INF
Wooster, Charles	33	5.04	DRK	LGT	DRK	Farmer	Wurtemburg GER	Detroit MI	PVT	COM D 1st MI INF
Wooster, John W.								Adrian MI	PVT	Adrian Guards
Worden, LeRoy	20	5.08	GRY	BWN	FIR	Carpenter	New York State		PVT	COM I 1st MI INF

ENROLLED	MUSTERED	DISCHARGED	REMARKS
04/01/47 Dearborn MI			
11/14/47 Detroit MI	11/14/47 Detroit MI	07/26/48 Detroit MI	Received pension
06/03/46 Detroit MI			VTS WNA
11/20/47 Monroe MI	12/01/47 Detroit MI	07/27/48 Detroit MI	PEN
04/01/47 Detroit MI	04/22/47 Detroit MI	07/31/48 Jefferson BKS MO	LIH at Vera Cruz MEX 06/03/47
03/18/47 Detroit MI	03/18/47 Detroit MI	07/25/48 East Pascagoula MS	PEN
10/30/47 St. Joseph MI	12/02/47 Detroit MI	07/28/48 Detroit MI	Died at Milwaukee 09/04/48 from war illness. PEN
11/14/47 Detroit MI	11/14/47 Detroit MI	07/26/48 Detroit MI	AKA Gotfried Wolheben
11/15/47 Marshall MI	12/01/47 Detroit MI	07/18/48 Detroit MI	
09/07/47 Detroit MI	Detroit MI	03/??/48 New Orleans LA	Discharged for disability
11/02/47 Jackson MI	11/12/47 Detroit MI	07/26/48 Detroit MI	
04/15/47 Jackson MI	04/27/47 Detroit MI		Died 05/06/48 at Jalapa MEX
04/07/47 Tecumseh MI	04/22/47 Detroit MI		Died of disease at Perote MEX 07/03/47
04/27/47 Ann Arbor MI	04/27/47 Detroit MI	08/06/48 Cincinnati OH	WIA at Mexico City 08/20/47. TRA COM E 12/26/47
06/01/46 Adrian MI			VTS WNA
06/01/46 Adrian MI			Drummer? VTS WNA
04/10/47 Detroit MI	04/30/47 Detroit MI		Died of diarrhea at Nopuluca MEX 05/30/48
11/02/47 Port Huron MI	11/12/47 Detroit MI	07/26/48 Detroit MI	MNI Allen
12/20/47 Marshall MI	01/01/48 Detroit MI	07/18/48 Detroit MI	PEN
12/15/47 Ann Arbor MI	01/01/48 Detroit MI		Died of diarrhea at Cordova MEX 05/20/48
04/27/48 Detroit MI	Detroit MI	06/20/48 Newport KY	
05/28/46 Detroit MI			VTS WNA
11/02/47 Port Huron MI	11/12/47 Detroit MI	07/26/48 Detroit MI	PMT 4SG 05/??/48
11/14/47 Detroit MI	11/14/47 Detroit MI	07/26/48 Detroit MI	PEN
06/01/46 Adrian MI			VTS WNA
11/15/47 Marshall MI	12/01/47 Detroit MI		Deserted at Detroit MI 01/07/48

NAME	AGE	HGT	EYE	HAIR	CPX	TRADE	BORN	HOME	RANK	UNIT
Wren, James								Detroit MI	2SG	Montgomery Guards
Wright, Elisha	32						Connecticut	Clinton MI	2LT	COM H 1st MI INF
Wright, George	24	5.09	BLU	LGT	FIR	Sailor	Seneca Co NY		RCT	US Army
Wright, Jackson	21	5.09	BLU	LGT	FIR	Sailor	Seneca Co NY		RCT	COM ? 3rd US DRG
Wright, Ralph Jr.	21	5.09	HZL	BWN	LGT	Printer	Livingston Co NY		PVT	COM A 15th US INF
Wright, William W.	27	5.10	BLU	BWN	FIR	Farmer	Ashtabula Co OH		PVT	COM F 1st MI INF
Wydner, Henry	21	5.06	GRY	LGT	LGT	Laborer	Chili NY	Pontiac MI	PVT	COM A 15th US INF
Wyman, Henry	40	5.10	BLU	LGT	LGT	Engineer	Cheshire ENG		PVT	COM B 1st MI INF
Yager, Peter								Adrian MI	PVT	Adrian Guard
Yaple, Chauncy	33	5.08	BLU	BWN	FLD	Farmer	Danby NY	Detroit MI	PVT	Brady Guards
Yearington, John	39	6.00	BLK	BLK	DRK	Laborer	Montgomery Co NY		PVT	COM E 15th US INF
Yinger, Michael	32	5.11	BLU	RED	DRK	Weaver	Darmstadt GER		PVT	COM G 15th US INF
York, William	26	5.04	BLK	DRK	DRK	Porter	London ENG	Detroit MI	PVT	COM E 1st MI INF
Yost, Abrahem	28	5.11	HZL	BWN	DRK	Laborer	Seneca Co NY		PVT	COM D 1st MI INF
Yost, Lewis	38	5.09	BLU	LGT	FIR	Tailor	Seneca Co NY	Pontiac MI	PVT	COM C 1st MI INF
Young, Andrew	24	5.05	HZL	BWN	FIR	Laborer	Berwickshire		PVT	COM B 3rd US INF
Young, Freeman	19	5.08	GRY	DRK	DRK	Laborer	Livingston Co NY		PVT	COM B 3rd US INF
Young, John	28	5.10	GRY	BWN	FIR	Farmer	Rutland VT		RCT	US Army
Young, Joseph Jr.	23	5.08	BLK	BWN	FIR	Farmer	Tyre NY		RCT	US Army
Youngs, Timothy	18	5.07	GRY	BWN	DRK	Farmer	Wayne Co MI		PVT	COM G 1st MI INF
Zimma, Peter	25	5.11	BLU	LGT	LGT	Laborer	Banagon GER		PVT	COM B 5th US INF

ENROLLED	MUSTERED	DISCHARGED	REMARKS
05/28/46 Detroit MI			VTS WNA
10/30/47 Clinton MI	12/01/47 Detroit MI	07/??/48 Detroit MI	Died of disease at Clinton MI 07/26/48
05/02/48 Detroit MI	Detroit MI		Deserted 06/24/48
05/02/48 Detroit MI	Detroit MI	07/16/48 East Pascagoula MS	
04/03/47 Ann Arbor MI	04/27/47 Detroit MI		PMT CPL 12/26/47. Died of typhus in MEX 01/15/48
11/15/47 Niles MI	12/02/47 Detroit MI	07/28/48 Detroit MI	PEN
03/26/47 Pontiac MI	04/27/47 Detroit MI		DOW 08/28/47 at Churubusco MEX. AKA Henry Widner
11/02/47 Port Huron MI	11/12/47 Detroit MI		Deserted at Detroit MI 12/26/47
06/01/46 Adrian MI			VTS WNA
06/18/47 Detroit MI	06/18/47 Detroit MI	06/30/48 Detroit MI	
04/08/47 Jackson MI	04/27/47 Detroit MI	04/13/48 New Orleans LA	Discharged for disability
04/30/47 Detroit MI	04/30/47 Detroit MI		LIH at New Orleans LA 07/12/48. PEN
11/20/47 Detroit MI	12/04/47 Detroit MI	07/18/48 Detroit MI	
11/14/47 Detroit MI	11/14/47 Detroit MI		Deserted at Detroit MI 12/20/47
11/30/47 Pontiac MI	12/01/47 Detroit MI	07/26/48 Detroit MI	
03/10/47 Detroit MI	03/10/47 Detroit MI	07/25/48 East Pascagoula MS	PEN. Born in Scotland
03/18/47 Detroit MI	03/18/47 Detroit MI	07/25/48 East Pascagoula MS	
09/07/47 Detroit MI	Detroit MI		Deserted 09/13/47
08/04/47 Detroit MI	Detroit MI		
02/20/48 Detroit MI	03/01/48 Detroit MI		Died on board steamer near Memphis TN 06/29/48
07/09/47 Detroit MI	Detroit MI	07/01/48 East Pascagoula MS	Born in Prussia

INDEX OF NAMES

Note: No names listed alphabetically in the rosters are included in this index. The entries found here include only those names that appear in the narrative portion of the text or in the "Remarks" column of the rosters.

INDEX OF PLACES AND SUBJECTS

Titles in the Great Lakes Books Series

Detroit Images: Photographs of the Renaissance City, edited by John J. Bukowczyk and Douglas Aikenhead, with Peter Slavcheff, 1989

Hangdog Reef: Poems Sailing the Great Lakes, by Stephen Tudor, 1989

Detroit: City of Race and Class Violence, revised edition, by B. J. Widick, 1989

Deep Woods Frontier: A History of Logging in Northern Michigan, by Theodore J. Karamanski, 1989

Orvie, The Dictator of Dearborn, by David L. Good, 1989

Seasons of Grace: A History of the Catholic Archdiocese of Detroit, by Leslie Woodcock Tentler, 1990

The Pottery of John Foster: Form and Meaning, by Gordon and Elizabeth Orear, 1990

The Diary of Bishop Frederic Baraga: First Bishop of Marquette, Michigan, edited by Regis M. Walling and Rev. N. Daniel Rupp, 1990

Walnut Pickles and Watermelon Cake: A Century of Michigan Cooking, by Larry B. Massie and Priscilla Massie, 1990

The Making of Michigan, 1820–1860: A Pioneer Anthology, edited by Justin L. Kestenbaum, 1990

America's Favorite Homes: A Guide to Popular Early Twentieth-Century Homes, by Robert Schweitzer and Michael W. R. Davis, 1990

Beyond the Model T: The Other Ventures of Henry Ford, by Ford R. Bryan, 1990

Life after the Line, by Josie Kearns, 1990

Michigan Lumbertowns: Lumbermen and Laborers in Saginaw, Bay City, and Muskegon, 1870–1905, by Jeremy W. Kilar, 1990

Detroit Kids Catalog: The Hometown Tourist, by Ellyce Field, 1990

Waiting for the News, by Leo Litwak, 1990 (reprint)

Detroit Perspectives, edited by Wilma Wood Henrickson, 1991

Life on the Great Lakes: A Wheelsman's Story, by Fred W. Dutton, edited by William Donohue Ellis, 1991

Copper Country Journal: The Diary of Schoolmaster Henry Hobart, 1863–1864, by Henry Hobart, edited by Philip P. Mason, 1991

John Jacob Astor: Business and Finance in the Early Republic, by John Denis Haeger, 1991

Survival and Regeneration: Detroit's American Indian Community, by Edmund J. Danziger, Jr., 1991

Steamboats and Sailors of the Great Lakes, by Mark L. Thompson, 1991

Cobb Would Have Caught It: The Golden Age of Baseball in Detroit, by Richard Bak, 1991

Michigan in Literature, by Clarence Andrews, 1992

Under the Influence of Water: Poems, Essays, and Stories, by Michael Delp, 1992

The Country Kitchen, by Della T. Lutes, 1992 (reprint)

The Making of a Mining District: Keweenaw Native Copper 1500–1870, by David J. Krause, 1992

Kids Catalog of Michigan Adventures, by Ellyce Field, 1993

Henry's Lieutenants, by Ford R. Bryan, 1993

Historic Highway Bridges of Michigan, by Charles K. Hyde, 1993

Lake Erie and Lake St. Clair Handbook, by Stanley J. Bolsenga and Charles E. Herndendorf, 1993

Queen of the Lakes, by Mark Thompson, 1994

Iron Fleet: The Great Lakes in World War II, by George J. Joachim, 1994

Turkey Stearnes and the Detroit Stars: The Negro Leagues in Detroit, 1919–1933, by Richard Bak, 1994

Pontiac and the Indian Uprising, by Howard H. Peckham, 1994 (reprint)

Charting the Inland Seas: A History of the U.S. Lake Survey, by Arthur M. Woodford, 1994 (reprint)

Ojibwa Narratives of Charles and Charlotte Kawbawgam and Jacques LePique, 1893–1895. Recorded with Notes by Homer H. Kidder, edited by Arthur P. Bourgeois, 1994, co-published with the Marquette County Historical Society

Strangers and Sojourners: A History of Michigan's Keweenaw Peninsula, by Arthur W. Thurner, 1994

Win Some, Lose Some: G. Mennen Williams and the New Democrats, by Helen Washburn Berthelot, 1995

Sarkis, by Gordon and Elizabeth Orear, 1995

The Northern Lights: Lighthouses of the Upper Great Lakes, by Charles K. Hyde, 1995 (reprint)

Kids Catalog of Michigan Adventures, second edition, by Ellyce Field, 1995

Rumrunning and the Roaring Twenties: Prohibition on the Michigan-Ontario Waterway, by Philip P. Mason, 1995

In the Wilderness with the Red Indians, by E. R. Baierlein, translated by Anita Z. Boldt, edited by Harold W. Moll, 1996

Elmwood Endures: History of a Detroit Cemetery, by Michael Franck, 1996

Master of Precision: Henry M. Leland, by Mrs. Wilfred C. Leland with Minnie Dubbs Mill-brook, 1996 (reprint)

Haul-Out: New and Selected Poems, by Stephen Tudor, 1996

Kids Catalog of Michigan Adventures, third edition, by Ellyce Field, 1997

Beyond the Model T: The Other Ventures of Henry Ford, revised edition, by Ford R. Bryan, 1997

Young Henry Ford: A Picture History of the First Forty Years, by Sidney Olson, 1997 (reprint)

The Coast of Nowhere: Meditations on Rivers, Lakes and Streams, by Michael Delp, 1997

From Saginaw Valley to Tin Pan Alley: Saginaw's Contribution to American Popular Music, 1890–1955, by R. Grant Smith, 1998

The Long Winter Ends, by Newton G. Thomas, 1998 (reprint)

Bridging the River of Hatred: The Pioneering Efforts of Detroit Police Commissioner George Edwards, by Mary M. Stolberg, 1998

Toast of the Town: The Life and Times of Sunnie Wilson, by Sunnie Wilson with John Cohassey, 1998

These Men Have Seen Hard Service: The First Michigan Sharpshooters in the Civil War, by Raymond J. Herek, 1998

A Place for Summer: One Hundred Years at Michigan and Trumbull, by Richard Bak, 1998

Early Midwestern Travel Narratives: An Annotated Bibliography, 1634–1850, by Robert R. Hubach, 1998 (reprint)

All-American Anarchist: Joseph A. Labadie and the Labor Movement, by Carlotta R. Anderson, 1998

Michigan in the Novel, 1816–1996: An Annotated Bibliography, by Robert Beasecker, 1998

"Time by Moments Steals Away": The 1848 Journal of Ruth Douglass, by Robert L. Root, Jr., 1998

The Detroit Tigers: A Pictorial Celebration of the Greatest Players and Moments in Tigers' History, updated edition, by William M. Anderson, 1999

Father Abraham's Children: Michigan Episodes in the Civil War, by Frank B. Woodford, 1999 (reprint)

Letter from Washington, 1863–1865, by Lois Bryan Adams, edited and with an introduction by Evelyn Leasher, 1999

Wonderful Power: The Story of Ancient Copper Working in the Lake Superior Basin, by Susan R. Martin, 1999

A Sailor's Logbook: A Season aboard Great Lakes Freighters, by Mark L. Thompson, 1999

Huron: The Seasons of a Great Lake, by Napier Shelton, 1999

Tin Stackers: The History of the Pittsburgh Steamship Company, by Al Miller, 1999

Art in Detroit Public Places, revised edition, text by Dennis Nawrocki, photographs by David Clements, 1999

Brewed in Detroit: Breweries and Beers Since 1830, by Peter H. Blum, 1999

Detroit Kids Catalog: A Family Guide for the 21st Century, by Ellyce Field, 2000

"Expanding the Frontiers of Civil Rights": Michigan, 1948–1968, by Sidney Fine, 2000

Graveyard of the Lakes, by Mark L. Thompson, 2000

Enterprising Images: The Goodridge Brothers, African American Photographers, 1847–1922, by John Vincent Jezierski, 2000

New Poems from the Third Coast: Contemporary Michigan Poetry, edited by Michael Delp, Conrad Hilberry, and Josie Kearns, 2000

Arab Detroit: From Margin to Mainstream, edited by Nabeel Abraham and Andrew Shryock, 2000

The Sandstone Architecture of the Lake Superior Region, by Kathryn Bishop Eckert, 2000

Looking Beyond Race: The Life of Otis Milton Smith, by Otis Milton Smith and Mary M. Stolberg, 2000

Mail by the Pail, by Colin Bergel, illustrated by Mark Koenig, 2000

Great Lakes Journey: A New Look at America's Freshwater Coast, by William Ashworth, 2000

A Life in the Balance: The Memoirs of Stanley J. Winkelman, by Stanley J. Winkelman, 2000

Schooner Passage: Sailing Ships and the Lake Michigan Frontier, by Theodore J. Karamanski, 2000

The Outdoor Museum: The Magic of Michigan's Marshall M. Fredericks, by Marcy Heller Fisher, illustrated by Christine Collins Woomer, 2001

Detroit in Its World Setting: A Three Hundred Year Chronology, 1701–2001, edited by David Lee Poremba, 2001

Frontier Metropolis: Picturing Early Detroit, 1701–1838, by Brian Leigh Dunnigan, 2001

Michigan Remembered: Photographs from the Farm Security Administration and the Office of War Information, 1936–1943, edited by Constance B. Schulz, with Introductory Essays by Constance B. Schulz and William H. Mulligan, Jr., 2001

This Is Detroit, 1701–2001, by Arthur M. Woodford, 2001

History of the Finns in Michigan, by Armas K. E. Holmio, translated by Ellen M. Ryynanen, 2001

Angels in the Architecture: A Photographic Elegy to an American Asylum, by Heidi Johnson, 2001

Uppermost Canada: The Western District and the Detroit Frontier, 1800–1850, by R. Alan Douglas, 2001

Windjammers: Songs of the Great Lakes Sailors, by Ivan H. Walton with Joe Grimm, 2002

Detroit Tigers Lists and More: Runs, Hits, and Eras, by Mark Pattison and David Raglin, 2002

The Iron Hunter, by Chase S. Osborn, 2002 (reprint)

Independent Man: The Life of Senator James Couzens, by Harry Barnard, 2002 (reprint)

Riding the Roller Coaster: A History of the Chrysler Corporation, by Charles K. Hyde, 2003

Michigan's Early Military Forces: A Roster and History of Troops Activated prior to the American Civil War, rosters compiled by Le Roy Barnett with histories by Roger Rosentreter, 2003

For an updated listing of books in this series, please visit our Web site at
http://wsupress.wayne.edu